T0398200

Targum Chronicles and Its Place among the Late Targums

Supplements to Aramaic Studies

Targum Chronicles and Its Place Among the Late Targums

By

Leeor Gottlieb

BRILL

LEIDEN | BOSTON

Library of Congress Cataloging-in-Publication Data

Names: Gottlieb, Leeor, author.
Title: Targum Chronicles and its place among the late Targums / by Leeor
  Gottlieb.
Description: Leiden ; Boston : Brill, 2020. | Series: Supplement to aramaic
  studies, 2468-2810 ; volume 16 | Includes bibliographical references and
  index.
Identifiers: LCCN 2020002412 (print) | LCCN 2020002413 (ebook) |
  ISBN 9789004416970 (hardback) | ISBN 9789004417632 (ebook)
Subjects: LCSH: Bible. Chronicles. Aramaic—Criticism, interpretation, etc.
  | Bible. Chronicles—Translating. | Bible. Old Testament.
  Aramaic—Criticism, interpretation, etc.
Classification: LCC BS1345.52 .G68 2020 (print) | LCC BS1345.52 (ebook) |
  DDC 222/.6042—dc23
LC record available at https://lccn.loc.gov/2020002412
LC ebook record available at https://lccn.loc.gov/2020002413

Typeface for the Latin, Greek, and Cyrillic scripts: "Brill". See and download: brill.com/brill-typeface.

ISSN 2468-2810
ISBN 978-90-04-41697-0 (hardback)
ISBN 978-90-04-41763-2 (e-book)

וּכְדוּן אֱלָהָנָא מוֹדִין אַנַן לָךְ וּמְשַׁבְּחִין לְשׁוּם תּוּשְׁבַּחְתָּךְ: וַאֲרוּם מָה אֲנָא וּמָה עַמִּי דְּנִסְגֵּי
חֵילָא לְאִתְנַדְבָּא כְּדָא אֲרוּם מִן־קֳדָמָךְ מִתְיְיהֵב כּוֹלָא וּמִן־בִּרְכַּת יְדָךְ יְהָבוּ לָךְ: אֲרוּם דַּיְירִין
אַנַן גַּבָּךְ וְתוֹתָבִין הֵי כְּכָלְהוֹן אֲבָהָתָנָא הֵי בְּטוּלָא דְּעוֹפָא דְּפָרַח בַּאֲוֵיר שְׁמַיָא הֵכְדֵּין יוֹמָנָא
עַל־אַרְעָא וְלֵית סִיבּוּר לְבַר־נָשָׁא דְּיֵיחֵי עַד־עָלָם:

•••

*Now, our God, we praise You and sing praises to Your praiseworthy
name. But what am I and what are my people that we should be able to
freely offer like this? For from before You everything is given, and from
the blessing of Your hand they have given back to You. For we are in your
presence sojourners and aliens, just as all of our fathers were. As the
shadow of the bird that flies in the air of the sky, so also are our days on
the earth, and there is no hope for a son of man that he should live forever.*

TARGUM 1 CHRONICLES 29:13-15; ENGLISH TRANSLATION
BY CHRISTOPHER DOST

∵

Contents

Acknowledgements

Etenim, iudices, cum omnibus virtutibus me affectum esse cupio, tum nihil est, quod malim quam me et gratum esse et videri. Haec est enim una virtus non solum maxima, sed etiam mater virtutum omnium reliquarum.

For indeed, gentlemen, while I would fain have some tincture of all the virtues, there is no quality I would sooner have, and be thought to have, than gratitude. For gratitude not merely stands alone at the head of all the virtues, but it is even mother of all the rest.

(Cicero, "Pro Cnaeo Plancio", 80; English translation by N.H. Watts)

I acknowledge with great joy and gratitude the generous support of my research that has allowed me to complete this elaborate study of Targum Chronicles. This book was published with the support of the Israel Science Foundation, to whom I extend my heartfelt thanks. I have also been privileged to receive support of the Beit Shalom-Japan fund for this study and I deeply thank them as well.

My colleagues and students in the Bible Department at Bar-Ilan University and in the Minerva Center for the Relations Between Israel and Aram in Biblical Times have been a continuous source of growth and inspiration. Their assistance – and at times the challenges they raised – helped sharpen arguments laid forth in this book.

I am blessed to have studied under outstanding scholars and teachers in the course of my Yeshiva education and academic training alike. I am indebted to each and every one of them. With regard to this particular study, I have benefited greatly from my esteemed teacher, Menahem Kister of Hebrew University in Jerusalem, who has generously shared his vast scholarly knowledge and keen insight with me from the time I took my first strides in Targum studies and to the present day. Shortcomings and fallacies in my arguments throughout this book are, however, mine to bear.

Though my hands sowed this book, its burden was shared by my family. Thank you, Sara, Moshe, Talia, Yoel, Yishai, Dan, Roey and Rachel. May you be blessed to reap in joy.

יהון לרעוא מימרי פומי וריננת רעיוני קדמך ה' תוקפי ופריקי:

(Targum Psalms 19:15)

Leeor Gottlieb
Bar-Ilan University
Ramat-Gan, Israel

Abbreviations

Names of biblical books, talmudic tractates and other rabbinic works are abbreviated as per *The SBL Handbook of Style—Second Edition*, Atlanta: SBL Press 2014.

b.	Bavli (Babylonian Talmud)
BDB	*The Brown-Driver-Briggs Hebrew and English Lexicon*, Peabody: Hendrickson 2000[5]
BHS	*Biblia Hebraica Stuttgartensia*, ed. K. Elliger, W. Rudolph, Stuttgart 1997[5]
BT	Babylonian Talmud
C	MS Ee. 5.9
CD	S. Schechter, *Documents of Jewish Sectaries*, Volume I, Cambridge 1910
DJD	*Discoveries in the Judaean Desert*, Oxford 1955–2009
E	MS Or. fol. 1211
FT	Fragments Targum
FTP	Fragments Targum, MS Paris
FTV	Fragments Targum, MS Vatican
GT	Targums from the Cairo Genizah
HALOT	L. Koehler, W. Baumgartner, *The Hebrew and Aramaic Lexicon of the Old Testament*, 5 vols. Leiden: Brill 1994–2000
JBA	Jewish Babylonian Aramaic
JPA	Jewish Palestinian Aramaic
LBH	Late Biblical Hebrew
LJLA	Late Jewish Literary Aramaic
LSJ	H.G. Liddell, R. Scott, H.S. Jones *A Greek-English Lexicon*, Oxford: Clarendon Press 1996
LXX	Septuagint
m.	Mishnah
MS	Manuscript
MT	Masoretic Text
NJPS	*Tanakh: A New Translation of the Holy Scriptures According to the Traditional Hebrew Text*, Philadelphia 1985
OTL	Old Testament Library
Pesh.	Peshiṭta
pr. n.	proper noun
SBL	Society of Biblical Literature
t.	Tosefta
TAD	B. Porten, A. Yardeni, *Textbook of Aramaic Documents from Ancient Egypt*, 4 volumes, Jerusalem 1986–1999

TC	Targum Chronicles
Tg.	Targum
Tg. Cant	Targum Canticles (Song of Songs)
Tg. Chr	Targum Chronicles
Tg. Eccl	Targum Ecclesiastes (Qohelet)
Tg. Esth	Targum Esther
Tg. Job	Targum Job
Tg. Lam	Targum Lamentations
Tg. Prov	Targum Proverbs
Tg. Ps	Targum Psalms
Tg. Ruth	Targum Ruth
TJ	Targum Jonathan
TL	Targum Lamentations
TN	Targum Neophyti
TNM	Marginalia of Targum Neophyti
TO	Targum Onqelos
TP	Targum Psalms
TPJ	Targum Pseudo-Jonathan
TT	Tosefta Targum
TY	Talmud Yerushalmi (Palestinian Talmud)
V	Cod. Vat. Urb. ebr. 1
y.	Yerushalmi (Palestinian Talmud)

CHAPTER 1

Introduction

1 The Book of Chronicles and Its Traditional Jewish Commentaries

The book of Chronicles is one of the latest books in the Hebrew Bible. Beginning with Adam and concluding with the declaration of Cyrus, it serves to some degree as a reflection of the entire biblical era.[1] The author of the book creates a historiographical tapestry by weaving earlier sources within a narrative framework and sequence. These earlier sources include biblical books alongside works that are not part of the biblical canon.[2] Particularly salient is the author's use of the books of Samuel and Kings, as well as certain chapters of Psalms, but the historical picture that emerges from Chronicles is by no means identical to that which arises from these books. Rather, despite heavy reliance on the Deuteronomistic histories, the author created a different historical picture by employing three kinds of editorial changes: 1) by omitting many details that appear in the books of Samuel-Kings; 2) by making changes within the units that are incorporated from these sources; 3) by adding narrative units of his own composition or of external sources.

The author's extensive use of other biblical works invites comparison between many units in Chronicles and their parallels in other books, and his selection of particular units and exclusion of others illuminates his narrative objectives.[3] Placing the parallel units side by side facilitates analysis of the differences and similarities between them. While many changes can be attributed to the author's adaptation of his sources according to his own objectives, style and language, others may indicate differences between the author's own *Vorlage* and the parallel Masoretic Text. Changes of both types have greatly contributed to our understanding of Chronicles, whether from a

---

1 In addition to the mention of Cyrus' proclamation, Chronicles contains many other data that indicate a relatively later period than most other biblical books. For example, MT Chronicles records David's genealogy till the sixth generation after Zerubabel (1 Chr 3:17–24), while LXX goes even further to the eleventh generation. Also, the Hebrew used throughout the book has been identified by many scholars as Late Biblical Hebrew; cf. Hurvitz *LBH*.

2 See a list of non-canonical sources mentioned in Chronicles in Curtis-Madsen, pp. 21–22. On the complexity of arriving at conclusions about the way the Chronicler used these sources and on the difficulty of even defining these sources, cf. Knoppers *vol. I*, pp. 118–128.

3 For an extensive discussion of the Chronicler's objectives cf. Japhet *Ideology*.

© KONINKLIJKE BRILL NV, LEIDEN, 2020 | DOI:10.1163/9789004417632_002

literary perspective or a textual-critical perspective of the book and its biblical sources.[4]

The historiographical framework convenes a variety of literary genres at the author's disposal. The book of Chronicles contains genealogies, anecdotes, speeches of various kinds (royal declarations, prophetic speeches, priestly pronouncements, among others), prayers and hymns.[5] Many of the latter are addressed to a communal assembly as a narrative strategy employed to convey the message of the text.

In his study of the development of midrashic literature, Zunz perceived the book of Chronicles as a final link in the chain of biblical literature, and the usher of post-biblical midrashic literature.[6] Ironically, however, Chronicles itself lies far from the center of post-biblical exegetic attention. While rabbinic literature indeed contains homiletic readings of several of its verses, a considerable part of Chronicles remained uncharted in this literature.[7] Despite the talmudic statement in *b. Pesaḥ.* 62b: "Mar Zutra said: Between 'Azel' (1 Chr 8:38) and 'Azel' (1 Chr 9:44), they have laden four hundred camels with exegetical interpretations," there is no complete, comprehensive midrashic compilation on Chronicles from rabbinic times. Intriguing evidence indicates that the book

---

4 Much has been written about the parallels between Chronicles and other biblical books. These units are displayed together in Vannutelli and Bendavid. Vannutelli also includes LXX, the Vulgate and relevant sections of Josephus' *Antiquities*. Bendavid graphically emphasizes textual variants in the MT parallels by inserting spaces and red ink.

5 See Japhet *OTL*, p. 33; Klein *1 Chronicles*, pp. 19–23.

6 Zunz, pp. 7–20. Zunz laid the foundation for further discussion of Chronicles' character and the relation between it and Ezra-Nehemiah. In rabbinic tradition Chronicles was attributed— at least in part—to Ezra the scribe. Thus in the well-known baraita in *b. B. Bat.* 15a: עזרא כתב ספרו ויחס של דברי הימים עד לו, *Ezra wrote the book that is called by his name and the genealogies of the book of Chronicles up to his own time.* The Amoraic discussion there attributes the rest of Chronicles to Nehemiah. For more on this enigmatic statement in the baraita and other understandings thereof, cf. Viezel *Author*. Zunz, however, flipped the matter entirely in his study and suggested not that Ezra composed Chronicles, but that the Chronicler composed Ezra-Nehemiah. This opinion—that one author composed Ezra-Nehemiah and Chronicles—was the prevailing one in the scholarly world for more than a century after Zunz (cf. e.g. Curtis-Madsen, pp. 2–5; interestingly, Geiger, p. 17, seemingly held the opinion that the books were composed by separate authors). As Rudolph, p. 1, states: "Dass Chr/Esr/Neh ein gemeinsames Werk darstellen, ist deshalb heute allgemein anerkannt". However, this wide-held opinion came under scrutiny in the late twentieth century. Sara Japhet pointed out fundamental differences between the two works, including linguistic and stylistic differences, but also differences in *Weltanschauung*, all indicating that the books were not written by one person; cf. Japhet *Authorship*; Japhet *OTL*, pp. 3–4. Consequently, there no longer exists a consensus that Chronicles and Ezra-Nehemiah were composed by one author; see Knoppers' survey of scholarly opinions on this matter, Knoppers *vol. 1*, pp. 73–89.

7 For an illustration of this, cf. the list of verses in Hyman, vol. 3, pp. 260–287.

was studied in the land of Israel during the Byzantine era, as a poetic summary of the book of Chronicles survives and is understood by Sokoloff and Yahalom as a *piyyut* written in honor of the completion of its being read or studied.[8] The scope and nature of this study is unknown, and in any event, we have not identified any other of its literary results.

The book did not fare much better in Jewish circles in medieval times, save for a few commentaries that we possess. Of these, particularly noteworthy is the commentary attributed to a student of R. Saadyah Ga'on (the author cites R. Saadyah Ga'on and R. Judah ibn Kuraish on a few verses); R. Samuel Masnuth, Pseudo-Rashi, R. David Qimḥi, and R. Benjamin the son of R. Judah.[9] Particularly illuminating is Don Isaac Abravanel's personal testimony of his search for sources which explain the striking disparity between the books of Samuel-Kings and Chronicles, which is found in the introduction to his commentary to the book of Samuel:[10]

> And it is impossible that all this shall remain without explanation, for these are great quandaries that arise from this immense question. As to the answer, I remain alone and no-one else besides me deals with this, for our Sages, of blessed memory, have said nothing great or small, convincing or unconvincing; neither the first scholars of the Talmud, nor the later authors and commentators; not one has stirred to the doubt at all, and not one has sought a path to the answer. And behold, the Lord has piled trouble upon my pain, for there is no commentary on the book of Chronicles in this land, but a few brief words by R. David Qimḥi, of blessed memory, and they are so brief as to be insignificant, and he did not delve deeply into the matter at all, and besides, that book—the book of Chronicles—does not feature in Jewish midrash. I must confess that I have never read it nor looked into its matters until now …

2 The Targum of Chronicles as an Object of Research

It is therefore not to be taken for granted that a Targum for Chronicles would even be composed, for the Hebrew book is not read publicly in the synagogue, nor is there a strong tradition of Jewish study and commentary on the book.

---

8   Sokoloff-Yahalom, 44, pp. 34, 252–257.

9   For a summary on Jewish exegesis of Chronicles in this period, cf. Kalimi *Interpretation*, pp. 33–38; Kalimi *Journey*, pp. 189–242.

10   Abravanel, pp. 4–5.

Nevertheless, a Jewish Aramaic translation of Chronicles does exist, though it has hardly left any mark upon history until the modern era.[11] This Targum is not mentioned in the medieval commentaries, and signs of its circulation among the Jewish population of this period are scarce. Three manuscripts of the Aramaic Targum Chronicles (= TC) that are extant today were written at the end of the thirteenth century and the mid fourteenth century, and while they are not identical, they certainly belong to the same textual family.[12] Statements made by medieval rabbinic scholars about the lack of a translation of Chronicles—even in books written after the aforementioned manuscripts; and the fact that TC is not quoted in any of the medieval commentaries on Chronicles, testify to its poor circulation.[13] Targum Chronicles has also received less modern scholarly attention than other translations. However, TC is

---

11   TC opens with a title heading (which is missing in MS C):

דין ספר יחוסיא פתגמי יומיא דמן יומי עלמא TC

Dost: This is the book of genealogies, the chronicles, which are from the days of old.

This title designates for the biblical book two purposes, a genealogy and a chronicle, standing grammatically in apposition to each other in the Aramaic text. Rosenberg-Kohler, p. 138, regarded this as an allusion to the two parts of the book of Chronicles, i.e. 1 Chr 1–9 was *the book of Genealogies* and the rest of the book was *the Chronicles*, however I am not convinced this is the original meaning of the title. The original may have been ספר יחוסי פתגמי יומיא (with the word יחוסי in construct form, as opposed to emphatic), which is somewhat similar to the language of the baraita in *b. B. Bat.* 15a mentioned above: עזרא כתב ספרו ויחס של דברי הימים עד לו.

12   Le Déaut–Robert, vol. 1, pp. 21–22.

13   Qimḥi, Pseudo-Rashi, R. Samuel Masnuth and others quote Targums often in their commentaries, but these excerpts are generally from Targum Jonathan to Samuel and Kings in chapters with parallel sections to these books, and occasionally from other Targums too, but nowhere has been found a clear reference to Targum Chronicles in these commentaries. On Pseudo-Rashi's unfamiliarity with TC, cf. Viezel *Pseudo-Rashi*, p. 41. On Qimḥi, cf. Berger, p. 13, n. 32. In addition to the lack of use of TC in medieval Jewish commentaries, there are also Jewish authorities who made explicit statements to the effect that an Aramaic Targum for Chronicles does not exist. R. Samuel Masnuth wrote on 1 Chr 8:29 (MS Vat. ebr. 97, col. 37; cf. Viezel *Pseudo-Rashi*, p. 40, n. 95)—

ולפיכך הקורא באותם השמות האמורים בזה הספר וביחוש המשפחות הוא משתבש בהם ואינו יכול למצוא להם טעם לפי שאינם נאמרין על פשטן ולפיכך לא נתן להתרגם כמו שאר עשרים וארבעה

Therefore, whosoever reads the names in this book and in the genealogy of families remains confounded and he cannot find for them rhyme or reason for they are not stated according to *peshat*. Consequently [the book of Chronicles] could not undergo translation as did the rest of the books of the Bible.

R. Abraham Zacuto wrote the following in his ספר יוחסין (p. 60)—

ואני ראיתי תרגום של כתובים חוץ מדניאל ועזרא ודברי הימים

I have seen a Targum for the Hagiographa, except for Daniel, Ezra and Chronicles.

R. Elijah Levita wrote in his *Meturgeman* (entry כור)—

ולא נמצא 'כורים' בלשון רבים במקרא רק בדברי הימים שאין בו תרגום

an intriguing research object for several reasons. The many parallels between
Chronicles and biblical historiographical works, mainly Samuel and Kings, invite comparison not only between the Hebrew accounts, but between their
Aramaic translations as well. Did the Aramaic translator of Chronicles refer
to the existing translations of the parallel chapters or not; and if so, what kind
of use was made of these earlier Targums? Did he agree with the conclusions
and interpretations of his predecessors? When, and in what cultural context,
did TC arise?

In eleven instances, the author of TC (= the targumist) or a scribe presents
an alternative translation for a word as it appears throughout the text, using
the abbreviation ל״א (= לישנא אחרינא, "Variant Text").[14] Double translations,
marked in the text with the abbreviation ל״א (or ת״א, "another translation")
are fairly common in the Targum of Job as well as that of Psalms.[15] However,
it is unclear if the alternative translations in Job are the copyist's handiwork,
or if this was the translator's method of preserving multiple traditions; while
the alternative translations in the table of nations in TC do not seem to be the
targumist's own creation. This is because the alternative translation in 1 Chr 1:7
is the same language that Pseudo-Jonathan uses in Gen 10:4, and the first translation differs from its alternative in a single detail (איטליון as opposed to אבזיה),
which itself is found in other Pentateuchal Targums. This indicates that none
of the alternatives are the targumist's original additions, but rather his—or a
copyist's—attempts to preserve more than one tradition he was familiar with.
In any case, this phenomenon hints to a certain connection between TC and
the Targums of Job and Psalms; the aforementioned example also points to the
Pentateuchal Targum Pseudo-Jonathan.

It is common knowledge that there is no translation without interpretation.
The Aramaic translations contain an array of ancient traditions and fascinat-
ing interpretations, and served as a biblical commentary for the medieval who
studied the Bible. These translations, therefore, are one of the most important keys to understanding the world of ancient biblical exegesis. Is it possible
to point out influences and connections between the translators' exegetical
statements and other ancient commentaries, first and foremost the translations and rabbinic literature? Does the targumist follow in the footsteps of rabbinic exegesis, or does he pave his own paths? Can lost exegetical traditions
be extracted from a translation? How does the targumist deal with the unique

---

The word כורים is not found in plural form in the Bible, except for in Chronicles, which
does not have a Targum.

14   1 Chr 1:5–7, 16; 9:40; 11:16; 18:3; 21:27; 2 Chr 6:10; 15:8; 16:9. Data as per MS V.

15   See discussion and bibliography included in Weiss, pp. 288–293; Stec *Job*, pp. 85–94.

material of Chronicles? Does he connect certain verses in the biblical work to figures or events he is familiar with?

3   The Text of Targum Chronicles: Manuscripts and Editions

There are three extant manuscripts of TC: The Vatican Manuscript (henceforth V) from 1294; the Erfurt Manuscript (= E) from 1343, and the Cambridge Manuscript (= C) from 1347.[16] A fourth manuscript was unfortunately destroyed in Dresden in 1945, and all that remains of it is an illegible, charred lump.[17] Over the years, the three manuscripts V, C and E have been published. M.F. Beck printed the E manuscript of 1 Chronicles in 1680, and 2 Chronicles in 1683, together with an introduction, a Latin translation, and annotation. C was published by D. Wilkins (the project was started by S. Clarke, but completed by Wilkins) in 1715. Wilkins' edition served as the basis for Ben Menaḥem's edition in 1815—which led to different printings in *Mikraot Gedolot*,[18] as well as the Rahmer Edition in 1866.[19] P. de Lagarde published an eclectic edition of Targum Chronicles in 1872, based mainly on E, but taking the C and Dresden texts into consideration as well. The 1968 Sperber edition is also purportedly based on E, although it is heavily influenced by de Lagarde's edition.[20] In the text itself, Sperber signified the translation's integration of rabbinic interpretations; long midrashic additions; (unclassified) emendations of the Masoretic text; words derived from Greek and Latin; and also used lines to signify double translations.

---

16   V = Cod. Vat. Urb. ebr. 1 (F726 in the JNL manuscript institute), from folio 898v and on.
      E = MS Or. fol. 1211, from folio 46or and on.
      C = MS Ee. 5.9 (F15862 in the JNL manuscript institute).

17   Le Déaut–Robert, vol. 1, p. 13, n. 19.

18   TC's inclusion in various editions of the rabbinic Bible (מקראות גדולות) was not uniform and in many places it was not accessible (cf. Z. Kokhab-Tob's edition of ibn-Farḥun's מחברת הערוך [Pressburg, 1844], p. 10b, entry ברר, n. 4). Even today not all rabbinic Bibles include TC. Some editions include it as an addendum in the back of the volume, while yet others include it in the same manner as any other Targum, accompanying the Hebrew verses.

19   Ben Menaḥem received the attribution of TC to Rab Joseph and identified him with the Rab Joseph of the Talmud Bavli, as did Rahmer, thereby apparently cementing this identification in later Jewish editions. This identification with a third generation Amora, however, is simply untenable, as the Targum in its current form is unquestionably post-talmudic.

20   Sperber, vol. 4a, p. VII.

FIGURE 1   First page of Chronicles in MS V (MS Urb. ebr. 1, p. 895r; courtesy of the
Biblioteca Apostolica Vaticana)

FIGURE 2   First page of Chronicles in MS E (MS or. fol. 1211,
            p. 460r; courtesy of the Staatsbibliothek zu Berlin,
            Orientabteilung)

Due to historical circumstances, the oldest, most complete manuscript, V, was only published in 1971, by R. Le Déaut and J. Robert.[21] This edition includes an introduction; a French translation (deviations from the Masoretic text are in italics); annotation; the Aramaic text, variants in C and E; and independent reading suggestions, as well as brief French and English dictionaries.

Consequently, our knowledge of the text of TC is based on three medieval manuscripts that are closely related from a chronological, geographical (Ashkenaz) and traditional perspective, which does not allow us to determine how the text developed from its time of compilation until their emergence.[22]

---

21   See Levine for a survey of the general nature of this manuscript.
22   This, despite Rosenberg-Kohler, p. 277, who tried to determine a stemmatic relation between E and C, the two versions they knew.

Throughout my study, I made use of the Le Déaut-Robert edition, which pri-
oritizes V but takes the other manuscripts into account, and at the same time,
I constantly referred to a copy of the V manuscript itself.[23] Through this double reading, I found that the editors took great pains to produce an accurate
work. Nonetheless, in the few places where I found textual considerations that
pointed to a possible reading that did not appear in their edition, I proposed a
different reading than that of Le Déaut and Robert.[24]

4 The *Vorlage* of Targum Chronicles

Careful study of the Aramaic text of Targum Chronicles reveals several apparent differences between the Hebrew source text upon which the targumist relied and the Masoretic Text of Chronicles. BHS should not be relied upon when
it utilizes TC in its *Apparatus Criticus*, because it did not rely upon MS V. In a
study devoted to the question of TC's Hebrew *Vorlage*, I identified and documented these differences, resulting in four categories: differences in consonantal orthography, differences in vocalization, differences in syntactic division
and the degree of conformity with *ketiv*/*qere*.[25] This, however, does not mean
that the Hebrew *Vorlage* our targumist used was a different version other than
the Masoretic Text. Rather, the differences identified reflect no more than common deviations from our conception of the Masoretic Text, as found in many
biblical manuscripts of the Masoretic text family. In fact, the degree of accu-
racy of the scriptural text that lay before the author of Targum Chronicles was
not materially different from that of many medieval Masoretic manuscripts
with which we are familiar, many details of which deviate from the principal
transmission of this version. Below are three concise lists of presumed textual
variants between MT and the Targum's *Vorlage*. For each reading in question
I will present MT, TC, the Septuagint and the Peshiṭta (and in a few cases the
Vulgate too), followed by my conclusion regarding the Hebrew *Vorlage* of TC. A
list of the Targum's conformity with Masoretic *ketiv* and *qere* is also provided.
Contra the more elaborate presentation of primary sources throughout this
book, the Hebrew verses and their classical translations in the following four
lists will not be accompanied by English translations. For more detail and a

---

23   The manuscript is held in the Biblioteca Vaticana. I was given permission by the library
      manager to use a photo of the manuscript for the purpose of this study.
24   Targum manuscripts differ on the way to abbreviate the Tetragrammaton (e.g. יי, ייי,
      ייי, ה׳). For purpose of graphical harmonization, I used the abbreviation ה׳ throughout
      MT, TC and all other Targums, without noting what form actually appears in this or that
      manuscript.
25   Gottlieb *Vorlage*.

discussion of TC and the accompanying textual versions, I refer the reader to my aforementioned article on this subject.

4.1   *Differences in Consonantal Orthography*

1 Chr 1:12 פְּלִשְׁתִּיִם וְאֶת־ כַּפְתֹּרִים: וְאֶת־ פַּתְרֻסִים   וְאֶת־ כַּסְלֻחִים אֲשֶׁר יָצְאוּ מִשָּׁם

TC   פלשתאי וית קפוטקאי: מנהון   נסיוטאי דנפקו   וית פנטפוליטאי וית

LXX   ἐκειθεν

Pesh.   ܡܢ ܗܢܐ

    TC reflects מֵהֶם.

1 Chr 4:8 הָרוּם: בֶּן־   אֲחַרְחֵל   וּמִשְׁפְּחֹת

TC   דמרים: בוכרא הוא   חור   אחרא[ל]   וגניסת

LXX   ἀδελφοῦ Ρηχαβ

Pesh.   ---

    TC reflects אחראל.

1 Chr 4:12   רֵכָה: אֵלֶּה אַנְשֵׁי

TC   רבתא: סנהדרין אלין אנשי

LXX   Ρηφα

Pesh.   ܪܟܐ܆   ܟܢܫܝ

    I believe TC reflects רַבָּה.

1 Chr 4:15   וּקְנַז: אֵלֶּה   וּבְנֵי

TC   קנז: אלה   ובני

LXX   Κενεζ Αλα· καὶ υἱοί

Pesh.   ---

    TC reflects קְנַז.

1 Chr 4:29 וּבְתוֹלָד: וּבְעֶצֶם   וּבְבִלְהָה

TC   ובתולד: ובעטם   ובבלהה

LXX   καὶ Βοασομ

Pesh.   ܘܒܥܛܡ

    TC reflects ובעטם.

1 Chr 4:30 וּבְצִיקְלָג: וּבְחָרְמָה   וּבִבְתוּאֵל

TC   ובצקלג: ובחרמה   ובביתאל

LXX   καὶ Βαθουηλ

Pesh.   ܘܒܝܬܝܠ

    TC reflects ובביתאל.

1 Chr 4:32   וְעָשָׁן וְתֹכֶן וְעַיִן רִמּוֹן וְעֶ֫טֶם עֵיטָם וְחַצְרֵיהֶ֫ם
TC   ועיטן ותכן ועין ורמון עיטם וקסטרוותהון
LXX   καὶ Αισαν
Pesh.   ܘܐܝܬܡ

     TC reflects ועיטן.

1 Chr 4:34:   אֲמַצְיָה בֶּן־ וְיוֹשָׁה וִימְלֵךְ וּמְשׁוֹבָב
TC   אמציה: בר ויוטה וימלך ומן שובב
LXX   καὶ Ιωσια
Pesh.   ---

     TC reflects ויוטה.

1 Chr 5:12   בַּבָּשָׁן: וְשָׁפָט וְיַעְנַי
TC   בבותנן: דיינא ויעני
LXX   ὁ γραμματεὺς
Pesh.   ܘܗܘܐ ܐܝܟ ܘܗܘܐ ܕܝܢܐ ܕܥܡܠ ܠܡܠܗ ܘ

     TC reflects שופט.

1 Chr 6:55   מִגְרָשֶׁ֫יהָ וְאֶת־ בִּלְעָם וְאֶת־
TC   פרוילה[א] ית יבלעם וית
LXX   Ιεβλααμ
Pesh.   ܘܒܠܡ

     TC reflects יִבְלְעָם.

1 Chr 7:1: אַרְבָּעָה וְשִׁמְרוֹן יָשׁוּב (ק׳) וּפוּאָה תּוֹלָע יִשָּׂשׂכָר וְלִבְנֵי
TC   ארבעא: ושמרון ויוב ופוה תולע ישׁשכר ולבני
LXX   καὶ Ιασουβ καὶ Φουα
Pesh.   ܘܝܫܘܒ ܘܦܘܐ

     TC reflects ופוה and ויוב, influenced by MT Gen 46:13.

1 Chr 7:6: שְׁלֹשָׁה וִידִיעֲאֵל וָבֶ֫כֶר בֶּ֫לַע בִּנְיָמִ֫ן בני
TC   תלתה: וידעיה ובכר בלע בנימין בני
LXX   καὶ Ιαδιηλ Βενιαμιν
Pesh.   ܘܒܟܪ ܘܒܠܥ

     TC reflects בני בנימן and וידעיה.

1 Chr 7:13: בִּלְהָה בְּנֵי וְשַׁלּוּם וְיֵצֶר וְגוּנִי יַחֲצִיאֵל נַפְתָּלִי בְּנֵי
TC   בלהה: בני ושלם ויצר וגני יחצאל נפתלי בני
LXX   καὶ Σαλωμ   Ιασιηλ
Pesh.   ܘܫܠܡ   ܝܚܨܝܐܝܠ

TC reflects יַחְצְאֵל and וְשַׁלֵּם, influenced by MT Gen 46:24.

1 Chr 7:28: וּבְנֹתֶיהָ עַד־עַיָּה וּבְנֹתֶיהָ וּשְׁכֶם גֶּזֶר וְלַמַּעֲרָב
TC   וכופרנהא עדיה ובנתיהא ושכם גזר ולמערבא
LXX   ἕως Γαιαν
Pesh.   ܘܥܝܬܐ

TC reflects עַד־עַיָּה.

1 Chr 8:8: נָשָׁיו בַּעְרָא וְאֶת־ חוּשִׁים אֹתָם שִׁלְּחוֹ מִן־ ... וְשַׁחֲרַיִם הוֹלִיד
TC   נשוהי בערה ית חושים ית ונסיבנון ותב יתהון דפטר בתר מן ... אוליד ושחרים
Pesh.   ---
LXX ... μετὰ τὸ ἀποστεῖλαι αὐτὸν   Ωσιμ καὶ τὴν Βααδα γυναῖκα αὐτοῦ

TC seems to reflect אֶת־חוּשִׁים.

1 Chr 8:12: וְשָׁמֶד וּמִשְׁעָם עֵבֶר אֶלְפַּעַל וּבְנֵי
TC   ושמר ומשעם עבר אלפעל ובני
LXX   Σεμμηρ
Pesh.   ܘܫܡܪ

TC reflects ושמר.

1 Chr 11:38: בֶּן־הַגְרִי מִבְחָר
TC   גדא: בר מבחר
LXX   Αγαρι
Pesh.   ܒܪ ܡܢ ܓܕܝ

TC reflects בֶּן־הַגְדִי.

1 Chr 27:25 עֲדִיאֵל בֶּן־ עַזְמָוֶת הַמֶּלֶךְ אֹצָרוֹת וְעַל
TC   עדיאל בר עזמות מלכא בית תסברי ועל
LXX   τοῦ βασιλέως   τῶν θησαυρῶν
Pesh.   ܕܡܠܟܐ   ܐܘܨܖܐ

TC reflects וְעַל אֹצָרוֹת בֵּית הַמֶּלֶךְ.

1 Chr 29:22 לְנָגִיד לַה' וַיִּמְשְׁחוּ בֶּן־דָּוִיד לִשְׁלֹמֹה שֵׁנִית וַיַּמְלִיכוּ
TC   למלכא קדם ה' ומשחוהי דוד בר שלמה תנינות ית ואמליכו
LXX   καὶ ἔχρισαν αὐτὸν
Pesh.   ---

TC reflects וַיִּמְשָׁחוּהוּ.

2 Chr 1:5   וּמִזְבַּח הַנְּחֹשֶׁת אֲשֶׁר עָשָׂה בְּצַלְאֵל בֶּן־אוּרִי בֶן־חוּר שָׁם   לִפְנֵי מִשְׁכַּן הֹ'

TC   ומדבחא דנחשא די עבד   בצלאל בר אורי בר חור שׁוי   קדם משכנא דה'

LXX   ἐκεῖ ἦν

Pesh.   ܗܘܐ ܬܡܢ

    TC reflects שָׁם.

2 Chr 3:11   כְּנַף הָאֶחָד ... וְהַכָּנָף הָאַחֶרֶת אַמּוֹת חָמֵשׁ מַגִּיעַ לִכְנַף הַכְּרוּב הָאַחֵר:

TC   גדפא חד ... וגדפא חורניתא אמין חמש מטי לגדפא דכרוביא חד:

LXX   τοῦ ἑτέρου

Pesh.   ܐܚܪܢܐ

2 Chr 3:12   וּכְנַף הַכְּרוּב הָאֶחָד ... וְהַכָּנָף הָאַחֶרֶת ... דְּבֵקָה לִכְנַף הַכְּרוּב הָאַחֵר:

TC   וגדפא דכרובא חד ... וגדפי חורניתא ... מדבקא לגדפא דכרוביא חד:

LXX   τοῦ ἑτέρου

Pesh.   ܐܚܪܢܐ

    In both adjacent verses, TC reflects הָאֶחָד.

2 Chr 13:3   ... אַרְבַּע מֵאוֹת אֶלֶף אִישׁ בָּחוּר ... בִּשְׁמוֹנֶה מֵאוֹת אֶלֶף אִישׁ בָּחוּר

TC   ... ארבע מאה אלפין גוברין עולימין ... בתמני מאה אלפין גוברין

LXX   δυνατοί

Pesh.   ܓܒܪܐ

    TC reflects the lack of the word בָּחוּר.

2 Chr 19:11   בֶּן־יִשְׁמָעֵאל הַנָּגִיד   וּזְבַדְיָהוּ

TC   בר ישמעאל ארכונא   וזכריהו

LXX   καὶ Ζαβδιας

Pesh.   ܘܙܟܪܝܐ

    TC reflects וּזְכַרְיָהוּ.

2 Chr 20:25   שְׁלָלָם   אֶת־   לָבֹז   וְעַמּוֹ   יְהוֹשָׁפָט   וַיָּבֹא

TC   עדאיהון   למבוז   וקם   יהושפט   ואתא

LXX   καὶ ὁ λαὸς αὐτοῦ

Pesh.   ܘܩܡ ܐܦ ܝܘܫܦܛ

    TC reflects וְעָמַד.

2 Chr 22:7   אֶל־יוֹרָם   לָבוֹא   אֲחַזְיָהוּ   תְּבוּסַת   הָיְתָה   וּמֵאֱלֹהִים

TC   לות יורם   למיתי   אחזיהו   תסקפת   הות   ומן קדם ה'

LXX   καταστροφῂ

Pesh.   ܬܒܬܐ

    TC reflects תסבת אחזיהו or תסובת אחזיהו (cf. 2 Chr 10:15).

2 Chr 26:5   הָאֱלֹהִים   בִּרְאֹת   הַמֵּבִין
TC   דה׳   בדחלתא   דמליף
LXX   ἐν φόβῳ
Pesh.   ܗܘܐ ܕܡܠܦ

    TC reflects בִּרְאַת.

2 Chr 26:6   יַבְנֶה   חוֹמַת   וְאֶת־   גַּת   חוֹמַת   אֶת־   וַיִּפְרֹץ
TC   דעזה   שורא   וית   דגת   שורא   ית   ותרע
LXX   Ιαβνη
Pesh.   ܘܕܐܒܢܐ   ܫܘܪܐ ܕܓܬ

    TC reflects חוֹמַת עַזָּה.

2 Chr 26:7   וְהַמְּעוּנִים: בָּעַל   בְּגוּר־   הַיֹּשְׁבִים   (ק׳)   וְעַל־הָעַרְבִים
TC   מעון: ובמישר   בגזר   דיתבין   ועל ערבאי
LXX   ἐπὶ τῆς πέτρας
Pesh.   ---

    TC reflects בְּגֶזֶר.

2 Chr 28:3   בָּאֵשׁ   אֶת־בָּנָיו   וַיַּבְעֵר
TC   באשתא   ית בנוהי   ואעבר
LXX   καὶ διῆγεν
Pesh.   ܘܐܥܒܪ

    TC reflects וַיַּעֲבֵר (cf. the parallel at 2 Kgs 16:3).

2 Chr 28:19   יִשְׂרָאֵל   מֶלֶךְ־   אָחָז   בַּעֲבוּר   אֶת־יְהוּדָה   ה׳   הִכְנִיעַ   כִּי־
TC   דיהודה   מלכא   אחז   מן בגלל   ית יהודה   ה׳   אמאיך   ארום
LXX   Ιουδα βασιλέα
Pesh.   ܕܝܗܘܕܐ ܡܠܟܐ

    TC reflects מֶלֶךְ יְהוּדָה.

2 Chr 29:36   לָעָם   הָאֱלֹהִים   הֵכִין   עַל   וְכָל־הָעָם   יְחִזְקִיָּהוּ   וַיִּשְׂמַח
TC   דלבהון   יצרא   לעמא   דאתקן ה׳   מן בגלל   וכל עמא   יחזקיה   וחדא
LXX   τῷ λαῷ
Pesh.   ---

    TC reflects הֵכִין הָאֱלֹהִים לְעָם לִבָּם (and then, secondarily, הֵכִין הָאֱלֹהִים לָעָם לִבָּם).

2 Chr 30:12   ה׳:   בִּדְבַר   וְהַשָּׂרִים   הַמֶּלֶךְ   מִצְוַת   לַעֲשׂוֹת
TC   דה׳:   הי־כפתגמא   ורבניא   דמלכא   תפקדתא   למעבד
LXX   κυρίου   ἐν λόγῳ
Pesh.   ܗܘܐ ܕܡܠܟܐ ܐܝܟ ܦܘܩܕܢ

    TC reflects כִּדְבַר ה׳.

2 Chr 30:19 הָאֱלֹהִ֖ים בִּדְבַ֑ר לִדְר֣וֹשׁ הֵכִ֖ין לְבָב֥וֹ כָּל־
TC דאלהא דחלתא למתבע אתקין לבביה ארום
LXX πάσης
Pesh. ܟܠܗ

TC reflects כִּי לְבָב֥וֹ הֵכִ֖ין.

2 Chr 30:26 כָזֹ֖את בִּירוּשָׁלָ֑ם לֹ֣א יִשְׂרָאֵ֑ל מֶ֥לֶךְ בֶּן־דָּוִ֛יד שְׁלֹמֹ֧ה מִימֵ֞י כִּ֣י
TC בירושלם כדא הות לא דישראל מלכא בר שלמה יומי מן ארום
LXX οὐκ ἐγένετο
Pesh. ܠܐ ܗܘܐ

TC reflects לֹא הָיְתָה כָזֹאת.

2 Chr 32:5 הַמִּגְדָּלֽוֹת עַל־ וַיַּ֥עַל הַפְּרוּצָ֖ה אֶת־כָּל־הַחוֹמָ֥ה וַיִּ֣בֶן
TC מוגדליא עלוהי ואסיק דמתרעא ית כל שורא ובנא
LXX ---
Pesh. ---
Vulg. et extruxit turres desuper

TC reflects וַיַּעַל עֲלֵיהָ מִגְדָלוֹת.

2 Chr 32:22 מִסָּבִֽיב׃ וַיְנַהֲלֵ֖ם ... יֹשְׁבֵ֣י יְרוּשָׁלָ֑ם| וְאֵ֧ת אֶת־יְחִזְקִיָּ֛הוּ ה֥' וַיּ֣וֹשַׁע
TC חֲזוֹר־חֲזוֹר׃ לרוחצן ואשרנון ... יתבי ירושלם וית ית יחזקיהו ה' ופרק
Pesh. ---
LXX καὶ κατέπαυσεν αὐτοὺς
Vulg. ei quietem

TC likely reflects וַיָּנַח לָהֶם.

2 Chr 35:9 חָמֵ֥שׁ מֵאֽוֹת׃ וּבָקָ֖ר חֲמֵ֣שֶׁת אֲלָפִ֔ים לַפְּסָחִ֗ים לַלְוִיִּ֜ם הֵרִ֨ימוּ
TC מאה׃ חמש ותורין אלפין חמשא עאן לפסחיא לליוָאי אפרישו
LXX πρόβατα εἰς τὸ φασεχ
Pesh. ܠܦܨܚܐ ܚܡܫ ܐܠܦܝܢ

TC reflects לַפְּסָחִים צֹאן חֲמֵשֶׁת אֲלָפִים.

2 Chr 35:15 עֲבֹדָתָֽם מֵעַ֖ל לָס֖וּר לָהֶ֛ם אֵ֥ין
TC פולחנהון מכל למעדי להון לית
LXX λειτουργίας ἁγίων ἀπὸ τῆς
Pesh. ܡܢ ܟܠ ܕܬܫܡܫܬܗܘܢ

TC reflects מִכֹּל.

2 Chr 35:25   בְּקִינוֹתֵיהֶם עַל־יֹאשִׁיָּהוּ   וְהַשָּׁרוֹת | כָּל־ הַשָּׁרִים   וַיֹּאמְרוּ

TC   והוון מתיבין באילייהון על יאשיהו   ומטרוניתא   רברביא   ואמרין עמיה כל

LXX   καὶ αἱ ἄρχουσαι οἱ ἄρχοντες

Pesh.   ܐܡܪ̈ܬܐ ܘܪܘܪ̈ܒܢܐ ܟܠ

     TC reflects הַשָּׁרִים וְהַשָּׁרוֹת.

2 Chr 36:10   הֹ   בֵּית־   חֶמְדַּת   כְּלֵי עִם־ בָּבֶלָה וַיְבִאֵהוּ

TC   דה'   מקדשא   בית   רוגגת   כל עם לבבל ואיתיה

LXX   τῶν σκευῶν

Pesh.   ܘܡܐܢ̈ܐ

     TC reflects כֹּל חֶמְדַּת.

Ezra 1:3   וְיָעַל   עִמּוֹ   אֱלֹהָיו   יְהִי מִכָּל־עַמּוֹ מִי־בָכֶם

2 Chr 36:23:   וְיָעַל   עִמּוֹ   אֱלֹהָיו   הֹ מִכָּל־עַמּוֹ מִי־בָכֶם

TC   בסעדיה ויסק: מימרא דה'   יהא עמיה מכל דאית ביניה בכון מן

LXX   ὁ θεὸς αὐτοῦ   ἔσται

Pesh.   ܘܐܠܗܐ   ܢܗܘܐ

     TC reflects יְהִי אֱלֹהָיו.

4.2   *Differences in Vocalization*

1 Chr 4:34:   בֶּן־אֲמַצְיָה   וְיוֹשָׁה   וַיָּמְלֵךְ   וּמְשׁוֹבָב

TC   בר אמציה: ויוטה   וימלך   ומן שובב

LXX   καὶ Μοσωβαβ

Pesh.   ---

     TC reflects וּמְשׁוֹבָב.

1 Chr 8:38; 9:44   וְיִשְׁמָעֵאל   בֹּכְרוּ | עַזְרִיקָם   שְׁמֹתָם   וְאֵלֶּה

TC   וישמעאל   ובוכריה   עזריקם שמהתהון ואלין

LXX   πρωτότοκος αὐτοῦ

Pesh.   ܘܫܡܗ̈ܬܐ ܗܠܝܢ   ܥܙܪܝܩܡ   ܚܙܘ

     TC reflects בְּכֹרוֹ.

1 Chr 11:18   אֶל־דָּוִיד   וַיָּבִאוּ   וַיִּשְׁאֲבוּ

TC   לות דוד   ואתו   ונסיבו ונטלו

LXX   καὶ ἦλθον

Pesh.   ܘܐܬܘ ܘܢܣܒܘ ܘܐܙܠܘ

     TC reflects וַיָּבִאוּ.

1 Chr 17:6   שֹׁפְטֵי יִשְׂרָאֵל   אֶת־אַחַד   דִּבַּרְתִּי   הַדָּבָר
TC   דישראל נגודיא   מן   עם חד   מלילית   האפשר דמללא
LXX   εἰ λαλῶν   ἐλάλησα
Pesh.   ܕܠܡܐ ܡܠܠܐ ܐܡܪܬ
TJ 2 Sam 7:7   מלילית   הפתגם
   TC reflects הַדָּבֶּר דִּבַּרְתִּי.

2 Chr 11:23 ... יְהוּדָה   לְכָל־אַרְצוֹת   מִכָּל־בָּנָיו   וַיִּפְרֹץ   וַיִּבֶן
TC   ... יהודה דבית ארעתא כל על בנוי ומני קרוין ושפיץ   ובנא
LXX   διενοεῖτο αὐτὸν
Pesh.   ---
   TC reflects וַיִּבֶן.

2 Chr 16:4   וְאֵת אָבֵל מָיִם   וְאֶת־דָּן   אֶת־עִיּוֹן   וַיַּכּוּ
TC   ממערבא אבל וית   דן וית   עיון ית   ומחו
LXX   καὶ τὴν Αβελμαιν
Pesh.   ܡܚܐܘ ܠܥܝܢ ܘܠܐܒܠ
   TC reflects מָיִם.

2 Chr 24:5   הַלְוִיִּם: מִהֲרוּ   וְלֹא   לְדַבֵּר   וְאַתֶּם תְּמַהֲרוּ
TC   ליואי: סרהיבו   ולא   למללא   ואתון תסרהבון
LXX   λαλῆσαι
Pesh.   ܠܡܡܠܠܘ
   TC reflects לְדַבֵּר.

2 Chr 35:12   לַבֹּקֶר: וְכֵן
TC   לצפרא: והכדין
LXX   εἰς τὸ πρωΐ
Pesh.   ܦܘܩ ܢܦܩ ܟܠ ܡܢ ܕܗܘܐ ܕܢܦܩܘܢ ܘܗܘ
   TC reflects לַבֹּקֶר.

4.3   *Differences in Syntactic Division*

1 Chr 7:12   אַחֵר: בְּנֵי חֻשִׁם בְּנֵי עִיר וְחֻפִּם וְשֻׁפִּם
TC   אחר: בני חשים יתבי קרית וחפים ושפים
   TC reflects עִיר חֻשִׁם as a single construct phrase.

1 Chr 7:14   אֶת־מָכִיר   הָאֲרַמִּיָּה יָלְדָה   פִּילַגְשׁוֹ   אֲשֶׁר יָלְדָה אַשְׂרִיאֵל מְנַשֶּׁה בְּנֵי
TC   ית מכיר   ארמיתא וילידת   פילקתיה   דילידת אשריאל מנשה בני
LXX   ἡ παλλακὴ αὐτοῦ   ὃν ἔτεκεν
Pesh.   ܘܠܕܬ ܠܡܟܝܪ   ... ܕܝܠܕܬ ܠܡ ܐܫܪܝܐܝܠ

TC reads ילדה (appearance I) as the predicate of פִּילַגְשׁוֹ, whose clause ends with the word הָאֲרַמִּיָּה. In order to open a new clause with the following word, ילדה (appearance II), Peshiṭta and TC added a conjunctive *waw* to the corresponding Aramaic word.

1 Chr 9:1   כְּתוּבִים   וְהִנָּם   הִתְיַחְשׂוּ   וְכָל־יִשְׂרָאֵל
TC   כתיבין   והא אנון   אתיחסו   וכולהון ישר[אל]

1 Chr (cont.)   בְּמַעְלָם: לְבָבֶל   הָגְלוּ   וִיהוּדָה   מַלְכֵי יִשְׂרָאֵל   עַל־סֵפֶר
TC   מטול שקריהון: לבבל   בגלותא ואזלו   יהודה דבית ומלכיא ישראל דבית מלכיא   ספר על
LXX   ... ἐν βιβλίῳ τῶν βασιλέων Ισραηλ καὶ Ιουδα μετὰ τῶν ἀποικισθέντων ...

TC reads the name of the book containing the names of all of Israel as the Book of the Kings of Israel and Judah. Because he read ישראל ויהודה within the same syntactic clause, the targumist was compelled to add a conjunctive *waw* to the verb אזלו (corresponding to הָגְלוּ).

1 Chr 22:7   בַּיִת   לִבְנוֹת   עִם־לְבָבִי   הָיָה   אֲנִי   (קר״) בְּנִי   (כתיב) בנו   לִשְׁלֹמֹה דָוִיד וַיֹּאמֶר
TC   מוקדשא בית למבני   לבבי עם   הוה   אנא   בריה   לשלמה דוד ואמר
LXX   Τέκνον

TC reads בנו in apposition with שלמה. See also the difference between *ketiv* and *qere*, below.

2 Chr 20:25   שְׁלָלָם   אֶת־   לָבֹז   וְעַמּוֹ   יְהוֹשָׁפָט   וַיָּבֹא
TC   עדאיהון   למבוז   וקם   יהושפט   ואתא
LXX   καὶ ὁ λαὸς αὐτοῦ
Pesh.   ܘܥܡܗ ܕܢܒܙܘܢ

TC reads וְעָמַד as the governing verb over the infinitive לָבֹז. This verse also reflects a consonantal variant, as mentioned above.

2 Chr 26:7   וְהַמְּעוּנִים: בְּעַל־   בְּגוּר־   הַיֹּשְׁבִים   (ק׳) וְעַל־הָעַרְבִים
TC   מעון: ובמישר   בגזר   דיתבין   ועל ערבאי
LXX
Pesh.   ---

TC reads בעל as the nomen regens of the following word (מעון/והמעונים).

4.4   *Ketiv and Qere*

There are some 80 *ketiv/qere* notations in MT Chronicles.[26] As is common in other Targums,[27] TC typically corresponds to the *qere*.[28] Sometimes TC can be read as corresponding both to the *ketiv* and to the *qere*. In only a few cases, however, generally concerning substitution of *waw* and *yod*, TC corresponds only to the *ketiv* in MT and not to the *qere*. These few variants, moreover, generally reflect the version found in MS V, whereas other MSS of *Tg. Chr* tend more heavily toward the *qere*. Following are these few cases:

1 Chr 7:34   (קרי) וְרָהְגָּה   (כתיב) ורוהגה   וּבְנֵי שֶׁמֶר אֲחִי
TC   ורוהגה

1 Chr 8:25:   בְּנֵי שָׁשָׁק: (קרי) וּפְנוּאֵל   (כתיב) ופניאל   וְיִפְדְיָה וּפְנִיאֵל
TC   ופניא[ל]

1 Chr 9:4   בְּנֵי־פֶרֶץ   (קרי) בֶּן־   (כתיב) בָּנִי   בֶּן־אַמְרִי בֶן־בְּנִימָן
TC   בני פרץ   מן   בר בנימן

1 Chr 22:7   לִבְנוֹת בֵּית   אֲנִי הָיָה עִם־לְבָבִי   (קרי) בְּנִי   (כתיב) בנו   וַיֹּאמֶר דָּוִיד לִשְׁלֹמֹה בנו
TC   אנא הוה עם לבבי למבני בית מוקדשא   ואמר דוד לשלמה בריה
LXX   Τέκνον

TC reflects בְּנוֹ.

1 Chr 24:24   (קרי) שָׁמִיר   (כתיב) שמור   שמור מִיכָה   לִבְנֵי
TC   שמור

---

26   1 Chr 1:11, 46, 51; 2:16, 55; 3:24; 4:7, 20, 41; 6:11, 20; 7:1, 10, 31, 34; 8:25; 9:4, 33, 35; 11:11, 17, 20, 44; 12:3, 6, 16, 19; 14:1, 10; 15:24; 18:10; 20:5; 22:7; 23:9; 24:24; 25:1; 26:25; 27:12, 29; 29:16; 2 Chr 3:17; 4:11; 5:12, 13; 7:6; 8:10, 18; 9:10, 29; 11:18; 13:14; 17:8; 18:8, 33; 24:25, 27; 25:17; 26:3, 7, 11, 21; 29:8, 13, 14, 28; 31:12, 13, 21; 33:16; 34:5, 6, 9, 22, 25; 35:3, 4, 9; 36:14, 17.

27   Cf. Sperber, vol. IVb, pp. 132–133. Note his short, but telling, remark (p. 133): "The Targum follows *qere* in the places that were not quoted here".

28   Churgin *Hagiographa*, p. 241, writes that TC adheres to the *ketiv* in only one instance, viz. 2 Chr 34:4. In point of fact, as we shall see below, there are additional cases. In any event, the rendering of the verse to which Churgin refers is not uniform in the manuscripts of TC. Churgin relied on de Lagarde, whose edition's ויתבי (as in MS C) indeed corresponds to the *ketiv* (as is the case with LXX and Peshiṭta). MSS V and E, however, read as follows, corresponding to the *qere*:

2 Chr 34:9:   יְרוּשָׁלָם: (קרי) וַיָּשֻׁבוּ   (כתיב) וישבי
TC   לירושלם: ותבו
LXX   καὶ οἰκούντων
Pesh.   ܒܐܘܪܫܠܡ

2 Chr 9:10 (קרי) חוּרָם֙ (כתיב) חירם וְגַם־עַבְדֵי֩
TC   חירם

2 Chr 13:19 (קרי) עֶפְרַ֔יִן (כתיב) עפרון וְאֶת־
TC   עפרון

2 Chr 35:9 (קרי) וְכָנַנְיָ֡הוּ (כתיב) וכוניה
TC   וכוניה

5   Survey of Literature of TC

Scholarly engagement with TC began in nineteenth century Germany amongst a circle of scholars devoted to *Wissenschaft des Judentums*, the scientific study of Jewish literature and culture. Zunz laid the cornerstone of familiarity with TC when he determined, according to its style and tendency to weave *Aggadot* into its thread, that the work was translated in the Land of Israel.[29] In general, he dated the Targums of the Hagiographa within a creative period that concluded in the mid-eighth century BCE.[30]

In 1869, J.H. Schorr published a list of places in TC that indicated discrepancies between the translation's Hebrew *Vorlage* and the Masoretic Text.[31] Over the years, additional examples were added to Schorr's list by others (notably Rosenberg and Kohler, as well as Churgin, whose contribution to TC research is discussed below).

In 1870, M. Rosenberg and K. Kohler published the first comprehensive study of TC.[32] The first to discuss the targumist's translation techniques, including the reasons that compelled him to deviate from literal translation, they traced TC's sources; compared the texts of the two manuscripts that had been published by their time (namely E and C); discussed TC's grammatical forms; investigated the identification of the author/s of the translation, its possible dating, and the *Sitz im Leben* that could have generated such a work.

Rosenberg and Kohler concluded that TC was compiled in the Land of Israel; that it was gradually compiled, first orally and then recorded in writing; that

---

29   Zunz, p. 40; p. 265, n. 88.
30   Zunz, p. 152. Here Zunz comments on all the Targums to the Hagiographa in general and does not provide examples or evidence for his claim. On p. 11 (in chapter 2) he notes that TC is a late composition, without going into detail, and that TJ precedes it.
31   Schorr, bibliography.
32   Rosenberg-Kohler, bibliography.

the translation was not the product of synagogues but rather of schools, where children were taught the Bible by rote; and that the text originated no earlier than the fourth century CE, but no later than the eighth century.[33] Thus, their conclusions supported Zunz's opinion. The importance of their study was the fruit of their scientific, systematic labor, which was not applied to TC before them. The study was divided into many categories, each supported with concrete examples from the Targum. This division allowed detection of the targumist's various objectives and what motivated the additions in his translation. The first study that allowed the reader to recognize many of TC's features and characteristics, Rosenberg and Kohler's work became the authoritative source of information about TC for those who succeeded them. Many encyclopedia editors' entries about TC, or introductions to works on the topic, repeat the material first brought by Rosenberg and Kohler, firsthand or even secondhand.[34] Without undermining the importance of their study, however, I believe that several of their conclusions call for reevaluation. Fixing the eighth century as the latest possible time of compilation is based on the assumption that a translation lacking Arabic words was necessarily compiled before Arabic replaced Aramaic as the spoken language of the Jews in Palestine. Moreover, a close reading of TC in its entirety raises several details—which will be discussed in the present work—which seem incompatible with the dating and place of compilation proposed by Rosenberg and Kohler.

In his 1945 book about the Targums of the Hagiographa, P. Churgin devoted a generous chapter to TC.[35] This study reinforced Rosenberg and Kohler's conclusions, but also advanced research beyond their achievements in several areas. Churgin's work contributed to understanding of TC's midrashic sources. He even compared TC to other Aramaic Targums (Palestinian Pentateuchal Targums, Targum Jonathan to the Prophets), and attempted to explain the affinity between the different translations. Churgin argued that TC follows Targum Jonathan in chapters parallel to Samuel and Kings, but still pointed out differences between the translation of individual words in each work. Churgin explained this phenomenon with the hypothesis that the targumist

---

33 Rosenberg-Kohler, pp. 273–277.

34 So, e.g., Bacher *JE*; Grossfeld *EJ*; Le Déaut—Robert, vol. 1, pp. 9–32; Komlosh *Bible*, pp. 97–99; Komlosh *EB*; Alexander *ABD*; McIvor, pp. 11–31; Kalimi *Interpretation*, pp. 29–30; Kalimi *Journey*, pp. 155–176. B. Eisenberg wrote a study on TC in 1938, which is mentioned in Komlosh *Bible*, pp. 97–98, who comments that it was written in Hungarian and refers to five pages in the study that discuss the text of the Targum. Grossfeld *Bibliography*, p. 46, mentions that this study is only on the 1 Chronicles part of TC.

35 Churgin *Hagiographa*, pp. 236–275.

used a different, earlier Palestinian version of Targum Jonathan, which was
lost, rather than the Babylonian version that exists today. This claim, in my
opinion, makes several unnecessary assumptions, and a reexamination of the
relationship between TC and Targum Jonathan will shed new light on the similarities and differences between them. Moreover, the relationship between TC
and Pentateuchal Targums is also in need of reappraisal, as well as the identification of the targumist's literary sources.

Sperber saw importance in comparison of TC and Targum Jonathan's parallel chapters in Samuel and Kings. In his edition, he added several pages in
which he arranged the parallel narratives in columns on the same page without making any actual conclusions, consciously and deliberately anticipating
the analysis of future scholars:[36]

> Of special interest is a comparison of the vocabulary used by the Targum
> of Chronicles with that of corresponding parallel passages in the Targum
> to the Former Prophets. Here I bring a number of such passages in the
> hope that this may induce a younger scholar to make it the subject of a
> more detailed investigation, which I firmly believe will lead to interesting
> results.

It is my hope that this book rises to this renowned scholar's challenge.

The Le Déaut-Robert edition includes, as mentioned, a critical apparatus
with textual variants from other manuscripts and footnotes throughout the
translation. The compilers' comments are, in a sense, a brief commentary on
the translation, and thus make an important contribution to the study. This edition has many advantages, and renders the TC text more accessible. However,
its contribution to understanding of the work's origins and techniques does
not exceed that of its predecessors, and its commentary fails to relate to many
of the translation's finer points.

In 1981, R.T. White wrote his doctoral dissertation on TC's language in comparison to different Aramaic dialects. White's study is chiefly a lexical comparison between TC and other Aramaic translations. White concludes that the
linguistic affinity between TC and the Pentateuchal Targum Pseudo-Jonathan is
greater than TC and the so-called Targum Neophyti.[37] White detects similarity

---

36   Sperber, vol. 4a, p. 72.

37   I say "so-called" because the name, Targum Neophyti, is misleading. Neophyti is, at best, a
      name that describes the manuscript in which this Targum is found (MS Neophyti 1, also
      spelled Neofiti), but it does not describe the text of this Targum. The manuscript itself
      describes this Targum as תרגום חומש ירושלמי, i.e. Palestinian Pentateuchal Targum. So

between Pseudo-Jonathan and TC's general vocabulary, and Imperial Aramaic. This study's strength lies in its meticulous examination of equivalent words in different Targums. Its weakness, however, lies in the fact that its proposed conclusions do not naturally stem from its findings. For example, the affinity between the Targums' language and Imperial Aramaic, together with several statements from the Talmud and the Zohar, lead him to backdate the original compilation date of Targum Pseudo-Jonathan by centuries in order to entertain the possibility that its author is none other than Jonathan the son of Uziel.[38] These conclusions, however, should not be accepted, seeing as these connections can be explained, more simply, as part of the features of the special dialect both Targums share.

In 1994, McIvor published an English translation of TC.[39] This rendered the work accessible to an English-speaking audience. The edition reviews the research about TC up to its own publication, and the influence of the Le Déaut-Robert edition is particularly salient. McIvor's commentary is more substantial than Le Déaut and Robert's, and he guides the reader through exegetical difficulties more assiduously, but he, too, leaves much untrodden ground for his successors.[40]

In 2009, H. Hamiel devoted an extensive chapter in his volume on the Targums to the Hagiographa to TC.[41] In his work, Hamiel discussed the targumist's treatment of names of people and nations, presenting units of TC together with their parallel units in other works, and commented on significant differences between them. Compiling a list of TC's aggadic additions, he attempted to determine their sources, identifying several sources which had not been mentioned by Churgin or others. Moreover, Hamiel reviewed several translation techniques, as well as terms the targumist used in order to avoid anthropomorphism of God. Hamiel's study is, to date, the most extensive collection of textual examples that illustrate TC phenomena. However, the discussions of the examples he brings are usually brief, presenting the reader with an incomplete picture. He refers to the Sperber edition, despite his awareness of

---

when scholars use the term Targum Neophyti, it should be as an abbreviation of, "The Palestinian Pentateuchal Targum found in MS Neophyti 1". It is in this sense that I use the term throughout this book.

38   White, p. 271.

39   McIvor, bibliography.

40   In addition to the aforementioned studies, some studies on singular verses or a small unit within TC were published as well; cf. Kalimi *Bibliography*, pp. 63–64. These studies are not enumerated here, as they do not influence this survey of literature.

41   Hamiel, pp. 357–490.

the more precise Le Déaut-Robert edition. In some cases, his use of the Sperber edition results in inaccurate explanations.

6 Research Tools

From the days of S.D. Luzzatto and A. Geiger, the Aramaic Targums were considered objects of scientific research that enriched biblical scholarship, but the latest generation has seen growing interest in these works in themselves, as well as studies and monographs that focus upon the Targums of individual books of the Bible. Some explore the translation techniques employed, others discuss the translators' beliefs, opinions and objectives, while yet others consider the criteria for exegetical influence upon the Targum in question.[42] As I began my task after interest in the Aramaic Targums had already gathered momentum, I was granted the privilege of learning from an entire range of scholarly approaches and methods as presented in the works of many great scholars; and the privilege of incorporating selected methods into this study, as need arose.

The various reference works and dictionaries used throughout this study are listed in the bibliography at the end of this work. Other study tools, whose importance cannot be overestimated, are the electronic databases at this generation's disposal. I made extensive and highly instrumental use of the texts and search tools developed by the Comprehensive Aramaic Lexicon Project (CAL), the Academy of the Hebrew Language's Historical Dictionary Project, the Accordance Bible Study program, the Saul Lieberman Institute's Babylonian Talmud Database, Bar Ilan University's Responsa Project, and the *Mikra'ot Gedolot Haketer* initiative.

In addition to these resources, I created two vital study tools of my own in preparation for my research: a concordance and a synopsis. The concordance records each word in the Targum with its meaning, the places it appears in the

---

42 There is a broad literature of commentaries to individual Targums and to the origins and nature of various Targums. Thus, to name a few, see (full details of the following in bibliography) Posen on Onqelos, Díez Macho on MS Neophyti 1, Shinan on Pseudo-Jonathan, Churgin on Jonathan to the Prophets and the Targums to the Hagiographa, Smelik on Jonathan to the book of Judges, van Staalduine-Sulman on Jonathan to Samuel, Dray on Jonathan to Kings, Weiss on Targum Job. *The Aramaic Bible* series (Collegeville 1987–2007) offers an English translation, an introduction and a commentary on most of the targumic literature, written by some of the most influential scholars of the last generation. On top of these, many individual articles have been published.

text, and, usually, its context. I compiled the synopsis by listing each word in Chronicles together with its Aramaic translation, its Syriac translation, and—in units parallel to other biblical works—its parallel Hebrew term together with its own Aramaic translation.[43] They remain unpublished as of yet.

7 Structure and Methods of This Work

Since Rosenberg and Kohler's time, different scholars have proposed that TC is a work that crystallized over the generations, accumulating several textual layers as the translation passed from hand to hand, until it was finally edited and concluded.[44] Churgin raised the possibility that a few of the Targum's aggadic additions were incorporated at a secondary stage.[45] I relate to TC as a single, unified work from start to finish, without making systematic attempts to differentiate between different redactive layers. I chose this approach because the Targum is such an intricate mosaic of sources that differentiation between redactive layers and use of other literary sources is problematic to the point of being counterproductive. It is even difficult to distinguish between the hand of translator and editor in regard to the aforementioned addition of alternate translations marked with the abbreviation ל״א. I therefore determined that scholarly prudence demanded that I study the work in its entirety, in its present form, although this does not rule out the possibility that different redactive layers may emerge through future research.

In the second chapter, I will describe principal translation techniques employed in TC, and the exegetic propensities they indicate. Methodologically, analysis of the translation is a gradual process: it should begin with description of the translation techniques used, followed by analysis of the interpretative dimension added through translation, and finally, it is possible to reach general conclusions about the entire work.[46] In his study of the Septuagint,

---

43 A current work in progress of mine is The Equivalent Project, which is intended to provide a synopsis and comprehensive list of equivalents for the Hebrew Bible and its ancient translations. The first stage of The Equivalent Project encompasses the Torah and its Targums. My comprehensive synopsis of Chronicles, its Targum, its Peshiṭta and its parallels is scheduled to be incorporated into this research project in the future.

44 Rosenberg-Kohler, p. 273, presume that the Targum was transmitted first in oral form and in a later stage it was put in writing.

45 Churgin Hagiographa, p. 244.

46 Cf., for example, Bernstein's comments (p. 30) on the desired methodology for the study of Targum.

E. Tov differentiates between literal and free translation.[47] The more literal the translation, the more difficult it becomes for the scholar to draw positive conclusions about the nature of the translation. Tov's observation serves both his analysis of the Hebrew *Vorlage* at the translator's disposal and his attempts to isolate the fingerprints that testify not to the original text but to characterization of the translator himself. While this model was developed to facilitate analysis of the Greek translation, it is also useful for Aramaic translations (stylistic differences considered). It allows me to offer an initial description of TC using its parameters:[48] while the work's frame inclines towards literal translation, it also contains short, freer extensions, as well as notable expansions protruding from its frame.

The Aramaic material equivalent to the Hebrew source—which is, in general, the vast majority of most Targums—serves as the main exploration grounds of the targumist's methodology. Even here, the translator's approach begins to emerge, as his selection of a particular Aramaic root to represent a particular Hebrew root reflects a particular propensity. In this chapter, I included a list of translation techniques that, to my mind, faithfully and consistently characterize TC. Some describe basic techniques employed throughout targumic literature; others reveal this specific targumist's approaches and objectives.

In the third chapter, I sketch out TC's relationship with Targum Jonathan. In such a work as TC, which contains many chapters that are parallel to Samuel and Kings, it was necessary to conduct an individual comparison of this parallel material. Scholars have already noted the close affinity between TC and the corresponding chapters of Targum Jonathan (TJ), but this proximity is by no means absolute. I therefore closely examined the translators' methods of the material in question, devoting the chapter to this comparison.

Chapter four surveys the units in Chronicles parallel with the Torah and compares TC with the Pentateuchal Targums in these units. The parallel verses are studied and cases of influence of the Pentateuchal Targums on TC are examined and ties between the individual works are established. This becomes most prominent with regard to Targum Pseudo-Jonathan.

The emerging connection between TC and TPJ—which was noticed to a certain degree by past scholars—is explored in great depth in chapter five. The vocabulary shared by these two Targums is studied, in order to determine if TPJ's influence on TC extends beyond the units that are parallel to the Pentateuch. Indeed, cases of direct dependence of TC upon TPJ are detected

---

47   Tov *LXX*, pp. 18–31.
48   Flesher *Scripture*, pp. 64–65, contains similar sentiments and refers to Barr's discussion of the Septuagint.

throughout the Torah. Due to recent developments in our understanding of TPJ's late origins, this has very important implications for determining the date of TC's composition.

Chapter six explores TC's relationship with the Targum of Psalms (TP). This study is divided into two distinct sections. The first part discusses just one word found in both Targums—הונגראי—which reveals much about the two works' time and place of composition. The second part is a systematic comparison of TC on 1 Chronicles 16 to the parallel chapters in Psalms. The purpose of this study is to determine if the many points of similarity between the two translations indicate a literary dependency between them or not.

The seventh chapter is devoted to a discussion of the many aggadic expansions TC that display a dependence on the Babylonian Talmud. TC's reliance on the Bavli is found to be relatively large, moreso than on all other rabbinic texts combined (excluding other Targums—depending on one's definition thereof). Of the seventy six expansions I isolated throughout TC, thirty three most probably rely on BT and another eight possibly rely on it.

Chapter eight studies the rest of the expansions with the purpose of discovering their source. Some are based on TPJ, others on traditions found also in MS Reuchlin, and yet others on various midrashic works. The sources of twelve expansions in TC remain unidentified and some of these may reflect the independent exegesis of the targumist.

The expansions studied in chapters seven and eight are potential windows to the world and objectives of the targumist, who did not merely convey the biblical source at hand, but embellished the Hebrew text with his own ideas or the ideas of others. There is great importance in identifying the general midrashic background on one hand, and his precise sources on the other; for both contribute to the understanding of the targumist's exegetical background and his world. These expansions illuminate the targumist's objectives, for even if they were brought from other sources, the decision to include them in the text and the way they were made to fit into the text reflect upon the targumist. Because many of these aggadic additions have not received due attention in previous studies, this discussion will serve as an opportunity to present new explanations for parts of the Targum and the way it interpreted its sources, thus contributing to our understanding of the work. Occasionally, I will even be able to pinpoint the version of the talmudic text the targumist had at his disposal. Once again, these details shed light on the targumist's textual and historical environment.

Comprehensive analysis of Targum Chronicles from different perspectives—the translation techniques employed; discussion of its lexicon; its ties to other Targums; tracing of its aggadic sources—and systematic presentation of its findings will award the due attention to a work that, while so impressive, has left to date so little an impression.

In the book's conclusion, chapter 9, I will attempt to connect many of the dots discovered throughout this book's various chapters with regard to TC's origins. I will attempt to offer novel ideas with regard to the following questions: When was TC composed? Where was TC composed? Why was TC composed? The conclusions I shall offer differ with those reached by previous scholars and may have implications for the study of other Targums as well. Indeed, to my mind they will warrant a rethinking of several key assumptions in the entire field of Targum studies.

CHAPTER 2

Principal Translation Techniques of Targum Chronicles

1   Opening

In this chapter we shall begin acquainting ourselves with the character of Targum Chronicles, drawing on concrete examples of several techniques employed by the targumist throughout his composition. Several methods characteristic of TC have been detailed in previous studies, each in the style of its particular author, and one need only consult them to find lists of the translation techniques and references to illustrative examples. I do not wish to reprise the work of my predecessors—indeed, in the present work I will not presume to provide a comprehensive list of all translation techniques used in TC. Nevertheless, several of the techniques employed in the translations of TC bear description here, for the following reasons:

1.   An account of the translation techniques used by the targumist is helpful for forming a fuller picture of the Targum itself and can be the first stage of a deeper consideration of the document.[1]

2.   There are aspects of TC that have not been described in previous scholarship or, at the least, have not been described sufficiently. This survey will provide some part of the discussion that is yet absent.

3.   Several of the phenomena described in this chapter prepare the ground for engagement in comparative scholarship between TC and other works. In this sense, the basis for the remaining chapters of this study is to be found in the present chapter. A wealth of references throughout the chapter will therefore direct the reader to more exhaustive discussions to be found elsewhere in this book.

Perusal of TC frequently brings the reader back to the Targums of the Torah and TJ to the Prophets. The latter is a valuable source due to the ample opportunities to compare its translations to verses in Samuel and Kings with those given by TC to parallel verses in Chronicles. The relationship between TC and TJ and other parallel Targums will be rigorously examined in chapters three through six (pp. 108–244 below). The main thrust of the present chapter, meanwhile, shall be an examination of how the author of TC coped with the large bulk of

---

1   Cf. the methodological comments by Bernstein, p. 30.

material in Chronicles that lacks parallels in other biblical books, where we
know the targumist did not have before him a pre-existing parallel Targum
upon which he could erect his own translation to the given verse. That is not
to say that targumic and midrashic traditions did not influence the targumist
in these cases, but these influences do not take the shape a fully formed existing translation of the given verse. Throughout this chapter, verses of TC will be
presented alongside their Hebrew counterparts. Due to the palpable influence
of the other translation traditions even in the case of verses of Chronicles that
lack parallels elsewhere, we shall make regular reference to these potential
sources of inspiration, comparing the translation techniques exhibited in TC
with those familiar to us from other translations.

2   Common Additions in the Aramaic Text

2.1   *Opening*

McIvor correctly asserted that the principal technique employed by the author
of TC is simply translation.[2] This statement is by no means trivial, although it
does not apply only to the author of TC. In reading TC, one senses that the author's underlying method was to offer a literal Aramaic edition of the Hebrew
text he had before him, as is the case with most of the Targums to biblical
prose. He does not busy himself, for the most part, with exposition of nonliteral strata, such as that found in the Targumim to Esther. To be sure, quite
a few verses in TC, in deviation from this rule, feature a midrashic-aggadic approach to the Hebrew *Vorlage*.[3] In quantitative terms, however, these comprise
a small minority next to the great majority of the verses of the book. In fact,
Targum Chronicles displays the lowest Growth Percentage of all the Targums
of the Hagiographa.[4] In the absence of a specific inclination on the targumist's

---

2   McIvor, p. 22.
3   These exceptions (or nearly all of them) will be presented and analyzed in chapters seven
    and eight of this book.
4   Growth Percentage is the term I use to express the ratio of words in a Targum to the words in
    the Hebrew source in the Bible it is purporting to translate. The higher the number of words
    in a Targum in comparison with the number of words in its Hebrew source, the higher that
    Targum's Growth Percentage will be. I gave a lecture on Growth Percentage in the Targums at
    the SBL 2017 Annual Meeting and an article of mine on this topic is at this time forthcoming.
    A full explanation of how the percentage figures were calculated will appear in that article.
    For the purpose of this book it will suffice to append the following list of Growth Percentage
    in all the Targums to the Hagiographa in order to illustrate Targum Chronicle's position at the
    bottom of this list. Obviously, it is not only the targumist's personal tendency to expansion
    alone that determines the resulting Growth Percentage, so the comparison between different
    books can be somewhat misleading and a close look at the details is necessary to ascertain

part to turn to midrashic interpretation, his tendency is to preserve the structure of the Hebrew verse, including both the literal meaning of each word and the number words and their order within the sentence.

Notwithstanding the targumist's aforementioned basic tendency to transmit an Aramaic text that parallels the Hebrew, the verses of TC diverge from the Hebrew with regard to many particulars. The author of TC systematically added specific elements to the Aramaic text to meet the demands of language, style, and expression. In instances where the diction of Chronicles is lacking, abbreviated, or not in keeping with the Aramaic dialect in which he wrote, the targumist inserted whatever elements were missing into the Aramaic as he went along. In the following paragraphs, I shall present examples of various types of supplementations and insertions that abound throughout TC.[5] What follows is not an exhaustive discussion of the ways in which TC deviates from its *Vorlage*, but will serve to draw attention to general and salient phenomena present throughout the Targum that together comprise one of the more pronounced features of its outer appearance.

2.2   *The Root* מנ״י *(to appoint)*

The Hebrew text of Chronicles frequently records officials' names while alongside them identifying their titles or responsibilities. Throughout the book, the title רֹאשׁ/הָרֹאשׁ (i.e. head or chief) is attached to men's names quite often. In some cases the book denotes the relationship between a person and his

---

the precise significance of these figures. Nevertheless, that Targum Chronicles appears at the bottom of the list is quite telling.

Growth Percentage in the Targums to the Hagiographa (in descending order):

Targum Song of Songs	425.27%
Targum Sheni of Esther	403.35%
Targum Ecclesiastes	154.51%
Targum Rishon of Esther	99.04%
Targum Lamentations	88.21%
Targum Ruth	68.56%
Targum Job	46.31%
Targum Proverbs	46.28%
Targum Psalms	44.28%
Targum Chronicles	24.15%

5   I have not included phenomena that go without saying in an Aramaic translation, such as frequent use of the subordinating particle ד-/ד״י to separate out Hebrew genitives. Regarding this I would note only that the usual structure "[pr. n.]-ד מלכא" as a parallel for the Hebrew "[pr. n.] מֶלֶךְ" occurs over seventy times in TC (1 Chr 3:2; 5:6, 17, 26; 14:1; 18:5, 9; 2 Chr 2:2, 10; 8:11; 12:2, 9; 16:1–3, 7; 18:3–5, 7–9, 17, 19, 25, 28–34; 21:2; 22:5–6; 25:17–18; 28:3, 5, 16, 19–21; 29:27; 30:26; 32:1, 7, 9–11, 21–22, 31; 33:11; 35:3–4, 20; 36:3–4, 6, 22–23). However, these are joined by the exception מליך מעכה at 1 Chr 19:17 as well as four references to מלכת שבא, all of the latter rendered as מלכת זמרגד rather than מלכתא דזמרגד (1 Chr 9:1, 3, 9, 12). See my discussion of זמרגד below, pp. 149–151.

area of responsibility with the preposition עַל. In instances of this sort, such as the examples that follow, the targumist inserts a verb of the root מנ״י (while adding ל-, עַל, or ב-):

1 Chr 5:15

MT   אָחִי֙ בֶּן־עַבְדִּיאֵ֔ל בֶּן־גּוּנִ֑י   רֹ֖אשׁ   לְבֵ֥ית אֲבוֹתָֽם׃

TC   אחי בר עבדאל בר גוני   מתמנא לרישא   לבית אבהתהון׃

NJPS: Ahi son of Abdiel son of Guni was chief of their clan.

Dost: Ahi son of Abdiel, son of Guni, who was *appointed* as the head of their fathers' house.

1 Chr 7:2

MT   וּבְנֵ֣י תוֹלָ֗ע עֻזִּ֤י וּרְפָיָה֙ ... וְיִבְשָׂ֖ם וּשְׁמוּאֵ֑ל   רָאשִׁ֖ים   לְבֵית־אֲבוֹתָ֥ם

TC   ובני תולע עזי ורפיה ... ויבשם ושמואל   ממנן רישין   על בית אבהתהון

NJPS: The sons of Tola: Uzzi, Rephaiah, Jeriel, Jahmai, Ibsam, Shemuel, chiefs of their clans

Dost: The sons of Tola: Uzzi, Rephaiah, Jeriel, Jahmai, Ibsam, and Samuel, who were *appointed* as chiefs over their ancestral houses

A verb from the root מנ״י with no corresponding verb in the Hebrew *Vorlage* is found in over fifty verses in TC.[6] Not included in this figure are the dozens of verses where the root מנ״י does in fact have a clear verbal equivalent in the Hebrew *Vorlage*, such as נת״ן, שי״ם, פק״ד, or צו״ה. In this respect the author of TC followed a path forged in equivalent cases in Targums that preceded him, such as those of Onqelos and Jonathan.[7] However, the great concentration of

---

6 Viz., 1 Chr 4:4, 42; 5:7, 15, 24, 36; 7:2–4, 7; 9:13, 17, 19, 21, 23,26–28, 31–32; 12:3; 16:7, 42; 18:15–17; 23:8, 11, 16–18; 25:2, 6; 26:24, 31; 27:3, 5, 7; 28:5; 29:11; 2 Chr 2:1; 7:6; 10:18; 11:23; 19:11; 20:27; 24:6, 11; 26:20–21; 28:7; 30:17; 31:10, 12; 34:10.

7 For example:

Gen 41:40

MT   אַתָּה֙ תִּהְיֶ֣ה   עַל־בֵּיתִ֔י וְעַל־פִּ֖יךָ   יִשַּׁ֣ק כָּל־עַמִּ֑י

TO   את תהי   ממנא על ביתי ועל מימרך יתזן כל עמי

NJPS: You shall be in charge of my court, and by your command shall all my people be directed; only with respect to the throne shall I be superior to you.

Clem: You will be *appointed* over my house, and at your word all my people will be fed. Only with regard to the throne of the kingdom will I be more honored than you.

Gen 41:33

MT   וְעַתָּה֙ יֵרֶ֣א פַרְעֹ֔ה אִ֥ישׁ נָב֖וֹן וְחָכָ֑ם   וִישִׁיתֵ֖הוּ עַל־   אֶ֥רֶץ מִצְרָֽיִם׃

TO   וכען יחזי פרעה גבר סוכלתן וחכים   וימנינה על   ארעא דמצרים׃

NJPS: Accordingly, let Pharaoh find a man of discernment and wisdom, and *set* him over the land of Egypt

verses containing lists of officials in Chronicles, relative to other biblical books, causes this element to stand out as a feature of TC more than of other scriptural translations.

2.3 *Group Markers*

As in several of the ancient targums, it is the translator's practice to indicate proper nouns that serve—in the context of Chronicles—as names of small groups within a larger nation, such as tribes or clans. Where a proper noun in Chronicles has the function of indicating a group and the targumist wishes to clarify that the entity in question is neither an entire nation nor an individual person, or else seeks to establish a logical correspondence between the noun and its verb in a sentence, he tends to precede these names with a word (and, on occasion, multiple words) precisely defining the function of the proper noun. The author of TC thus follows in the footsteps of TJ to the Prophets.[8] The three words most commonly added to a verse in Aramaic against such a backdrop are שבט, בית (sometimes in combination as שבטא דבית), and אנש/אנשי. For purposes of an initial illustration, we shall look to the paragraph at 1 Chr 27:16–22 listing the princes of the tribes of Israel, which features several such adjustments to the text:

1 Chr 27:16

MT	אֱלִיעֶ֖זֶר בֶּן־זִכְרִ֑י	נָגִ֔יד	לָרֽאוּבֵנִ֖י	יִשְׂרָאֵ֔ל	וְעַל֙ שִׁבְטֵ֣י
TC	אליעזר בר זכרי	נגודא	ראובן לשיבט	דישראל	ועל שבטיא
	בֶּן־מַעֲכָֽה:	שְׁפַטְיָ֖הוּ		לַשִּׁמְעוֹנִ֔י	
	בר מעכה:	שפטיהו	לשיבט	שמעון	

Clem: And now, let Pharaoh choose an intelligent and wise man and *appoint* him over the land of Egypt

1 Sam 12:13

MT	וְהִנֵּ֗ה נָתַ֨ן הַ֤' עֲלֵיכֶ֖ם מֶֽלֶךְ:
TJ	והא מני ה' עליכון מלכא:

NJPS: Well, the LORD has *set* a king over you!

Clem: behold, the Lord has [*appointed*—L.G.] over you as king

1 Kgs 4:6

MT	וַאֲחִישָׁ֖ר עַל־הַבָּ֑יִת וַאֲדֹנִירָ֥ם בֶּן־עַבְדָּ֖א עַל־ הַמַּֽס:
TJ	ואחישר ממנא על ביתא ואדונירם בר עבדא ממנא על מסקי מסין:

NJPS: Ahishar—in charge of the palace; and Adoniram son of Abda—in charge of the forced labor.

Clem: And Ahishar was *appointed* over the palace; and Adoniram son of Abda was *appointed* over the levying of taxes.

8 Smelik, pp. 330–331; van Staalduine-Sulman *TJ Samuel*, אנשא: pp. 157–158; ביתא: pp. 159–160.

NJPS: Over the tribes of Israel: Reuben: the chief officer, Eliezer son of Zichri. Simeon: Shephatiah son of Maaca.

Dost: Over the tribes of Israel: For *the tribe of Reuben*, the officer was Eliezer son of Zichri; for *the tribe of* Simeon, Shephatiah son of Maachah

1 Chr 27:17

MT   צָדֽוֹק: לְאַהֲרֹ֖ן   חֲשַׁבְיָ֥ה בֶן־קְמוּאֵ֑ל   לְלֵוִ֔י

TC   לשיבט לוי   חשביה בר קמואל   לבית אהרן   צדוק:

NJPS: Levi: Hashabiah son of Kemuel. Aaron: Zadok.

Dost: for *the tribe of* Levi, Hashabiah son of Kemuel; for *the house of* Aaron, Zadok

1 Chr 27:18

MT   עָמְרִ֖י בֶּן־מִיכָאֵֽל: אֱלִיה֖וּ מֵאֲחֵ֣י דָוִ֑יד לְיִ֨שָּׂשכָ֔ר   לִֽיהוּדָ֕ה

TC   לשיבט יהודה אליהו מאחי דוד   לשיבט ישישכר   עמרי בר מיכה:

NJPS: Judah: Elihu, of the brothers of David. Issachar: Omri son of Michael.

Dost: for *the tribe of* Judah, Elihu, one of the brothers of David; for *the tribe of* Issachar, Omri son of Micah

1 Chr 27:19

MT   לְעַזְרִיאֵֽל: יְרִימ֖וֹת בֶּן־   לְנַ֨פְתָּלִ֔י   יִשְׁמַֽעְיָ֖הוּ בֶּן־עֹבַדְיָ֑הוּ   לִזְבוּלֻ֕ן

TC   לשיבט זבולן   ישמעיהו בר עובדיהו לשיבט נפתלי   ירימות בר עזריאל:

NJPS: Zebulun: Ishmaiah son of Obadiah. Naphtali: Jerimoth son of Azriel.

Dost: for *the tribe of* Zebulun, Ishmaiah son of Obadiah; for *the tribe of* Naphtali, Jerimoth son of Azriel

1 Chr 27:20

MT   יוֹאֵ֖ל בֶּן־פְּדָיָֽהוּ:   לַחֲצִ֕י שֵׁ֣בֶט מְנַשֶּׁ֔ה   הוֹשֵׁ֖עַ בֶּן־עֲזַזְיָ֑הוּ   לִבְנֵ֣י אֶפְרַ֔יִם

TC   לבני אפרים   הושע בר עזיהו   לפלגות שבטא דמנשה   יואל בר פדהיהו:

NJPS: Ephraimites: Hoshea son of Azaziah. The half-tribe of Manasseh: Joel son of Pedaiah.

Dost: for the children of Ephraim, Hoshea son of Azaziah; for the half-tribe of Manasseh, Joel son of Pedaiah

1 Chr 27:21

MT   יַעֲשִׂיאֵ֖ל בֶּן־אַבְנֵֽר: זְכַרְיָ֑הוּ לְבִ֨נְיָמִ֔ן   גִּלְעָ֔דָה יִדּ֖וֹ בֶּן־   הַֽמְנַשֶּׁ֣ה   לַחֲצִ֞י

TC   לפלגות שבטא דמנשה דבגלעד ידו בר זכריהו לשיבט בנימן יעשיאל בר אבנר:

NJPS: Half Manasseh in Gilead: Iddo son of Zechariah. Benjamin: Jaasiel son of Abner.

Dost: for the half-*tribe of* Manasseh that is in Gilead, Iddo son of Zechariah; for *the tribe of* Benjamin, Jaasiel son of Abner

1 Chr 27:22

MT לְדָ֕ן עֲזַרְאֵ֖ל בֶּן־יְרֹחָ֑ם אֵ֥לֶּה שָׂרֵ֖י שִׁבְטֵ֥י יִשְׂרָאֵֽל׃

TC לשיבט דן עזראל בר ירוחם אלין רברבי שבטיא דישראל׃

NJPS: Dan: Azarel son of Jeroham. These were the officers of the tribes of Israel.

Dost: for *the tribe of* Dan, Azarel son of Jeroham. These were the leaders of the tribes of Israel.

The author of TC rendered the list with precision, systematically adding the word שבט before every tribal name not preceded by a modifier. He did the same in instances where a tribe's name appears with the adjectival sufformative *yod*, e.g. רְאוּבֵנִי and שִׁמְעֹנִי of v. 16, as is conventional in the targums of his predecessors Onqelos and Jonathan.[9] Upon encountering a name used to designate a group other than a traditional tribe—אַהֲרֹן of v. 17—he selected an alternative word that he found more appropriate to reflect the name's function as the designation of a group: בית אהרן (*house of* Aaron).[10]

This practice of the targumist is altogether common throughout TC, but does not comprise an absolute rule. Thus, for instance:

1 Chr 19:18 וַיָּ֣נָס אֲרָ֗ם מִלִּפְנֵ֣י יִשְׂרָאֵל֮ וַיַּהֲרֹ֣ג דָּוִ֗יד מֵאֲרָ֥ם ...

TC ואפכו אנשי ארם מן קדם ישראל וקטל דוד מאנשי ארם ...

TJ 2 Sam 10:18 ואפכו אנש ארם מן קדם ישראל וקטל דויד מארם ...

NJPS: But [Aram was] put to flight by Israel. David killed [of Aram]...

Dost: Then *the men of* Aram fled from before Israel, and David killed of *the men of* Aram ...

Clem: Then *the men of* Aram fled from before Israel, and David killed [of Aram]...

---

9   For example:

Deut 3:16

MT וְלָרֽאוּבֵנִ֣י וְלַגָּדִ֗י נָתַ֤תִּי מִן־הַגִּלְעָד֙ וְעַד־נַ֣חַל אַרְנֹ֔ן

TO ולשיבט ראובן ולשיבט גד יהבית מן גלעד ועד נחלא דארנון

NJPS: And to the Reubenites and the Gadites I assigned the part from Gilead down to the wadi Arnon

Clem: And to the *tribe of* Reuben and to the *tribe of* Gad I have given some of Gilead as far as the Wadi Arnon

Josh 22:1

MT אָ֚ז יִקְרָ֣א יְהוֹשֻׁ֔עַ לָרֽאוּבֵנִ֖י וְלַגָּדִ֑י וְלַחֲצִ֖י מַטֵּ֥ה מְנַשֶּֽׁה׃

TJ בכין קרא יהושע לשיבט ראובן ולשיבט גד ולפלגות שבטא דמנשה׃

NJPS: Then Joshua summoned the Reubenites, the Gadites, and the half tribe of Manasseh

Clem: Then Joshua summoned the *tribe of* Reuben, and the *tribe of* Gad, and the half-tribe of Manasseh

10   Cf. Ps 115:10, 12; 118:3; 135:19.

Following TJ to the parallel verse, the author of TC prefaced ארם where it appears at the beginning of the verse with the word אנשי. While TJ was content to employ only the first marker, the author of TC appended another such marker at the next appearance of ארם in the verse. Notwithstanding, the targumist did not feel compelled to add a similar marker to the word ישראל in this verse. This is not due to a general unsuitability of the noun ישראל to receive markers, as evidenced by the targumist's addition of the marker אנש prior to ישראל at 2 Chr 25:22—despite Jonathan's failure to do so in the parallel verse at 2 Kgs 14:12. A further difference between TJ and TC at the above verse concerns the number of the marker אנש/אנשי, which in TC appears in the plural and in TJ in the singular. Jonathan consistently uses this word thus;[11] in TC, however, though the word generally used is אנש, there are cases, such as in the present verse, where the word chosen is אנשי. It is clear from a survey of the targums to the Torah that the singular form, אנש, is characteristic of TO, while the plural, אנשי, is characteristic of TN. TJ maintains the tradition of TO, while the author of TC appears to have been influenced by both of these targumic traditions.

2 Chr 28:7

MT   וַיַּהֲרֹ֣ג זִכְרִ֣י ׀ גִּבּ֣וֹר   אֶפְרַ֗יִם   אֶת־מַעֲשֵׂיָ֙הוּ֙ בֶּן־הַמֶּ֔לֶךְ
TC   וקטל זכרי   גברא   דבית אפרים ית מעשיהו בר מלכא

NJPS: Zichri, the champion of Ephraim, killed Maaseiah the king's son,
Dost: Zichri, a warrior of [*the house of*—L.G.] Ephraim, killed Maaseiah, the son of the king.

1 Chr 5:41

MT   בְּהַגְל֣וֹת ה' אֶת־   יְהוּדָ֖ה וִירוּשָׁלִָ֑ם   בְּיַ֖ד נְבֻכַדְנֶאצַּֽר׃
TC   כד אגלי ה' ית אנש יהודה ויתבי ירושלם ביד נבוכ[ד]נצר׃
NJPS: and Jehozadak went into exile when the LORD exiled Judah and Jerusalem by the hand of Nebuchadnezzar.
Dost: Jehozadak went into exile when the Lord exiled by the hand of Nebuchadnezzar *the people of* Judah and *the inhabitants of* Jerusalem

In some cases we see that the author of TC prefaced a Hebrew word denoting a place (country, city, or otherwise) with the word יתבי (such as יתבי ירושלים at 1 Chr 5:41, above), in the interest of avoiding monotony. This practice is

---

11   The word אנשי (in the plural) appears dozens of times in TJ, but always corresponding to אנשי in the Hebrew *Vorlage*, with only a single exception (1 Sam 5:3, אנשי אשדוד for אַשְׁדּוֹדִים). This exception, however, appears in the plural in order to reflect the plural morpheme at the conclusion of the Hebrew word.

characteristic of neither TO[12] nor TN, but is common in TPJ.[13] TJ also contains usage of the insertion יתבי.[14] Addition of the word אנש is characteristic of TO; TJ (in these two instances, in the singular, אנש); TN (in the plural, אנשי), and TPJ.[15]

Let us consider the following statistical observation: the Book of Chronicles contains 40 appearances of the words שֵׁבֶט and מַטֶּה, while in the translation the word שבט appears no fewer than 120 times. In effect, the number of times the word appears in the Targum in the absence of an equivalent in the *Vorlage* is twice the number of times it directly reflects the Hebrew *Vorlage*.

The targumist's practice of inserting group markers in the text prior to nouns that may have any of several functions is responsible for an interesting peculiarity in the translation of the phrase "[pr. n.] מֶלֶךְ" in Chronicles.

Where the nation in question is Moab, Assyria, Babylonia, or any other foreign people, it is the targumist's practice to render, "[pr. n.]-ד מלכא", because from the vantage point of the targumist, these names may be understood only as names of nations.[16] So, too, when the proper noun is Israel, the targumist tends to translate the term as מלכא דישראל, as this name, as well, is understood strictly as the name of a nation.[17] When the proper noun is יהודה, however, the tendency of the author of TC is to employ an expanded translation—מליך שבטא דבית יהודה (i.e., king of the tribe of the house of Judah)—so as to avoid an eventuality where the name יהודה might be understood as the name of a nation independent and separate from the people of Israel.[18] This convention,

---

12   An exception to this rule is TO to Num 33:53. The addition in that v., however, results from the influence of vv. 52, 55.

13   Cf., for instance, the various translations to the following verse from the Torah:
Ex 8:20

MT	הֶעָרֹב׃	הָאָרֶץ מִפְּנֵי	תִּשָּׁחֵת	וּבְכָל־אֶרֶץ מִצְרַיִם
TO	ערובא׃	ארעא מן קדם	אתחבלת	ובכל ארעא דמצרים
TN	ערברובא׃	ארע מן קדם	אתחבלת	ובכל ארעא דמצרים
TPJ	חיות ברא׃	ארעא מן קדם עירבוב	אתחבלו יתבי	ובכל ארעא דמצרים

14   Thus, e.g., in Judg 1:2; 18:30; 1 Sam 27:9; 2 Kgs 8:22; 18:22; Isa 1:1; 2:1.

15   The plural and the singular form both appear alternately in TC; it may be that the targumist's approach reflects the influence of two targumic traditions, such as those of TO and TN.

16   Exceptions to this rule are listed above, p. 31, n. 5.

17   Thus 30 times: 1 Chr 5:17; 2 Chr 8:11; 16:1, 3; 18:3–5, 7–8, 17, 19, 25, 28–34; 21:2; 22:5; 25:17–18; 28:5; 29:27; 30:26; 35:3–4. In four instances he deviates from this pattern, rendering, מלכא דבית ישראל (2 Chr 20:35; 25:21, 23, 25), but in these cases the term appears alongside the phrase מלכא דבית יהודה/מליך שבטא.

18   Thus 22 times in the book: 1 Chr 5:17; 2 Chr 11:3; 16:1, 7; 18:3, 9, 28; 19:1; 20:35; 21:12; 22:1, 6; 25:17, 21, 23; 30:24; 32:8–9, 23–24, 26; 35:21. The phrase מלכא דבית יהודה appears twice

hardly an original device conceived by the author of TC, is found as early as TJ; the author of TC, for his part, chose to be a faithful adherent to the path that had been forged before his time.[19]

2.4   *The House of the Lord's Sanctuary*

It is well known that the targumists' practice was to translate the phrase בית ה׳ (house of the Lord, i.e. the Temple) and similar terms in an expanded fashion: בית מקדשא (דה׳) (house of the Lord's sanctuary, or site of the Lord's sanctuary).[20] The author of TC is a faithful representative of this targumic tradition, using the expression a total of 177 times.

2.5   *Differentiation of Hebrew Doublets and Pairs*

Where the Hebrew verse contains a pair both of whose components appear to serve a single function, the targumist tends to disassemble the pair and propose a distinction between the two elements. The distinction sometimes is in keeping with the simple sense of the scripture, while on other occasions the distinction is midrashic in nature. What is consistent across expansions of this type is the need to assign a distinct province to each of the elements of the expression, thus saving Scripture from redundancy. For instance:

1 Chr 12:19

MT		לְעֹזְרֶ֑ךָ	לְךָ֣ וְשָׁל֖וֹם	שָׁל֔וֹם	שָׁל֧וֹם ׀
TC	לדמסיעין לך	ושלמא לך	בליליא	ושלמא ביממא	שלמא

NJPS: At peace, at peace with you, And at peace with him who supports you,
Dost: May you have well-being *during the day* and well-being *during the night*, and may those who aid you have well-being

In the quotation spoken by Amasa, the word שָׁל֔וֹם twice refers to David. The targumist is careful to establish that the first appearance applies to the daylight

---

19   (2 Chr 25:18, 25). The phrase מליך שבטא דיהודה appears once (1 Chr 4:41). The phrase מלכא דיהודה also appears once in TC (2 Chr 28:19).

Cf., for instance:

1 Kgs 22:10

MT		וִיהוֹשָׁפָ֣ט מֶ֔לֶךְ־	יְהוּדָ֗ה	יֹשְׁבִ֜ים אִ֣ישׁ עַל־כִּסְא֗וֹ	וּמֶ֣לֶךְ יִשְׂרָאֵ֡ל
TJ	גבר על כרסוהי	שבטא דבית יהודה יתבין	ויהושפט מלך	ומלכא דישראל

NJPS: The king of Israel and King Jehoshaphat of Judah were seated on their thrones,
Clem: Now the king of Israel and Jehoshaphat king of *the tribe of the House of* Judah were sitting, each on his throne

20   This expansion bears the hallmark of rabbinic parlance; cf. Hurvitz-Gottlieb, pp. 62–64, and bibliography cited there.

hours and the second to nighttime, so that Amasa's comments contain no needless redundancy. This phenomenon of doublet differentiation doublets may be found in several places in TJ.[21] It thus stands to reason that the author of TC was influenced in his work by targumic techniques already familiar to him.

1 Chr 24:6

MT   לְאִיתָמָר׃   אָחֻז   ... לְאֶלְעָזָר   אֶחָד אָחֻז   בֵּית־אָב אֶחָד

TC   בֵּית־אָב אֶחָד דמתאחד תמניא למטרת אלעזר ... מתאחד אשתה עסרי לאיתמר׃

NJPS: one clan more taken for Eleazar for each one taken of Ithamar.

Dost: one ancestral house, which was chosen *eight* (*times*) for the watch of Eliezer, and what was chosen was chosen *sixteen* (*times*) for Ithamar

The families of Eleazar and Itamar are presented equivalently in this Hebrew verse. Previously, however, in v. 4, it was stated that the sons of Eleazar were more numerous than those of Itamar, resulting in the designation of sixteen leaders of Eleazar and eight of Itamar. In this verse, therefore, the targumist took pains to detail that what in the Hebrew appear as two similar elements of

---

21   Examples in which doublets are expanded:

Isa 6:3

MT   ה׳ צְבָאוֹת   קָדוֹש   קָדוֹש   קָדוֹש |

TJ   קדיש   בשמי מרומא בית שכינתיה קדיש על ארעא עובד גבורתיה קדיש לעלם עלמיא ה׳ צבאות

NJPS: Holy, holy, holy! The LORD of Hosts!

Clem: Holy *in the heavens on high is the temple of his Shekhinah*; holy *on the earth is the work of his power*; holy *in eternity* is the Lord of Hosts.

Isa 21:9

MT   לָאָרֶץ׃   שֻׁבַּר אֱלֹהֶיהָ וְכָל־פְּסִילֵי בָּבֶל נָפְלָה   נָפְלָה

TJ   נפלת ואף עתידא למיפל בבל וכל צלמי טעותהא ידקדקון לארעא׃

NJPS: Fallen, fallen is Babylon, And all the images of her gods Have crashed to the ground!

Clem: Fallen, *and even is about* to fall, Babylon; and they will crush all the images of her idols to the ground.

Isa 57:19

MT   וְלַקָּרוֹב   לָרָחוֹק   שָׁלוֹם   שָׁלוֹם |

TJ   שלמא   יתעביד לצדיקיא דנטרו אוריתי מלקדמין ושלמא יתעביד לתביא דתבו לאוריתי קריב

NJPS: It shall be well, Well with the far and the near

Clem: peace *will be done for the righteous who kept my Torah from of old*, and peace *will be done for those who repent, who have come back to my Torah* recently

Jer 22:29

MT   שִׁמְעוּ דְּבַר־ה׳׃   אֶרֶץ   אֶרֶץ   אֶרֶץ

TJ   מארעיה אגליוהי לארע אוחרי ארעא דישראל קבילי פתגמא דה׳׃

NJPS: O land, land, land, Hear the word of the LORD!

Gottlieb: *From his* land *they exiled him to another* land, O land *of Israel* obey the word of the Lord.

a pair in fact were proportionally divided according to family size—eight and sixteen—for a total of twenty-four priestly watches (the same reason for which the word מטרת was added). Notwithstanding, the text of this verse in all MSS of TC assigns eight to Eleazar and sixteen to Itamar. It thus appears that the two numbers were transposed in TC early on.

1 Chr 28:2

MT	וְעַמִּי	וַיָּקָם דָּוִיד הַמֶּלֶךְ עַל־רַגְלָיו וַיֹּאמֶר שְׁמָעוּנִי אַחַי
TC	ועמי	וקם דוד מלכא על רגלוי ואמר קבילו מני אחיי
		אחי בית ישראל ועמי גיוריא די בקרויהון

NJPS: King David rose to his feet and said, "Hear me, my brothers, my people! Dost: Then King David rose upon his feet and said, "Receive from me, my brethren, my people, *my brethren the house of Israel, and my people the proselytes who are in their cities*

The targumist preferred not to attribute needless redundancy to David in his address to the people: if they are addressed as אֲחַי, my brethren, then what further need is there for עַמִּי, my people? The author of TC therefore distinguished between the two terms, applying them to different groups. David's brethren are the House of Israel, with whom he shares blood ties. With the term עַמִּי, David further includes non-natives, who share no family ties with the king but have become a part of the nation by casting their lot with the people of Israel.

1 Chr 29:12

MT	וְאַתָּה מוֹשֵׁל בַּכֹּל	מִלְּפָנֶיךָ	וְהַכָּבוֹד		וְהָעֹשֶׁר
TC	ועותרא דעתיריא ויקרא	דמלכיא ושליטיא	מן קדמך מתיהב להון ואת שליט בכולא

NJPS: Riches and honor are Yours to dispense; You have dominion over all;
Dost: The wealth *of the wealthy* and the glory *of kings and rulers* are given from before You to them, and You rule over all

The components of the Hebrew pair עֹשֶׁר וְכָבוֹד are not identical in meaning, but when appearing concurrently they serve as a kind of *hendiadys*.[22] The targumist sought to avoid giving the components of the pair overlapping functions and so divided them, ascribing each to a reference group he found appropriate: "wealth" alludes to the rich, while "glory" refers to kings and rulers. This verse follows one whose interpretation entails a significant expansion (regarding which see the discussion below, pp. 325–327), and it may be that the expansion noted here is in some degree owed to that previous verse. Even

---

22   Cf. the definition and examples given by Melamed, pp. 142–159.

if this is the case, the manner of expansion here, i.e., breaking apart a pair, is similar to that seen in the examples above.

2.6   *Insertion of "Missing" Words*

The diction of the Book of Chronicles is sparing at times, or even lacking in its use of words that might be expected to appear in a given sentence from the perspective of the targumist and our own. In general, it is easy enough to fill in whatever is absent and gain an understanding of the verse. Where the Hebrew transmission includes a sparse verse of this sort, the targumist tends to insert what is lacking. He preserves the sentence structure and the general verbal framework, but adds to the sentence a word or expression that suffices to fill in what is missing and more precisely establish the meaning of the text. We might say that the targumist's additions in these instances result from clear necessity. Thus, for instance:

1 Chr 11:23

MT   כִּמְנוֹר אֹרְגִים   חֲנִית   וּבְיַד הַמִּצְרִי

TC   כְּאַכְסָן דְּגַרְדָּאִין   דְּסוֹמְכֵיהּ   מוֹרַנִיתָא   וּבִידָא דְמַצְרָאָה

NJPS: The Egyptian had a spear in his hand, like a weaver's beam,

Dost: In the hand of the Egyptian was a spear, *whose thickness was* as a weaver's beam

1 Chr 17:25

MT   לְהִתְפַּלֵּל לְפָנֶיךָ:   מָצָא עַבְדְּךָ   עַל־כֵּן

TC   לְצַלָּאָה קְדָמָךְ:   פִּתְחָא דְּפוּמָא   אַשְׁכַּח עַבְדָּךְ   בְּגִין כֵּן

NJPS: ... Your servant has ventured to pray to You.

Dost: Therefore, Your servant was able *to open his mouth* to pray before You.

2 Chr 32:16

MT   הָאֱלֹהִים וְעַל יְחִזְקִיָּהוּ עַבְדּוֹ:   עַל־הֹ'   וְעוֹד דִּבְּרוּ עֲבָדָיו

TC   אֱלֹהִים וְעַל יְחִזְקִיָּה עַבְדֵּיהּ:   עַל מֵימְרָא דַּה'   סְטַיָּא   וְתוּב מַלִּילוּ עַבְדּוֹהִי

NJPS: His officers said still more things against the LORD God and against His servant Hezekiah.

Dost: Yet again his servants incited *rebellion* against the Memra of the Lord God and against Hezekiah His servant.

The negative tone of the words spoken by the servants of Assyrian king is implicitly understood from the Hebrew verse, but the targumist saw fit to add a word to explicate the character of these comments, clarifying that in the context of the present verse, the phrase דב"ר על ה' is not to be understood

neutrally. This addition by the author of TC is based on the words דִּבֶּר־סָרָה
עַל־יהֹ' (he urged disloyalty to the LORD) of Deut 13:6, rendered by both TO and
TPJ as מליל סטיא על ה'.[23] In effect, the author of TC seeks to clarify that the
meaning of the verse is that the servants of the king of Assyria spoke demean-
ingly of God and of Hezekiah.

1 Chr 12:9

MT   וְכִצְבָאִים עַל־הֶהָרִים לְמַהֵר:
TC   והי כטביא על טוריא רהיטין לאוחאה:

NJPS: as swift as gazelles upon the mountains.

Dost: and just like the gazelles *sprinting* upon the mountains

2 Chr 34:22

MT   וַיֵּלֶךְ חִלְקִיָּהוּ וַאֲשֶׁר הַמֶּלֶךְ אֶל־חֻלְדָּה הַנְּבִיאָה
TC   ואזל חלקיה ודהוו עם מלכא לות חלדה נביאתא

NJPS: Hilkiah and those whom the king [had ordered] went to the prophetess
Huldah[24]

Dost: So Hilkiah and those *who were with* the king went to Huldah the
prophetess

2 Chr 35:14

MT   כִּי הַכֹּהֲנִים בְּנֵי אַהֲרֹן בְּהַעֲלוֹת הָעוֹלָה וְהַחֲלָבִים עַד־לָיְלָה
TC   ארום כהניא בני אהרן מתעסקין באסקות עלתא ותריביא עד ליליא

NJPS: for the Aaronite priests [were busy] offering the burnt offerings and the
fatty parts until nightfall,[25]

Dost: because the priests, the sons of Aaron, *were busy* with the offering up of
the brunt offering and the fat portions until night.

1 Chr 9:26

MT   כִּי בֶאֱמוּנָה הֵמָּה אַרְבַּעַת גִּבֹּרֵי הַשֹּׁעֲרִים הֵם הַלְוִיִּם
TC   ארום בהימנותא הנון עבדין ארבעתי גבריא תרעיא הנון ליואי

NJPS: the four chief gatekeepers, who were Levites, were entrusted ...

Dost: but four men *served* as gatekeepers permanently. They were Levites,

---

23   The targumist proceeded to add the word סטיא in the next v., 2 Chr 32:17, as well. The
     word סרה is translated as סטיא in TO, TPJ, and TJ (respectively) in the following locations,
     as well: Deut 19:16; Isa 59:13; Jer 28:16; 29:32. Cf. *Tg. Cant* 7:1.
24   The words in the brackets were inserted by NJPS specifically because they have no equiva-
     lent in the Hebrew of MT.
25   The words "were busy" appear in NJPS without brackets. I added the brackets because
     these words have no equivalent in the Hebrew of MT.

The addition of the verb עב״ד produces a phrase parallel to that appearing in 2 Kgs 12:16 22:7; 2 Chr 34:12.

The following verses enumerate tasks associated with the Temple service with which the Levitical families were charged. Scripture recounts their areas of responsibility in a generally succinct manner. The targumist added words throughout the verses in order to clarify them as well as to correlate the various aspects of the Temple service enumerate in them with those familiar to him from the Torah.

1 Chr 9:27

| MT | וְלַבֹּקֶר לַבֹּקֶר: | עַל־הַמַּפְתֵּחַ | וְהֵם |
| TC | בצפר: צפר | למיחד ולמפתח בעדן על אקלידיא | והנון ממנן |

NJPS: and they were in charge of opening it every morning.

Dost: and they were appointed over the keys *for shutting and opening* in the morning every morning.

The Targum here seeks to clarify the relationship between the key (מַפְתֵּחַ)[26] and the end of the verse: since the Levites opened the Temple with the key every morning, it follows that they similarly employed the key to close (למיחד) the Temple at night.

1 Chr 9:29

| MT | וְהַבְּשָׂמִים: | וְהַשֶּׁמֶן וְהַלְּבוֹנָה | וְהַיַּיִן | וְעַל־הַסֹּלֶת |
| TC | דקטורתא: ובושמיא אדכרתא ולבונת | וחמר נסוכא | דמנחתא | ועל סלתא |

NJPS: and of the flour, wine, oil, incense, and spices.

Dost: and over the fine flour *of the grain offerings*, the wine *of the libations*, the *memorial* incense, and the spices *of incense*.

In his translation, the targumist systematically adds the function fulfilled in the Temple service by each of the various items named in the Hebrew verse, in keeping with the instructions of the Torah.[27]

---

26   Contra TC, many translators—such as NJPS, Japhet *OTL*, p. 201, and Knoppers *vol. 1*, p. 15—read this word as a gerund.

27   Fine flour for meal offerings, e.g., Lev 6:8 (cf. TO and TN ibid.); wine for libations, e.g., Num 15:5 (cf. TO and TN ibid.). The phrase לבונת האזכרה does not occur in Scripture; TC constructs it on the basis of a verse such as Lev 24:7 (cf. TO and TN ibid.). TC similarly constructs the phrase בושמיא דקטורתא ("the spices of the incense offering") on the basis of a verse such as Exod 25:6 (cf. TO and TN ibid.). Though there is no translation for וְהַשֶּׁמֶן in any of the various MSS of TC, it is improbable that the targumist purposely declined to translate the reference to oil. We therefore may assume that the translation of this word

1 Chr 9:31

MT   הַחֲבִתִּֽים׃   עַל מַעֲשֵׂה   ... מִן־הַלְוִיִּ֔ם   וּמַתִּתְיָ֙ה

TC   מנחת מסריתא   על עובד   ... מן ליואי   ומתתיה

NJPS: Mattithiah, one of the Levites ... was entrusted with making the flat cakes.

Dost: Mattithiah of the Levites ... was appointed permanently over the service *of the offering* of the pan.

The targumist associated the hapax legomenon חֲבִתִּים with the pentateuchal word מַחֲבַת (Lev 2:5; 6:14; 7:9), which is translated as מסריתא in TO, TN, and TPJ and the context of whose three occurrences is that of flour offerings. TC thus stresses that the חֲבִתִּים named here are a variety of flour offering.

1 Chr 9:32

MT   שַׁבַּת שַׁבָּֽת׃   לְהָכִ֑ין   הַֽמַּעֲרֶ֖כֶת   עַל־לֶ֥חֶם   מִן־אֲחֵיהֶ֛ם   הַקְּהָתִ֧י   וּמִן־בְּנֵ֣י

TC   שבא בשבא   על פתורא   לתקנא   על לחם סדורא   וּמן אחוהון ממנן   בני קהת   ומן

NJPS: Also some of their Kohathite kinsmen had charge of the rows of bread, to prepare them for each sabbath.

Dost: Some of the sons of Kohath and from the sons of their brethren were appointed over the showbread to prepare *on the table* every Sabbath.

TC goes out of its way to specify that the showbread was placed on the Table, as required by Lev 24:6.

The language of the Book of Chronicles features several constructions combining אֵין + infinitive or verbal noun, which carry various modal shades of meaning from the semantic field of prohibition.[28] In order to express these shades of meaning, the targumist supplements the construction with a word more precisely defining the prohibition, as indicated by the context of the Hebrew verse. Thus, for instance:

2 Chr 35:3

MT   מַשָּׂ֣א בַּכָּתֵ֑ף   אֵֽין־לָכֶ֥ם   ... שְׁלֹמֹ֑ה   בָּנָ֥ה   אֲשֶׁ֤ר   בַּבַּ֗יִת   תְּנ֣וּ אֶת־אֲרֽוֹן־הַקֹּ֜דֶשׁ

TC   רשותא למטל בכתף   לית לכון   ... שלמה   בנא   די   דקודשא בביתא   הבו ית ארונא

NJPS: Put the Holy Ark in the House that Solomon ... built; as you no longer carry it on your shoulders,

---

was omitted at an early stage due to scribal error. Given the approach in TC to the remainder of the items listed in the verse, the translation here presumably read משח רבותא or משח דרבותא, corresponding to שמן המשחה (oil used for anointing).

28   This structure is characteristic of late biblical Hebrew. See van Peursen, pp. 227–230; Seow, pp. 18–19; Hurvitz-Gottlieb, pp. 36–39.

Dost: Put the holy ark into the temple that Solomon son of David, the king of Israel, built. You do not have *permission* (*any longer*) to carry it on (your) shoulder(s).

1 Chr 23:26

MT וְגַם לַלְוִיִּם אֵין־ לָשֵׂאת אֶת־הַמִּשְׁכָּן וְאֶת־כָּל־כֵּלָיו לַעֲבֹדָתוֹ:

TC ולחוד אוף לליואי לא כשר למטל ית משכנא דה׳ וית כל מנוהי לפולחניה:

NJPS: Therefore the Levites [need] not carry the Tabernacle and all its various service vessels.[29]

Dost: So for the Levites it is not *longer necessary* to carry the tabernacle of the Lord and all of its vessels for its worship.

2 Chr 5:11

MT כִּי כָּל־הַכֹּהֲנִים ... הִתְקַדָּשׁוּ אֵין לִשְׁמוֹר לְמַחְלְקוֹת:

TC ארום כל כהנא ... אתקדשו לית להון עסקא במטרת ביתא לפלוגת ליואי:

NJPS: all the priests ... had sanctified themselves, without keeping to the set divisions

Dost: for all of the priests ... were consecrated, (for) they did not *have the responsibility of* guarding *the house* like the division of *the Levites*

In the last of these examples, the targumist goes out of his way to fill in several elements that, to his mind, were lacking. He sublimates the element of prohibition by indicating that the verse here gives not a prohibition pertaining to the priests, but a statement negating the relevance of guard duty to the priests. The targumist uses a verbal noun (taking the place of the Hebrew infinitive form) to represent the element of guarding and adds the word ביתא to define the purpose of this activity. After treating the final word of the verse, viz. לְמַחְלְקוֹת, he adds the positive alternative (לפלוגת ליואי) to the negation of the priests from the duty of guarding the Temple. The priests do not guard the Temple, but rather this duty is the province of the Levitical divisions.

The targumist, however, does not insert words at every opportunity:

2 Chr 35:15

MT וְהַשֹּׁעֲרִים לְשַׁעַר וָשַׁעַר אֵין לָהֶם לָסוּר מֵעַל עֲבֹדָתָם

TC ותרעיא לתרע ותרע לית להון למעדי מכל פולחנהון

NJPS: and the gatekeepers were at each and every gate. They did not have to leave their tasks, because their Levite brothers provided for them

---

29   The word "need" appears in NJPS without brackets. I added the brackets to illustrate that this word has no equivalent of its own in the Hebrew of MT.

Dost: And the gatekeepers were at each and every gate. They did not leave off from all of their service

The sense of the Hebrew formation could have led the targumist to add some type of modification that would render the translation as, "They did not *need to* leave ...", but in this case he did not do so.

3   Translation Consistency

3.1   *Opening*

In the final example above, we saw the targumist deviate from the style of translation that he had employed in similar cases elsewhere in his work. This peculiarity in its own right is cause for discussion. As noted, the targumist's basic tendency is to transmit a literal translation, subject to the requirements of language, expression, and style. Naturally, as he proceeds with his work, he develops something of a lexicon of Aramaic equivalents for Hebrew words that recur on a number of occasions in the source text. Indeed, one who is thoroughly familiar with the diction and preferences of the targumist often can predict his translation of a given verse in advance. Yet the targumist is not wholly consistent. In some cases he chooses an equivalent other than the accustomed word although it is difficult to arrive at any conscious reason he may have had for such a deviation, such as the need to generate a distinction between meanings or else stylistic demands. Following are a few examples of such deviations:

3.2   ארום / (י)מטול ד

The Hebrew word כִּי is generally rendered in TC as ארום, which appears in TC a total of 259 times. The phrase מטול ד(י), however, appears in TC 35 times, including 22 instances where it takes the place of the word כִּי.[30] Use of the ארום (as opposed to ארי) is a familiar characteristic of Palestinian Targums of the Torah and TPJ, as well as several Targums of the Writings.[31] Use of the phrase מטול ד(י), meanwhile, is typical of *Tg. Prov* (an observation consistent with that Targum's presumed Syrian origins) and *Tg. Esth II*.[32] Notwithstanding, a select

---

30   1 Chr 5:2; 9:28; 12:22, 41; 16:25–26, 34, 41; 19:2; 28:6; 2 Chr 7:7; 12:2; 17:4; 18:7; 21:10; 22:4; 25:16; 28:21; 30:3, 5; 31:18; 36:15.

31   Aside from TC, the word appears in the Targums to Psalms, Job, Ruth, Canticles, Ecclesiastes, and Lamentations, as well as *Tg. Esth I*. See Weiss, p. 307; White, pp. 50–51.

32   See Dan, p. 360, who includes מטול in his list of vocabulary common to *Tg. Ps* and the Syriac. Notwithstanding, *Tg. Prov* does not altogether eschew use of the word ארום.

few targumic works, among them TC, employ both forms, making extensive use of ארום alongside occasional resort to the phrase מטול ד(י). Aside from TC, this group includes TPJ, *Tg. Ps*, and *Tg. Job*.[33] It may be that use of both alternatives is characteristic of the Late Jewish Literary Aramaic dialect,[34] but I can offer no explanation of why the targumist would have chosen one word over the other in each given case. Still, I shall note a feature of TC that may in the future provide part of the answer to this quandary. Of the 35 instances where TC uses the phrase מטול ד(י), in only three does it correspond to the word כִּי, when כִּי appears in both Chronicles and Samuel/Kings.[35] The significance of this figure lies in that that the frequency with which the phrase מטול ד(י) occurs where the corresponding verse in TJ has ארי is far less than that with which the phrase occurs elsewhere in TC. The author of TC thus seems to have hesitated less in choosing one of the two alternate translations for the word כִּי where TJ gave the corresponding word as ארי, for which he almost always substituted ארום. What is more, there may be what to learn from this phenomenon about the targumist's Aramaic dialect. It may be that his tendency to use ארום as the equivalent of כִּי may reflect his faithfulness to the targumic tradition that had been transmitted to him, while his own predilection to use the phrase מטול ד(י) reflects penetration of the targumic idiom by a new linguistic element.

3.3   רב / אב

The nomen regens form אֲבִי is quite common in the genealogical lists in Chronicles, where it appears no fewer than 35 times. The word sometimes signifies that one person biologically sired another, whose name is given as the nomen rectum. On other occasions it signifies that a person was the leader or founder of the settlement whose name follows the word.[36] Determining whether the proper noun appearing as nomen rectum is a personal name or a toponym is not always an easy task, but the very fact of the difference in meaning provides an opportunity for the targumist to establish a distinction

---

33   Following is a table showing the frequency with ארום and מטול ד(י) occur in these Targums. The numbers ought not be given undue significance, as in the case of several Targumim they vary from one MS to another. The table does, however, give a helpful general picture of the proportional use of the two alternatives within these Targums.

	ארום	מטול ד(י)
TPJ	883	87
Tg. Ps	375	82
Tg. Job	191	13
TC	259	35

34   Cf. Kaufman *TPJ*, pp. 379, 382.

35   2 Chr 7:7 (|| 1 Kgs 8:64); 18:7 (|| 1 Kgs 22:8); 22:4 (|| 2 Kgs 8:27).

36   See Oeming, pp. 127–129, for a survey of the development of scholarship on this term.

in his translation, selecting different words to correspond to the single Hebrew source word. Namely, the word generally is translated as either אב or רב, with אב apparently used where—in the targumist's view—the Hebrew word denotes biological fatherhood, and the word רב, meaning master or ruler, where the targumist believed that Scripture sought to indicate leadership of a given community.[37] The list of occurrences includes a few instances that are clearly subject to interpretation in light of each given verse's context, such that different translators would tend to arrive at different decisions, but the targumist's rationale for translating one appearance as אב and another as רב are for the most part readily discernable. Here we shall give our attention to a few instances that appear idiosyncratic and inconsistent:

1 Chr 2:45

| MT | וּבֶן־שַׁמַּי | מָעוֹן | וּמָעוֹן | אֲבִי | בֵית־צוּר׃ |
| TC | וברי דשמי | מעון | ומעון | אבא | דבית צור׃ |

NJPS: The son of Shammai: Maon, and Maon *begot* Bethzur.

Dost: The son of Shammai was Maon, and Maon was *the father of* Beth-zur.

It is difficult to believe that the targumist read בית צור as a personal name (cf. 1 Chr 2:51; 4:4)—the expected translation would be רבא דבית צור. It may be that an error crept in during transcription of TC, but all of the extant MSS are in agreement concerning the orthography of this word.

---

37   Phrases translated with אב: וְאַבִי עֲמָשָֹא ‖ ואבא דעמשא ‖ אֲבִי גִלְעָד ‖ אבא דגלעד (1 Chr 2:17); אֲבִי מַדְמַנָּה ... אבא דירקעם ‖ אֲבִי בֵית־צוּר ‖ אבא דבית צור ‖ אֲבִי־גִלְעָד ‖ אבא דגלעד (1 Chr 2:23); אֲבִי חֶבְרוֹן ‖ אבא דחברון (1 Chr 2:42); (1 Chr 2:45); ... אֲבִי גֵדֹר אבי עיר נחש ‖ אֲבִי עִיר נָחָשׁ ‖ אבא דאשתון ‖ אֲבִי אֶשְׁתּוֹן (1 Chr 4:11); אבא דמכבנא ואבא דגבעא ‖ אֲבִי מַכְבֵּנָה וַאֲבִי גִבְעָא (1 Chr 2:49); אֲבִי לְכָה ‖ אבי לכה ‖ אֲבִי אֶשְׁתְּמֹעַ ‖ אבא דאשתמע (1 Chr 4:17); (1 Chr 4:12); אֲבִי חוּשָׁה (1 Chr 4:4); || אֲבִי־גִבְעוֹן ‖ גִלְעָד ‖ אבוהון דגלעדאי ‖ אֲבִי בְרֶחָיָת (ק׳) (1 Chr 7:14); אבא דברזית ‖ (1 Chr 7:31); אֲבִי לֶחֶם אֲבִי־גִבְעוֹן (1 Chr 4:21); אבהתהון דגבעונאי (1 Chr 9:35).

Phrases translated with רב: רב תְּקוֹעַ ‖ אֲבִי תְקוֹעַ ‖ רבהון דתקועאי ‖ אֲבִי־זִיף ‖ רבהון דזיפאי (1 Chr 2:24); אֲבִי קִרְיַת יְעָרִים ‖ רבהון דקרית יערים ‖ אֲבִי ... אֲבִי בֵית־לָחֶם (1 Chr 2:50); רב קרית ‖ אֲבִי קִרְיַת יְעָרִים ‖ רבהון דבית לחם ... רבהון דבית גדר ‖ בֵית־גָּדֵר (1 Chr 2:51); (1 Chr 2:42); רבא בבית ‖ אֲבִי בֵית לָחֶם ‖ רבניא דיתבין בעיטם ‖ אֲבִי עֵיטָם (1 Chr 4:3); יערים (1 Chr 2:52); רב חילא דאומניא ‖ אֲבִי גֵיא חֲרָשִׁים ‖ רבא דתקוע ‖ אֲבִי תְקוֹעַ (1 Chr 4:5); לחם (1 Chr 4:4); רבא דמרשה ‖ אֲבִי מָרֵשָׁה ‖ רבא דקעילה ‖ אֲבִי קְעִילָה (1 Chr 4:19); (1 Chr 4:21); רבני דגבעון ‖ אֲבִי גִבְעוֹן (1 Chr 8:29).

1 Chr 8:29; 1 Chr 9:35

MT:	מַעֲכָה		וְשֵׁם אִשְׁתּוֹ		גִּבְעוֹן	אֲבִי	יָשְׁבוּ	וּבְגִבְעוֹן
TC:	מעכה	דגבען מעכה	ושום אנתתיה		דגבעון	רבני	יתיבו	ובגבעו[ן]
MT:	מַעֲכָה		וְשֵׁם אִשְׁתּוֹ	(ק) יְעִיאֵל	גִּבְעוֹן	אֲבִי	יָשְׁבוּ	וּבְגִבְעוֹן
TC:	מעכה		ושום אתתיה	יעיאל דגבעונאי	אבהתהון	יתיבו	ובגבעון

NJPS (1 Chr 8:29): *The father of Gibeon* dwelt in Gibeon, and the name of his wife was Maacah.

Dost: *The leaders of* Gibeon dwelt in Gibeon, and the name of Gibeon's wife was Maacah.

NJPS (1 Chr 9:35): *The father of* Gibeon, Jeiel, lived in Gibeon, and the name of his wife was Maacah.

Dost: In Gibeon lived *the fathers of* the Gibeonites: Jeiel, whose wife's name was Maacah

The distance between these two nearly identical verses (which introduce two nearly identical lists) is only one chapter, and why the targumist translated אֲבִי differently in the two similar verses is unclear. Also unclear is why, in several translations of the word אֲבִי, he oscillates between singular and plural. This is the case, for example, with the phrase מָכִיר אֲבִי גִלְעָד which appears in both 1 Chr 2:23 and 1 Chr 7:14. In the first instance we find a translation in the singular, אבא דגלעד, while in the second the plural form אבוהון דגלעדאי is used, while we are left with no obvious contextual reason to which to attribute the disparity.

3.4   סימא / כספא

The word כסף appears 38 times in TC, serving as the typical equivalent for its parallel in Hebrew, כֶּסֶף.[38] Thirteen times, however, the targumist prefers to use the equivalent סימא for כֶּסֶף, despite the absence of obvious cause for choosing a different word from that found elsewhere.[39] Both equivalents of כֶּסֶף are found concurrently in *Tg. Ps*, as well.[40]

3.5   עגיל / תריס

The words מָגֵן, צִנָּה, and שֶׁלֶט appear 21 times in Chronicles. They are variously translated as תריס or עגיל, but there is no clear consistency in the choice of one

---

38   1 Chr 1:50; 18:10–11; 19:6; 21:22, 24; 22:14, 16; 28:14–17; 29:2–5, 7; 2 Chr 1:15, 17; 2:6, 13; 5:1; 9:14, 20; 21:3; 24:5, 11, 14; 25:6, 9, 18, 24; 27:5.

39   2 Chr 9:20–21, 24, 27; 15:18; 16:2–3; 17:11; 32:27; 34:9, 14, 17; 36:3.

40   Cf. Dan, p. 360, who includes סימא in his list of vocabulary common to *Tg. Ps* and Syriac.

over the other. The word מָגֵן is rendered as תריס in eight verses,[41] but as עגיל in one other.[42] The word צִנָּה is rendered as עגיל in four verses,[43] but as תריס in three.[44] The word שֶׁלֶט is rendered once as תריס,[45] and in one other instance as עגיל.[46] Even TJ, in point of fact, is not wholly consistent in its rendering of these words in the prophetic books, and it may be that the author of TC was influenced by this inconsistency.[47] As for translation of the word שֶׁלֶט, TC does not appear to be similar to any other Targum. TJ thrice leaves the word in its Hebrew form, שלט (2 Kgs 11:10; Jer 51:11; Ezek 27:11), while in *Tg. Cant* 4:4 it is translated as מיני זינין, i.e., weapons in general.

3.6   פיילי / מזרק

The Hebrew word מִזְרָק appears four times in Chronicles. Twice it is translated with the Hebrew form מזרק,[48] as in the various Targums of the Torah and in accord with the typical rendering of the word in TJ, but on two other occasions it is translated with the Greek loanword פיילי.[49] The word פיילי functions in Palestinian Targums as a counterpart of the word קְעָרָה. In TJ is appears once as a parallel of סֵפֶל (Judg 5:25); twice for קַבַּעַת (Isa 51:17, 22); and once for מִזְרָק (Amos 6:6). It is difficult to believe that the text of *Tg. Amos* is behind the decision of the author of TC to deviate from the Targums of the Torah; thus it may be that the targumist's choice of diction reflects another targumic tradition as yet unknown to us.

3.7   חמת / אנטיוכיה

The toponym חֲמָת appears in Chronicles seven times. In four verses, TC substitutes for it the Hellenistic name אנטיוכיה; in the three other verses it simply

---

41   2 Chr 9:16; 12:9; 14:7; 17:17; 23:9; 26:14; 32:5, 27.

42   2 Chr 12:10.

43   2 Chr 9:15; 11:12; 14:7; 25:5.

44   1 Chr 12:9, 25, 35.

45   1 Chr 18:7.

46   2 Chr 23:9.

47   Where מָגֵן signifies a concrete defensive apparatus (as opposed to verses where is indicates divine protection of a person), it is variously translated in TJ: תריס (Judg 5:8; 2 Sam 1:21; 2 Kgs 19:32; Isa 22:6; 37:33; Jer 46:6; Ezek 38:4; Nah 2:4); עגיל (Jer 46:3; Ezek 27:10; 38:5; 39:9); זינא (Isa 21:5); or the transcription מגן (1 Kgs 10:17; 14:26–27). צִנָּה typically is represented in TJ by תריס (1 Sam 17:7, 41; 2 Kgs 10:16; Jer 46:3; Ezek 26:8; 39:9), but in Ezek 38:4 is translated as עגיל. In Ezek 23:24, עגיל corresponds to both the words צִנָּה and מָגֵן.

48   1 Chr 28:17; 2 Chr 4:22.

49   2 Chr 4:8, 11.

transcribes the Hebrew חמת.[50] The two major targumic schools are at odds regarding these two equivalents, with TO and TJ consistently using חמת and the Palestinian Targums of the Torah preferring אנטיוכיה.[51] The author of TC has apparently been influenced by both traditions, but there seems to be no clear, consistent criterion for the targumist's various decisions on the matter.

4   Proper Nouns in Targum Chronicles

4.1   *Opening*

Scattered among rabbinic literature are several dicta extoling the uniqueness of the Book of Chronicles as fertile ground for homiletic interpretation of names. It is well known that "the Book of Chronicles was given for naught but that it be expounded" (*Lev. Rab.* 1:3)—a statement first put forward in connection with the many names in the book's genealogical lists, some of which are the subject of midrashic homiletics appearing in rabbinic literature. The introduction to a talmudic homily on 1 Chr 4:18 is phrased thus: "rabbi Simon b. Pazi, upon commencing a discussion of Chronicles, would say thus: 'All Your words are one, and we know how to expound them'" (*b. Meg.* 13a). With this introduction under his belt, the talmudic exegete embarks on a detailed homiletic discussion of the names appearing in the above verse. The Talmud (b. Pes. 62b) states that the vast majority of homilies to the book did not reach the Rabbis of the Talmud, but were lost:

> From the day on which the Book of Genealogies was suppressed, the power of sages has grown feeble, and the light of their eyes has dimmed ... On the passage beginning with 'And Azel had six sons' (1 Ch. 8:38) and the one ending 'these were the sons of Azel' (1 Ch. 9:44), they were burdened with four hundred camels loaded with [books of] interpretations [of those few verses alone].

This last statement describes the tremendous number of homiletic renderings of names concerning a small section of Chronicles—that between the two appearances of the name Azel at 1 Chr 8:38 and 1 Chr 9:44—as recorded by rabbinic tradition. These rabbinic dicta make clear that names found in Chronicles were seen as riddles and allusions of a sort, containing meaning

---

50   Instances where the translation אנטיוכיה is given: 1 Chr 1:16; 13:5; 18:9; 2 Chr 7:8. Instances where the word חמת is transcribed: 1 Chr 18:3; 2 Chr 8:3–4.

51   TPJ once renders אנטיוכיה (Num 13:21) and once טבריה (Num 34:8).

far broader than the mere personal names they signify in the context of their respective verses.

The targumist, carrying forward this tradition, proposes a plethora of midrashic treatments of names found in Chronicles throughout his Targum. Many of these *derashot* are familiar from rabbinic literature and other Targums; these shall be identified and discussed in due course, in chapters seven and eight. Sometimes the targumist explicates his agenda of explaining the meaning of a name, while on other occasions the exegesis is intimated by the presence in the translation of a word resembling the name. Following these two midrashic categories, we shall present here two lists enumerating the midrashic treatments of names in TC.

4.2 *Explicit Midrashic Renderings of Names*

1. **Joqtan** (1 Chr 1:19)[52]

    יקטן—מטול דביומוי שריאו שניהון דבני נשא ל**אתקטעא** מן בגלל חוביהון

    Joktan, for in his days the years of the children of men began *to diminish* on account of their sins.

2. **Almodad** (1 Chr 1:20)[53]

    אלמודד—ד**משח** ופליג ית ארעא באושליא

    Almodad, *who measured* and divided the land with ropes

3. **Sheleph** (ibid.)

    שלף—ד**שלף** ית נהרוותא לתחומיא

    Sheleph, *who diverted* the rivers to (their) borders

4. **Hazarmaveth** (ibid.)

    חצרמות—דאתקן **אתר כמניא לקטלא** עדי אורחא

    Hazarmaveth, who set *the place of the ambushes for the slaying of* those who pass by on the road

5. **Jerah** (ibid.)

    ירח—דאתקן **פונדוקין** והוה כל דעליל למיכל ולמשתי הוה מוכיל ליה סמא דקטול
    ונסיב כל מה דהוה בידוי

    Jerah, who established *inns*—and so it was, to each one who would enter to eat and to drink he would feed lethal poison and would take all that was in his hands

6. **Hadad, Matred, Mei-Zahav** (1 Chr 1:50)[54]

    הדד ... מטרד ... מי זהב—ד**הוה לעי במטרדותא** ובסרדותא ומן דעתר וקנא נכסין
    הוה מתגאה ו**הדר** למימר מה הוא כספא ו**מה הוא דהבא**

---

52 See discussion below, p. 470.

53 The four homiletic interpretations of names in this verse will be discussed below, pp. 387–392.

54 See discussion below, pp. 168–170.

Hadad ... Matred ...[Mei-Zahav—L.G.], who worked with the hunter's spear and the hunter's net, on account of which he became rich and acquired possessions. He became proud and *puffed up*, saying, "What is silver, and *what is gold*?"

7. **Jether the Ishmaelite** (1 Chr 2:17)[55]

 והוו צווחין ליה יתר ישמעאלא מטול דזריז ית חרצוי בסיפא למסייעא ית דוד הי־כערבאה

but they would call him Jether the Ishmaelite because he girded his loins with a sword to help David *like an Arab*

8. **Azubah, Jerioth** (1 Chr 2:18)[56]

ומאי צווחין לה עזובה מן בגלל דהות עקרה [וכאירתא] וגלי קדם ה' עולבנה ואתרווחת ואשתבהרת בחכמתא והות עזלא בחכמתא ית מעזי על גויתהון דעזיא כדלא גזין מטול יריעת משכנא

Why do they call her Azubah? Because she was *infertile and despised*. But her affliction was revealed before the Lord, and she was healed and was honored with wisdom. With skill she would spin the goat hair on the body of goats without sheering (them) because of *the curtains of the tabernacle.*

9. **Jabez** (1 Chr 2:55)[57]

יעבץ—דאוקים בעיצתיה תרביצא לתלמידיא

They called him Jabez because he established *by his counsel the study halls* for the disciples.

10. **Tirathim** (ibid.)

תרעתים—דהוה קלהון במשבחיהון הי־כיבבא

They were called Terathites because when they were praising their voice was *as a clamor.*

11. **Shimeathim** (ibid.)

שמעתים—דהוון מסברין אפין בשמעתתא

Shimeathites, because they were hopeful while (studying) *the legal tradition.*

12. **Sucathim** (ibid.)

סוכתים—דהוון מטללין ברוח נבואה

Sucathites, because they were *overshadowed* by the spirit of prophecy.

---

55 See discussion below, pp. 247–252.
56 See discussion below, pp. 356–362.
57 The homiletic interpretations of names in this verse will be discussed below, pp. 253–256, 364–371.

13. **Chileab** (1 Chr 3:1)[58]

כלאב—דדמי כוליה לאבא דיליה

Chileab—who *completely* resembled his *father*

14. **Shallum** (1 Chr 3:15)[59]

שלום—דשלימת מלכותא דבית דוד ביומוי

Shallum, in whose days the kingdom of the House of David *came to an end.*

15. **Jered** (1 Chr 4:18)[60]

ירד—דאוחית מנא לישראל

Jered because he *brought* manna to Israel

16. **Gedor** (ibid.)

גדור—דבנא חורבנהון דישר[אל]

Gedor, because he *rebuilt* the ruins of Israel

17. **Heber** (ibid.)

חבר—דחבר ישראל לאבוהון דבשמיא

Heber because he *bound* Israel to their Father who is in heaven

18. **Soco** (ibid.)

שוכו—דטליל על בית ישר[אל] בזכותיה

Soco, because he *covered* the house of Israel by his merit

19. **Jekuthiel** (ibid.)

יקותיאל—דאמתינו ישראל לאלהא דבשמי[א] ביומוי ארבעין שנין במדברא

Jekuthiel because in his days Israel *waited* forty years in the wilderness for their *God*, who is in heaven

20. **Zanoah** (ibid.)

זנוח—דשבק אלהא על חובי ישראל אמטולתיה

Zanoah because God *forgave* the sins of Israel on his account

21. **Mered** (ibid.)

מרד—דמרד במלכת מאלליא

Mered ... who *opposed* the counsel of the spies

22. **Sheerah** (1 Chr 7:24)[61]

שארה—דאשתיירת מן קטיליא

Sheerah, who *was left* from the slain

---

58   See discussion below, pp. 432–434.

59   See discussion below, pp. 252–253.

60   In keeping with rabbinic midrashic interpretations, names 15–20 are understood as various appellations of Moses. These homiletic interpretations of names will be discussed below, pp. 262–269.

61   See discussion below, p. 474.

23. **Hodeshah** (1 Chr 8:9)[62]

חדשה—דאתחדתא בנשואה

Hodeshah, ... for a *novel* interpretation of the law was established through her marriage

24. **Ner** (1 Chr 8:33)[63]

נר—מטול דהוה מדליק שרגיא בבתי מדרשיא ובבתי כנישייתא והיא זכותא גרמת לשאול בר בריה למהוי מלכ[א] ארום מלכותא אמתילא לשרגא

Ner because he would light the *lamps* in the academies and in the synagogues. That merit caused his grandson Saul to become king, for kingship was compared to the *lamp*.

25. **Meribbaal** (1 Chr 9:40)[64]

מריב בעל—מן בגלל דעבד פלוגתא עם מרי עלמא

Meribaal because he *disputed* with the *Lord of the World*

26. **Jachin** (2 Chr 3:17)

יכין—דאתקנת מלכותא דבית דוד

Jachin, because the kingdom of the dynasty of David was *established*,

27. **Boaz** (ibid.)

בעז—על שום בעז רב בית אבא לבית יהודה דמניה נפקו כל מלכיא דבית יהודה

Boaz, because *Boaz* was the greatest of the ancestral house of the house of Judah, from whom all the kings of the house of Judah descended

28. **Micaiah** and **Uriel** (2 Chr 13:2)[65]

מיכיהו בת אוריאל ... —מיכיהו, שמא דמעלי ... אוריאל ..., דלא למדכר שמיה דאבשלום

Micaiah daughter of Uriel ... Micaiah, a name that is excellent.... Uriel, ... so as not to remember the name of Absalom

4.3 *Implicit Midrashic Renderings of Names*

1. **Nimrod** (1 Chr 1:10)[66]

נמרוד—הוא שרי למהוי גבר בחטאה שדי אדם זכאי ומרוד קדם ה'

Nimrod. He became a mighty man in sin. He shed innocent blood and was a *rebel* before the Lord

2. **Dinhabah** (1 Chr 1:43)[67]

דנהבה—ואיתיהיבת ליה מגן

Dinhabah, and *it was given* to him freely

---

62 See discussion below, pp. 474–476.
63 See discussion below, pp. 445–449.
64 See discussion below, pp. 283–285.
65 See discussion below, pp. 482–484.
66 See discussion below, pp. 151–153.
67 See discussion below, p. 471.

3. **Ja'ir** (1 Chr 20:5)[68]

יעיר—דהוה <u>מתער</u> משנתיה בפלגות ליליא לשבחא קדם ה'

who would *arise* from his sleep in the middle of the night to sing praise before the Lord

4. **Shebuel** (1 Chr 23:16)[69]

שבואל—ובסיבותיה עבד <u>תתובא</u> ומני יתיה דוד לרישא על אוצריא

but in his old age *he repented*, so David appointed him as head over his treasuries.

5. **Shebuel** (1 Chr 26:24)

שבואל—<u>תב</u> לדחלתא דה'

... Shebuel ... he *returned* to the fear of *the Lord*

4.4 *Translation of Proper Nouns*

The author of TC generally transcribes proper nouns from the Hebrew.[70] In a few cases, however, he deviates from this practice, instead translating a Hebrew name into Aramaic: toponyms, such as names containing geographic terms (Valley of *X*, Mount *Y*), are often easier to understand with reference to their literal meaning, and literal translation of names can sometimes be a source of linguistic enrichment. The phenomenon is cause for greater surprise, though, when it manifests in the translation of personal names, as such a rendering is contrary to our assumption that a person's name is nothing more than a means of identification. Indeed, the list of translated personal names is quite short, and for most names on the list a literary source earlier than TC has been identified. In the final analysis, the only personal name translated for no apparent reason is that of Mehir son of Kelub, whose name is given as Perug (see below; 1 Chr 4:11). Below we shall present the translated names appearing in TC, discussing names of people and of places separately.

---

68 See discussion below, pp. 315–318.

69 This verse and 1 Chr 26:24 (the next example) will be discussed below, pp. 371–375.

70 The orthography of these names given in our texts of TC is not always consistent with that in MT. דָּוִיד of MT is spelled defectively in the Targum as דוד. Many names containing the suffix יָהוּ- in MT appear in the Targum with the suffix יה-, although these disparities do not appear to be systematic in nature.

4.4.1 Personal Names[71]

1 Chr 1:30–31[72]

MT	מִשְׁמָע וְדוּמָה מַשָּׂא חֲדַד וְתֵימָא: יְטוּר נָפִישׁ וָקֵדְמָה
TC	צייתא ושתוקא ומסוברא חריפא ואדרומא: יטור נפיש וקדמא

NJPS: *Mishma, Dumah, Massa, Hadad, Tema*: Jetur, Naphish, and *Kedmah*

Dost: *Listening, Silence, Endurance, Haripha, South*: Jetur, Naphish, and *Kadoma*

1 Chr 4:11

MT	וּכְלוּב אֲחִי־שׁוּחָה הוֹלִיד אֶת־מְחִיר הוּא אֲבִי אֶשְׁתּוֹן:
TC	וכלוב אחוי דשוחא אוליד ית פירוג הוא אבא דאשתון:

NJPS: Chelub the brother of Shuhah begot *Mehir*, who was the father of Eshton

Dost: Chelub, the brother of Shuhah, fathered *Perug*, who was the father of Eshton

The word פירוג is a Judean Aramaic common noun meaning *price* or *consideration*.[73] I have no satisfactory explanation of why the author of TC chose to translate this particular name literally where it appears here.

2 Chr 35:20

MT	אַחֲרֵי כָל־זֹאת ... עָלָה נְכוֹ מֶלֶךְ־מִצְרַיִם לְהִלָּחֵם בְּכַרְכְּמִישׁ
TC	בתר כל דנא ... סליק פרעה חגירא מלכא דמצרים לאגחא קרבא בכרכמיש

NJPS: After all this ... King *Necho* of Egypt came up to fight at Carchemish

Dost: After all of this ... the *lame* pharaoh, the king of Egypt, went up to wage war at Carchemish

This translation appears in TC in two additional locations: 2 Chr 35:22; 36:4. In rendering the name נְכוֹ as חגירא, lame, in these verses, the targumist follows in the footsteps of TJ in 2 Kgs 23:29, 33–35; Jer 46:2; Zech 12:11 (cf. *Tg. Lam* 1:18), as well as several rabbinic sources, such as *b. Meg.* 3a; *Mo'ed Qaṭ.* 28b. He added the title פרעה at 2 Chr 35:20, in accordance with the presentation of the figure's name with his title in other scriptural books and their Targums, but at the other two points where the name appears (2 Chr 35:22; 36:4) he no longer felt

---

71   1 Chr 5:12 (דיינא for וְשָׁפָט) is excluded from this list due to the probability that the translation is based on the Hebrew *Vorlage* שׁוֹפֵט, which follows and defines the name יַעֲנִי; see p. 11 above.

      The translation בר גדא for בֶּן־הַגְרִי reflects the Hebrew reading בן הגדי. The targumist here understood the verse as describing a tribal affiliation; see p. 12 above.

72   The translations of these names will be discussed below, pp. 392–395.

73   See discussion below, p. 185.

a need to expand the structure of his translation beyond that of the Hebrew verse and translated simply חגירא, without the monarch's title.

4.4.2 Toponyms

1 Chr 1:48

MT: הַנָּהָר   שָׁאוּל מֵרְחֹבוֹת   וַיִּמְלֹךְ תַּחְתָּיו

TC: ומליך תחותוי פרעה שאול דמן פל[ט]יותא[74] קרתא רבתא דמתבניא על־כיף פרת:

NJPS: Saul of *Rehoboth*-on-the-River succeeded him as king

Dost: and in his stead reigned Saul, who was from *Paltyutha* [literally, width—L.G.], the great city, which was built on the shore of the Euphrates

1 Chr 4:14

MT: חֲרָשִׁים הָיוּ   כִּי   גֵּיא חֲרָשִׁים אֲבִי   אֶת־יוֹאָב   הוֹלִיד   וּשְׂרָיָה

TC: ושריה אוליד ית יואב רב חילא דאומניא ארום אומניא הוו:

NJPS: Seraiah begot Joab father of *Ge-harashim*, so-called because they were craftsmen

Dost: Seraiah fathered Joab, the chief of the *Valley of Artisans*, for they were artisans

Where the word גיא serves as part of a toponym, it is typically translated as a nomen regens form, חילת, as in 1 Chr 18:12, חילת מלח; 2 Chr 14:9, חילת צפת; 25:11, חילת מלחא. 28:3, חילת בר הנם; 33:6, חילת בר הנם.

We find similar renderings throughout TJ (e.g. 1 Sam 13:18, חלת ‖ גֵּי הַצְּבֹעִים אפעיא),[75] and in the present verse would thus expect to find the construct phrase חילת אומניא or (with the inclusion of the words preceding the toponym) יואב רב חילת אומניא. This title of Joab is quite similar to the title רב חילא that appears frequently in TC after proper nouns (and corresponds to the title גבר חילא).[76] It may be that a scribal error brought about the transcription of the common phrase רב חילא and this error in turn required the addition of the particle ד- to the word אומניא to form a logical word pair.

1 Chr 4:28

MT: שׁוּעָל   וַחֲצַר   וּמוֹלָדָה   בִּבְאֵר־שֶׁבַע   וַיֵּשְׁבוּ

TC: ויתיבו בבירא־דשבע ומולדה וחצר תעלא:

NJPS: They dwelt in Beersheba, Moladah, Hazar-*shual*

Dost: They lived in Beersheba, Moladah, and Hazar *Taala* [literally, fox—L.G.]

---

74   MS V has פלייותא, but this presumably is a corruption of פלטיותא; see below, pp. 167–168.

75   In a number of instances the term is transliterated, e.g., TJ 2 Sam 8:13: גיא מלח.

76   Cf. 1 Chr 4:42; 11:6; 12:22; 19:16, 18; 25:1; 26:7, 26; 27:3, 5, 34; 2 Chr 16:4; 18:33; 33:11, 14.

The targumist alternately could have rendered דרת תעלא (cf. 1 Chr 4:31, דרת סוסיא).

1 Chr 4:31

MT וּבְבֵית מַרְכָּבוֹת וּבַחֲצַר סוּסִים וּבְבֵית בִּרְאִי וּבְשַׁעֲרָיִם אֵלֶּה עָרֵיהֶם

TC ובאורייות ארתיכא ובדרת סוסיא ובבית־בראי ובשערים אלין קרויהון

NJPS: Beth-marcaboth, Hazar-susim, Beth-biri, and Shaaraim. These were their towns

Dost: and in *Uryawat Arikaya* [literally, chariots' stables—L.G.], *Darath Susaya* [literally, horses' courtyards—L.G.], Beth-biri, and Shaaraim. These are their cities

The targumist chose to translate the Hebrew בית contextually (stables) rather than literally (houses).

1 Chr 4:41

MT וַיָּבֹאוּ אֶת־אָהֳלֵיהֶם וְאֶת־הַמְּעוּנִים (קרי) אֲשֶׁר נִמְצְאוּ־שָׁמָּה וַיַּחֲרִימֵם עַד־הַיּוֹם הַזֶּה

TC ומחו ית משכניהון וית מרודיא דאשכחו תמן וגמרונון עד יומא הדין

NJPS: and attacked their encampments and the *Meunim* who were found there, and wiped them out forever

Gottlieb: and they smote their tents and the *rebels* that they found there, and they destroyed them as unto this day

The ethnonym מעונים, whose meaning is not altogether clear, appears in several of the later biblical books.[77] Targumic textual witnesses are divided as to the correct form of the word: MSS V and E have מרודיא, as appears above, while MS C reads מדוריי (and deLagarde and Sperber's editions have מדוריא), dwelling places. The logic behind the version in C appears to be that מעונים is a plural form of מָעוֹן, in the sense of a place of residence. This is indeed the interpretation given the word by Beck, although his Aramaic text read מרודיא, and his position was subsequently taken up by Le Déaut and Robert and by McIvor.[78] These scholars apparently rejected the version מרודיא because they did not see what relevance rebellion might have to the Meunites, and their view appears quite justified. The reading found in C and E may be understood not as denoting rebellion, but as an Aramaic form resembling another Hebrew word always accompanied in Scripture by the root ענ״י. In Isa 58:7 we encounter the word pair עֲנִיִּים מְרוּדִים (the wretched poor); in Lam 1:7, עָנְיָהּ וּמְרוּדֶיהָ (woe and sorrow); in Lam 3:19, עָנְיִי וּמְרוּדִי (my distress and my misery). Rosenthal collated rabbinic

---

77   See Knoppers *vol. 1*, p. 369, for a survey of various views.

78   Beck *1*, p. 83; Le Déaut-Robert, vol. 1, p. 51; McIvor, p. 63.

sources indicating that the Rabbis understood the root מר״ד in such contexts as synonymous with גל״ה, so that in their parlance an impoverished person described with the root מר״ד is a destitute, homeless vagabond.[79] Possibly this Hebrew passive participle found its way from Hebrew into the Jewish-Aramaic dialect of the author of TC as a counterpart of the passive participle of ענ״י found in our verse, and the reading מדורײ of MS C reflects an emendation of the original reading מרודיא found in MSS V and E to a more familiar form. In any event, although the meaning of the word varies from one MS to another, both the reading in MS C and that in MSS V and E appear to be literal translations of the name found in the verse. Thus the targumist may not have understood the term to be an ethnonym—although elsewhere in his work, in the Targum to 2 Chr 26:7 (וְהַמְּעוּנִים), he does in fact understand the term as an ethnonym and accordingly renders it as מעון.

1 Chr 5:23

MT	וְהַר־חֶרְמוֹן	וּשְׂנִיר	חֶרְמוֹן	עַד־בַּעַל	מִבָּשָׁן		
TC	וטור חרמון	מסרי פירוי[80]	חרמון וטור	עד מישר	מן בותנן		

NJPS: from Bashan to Baal-hermon, *Senir*, and Mount Hermon

Dost: in the land of Buthnan unto the plain of Hermon, the mountain of *insipid fruit*, and Mt. Hermon

1 Chr 11:15

MT	בְּעֵמֶק רְפָאִים:	חֹנָה	פְלִשְׁתִּים	וּמַחֲנֵה	
TC	במישר גבריא[81]:	שרייה	פלשתאי	ומשריית	

NJPS: while a force of Philistines was encamped in the *Valley of Rephaim*

Dost: while the camp of the Philistines were encamping in the *plain of the warriors*

מישר גבריא is the translation typically found in TJ for the name עֵמֶק רְפָאִים.[82] The author of TC inherited this targumic tradition from TJ (1 Chr 11:15 || 2 Sam 23:13; 1 Chr 14:9 || 2 Sam 5:18).

---

79   Rosenthal *Inscription*, pp. 355–356.
80   See below, pp. 209–212, for a discussion of טור מסרי פירוי as an equivalent of שניר.
81   This toponym translation appears at 1 Chr 14:9, as well.
82   Josh 15:8; 18:16; 2 Sam 5:18, 22; 23:13; Isa 17:5.

2 Chr 8:17

MT אָ֚ז הָלַ֣ךְ שְׁלֹמֹ֔ה לְעֶצְיֽוֹן־גֶּ֖בֶר וְאֶל־אֵיל֑וֹת

TC הא בכין הליך שלמה לכרך תרנגולא ולאילות

NJPS: At that time Solomon went to *Ezion-geber* and to Eloth

Dost: Behold, then Solomon went to the *Fortress of the Rooster* and to Eloth

The toponym עציון גבר appears in the Torah in Num 33:35–36 and Deut 2:8. TO transcribes the name verbatim, whereas TN and TPJ ad loc. translate it as כרד תרנגולא.[83] The author of TC was a recipient of this targumic tradition.

2 Chr 16:6

MT וַיִּשְׂא֣וּ אֶת־אַבְנֵ֤י הָרָמָה֙ וְאֶת־עֵצֶ֔יהָ ... וַיִּ֤בֶן בָּהֶם֙ אֶת־גֶּ֔בַע וְאֶת־הַמִּצְפֶּֽה׃

TC ונטלו ית אבני רמתא וית קיסייהא ... ובנא בהון ית גבישתא וית סכותא׃

NJPS: and they carried away the stones and timber ... with these [King Asa] built up *Geba* and *Mizpah*

Dost: and they carried away the stones of Ramatha and its trees ... and with them he built *Gebishta* [literally, hill—L.G., but see below] and *Sacutha* [literally, observation point—L.G.]

גבישתא: The various MSS of TC are divided with regard to the targumic text here. MSS C and E here read גבעתא, hill, which is readily understood in the present context and appears in TJ to the parallel verse at 1 Kgs 15:22. MS V and an alternate reading in the margin of MS C give גבישתא. The meaning of the word גבישתא is not entirely clear. It is not documented elsewhere in TC, nor in other major targumic recensions, nor other Aramaic texts. Still, it is my view that גבישתא—the *lectio difficilior*—is the primary reading and גבעתא is a secondary reading reflecting an effort to provide a more familiar form. As much is indicated by the appearance of the word גבישתא in several MSS of TJ Zeph 1:10, corresponding to the Hebrew word גִּבְעוֹת.[84] I believe it is reasonable to associate this word with גבשושית, which is familiar to us from Rabbinic Hebrew and Aramaic as signifying a hillock or a mound of rocks.[85] The reading given in MS V thus appears the most well-founded, an outcome of the targumist's

---

83   The translation of the word גבר as תרנגול, taken independently, accords with one of the meanings of this word in rabbinic parlance, e.g., *m. Yoma* 1:8: "Ash is taken from the altar every day from the cock's crow (*qerot ha-gever*) or in immediate proximity thereto." See Jastrow, p. 208.

84   See Sperber, vol. 3, p. 468, for variant readings, including the forms גבשותא and גיבשתא. Sperber, ibid., has גבעתא as his preferred reading.

85   Jastrow, p. 209; Sokoloff *JPA*, p. 108.

familiarity with the word גבישתא, in the sense of a hill, in his own dialect of Aramaic.

סכותא: The author of TC translated the Hebrew word הַמִּצְפָּה by substituting the Aramaic root סכ״י for the Hebrew root צפ״י. Translation of הַמִּצְפָּה as סכותא occurs as early as TO and TPJ Gen 31:49, and it stands to reason that this tradition informed the targumist's decision here.

2 Chr 20:2

| MT | | | | בְּחַצְצוֹן תָּמָ֖ר | הִ֣יא | עֵ֥ין גֶּֽדִי׃ | וְהִנָּם֙ |
| TC | | | | בסביך דקלייה | היא | עין־גדי׃ | והא אנון |

NJPS: and is now in *Hazazon-tamar*—that is, Ein-gedi
Dost: and behold, they are in *Thicket of the Palms*, which is En-gedi

The toponym Hazazon Tamar appears elsewhere in Scripture in Gen 14:7. The various Targums of the Torah to that verse, influenced by the Hebrew, render the name as עין גדי.[86] In TC, however, the targumist unsurprisingly does not take a cue from the Targums to the Torah, because doing so would entail writing עין גדי twice in the present verse. This being said, I cannot determine whether he obtained the phrase סביך דקלייה from another source, or what basis he had for understanding חצצון as indicating a thicket.[87]

2 Chr 20:16

| MT | הַצִּ֗יץ | | בְּמַעֲלֵ֣ה | עֹלִ֤ים | הִנָּ֣ם | עֲלֵיהֶ֔ם | רְד֖וּ | מָחָ֗ר |
| TC | כלילא | דאודיקות | במסקנא | סלקין | האנון | עליהון | חותו | יומא־אחרא |

NJPS: March down against them tomorrow as they come up by the *Ascent of Ziz*
Dost: Descend upon them tomorrow. Behold, they are going up the *ascent of Odikuth Kelila* [literally, Diadem View—L.G.]

The word מַעֲלֵה, forming part of a construct phrase that describes a place, also is literally translated as מסקנא in TJ 1 Sam 9:11; 2 Sam 15:30. The phrase אודיקות כלילא is somewhat surprising, but Levy has already observed that it is in fact a double translation of the Hebrew word הַצִּיץ.[88] The first element of the double translation, אודיקות, takes the word הציץ in the verse as denoting the act

---

86   TN ad loc. somewhat expansively renders עין גדי תמריא, *Ein Gedi of the date-palms*, thus bringing the translation slightly closer to the Hebrew.

87   Churgin *Hagiographa*, p. 239, suggests that the phrase סביך דקלייה may have appeared in TPJ Genesis and the author of TC taken it from there, and that the phrase was subsequently omitted from TPJ. Though this hypothesis does explain the reading in TC, it does not explain the translation of חצצון as סביך by the original translator, whoever that may have been.

88   Levy, vol. 1, p. 11. On double translation in TC, see also pp. 67–76, below.

of viewing, a usage found in מֵצִיץ מִן־הַחֲרַכִּים (Cant 2:9) and often in rabbinic sources.[89] The second element, כלילא, renders הציץ as denoting a crown—specifically, that of the high priest, which is called צִיץ נֵזֶר־הַקֹּדֶשׁ (Exod 39:30). The Targums of the Torah in fact simply transcribe the word צִיץ, but translate the accompanying word נֵזֶר as כלילא; Peshiṭta, moreover, renders צִיץ as ܟܠܝܠܐ (Exod 28:36; 39:30; Lev 8:9). I therefore conclude that the text we have before us in TC preserves two alternate translations for the word צִיץ in its role as part of the toponym in the verse. According to the first, the place is called מסקנא דאודיקותא (literally, Watching Rise, i.e., a lookout point or elevated space from which one can observe the surrounding terrain), while according to the second it is known as מסקנא דכלילא (Diadem Rise). The two competing translations were combined as מסקנא דאודיקות כלילא, resulting in a challenging, opaque reading.

2 Chr 28:3

MT				
	וְהוּא	הִקְטִיר	בְּגֵיא	בֶן־הִנֹּם
TC	והוא	אסיק קטרתא	בחילת	בר הנם[90]

NJPS: He made offerings in the *Valley of Ben*-hinnom

Dost: He offered up incense in the *Valley of the Son of* Hinnom

This name is translated as rendered by TJ (Josh 15:8; 18:16; 2 Kgs 23:10; Jer 7:31–32; 19:2, 6; 32:35).

Other toponyms that TC translates, rather than transcribes, include: חושבנא (for חֶשְׁבּוֹן, 1 Chr 6:66); מישר ברכתא (for עֵמֶק בְּרָכָה, 2 Chr 20:26); חילת מלחא (for גֵּיא הַמֶּלַח, 2 Chr 25:11).

1 Chr 6:66

MT	וְאֶת־חֶשְׁבּוֹן	וְאֶת־מִגְרָשֶׁיהָ	וְאֶת־יַעְזֵיר	וְאֶת־מִגְרָשֶׁיהָ׃
TC	וית חושבנא	וית פרוילה׳	וית יעזר	וית פרוילהא׃

NJPS: *Heshbon* with its pasturelands, and Jazer with its pasturelands

Gottlieb: *Calculation* and its outlying areas, and Jazer and its outlying areas

---

89 The nomen regens אודיקות is a verbal noun in the *aph'el* from the root דו״ק, in this instance declined as if its root began with *yod*, as noted by Dan, p. 150, in his discussion of the occurrences of the verb in *Tg. Ps* Dan, ibid., is unsure of whether this tendency stems from the influence of Babylonian Aramaic or is an indigenous development of Palestinian Aramaic. Without weighing in on the matter, let it be noted that the targumic works in which the verb is thus declined include TPJ, *Tg. Ps*, and TC, with one instance toward the end of TN, as well. Based on this distribution, the phenomenon may be linked to Late Jewish Literary Aramaic; cf. Kaufman *TPJ*.

90 The name is thus translated in 2 Chr 33:6, as well.

The Aramaic חושבנא for the Hebrew proper noun חֶשְׁבּוֹן is found in TPJ to Deut 29:6.

2 Chr 20:26

MT וּבַיּוֹם הָרְבִעִי נִקְהֲלוּ לְעֵמֶק בְּרָכָה כִּי־שָׁם בֵּרֲכוּ אֶת־הֹ׳

TC וביומא רביעאה אתכנשו למישר ברכתא ארום תמן בריכו ית ה׳

NJPS: On the fourth day they assembled in the *Valley of Blessing*—for there they blessed the Lord

Dost: Now on the fourth day they were assembled at the *Valley of Blessing*—for there they blessed the Lord

2 Chr 25:11

MT וַאֲמַצְיָהוּ הִתְחַזַּק וַיִּנְהַג אֶת־עַמּוֹ וַיֵּלֶךְ גֵּיא הַמֶּלַח

TC ואמציהו אתקף ודבר ית עמיה ואזל לחילת מלחא

NJPS: Amaziah took courage and, leading his army, he marched to the *Valley of Salt*

Dost: When Amaziah became resolute, he led his people and went to the *Valley of Salt*

4.4.3 Conversion of Nouns to the Plural

The targumist frequently gives national names in plural form despite the singular form of the source words in his Hebrew *Vorlage*. In some instances he thus establishes agreement between a plural verb (or other accompanying word) and what is a singular noun in the Hebrew *Vorlage* (e.g., וַיִּהְיוּ מוֹאָב, 1 Chr 18:2), while in other cases the targumist engages in this practice even in the absence of any lack of agreement in the Hebrew verse, whether no verb is associated with the national name or the verb, too, is given in singular form. In these instances the targumist pluralizes the verb as well as the name. When a name appears with the adjectival sufformative *yod* in singular form (e.g., 1 Chr 1:14–16; 2:53; 2 Chr 8:7), the targumist typically gives the national name in the plural.

Following are a few examples of substitution of the singular with the plural:

1 Chr 19:12

MT אִם־תֶּחֱזַק מִמֶּנִּי אֲרָם וְהָיִיתָ לִּי לִתְשׁוּעָה וְאִם־בְּנֵי עַמּוֹן יֶחֱזְקוּ מִמְּךָ וְהוֹשַׁעְתִּיךָ:

TC אין מתקפין מני ארמאי ותהי לי לפריק ואין בני עמון יתקפון מנך ואפרקנך:

NJPS: If the *Arameans prove* too strong for me, you come to my aid; and if the Ammonites prove too strong for you, I will come to your aid

Dost: If the *Arameans are* stronger than me, then you can become my deliverer, and if the children of Ammon are stronger than you, then I will deliver you

The conversion from singular to plural in the Targum establishes agreement between the beginning and the end of the verse. The same holds true in the next example:

2 Chr 21:8

MT בְּיָמָיו֙ פָּשַׁ֣ע אֱד֔וֹם מִתַּ֖חַת יַד־ יהודה וַיַּמְלִ֥יכוּ עֲלֵיהֶ֖ם מֶֽלֶךְ׃

TC ביומי מרדו אדומאי ואשתמיטו מתחות ידא דבית יהודה ואמליכו עליהון מלכא:

NJPS: During his reign, the *Edomites rebelled* against Judah's rule and *set up* a king of *their* own

Dost: In his days the *Edomites rebelled* and withdrew from under the power of the house of Judah and *appointed* a king over *themselves*

Here, as well as twice in v. 10 below, the targumist added the verb אשתמיטו prior to the phrase מתחות יד. Finding the Hebrew phrase תחת יד + פש״ע overly abstract, he saw a need to clarify that the act of rebellion was that of the nation's slipping off the yoke of Judea. These verses parallel 2 Kgs 8:20, 22, but no verb is added in TJ ad loc., and the phrase that results in TC is unfamiliar from other sources. This choice of translation thus appears to be an independent initiative on the part of the author of TC.

2 Chr 21:10

MT וַיִּפְשַׁ֨ע אֱד֜וֹם מִתַּ֣חַת יַד־ יְהוּדָ֔ה עַ֖ד הַיּ֣וֹם הַזֶּ֑ה

TC ומרדו אדומאי דאשתמיטו מתחות ידא דבית יהודה עד יומא הדין

NJPS: *Edom has been in rebellion* against Judah, to this day

Dost: *So the Edomites who withdrew* from under the power of the house of Judah *have rebelled* until this day.

(cont.) אָ֣ז תִּפְשַׁ֧ע לִבְנָ֛ה בָּעֵ֥ת הַהִ֖יא מִתַּ֥חַת יָדֽוֹ

TC הא בכין מרדת לבנה בעדנא ההיא ואשתמיטת מתחות ידיה

NJPS: *Libnah also rebelled* against him at that time

Dost: *Behold, then Libnah rebelled* at that time *and withdrew* from under his power

This verse uses similar terminology to describe two rebellions in both the Hebrew (פש״ע) and the Aramaic (מר״ד, שמ״ט, regarding which see earlier discussion of v. 8). TJ to the parallel verse at 2 Kgs 8:22 converts both parts to the plural, rendering בכין מרדו יתבי לבנה). TC pluralizes only the first part. Why the author of TC deviated from the example of TJ in its treatment of the city of Libnah is unclear, given his tendency elsewhere to explicate that it is the residents of a city, rather than the city per se, who perform an action.

The following plural forms also are translations of singular nouns:

‏,ארפכסדאי, אתוראי, עילמאי ‏(1 Chr 1:9); ‏זינגאי, לובאי, סמראי, בנדקאי, סינידאי‏
‏(1 Chr 1:18); ‏ארפכסדיי‏ (1 Chr 1:17); ‏משכאי, גתראי, חולאי, ארמניאי, ארמאי, לודאי‏
‏(1 Chr 1:54; ‏אדומאי‏ (1 Chr 1:46); ‏מואבאי, מדיינא‏ (1 Chr 1:38); ‏שובלאי, לוטאי‏
‏(1 Chr 2:42); ‏זיפאי‏ (1 Chr 2:24); ‏תקועא‏ (1 Chr 2:23); ‏ארמא, גשוראי‏ ,2 Chr 24:23);
‏גלעדאי‏ (1 Chr 7:14);[91] ‏גבעונא‏ (1 Chr 9:35);[92] ‏עמלקא‏ (1 Chr 18:11).[93]

4.4.4 Identification of Characters

The targumist identifies figures named in Chronicles with characters familiar from other books, thus adding an additional layer of connections and ties between his composition and a number of scriptural protagonists familiar to his readership from other biblical books as well as from the aggadic world. Many of these identifications have their origins in rabbinic sources, which will be discussed in chapters seven and eight. A few identifications serve to bridge the gap left by the disparity between the orthography of some characters' names familiar from other scriptural books and the different form in which they appear in Chronicles. In these cases, the author of TC is careful to clarify that the figure appearing here with a less familiar orthography (e.g., Achar of the second example below) is identical to one who is familiar from a different book with a different spelling. We shall present here a consolidated list of identifications of characters and names throughout TC.

1. Bela son of Beor is translated as Balaam son of Beor and identified with Laban the Aramean (1 Chr 1:43.)
2. Carmi is identified with Zimri; it is clarified that Achar is Achan (1 Chr 2:7).
3. Ephrath is identified with Miriam (1 Chr 2:19; 4:4, 17).
4. Joab is identified with Joab son of Zeruiah (1 Chr 2:54).
5. The scribal families are identified with the sons of Rehabiah grandson of Moses, and Jabez with Othniel son of Kenaz; the Kenites are identified with the sons of Zipporah, and the father of the House of Rechab with Moses (1 Chr 2:55; Jabez is identified with Othniel at 1 Chr 4:9, 13, as well).
6. Daniel son of David is identified with Chileab son of David (1 Chr 3:1).
7. Eglah is identified with Michal daughter of Saul (1 Chr 3:3).
8. It is clarified that Bathshua is Bathsheba (1 Chr 3:5).

---

91 In this verse ‏מָכִיר אֲבִי גִלְעָד‏ is translated as ‏מכיר אבוהון דגלעדאי‏, whereas in 1 Chr 2:21, 23 the targumist leaves the phrase in the singular.

92 In this verse ‏אֲבִי־גִבְעוֹן‏ is translated as ‏אבהתהון דגבעונאי‏, whereas in 1 Chr 8:29 the targumist leaves the name ‏גבעון‏ in the singular.

93 Pluralization of the noun ‏עמלק‏ in this verse is in accordance with the noun ‏פלשתים‏, as in the parallel verse at TJ 2 Sam 8:12.

9.   It is clarified that Azariah is Uziah (1 Chr 3:12).

10. Anani is identified with the messiah (1 Chr 3:24).

11. Aharhel is identified with Hur (1 Chr 4:8).

12. Jephunneh is identified with Hezron (1 Chr 4:15).

13. An anonymous woman is identified with Bithiah daughter of Pharaoh; Jered father of Gedor, Heber father of Socho, and Jekuthiel father of Zanoah are identified with Moses; Mered is identified with Caleb (1 Chr 4:18).

14. Jokim is identified with Joshua; the men of Chozeba are identified with the Gibeonites; Joash and Saraph are identified with Mahlon and Chilion (1 Chr 4:22).

15. Saul is identified with Zimri (1 Chr 4:24).

16. Beerah is identified with Beerah the Prophet (i.e., the father of Hosea; 1 Chr 5:6).

17. Hodesh is identified with Beerah (1 Chr 8:9).

18. Ner is identified with Abiel (1 Chr 8:33).

19. It is clarified that Meribbaal is Mephibosheth (1 Chr 9:40).

20. Elhanan son of Jair is identified with David son of Jesse (1 Chr 20:5).

21. the giant(ess) is identified with Orpah (1 Chr 20:6, 8).

22. Shebuel is identified with Jonathan grandson of Moses (1 Chr 23:16; 26:24).

23. Shemaiah is identified with Moses (1 Chr 24:6).

24. The unnamed daughter of Pharaoh is identified with Bithiah daughter of Pharaoh (2 Chr 8:11).

25. Michaiah daughter of Uriel is identified with Maachah daughter of Absalom (2 Chr 13:2; 15:16).

26. An anonymous man is identified with the Aramean general Naaman (2 Chr 18:33).

5   Double Translations

The author of TC normally gives a single continuum of Aramaic text in translation of each individual continuum of Hebrew text, although the demands of translation are such that the length of the Aramaic continuum sometimes exceeds that of its Hebrew source. There are some instances, however, where the targumist presents two different, parallel translations for a single Hebrew continuum.[94] These are distinct from those cases where TC gives an alternate

---

94   Cf. Churgin *Hagiographa*, pp. 241–244.

translation marked ל״א (לישנא אחרינא, alternate version), in which the author or scribe announce a double translation;[95] I also do not include under this rubric the many instances where aggadic elements expressing a verse's literal or midrashic translation are interspersed within the parallel translation. Following are several examples of double translations of this description:

1 Chr 11:18

MT			וַיִּשְׂא֤וּ וַיָּבִ֙אוּ֙ אֶל־דָּוִ֔יד
TC			ונטלו
			ונסיבו ואתו לות דוד

NJPS: and they *carried* it back to David
Gottlieb: they *lifted* it and *took* it, and came to David

This verse parallels 2 Sam 23:16, where TJ renders the verb וַיִּשְׂא֤וּ as ונסיבו. Notably, the use of the root נס״ב here diverges from the author's accustomed use of that root elsewhere, where the Hebrew root נש״א denotes physical lifting of an object.[96] In those cases, it is the root נט״ל that generally appears. Therefore, TC here includes two translations for the root נש״א: one in accordance with the targumist's accustomed practice, and a second conforming to TJ to the parallel verse.

1 Chr 18:2

MT	מִנְחָֽה׃	נֹשְׂאֵ֥י	לְדָוִ֖יד	עֲבָדִ֔ים	מוֹאָב֙	וַיִּהְי֤וּ
TC	פרס	נטלי	לדוד	לעבדין	מואבאי	והוו
	דורון׃	מקרבי				

NJPS: the Moabites became *tributary vassals* of David
Dost: so the Moabites became for David servants who *bear tribute*, who *offer gifts*

1 Chr 18:6

MT	מִנְחָ֑ה	נֹשְׂאֵ֣י	עֲבָדִ֖ים	לְדָוִ֔יד	אֲרָם֙	וַיְהִ֤י
TC	פרס	נטלי	לעבדין	לדוד	ארמאי	והוו
	מיסין	מסקי				

NJPS: and the Arameans became *tributary vassals* of David
Dost: and the Arameans became to David servants who *bear tribute*, who *pay taxes*

---

95 On this topic, see Introduction, p. 5, above.
96 As opposed, e.g., to marrying a woman, which in TC is translated with the root נס״ב, as is the conventional targumic practice for the more common scriptural phrase, לק״ח אשה. See also Posen, pp. 25–28.

The phrase נֹשְׂאֵי מִנְחָה appears twice in Samuel (2 Sam 8:2, 6), and in both instances is translated by TJ as נְטלי פרס. The word פרס has its origins in the Greek φόρος,[97] which denotes a tax or tribute paid to the king or, alternately, the consideration for work performed. The two verses cited above parallel the two verses of Chronicles excerpted here. It is thus no surprise that the phrase נטלי פרס appears in their rendering in TC, as well. Nevertheless, aside from this phrase, TC to each of the verses gives an additional translation: in one מקרבי דורון and in the other מסקי מיסין. TC, then, gives a double translation for each of the two verses and—although a mere four verses intervene between them— TC gives two different alternate translations for the Hebrew phrase נֹשְׂאֵי מִנְחָה.

The phrase מסקי מיסין, denoting tributaries, appears in TO and TN as part of the translation of the Hebrew expression הי"ה למס (Gen 49:15; Deut 20:11) and functions similarly in TJ (Josh 16:10; 17:13; Judg 1:28, 30, 33, 35; 2 Sam 20:24; 1 Kgs 4:6; 5:27–28; 9:15, 21; 12:18). TC also makes use of this phrase at the two points in Chronicles where the word מַס appears (2 Chr 8:8; 10:18). The addition of the phrase in v. 6 thus appears intended to identify נֹשְׂאֵי מִנְחָה with the terminology (מַס) used elsewhere in Scripture to signify tribute.

The phrase מקרבי דורון is unique in targumic literature. The word דורון, however, is given as a translation of מִנְחָה at several points in TN and TPJ.[98] This unique targumic rendering, preserved within a double translation in TC, therefore would seem to reflect an effort to translate נֹשְׂאֵי מִנְחָה literally, without the influence of TJ. I cannot say why the targumist treated the Aramean bearers of tribute differently from those hailing from Moab.

We might ask what defect there is in the translation of this expression's two appearances in TJ that necessitated a double translation in TC. As noted earlier, the Aramaic נט"ל is a conventional equivalent of the Hebrew נש"א that is used in TC to denote delivery of tribute to a king. Yet be that as it may, the reader may be liable to understand the Hebrew form of this expression inversely, as we find with van Staalduine-Sulman's hesitation regarding the precise meaning of the word פרס in TJ due to the word's absence from the remainder of targumic literature and its talmudic denotation of a consideration for work performed, rather than tribute to a king.[99] The double translation in TC may be intended to avoid such vagueness in the term's meaning, as individuals well-versed in rabbinic parlance are familiar with the phrase נט"ל פרס in the sense

97   Krauss *Lehnwörter*, p. 491; Sokoloff *Syriac*, pp. 1244–1245.

98   TN Gen 4:3; 32:14, 19, 21–22; 33:10; 43:11, 15, 25–26; TPJ Gen 32:14, 19, 21–22; 43:11, 15, 25, 26; Num 16:15; 28:8, 26.

99   Van Staalduine-Sulman *TJ Samuel*, p. 535, and literature cited ibid.

of receiving a stipend from the king, rather than bringing tribute to him, as indicated in several locations in the Talmud, such as *b. Meg.* 6b:

איטליא שליון זה כרך גדול שלרומי ... הנולד בו אע״פ שלא דר בו והדר בו אע״פ
שלא נולד בו—נוטל פרס מאת המלך.

Italy of Greece (Magna Graecia) is a large city of Rome ... and [every] resident, even if not born there, receives a gift [from the king].

The author of TC exhibits broad knowledge of the Babylonian Talmud, as we shall see in the chapter seven, and certainly was familiar with this and related talmudic expressions. It is not self-evident, but perhaps the double translation of נטלי פרס, which the author of TC inherited from TJ, came about on account of the potential for misunderstanding this rare expression and the targumist's desire to clarify that the meaning is payment of tribute to the king.

1 Chr 21:2

MT   לְכוּ סִפְרוּ אֶת־יִשְׂרָאֵל ... וְהָבִיאוּ אֵלַי וְאֵדְעָה אֶת־מִסְפָּרָם:
TC   איזילו מנו ית ישראל ... ואייתיאו לותי   ית סכומהון
     וית מנינהון:

NJPS: Go and count Israel ... and bring me information as to *their number*
Dost: Go, number Israel ... and bring to me *their tally* and *their number*

1 Chr 21:16

MT   וַיִּפֹּל דָּוִיד וְהַזְּקֵנִים
TC   ונפל דוד וספריא
     וסביא

NJPS: David and the *elders* ... threw themselves
Dost: And David, together with the *scribes* and the *elders* ... fell

The word זְקֵנִים typically is translated as סביא in TO and TJ, as well as throughout TC.[100] Translation of the word זָקֵן, elder, as סְפֵר, scribe, is unfamiliar from other Targums or elsewhere in TC, and occurs only here.[101] I do not know why

---

Aside from the present verse: 1 Chr 11:3; 15:25; 2 Chr 5:2, 4; 10:6, 8, 13; 34:29; 36:17.

The word וספריא is absent in MS E, but its appearance in the present verse as part of a double translation in the other MSS indicates that it was omitted from E.

this word was used at this specific point, but its appearance results in what appears to be a double translation.[102]

2 Chr 4:10

| MT | וְאֶת־הַיָּם נָתַן מִכֶּתֶף הַיְמָנִית קֵדְמָה מִמּוּל נֶגְבָּה: |
| TC | וית ימא יהב מן עיבר ביתא ימינא לרוח קדומא מדינחא מקביל דרומא: |

NJPS: He set the sea on the right side, at the *southeast* corner
Dost: He put the sea on the right side of the house on the *east* side, *to the east,* facing south

This double translation was influenced by TO and TPJ Exod 38:13: ולרוח קדומא מדינחא חמשין אמין.

2 Chr 5:6

| MT | וְהַמֶּלֶךְ שְׁלֹמֹה וְכָל־עֲדַת יִשְׂרָאֵל ... מְזַבְּחִים צֹאן וּבָקָר אֲשֶׁר לֹא־ יִסָּפְרוּ |
| TC | ומלכא שלמה וכל כנשתא דישראל ... מנכסין ודבחין עאן ותורין דלית להון סכימא |

NJPS: King Solomon and the whole community of Israel ... were *sacrificing* sheep and oxen in such abundance that they could not be numbered
Dost: King Solomon and all of the congregation of Israel ... (were) *slaughtering* and *sacrificing* sheep and oxen, which were innumerable

TJ to the parallel verse at 1 Kgs 8:5 reads מנכסין. Both TO and TJ persistently alternate between the Aramaic roots נכ״ס and דב״ח in their translations of the Hebrew root זב״ח. The author of TC, conversely, uses the root דב״ח frequently but renders זב״ח as נכ״ס in only one of sixteen appearances (aside from the present verse).[103] The author of TC seems in our verse to have taken the translation used in TJ and preceded it with the verb he was accustomed to using, viz., דבחין.[104]

---

102   The word ספר serves as the translation of the Hebrew סוֹפֵר, but also as that of the word נָבִיא in many instances in TJ. Cf. van Staalduine-Sulman *TJ Samuel,* pp. 150–151. With this in mind, we might suppose that the targumist sought to attribute prophetic status to the elders indicated here (so that perhaps their falling earthward like David signals that they, too, saw the angel of the Lord), but this is improbable given that it is not the practice of TC to translate נָבִיא as ספר.

103   זב״ח is translated as דב״ח in the following 15 instances: 1 Chr 15:26; 21:28; 29:21; 2 Chr 5:6; 7:4–5; 11:16; 15:11; 28:4, 23; 30:22; 33:16–17, 22; 34:4.
        Translation of זב״ח as נכ״ס: 2 Chr 18:2 (MS E here has a verb from the root נס״ב, but this appears to be the result of corruption).

104   TJ itself contains a variant reading, מדבחין, in this verse. See Sperber, vol. 2, p. 231.

2 Chr 6:2

MT: עוֹלָמִים   לְשִׁבְתְּךָ   וּמָכוֹן   לָךְ   בֵּית־זְבֻל   בָּנִיתִי   וַאֲנִי

TC: לבית שכנתך   אתר מתקן   בית מקדשא קדמך   ואנא בניתי

כל קבל כורסי בית מותבך   דבשמיא לעלמין: ומכוון

NJPS: I have built for You a stately House, *and a place where You may dwell* forever.

Dost: I, indeed, have built a temple before You, *a place prepared as an abode for Your Shekhinah* and built *according* to the throne of the *house of Your habitation*, which is in the heavens forever.

This double translation draws from TJ to the parallel verse (1 Kgs 8:13) while appending to it an additional exegetical tradition.[105]

2 Chr 6:28

MT   בָּאָרֶץ   כִּי־יִהְיֶה   רָעָב

TC   אולצן

כפנא   כד יהי   בארעא

NJPS: if there is a *famine* in the land

Dost: When *distress* of *famine* is in the land

TO and TJ typically translate רָעָב as כפן, and this word indeed is that which appears in TJ to the parallel verse at 1 Kgs 8:37. The word רְעָבוֹן/רָעָב is translated as אולצן in *Tg. Ps* 33:19; 37:19.[106] Only in TC do אולצן and כפנא appear concurrently. The Targum appears to contain two possible translations that have been spliced together as an artificial construct phrase: one in accordance with the targumic tradition of TJ, and another following the Aramaic dialect of the targumist, which is close to that of *Tg. Ps*[107]

2 Chr 19:9

MT   שָׁלֵם: וּבְלֵבָב   בֶּאֱמוּנָה   ה'   בְּיִרְאַת   תַּעֲשׂוּן   כֹּה

TC   בהימנותא   דה'   בדחלתא   תעבדון   הכדין

וקשטא   ובלב   שלים:

NJPS: This is how you shall act: in fear of the LORD, *with fidelity*, and with whole heart.

---

105   On this topic, see below, pp. 135–136.

106   In Job 5:22; 30:3, the Hebrew word כָּפָן is translated as אולצן.

107   Weiss, p. 94, n. 135, suggests a somewhat different solution, taking the view that כפנא is a gloss for אולצן. Yet if indeed אולצן constituted a natural equivalent in the Aramaic dialect of the targumist, there would be no need for a gloss. I therefore prefer to explain that כפנא reflects the influence of TJ, rather than a need to explain אולצן.

McIvor: Thus you will act, in the fear of the Lord, *in faithfulness and truth*, and in sincerity of heart.[108]

The two most common equivalents of Hebrew אֱמוּנָה in targumic literature are הימנותא and קשוט.[109] In TC in particular, though, this is not the case. הימנותא is the expected equivalent of אֱמוּנָה in TC, while קשוט tends to translate אֱמֶת.[110] 2 Chr 19:9 would be the only place in TC where קשוט translates אֱמוּנָה, which calls for an explanation.

A possible explanation is that the Aramaic text before us is the result of two stages of translation. The particular Hebrew expression at hand, בֶּאֱמוּנָה וּבְלֵבָב שָׁלֵם, is very similar to another one, בֶּאֱמֶת וּבְלֵבָב שָׁלֵם, which appears in 2 Kgs 20:3 (note also its nearly identical parallel in Isa 38:3). TJ there translates בקשוט ובלבב שלים. A translator of TC may have had this verse in his mind (or perhaps even in his Hebrew manuscript) leading him to render קשטא, as he did regularly when אֱמֶת appeared in Chronicles.

In a second stage, when the Hebrew text was recognized to be אֱמוּנָה, the regular equivalent for אֱמוּנָה in TC—הימנותא—was introduced into the Targum, while קשטא of the first stage was not eliminated, resulting in a rather charming hendiadys, בהימנותא וקשטא.[111]

2 Chr 24:22

| MT | וּכְמוֹתוֹ | אָמַר | יֵרֶא | ה' | וְיִדְרֹשׁ: |
| TC | וכד מטא לממת | אמר | יתגלי | קדם ה' | ויתפרע ויתבע: |

NJPS: As he was dying, he said, "May the LORD see and *require it*."

Dost: As he was dying he said, "Let it be revealed before the Lord, and let Him *exact revenge* and *seek (it) out*."

108 In this instance I quoted McIvor because Dost did not give representation to the double translation (rendering both together as "in faithfulness").

109 אֱמוּנָה translated by הימנותא: TN FT TPJ Exod 17:12; TJ 2 Kgs 12:16; 22:7; Isa 11:5; 59:4; Jer 5:1, 3; 7:28; 9:2; Hos 2:22; *Tg. Ps* 33:4; 36:6; 37:3; 89:34, 50; 96:13; 100:5; 119:30, 90, 138; *Tg. Prov* 12:17, 22; *Tg. Lam* 3:23; 1 Chr 9:22, 26, 31; 2 Chr 19:9 (the example under discussion); 31:12, 15, 18; 34:12.

      אֱמוּנָה translated by קשוט: TJ 1 Sam 26:23; Hab 2:4; *Tg. Ps* 40:11; 88:12; 89:2–3, 6, 9, 25; 92:3; 98:3; 119:75, 86; 143:1.

110 הימנותא is the equivalent of אֱמוּנָה in TC in the places mentioned in the above footnote. קשוט as an equivalent of אֱמֶת in TC: 2 Chr 9:5; 15:3; 18:15; 31:20; 32:1.

111 הימנותא וקשוט appear together as a double translation for אֱמֶת in *Tg. Ps* 45:5. However, I don't see cause or reason for any direct influence of one verse on the other in this case.

This is not a routine case of double translation, as פר״ע is not used else-where as a regular translation of דר״ש. I believe that the surprising translation found here is a product of its resemblance to another verse and its targum. In Exod 5:21, the Israelite foremen say to Moses and Aaron, יֵרֶא הֲ׳ עֲלֵיכֶם וְיִשְׁפֹּט. That sentence is rendered in TO as אתגלי ה׳ עליכון ויתפרע, and in TPJ as יתגלי קדם ה׳ עולבננא ולחוד יתפרע מינכון.

The structure indicated by this verse is that the sight of God, expressed by גל״י קדם, brings judgment, and judgment is expressed with the root פר״ע in the *etpaʿal*.[112] A similar structure may be found in other scriptural verses:

1 Sam 24:16

MT: וְהָיָה ה׳ לְדַיָּן וְשָׁפַט בֵּינִי וּבֵינֶךָ וְיֵרֶא וְיָרֵב אֶת־רִיבִי וְיִשְׁפְּטֵנִי מִיָּדֶךָ׃

TJ: ויהי ה׳ לדיין ועביד דין בינא ובינך וגלי קדמוהי דידין דיני ויתפרע עלבני מנך׃

NJPS: May the LORD be arbiter and may He judge between you and me! May He take note and uphold my cause, and vindicate me against you."

Clem: And may the Lord be for a judge and may He execute judgment be-tween me and you, and may it *be revealed before Him* who will plead my cause, and may my affliction be *avenged* on you."

2 Kgs 19:16

MT: הַטֵּה ה׳ | אָזְנְךָ וּשֲׁמָע פְּקַח ה׳ עֵינֶיךָ וּרְאֵה וּשְׁמַע אֵת דִּבְרֵי סַנְחֵרִיב

TJ: גלי קדמך ה׳ ודין ושמיע קדמך ואתפרע ועביד על כל פתגמי סנחריב

NJPS: O LORD, incline Your ear and hear; open Your eyes and see. Hear the words that Sennacherib

Clem: *It is revealed before You*, O Lord, and judged and heard before You, *so take vengeance* and do against all the words of Sennacherib

The targum of this last verse is indeed far from the literal meaning of the Hebrew (as well as its parallel at Isa 37:17), but nevertheless faithfully reflects the expectation that God will witness the injustice and consequently exact ret-ribution from the malfeasor.

This linguistic structure, which we have seen in TO, TPJ, and TJ, also appears elsewhere in TC:

---

112 This is the place to note that the root גל״י commonly serves in targumic literature to cor-respond to various Hebrew verbs describing divine actions in human terms. Chester dedi-cated much of his research to the manner in which the root גל״י is used in the Targums; see Chester, pp. 264–268.

1 Chr 12:18

MT   יֵרֶא   אֱלֹהֵי   אֲבוֹתֵינוּ   וְיוֹכַח:

TC   יתגלא קדם אלהי דאבהתנא ויתפרע:

NJPS: then let the God of our fathers take notice and give judgment

Dost: *it will be revealed before* the God of our fathers, and *He will repay* (you)

The author of TC chose to translate the verb וְיוֹכַח nonliterally, as ויתפרע, because the structure of the Hebrew verse reminded him of such verses as Exod 5:21. It seems to me that such a thing happened with regard to the present verse, as well. I believe that these targumic structures, particularly that at Exod 5:21, caused the targumist to render our verse in Chronicles such that וְיִשְׁפֹּט is echoed by ויתפרע. The verb ויתבע appearing in the Targum constitutes a literal translation of וְיִדְרֹשׁ. The result is a kind of double translation of the word וְיִדְרֹשׁ.

2 Chr 32:28

MT   וְיִצְהָר   וְתִירוֹשׁ   דָּגָן   לִתְבוּאַת   וּמִסְכְּנוֹת

TC   ובית אוצרין

    ומשח   וחמר   עיבור   לעללת   ואורייאות

NJPS: and *store-cities* with the produce of grain, wine, and oil,

Dost: and the *storehouses* and *granaries* for the harvest of grain, wine, and oil

TC generally translates מסכנות as בית אוצר, as do TO, TPJ, and TJ.[113] In one *aggadic* expansion in TC, the targumist uses the term אוריא to signify a granary (1 Chr 21:13, אוריאיא דדויד מליין עיבורא). The word מסכנות appears in our verse in a context indicating that these are storage facilities for grain, wine, and oil. In all other appearances of the word in Scripture, the context does not indicate the precise function of the storage facilities. It may be for this reason that the word was translated using both the accustomed equivalent of TO and the denotation indicated by the present context.

2 Chr 36:6

MT   בְּבֶלָה: לְהֹלִיכוֹ   בַּנְחֻשְׁתַּיִם   וַיַּאַסְרֵהוּ   בָּבֶל   מֶלֶךְ   נְבוּכַדְנֶאצַּר   עָלָה   עָלָיו

TC   עלוהי סליק נכבוד נצר מלכא דבבל ואסריה בכירומנקיא

    בשושלון דנחשא לאובלא יתיה לבבל:

NJPS: King Nebuchadnezzar of Babylon marched against him; he bound him in *fetters* to convey him to Babylon

Dost: Nebuchadnezzar king of Babylon came up against him and bound him in *manacles*, in *bronze chains*, to lead him to Babylon

---

113   2 Chr 8:4, 6; 16:4; 17:12; and the present verse. See also TO and TPJ Exod 1:11 and TJ 1 Kgs 9:19.

The phrase שושלון דנחשא is the habitual translation of נחשתים.[114] The word כירומנקיא (lit., handcuffs; see p. 467) appears once more in TC, in 2 Chr 33:11 (and nowhere else in targumic literature), corresponding to חחים, which parallels the Hebrew נחשתים, the last of which is translated, as in the present verse, as שושלון דנחשא:[115]

2 Chr 33:11

MT וַיִּלְכְּד֤וּ אֶת־מְנַשֶּׁה֙ בַּחֹחִ֔ים וַיַּאַסְרֻ֙הוּ֙ בַּֽנְחֻשְׁתַּ֔יִם וַיּוֹלִיכֻ֖הוּ בָּבֶֽלָה׃

TC ואחדו ית מנשה בכירומנקייא ואסרוהי בשושלון דנחשא ואובלוהי לבבל׃

NJPS: who took Manasseh captive in manacles, bound him in fetters, and led him off to Babylon

Dost: and they seized Manasseh with manacles, and they bound him with chains of bronze, and led him away to Babylon

The clear similarity between the two verses may have caused the targumist to insert the parallel of the phrase שושלון דנחשא in our verse, as well, thus producing a double translation.[116]

6 Harmonization

6.1 *Reconciliation of Conflicts between Biblical Books*

The content of the Book of Chronicles, which so often parallels that of other biblical books, frequently compels the targumist to contend with contradictions posed by these other books. In a few instances the targumist seeks to harmonize the books, i.e., to proffer a solution according to which there is no real contradiction between the sources, but rather each provides partial information and both are accurate. This approach of accepting all relevant information without criticism required the targumist concurrently to elucidate both truths by establishing distinctions between the statements of the two books that appear mutually exclusive. Thus, for instance, it is stated in 2 Chr 9:12 that Solomon gave the queen of Sheba all that she sought and that she, too, bestowed gifts on Solomon. The parallel verse at 1 Kgs 10:13 states that Solomon

---

114 The other appearances of נחשתים in Scripture are translated with phrases similar to that in our verse: שישלן דנחש (TJ Judg 16:21; 2 Kgs 25:7; Jer 39:7; 52:11); זיקין דנחש (2 Sam 3:34); שושלון דנחשא (2 Chr 33:11).

115 The targumist's choice of the word כירומנקייא reflects the influence of rabbinic literature, as noted below, p. 467.

116 White, pp. 246, 254, notes that the targumist borrowed the word כירומנקיא in 2 Chr 36:6 from 2 Chr 33:11, without offering an explanation of what caused him to do so.

not only gave her all that she sought, but also gave her even things that she had not requested, in accordance with the king's means. TC explains that those things that he gave her in addition to those she sought were in consideration of the gifts she had brought him:

2 Chr 9:12	אֲשֶׁר־	מִלְּבַד	שָׁאָלָה אֲשֶׁר אֶת־כָּל־חֶפְצָהּ לְמַלְכַּת־שְׁבָא נָתַן שְׁלֹמֹה וְהַמֶּלֶךְ
TC	די ממה בר מניה	בעת	ית כל רעותה די למלכת זמרגד יהב שלמה ומלכא
1 Kgs 10:13	אֲשֶׁר	מִלְּבַד	שָׁאָלָה אֲשֶׁר אֶת־כָּל־חֶפְצָהּ לְמַלְכַּת־שְׁבָא נָתַן שְׁלֹמֹה וְהַמֶּלֶךְ

(cont.) וַתֵּלֶךְ לְאַרְצָהּ הִיא וַעֲבָדֶיהָ:	וַתִּפֶן וַתַּהֲפֹךְ	הַבִּיאָה אֶל־הַמֶּלֶךְ
TC	לארעא היא ועבדהא: ואזלת ואתפניאת	מניה דאייתיאת לות מלכא מה חלופי לה יהב
(cont.) וַתֵּלֶךְ לְאַרְצָהּ הִיא וַעֲבָדֶיהָ:	וַתֵּפֶן שְׁלֹמֹה הַמֶּלֶךְ כְּיַד	נָתַן־לָהּ

NJPS: King Solomon, in turn, gave the queen of Sheba everything she expressed a desire for, exceeding a return for what she had brought to the king. Then she and her courtiers left and returned to her own land.

TC: King Solomon gave to the queen of Zemargad every desire that she requested from him, excluding what he gave to her in exchange for what she brought to the king. Then she turned and went to her own land, she and her servants.

NJPS (Kgs): King Solomon, in turn, gave the queen of Sheba everything she wanted and asked for, in addition to what King Solomon gave her out of his royal bounty. Then she and her attendants left and returned to her own land.

The words ‫יהב לה חלופי מה ד-‬ constitute a targumic addition to the text in Chronicles, but correspond partially to the wording found in Kings (‫יהב לה‬). The targumist's agenda is straightforward: to use the supplementary text to unify the disparate reports of 1 Kings and 2 Chronicles and thus unify them as a single, harmonious account.

Additional examples of harmonization between Chronicles and other biblical books:

> 1 Chr 11:13 with 2 Sam 23:11 (half lentils and half barley).[117]
> 2 Chr 2:13 with 1 Kgs 7:14 (she is of the daughters of Dan, but her father is descended from Naphtali).[118]

---

117 See broader discussion of the targum to this verse and its sources, pp. 299–301 below.

118 See broader discussion of this solution by the targumist and his sources, pp. 333–336, below.

2 Chr 4:5 with 1 Kgs 7:26 (2,000 liquid units, 3,000 dry).[119]

2 Chr 11:20; 13:2; 15:16 with 2 Kgs 15:2, 10 (Michaiah daughter of Uriel was the name used by Maachah daughter of Absalom after her resumption of her seemly ways).[120]

6.2   *Synthesis of Competing Views in Extra-Biblical Source Material*

In dozens of cases throughout TC, the targumist premises his work on rabbinic literary sources, first and foremost among them the Babylonian Talmud. This phenomenon will be discussed comprehensively in chapters seven and eight. For now, we will make do with an observation regarding his approach to these sources. The Babylonian Talmud commonly presents varying opinions or exegeses regarding a given verse. Sometimes the author of TC bases his comments on the Talmud and inserts its insights within his translation in the form of a synthesis of disparate talmudic opinions. In other instances the targumist bases his work on two different sources that he integrates within his composition. Following are several examples of the targumist's technique of synthesizing different views contained in his sources:

1 Chr 4:10 (the prayer of Jabez): The Targum synthesizes various homilies from *b. Tem.* 16a.[121]

1 Chr 11:22 (the exploits of Benaiah son of Jehoiada): TC includes various opinions recorded in *b. Ber.* 18b.[122]

1 Chr 16:3: The translation of אֲשִׁישָׁה is based on two interpretations of the word given in *b. Pesaḥ.* 36b.[123]

1 Chr 21:15: The objects of God's vision in the Targum appear as different suggestions in *b. Ber.* 62b.[124]

1 Chr 29:11: TC is based on two exegeses in *b. Ber.* 58a.[125]

2 Chr 23:11: The account of the coronation of Joash brings together *b. ʾAbod. Zar.* 44a and an aggadic tradition similar to that found in the Reuchlin MS on 2 Kgs 11:12.[126]

---

119 See broader discussion of this matter in the Targum and its sources, pp. 336–337, below.

120 See broader discussion of the woman's name and the sources informing TC on the matter, pp. 482–484, below.

121 See broader discussion of these expansions and their relationship with the Talmud, pp. 257–261, below.

122 See discussion and analysis of this expansion in TC, pp. 301–306, below.

123 See detailed discussion of this topic, pp. 309–311, below.

124 See detailed discussion of this topic, pp. 318–323, below.

125 See detailed discussion of this topic, pp. 327–333, below.

126 See detailed discussion of this topic, pp. 409–412, below.

7 Trends in Targum Chronicles

7.1 *Lexicon of Divine Honor*

7.1.1 Opening

It is well known that the Aramaic Targums tend to deviate from the literal meaning of the Hebrew in their treatment of a great many terms concerning God, in effect forming a lexicon, or a collection of specialized expressions, for this area. Across the generations, sages and scholars have deliberated on the precise purpose of this targumic convention—to avoid anthropomorphism, perhaps, or to serve as a token of respect in discussions of God?[127]—but the phenomenon per se of these specialized expressions for description of God is highly conspicuous throughout targumic literature, including TC. The author of TC was well-versed in the various translation techniques used in descriptions of God and put them to use throughout his opus. Below we shall list a selection of such expressions appearing in TC and consider how the targumist employed them, while casting a comparative gaze toward the approach taken by the earlier Targums.

7.1.2 מימרא דה׳

The question of this phrase's function in various targumic works has been scrutinized over many generations, and has occupied modern scholarship since the start of the last century. Some scholars compare the term to the theological concept *logos* (λόγος), a central idea in Hellenic Judaism (Philo) and Christianity, and see מימרא דה׳ as a hypostasis of God. Others opine that the expression is merely a linguistic convention, a translation technique in use among the targumists to express respect for the Creator but lacking any inherent theological significance. The former view has been advocated by Weber in the previous century and in the present by Boyarin and, with some reservations, Hayward, who points to development in this respect across targumic works. The latter view has been espoused by Moore, Billerbeck, and Klein.[128] Whatever the origins of the term in early targumic literature, the use of the

---

127   There is a wide-ranging literature concerning this question; see Kadushin, pp. 325–336; Smolar-Aberbach, pp. 130–150; Smelik, pp. 99–111; van Staalduine-Sulman *TJ Samuel*, pp. 121–126, and literature cited ibid.

128   See survey in Chester, pp. 293–312, including the essential views of Saadyah Ga'on, Maimonides, and Naḥmanides, proceeding with Weber, the contrary opinions of Moore and Billerbeck, and a discussion of the current (1986) state of scholarship. See also Hayward *Memra*, pp. 9–10; Klein *Anthropomorphism*; Boyarin *Memra*; Boyarin *Border Lines*, pp. 112–127.

expression in TC is not necessarily instructive regarding its development or the manner of its use in earlier targumic compositions.

The word מימרא precedes the name of the Lord, or else a suffixed pronoun substituting for it (such as מימריה), over 100 times in TC. Certain verbs are translated literally along with the name of God without insertion of the word מימרא, while other verbs and parts of speech tend to appear accompanied by the added word. Thus, for instance, the targumist does not add the word מימרא when God's name functions as the subject (and sometimes the object) of verbs with the stems אמ״ר, בר״ך, נת״ן, יה״ב, רע״י, and מל״ל, inter alia.[129] The targumist was inconsistent in his treatment of the roots נו״ח and מס״ר, as with the expression מל״ל על ה׳ (not to be confused with verses where God's name is the subject of this verb).[130] In several instances the targumist added the word מימרא to the phrase שֵׁם ה׳ (or the word שֵׁם appearing with a suffixed pronoun referring to God): 1 Chr 16:2; 29:1; 2 Chr 6:1, 10; 14:10; 18:15; 20:8; 33:17–18. Meanwhile, elsewhere the targumist did not add the word מימרא to the phrase שֵׁם ה׳, but instead translated שמא דה׳: 1 Chr 21:19; 22:7, 19; 2 Chr 1:18; 2:3; 6:7. In several

---

129 בר״ך: 1 Chr 16:36; 17:27; 26:5; 29:10, 20; 2 Chr 2:11; 9:8; 20:26; 25:24; 31:8.

יה״ב: 1 Chr 25:5; 28:5; 2 Chr 13:16; 18:11; 28:5; 32:29.

רע״י: 1 Chr 15:2; 28:4; 2 Chr 12:13; 29:11.

מל״ל: 1 Chr 21:9; 2 Chr 6:10; 23:3; 33:10; 35:6.

אמ״ר: 2 Chr 18:9; 21:12; 33:4, 7.

נת״ן: 1 Chr 22:12.

130 מס״ר (for Hebrew נת״ן):

ואפכו בני ישראל מן קדם דבית יהודה ומסרנון ה׳ בידיהון 2 Chr 13:16

Dost: Then the children of Israel fled from before those of the house of Judah, and *the Lord delivered them* into their hands.

ומסריה ה׳ אלהיה בידא דמלכא דארם 2 Chr 28:5

Dost: So *the Lord*, his God, *handed him over* into the hand of the king of Aram

כל מלכוותא דארעא מסר לי מימרא דה׳ אלהא דשמיא 2 Chr 36:23

Dost: The *Memra of the Lord*, the God of the heavens, *has delivered* unto me all of the kingdoms of the earth

נו״ח (in Hebrew and Aramaic):

אניח מימרא דה׳ אלהא דישראל לעמיה 1 Chr 23:25

Dost: The *Memra of the Lord*, the God of Israel, *has given rest* to His people

ולית עמיה קרבא בשניא האלין ארום אנח ה׳ ליה 2 Chr 14:5

Dost: and he did not have war in those years, for *the Lord gave rest* to him

ואניח ה׳ להון מן חזור חזור 2 Chr 15:15

Dost: and the Lord gave rest to them from round about

מל״ל על (for Hebrew דב״ר):

ותוב מלילו עבדוהי סטיא על מימרא דה׳ אלהים ועל יחזקיה עבדיה 2 Chr 32:16

Dost: Yet again his servants *incited* rebellion *against the Memra of the Lord* God and against Hezekiah His servant.

ומלילו על אלהא דשכנתיה שריא בירושלם היכמא דמלילו על טעות עממי ארעא 2 Chr 32:19

Dost: And they *spoke about the God* whose Shekhinah was dwelling in Jerusalem just as they spoke about the idols of the gentiles of the land

places the targumist wrote שמא דה' as corresponding to the unattached name ה' in the Hebrew: 1 Chr 21:24, 26; 22:5–6; 2 Chr 2:11; 5:13; 6:4; 35:3. At one point, 2 Chr 3:1, he wrote שמא דה' in an expansion. I have not found any reason for the inconsistency. Here we shall note several Hebrew expressions to which the word מימרא frequently is added:

The Hebrew expression X אלהים עם/הי"ה ה' (used in either a blessing or a description), is translated as הו"ה מימרא דה' בסעדיה, as in:[131]

2 Chr 22:11

| MT | עִמָּךְ | ה' | יְהִי | בְנִי | עַתָּה |
| TC | בסעדך | דה' | מימרא | יהא | ברי | כדון |

NJPS: Now, my son, *may the LORD be with you*
Dost: Now, my son, *may the Memra of the Lord be at your aid*

TC here follows in the footsteps of TO, TPJ (Gen 26:28; Exod 10:10; Num 14:43), and TJ (Judg 2:18; 1 Sam 18:12, 14; 20:13; 1 Kgs 1:37; 2 Kgs 18:7; Zech 10:5).

באלהים/בה': When the preposition בְּ precedes a divine name (or a suffixed pronoun referring to God), the resulting phrase is rendered as במימרא דה':[132]

1 Chr 5:20

| MT | בּוֹ: | כִּי־בָטְחוּ | לָהֶם | וְנַעְתּוֹר | בַּמִּלְחָמָה | זָעֲקוּ | לֵאלֹהִים | כִּי |
| TC | במימריה: | אתרחיצו | ארום | צלותהון | וקבל | בקרבא | צלו | קדם ה' | ארום |

NJPS: for they cried to God in the battle, and He responded to their entreaty because they trusted *in Him*
Dost: For they prayed before the Lord during the battle, and He received their prayer because they trusted *in His Memra*

1 Chr 10:13

| MT | בַּה' | אֲשֶׁר מָעַל | בְּמַעֲלוֹ | שָׁאוּל | וַיָּמָת |
| TC | דה' | במימרא | דשקר | שקריה | מטול | שאול | ומית |

NJPS: Saul died for the trespass that he had committed *against the LORD*
Dost: So Saul died because of his treachery that he committed *against the Memra of the Lord*

---

131   The phrase X עם (הי"ה/ה' אלהים) appears in Chronicles at the following points, in each case translated as הו"ה מימרא דה' בסעדיה: 1 Chr 9:20; 11:9; 17:2; 22:11, 16, 18; 28:20; 2 Chr 1:1; 15:2, 9; 17:3; 19:11; 20:17; 25:7; 36:23.

132   The phrase במימרא דה' (or else an equivalent phrase with a suffixed pronoun substituted for God's name) appears at the following points in TC: 1 Chr 5:20; 10:13; 14:10, 14; 21:15; 2 Chr 6:4, 15; 7:16; 12:2; 20:7, 20; 26:16; 28:19, 22; 29:19; 30:7, 9; 32:1, 24; 33:13; 36:13. Sometimes it appears in expansions (those not corresponding to any word in the Hebrew *Vorlage*).

1 Chr 14:10

MT   וַיִּשְׁאַל דָּוִיד בֵּֽאלֹהִים֮ לֵאמֹר֒ הַאֶֽעֱלֶה֙ עַל־פְּלִשְׁתִּ֔ים (ק׳) ... וַיֹּאמֶר לוֹ֨ ה׳ עֲלֵ֔ה

TC   ושאל דוד במימרא דה׳ למימר האסק על פלשתאי ... ואמר ליה ה׳ סק

NJPS: David inquired *of God*, "Shall I go up against the Philistines?..." And the
LORD answered him, "Go up ..."

Dost: So David inquired *of the Memra of the Lord*, saying, "Shall I go up against
the Philistines ...?" Then the Lord said him, "Go up ..."

(1 Chr 14:10 ‖ 2 Sam 5:19, where TJ similarly renders מימרא דה׳)

2 Chr 20:20

MT   הַאֲמִ֜ינוּ בַּה׳ אֱלֹהֵיכֶם֙ וְתֵאָמֵ֔נוּ   וַיֹּ֗אמֶר הַאֲמִ֤ינוּ בִנְבִיאָיו֙ וְהַצְלִֽיחוּ:

TC   הימינו במימרא דה׳ אלהכון והימינו באוריתיה ואמר והימינו בנביוהי ותצלחון:

NJPS: Trust firmly in *the LORD* your God and you will stand firm; trust firmly in
His prophets and you will succeed

Dost: Believe in *the Memra of the Lord* your God, believe in His Torah, and believe in His prophecies, so that you may be successful

The addition of במימרא in deference to God is particularly conspicuous here in
view of the word's absence prior to בִּנְבִיאָיו, at the end of the verse, which in the
Hebrew is structured similarly to its beginning (האמינו בX).[133]

   This targumic convention is quite common in TO, but even more so in TJ. TO
translates the phrase מע״ל בה׳ as שקק״ר קדם ה׳ (Lev 5:21; Num 5:6; 31:16), while TJ
translates the term as שקק״ר במימרא דה׳ (Josh 22:16, 22, 31). TC follows the latter
at 1 Chr 10:13, above.

---

133   The Hebrew verse is comprised of two parallel elements containing a demand for faith
      and the promise of a certain outcome. If you have faith (תאמינו) in the Lord, then you
      will enjoy stability (תֵּאָמְנוּ; cf. NJPS: "you will stand firm"); if you believe in His prophets,
      you will enjoy prosperity. TC adjusts the structure of the sentence by rendering וְתֵאָמֵנוּ
      as והימינו באוריתיה. The resulting Aramaic sentence contains three demands for faith
      (in the word of the Lord, in His Torah, and in His prophets) and one outcome: תצלחון.
      I do not believe that this deviation in TC necessarily reflects a different reading in the
      Hebrew (ותאמינו), although this is not impossible. Rather, it seems to me that the tar-
      gumist encountered a challenge when called upon to interpret the form וְתֵאָמֵנוּ. Other
      niph'al forms of verbs from the root אמ״ן appear in 1 Chr 17:23–24; 2 Chr 1:9; 6:17. In each
      case, the subject of the verb is the word of the Lord or the name of the Lord, and the refer-
      ence is not to the outcome of faith, but anticipation of the fulfillment of promises. In our
      verse, however, the subject of the verb is the men of Judah, and given this context, the
      usual meaning of the verb in the *niph'al* form is irrelevant. The targumist found it difficult
      to understand the verb as indicating a result of faith in God and therefore gave a more
      expansive rendering, adding a middle member containing a threesome of objects of faith
      consistent with his beliefs (God, the Torah, and the prophets).

Notwithstanding the preceding, the phrase דר״ש בה׳ appears twice in the book (1 Chr 10:14; 2 Chr 34:26; there are no more occurrences in Scripture), and in both cases the author of TC declines to translate במימרא דה׳. The reason, it would seem, is that the targumist took the same approach to this phrase as he did to the words דר״ש את ה׳, which are assigned a special translation: תב״ע אולפן מן קדם ה׳ (regarding which see below, p. 91). The verse at 1 Chr 5:25 also is anomalous and does not include the word מימרא as expected:

1 Chr 5:25

| MT | וַיִּמְעֲלוּ בֵּאלֹהֵי אֲבֹתֵיהֶם |
| TC | ושקרו באלהא אבהתון |

NJPS: But they trespassed against the God of their fathers
Gottlieb: But they acted unfaithfully with the God of their fathers

In 2 Chr 25:8, instead of מימרא, we find a different (and surprising) word added—יד *hand*:

2 Chr 25:8

| MT | כִּי יֶשׁ־כֹּחַ בֵּאלֹהִים |
| TC | ארום אית חילא בידא דה׳ |

NJPS: For in God there is power
Dost: for there is power in the Lord's *hand*

—שע״ן על ה׳

| 2 Chr 16:7 | בְּהִשָּׁעֶנְךָ עַל־מֶלֶךְ אֲרָם הַ׳ וְלֹא נִשְׁעַנְתָּ עַל־ הַ׳ אֱלֹהֶיךָ |
| TC | כד אסתמכתא על מלכא ה׳ דארם ולא אסתמכתא על מימרא דה׳ אלהך |

NJPS: Because you relied on the king of Aram and did not rely on the LORD your God
Dost: Because you leaned upon the king of Aram and did not lean *on the Memra of the Lord*, your God

In this verse we find two objects of reliance. Where the king of Aram is concerned the targumist makes no addition, but when the object is God, TC renders (סמ״ך על) מימרא דה׳. The targumist renders similarly the other three instances of the phrase שע״ן על ה׳ that occur in the book (2 Chr 13:18; 14:10; 16:8). The phrase שע״ן על ה׳ appears twice more in Scripture—Isa 10:20; Mic 3:11—and in both cases TJ renders סמ״ך על מימרא דה׳. The author of TC thus appears to take after his predecessor in his translation of the phrase.

7.1.3   שכינה

This word, like the preceding one, has been the subject of a multitude of studies, both within rabbinic literature and in targumic scholarship, and the same basic question that we encountered regarding the use of מימרא recurs here: does use of the word שכינה in the Targum indicate a theological position taken by the targumist, or is it a part of the effort to guard God's dignity by linguistic means? Moore, true to form, argued that "the Shekhinah is not separate from God, but an honorific equivalent for God."[134] Urbach, following his examination of the term's use in TO and rabbinic sources, concluded that "a survey of all places where the Shekhinah is discussed shows definitively that the Shekhina is not a 'hypostasis' and has no separate existence alongside that of God."[135] "The concept of the Shekhina," he argued, "serves not to answer any question concerning God's identity, but to give expression to the feeling of His presence in the world and his closeness to man without contemporaneously losing the sense of distance."[136]

TC uses the word שכינה systematically, following the tradition of TO.[137] The word occurs in TC a total of 27 times—none as a literal translation of the Hebrew *Vorlage*.[138] The targumist uses the word שכינה when translating Hebrew expressions conveying God's presence in physical space. I believe, much in keeping with Urbach, that the addition of the word שכינה in TC serves to moderate Scripture's anthropomorphic language and permits the reader to appreciate God's revelation while maintaining a dignified distance from Him. Thus, for example, when the Hebrew verse describes the place where the God of Israel is enthroned—whether a heavenly throne or the Temple in Jerusalem—God's presence is expressed with the word שכינה (sometimes supplemented by additional verbiage):

---

134   Moore, vol. 1, p. 436.

135   Urbach, p. 50. See also survey by Smelik, pp. 99–111.

136   Urbach, p. 52.

137   On the question of TO's consistency in the use of the word שכינה, see discussion by Posen, pp. 132–134, and literature cited ibid. See also Muñoz León. Aufrecht, p. 87, suggested that the more methodical and systematic the use of the concept שכינה (as well as other terms) in a targumic work, the later its composition, reflecting increased formalization of the term's use. He thus argued that Onqelos, whose use of the term is relatively consistent, represents a later stage of redaction than do the Palestinian Targums of the Torah. Aufrecht's argument regarding TO—and its ramifications for the question of the interrelationships of the various Targums of the Torah—requires further consideration, but in any event rings true with regard to TC, as this Targum is later than most and indeed uses the term שכינה consistently, as discussed below.

138   1 Chr 4:23; 13:6; 17:4–6; 23:25; 2 Chr 6:1–2, 5–6, 14, 18, 20–21, 30, 33, 39; 7:1–3, 10, 16, 20; 12:13; 18:18; 19:6; 20:6, 9; 30:9, 27; 32:19; 33:4, 7; 36:15.

1 Chr 13:6

MT   אֲרוֹן הָאֱלֹהִים | הֵ' יוֹשֵׁב הַכְּרוּבִים אֲשֶׁר־נִקְרָא שֵׁם:

TC   ארונא דה' הוא ה' דשכנתיה שריא עיל מן כרובי[א] דאתקרי שמיה עלוהי:

NJPS: the Ark of God, the LORD, *Enthroned on the Cherubim*, to which the Name was attached

Dost: the ark of the Lord, who is the Lord, *whose Shekhinah dwells above the Cherubim*, over which His name was called

The distance between the literal Hebrew and the Aramaic translation is profound. In the Hebrew verse God is honored with the title יוֹשֵׁב הַכְּרוּבִים. In the Aramaic translation, it is not God but His Shekhinah that is associated with the cherubim; it is not seated, but resting or poised; and, far from touching the cherubim, it is stationed above them. The anthropomorphic elements of the Hebrew verse are thus moderated by the Aramaic translation.

   Additional examples of the use of שכינה in TC:

1 Chr 17:4–5

MT   לֹא אַתָּה תִּבְנֶה־לִּי הַבַּיִת לָשָׁבֶת: כִּי לֹא יָשַׁבְתִּי בְּבַיִת

TC   לא את תבנה קדמי ביתא לאשראה שכנתי ביה: ארום לא אשריתי שכנתי בביתא

NJPS: You are not the one to build *a house* for Me *to dwell in ... I have not dwelt in a house*

Dost: You will not build a *house* before Me *in which to house My Shekhinah*. For *I have not caused My Shekhinah to dwell in a house*

2 Chr 6:21

MT   וְאַתָּה תִּשְׁמַע מִמְּקוֹם שִׁבְתְּךָ מִן־הַשָּׁמַיִם וְשָׁמַעְתָּ וְסָלָחְתָּ:

TC   ואת תקבל מאתר בית שכנתך מן שמיא ותקבל צלותהון ותשתביק לחוביהון:

NJPS: give heed in *Your heavenly abode*—give heed and pardon

Dost: and receive from *the place of the abode of Your Shekhinah*, from the heavens, and receive their prayer and forgive their sins

2 Chr 36:15

MT   כִּי־חָמַל עַל־עַמּוֹ וְעַל־מְעוֹנוֹ:

TC   מטול דחאיס על עמיה ועל מדור בית שכינת קודשיה:

NJPS: for He had pity on His people and *His dwelling-place*

Dost: that he might have compassion on His people and upon *the dwelling of the abode of His holy Shekhinah*

When visible to the eye, כְּבוֹד ה'—literally, the glory of the Lord—is translated as (א)יקר שכנתא דה'—the glory of the Lord's Shekhinah, as in:

2 Chr 7:3   עַל־הַבַּ֫יִת   ה'   וּכְב֣וֹד   הָאֵ֗שׁ   בְּרֶ֫דֶת   רֹאִים֙   יִשְׂרָאֵ֤ל   בְּנֵ֣י   וְכֹ֣ל

TC   שרא על ביתא   וכל בני ישראל חמיין כד נחתת ... אשתא על ביתא ואיקר שכנתא דה' שרא על ביתא

NJPS: All the Israelites witnessed the descent of the fire and *the glory of the LORD* on the House

Gottlieb: All of the children of Israel were watching when the fire descended ... upon the temple, and *the glory of the Lord's Shekhinah* rested over the temple.

This phrase is also common in TN as well as TPJ.

Sometimes the Hebrew text refers not to God's manifestation in the physical world, but to that of His name. This means of expression is also translated by reference to the Shekhinah:

2 Chr 12:13

MT   יִשְׂרָאֵ֜ל שִׁבְטֵ֣י מִכֹּל֙ שָׁ֗ם שְׁמ֜וֹ אֶת־ לָשׂ֨וּם ה' בָּחַ֨ר־ אֲשֶׁר֩ הָעִ֨יר בִּירוּשָׁלַ֖ם

TC   דישראל שבטיא מכל תמן שכנתיה לאשראה ה' אתרעי די קרתא בירושלם

NJPS: in Jerusalem—the city the LORD had chosen out of all the tribes of Israel *to establish His name* there.

Dost: in Jerusalem, the city out of all the tribes of Israel where the Lord chose *to make His Shekhinah dwell.*

2 Chr 20:9

MT   וְתוֹשִֽׁיעַ׃ וְתִשְׁמַ֥ע מִצָּרָתֵ֖נוּ אֵלֶ֛יךָ וְנִזְעַ֥ק הַזֶּ֖ה בַּבַּ֥יִת שִׁמְךָ֩ כִּ֣י

TC   ותפרקיננא׃ צלותנא ותקבל מעיקתנא לותך ונצוח הדין בביתא שכנתך ארום

NJPS: for *Your name* is in this House—and we shall cry out to You in our distress, and You will listen and deliver us.

Dost: for *Your Shekhinah* is in this house—and we shall cry out to You in our distress, You will receive our prayer and redeem us.

The following is an intriguing use of the word Shekhinah as a means of avoiding the appearance of any geographic limitation of God's domain:

2 Chr 32:19

MT   וַֽיְדַבְּר֔וּ אֶל־אֱלֹהֵ֖י יְרוּשָׁלָ֑ם כְּעַ֗ל אֱלֹהֵי֙ עַמֵּ֣י הָאָ֔רֶץ

TC   ארעא עממי טעות על דמלילו היכמא שריא דשכנתיה אלהא ה' על ומלילו

NJPS: They spoke of the God of Jerusalem as though He were like the gods of the other peoples of the earth

Dost: And they spoke about the Lord, the God *whose Shekhinah was dwelling* in Jerusalem just as they spoke about the idols of the gentiles of the land

The targumist declines to use the succinct translation אלהא דירושלם, the God of Jerusalem, instead expanding the text so that only God's Shekhinah is directly associated with Jerusalem. Apparently the targumist was concerned that the title אֱלֹהֵי יְרוּשָׁלָם might be understood as limiting the sphere of God's dominion to Jerusalem alone.[139] He therefore employed flexible diction allowing the entire earth to be filled with God's glory, and limited only the presence of His Shekhinah to Jerusalem.

7.1.4   דחלתא דה׳

In many cases where a Hebrew verse mentions or alludes to God, the targumist substitutes the phrase דחלתא דה׳ for God's name.[140] דחלתא דה׳ literally signifies fear of God, but in the targumic context also includes worship of God and/or acceptance of His yoke.[141] The phrase and its usage also are not an innovation of TC, but follow the path previously forged by TO, TJ, and TPJ.[142] Substitution

---

139   The phrase is unique in biblical Hebrew. A similar, Aramaic phrase, אֱלָהּ יְרוּשְׁלֶם, appears once, in the comments of King Artaxerxes of Persia given in Ezra 7:19.

140   1 Chr 26:24; 28:9; 2 Chr 6:37; 12:5; 13:10–11; 14:3, 6; 15:2, 12, 15; 17:7; 19:4, 7, 9; 20:33; 21:10; 22:9; 24:24; 25:26; 26:5; 28:6; 30:6, 8–9, 19; 33:13; 34:25, 31; 36:13.

141   The word דחלא also has additional meanings in TC. It signifies other gods (as objects of reverence despite their lack of substance; see discussion of differential translation, p. 98) in 1 Chr 16:26; 2 Chr 2:4; 13:8; 25:14, 20. It serves in its literal sense, denoting fear, in 1 Chr 14:17; 2 Chr 14:13; 17:10; 20:29. In the last of these we find the complete phrase, דחלתא דה׳, despite its special standing in the lexicon of divine honor, signifying terrestrial or existential fear of God:

   2 Chr 20:29

   MT   וַיְהִי פַּחַד אֱלֹהִים עַל כָּל־מַמְלְכוֹת הָאֲרָצוֹת ... כִּי נִלְחַם ה׳ עִם אוֹיְבֵי יִשְׂרָאֵל

   TC   והות דחלתא דה׳ על כל מלכוות ארעא ... ארום אגיח קרבא מימרא דה׳ עם בעלי דבבהון דישראל׃

   NJPS: The *terror of God* seized all the kingdoms of the lands ... that the LORD had fought the enemies of Israel.

   Dost: And the *fear of the Lord* was upon all of the kingdoms of the land when they heard that the Memra of the Lord had waged war with the enemies of Israel.

142   Notably, the convention is absent in TN. However, TO, TJ, and TPJ regularly employ the expression. For instance:

   Gen 5:22

   MT   וַיִּתְהַלֵּךְ חֲנוֹךְ אֶת־הָאֱלֹהִים

   TO   והליך חנוך בדחלתא דה׳

   NJPS: Enoch walked with *God*

   Clem: And Enoch was walking in *the fear of the Lord*,

   Deut 7:4

   MT   כִּי־יָסִיר אֶת־בִּנְךָ מֵאַחֲרַי וְעָבְדוּ אֱלֹהִים אֲחֵרִים

   TO   ארי יטעין ית בנך מבתר דחלתי ויפלחון לטעות עממיא

   NJPS: For they will turn your children away *from Me* to worship other gods

   Clem: For they will lead your son astray *from after the fear of Me*, and they will worship the idols of the nations

   2 Kgs 18:6

   MT   וַיִּדְבַּק בַּה׳ לֹא־סָר מֵאַחֲרָיו

   TJ   ואדבק בדחלתא דה׳ לא סטא מבתר פלחניה

   NJPS: He clung *to the LORD*; he did not turn away from following Him

of fear of God for God Himself distances linguistic expression from direct contact with God, in favor of engagement with man's conformance to God's ways and human submission to His dominion. For instance:

2 Chr 12:5

MT   כֹּה־אָמַר ה' אַתֶּם עֲזַבְתֶּם אֹתִי וְאַף־אֲנִי עָזַבְתִּי אֶתְכֶם

TC   כדנן אמר ה' אתון שבקתון ית דחלתי וברם אנא אשבוק יתכון

NJPS: Thus said the LORD: You have abandoned *Me*, so I am abandoning you

Dost: This is what the Lord says, You have left *the fear of Me*; therefore, I shall leave you

This Hebrew verse features a symmetric linguistic structure that goes hand-in-hand with the message conveyed by God's words. *Justitia suum cuique distribuit.* The authorities in Jerusalem abandoned God; He therefore has abandoned them. The targumic rendering, however, voids the balance of the original sentence. Due to the familiar targumic device of using דחלה as an object, the God of Israel remains aloft and man is left only to decide whether to heed His voice. In one instance this meaning comes together with three different means of expression employed by the Hebrew scripture in a single unit:

2 Chr 19:4

MT   וַיֵּשֶׁב יְהוֹשָׁפָט בִּירוּשָׁלָ͏ִם וַיָּשָׁב וַיֵּצֵא בָעָם ... וַיְשִׁיבֵם אֶל־ ה'

TC   ויתיב יהושפט בירושלם ותב ונפק לאלפא בעמא ... ואתיבנון לדחלתא דה'

NJPS: Jehoshaphat remained in Jerusalem a while and then went out among the people ... he brought them back to *the LORD*

Dost: And Jehoshaphat dwelt in Jerusalem, and he returned and went out to teach the people ... And he returned them to *the fear of the Lord*

2 Chr 19:7

MT   וְעַתָּה יְהִי פַחַד־ה' עֲלֵיכֶם שִׁמְרוּ וַעֲשׂוּ

TC   וכדון יהי דחלתא דה' עליכון אסתמרו ועבידו

NJPS: Now let *the dread of the LORD* be upon you; act with care

Dost: So now, let *the fear of the Lord* be upon you; watch how you act.

Clem: And he adhered *to the fear of the Lord*; he did not turn aside from after His worship
Deut 6:12

MT   הִשָּׁמֶר לְךָ פֶּן־תִּשְׁכַּח אֶת־ ה'

TPJ   אסתמרו לכון דילמא תתנשון דחלתא דה' אלקכון

NJPS: take heed that you do not forget *the LORD*

Clem: take care lest you forget the *fear of the Lord* your God

2 Chr 19:9

MT וַיְצַו עֲלֵיהֶם לֵאמֹר כֹּה תַעֲשׂוּן בְּיִרְאַת ה' בֶּאֱמוּנָה וּבְלֵבָב שָׁלֵם:

TC ופקיד עליהון למימר הכדין תעבדון בדחלתא דה' בהימנותא וקשטא ובלב שלים:

NJPS: He charged them, "This is how you shall act: *in fear of the LORD*, with fidelity, and with whole heart.

Dost: He commanded them, saying, "Do thus in *the fear of the Lord*, in faithfulness, and with a whole heart.

In TC, Jehoshaphat returns the people not to God, but to His fear. The two additional Hebrew equivalents of דחלתא דה' in this selection—פַּחַד and יִרְאַת ה'—are accompanied by actions (תעבדון, אסתמרו ועבידו ... בהימנותא). The three expressions found in Chronicles are but one in TC.

7.1.5   קדם ה'

Another means used in TC—and quite widely in targumic literature in general—to establish a dignified distance from the Creator is addition of the preposition קדם prior to God's name when the latter appears as an indirect or direct object.[143] The phrase לה'/אלהים appears 106 times in Chronicles in reference to the God of Israel, but in Aramaic translation in only 6 instances, in all of which the targumist used אלהא (rather than ה').[144] The phrase את ה'/ (ה)אלהים appears 28 times in Chronicles,[145] but is rendered as ית ה'/אלהא only 8 times, solely in conjunction with the verbs בר"ך (bless), פל"ח (worship), and

---

143   As demonstrated by Klein *Preposition*, the targumists use the word קדם not to avoid anthropomorphism, but as an honorific buffer. Klein further demonstrates that the targumists employed this word honorifically with regard to human beings, as well, albeit the term most often appears with reference to God. See also van Staalduine-Sulman *TJ Samuel*, pp. 123–124, 177–178.

    There are a total of 141 appearances of קדם ה' in TC, but only 18 of these correspond to the literal Hebrew parallel of the phrase, viz., לפני ה'/אלהים.

    These figures do not include occurrences of מן קדם ה', which will be considered separately below.

    קדם ה' for לפני ה'/אלהים: 1 Chr 11:3;13:6, 8; 16:1; 17:16; 22:18; 23:13, 31; 29:22; 2 Chr 1:6; 7:4; 14:12; 18:20; 20:13, 18; 27:6; 31:20; 34:31.

    Additional appearances of קדם ה': 1 Chr 1:10; 2:3, 18; 5:20; 11:18; 13:10; 16:4, 7–8, 23, 28–29, 34, 36, 40–42; 18:11; 20:5; 21:7–8, 17–18, 22, 26; 23:5, 30; 24:5; 25:3, 7; 29:5, 9, 20–21; 2 Chr 1:8; 3:1; 5:13; 7:3, 6, 9; 8:12; 9:8; 11:14, 16; 12:7; 13:10–12, 14; 14:1, 10; 15:11, 14; 17:6, 16; 18:6; 19:7–8, 10; 20:15, 19, 21, 32; 21:6; 22:4; 23:16, 18; 24:2, 9, 22; 25:2, 9, 26; 26:4, 18; 27:2; 28:1, 3, 10, 13, 25; 29:2, 6, 30–32; 30:1, 5, 8, 17, 21–22; 31:6, 14; 32:17, 23–24; 33:2, 6, 12–13, 18–19, 22; 34:2; 35:1, 12, 17; 36:5, 9, 12.

144   1 Chr 4:10, 18; 17:22; 2 Chr 15:3; 17:4; 29:7.

145   1 Chr 28:9; 29:10, 20; 2 Chr 7:22; 11:16; 12:14; 14:3, 6; 15:12; 16:12; 18:7, 18; 20:4, 26; 21:10; 22:9; 24:20, 24; 26:5; 28:6, 25; 30:8; 31:8; 33:16; 34:21, 33; 35:3.

יד״ע (know).[146] In the bulk of the remaining cases as well as in expansions, we find the phrase קדם ה׳.[147] Thus, for instance:

1 Chr 23:5

MT		אֲשֶׁר עָשִׂיתִי לְהַלֵּל:	בַּכֵּלִים	מְהַלְלִים לַה׳	וְאַרְבַּעַת אֲלָפִים
TC		לשבחא:	זמר דעבדי[ת]	בזיני משבחיא קדם ה׳	וארבעת אלפין

NJPS: 4,000 gatekeepers, and 4,000 for praising *the LORD* "with instruments I devised for singing praises."

Dost: 4000 shall be gatekeepers, and 4000 shall be those who sing praise *before the Lord* with musical instruments, which I have made for praise.

7.1.6   מן קדם ה׳

TC, as other Targums, uses the prepositional phrase מן קדם where the Hebrew scripture attributes certain actions to God, as an honorific substitute for the preposition מן. Following are Hebrew expressions whose translation includes an appearance of the phrase מן קדם that does not correspond literally to the source:[148]

---

146 בר״ך ית ה׳ in TC: 1 Chr 29:10, 20; 2 Chr 20:26; 31:8. In this TC hews close to TO and TPJ Gen 24:48, וברִיכִית ית ה׳, contra TN ibid., וצלית קדם אלהה דריבוני, and TO Deut 8:10, ותבריך ה׳ אלהך, contra TPJ ibid., הוון מודין ומברכין קדם ה׳ אלקנך. The phrase is commonplace in *Tg. Ps* (16:7; 34:2; 134:1–2; 135:19–20), but that Targum sometimes uses the distancing phrase שמא דה׳ (103:1–2, 22; 104:1, 35).

פל״ח ית ה׳ in TC: 2 Chr 33:16; 34:33; 35:3. This convention in TC is somewhat surprising in light of the other Targums' tendency to translate the Hebrew phrase עב״ד את ה׳ as פל״ח קדם ה׳. The only instance I have located of the unconventional translation פל״ח ית ה׳ outside TC is in TJ Josh 24:24.

יד״ע ית אלהא in TC: 1 Chr 28:9. Concerning the last verb, it also is not logical on the fundamental level that its translation be given in conjunction with the preposition קדם.

147 Usage is a function of meaning and context. Thus, for instance, where לה׳ signifies for the sake of the Lord, the targumist prefers a different translation:

1 Chr 22:6

MT	לה׳			בַּיִת לִבְנוֹת וַיְצַוֵּהוּ
TC	לשמא דה׳ מקדשא בית למבני ופקדיה			

NJPS: and charged him with building the House *for the LORD*

Dost: and commanded him to build the temple *for the name of the Lord*

148 Appearances of מן קדם ה׳ in TC (51 occurrences): 1 Chr 10:14; 11:19; 13:2, 12; 14:15; 16:33; 17:3, 21; 21:12, 15, 18, 30; 22:8, 19; 25:5; 2 Chr 10:15; 11:2, 4, 16; 12:7, 14; 13:8; 14:13; 15:1, 13; 16:12; 18:9, 22–23; 19:2–3; 20:3–4, 14; 21:7; 22:7; 24:20; 25:20; 26:5; 30:12; 31:21; 33:12, 23; 34:3, 21, 26; 35:23; 36:21.

Appearances in TC of מן קדם with a suffixed pronoun referring to God (12 occurrences): 1 Chr 16:30; 29:12, 14; 2 Chr 6:31, 33, 40; 7:14, 20; 14:6; 15:2, 4; 34:27.

Appearances in TC of מן קדם מימרא דה׳ (or equivalents with a pronominal suffix referring to God; 4 occurrences):

דר״ש/בק״ש + ה׳/אלהים (15 occurrences corresponding to this terminology and 2 in an expansion reflecting this terminology), e.g.:

1 Chr 21:30

MT אֱלֹהִים   לִדְרֹשׁ לְפָנָיו לָלֶכֶת דָּוִיד וְלֹא־יָכֹל

TC ה׳ אולפן מן קדם למתבע קדמוהי למיזל דוד ולא ספיק

NJPS: and David was unable to go to it *to worship God*

Dost: David was not able to go before him *to seek instruction from before the Lord*

The phrase תב״ע אולפן מן קדם ה׳, seeking instruction from before the Lord, serves to broaden the two Hebrew elements that are behind it. The object sought in the Aramaic phrase is not God, but His counsel or instruction.[149] The word אולפן (not ה׳ or אלהים as in the Hebrew) functions as the object of the act of seeking,[150] and the prepositional phrase מן קדם now precedes ה׳, as in similar cases in TO and TJ.[151]

---

1 Chr 5:22; 2 Chr 7:15; 34:27; 36:12.

מן קדם ה׳ occurs only 10 times as a literal translation (for מ]לפני ה׳] and מעל פני ה׳).

149   A shift of another sort concerning the root דר״ש—from seeking God to seeking His Torah or His commandments—took place in the late biblical period. See Heinemann *Terms*, p. 185; Hurvitz *BLL*, pp. 131–134; Mandel, p. 24.

150   This nonliteral translation stands out against verses where the objects of the seeking verb are not God and therefore are translated without expansion. Following are two illustrative examples. In one the object of seeking is the Ark; in the second, it is other gods. TC translates literally in both instances:

1 Chr 13:3

MT שָׁאוּל: בִּימֵי דְרַשְׁנֻהוּ כִּי־לֹא אֵלֵינוּ אֱלֹהֵינוּ אֶת־אֲרוֹן וְנָסֵבָּה

TC שאול: ביומי יתיה תבענא לא ארום לותנא דאלהנא ארונא ית ונחזור

NJPS: in order to transfer the Ark of our God to us, for throughout the days of Saul *we paid* no *regard* to it.

Dost: Let us bring back the ark of our God to ourselves, for *we have* not *sought it* in the days of Saul.

2 Chr 25:15

MT מִיָּדֶךָ: אֶת־עַמָּם לֹא־הִצִּילוּ אֲשֶׁר הָעָם אֶת־אֱלֹהֵי דָרַשְׁתָּ לָמֶה

TC ידך: מן עמהון ית שיזיבו לא די עמא טעות ית תבעתא למא

NJPS: Why *are you worshiping* the gods of a people who could not save their people from you?

Dost: Why *have you sought* the people's idols, which did not save their people from your hand?

151   TO Gen 25:22; Exod 18:15, 19; 33:7; TJ 1 Sam 9:9; 2 Kgs 22:18; Jer 37:7; Ezek 20:1, 3.

מן/מאת/מעם/ מפי+ /אלהים/ה' (10 occurrences)

דְּבַר ה'/אלהים (6 occurrences): as part of the expression פתגם נבואה מן קדם ה'.
The author of TC obtained this device from TJ, where the expanded translation
occurs over 100 times throughout the Prophets.[152]

רוח ה'/אלהים (4 occurrences): As part of the expression רוח נבואה מן קדם ה'.
This translation was already in use in TO, TPJ, and TJ.[153]

יר"א את ה'/אלהים (3 occurrences): There is one instance in TO where ירא את
ה' is translated as דח"ל מן קדם ה' (Deut 25:18), but this rendering is common in
TN and TPJ and occurs over thirty times in TJ.[154] It also appears in the Targums
to Psalms, Job, and Ecclesiastes.[155]

Additional occurrences of מן קדם ה' in TC, corresponding to various assorted phrases: 1 Chr 14:15; 17:21; 21:12; 2 Chr 13:8; 14:13; 18:22; 21:7; 30:12.

7.1.7   מלאך שליח מן קדם ה'
TC employs this unusual expression incorporating the phrase מן קדם on five
occasions. To appreciate the expression's peculiarity, let us first examine two
parallel verses in Samuel and Chronicles and their treatment in the Targum:

2 Sam 5:24 || 1 Chr 14:15

MT (Sam)	לְפָנֶיךָ		ה'			יָצֵא	אָז	כִּי
TJ	קדמך	לאצלחא	דה'	מלאכא	נפק	בכין	ארי
MT (Chr)	לְפָנֶיךָ		הָאֱלֹהִים			יָצָא		כִּי־
TC	קדמך	לאצלחא	ה'	שליח מן קדם	מלאך	נפק	ארום

NJPS (Sam): for the LORD will be going in front of you
Clem: for then the angel of the Lord will have gone out before you
NJPS (Chr): for God will be going in front of you
Dost: for the angel sent from before the Lord will have gone out to give success
before you

Both Targums share a desire to distance themselves from the anthropomorphism of the shared Hebrew *Vorlage*: it is not God Himself who emerges before
David (cf. the literal translation given in Peshiṭta to Chronicles: ܢܦܩ ܡܪܝܐ
ܩܕܡܝܟ, *the Lord has gone out before you*), but His emissary, and the action

---

152   See, e.g., 1 Sam 15:10.
153   TO Gen 41:38; Num 24:2; TPJ Gen 41:38; Exod 35:31; Num 24:2; TJ Judg 3:10; 1 Sam 10:6, 10;
      19:20, 23; 1 Kgs 22:24; Isa 61:1; Ezek 11:5; Mic 3:8. TJ tends thus to translate the expression
      יד ה', as well: 2 Kgs 3:15; Ezek 1:3; 3:22; 8:1; 37:1; 40:1.
154   TN Gen 22:12; Exod 18:21; Deut 4:10; 5:29; 6:24; 8:6; 10:12; 14:23; 17:19; 31:12–13.
      TPJ Deut 4:10; 5:29; 6:24; 10:12; 14:23; 17:19; 31:13.
155   Ps 25:12; 34:10; 55:20; 128:4; Job 1:1, 8; 2:3; Eccl 7:18; 8:12.

described is not physical ambulation by God, but His granting success to David's endeavor. The disparity between the two Targums concerns the means by which the member representing the angel is added. TJ summarily translates מלאכא דה׳, *the angel of the Lord*, while TC more expansively renders מלאך שליח מן קדם ה׳, *an angel sent from before the Lord*. This expanded translation in TC is surprising in several respects:

1:    The root של״ח is rarely used in TC, as we shall see below (p. 131). TC generally prefers the root שד״ר.

2:    TC does not consistently use this translation wherever an angel is mentioned, but only in five such instances.[156] Elsewhere he is not disinclined to employ the shorter phrase מלאכא דה׳,[157] or else describe the angel according to its particular assignment (מלאכא דמותנא, *angel of plague/ death*, מלאכא מחבלא, *destroying angel*)[158] or with the use of other phrases.

3:    מלאך שליח מן קדם ה׳ is an unfamiliar phrase in targumic literature. It does not appear in the Targums of the Torah or elsewhere in the Targums to the Writings, but only in TJ Josh 5:14–15, representing Hebrew שַׂר־צְבָא ה׳, *commander of the Lord's host*, and with some change in inflection (such as מלאך שליח מן קדמי) in Isa 10:5 for (וּמַטֶּה־)הוּא בְיָדָם, *and a staff (in their hand)*; 63:9 for פָּנָיו (וּמַלְאַךְ), *(and the angel of) His Presence*; Ezek 16:12 for וַעֲטֶרֶת תִּפְאֶרֶת, *and a splendid crown*; Hos 11:3 in an expansion.

The phrase מלאך שליח מן קדם ה׳ is twice used in TC to correspond to האלהים (1 Chr 14:15; 17:21) and three times in the story of Ornan's threshing floor to correspond to מלאך ה׳ (1 Chr 21:15, 18, 30). It may be that the appearance of this unusual expression in Joshua for שַׂר־צְבָא ה׳ offers us an avenue for understanding the expression in TC, and that the expression's appearance in TC results from a secondary use of the phrase appearing there. As noted, TJ to 2 Sam chose to use מלאכא דה׳ instead of ה׳ in order to maintain distance. The author of TC sought to be more precise in his description of the angel. He took the view that the martial mission of the putative angel, described with the words, כִּי־יָצָא הָאֱלֹהִים לְפָנֶיךָ לְהַכּוֹת אֶת־מַחֲנֵה פְלִשְׁתִּים, *for God will be going in front of you to attack the Philistine forces*, suffices to identify him with the commander of the Lord's host who appears in Joshua[159]—and if the figure in question is the commander of

---

156   Three of the five occurrences are in the story of Ornan the Jebusite's threshing floor. The places in TC where the expression appears are: 1 Chr 14:15 (the verse discussed here); 17:21; 21:15, 18, 30.

157   Thus in three instances: 1 Chr 12:23 (in the plural); 1 Chr 21:16; 2 Chr 3:1.

158   Thus in four instances: 1 Chr 21:15 (×2), 27; 2 Chr 7:13.

159   On the characterization of the revelation of the commander of the Lord's host in Joshua and its literary function, see Rofé, pp. 216–219. Rofé, ibid., relates to Scripture, rather than targumic literature, but his comments, particularly on p. 219, lend credence to the

the Lord's host, it is only fitting to signify this with the translation given there in TJ for this particular title: מלאך שליח מן קדם ה'. The targumist's use of the root של"ח (rather than שד"ר, the more common root in TC) lends further credence to the argument that he copied the phrase wholesale from the only other work in which it appears in this form, viz., TJ Joshua.

The use of the phrase מלאך שליח מן קדם ה' in 1 Chr 17:21 also strengthens this thesis, but there another textual consideration is at play. The verse parallels 2 Sam 7:23, and the difference between the Hebrew *Vorlage* of the two books also influences the Targum:

1 Chr 17:21 ‖ 2 Sam 7:23

MT (Chr)	... עָם לוֹ לִפְדּוֹת הָאֱלֹהִים	אֲשֶׁר הָלַךְ ...	וּמִי כְעַמְּךָ יִשְׂרָאֵל
TC	... למפרק ליה עם ה'	מלאך שליח מן קדם	דאתגלי ... ומן כעמך ישראל
MT (Sam)	... לְעָם לִפְדּוֹת־לּוֹ אֱלֹהִים	אֲשֶׁר הָלְכוּ־ ...	וּמִי כְעַמְּךָ כְּיִשְׂרָאֵל
TJ	... למפרק ליה עם ה'	שליחין מן קדם	דאזלו ... ומן כעמך ישראל

NJPS (Chr): And who is like Your people Israel ... whom God went and redeemed as His people

Dost: Who is like Your people Israel ... (for) whom appeared an angel sent from before the Lord to deliver for Himself a people

NJPS (Sam): And who is like Your people Israel ... whom God went and redeemed as His people

Clem: And who is like Your people Israel ... who went off, sent by the Lord so as to deliver for Himself a people

The Hebrew *Vorlage* of 2 Samuel associates the plural verb הָלְכוּ with the word אֱלֹהִים where that word seems to signify the God of Israel. The translation in TJ does away with this theological difficulty by attributing the verb to God's agents, rather than to God Himself. Who are these agents? Were TJ of the opinion that these were divine angels, its translation presumably would employ the word מלאך, rather than שליח, as is the case in 2 Sam 5:24. One therefore may conclude that TJ reflects the interpretation—found in *Eccl. Rab.*; *Midr. Sam*; and, later, Rashi and Qimḥi in their commentaries to Samuel—that the subject of the verb הָלְכוּ is Moses and Aaron.[160] In none of targumic literature is there

---

proposal presented here that the author of TC associated the commander of the Lord's host in Joshua with revelations of a threatening, martial character in Chronicles.

160 *Eccl. Rab.* 7:1 (p. 34); *Midr. Sam* 27:3 (p. 89). Following is the text given in *Midr. Sam*:
"And who is like your nation, Israel ...?" R. Berekhyah [said] in the name of R. 'Abba' b. Kahana: One scripture states, "who went" [in the singular], and another scripture states, "who went" [in the plural]. "Who went" [singular]—this is the holy One, blessed is He; "who went" [plural]—this is Mose and Aaron.
See Komlosh *Bible*, p. 314; van Staalduine-Sulman *TJ Samuel*, p. 531.

another such occurrence of שליחין מן קדם ה׳, but the diction is well suited to this interpretation, and perhaps further inspired by Ps 105:26, שָׁלַח מֹשֶׁה עַבְדּוֹ אַהֲרֹן אֲשֶׁר בָּחַר־בּוֹ, *He sent His servant Moses, and Aaron, whom He had chosen.*

The difficulty of interpreting the text in Samuel does not pertain to the parallel verse in Chronicles, as the verb in the latter book is in the singular: הָלַךְ. Still, the characterization of the God of Israel as moving and acting in physical space is incompatible with the style of expression typical of TC. The author of the Targum therefore declines to apply the aforementioned midrashic tradition attributing the action of walking to God. The targumist's solution for this anthropomorphism is to identify an angel as the verb's subject while adopting the translation given the parallel verse in TJ, mutatis mutandis.[161] In keeping with the verb הָלַךְ—now understood to denote revelation rather than walking[162]—TC adapts שליחין מן קדם ה׳ from TJ by singularizing the word and preceding it with the word מלאך. The resulting phrase, resembling that describing the commander of the Lord's host in Joshua, is well-suited here, as our verse, like 1 Chr 14:15, uses physical terminology (הָלַךְ) to describe the figure hiding behind the word הָאֱלֹהִים as engaging in military activities against the enemies of Israel: לִפְדּוֹת לוֹ עָם ... לְגָרֵשׁ מִפְּנֵי עַמְּךָ ... גּוֹיִם, (He) *redeemed as His people ... driving out nations before Your people.*

The remaining three occurrences of מלאך שליח מן קדם ה׳, all in the story of Ornan the Jebusite's threshing floor, correspond to the Hebrew phrase מלאך ה׳, which is much closer to this Aramaic phrase. It is reasonable to imagine that this angel, too, is conceived by the targumist to be the commander of the host of the Lord, performing as he does military actions and appearing to mortal man with sword in hand. The great similarity between certain expressions in Joshua and those in the story of the threshing floor further buttresses the presumption that the author of TC identified the angel with the commander of the Lord's host found in Joshua:

Josh 5:13 ... וְחַרְבּוֹ שְׁלוּפָה בְּיָדוֹ ... עֹמֵד לְנֶגְדּוֹ ... וְהִנֵּה־אִישׁ וַיַּרְא עֵינָיו וַיִּשָּׂא
1 Chr 21:16 ... וְחַרְבּוֹ שְׁלוּפָה בְּיָדוֹ עֹמֵד ה׳ אֶת־הַמַּלְאַךְ עֵינָיו וַיַּרְא אֶת־ דָוִיד וַיִּשָּׂא

Josh 5:14 וַיִּשְׁתָּחוּ אַרְצָה אֶל־פָּנָיו יְהוֹשֻׁעַ וַיִּפֹּל ...
1 Chr 21:16 עַל־פְּנֵיהֶם: בַּשַּׂקִּים מְכֻסִּים וְהַזְּקֵנִים דָוִיד וַיִּפֹּל ...

---

161   On the use of TJ by TC as the backbone of his translation of parallel chapters, see Chapter 3, pp. 108–141

162   On targumic use of the verb אתגלי for physical verbs, see Chester, pp. 264–268.

NJPS (Josh): he looked up and saw a man standing before him, drawn sword in hand ... Joshua threw himself face down to the ground and, prostrating himself ...

NJPS (Chr): David looked up and saw the angel of the LORD standing ... with a drawn sword in his hand ... David and the elders, covered in sackcloth, threw themselves on their faces.

This unusual term thus has a place in quite a number of honorific expressions used by TC in reference to God. While the other targumic conventions employed in honorifics for God are found in other targumic works to one extent or another, the manner in which the expression מלאך שליח מן קדם ה׳ is used, influenced by TJ to Josh 5:14–15, is unique to TC.

7.2 *Differential Translation*

7.2.1 Opening

The theological agenda of the author of TC has yet another intriguing manifestation. It is the custom way of the Targums to distinguish between meanings that carry different theological implications upon encountering certain words that lack any such distinction in the original Hebrew.[163] Here we shall refer to this phenomenon as differential translation. The author of TC, following the best of the targumic tradition that preceded him, also distinguished between different meanings within a set of theologically sensitive words.[164] By painstakingly choosing different equivalents for a group of words hailing from the religious-ritual sphere, the targumist succeeded in imposing a distinction between holy and mundane, impure and pure, in accordance with the tradition established by the targumists who had come before him.

7.2.2 אלהים

Throughout TC, when the targumist reads this word in Chronicles as referring to the God of Israel, he uses the designation ה׳, the transcription אלהים, or the word אלהא. Where the word signifies any other entity (generally, a foreign god), TC renders it variously:[165]

7.2.2.1 טעוון

In keeping with the practice of the ancient targumists, TC generally avoids allowing any legitimacy to the divinity of other gods, which are dubbed טעוון,

---

163   See general insights in Churgin *TJ*, pp. 339–344; Posen, pp. 135–142; Samet.

164   Rosenberg-Kohler, pp. 143–144, recorded distinctions between the meanings of several of the words listed below where they appear in TC.

165   Cf. Churgin *TJ*, pp. 339–340.

literally, errors.[166] This is the most common translation in TC for gods other than the God of Israel. For example:[167]

1 Chr 5:25

MT   וַיִּזְנ֗וּ אַחֲרֵ֞י אֱלֹהֵ֤י עַמֵּֽי־הָאָ֨רֶץ֙ אֲשֶׁר־הִשְׁמִ֥יד אֱלֹהִ֖ים מִפְּנֵיהֶֽם׃

TC   וטעו בתר טעות עמי ארע[א] דישיצי ה' מן קדמיהון׃

NJPS: by going astray after *the gods* of the peoples of the land, whom God had destroyed before them

Dost: and they went astray after *the idols* of the people of the land, which the Lord destroyed from before them

In this context, I would draw the reader's attention to a targumic turn of phrase that includes an intriguing addition. In TO, TJ, and TPJ, the Hebrew phrase אלהים אחרים normally is rendered nonliterally as טעות עממיא, *errors of the nations*.[168] Of the four appearances of the phrase in Chronicles, two are translated in TC in the style of its predecessors (טעות עממיא),[169] but for the two remaining occurrences TC gives the more expansive rendering טעות עממין נוכראין, *errors of foreign nations*.[170] The author of TC, it would seem, sought to supplement the typical translation he had inherited from his predecessors with a word corresponding to אחרים, *other/foreign*. In the resulting phrase, the adjective נוכראין/אחרים modifies not the word אלהים, but the nations—hence, the gods/errors of other/foreign nations.[171] A similar phenomenon occurs in TC at 2 Chr 14:2, where מִזְבְּחֹות הַנֵּכָר, *foreign altars*, is translated with the phrase אגורי עממין נוכראין, *altars of foreign nations*.[172]

Another such choice of translation that bears note appears at 2 Chr 32:13, 15, where the targumist renders אלהים as טעות despite the fact that the speaker in

---

166   On the similar tendency of the Targums of the Torah, see Chester, p. 332. See also Churgin *TJ*, p. 341; Smolar-Aberbach, p. 154; van Staalduine-Sulman *TJ Samuel*, pp. 141–142.

167   Thus also at 1 Chr 10:10; 14:12; 16:26; 2 Chr 7:19, 22; 25:14–15; 28:23, 25; 32:13–14, 17, 19, 21; 33:15; 34:25; 35:21–22.

168   Thus dozens of times in the Torah and the Prophets. The exceptions to this rule are in the two appearances of the Ten Commandments, in Exod 20:3; Deut 5:7. TN customarily gives a more literal translation: טעוון אחרניין, *other errors*.

169   2 Chr 7:22; 34:25.

170   2 Chr 7:19 (in the verse paralleling 1 Kgs 9:6, TJ renders טעות עממיא); 28:25.

171   Churgin *TJ*, p. 340, associates this targumic practice with rabbinic interpretation, as reflected by *Mek. RY, Yitro* 6 (p. 223): "And what is to be learned from the statement, "other gods"? It is only that others refer to them as deities."

172   A similar phenomenon pertains at TPJ Exod 30:9, where the phrase קְטֹרֶת זָרָה, *foreign incense*, is translated as קטרת בוסמין דעממין נוכראין, i.e., *spiced incense of foreign nations*. See also Ps 44:21, where אֵל זָר, *foreign god*, is translated as טעות עמין נוכראין, *errors of foreign nations*.

the verse is not a God-fearing Jews, but the Assyrian king Sennacherib (via his emissaries). The author of TC thus lends an artificial perspective to the comments reported in the Hebrew text, as one cannot very well expect a gentile king to define other gods as טעוון. By rendering thus, TC departs from the style used in TJ, where an effort is made to avoid placing this derogatory description in the mouths of gentiles.[173] This artificiality continues on into the following two verses, where the targumist has Sennacherib use the word אלהא to refer to the God of Israel. At 2 Chr 35:21, the targumist seeks to establish that the gods of Necho (אֱלֹהִים אֲשֶׁר־עִמִּי) are false gods, and therefore artificially places the word טעות in the mouth of King Necho of Egypt.

7.2.2.2   דחלן

Despite the targumist's tendency to describe foreign gods as טעוון, in five instances he uses the word דחלה, *fear/awe*, signifying an object of reverence. Thus, for instance:[174]

2 Chr 13:8

MT   וְאַתֶּם הָמוֹן   רָב   וְעִמָּכֶם עֶגְלֵי זָהָב   אֲשֶׁר עָשָׂה לָכֶם יָרָבְעָם   לֵאלֹהִים:

TC   ואתון ריכפת עממין סגיעין ועמכון עגלין דדהבא די   עבד לכון ירבעם בר נבט לדחלן:

NJPS: because you are a great multitude and possess the golden calves that Jeroboam made for you *as gods*.

Dost: because you are a great multitude of peoples and (because) you have calves of gold that Jeroboam son of Nebat made for you *to fear*.

Much as Churgin wrote regarding the style of TJ, the reason for the deviation in these cases appears to be that the verses' context demands that the other gods be viewed as the objects of reverence that they in fact are, despite their lack of substance in reality.[175] In these five instances, upholding the tradition of earlier targumic works, TC describes the other gods as entities that, in point of fact, are objects of reverence by describing them as דחלן, while seeking to avoid granting them the legitimacy that would be conveyed by the literal translation אלהיא.

---

173   Smelik, p. 590. TJ to the parallel verse, 1 Kgs 18:33, has דחלן (see discussion of that term in this chapter). Rabshakeh, an emissary of the king of Assyria, nevertheless does not decline to use the term מימרא דה׳ several times in his comments; see Dray, pp. 99–101.

174   Thus also at 1 Chr 16:26; 2 Chr 2:4; 25:14, 20.

175   Churgin TJ, pp. 340–341. Other proposed distinctions between טעוון and דחלן—though not admissible with regard to TC—appear in the discussion by Posen, TO, pp. 138–140, and literature cited ibid.

7.2.2.3 מַלְאָךְ

In one case the word אלהים (as a plural noun) is used, as dictated by the context and the targumist's preference to interpret it as referring to angels rather than to other gods:

1 Chr 16:25

MT   כִּי גָדוֹל יְהוָה וּמְהֻלָּל מְאֹד וְנוֹרָא הוּא עַל־כָּל־אֱלֹהִים׃

TC   מטול דרב ה' ומשבח לחדא ודחיל הוא על כולהון מלאכייה׃

NJPS: For the LORD is great and much acclaimed, He is held in awe by all *divine beings*.

Dost: For great is the Lord and greatly to be praised; and He is more to be feared than all *the angels*.

As far as the targumist is concerned, the powers indicated in the verse cannot be other gods: in his view, all foreign gods lack substance and the only true deity is the Lord. Subordinating them to the God of Israel by describing them as revering the Lord therefore would be problematic for its acknowledgment of their very existence. There thus arises an exegetic need to identify the powers invoked by the verse with entities whose existence poses no theological threat to the uniqueness of the Lord.[176] The targumist therefore identifies these powers with God's agents the angels, who may be said to fear Him, without producing any difficulty.

7.2.3 בָּמָה

The targumist distinguishes between what he perceives as a legitimate high place dedicated to the Lord and one that functions in idolatrous worship. The latter he dubs בימס,[177] as do TN and TPJ, unlike TO and TJ, which use the word במה in Aramaic, as well.[178] The Book of Chronicles makes mention of a single licit high place—that in Gibeon—and references to this site are translated in three different ways. In the account of God's revelation to Solomon, it is twice named as רמתא:

---

176   This runs contrary to the parallel translation, *Tg. Ps* 96:4, which translates literally: אלהיא.

177   2 Chr 11:15; 14:2, 4; 15:17; 17:6; 20:33; 21:11; 28:3 (contra Hebrew *Vorlage* in Chronicles), 4, 25; 31:1; 32:12; 33:3, 17, 19; 34:3.

178   Van Staalduine-Sulman *TJ Samuel*, p. 143. In one instance (Num 21:28), TO translates the word במה as רמתא.

2 Chr 1:3

MT וַיֵּלְכֹ֣וּ שְׁלֹמֹ֗ה וְכָל־הַקָּהָ֛ל עִמֹּ֖ו לַבָּמָ֥ה אֲשֶׁ֣ר בְּגִבְעֹ֑ון כִּי־שָׁ֗ם הָיָ֞ה אֹ֤הֶל מֹועֵד֙ הָֽאֱלֹהִ֔ים

TC ואזלו שלמה וכל קהלא עמיה לרמתא די בגבעון ארום תמן הוה משכן זמנא דה׳

NJPS: Then Solomon, and all the assemblage with him, went *to the shrine* at Gibeon, for the Tent of Meeting,

Dost: Then Solomon, and all the assembly with him, went *to the high place* of Gibeon, for there was the tent of meeting of the Lord

2 Chr 1:13

MT וַיָּבֹ֨א שְׁלֹמֹ֜ה לַבָּמָ֤ה אֲשֶׁר־בְּגִבְעֹון֙

TC ואתא שלמה לרמתא די בגבעון

NJPS: From *the shrine* at Gibeon ... Solomon went to ...

Dost: Then Solomon went to *the high place* that is in Gibeon

רמתא is commonly used in TO and TN as a translation of גבעה, *hill*, פסגה, *summit*, and similar words. The choice of this equivalent in TC takes away something of the Hebrew word's cultic sense, instead focusing on the literal, topographic aspect of the word.

The high place of Gibeon is once rendered in translation as מקדש, *temple*:

1 Chr 21:29

MT וּמִשְׁכַּ֣ן ה֗' אֲשֶׁר־עָשָׂ֤ה מֹשֶׁה֙ בַמִּדְבָּ֔ר ... בָּעֵ֖ת הַהִ֑יא בַּבָּמָ֖ה בְּגִבְעֹֽון׃

TC ומשכנא דה׳ דעבד משה במדברא ... בעדנא ההיא במקדש]א[דבגבעון׃

NJPS: for the Tabernacle of the LORD, which Moses had made in the wilderness, and the altar of burnt offerings, were at that time *in the shrine* at Gibeon.

Dost: Now the tabernacle of the Lord, which Moses made in the wilderness, and the altar of burnt offering were at that time *at the temple* of Gibeon.

Neither have we found another such equivalent in any of targumic literature, nor is this a literal rendering. It may be, though, that the targumist thus seeks to stress that Scripture in no ways objects to the presence of the Tabernacle in a location described as a high place.

In one instance, the translation used is the surprising term בית כנישתא, literally, *house of assembly*, which is the standard Jewish Aramaic term for *synagogue*:

1 Chr 16:39

MT וְאֵת֙ צָדֹ֣וק הַכֹּהֵ֔ן וְאֶחָיו֙ הַכֹּ֣הֲנִ֔ים לִפְנֵ֖י מִשְׁכַּ֣ן ה֑' בַּבָּמָ֖ה אֲשֶׁ֥ר בְּגִבְעֹֽון׃

TC וית צדוק כהנא ואחוהי כהניא קדם משכנא דה׳ בבית כנישתא די בגבעון׃

NJPS: also Zadok the priest and his fellow priests before the Tabernacle of the LORD *at the shrine* which was in Gibeon

Dost: (He left) Zadok the priest and his brothers the priests before the tent of the Lord *in the House of the Congregation*, which was at Gibeon

Le Déaut and Robert regard this targumic reference to a gathering place—a synagogue—as an attempt to peg the early development of this late institution in the days of David and Solomon.[179] No doubt the usage here is anachronistic, but I do not believe that we ought to read into it any conscious agenda on the part of the author. The targumist may have simply chosen this word in order to signify a place of divine worship using a word with the connotation of something less than a temple. Regardless, the three different translations selected in TC for the licit high place of Gibeon appear to open a window into a tendency that is among the basic impulses of the author of this Targum.

7.2.4   כֹּהֵן

When the word כֹּהֵן appears in Chronicles in the sense of a descendant of Aaron who serves (or is fit to serve) in the Temple, its translation in TC preserves the root כה"ן.[180] When the word appears in Chronicles in the sense of one who officiates in idolatrous worship, a translation from the root כמ"ר is used. This distinction, too, is present in previous targumic works.[181] It is particularly conspicuous in 2 Chr 13:9, where the Hebrew verse contrasts the Aaronide priests of the Lord with unfit priests, using the word כֹּהֵן for both, whereas in the Aramaic each type of priest is given its own translation.

2 Chr 13:9

MT   הֲלֹא הִדַּחְתֶּם אֶת־כֹּהֲנֵי ה'   אֶת־בְּנֵי אַהֲרֹן ... וַתַּעֲשׂוּ לָכֶם כֹּהֲנִים כְּעַמֵּי הָאֲרָצֹות

TC   הלא תריכתון ית כהניא דה'   בני אהרן ... ועבדתון לכון כומרין היך עמי ארעתא

NJPS: Did you not banish the *priests* of the LORD, the sons of Aaron and the Levites, and, like the peoples of the land, appoint your own *priests*?

Dost: Have you not driven out the *priests* of the Lord, the sons of Aaron, and the Levites, and made for yourselves *pagan priests* just as the peoples of the lands?

---

179   Le Déaut-Robert, vol. 1, p. 78, n. 12; their lead is followed by McIvor, p. 103, n. 28.

180   1 Chr 9:2, 10, 30; 13:2; 15:11, 14, 24; 16:6, 39; 23:2; 24:6, 31; 27:5; 28:13, 21; 29:22; 2 Chr 4:6, 9; 5:5, 7, 11–12, 14; 6:41; 7:2, 6; 8:14–15; 11:13; 13:9–10, 12, 14; 15:3; 17:8; 19:8, 11; 22:11; 23:4, 6, 8–9, 14, 18; 24:2, 5, 11, 20, 25; 26:17–20; 29:4, 16, 21–22, 24, 26, 34; 30:3, 15–16, 21, 24–25, 27; 31:2, 4, 9, 15, 17, 19; 34:9, 14, 18, 30; 35:2, 8, 10–11, 14, 18; 36:14. Similarly, when the word כהן appears in the Targum but not in the Hebrew *Vorlage* (1 Chr 1:24; 2:52, 54; 4:21; 5:36; 10:14; 11:22; 27:34; 2 Chr 24:27; 28:3) this meaning is generally preserved. An exception is the instance of שם כהנא רבא (*Shem the High Priest*, 1 Chr 1:24), who in the rabbinic interpretation, here taken up by TC, is understood to be a legitimate priest, although of course he was not a descendant of Aaron. See further discussion below, pp. 195–196.

181   See Churgin *TJ*, pp. 343–344; Smolar-Aberbach, pp. 36–37, 154; van Staalduine-Sulman *TJ Samuel*, p. 146; Posen, p. 140. Appearances of כמ"ר in TC: 2 Chr 11:15; 13:9; 15:3; 23:17; 34:5.

7.2.5   מִזְבֵּחַ

As in previous Targums, our author differentiates between an altar intended
for worship of the Lord (מדבח) and one used in idolatrous worship (אגור).[182]
Thus, for instance, the following example distinguishes between rejected altars
and the licit altar in Jerusalem:[183]

2 Chr 32:12

MT   הֲלֹא־הוּא יְחִזְקִיָּהוּ הֵסִיר אֶת ... מִזְבְּחֹתָיו וַיֹּאמֶר ... לִפְנֵי מִזְבֵּחַ אֶחָד תִּשְׁתַּחֲווּ

TC   הלא הוא יחזקיהו דעטר ית ... אגורוהי ואמר ... קדם מדבח חד תסגדון

NJPS: But is not Hezekiah the one who removed ... His *altars* and command-
ed ..., 'Before this one *altar* you shall prostrate yourselves'
Dost: Is he not the Hezekiah who abolished ... his *pagan altars*, and who said ...
'Before one *altar* you shall worship'

7.2.6   אֵשׁ

The Targum differentiates between earthly fire (נור) and fire that descends
from heaven (אשה). Something approaching such a distinction is discernable
in TO, where אשה and נור are used to distinguish between holy fire (even of
earthly origin) and non-holy fire. In TJ, too, a distinction is drawn between
אשה and נור.[184]

Example of earthly fire:[185]

1 Chr 14:12

MT   וַיַּעַזְבוּ שָׁם אֶת־אֱלֹהֵיהֶם וַיֹּאמֶר דָּוִיד וַיִּשָּׂרְפוּ בָּאֵשׁ:

TC   ושבקו תמן ית טעוותהון ואמר דוד ואתוקדו בנורא:

NJPS: They abandoned their gods there, and David ordered these to be burned
[*by fire*—L.G.].
Dost: and they left their idols there. Then David commanded, and they burned
them with *fire*.

---

182   Churgin *TJ*, p. 341; Smolar-Aberbach, p. 154; Posen, p. 140.
183   Verses of TC with the translation מדבח: 1 Chr 6:34; 16:40; 21:15, 18, 22, 26, 29; 22:1; 28:18;
         2 Chr 1:5–6; 3:1; 4:1, 19; 5:12; 6:12, 22; 7:1, 7, 9–10; 8:12; 15:8; 23:10; 24:20; 26:16, 19; 29:18–19,
         21–22, 24, 27; 32:12; 33:16; 35:16.
              Verses of TC with the translation אגור: 2 Chr 14:2; 23:17; 28:24; 30:14; 31:1; 32:12; 33:3–5,
         15; 34:4–5, 7.
184   Cf. Samet, pp. 81–84, for the distinction between אש and נור in Onqelos. Litke, *Semantics*,
         examined this distinction throughout the various Targums.
185   Complete list of appearances of earthly fire (נור) in TC: 1 Chr 8:12; 14:12; 2 Chr 28:3; 33:6, 12;
         35:13 (with regard to cooking of the paschal sacrifice); 36:19.

Example of heavenly fire:[186]

1 Chr 21:26

MT וַיִּקְרָא אֶל־ה' וַיַּעֲנֵהוּ בָאֵשׁ מִן־הַשָּׁמַיִם עַל מִזְבַּח הָעֹלָה:

TC וצלי קדם ה' וקביל צלותיה באשא דנחתת מן שמיא על מדבח עלתא:

NJPS: He invoked the LORD, who answered him *with fire* from heaven on the altar of burnt offerings.

Dost: and he prayed before the Lord. And the Lord accepted the prayer *by fire* that came down from heaven upon the altar of burnt offering.

7.2.7 מַלְאָךְ

The word מַלְאָךְ in the Hebrew Bible sometimes signifies a human messenger, while at others it refers to a divine angel.[187] TO, TJ, and TPJ distinguished between heavenly and earthly agents through the respective use of מלאך and אזגד, and TC does the same.[188]

Example of heavenly messenger:[189]

1 Chr 21:20

MT וַיָּשָׁב אָרְנָן וַיַּרְא אֶת־הַמַּלְאָךְ וְאַרְבַּעַת בָּנָיו עִמּוֹ מִתְחַבְּאִים

TC ותב ארון וחמא ית מלאכא וארבעתי בנוי מטמרן מן קדם מלאכא

NJPS: Ornan too saw the *angel*; his four sons who were with him hid themselves

Dost: Now Arwan turned and saw the *angel*. His [four—L.G.] sons were hiding from before the *angel*

---

186 Complete list of appearances of heavenly fire (אשה) in TC: 1 Chr 21:26; 2 Chr 7:1, 3, 10; 32:21.

187 Cf. BDB, p. 521.

188 See Azuelos for a monograph on the rendition of מלאך in the Pentateuchal Targums. On this distinction in TJ, see discussion by van Staalduine-Sulman *TJ Samuel*, pp. 147–148.

189 Appearances of מלאך in TC: 1 Chr 12:23; 14:15; 16:25; 17:21; 21:15–16, 18, 20, 27, 30; 29:11; 2 Chr 3:1; 7:13; 32:21; 33:13. This is the place to note that various titles frequently accompany the word מלאך in TC, in accordance with the role of the angel in the given verse. Thus we find *angel of the Lord* (מלאכא דה'), *angel sent from before the Lord* (מלאך שליח מן קדם ה'), *angel of death* (מלאכא דמותנא), and *destructive angel* (מלאכא מחבלא). The common feature of all such descriptions is the targumist's use of the word מלאך to signify that they are not human beings.

Example of human messenger:[190]

1 Chr 14:1

MT וַיִּשְׁלַח חוּרָם (ק) מֶלֶךְ־צֹר מַלְאָכִים אֶל־דָּוִיד ... לִבְנוֹת לוֹ בָּיִת:

TC ושדר חורם מלכא דצור עזגדין לות דוד ... למבני ליה היכלא:

NJPS: King Hiram of Tyre sent *envoys* to David ... to build a palace for him.

Dost: Hiram king of Tyre sent *messengers* to David ... in order to build a palace for him.

7.3 *The Rabbinic World in Targum Chronicles*

The vast distance between the world of Scripture and that of the talmudic Sages not infrequently is a source of exegetic challenges for one who wishes to base his worldview on two different realities, seeing the Rabbis and their conceptual world as a direct and faithful extension of the scriptural period. One means of bridging this gap is introduction of the discourse and paraphernalia of the talmudic period to the scriptural era using midrashic devices. TC, which shares this agenda, frequently furnishes its biblical protagonists with rabbinic trappings. One who learns about characters such as Jabez, David, and Benaiah son of Jehoiada from TC receives the impression that they were Torah scholars of the talmudic model, founding talmudic academies, training many disciples, and occupying themselves with the study of the Torah. The author of TC accomplished this, for the most part, by working with specific rabbinic legends, the bulk of which are known to us from other sources. The targumist's sources will be discussed at length not here, but in chapters seven and eight, which will be dedicated to the topic. Here we shall make do with itemizing those instances where the scriptural description is colored by TC with concepts clearly taken from the talmudic world.

Several characters in Chronicles are represented by the Targum as sages who occupied themselves with the study of the Torah. Jabez—a scriptural figure known only from Chronicles—is presented by the Targum as a sage who trains many disciples and builds them an academy (תרבע).[191] King David is presented in the Targum as a king who occupies himself with Torah study, and his occupation with the Torah is no private endeavor; rather, he teaches the entire

---

190 Also at 1 Chr 9:2, 16; 2 Chr 18:12; 35:21; 36:15–16. (In these final two verses, although the beings are sent by God, the targumist correctly understands from the context that they are human agents. He therefore refers to them as עזגדין.) The orthography of the word עזגד, with an *ayin* (rather than אזגד, with an *aleph*) is characteristic of Late Jewish Literary Aramaic.

191 1 Chr 2:55; 4:9–10.

nation of Israel.[192] His great-grandfather Boaz, too, occupied himself with Torah study as the dean of the Bethlehem academy.[193] Benaiah son of Jehoiada, one of David's warriors, is represented in TC as a prime example of a religious scholar. The descriptions given him in the Targum include: sin-fearing; a performer of good deeds; a greatly righteous man; the dean of an academy. The military and natural prowess with which he is described in the scriptural description becomes, in the Targum, prowess in worship of God and in Torah study, including mention of the midrashic work, *Siphra debei Rab* (also known as *Torat Kohanim*). He is appointed by David as the dean of an academy as well as bears responsibility for the Great and Small Sanhedrin.[194] Torah scholars as a group are portrayed as bearing responsibility for the judicial system and calculation of the religious calendar—a competence demanding a great degree of knowledge and expertise. In effect, the entire world was created for Torah scholars, who continuously improve the world by engaging in their particular occupation.[195]

Various verses of TC, some of them in the genealogical lists, make mention of several institutions corresponding o the reality of the sages of the Oral Torah. The Sanhedrin is named in various contexts, including in connection with figures unfamiliar from any other source.[196] The synagogue (בית כנישתא) is mentioned both as a substitute for the word בָּמָה and, in an expansion, within a description indicating that Saul was privileged to reign on account of the righteousness of his grandfather Ner, who is represented as an exemplary figure who donated oil for use in synagogues and study halls.[197] Aside from this expansion, the *bet midrash, study hall*, appears in one other passage.[198] In both instances the word מִשְׁנֶה is translated as בית אולפן, i.e., a place of Torah study (associating the Hebrew with the root שנ"ה, *to study*).[199] מתיבה (equivalent to Hebrew ישיבה), which indicates a place of Torah study, and ריש מתיבה (equivalent to Hebrew ראש ישיבה), the title of the leader of such an institution, also appear in TC.[200] The targumist's use of the institution of the academy as a place of Torah study and the title of dean as denoting leadership of this

---

192 1 Chr 11:2, 11.

193 1 Chr 4:22.

194 1 Chr 11:22, 25; 18:17. His son later succeeds him as head of the Sanhedrin; 1 Chr 27:34.

195 1 Chr 4:23; 12:33; 2 Chr 20:20.

196 1 Chr 4:12; 5:12; 12:33; 18:17; 27:34; 2 Chr 23:5.

197 1 Chr 8:33; 16:39.

198 1 Chr 11:2.

199 1 Chr 5:12; 2 Chr 34:22 (influenced by TJ 2 Kgs 22:14).

200 1 Chr 4:22; 11:11, 25. The institution of מתיבה (ריש) appears elsewhere in targumic literature only in *Tg. Cant* 2:4; 4:4; 7:3; 8:13.

institution reflect, by all appearances, a reality postdating that of the Talmud, as these concepts date to the Geonic Period.[201]

In three instances in TC, the talmudic sages' belief in the World to Come is placed in David's mouth.[202] The Evil Inclination and subjugation thereof also appear in the Targum.[203] In various contexts, the targumist attributes to the word זכות, *merit*, the religious associations it takes on in rabbinic literature. Thus Moses' merit is responsible for auspicious outcomes both during his lifetime and posthumously,[204] the gates of the Temple open in recognition of David's merit,[205] and the merit of Joshua son of Jehozadak saves him from incineration.[206] With the targumist's use of such concepts, TC becomes a composition deeply rooted in the world of the Rabbis, and the distance between biblical literature and that of the Rabbis is effectively bridged.

8   Conclusion

In this chapter we have addressed several of the elements that informed the targumist's style in the composition of his translation. On one hand, we saw in this chapter that the author of TC sought to hew close to the Hebrew text and transmit an Aramaic translation tending toward the literal. On the other hand, the targumist did not keep to a high degree of literalness when he found cause within the Hebrew text to deviate from a literal rendering. Indeed, the targumist had ample reasons and opportunities to add various elements to his text.

The vast majority of translation techniques described in this chapter, as we have seen, have roots and sources among the Targums of the Torah and the Prophets. In this sense, the author of TC should be seen as a faithful student of the targumic tradition that preceded him. He seeks not to forge new paths or a new approach, but to apply the principles of translation that he inherited from his predecessors to a scriptural book for which no Aramaic translation was known to exist in his day. The same holds true for what we have here designated the lexicon of divine honor and for differential translation. In TC, these phenomena, too, take the form of translation techniques. Still, it is evident that the targumist has more than a passing understanding of the principles of this

---

201   See Sokoloff *JBA*, pp. 720, 1081, and literature cited in both these locations.
202   1 Chr 16:36; 17:17; 29:10.
203   1 Chr 4:10; 8:40. For more on this, see my forthcoming article, Gottlieb *Yetzer*.
204   1 Chr 2:55; 4:18; 23:17.
205   2 Chr 7:10.
206   2 Chr 28:3.

technique and is capable of distinguishing between those passages of Scripture that justify its application and those where this would be inappropriate.

The world of the targumist begins to open up to a reader who can interpret his systematic divergences from the Hebrew *Vorlage*. The targumist works in an environment that is familiar with the tradition of the Targums of the Torah and the Prophets. He is immersed in the world of the talmudic sages, as expressed by his efforts to bridge the distance between the scriptural world and that of the Rabbis. The targumist's diction shows familiarity with that of the targumic works that preceded him (as we shall explore in greater depth in the following chapters), but contains a greater quantity of Greek loanwords. TC thus is fully a partner to the classical tradition of Aramaic scriptural translations (viz., TO and TJ), but its diction makes clear that the author is neither a contemporary nor a compatriot of theirs. Particular similarities have been detected throughout this chapter between TC and TPJ, and suggest an affinity between the two. A more precise definition of this relationship requires a different sort of analysis, for which reason we now shall turn to specific comparisons of TC and a number of other translations.

The Relationship of Targum Chronicles and Targum Jonathan

1 Opening

A great deal of the Book of Chronicles consists of chapters to which parallel units exist in Samuel or Kings.[1] Many biblical scholars have occupied themselves with these parallel units, comparing the Hebrew text of Samuel and Kings to that of the corresponding sections of Chronicles. Yet aside from the opportunity they afford for analysis of the Hebrew text, these parallel units also allow us more precisely to comprehend the character of TC. As we shall see below, the parallel units provide clear evidence that the targumist did not embark on his translation of these chapters in a vacuum, but first carefully studied the Targum to Samuel and Kings—viz., TJ.

2 Adherence in TC to the Hebrew Text of Chronicles

In comparing TJ and TC, we find that even where chapters run parallel to each other, TC translates the Hebrew text of Chronicles, rather than that of Samuel and Kings. This determination is a facile one, because in the vast majority of instances TC reflects the variant readings of Chronicles relative to that of Samuel or Kings. A few examples will suffice to demonstrate that the targumist's work on these chapters does not consist of mere transcription from his predecessors. Rather, his is a work that clearly uses preexisting documents as a foundation, but seeks to present an independent Aramaic translation of the Hebrew Book of Chronicles.

1 Chr 17:10 / 2 Sam 7:11

MT Chr	וּלְמִיָּמִים אֲשֶׁר צִוִּיתִי שֹׁפְטִים עַל־עַמִּי יִשְׂרָאֵל וְהִכְנַעְתִּי אֶת־כָּל־אוֹיְבֶיךָ
TC	ולמן יומיא דפקידית נגודיא על עמי ישראל ותברית ית כל בעלי־דבבך
MT Sam	וּלְמִן־הַיּוֹם אֲשֶׁר צִוִּיתִי שֹׁפְטִים עַל־עַמִּי יִשְׂרָאֵל וַהֲנִיחֹתִי לְךָ מִכָּל־אֹיְבֶיךָ
TJ	ולמן יומא דפקידית נגודין על עמי ישראל ואנחית לך מכל בעלי־דבבך

---

1 See detail of parallel units in Bendavid; Klein *1 Chronicles*, pp. 30–37.

NJPS Chr: ever since I appointed judges over My people Israel. I will subdue all your enemies

Dost: From the days that I appointed leaders over My people Israel, I have defeated all of your enemies

NJPS Sam: ever since I appointed chieftains over My people Israel. I will give you safety from all your enemies.

Clem: And from the day that I appointed leaders over My people Israel, I have given you rest from all your enemies.

The similarity between the two Hebrew verses as well as their translations is significant, but where the Hebrew text of Chronicles deviates from that of Samuel given above, the targumist follows the reading in Chronicles: יומיא, *the days*, in the plural, instead of יומא as in TJ, and ותברית ית instead of ואנחית לך מ- as in TJ.

1 Chr 10:12 / 1 Sam 31:13

1 Chr	וַיִּקְבְּרוּ אֶת־עַצְמוֹתֵיהֶם	תַּחַת הָאֵלָה	בְּיָבֵשׁ	וַיָּצוּמוּ שִׁבְעַת יָמִים:	
TC	וקברו ית גרמיהון	תחות בוטמא דיבש	וצמו	שובעא יומין:	
1 Sam	וַיִּקְחוּ אֶת־עַצְמֹתֵיהֶם וַיִּקְבְּרוּ תַּחַת־הָאֶשֶׁל	בְּיָבֵשָׁה	וַיָּצֻמוּ שִׁבְעַת יָמִים:	
TJ	ונסיבו ית גרמיהון	וקברו תחות אשלא	ביביש	וצמו	שבעא יומין:

NJPS Chr: They buried the bones under the oak tree in Jabesh, and they fasted for seven days

Dost: Then they buried their bones beneath the terebinth of Jabesh and fasted for seven days

NJPS Sam: Then they took the bones and buried them under the tamarisk tree in Jabesh, and they fasted for seven days.

Clem: Then they took their bones and they buried them under the tamarisk tree in Jabesh, and they fasted for seven days

To the extent that the Hebrew text of Chronicles mirrors that of 1 Samuel, TC mirrors TJ—but TC conscientiously places the verb וקברו where its presence is dictated by Chronicles, and not by 1 Samuel. The targumist also acted deliberately in his selection of the word בוטמא, the common Aramaic equivalent of the word אֵלָה.[2] The usage of the relative particle in דיבש instead of the preposition may also be the result of this.

---

2   See TO and TPJ Gen 35:4; TJ Judg 6:11, 19; 2 Sam 18:9–10, 14; 1 Kgs 13:14; Isa 1:30; 6:13; Ezek 6:13; Hos 4:13.

2 Chr 18:31 / 1 Kgs 22:32

2 Chr	וְהֵמָּה אָמְרוּ	מֶלֶךְ יִשְׂרָאֵל	הוּא וַיָּסֹבּוּ עָלָיו לְהִלָּחֵם
TC	ואנון אמרו	מלכא דישראל הוא ואסחרו עלוי לאגחא קרבא	
1 Kgs	וְהֵמָּה אָמְרוּ אַךְ	מֶלֶךְ־יִשְׂרָאֵל	הוּא וַיָּסֻרוּ עָלָיו לְהִלָּחֵם
TJ	ואנון אמרו ברם מלכא דישראל הוא וזרו עלוהי לאגחא		

NJPS Chr: whom they took for the king of Israel, they wheeled around to attack him

Dost: they said, "It is the king of Israel," and they turned aside after him to do battle.

NJPS Kgs: whom they took for the king of Israel, they turned upon him to attack him

Clem: then they said, "Indeed, it is the king of Israel," and they turned aside after him to fight

Here, too, the text of the two Hebrew verses is largely identical. Chronicles differs from Kings only in its omission of the word אַךְ and its reading of וַיָּסֹבּוּ, a verb that differs by one letter from the parallel verb, וַיָּסֻרוּ. The author of TC translated the Hebrew text of Chronicles, and the resulting translation therefore differs from TJ precisely at these two points.

The general rule illustrated by these examples, and evident from parallel chapters in TC in general, is that TC is content to accept TJ as a foundation text when it corresponds to the Hebrew text of Chronicles, but parts ways with his predecessor when the reading in Chronicles differs from that in Samuel or Kings.

3   Similarity of TC and TJ

Although the final product constituting TC should generally be taken as a comprehensive and independent work, it is clear from a comparative analysis of TJ and TC that the two are intimately related. The nature of this relationship, then, is in need of definition. Rosenberg and Kohler's study provides no answer to the question here posed. The first scholar to discuss the matter at length was Churgin.[3] He conjectured that TC had inherited his translation of the parallel chapters from a Palestinian version of TJ. This version used the familiar dialect of the other Palestinian targums and contained a greater number of aggadic expansions than the version of TJ known to us.

Sperber, too, noted the relationship between the two targums and presented a number of parallel verses in his edition. He eschewed, however, any

---

3 Churgin *Hagiographa*, pp. 266–272.

discussion of conclusions to be drawn from a comparison of the two books, preferring to leave the task to his successors (his comments on the matter are excerpted above, p. 22).

White expressed an opinion similar to Churgin's, as well as held out the possibility that far-reaching historiographical conclusions might be drawn.[4] Le Déaut and Robert,[5] and after them McIvor,[6] forwent an independent analysis of the topic, and in their surveys quoted Churgin, leaving his as the only view given on the matter. Hamiel set the parallel verses side-by-side and, for certain words, provided some degree of comparative information based on other chapters, but his discussion does not address the nature of the relationship between the two Targums.[7]

Churgin's hypothesis cannot suffice to provide a complete answer to the question posed here. By attributing all of the dialectal respects in which TC differs from TJ to a presumed Palestinian Targum to the Prophets, Churgin avoids the need to adopt the view that the author of TC had actively tampered with the dialectal elements of his sources, but ultimately fails to explain how two so highly similar Targums to the Prophets came into being and what author adapted the dialect of the other. The question of the relationship between TC and TJ thus deserves to be considered anew. Below we shall consider similarities and differences between TC and TJ within the parallel chapters, and seek to draw conclusions from these phenomena.

3.1   *Unexpected Choice of Identical Words*

The resemblance between TC and TJ in parallel chapters is not solely a function of the affinity of their Hebrew sources. The existence of a relationship between the Targums is easily proven where they deviate from the anticipated literal translation, whether through a surprising choice of diction or by inserting additional words in the text. In the following examples, we will see a few of the many instances that demonstrate such a relationship between TC and TJ.

2 Chr 6:15 / 1 Kgs 8:24

2 Chr	מִלֵּֽאתָ	וּבְיָדְךָ֥	בְּפִ֖יךָ	לֹ֑ו וַתְּדַבֵּ֥ר	אֲשֶׁר־דִּבַּ֖רְתָּ	אֵ֥ת	דָּוִ֣יד אָבִ֗י	לְעַבְדְּךָ֙	אֲשֶׁ֣ר שָׁמַ֔רְתָּ
TC	קיימתא	וברעותך	במימרך	ית די מלילתא ליה וגזרתא		ית די מלילתא ליה	דוד אבא	לעבדך	די נטרתא
1 Kgs	מִלֵּֽאתָ	וּבְיָדְךָ֥	בְּפִ֖יךָ	לֹ֑ו וַתְּדַבֵּ֥ר	אֲשֶׁר־דִּבַּ֖רְתָּ	אֵ֥ת	דָּוִ֣ד אָבִ֗י	לְעַבְדְּךָ֙	אֲשֶׁ֣ר שָׁמַ֔רְתָּ
TJ	קיימתא	וברעותך	במימרך	ית דמלילתא ליה וגזרתא		ית דמלילתא ליה	דוד אבא	לעבדך	דנטרתא

NJPS Chr: You who have kept the promises You made to Your servant, my father David; You made a promise and have fulfilled it

Dost: You kept for Your servant David, (my) father, what You had promised to him. You decreed by Your Memra, and by Your will You have fulfilled (it)

NJPS Kgs: You who have kept the promises You made to Your servant, my father David, fulfilling with deeds the promise You made

Clem: And You kept for Your servant David my father what You had spoken to him. And (what) You have decreed by Your Memra and by Your will

In the above unit, TC and TJ are identical even in the nonliteral translation וגזרתא במימרך וברעותך קיימתא (cf. literal translation in Peshiṭta, ܘܡܠܠܬ ܒܐܝܕܝܟ[8]). This example is particularly telling in light of the dual appearances of the verb דב״ר in the verse. In the first instance, TJ and TC chose the verb מל״ל as a literal translation; in the second, both preferred a farther-removed meaning, from the root גז״ר. This root, accompanied by the loaded word במימר, forms the typical translation in TJ for דב״ר in such expressions as אני ה' דברתי and כי ה' דבר, where the context indicates an oath or judgment by God (cf. lexicon of divine honor, pp. 79–80, above).[9] Because this is a nonliteral translation characteristic of TJ and uncommon in other targumic works, we cannot simply assume that the author of TC chose these words independently.

1 Chr 14:15 / 2 Sam 5:24

1 Chr	לְפָנֶיךָ		הָאֱלֹהִים		יָצָא	כִּי־
TC	קדמך	לאצלחא	שליח מן קדם ה'	נפק מלאך		ארום
2 Sam	לְפָנֶיךָ		ה'		יָצָא אָז	כִּי
TJ	קדמך	לאצלחא	דה'	נפק מלאכא	בכין	ארי

NJPS Chr: for God will be going in front of you

Dost: for the angel sent from before the Lord will have gone out to give success before you

NJPS Sam: for the LORD will be going in front of you

Clem: for then the angel of the Lord will have gone out before you

---

8 Even Peshiṭta's deviation from literalness in its rendering of the word וּבְיָדְךָ (as ܘܒܝܕܝܟ), whose meaning is similar to that of the Aramaic translations, differs from them in lexical choice.

9 Such a translation is found once in TO and TPJ (Num 14:35), but dozens of times in TJ: 1 Kgs 8:15, 24; 14:11; Isa 1:20; 21:17; 22:25; 25:8; 40:5; 48:15; 58:14; Jer 4:28; 13:15; Ezek 5:13, 15, 17; 6:10; 17:21, 24; 21:22, 37; 22:14; 23:34; 24:14; 26:5, 14; 28:10; 30:12; 34:24; 36:5–6, 36; 37:14; 38:19; 39:5, 8; Joel 4:8; Obad 18; Mic 4:4.

TC conforms to TJ in adding the word לאצלחא, although in other respects the two translations diverge, both on account of variant Hebrew *Vorlagen* (the word אָז is absent in Chronicles and, therefore, was not translated into Aramaic) and due to different solutions found for the theological challenge posed by the Hebrew verse (with TC using not only מלאכא דה׳, as in TJ, but מלאך שליח מן קדם ה׳).[10] The addition לאצלחא, common to both Targums, is unexpected and bespeaks familiarity on the part of one targumist with the work of the other.

2 Chr 2:9 / 1 Kgs 5:25

2 Chr	כֹּרִים עֶשְׂרִים אֶלֶף	חִטִּים ׀ מַכֹּות לַעֲבָדֶיךָ		נָתַתִּי
TC	כורין עשרין אלפא	חטין פרנוס לעבדך		יהבית
1 Kgs		עֶשְׂרִים אֶלֶף כֹּר חִטִּים מַכֹּלֶת לְבֵיתֹו		
TJ		עסרין אלפין כורין חטין פרנוס לאנש ביתיה		

NJPS Chr: I have allocated for your servants ... 20,000 kor of crushed wheat
Dost: I will give as wages to your servants 20,000 kors of wheat
NJPS Kgs: 20,000 kors of wheat as provisions for his household
Clem: twenty thousand cors of wheat as support for the men of his house

The word מַכֹּות in 2 Chronicles poses a difficulty for any reader, in contrast with מַכֹּלֶת in 1 Kings. We have no witnesses to the reading מַכֹּלֶת in medieval Hebrew MSS of Chronicles. Yet even if we were to assume that the Hebrew Vorlage of TC read מַכֹּלֶת, as in 1 Kings, we would be hard-pressed to believe that the two targumists had independently arrived at the Aramaic word פרנוס, given that the word פרנוס is rare in targumic literature and מַכֹּלֶת is a hapax legomenon. The most logical explanation is that one targumist had reference to the work of his predecessor and his inclusion of the word פרנוס in his translation reflected its presence in the other.

2 Chr 6:21 / 1 Kgs 8:30

2 Chr	וְסָלָחְתָּ׃		וְשָׁמַעְתָּ מִן-הַשָּׁמַיִם	שִׁבְתְּךָ	בֵּית	מִמְּקֹום	וְאַתָּה תִּשְׁמַע
TC	ותשתביק לחוביהון	צלותהון	ותקבל מן שמיא	שכנתך	בית	מאתר	ואת תקבל
1 Kgs	וְסָלָחְתָּ׃		וְשָׁמַעְתָּ אֶל-הַשָּׁמַיִם	שִׁבְתְּךָ	אֶל-מְקֹום		וְאַתָּה תִּשְׁמַע
TJ	ותשבוק לחוביהון	צלותהון	ותקביל מן שמיא	שכינתך	בית	מאתר	ואת תקביל

NJPS Chr: give heed in Your heavenly abode—give heed and pardon
Dost: and receive from the place of the abode of Your Shekhinah, from the heavens, and receive their prayer and forgive their sins
NJPS Kgs: give heed in Your heavenly abode—give heed and pardon

---

10   Regarding this last divergence, see my discussion above, pp. 92–96.

Clem: and receive from the place of the temple of Your Shekhinah, from the heavens, and receive their prayer and forgive their sins

The great similarity between the two translations (even with the divergence in the stem of the verb ותשבוק/ותשתביק) is amplified by the similarity of the two additional words that do not reflect the Hebrew text, viz., צלותהון and חוביהון. The Targums here not only contain identical exegesis, but make identical lexical decisions with regard to elements that are not present in the *Vorlage* and thus are unexpected. This finding gives ample credence to the argument that one Targum was acquainted with the other.

1 Chr 21:17 / 2 Sam 24:17

1 Chr	מֶה עָשׂוּ	הַצֹּאן	וְאֵלֶּה	וְהָרֵעַ הֲרֵעוֹתִי אֲשֶׁר־חָטָאתִי וַאֲנִי־הוּא	
TC	וְאֵלִין עַמָּא דְּאָנוּן הִי כְּעָנָא בִּיד רַעְיָא מַה עֲבַדוּ ואבאשא אבאשית ואנא הוא דחבית
2 Sam	מֶה עָשׂוּ	הַצֹּאן	וְאֵלֶּה	וְאָנֹכִי הֶעֱוֵיתִי הִנֵּה אָנֹכִי חָטָאתִי
TJ	כְּעָנָא בִּיד רַעְיָא מָא עֲבַדוּ ואלין עמא דאנון ואנא סרחית חבית הא אנא

NJPS Chr: I alone am guilty, and have caused severe harm; but these sheep, what have they done?

Dost: and I who sinned and acted evilly? But these people, who are as sheep in the hand of the shepherd, what have they done, O Lord, my God?

NJPS Sam: I alone am guilty, I alone have done wrong; but these poor sheep, what have they done?

Clem: Behold, I have sinned and have become guilty, and these people who are like sheep in the hand of a shepherd, what have they done?

The two Hebrew verses clearly parallel each other, albeit there are textual differences between them. TC adheres to the reading in Chronicles in its translation of the variant readings וַאֲנִי־הוּא אֲשֶׁר and וְהָרֵעַ הֲרֵעוֹתִי, and at these points bears no resemblance to TJ. However, in the expanded translation based on the word הַצֹּאן—viz., עמא דאנון הי כענא ביד רעיא—TC mirrors TJ in every detail except the dialectal choice of הי כ instead of כ. The similarity of the expansion in the two documents cannot have arisen from the content of the verse, but must be understood as clear evidence of one targumist's reliance on the other. Where the text of Chronicles diverges from 2 Samuel, the targumist follows his Hebrew *Vorlage*, but where the two books are in agreement he relies on the work of his predecessor.

3.2   *Influence of Samuel/Kings Where the Text of Chronicles Diverges*

As we saw above, TC generally adheres to the Hebrew *Vorlage* of Chronicles, diverging from the text of Samuel/Kings in the event of a difference between the books. Notwithstanding, one can identify instances where the targumist deviated from this rule by including in his translation words from the parallel verses of Samuel/Kings that do not appear in Chronicles. It may be that in these cases (or, at least, in some of them) the author of TC was influenced by the Hebrew verses in Samuel/Kings. More likely, however, is that TJ to these chapters was the source of the targumist's inspiration, and made its way into the Targum to Chronicles despite the absence in the independent Hebrew text of that book of any justification for such an insertion. Churgin opined that this phenomenon pertained to the translation of 1 Chronicles but not that of 2 Chronicles.[11] I, however, believe that the data demonstrate the existence of this phenomenon in both sections of the book. Below are examples of these data:

2 Chr 9:11 / 1 Kgs 10:12

2 Chr	וּלְבֵית הַמֶּלֶךְ	ה'	לְבֵית־	מְסִלּוֹת	הָאַלְגּוּמִּים	אֶת־עֲצֵי הַמֶּלֶךְ וַיַּעַשׂ
TC	ועבד מלכא מן קיסי אלמוגיא כיבשייה לסעיד לבית מקדשא דה' ולבית מלכא
1 Kgs	וּלְבֵית הַמֶּלֶךְ	ה'	לְבֵית־	מִסְעָד	הָאַלְמֻגִּים	אֶת־עֲצֵי הַמֶּלֶךְ וַיַּעַשׂ
TJ	ועבד מלכא ית אעי אלמוגיא סעיד לבית מקדשא דה' ולבית מלכא

NJPS Chr: The king made of the algum-wood ramps for the House of the LORD and for the royal palace,

Dost: The king made from the almug wood ramps for the support of the temple of the Lord and for the king's palace

NJPS Kgs: The king used the almug wood for decorations in the House of the LORD and in the royal palace

Clem: And the king made the almug wood into supports for the house of the sanctuary of the Lord and for the royal palace

The word מִסְעָד in 1 Kings is paralleled in Chronicles by מְסִלּוֹת. This is rendered by TC with the two words כיבשייה לסעיד. The word כיבשייה, the literal translation of מְסִלּוֹת, requires no supplementation; the second word, לסעיד, represents nothing more than the infiltration of a word from TJ.

2 Chr 9:18 / 1 Kgs 10:19

2 Chr	וְיָדוֹת...	מָאֳחָזִים	לַכִּסֵּא		וְכֶבֶשׁ בַּזָּהָב	לַכִּסֵּא מַעֲלוֹת	וְשֵׁשׁ
TC	ואשדית... מדבקין ביה כורסא סגלגלי		וכיבש בדהבא לכורסיא מסוקין ואשתה
1 Kgs	וְיָדֹת...	מֵאַחֲרָיו	לַכִּסֵּה	עָגֹל־	וְרֹאשׁ־	לַכִּסֵּה מַעֲלוֹת	שֵׁשׁ
TJ	ואשדתא... מאחורוהי לכרסיא סגלגל וריש		דרגין לכרסיא שתא

NJPS Chr: Six steps led up to the throne; and the throne had a golden footstool attached to it, and arms

---

11   Churgin Hagiographa, p. 272.

Dost: The throne had six steps and a golden footstool all around the throne attached to it. Arms

NJPS Kgs: Six steps led up to the throne, and the throne had a back with a rounded top, and arms

Clem: he throne had six stairs, and the throne had a round head in back, and arms

TC prefers מסוקיין over דרגין as the translation of the word מַעֲלוֹת,[12] but this is no proof that its rendering of the verse is unaffected by TJ. One would have expected the translation of the words וְכֶבֶשׁ בַּזָּהָב לַכִּסֵּא to read וכיבש בדהבא לכורסא. The word סגלגלי in TC comes directly from TJ, which in the parallel verse gives סגלגל for the word עָגֹל.

2 Chr 6:13

2 Chr						
	הַשָּׁמָיְמָה:	כַּפָּיו	וַיִּפְרֹשׂ	יִשְׂרָאֵל	כָּל־קְהַל	נֶגֶד	עַל־בִּרְכָּיו	וַיִּבְרַךְ	עָלָיו	וַיַּעֲמֹד

TC: וקם עלוי וכרע על ברכוי   כל קבל כל קהלא דישר[אל] ופרש ידוי   בצלו לצית שמיא:

NJPS: He stood on it; then, kneeling in front of the whole congregation of Israel, he spread forth his hands to heaven

Dost: He stood over it, and he knelt on his knees in the presence of all of the assembly of Israel, and he spread his hands in prayer toward the heavens.

The targumist expands the verse in his translation, explaining that Solomon's act of spreading his hands in 2 Chr 6:13 was one of prayer. The verse in Chronicles serves as a kind of amplification of that preceding it, which is paralleled by 1 Kgs 8:22:

1 Kgs 8:22 / 2 Chr 6:12

1 Kgs	הַשָּׁמָיִם:	כַּפָּיו	וַיִּפְרֹשׂ	יִשְׂרָאֵל	כָּל־קְהַל	נֶגֶד	... שְׁלֹמֹה	וַיַּעֲמֹד
TJ	לצית שמיא:	בצלו	ידוהי	ופרס	דישראל	כל קהלא	לקביל	שלמה...	וקם
2 Chr		כַּפָּיו	וַיִּפְרֹשׂ	יִשְׂרָאֵל	כָּל־קְהַל	נֶגֶד		...וַיַּעֲמֹד
TC	בצלו:	ידוי	ופרש	דישראל	כל קהלא	כל קבל		...וקם

NJPS Kgs: Then Solomon stood ... in the presence of the whole community of Israel; he spread the palms of his hands toward heaven

Clem: Then Solomon stood ... in front of all the congregation of Israel, and he spread out his hands in prayer to the heavens

---

12   Thus also in 2 Chr 32:33. The author of *Tg. Ps* followed this convention in all of the Songs of Ascents (Ps 120–134). This difference between TC and TJ is comparable to that between TO and TPJ Exod 20:26, and appears to reflect the divergent Aramaic dialects of the targumists.

NJPS Chr: Then, standing ... in front of the whole congregation of Israel, he spread forth his hands

Dost: Then he stood before the altar of the Lord in the presence of all the congregation of Israel, and he spread out his hands in prayer

TJ supplements Solomon's act of spreading his hands with the word בצלו and defines the direction in which they are spread as לצית שמיא, following the accepted practice in other targumic works where שְׁמַיִם indicates a direction.[13] TC, following TJ, translates ופרש ידוי בצלו, but declines to indicate a direction because its Hebrew *Vorlage* does not do so. In the following verse—although it is essentially an addition to the text in Kings—where the Hebrew *Vorlage* describes Solomon as spreading his hands heavenward, TC incorporates the entire text found in TJ 1 Kgs 8:22, including both the addition בצלו and the preposition לצית.

1 Chr 17:18 / 2 Sam 7:20

1 Chr	אֵלֶיךָ	עוֹד דָּוִיד		מַה־יּוֹסִיף
TC	קדמך	תוב דוד למלל[א]		מה יוסיף
2 Sam	אֵלֶיךָ	עוֹד לְדַבֵּר דָּוִד		וּמַה־יּוֹסִיף
TJ	קדמך	עוד דויד למללא		ומא יוסיף

NJPS Chr: What more can David add

Dost: What more can David speak before You?

NJPS Sam: What more can David say to You?

Clem: And what more can David speak before You?

The targumist preserved the word order of Chronicles, rather than the variant order found in 2 Samuel (עוֹד דָּוִיד), but nonetheless felt it necessary to include the verb left absent in Chronicles, and did so in accordance with TJ (למללא). Thus in this instance we can identify the direction of the influence exerted: it would seem that TJ was known to the author of TC.

2 Chr 7:7 / 1 Kgs 8:64

2 Chr	אֶת־הָעֹלָה	לְהָכֵיל לֹא יָכֹל	עָשָׂה שְׁלֹמֹה		אֲשֶׁר הַנְּחֹשֶׁת		כִּי־מִזְבַּח
TC	ית עלתא	דחיק ולא יכיל לסוברא	עבד שלמה		די דנחשא		מטול דמדבחא
1 Kgs	אֶת־הָעֹלָה	מֵהָכִיל	קָטֹן	לִפְנֵי ה'	אֲשֶׁר הַנְּחֹשֶׁת		כִּי־מִזְבַּח
TJ	ית עלתא	מלסוברא	דחיק	קדם ה'	ד דנחשא		ארי מדבחא

---

13   At issue is a prepositional phrase consisting of צית +ב/ל/על/עד that is added to the word שמיא or various manifestations of the divine glory. See, e.g., TO Exod 9:8; TN Gen 28:12; TPJ Deut 4:19. Cf. Sokoloff *JPA*, p. 445.

NJPS Chr: since the bronze altar that Solomon had made was not able to hold the burnt offerings

Dost: because the bronze altar that Solomon had made was too small and could not accommodate a burnt offering

NJPS Kgs: because the bronze altar that was before the LORD was too small to hold the burnt offerings

Clem: for the altar of bronze that was before the Lord was too small to bear the burnt offerings

The word דחיק appears in TC and TJ, but only in 1 Kings does the *Vorlage* contain a corresponding word. There is no reason to assume that the Hebrew *Vorlage* of TC also contained the word קָטֹן, because the Hebrew expression לֹא יָכוֹל לְ used in Chronicles fulfills a function similar to that of קָטֹן מֵ in 1 Kings. It follows that this alteration ought to be viewed as one of the textual adjustments performed by the author of Chronicles itself. The same is indicated by LXX, which translates the expression in accordance with MT: οὐκ ἐξεποίει δέξασθαι.[14] It is more reasonable to assess that here, too, the targumist generally followed the Hebrew text of Chronicles, but also included the word דחיק, in accordance with TJ. This addition further required the insertion of a *waw* at the beginning of the following word (ולא).

2 Chr 7:10 / 1 Kgs 8:66

2 Chr			לְדָוִיד	ה'	עָשָׂה	אֲשֶׁר	הַטּוֹבָה	עַל-
TC	עבדיה	לדוד	ה'	דעבד	טבתא	כל	על
1 Kgs	עַבְדּוֹ	לְדָוִד	ה'	עָשָׂה	אֲשֶׁר	הַטּוֹבָה	כָּל-	עַל
TJ	עבדיה	לדויד	ה'	דעבד	טבתא	כל	על

NJPS Chr: over the goodness that the LORD had shown to David

Dost: over all the good that the Lord had done for David His servant

NJPS Kgs: over all the goodness that the LORD had shown to His servant David

Clem: over all the good that the Lord had done for David His servant

In MT and LXX Chronicles we find a truncated version of the text, which omits כָּל and עַבְדּוֹ. Here TC adheres to the text of Kings and TJ, incorporating the words כל and עבדיה. In this case, as in the previous one, it seems clear that TC

---

14 Though Peshiṭta Chronicles has ܗܘܐ ܙܥܘܪ, this is best viewed as a result of the direct influence of the Hebrew text of 1 Kings, rather than a witness to a variant Hebrew *Vorlage* of 2 Chronicles. This accords with the character of the Syriac translation of Chronicles in general. On this topic, see Weitzman, p. 111.

was influenced by TJ. True, based on this case alone, one might argue that TC
was influenced simply by the Hebrew text of Kings, rather than by TJ, but the
potency of such an argument should be evaluated against the entire Targum
and in light of other examples.

2 Chr 9:14 / 1 Kgs 10:15

2 Chr	מְבִיאִים		וְהַסֹּחֲרִים	אַנְשֵׁי הַתָּרִים		מֶ	לְבַד
TC	דמובלין	תגריא	וסחורת	אומניא	אגר	מ	בר
1 Kgs	הָרֹכְלִים	וּמִסְחַר	אַנְשֵׁי הַתָּרִים		מֶ	לְבַד
TJ	תגריא	וסחורת	אומניא	אגר	מ	בר

NJPS Chr: besides what traders and merchants brought
Dost: apart from the wages of the craftsmen, and the merchandise of the trad-
ers, which they brought
NJPS Kgs: besides what came from tradesmen, from the traffic of the merchants,
Clem: apart from the wages of the craftsmen, and the merchandise of the
traders,

The reading in MT Chronicles is supported by LXX, Peshiṭta, and findings from
the available Hebrew MSS, and it stands to reason that this text lay before the
author of TC. TC renders the first five words of the verse similarly to TJ despite
the differences between the *Vorlagen* of the two books. TJ added the word אגר
(i.e., wages), which corresponds to no part of the Hebrew, under the influence
of the Hebrew word וּמִסְחַר in the parallel verse. The author of TC had no independent reason to use this translation, as the word וּמִסְחַר does not appear
in the text of Chronicles, but instead is replaced by וְהַסֹּחֲרִים. The appearance
of the word אגר in TC results not from an inherent requirement in Chronicles,
but from the direct influence of TJ. By the same token, the words וסחורת תגריא,
which serve in TC as the translation of וְהַסֹּחֲרִים, are not a literal translation, but
drawn from TJ.

1 Chr 13:9 / 2 Sam 6:6

1 Chr	כִּידֹן	עַד־גֹּרֶן	וַיָּבֹאוּ
TC	מתקן	עד אתר	ואתו
2 Sam	נָכוֹן	עַד־גֹּרֶן	וַיָּבֹאוּ
TJ	מתקן	עד אתר	ואתו

NJPS Chr: But when they came to the threshing floor of Chidon
Dost: When they came to (the) appointed place
NJPS Sam: But when they came to the threshing floor of Nacon
Clem: And they came to the prepared place

TJ to 2 Samuel understands the nomen rectum of the genitive גֹּרֶן נָכוֹן literally, as signifying *prepared*, and thus translates מתקן. In 1 Chronicles, however, there is no indication of why כִּידֹן (a reading supported by the evidence available to us from medieval Hebrew MSS) might be translated as מתקן—barring direct influence of TJ on TC.

2 Chr 7:21 / 1 Kgs 9:8

2 Chr		יִשֹּׁם	לְכָל־עֹבֵר עָלָיו	עֶלְיוֹן הָיָה אֲשֶׁר	וְהַבַּיִת הַזֶּה
TC		עלוי יכלי	כל מן דייעבר	עלאה יהא חרוב	דהוה הדין וביתא
1 Kgs	וְשָׁרַק	יִשֹּׁם	כָּל־עֹבֵר עָלָיו	עֶלְיוֹן	יִהְיֶה וְהַבַּיִת הַזֶּה
TJ	וינוד יכלי	עלוי דייעבר מן כל	חרוב יהא עלאה	דהוה הדין וביתא

NJPS Chr: And as for this House, once so exalted, everyone passing by it shall be appalled

Dost: And this temple, which was exalted, will be laid low; all those who pass by it will cry out

NJPS Kgs: And as for this House, [once] so exalted, everyone passing by it shall be appalled and shall hiss

Clem: And this temple that was most high will be ruined; all those who pass by it will cry out and nod

The Hebrew text of 1 Kings is problematic: the word עֶלְיוֹן appears to stand in contradiction to the negative message of the sentence in which it appears.[15] TJ met this challenge by emending and expanding the text: עֶלְיוֹן in TJ reflects the glory of the past (with the verb יִהְיֶה transformed into a past form, דהוה, as in the Hebrew text of Chronicles), while the adversity of the future is expressed by the words יהא חרוב. The Hebrew text of Chronicles poses no challenge requiring such a solution, because the difficulty described is no longer in evidence: the verse describes the glory of the past—וְהַבַּיִת הַזֶּה אֲשֶׁר הָיָה עֶלְיוֹן—in contradistinction to the adversity of the future: יִשֹּׁם. The author of TC nevertheless failed to decline the solution proffered by TJ in 1 Kings, adding the words יהא חרוב (and translating כל, rather than לכל) in his composition, as well.

---

15   The process of textual transmission appears to have been attended by a number of changes to the text; cf. Cogan *Kings*, p. 269. The original text read, roughly, והבית הזה יהיה לְעִיִּין (cf. Mic 3:12; Jer 26:18; Ps 79:1). לְעִיִּין became corrupted to עֶלְיוֹן at a secondary but very early stage, and remains in this form in MT 1 Kgs. The text of Chronicles reflects both familiarity with the text of MT 1 Kgs and an effort to ameliorate the difficulty it poses by changing the verse to the past tense: אֲשֶׁר הָיָה עֶלְיוֹן.

1 Chr 17:22 / 2 Sam 7:24

1 Chr	וַתִּתֵּ֠ן	אֶת־עַמְּךָ֙ יִשְׂרָאֵ֤ל ׀	לְךָ֙	לְעָ֖ם עַד־עוֹלָ֑ם	
TC	ואתקינתא	ית עמך ישראל	לך	לעם עד עלמא	
2 Sam	וַתְּכוֹנֵ֣ן	לְךָ֡ אֶת־עַמְּךָ֙ יִשְׂרָאֵ֤ל ׀	לְךָ֙	לְעָ֖ם עַד־עוֹלָ֑ם	
TJ	ואתקינת	לך ית עמך ישראל	קדמך	לעם עד עלמא	

NJPS Chr: You have established Your people Israel as Your very own people forever

Dost: You have established Your people Israel before Yourself as a people forever

NJPS Sam: You have established Your people Israel as Your very own people forever

Clem: And You have established Your people Israel before You for a people forever

The use of the verb תק״ן in both TC and in TJ is surprising in light of the two disparate verbs, נת״ן and כו״ן, that they represent in the two Hebrew books. We would expect TC to give the translation ויהבת or ושוית, in accordance with the typical equivalents in TC for the root נת״ן. The verb תק״ן appears in TC over fifty times,[16] but takes the place of the Hebrew verb נת״ן exclusively in the present verse. The only explicable reason for this phenomenon is that the author of TC was influenced by the text of TJ to 2 Samuel.

2 Chr 18:23 / 1 Kgs 22:24

2 Chr	אֵ֣י זֶ֤ה	הַדֶּ֙רֶךְ֙	עָבַ֣ר	ר֖וּחַ־	יְהֹוָ֑ה מֵאִתִּ֖י לְדַבֵּ֥ר אֹתָֽךְ׃	
TC	אידא שעתא		אסתלקא רוח	נבואה מן קדם ה'	מני לממלא עמך׃	
1 Kgs	אֵי־זֶ֨ה		עָבַ֧ר	רֽוּחַ־	יְהֹוָ֛ה מֵאִתִּ֖י לְדַבֵּ֥ר אוֹתָֽךְ׃	
TJ	אידא שעא		אסתלק רוח	נבואה מן קדם ה'	מני לממלא עמך׃	

NJPS Chr: However did the spirit of the LORD pass from me to speak with you!

Dost: (At) which hour was the spirit of prophecy taken from before the Lord from me to speak with you?

NJPS Kgs: Which way did the spirit of the LORD pass from me to speak with you?

Clem: In which hour was the spirit of prophecy taken from before the Lord from me to speak with you?

---

16   1 Chr 1:20; 9:22, 32; 11:11; 13:9; 14:2; 15:1; 16:30; 17:9, 11–12, 14, 22, 24; 22:3, 5, 10, 14; 28:7; 29:2–3, 16, 18–19; 2 Chr 1:4; 2:6, 8; 3:1, 17; 4:4; 5:7; 6:2, 8; 8:16; 12:1; 16:14; 17:5; 20:33; 26:14; 27:6; 29:19, 35–36; 30:19; 31:11; 32:30; 35:4, 6, 10, 14–16, 20.

After striking Micaiah son of Imlah on the cheek, Zedekiah son of Chenaanah posed a sarcastic question with the intent of ridiculing him. The version given in 1 Kings begins with the interrogative אֵי־זֶה, a device intended to depict as ridiculous the idea that the spirit of the Lord might leave Zedekiah, although the referent of the interrogative is left unspecified. The translation given by TJ adds the word שעא, turning the question into one concerning time, i.e., asking *when* the spirit of the Lord left Zedekiah. In Chronicles the function of the interrogative no longer poses any difficulty, as in that book the interrogative is supplemented by an additional word: אֵי זֶה הַדֶּרֶךְ: *however* did the spirit of the Lord leave Zedekiah? The reading in TC, אידא שעתא, adheres to the meaning of the question as understood by TJ, rather than that indicated by the Hebrew of 2 Chronicles.

3.3   *Influence of TJ even when TC Adds and Emends*

Though TC is highly influenced by TJ in parallel units, the author of the former did not simply copy the text of TJ without adapting the text to his own translation's context and his preferred interpretations according to his own discretion. Nevertheless, there are discernible instances where TC diverged from the text of TJ for any of a variety of reasons while leaving clear evidence that TJ had served as his foundation text.

1 Chr 11:2 / 2 Sam 5:2

1 Chr	אֶת־יִשְׂרָאֵל		אֶת־עַמִּי		תִרְעֶה אַתָּה לְךָ אֱלֹהֶיךָ ה' וַיֹּאמֶר		
TC	[ישר[אל ית ותפרנס	עמי על ותשלוט סרכן תהא	אנת לך אלהך ה' ואמר					
2 Sam	אֶת־יִשְׂרָאֵל		אֶת־עַמִּי		תִרְעֶה אַתָּה לְךָ		ה' וַיֹּאמֶר
TJ	ישראל ית		עמי ית		תפרניס את לך		ה' ואמר

NJPS Chr: and the LORD your God said to you: You shall shepherd My people Israel

Dost: The Lord your God said to you, 'You will be a leader, you will rule over My people, and you will govern Israel

NJPS Sam: and the LORD said to you: You shall shepherd My people Israel

Clem: Then the Lord said to you, 'You will support My people Israel

TC chose to underscore the authoritarian dimension of the text in translating the Hebrew verb תִרְעֶה, while TJ accentuated David's responsibility for the welfare of his flocks upon assuming their custodianship. Nevertheless, TC succeeded in preserving something of the text of TJ with the addition of the verb ותפרנס between the two elements of the apposition אֶת־עַמִּי אֶת־יִשְׂרָאֵל.[17]

---

17   White, p. 235, proposes that the word סרכן is a corruption of the word ארכון, which appears later in the verse. I do not concur with his proposal, but this is immaterial to our

1 Chr 17:18 / 2 Sam 7:20

1 Chr		יָדָעְתָּ:	עַבְדְּךָ	אֶת־	וְאַתָּה אֶת־עַבְדְּךָ לְכָבֹוד	
TC		ידעתא:	עבדך	ית	ואנת	ואת עבדתא בעותא דעבדך ליקרא יתיה
2 Sam		עַבְדְּךָ	אֶת־	יָדָעְתָּ	וְאַתָּה	
TJ		עבדך	בעות	עבדתא	ואת	

NJPS Chr: regarding the honoring of Your servant? You know Your servant

Dost: For You have done the request of Your servant by honoring him, for You know Your servant

NJPS Sam: You know Your servant

Clem: And You have done the request of Your servant

TJ translated the words יָדַעְתָּ אֶת־עַבְדְּךָ nonliterally (עבדתא בעות עבדך). TC, meanwhile, kept to a literal translation while also maintaining the order in which the words are given in the text of Chronicles (ית עבדך ידעתא). Notwithstanding, TC managed to preserve the translation given in TJ by using it to supplement the expression לְכָבֹוד אֶת־עַבְדְּךָ, which does not appear in 2 Samuel.

2 Chr 5:6 / 1 Kgs 8:5

2 Chr	צֹאן וּבָקָר	מְזַבְּחִים	עָלָיו...	הַנֹּועָדִים	יִשְׂרָאֵל וְכָל־עֲדַת	וְהַמֶּלֶךְ שְׁלֹמֹה
TC	עאן ותורין ודבחין	מנכסין	עלוהי...	דאזדמנו	ומלכא שלמה וכל כנשתא דישראל	
1 Kgs	צֹאן וּבָקָר	מְזַבְּחִים	עָלָיו...	הַנֹּועָדִים	יִשְׂרָאֵל וְכָל־עֲדַת	וְהַמֶּלֶךְ שְׁלֹמֹה
TJ	עז ותורין	מנכסין	עלוהי...	דאזדמנו	ומלכא שלמה וכל כנשתא דישראל	

NJPS Chr: Meanwhile, King Solomon and the whole community of Israel, who had gathered to him ... were sacrificing sheep and oxen

Dost: King Solomon and all of the congregation of Israel who were assembled to him ... (were) slaughtering and sacrificing sheep and oxen,

NJPS Kgs: Meanwhile, King Solomon and the whole community of Israel, who were assembled with him ... were sacrificing sheep and oxen

Clem: And King Solomon and all the congregation of Israel who were assembled to him were standing with him ... slaughtering sheep and bulls

TJ used the word מנכסין to translate מְזַבְּחִים. TC, meanwhile, employed both מנכסין (in accordance with TJ) and the root דב״ח in a way unparalleled in targumic literature. Though it is difficult to find a single, overriding rule to explain the distribution of these two verbs in TJ to the Former Prophets, there certainly are discernible trends.

Let us first consider the use of the verb נכ״ס, which appears 28 times in TJ to the Former Prophets. The Hebrew verb שח״ט consistently is translated as נכ״ס

---

conclusion here, viz., that the word ותפרנס in TC is an addition made under the influence of TJ to 2 Samuel.

(9 times). When an Aramaic verb joins the noun נכסה as its predicate (10 times, 9 of which have the Hebrew root זב״ח), it, too, always has נכ״ס as its stem. In the remaining nine instances where the root נכ״ס occurs in TJ to the Former Prophets, one is a targumic expansion,[18] while in all eight others it corresponds to the Hebrew root זב״ח.

The verb דב״ח occurs 26 times in TJ to the Former Prophets: 24 times for the Hebrew root זב״ח and twice as a supplementary word.[19]

2 Chr 7:10 / 1 Kgs 8:66

2 Chr	שְׂמֵחִים וְטוֹבֵי לֵב	לְאָהֳלֵיהֶם	שִׁלַּח אֶת־הָעָם
TC	וּשְׁפִירֵי לבא	למשכניהון ואזלו לקרויהון חדן	פטר ית עמא
1 Kgs	שְׂמֵחִים וְטוֹבֵי לֵב	לְאָהֳלֵיהֶם וַיְבָרֲכוּ אֶת־הַמֶּלֶךְ וַיֵּלְכוּ	שִׁלַּח אֶת־הָעָם
TJ	כד חדן וּשְׁפִיר לבהון	לקרויהון וברִיכוּ ית מלכא ואזלו	שלח ית עמא

NJPS Chr: he dismissed the people to their homes, rejoicing and in good spirits

Dost: he sent away the people to their tents, and they went to their cities rejoicing and glad-hearted

NJPS Kgs: he let the people go. They bade the king good-bye and went to their homes, joyful and glad of heart

Clem: he sent the people away, and they blessed the king. Then they went to their cities rejoicing and glad hearted

Here we see how TC preserved the continuum of the Hebrew *Vorlage* of 2 Chronicles—rather than that of 1 Kings—but nevertheless felt a need to insert a verb referring to departure of the people. TC copied this verb, along with its indirect object, from TJ, where they are given as part of the literal continuum of the text, rather than as an addition.

2 Chr 25:24 / 2 Kgs 14:14

2 Chr	וְאֵת בְּנֵי הַתַּעֲרֻבוֹת	
TC	וית בני רברבניא דמתמשכנין גביה	
2 Kgs	וְאֵת בְּנֵי הַתַּעֲרֻבוֹת	
TJ	וית בני רברביא	

NJPS Chr: and with the hostages,

Dost: and the leaders who were taken as a pledge with him

NJPS Kgs: as well as hostages

Clem: and the leaders

---

18   2 Sam 24:15.

19   1 Sam 2:14; 2 Kgs 23:9.

The expression בְּנֵי הַתַּעֲרֻבוֹת appears in Scripture only in these two instances. The word תַּעֲרֻבוֹת, from the root ער"ב, to give in pledge, and refers to children of vassals that were kept by the ruling king to insure loyalty. TJ translated בני רבר־ בניא, which indeed conveys their aristocratic status. TC followed TJ's בני רברביא, but added דמתמשכנין גביה, who were taken as a pledge with him, in order to provide literal representation of the word תַּעֲרֻבוֹת.

1 Chr 17:16 / 2 Sam 7:18

1 Chr	אֱלֹהִים ה'		מִי־אָנִי וַיֹּאמֶר ה' לִפְנֵי		וַיֵּשֶׁב דָּוִיד הַמֶּלֶךְ וַיָּבֹא
TC	אלהים כמסת ה' אנא לית ואמר ה' [קד]ם בצלותא ואשתהי דוד מלכא ואתא				
2 Sam	ה' אֲדֹנָי אָנֹכִי מִי וַיֹּאמֶר ה' לִפְנֵי		וַיֵּשֶׁב דָּוִד הַמֶּלֶךְ וַיָּבֹא
TJ	אלהים כמסת ה' אנא לית ואמר ה' קדם		ויתיב דויד מלכא ואתא

NJPS Chr: Then King David came and sat before the LORD, and he said, "What am I, O LORD God

Dost: Then King David came and tarried in prayer before the Lord and said, "I am not worthy, O Lord God

NJPS Sam: Then King David came and sat before the LORD, and he said, "What am I, O Lord GOD

Clem: Then King David came and sat before the Lord and said, "I am not worthy, O Lord God

The influence of TJ is felt in TC's deviation from literal translation, giving לית אנא כמסת as its rendering of מִי־אָנִי. TC nevertheless diverged from the text of TJ in its translation of the verb וַיֵּשֶׁב. Where TJ gave the literal translation ויתיב, TC described the act as not one of sitting per se, but one of being occupied with prayer. Most probably TC preferred not to give a literal translation of this verb out of deference to rabbinic tradition: the verse stands at the center of a debate, found at several points in rabbinic literature, concerning whether kings of the Davidic dynasty may sit in the courtyard of the Temple. The unambiguous diction of the verse—וַיֵּשֶׁב לִפְנֵי ה'—is cited as support for the view that permits Davidic kings to be seated. In y. Yoma 3:2 (40b, p. 572) and Midr. Ps 1 (p. 3), the verb וַיֵּשֶׁב found here is interpreted, following the view that even Davidic kings may not sit in the courtyard, in a manner similar to that found in TC: he settled himself in prayer.[20] The choice of the verb ואשתהי for וַיֵּשֶׁב is uncommon in targumic literature, but occurs elsewhere in TC itself. In 1 Chr 13:14, which discusses the time during which the Ark remained in the household of Obed-edom the Gittite, וַיֵּשֶׁב is translated as ואשתהי, rather than

---

20   The question stemming from the present verse also arises in b. Soṭah 40b, 41b, but there the verse is explained otherwise, viz., David did indeed sit, but not within the courtyard.

וּשְׁרָא, the rendering found in TJ. TC apparently chose this verb to express the length of the stay. Cf. *b. Meg.* 21a: "sitting (i.e. the word יְשִׁיבָה) denotes naught but lingering."

4   Disagreement of TC and TJ

4.1   *Dialect*

Against the clear substantive similarities linking TC and TJ, the linguistic-dialectal disparity between the two stands out in relief. Although the vocabulary of TJ is highly similar to that of TO, the language of TC is deeply rooted in the tradition of the Palestinian Targums, particularly the later among them. Though the literal continuum, sentence structure, and even lexical choices of TC in parallel chapters are greatly influenced by TJ, when the two translations are compared on a word-to-word basis, it is plain that TC employs certain Palestinian forms instead of the forms that are routine in TJ.[21]

Thus instead of TJ's אֲרֵי, TC uses אֲרוּם. Instead of TJ's כְּעַן, TC employs כְּדוֹן. Instead of TJ's כֵּין, TC offers כְּדֵין. The expression סְחוֹר סְחוֹר of TJ in TC appears as חֲזוֹר חֲזוֹר. The preposition כ in TJ manifests in TC as הֵיך (though not consistently). In many cases, עַל of TJ becomes מְטוֹל in TC. For instance:

'אֲרוּם' / 'אֲרֵי'

1 Chr 17:2 / 2 Sam 7:3

1 Chr		הָאֱלֹהִים עִמָּךְ:		כִּי
TC	בְּסַעְדָּךְ:	מֵימְרָא דַה'	אֲרוּם	
2 Sam	עִמָּךְ:	ה'		כִּי
TJ	בְּסַעְדָּךְ:	מֵימְרָא דַה'	אֲרֵי	

NJPS Chr: for God is with you

Dost: for the Memra of the Lord is at your aid

NJPS Sam: for the LORD is with you

Clem: for the Memra of the Lord is at your aid

אֲרוּם appears 258 times in TC; אֲרֵי does not appear even once.[22]

---

21   Rosenberg-Kohler, p. 272.

22   See discussion regarding distribution of the word אֲרוּם, pp. 46–47, above; White, pp. 50–51, 95.

'כדון' / 'כען'

2 Chr 6:16 / 1 Kgs 8:25

2 Chr	וְעַתָּ֞ה ה׳ אֱלֹהֵ֣י יִשְׂרָאֵ֗ל
TC	וכדון ה׳ אלהא דישראל
1 Kgs	וְעַתָּ֞ה ה׳ אֱלֹהֵ֣י יִשְׂרָאֵ֗ל
TJ	וכען ה׳ אלהא דישראל

NJPS Chr: And now, O LORD God of Israel
Dost: Now, O Lord, God of Israel
NJPS Kgs: And now, O LORD God of Israel
Clem: And now, O Lord God of Israel

כדון appears 54 times in TC; כען does not appear even once.

'כדין' / 'כין'

1 Chr 19:1 / 2 Sam 10:1

1 Chr	וַיְהִי֙ אַחֲרֵי־כֵ֔ן וַיָּ֕מָת נָחָ֖שׁ מֶ֣לֶךְ בְּנֵי־עַמּ֑וֹן
TC	והוה מן בתר כדין ומית נחש מלכא דבני עמון
2 Sam	וַיְהִי֙ אַחֲרֵי־כֵ֔ן וַיָּ֕מָת מֶ֣לֶךְ בְּנֵ֣י עַמּ֑וֹן
TJ	והוה בתר כין ומית מלכא דבני עמון

NJPS Chr: Sometime afterward, Nahash the king of the Ammonites died
Dost: Then it came about afterwards that Nahash king of the children of Ammon died
NJPS Sam: Some time afterward, the king of Ammon died
Clem: Then it came about afterwards that the king of the children of Ammon died,

כדין appears in TC 15 times, in 13 of which as part of the expression מן בתר כדין.
The form כין (also כן) in TC seems to be used principally as part of longer expressions, e.g., בגין כן (4 times) and בכין (הא־) (18 times, 14 of which corresponding to the Hebrew word אָז).

'חזור חזור' / 'סחור סחור'

1 Chr 10:9 / 1 Sam 31:9[23]

1 Chr	וַיְשַׁלְּח֞וּ בְאֶֽרֶץ־פְּלִשְׁתִּ֤ים סָבִ֔יב
TC	ושדרו בארע פלשתא׳ חזור חזור
1 Sam	וַיְשַׁלְּח֞וּ בְאֶֽרֶץ־פְּלִשְׁתִּ֤ים סָבִ֔יב
TJ	ושלחו בארע פלשתאי סחור סחור

---

23   This verse is also an example of the שלח/שד"ר pair; see p. 131, below.

NJPS Chr: and sent them throughout the land of the Philistines

Dost: and they sent throughout the land of the Philistines all around

NJPS Sam: and they sent them throughout the land of the Philistines

Clem: and they sent them throughout the land of the Philistines all around

The Aramaic root סח״ר commonly appears in TO and TJ as an equivalent of the Hebrew root סב״ב. The Palestinian Targums, meanwhile, tend to substitute the Aramaic חז״ר for the Hebrew סב״ב. TC nowhere contains the phrase סחור סחור, but does feature verbs of the root סח״ר corresponding to the Hebrew סב״ב, as well as verbs from the root חז״ר. Further, סח״ר is used in parallel units, non-parallel units, and nonliteral additions.[24] The absence of the expression סחור סחור thus stems not from a blanket predilection to do without that stem, but from a specific preference for חזור חזור over סחור סחור.

'כ' / 'היד'

2 Chr 1:15 / 1 Kgs 10:27

2 Chr	וְאֵת הָאֲרָזִים נָתַן כַּשִּׁקְמִים אֲשֶׁר־בַּשְּׁפֵלָה לָרֹב:
TC	וית ארזיא יהב הי־כשקמיא די בשפלתא לסוגי:
1 Kgs	וְאֵת הָאֲרָזִים נָתַן כַּשִּׁקְמִים אֲשֶׁר־בַּשְּׁפֵלָה לָרֹב:
TJ	וית ארזיא יהב כשקמיא דבשפלתא לסגי:

NJPS Chr: and cedars as plentiful as the sycamores in the Shephelah

Dost: and he caused cedars, which were in the Shephelah in abundance, (to be regarded) as sycamores

NJPS Kgs: and cedars as plentiful as sycamores in the Shephelah

Clem: and he gave cedars like sycamores of the lowlands for abundance

'מטול' / 'על'

1 Chr 19:13 / 2 Sam 10:12

1 Chr	חֲזַק וְנִתְחַזְּקָה בְּעַד־עַמֵּנוּ וּבְעַד עָרֵי אֱלֹהֵינוּ
TC	אתקף ונתקפה מטול עמנא ומטול קרוי אלהנא
2 Sam	חֲזַק וְנִתְחַזַּק בְּעַד־עַמֵּנוּ וּבְעַד עָרֵי אֱלֹהֵינוּ
TJ	תקף ונתקף על עמנא ועל קרוי אלהנא

NJPS Chr: Let us be strong and resolute for the sake of our people and the towns of our God

Dost: Be strong, and let us be strong for our people and for the cities of our God

NJPS Sam: Let us be strong and resolute for the sake of our people and the land of our God;

Clem: May we indeed be strong for our people and for the cities of our God

---

24   The root also appears as an addition in a verse with חז״ר, 2 Chr 35:22.

'אוּף' / 'אַף'

1 Chr 10:5 / 1 Sam 31:5

1 Chr				גַּם־הוּא עַל־הַחֶרֶב וַיָּמֹת׃	וַיִּפֹּל
TC				ואתרמא אוּף הוא על סייפא ומית׃	
1 Sam	עִמֽוֹ׃	וַיָּמָת	עַל־חַרְבּֽוֹ	גַּם־הוּא	וַיִּפֹּל
TJ	עמיה׃	ומית	על חרביה	אַף הוא	ונפל

NJPS Chr: he too fell on his sword and died

Dost: he also fell on his sword and died

NJPS Sam: he too fell on his sword and died with him

Clem: then he also fell on his sword and died with him

TC also features specific verbs that take the place of other verbs found in TJ:

'חמי' / 'חזי'

2 Chr 18:32 / 1 Kgs 22:33

2 Chr		הָרֶכֶב	שָׂרֵי	כִּרְאוֹת	וַיְהִי
TC	ארתיכא	רבני	חמון	כד	והוה
1 Kgs		הָרֶכֶב	שָׂרֵי	כִּרְאוֹת	וַיְהִי
TJ	רתכיא	רבני	חזו	כד	והוה

NJPS Chr: And when the chariot officers realized

Dost: It came about when the chariot commanders saw

NJPS Kgs: And when the chariot officers became aware

Clem: And it came about when the chariot commanders saw

The verb חמ״י appears 45 times in TC, 5 occurrences of which are in the passive participle form חֲמֵי. The verb חז״י appears in TC only 4 times, all in verses paralleling TJ.[25] The passive participle form חֲזֵי appears 6 times, all in verses with no parallel in Samuel or Kings.[26] We may explain the above findings by positing that, while the author of TC regarded חמ״י as the primary equivalent of Hebrew רא״ה for perfect or imperfect verbs, the four appearances of חז״י made their way into his composition under the influence of TJ. The passive participle form חֲזֵי, meanwhile, achieved an independent status of its own in the language of TC and existed alongside the parallel form חֲמֵי.

---

25   1 Chr 10:5; 17:17 and twice in 2 Chr 5:9.

26   Aside from the verb and adjective, we find the noun חֲזְוָה (once, 1 Chr 11:11, paralleling TJ); חֲזָון (once, in the sense of a seer, 1 Chr 29:29, and once in the sense of a vision, 2 Chr 9:29).

'מחי' / 'קטל'

1 Chr 18:9 / 2 Sam 8:9[27]

1 Chr	כִּי	הִכָּה דָוִיד אֶת־כָּל־חֵיל הֲדַדְעֶזֶר
TC	ארום	קטל דוד ית כל משרית הדרעזר
2 Sam	כִּי	הִכָּה דָוִד אֶת כָּל־חֵיל הֲדַדְעָזֶר:
TJ	ארי	מחא דויד ית כל משרית הדדעזר:

NJPS Chr: that David had defeated the entire army of King Hadadezer
Dost: that David had killed all the army of Hadarezer
NJPS Sam: that David had defeated the entire army of Hadadezer
Clem: that David had smitten all the armies of Hadadezer

This word pair exhibits not a consistent technique, but the trends of two Targums. Both make use of both קט״ל and מח״י, but TC tends to prefer קט״ל. White notes that nothing can be gleaned from this word pair that might help distinguish between the dialects of the Targums of the Torah.[28]

'משח' / 'רבי'

1 Chr 11:3 / 2 Sam 5:3

1 Chr	וַיִּמְשְׁחוּ אֶת־דָּוִיד לְמֶלֶךְ	עַל־יִשְׂרָאֵל
TC	ורביאו ית דוד למלכא	על ישראל
2 Sam	וַיִּמְשְׁחוּ אֶת־דָּוִד לְמֶלֶךְ	עַל־יִשְׂרָאֵל:
TJ	ומשחו ית דויד למהוי מלכא	על ישראל:

NJPS Chr: And they anointed David king over Israel
Dost: and they anointed David king over Israel
NJPS Sam: And they anointed David king over Israel
Clem: and they anointed David to be king over Israel

TC uses the verb מש״ח only in 1 Chr 29:22,[29] corresponding to the Hebrew *Vorlage* וַיִּמְשְׁחוּ.[30] In all other instances, TC makes use of the root רב״י. TJ, meanwhile, uses מש״ח almost exclusively.

---

27   This verse is another example of the ארי/ארום pair, above.
28   White, p. 50.
29   The noun שֶׁמֶן is translated as משח, and the word משיח appears twice.
30   Many have already suggested that an omission occurred in MT and the correct reading is וימשחוהו (see BHS' comment ad loc.). The translation given in TC, ומשחוהי, supports this thesis, although this alone is not strong evidence of the argument.

‏'שלח' / 'שדר'‏

2 Chr 25:18 / 2 Kgs 14:9

2 Chr	וַיִּשְׁלַ֞ח יוֹאָ֣שׁ מֶֽלֶךְ־יִשְׂרָאֵ֗ל		
TC	ושדר יואש מלכא דישראל		
2 Kgs	וַיִּשְׁלַ֞ח יְהוֹאָ֣שׁ מֶֽלֶךְ־יִשְׂרָאֵ֗ל		
TJ	ושלח יהואש מלכא דישראל		

NJPS Chr: King Joash of Israel sent
Dost: Then Joash king of Israel sent
NJPS Kgs: King Jehoash of Israel sent
Clem: Then Jehoash king of Israel sent

The root ‏שד"ר‏ appears 48 times in TC, including instances where the parallel verse in TJ has the root ‏של"ח‏, as in the above example. All occurrences of the stem ‏שד"ר‏ in TC are verbal forms in the *paʿel*. The root ‏של"ח‏ does exist in TC, but its usage is quite limited. Of ten appearances in TC, five occur in the rare expression ‏מלאך שליח מן קדם ה'‏, which in my estimation was borrowed directly from Josh 5:14 (on which see pp. 92–96, above). In two other occurrences, the root has the sense of removing hides (2 Chr 29:34; 35:11). In yet two other cases, the root is in verbal forms for which TC has no counterpart from the root ‏שד"ר‏: one, ‏דאשתלחון‏ (2 Chr 32:31), is passive, while the other, ‏אקדים‏ ‏ושלחא‏ (2 Chr 36:15), is an infinitive form. One final occurrence accords with the parallel in TJ (2 Chr 6:34).[31] The targumist thus used the root ‏שד"ר‏ often, even substituting it for ‏של"ח‏, but employed ‏של"ח‏ only in a few exceptional cases.

‏'שמ"ש' / 'קו"ם ושמ"ש'‏

2 Chr 10:6 / 1 Kgs 12:6

2 Chr	וַיִּוָּעַ֞ץ הַמֶּ֣לֶךְ רְחַבְעָ֗ם אֶת־הַזְּקֵנִים֙ אֲשֶׁר־הָי֣וּ עֹמְדִ֗ים לִפְנֵ֨י שְׁלֹמֹ֤ה אָבִיו֙						
TC	ואתמליך מלכא רחבעם עם סביא דהוון קיימין ומשמשין קדם שלמה אבוי						
1 Kgs	וַיִּוָּעַ֞ץ הַמֶּ֣לֶךְ רְחַבְעָ֗ם אֶת־הַזְּקֵנִים֙ אֲשֶׁר־הָי֣וּ עֹמְדִ֗ים אֶת־פְּנֵ֨י שְׁלֹמֹ֤ה אָבִיו֙						
TJ	ואתמליך מלכא רחבעם ית סביא דהוו משמשין קדם שלמה אבוהי						

NJPS Chr: King Rehoboam took counsel with the elders who had served ... his father Solomon
Dost: Then King Rehoboam took counsel with the elders that were attendant and had served before Solomon his father
NJPS Kgs: King Rehoboam took counsel with the elders who had served his father Solomon

---

31   For a distinction in meaning between ‏של"ח‏ (to send a message or order) and ‏שד"ר‏ (to send a person or object) in TJ (of Samuel), cf. van Staalduine-Sulman *TJ Samuel*, p. 181. This distinction, however, does not apply to TC.

Clem: Then King Rehoboam took counsel with the elders that had been serving before Solomon his father

The Hebrew expression לעמוד לפני (or על, את פני) can have the physical sense of standing per se, but may also signify service.[32] In Samuel and Kings, when the expression has a physical meaning, TJ renders it literally using the root קו״ם. Where it signifies service, TJ renders it using שמ״ש, according to context.[33] In the three instances in Chronicles where the root עמ״ד has the sense of service (2 Chr 10:6, 8; 18:18), TC translates it using both roots, viz., קו״ם and שמ״ש. If this phenomenon were limited to TC, it might be argued that the targumist had declined to make do with the sense indicated by the context (שמ״ש) and sought also to give expression to a root that corresponded literally to the Hebrew עמ״ד, viz., קו״ם. A more complicated reality arises, however, upon examination of the use of these roots in other targumic works, as the Palestinian Targums commonly express the sense of service with the phrase קו״ם ושמ״ש. What is more, these words generally were added by the targumist to the anticipated, literal continuum.[34] Aside from the Palestinian Targums of the Torah (and their

---

32   BDB, pp. 763–764.

33   Thus in 1 Sam 16:21; 1 Kgs 1:2; 12:6, 8 (discussed here); 17:1; 18:15; 2 Kgs 3:14; 5:16.

34   The common context of this linguistic expression is the priests' service in the Temple. An earlier, similar expression—though one not identical in its construction—exists in Biblical Hebrew, e.g. Deut 17:12: הַכֹּהֵן הָעֹמֵד לְשָׁרֶת שָׁם אֶת־ה׳. The expression is familiar in Rabbinic Hebrew, e.g., m. Yebam. 7:6: הרי זה ראוי להיות כהן גדול עומד ומשמש על גבי המזבח ("Indeed, he is worthy of being a high priest who stands and serves atop the altar"). Examples of קו״ם ושמ״ש in the Palestinian Targums (and their successor, TPJ):

Gen 14:18

MT	וְהוּא	כֹהֵן	לְאֵל	עֶלְיוֹן:
FTP	והוא קאים ומשמש בכהונתא רבתא קדם אל עילאה:			

NJPS: he was a priest of God Most High

Clem: standing and serving in the high priesthood before God Most High

Exod 19:22

MT	וְגַם	הַכֹּהֲנִים	הַנִּגָּשִׁים	אֶל־	ה׳	יִתְקַדָּשׁוּ
TN	ולחוד כהניא דקיימין ומשמשין קדם ה׳ יתקדשון					

NJPS: The priests also, who come near the LORD, must stay pure

Clem: And also the priests who stand and serve before the Lord should sanctify themselves

Cf. also FTP, FTV and GT MS F.

Exod 20:26

MT	וְלֹא־תַעֲלֶה בְמַעֲלֹת עַל־מִזְבְּחִי
GT MS F	ואתון כהניה בני דאהרון דקיימין ומשמשין על גבי מדבחי לא תסקון בדרגין על מדבחי

NJPS: Do not ascend My altar by steps

Clem: And you priests, the sons of Aaron who stand and serve upon my altar, you shall not go up on steps onto my altar.

Cf. also TN, FTP, FTV.

successor TPJ), the phrase קו״ם ושמ״ש occurs in targumic literature only in TC, in the three locations noted above. It therefore appears that what we have here is a systematic language shift undergone under the influence of the Palestinian targumic tradition.

4.2   *Aggadic Expansions in Parallel Units of TC*

Generally speaking, one might say that TC's tendency to insert aggadic expansions in the translational continuum is much greater than that of TJ. This phenomenon is particularly conspicuous in parallel chapters, which afford an opportunity to compare the two translations verse by verse.[35] TC often holds forth at length where TJ is brief; even where TJ itself is protracted, TC tends to be yet longer. We now will consider a few examples of such expansions, as well as how TJ and TC compare in their treatment of these passages. Generally speaking, these examples show that once the expansions introduced by TC in the parallel chapters are peeled away, what remains is a translational framework based directly on TJ.

Exod 21:14

MT   מֵעִם מִזְבְּחִי תִּקָּחֶנּוּ לָמוּת:

FTV   אפילו הוא כהנא רבא דקאים משמיש קודמוי על גבי מדבחא מן תמן תסבון יתיה ותקטלון יתיה:

NJPS: you shall take him from My very altar to be put to death

Clem: even if he is the high priest who stands and ministers before Me on the altar, you shall take him from there and execute him

Cf. also TN, FTP.

Exod 33:23

MT   וַהֲסִרֹתִי אֶת־ כַּפִּי וְרָאִיתָ אֶת־ אֲחֹרָי

TPJ   ואעבר ית כיתי מלאכיא דקימין ומשמשין קדמי ותחמי ית קטר דבירא דתפילי איקר שכינתי

NJPS: Then I will take My hand away and you will see My back

Clem: And I will cause to pass over a troop of angels who are standing and ministering before Me, and you will see the knot of the Dibbera of the tefillin of the glory of My Shekhinah

Cf. also TN, FTP, FTV.

Deut 18:7

MT   וְשֵׁרֵת בְּשֵׁם ה׳ אֱלֹהָיו כְּכָל־אֶחָיו הַלְוִיִּם הָעֹמְדִים שָׁם לִפְנֵי ה׳:

TN   וישמש בשם מימרה דה׳ אלהיה ככל אחוי ליווי דקיימין ומשמשין תמן קדם ה׳:

NJPS: He may serve in the name of the LORD his God like all his fellow Levites who are there in attendance before the LORD

Clem: he may serve in the name of the Memra of the Lord his God, like all his brothers the Levites who stand there and serve before the Lord

35   These expansions will not be discussed in depth here, but will be given their due treatment in Chapters 7 and 8, below. The present discussion will focus on the relationship between TC and TJ.

1 Chr 16:3 / 2 Sam 6:19

1 Chr   כִּכַּר־ לֶחֶם וְאֶשְׁפָּר וַאֲשִׁישָׁה:

TC   טולמא דלחמא חדא ופלוג חד מן אשתה בתורא ומנא חד מן אשתא בהינא דחמרא:

2 Sam   חַלַּת לֶחֶם אַחַת וְאֶשְׁפָּר אֶחָד וַאֲשִׁישָׁה אֶחָת

TJ   גריצתא דלחים ופלוג חד ומנתא חדא

NJPS Chr: a loaf of bread, a cake made in a pan, and a raisin cake

Dost: one loaf of bread, and a one-sixth share of a bull, and a one-sixth portion of a hin of wine

NJPS Sam: a loaf of bread, a cake made in a pan, and a raisin cake

Clem: a cake of bread, one portion and one share

TJ offers its audience a near-literal translation of a verse containing two rare words (אֲשִׁישָׁה, אֶשְׁפָּר). TC writes at great length, offering a translation based on talmudic interpretation of the verse.[36] Nonetheless, despite the different explanation offered, he does not disregard TJ, but takes from it the basic foundation of the translation: פלוג, *portion*, for אֶשְׁפָּר and מנה, *share*, for אֲשִׁישָׁה. To this matrix he adds the talmudic exegesis interpreting אֶשְׁפָּר as one-sixth of a bull and אֲשִׁישָׁה as one-sixth of a hin of wine. 2 Samuel adds the numeral אֶחָד/ אַחַת to describe the quantity of the various food items listed in the verse, while Chronicles does not. TC, however, incorporates the description חד, due to a somewhat complex influence exerted by TJ. TC took the first appearance, חדא, verbatim from TJ. In incorporating the two further appearances, however, he altered the words' functions: while in TJ the qualifier indicates a whole number declined according to the gender of the noun, in TC the word חד functions as the numerator of a fraction.

1 Chr 21:13 / 2 Sam 24:14

MT   וַיֹּאמֶר דָּוִיד אֶל־גָּד צַר־לִי מְאֹד אֶפְּלָה־נָּא בְיַד־ ה׳

TC   ואמר דויד לגד אין אנא בריר ית כפנא ימרון דבית ישראל אוריאיא דדויד
מליין עיבורא ולא אכפת ליה אין אין ימותון עמא ית בית ישר[אל] בכפנא
ואין אנא בריר ית קרבא ולמימפך מן־קדם דסנאיי ימרון דבית ישראל
דוד גברא גברא ומרי קרבא ולא אכפת ליה אין יפלון עמא בית ישראל
קטלין בחרבא הא עיק לי לחדא אתמסר כדון ביד מימרא דה׳

2 Sam   וַיֹּאמֶר דָּוִד אֶל־גָּד צַר־לִי מְאֹד נִפְּלָה־נָּא בְיַד־ה׳ כִּי־רַבִּים רַחֲמָו וּבְיַד־אָדָם אַל־אֶפֹּלָה:

TJ   ואמר דויד לגד עקת לי לחדא נתמסר כען ביד מימרא דה׳ ארי סגיאין רחמוהי
ובידא דאנשא לא אתמסר:

<hr>

36   See detailed discussion of this expansion and its talmudic source, pp. 309–311, below. The disparity between TJ and TC in their treatment of the first word of the excerpt (גריצתא, טולמא) stems, of course, from the difference between the *Vorlage* of the two books.

NJPS Chr: David said to Gad, "I am in great distress. Let me fall into the hands of the LORD, for His compassion is very great; and let me not fall into the hands of men."

Dost: Then David said to Gad, "If I choose famine, those of the house of Israel will say, 'The mangers of David are full of grain, so he does not care if the people the house of Israel die by famine.' But if I choose battle and fleeing from before my enemies, those of the house of Israel will say, 'David is a mighty warrior and master of war, but he does not care if the people, the house of Israel, fall slain by the sword.' Behold, I am greatly distressed. Let me be handed over now into the hand of the Memra of the Lord, for His mercies are great, but let me not be handed over into the hand of the children of man."

NJPS Sam: David said to Gad, "I am in great distress. Let us fall into the hands of the LORD, for His compassion is great; and let me not fall into the hands of men."

Clem: Then David said to Gad, "It is pressing on me very much. Let us be handed over now into the hand of the Memra of the Lord, for His mercies are great, but let me not be handed over into the hand of man."

TC here is far lengthier than TJ due to inclusion of an aggadic expansion (colored red above) detailing David's irresolution, but the two Targums are nearly identical at the beginning and the end of the verse.[37] In fact, the differences between the Targums in these segments may be explained as stemming from differences in the Hebrew *Vorlage* or as dialectal differences, as described above. Thus TC here contains a translational continuum similar to that in TJ with the exception of the lengthy aggadic expansion implanted within it. The expansion was inserted in an appropriate place relative to the sequence of events described, i.e., within David's comments but prior to his expression of pain and his decision.

2 Chr 6:2 / 1 Kgs 8:13

2 Chr	עוֹלָמִֽים׃	לְשִׁבְתְּךָ֖	וּמָכ֥וֹן	לָ֑ךְ	בֵּֽית־זְבֻ֖ל בָּנִ֥יתִי וַאֲנִ֛י
TC		לבית שכנתך	מתקן אתר קדמך מקדשא בית	בניתי ואנא	
	דבשמיא לעלמין׃	מותבך בית כורסי קבל כל ומכוון			
1 Kgs	עוֹלָמִֽים׃	לְשִׁבְתֶּֽךָ׃	מָכ֥וֹן	לָ֑ךְ	זְבֻ֖ל בֵּ֥ית בָּנִ֥יתִי בָּנֹ֨ה
TJ	עלמין׃	לבית שכינתך	מתקן אתר קדמך מקדשא בית	בניתי מבנה	

---

37   See detailed discussion of this expansion and its source, pp. 449–452, below.

NJPS Chr: I have built for You a stately House, And a place where You may dwell forever.

Dost: I, indeed, have built a temple before You, a place prepared as an abode for Your Shekhinah and built according to the throne of the house of Your habitation, which is in the heavens forever.

NJPS Kgs: I have now built for You a stately House, a place where You may dwell forever.

Clem: I indeed built the temple before You, a place prepared for the house of Your Shekhinah forever.

Each of the two words מָכוֹן לְשִׁבְתְּךָ is doubly represented in TC. In the first translation, the word מָכוֹן describes Solomon's Temple as a place that is ready (מוכן) to host the divine presence, which dwells (יש"ב) among the Children of Israel.[38] In the second translation, מָכוֹן intimates that the terrestrial Temple is located parallel (מכוון) to the heavenly throne on which God is seated (יש"ב). It is clear from a perfunctory survey of TJ that it is the source of the first translation given these words in TC. TC apparently retained TJ as a foundation for the verse's translation while remaining attentive to the slight divergence in the verse's Hebrew *Vorlage* and adding to it another translation/interpretation that was available to him.

2 Chr 23:11 / 2 Kgs 11:12

| 2 Chr | אֹתוֹ | וַיַּמְלִיכוּ | וְאֶת־הָעֵדוּת | עָלָיו | וַיִּתְּנוּ | אֶת־הַנֵּזֶר | אֶת־בֶּן־הַמֶּלֶךְ | וַיּוֹצִיאוּ |
| TC | מעל | די דבר דוד | דמלכותא | כלילא | ית עלוי | ויהבו | ברא דמלכא | ואפיקו ית |

רישא דמלכא דבני עמון ובה אבן טבא שייבה דהוה חקיק ומפרש עלה שמא רבא ויקירא דקבעה תמן
דוד ברוח קודשא והוה טימין דידה מתקל קנטינר דדהבא וסהדותא היא לבית דוד דכל מלכא
דלא הוה מזרעיה דדוד לא הות מתקבלא על רישיה ולית איפשר דיסובר יתה וכד חמן עמא דאתקבלת
על רישיה דיהואש וסובר ית כלילא הימינו דמזרעיה דדוד הוא ומן־יד אמליכו יתיה

| 2 Kgs | אֹתוֹ | וַיַּמְלִכוּ | וְאֶת־הָעֵדוּת | עָלָיו | וַיִּתֵּן | אֶת־הַנֵּזֶר | אֶת־בֶּן־הַמֶּלֶךְ | וַיּוֹצִא |
| TJ | יתיה | ואמליכו | וית סהדותא | כלילא | עלוהי ית | ויהב | בר מלכא | ואפיק ית |

NJPS Chr: Then they brought out the king's son, and placed upon him the crown and the insignia. They proclaimed him king

Dost: Then they brought out the king's son, and he put on him the royal crown that David took from upon the head of the king of the children of Ammon, in which was the lodestone, upon which was clearly engraved the great and glorious name, where David placed it by the spirit of holiness. Its price was the

---

38 On the function of the word שכינה in targumic literature in general and TC in particular, see discussion of the lexicon of divine honor, pp. 84–87, above.

weight of a centenarius of gold, and it was a testimony to the house of David that every king that was not from the seed of David could not fit it on his head and it was impossible for him to wear it. And when the people saw that it fit the head of Jehoash and (that) he was wearing the crown, they believed that he was from the seed of David. So they immediately made him king

NJPS Kgs: [Jehoiada] then brought out the king's son, and placed upon him the crown and the insignia. They ... proclaimed him king;

Here, too, we see that all words present in TJ are represented in TC (all others are colored red); the text derived by extruding these words from the additional verbiage deviates from TJ only where such is dictated by differences in the Hebrew *Vorlage* of Chronicles.[39] This is the case because TJ served the author of TC as a basic structure, to which he added aggadic elements of his own choosing.

1 Chr 11:11 / 2 Sam 23:8

2 Sam אֵלֶּה שְׁמוֹת הַגִּבֹּרִים אֲשֶׁר לְדָוִד יֹשֵׁב בַּשֶּׁבֶת תַּחְכְּמֹנִי | רֹאשׁ הַשָּׁלִשִׁי הוּא עֲדִינוֹ הָעֶצְנִי עַל־שְׁמֹנֶה מֵאוֹת חָלָל בְּפַעַם אֶחָת:

TJ אלין שמהת גבריא דהוו עם דויד גברא ריש משריתא יתיב על כרסי דינא וכל נבייא וסבייא מקפין ליה משיח במשח קדשא בחיר ומפנק שפיר ברויוה ויאי בחזויה חכים בחכמתא וסכלתן בעיצא גבר בגברותא ריש גבריא הוא מתקן במני זינא נפיק בפום קלא ונצח בקרבא ומתביב על ידי מורניתיה תמני מאה קטילין בזמן חדא:

NJPS Sam: These are the names of David's warriors: Josheb-basshebeth, a Tahchemonite, the chief officer—he is Adino the Eznite; [he wielded his spear] against eight hundred and slew them on one occasion

Clem: These are the names of the mighty men who were with David the mighty, the head of the armies. Enthroned on the throne of judgment, and all the prophets and elders surround him, anointed with holy anointing, chosen and pampered, beautiful in his presence, and comely in his appearance, wise in wisdom and intelligent in counsel, mighty in strength, the head of the mighty men. He was equipped with weapons, going out with a loud shout and victorious in battle, and bringing back with his spear eight hundred slain at one time.

The Aramaic verse is thrice the length of the Hebrew. TJ dilates the verse with exegetical bulk to the point that a Hebrew verse listing several of David's warriors, in its Aramaic translation, lengthily extolls David himself, rather than his warriors. What moved the targumist to make such a change to the topic of the verse? He apparently found himself contending with an objective exegetical

---

39   See detailed discussion of this expansion and its sources, pp. 409–412, below.

challenge: the lemma of the verse promises warrior's names, but what follows does not appear to be a list of names.[40] What is more, the thrust of the entire continuum following the word לְדָוִד is unclear. TJ treated all of the expressions in this section of the verse (עֲדִינוֹ הָעֶצְנִי, רֹאשׁ הַשָּׁלִשִׁי, יֹשֵׁב בַּשֶּׁבֶת, תַּחְכְּמֹנִי, עַל־שְׁמֹנֶה מֵאוֹת חָלָל) as sobriquets for a single individual: because the series of epithets is juxtaposed to David's name, they are exegetically deciphered as describing him.[41]

Now let us see the parallel verse in Chronicles (1 Chr 11:11) and its Targum:

וְאֵלֶּה מִסְפַּר הַגִּבֹּרִים אֲשֶׁר לְדָוִיד יָשָׁבְעָם בֶּן־חַכְמוֹנִי רֹאשׁ הַשָּׁלִישִׁים הוּא־עוֹרֵר 1 Chr
אֶת־חֲנִיתוֹ עַל־שְׁלֹשׁ־מֵאוֹת חָלָל בְּפַעַם אֶחָת:

ואליין סכומי גבריא דהוו עם דוד גברא ריש משריתא יתיב על כורסי דינא וכל TC
נבייא וחכימיא מקפין ליה מרבי במשח קודשא כד הוה נפיק לקרבא הוה מסתייע מל־
עילא ובמתביה לאולפן אוריתא הות סלקא שמעתה אלביה בחיר ומפנק שפיר ברויה
ויאה בחזוה בקי בחכמתא וסוכלתן בעצתא גבר בגבורתה ריש מתיבתה בסים בקלא
ורבן בשירתה וסרכן על כל גברייה והוא מתקן במאני זינא ונטיל מורניתה דביה תלי
אתא דטיקס משריית יהודה ונפיק על פס[42] קל רוחא דקודשא ונצח בקרבא ומתביב
על ידא דמורניתא תלת מאה קטילין בזמנא חדא:

NJPS Chr: This is the list of David's warriors: Jashobeam son of Hachmoni, the chief officer; he wielded his spear against three hundred and slew them all on one occasion.

Dost: Now these are the tallies of the warriors who were with David the warrior, the head of the camp, enthroned on the throne of judgment, and all the prophets and sages surrounding him, anointed with holy oil. When he went out to war he was helped from above, and when he sat for Torah instruction in the Torah the legal tradition come to his mind. (He was) distinguished and erudite, handsome in his appearance, comely in his looks, an expert in wisdom and intelligent in counsel, mighty in strength, the head of the academy, sweet of voice, a teacher of song, and an officer over all the warriors. He was equipped with weapons, carrying a spear on which was hung a sign of the battle standard of the camp of

---

40   This statement naturally pertains to the verse as it appears in MT, rather than its presumed original form. On this matter, as well as the aggadic expansions in TC to this verse and their sources, see pp. 285–299, below.

41   The verse is thus understood in *b. Moʿed Qaṭ.* 16b and elsewhere in rabbinic literature, although specific exegeses differ from one source to the next.

42   Sic in MS V. Le Déaut and Robert in their edition, vol. 2, p. 38, propose the reading פס.

Judah, going forth according to the voice of the holy spirit, victorious in battle, and executing with the spear 300 slain at one time.

The parallel verse in Chronicles (1 Chr 11:11) resembles that of 2 Samuel in a number of textual respects, but the major challenge posed by the text of 2 Samuel is here absent. The word לְדָוִיד is in fact followed by the name of a warrior (יָשָׁבְעָם בֶּן־חַכְמוֹנִי), accompanied by his capacity (רֹאשׁ הַשָּׁלִישִׁים) and an account of one of his military exploits (הוּא־עוֹרֵר אֶת־חֲנִיתוֹ עַל־שְׁלֹשׁ־מֵאוֹת חָלָל בְּפַעַם אֶחָת). When reading the Hebrew version of Chronicles, there is no need to interpret this section of the verse as consisting of titles for David.[43] Yet TC here awards him a lengthy series of accolades, enumerating a list in many respects indisputably similar to TJ, but much longer than the version given there. The expansions in TC that do not appear in TJ are colored red above.

The common elements of the expansions found in the Targums point to an unmistakable relationship between the two. What is more, we can identify the direction of the influence exerted: it necessarily was TJ that influenced TC, because there is no cause in the text of Chronicles for the lengthy translation we have before us. It appears here because the author of TC had TJ before him and used the homiletically enhanced translation in that composition as the basis of his work. The lengthy expansion in TJ glorifies David as an ideal Jewish king graced with wisdom, handsomeness, and heroism on the battlefield. The expansion added by TC to that in TJ gives David, inter alia, the additional characteristic of a religious scholar who occupies himself with Torah study.

5   Discussion and Conclusions

All of the information presented here attests to the existence of a direct relationship between TC and TJ in their parallel chapters. All early scholars of TC evinced an awareness of the existence of this relationship and the need for a comparison of parallel verses, but Churgin was the first to formulate a proposal seeking to tease out the nature of the relationship between the two Targums.

As noted, Churgin argued that the author of TC had utilized a pre-existing Targum of Samuel and Kings: not the version of TJ that we have today, but a kind of "Palestinian Targum Jonathan," in his words, whose dialect differed

---

43   If any part of the verse poses a difficulty, it is the words מִסְפַּר הַגִּבֹּרִים at its beginning, corresponding to שְׁמוֹת הַגִּבֹּרִים in 2 Sam. Yet here, rather than offer an expanded translation, TC translates, almost literally, סכומי.

from that in the version of TJ with which we are familiar.[44] He further suggested that the Targum Toseftot to the Former Prophets that had survived in
various MSS (ultimately compiled in Kasher's edition) were in fact surviving
fragments of this Palestinian Targum Jonathan, and that the aggadic expansions in TC might be remnants of that presumed lost Targum.

Churgin thus sought to explain the dialectal difference between TJ and TC
and to assign an early date to the traditions integrated within TC. His proposal,
however, cannot adequately realize these goals. With regard to the difference
in dialect, Churgin did not solve the problem, but merely set it at an earlier
point in time. What does it matter if the author of TC systematically tampered
with the dialect of TJ or the change came about earlier and in the opposite
direction? One way or the other, we are left to say that the original translation
(whatever its dialect might have been) was altered by a later targumist! As for
the aggadic traditions found within TC, does Churgin himself not agree that
the Babylonian Talmud was the source of many of these additions—in which
case the Targum must be post-talmudic even in his view? To these points we
must add those expansions that prove by their very linguistic content that they
belong to a later period and bear the influence of the Babylonian Aramaic of
the Talmud.

How, then, can we make sense of the relationship between TJ and TC? In all
of the examples given above, TC was similar to TJ or lengthier. However, even
where it was lengthier, whether by far or only slightly, it exhibited a clearly evident underlying framework that, aside from dialectal differences, resembled
the text of TJ. The dialect of the parallel chapters of TC is not fundamentally
different from that of unparalleled chapters. There are indeed differences between these units, but these do not concern the dialect typical of the text in its
entirety. If we were to accept Churgin's thesis, we would be compelled to take
the view that the author of TC had used a presumed version of TJ to the parallel chapters, but in his work on non-parallel chapters written independently
in a dialect similar to that of the presumed version of TJ! This argument is implausible; at the very least, it is an idea whose proposal ought to be supported
by stronger evidence, as even in Churgin's view, TJ and TC were separated by
hundreds of years' time.

The probable explanation is that in his translation of parallel chapters, TC
used TJ as a foundation for his own work. The author of TC had before him a text
with an unmistakable similarity to the TJ with which we are familiar, and that
targumist consciously made TJ the basis of his own Targum. Notwithstanding,
the author of TC was no prisoner of TJ, and altered that text to suit his own

---

44   Churgin *Hagiographa*, p. 266.

needs. He adjusted the dialect of TJ to match the Aramaic used in the remainder of the translation. Where the Hebrew *Vorlage* of Chronicles differed from that of Samuel or Kings, the targumist generally made changes to the text of TJ that served as his foundation to render it appropriate for the Hebrew *Vorlage* of Chronicles. Still, there are other instances where the text of TJ was preserved in TC despite its non-conformity with the Hebrew *Vorlage* of Chronicles, and in other cases the targumist altered TJ to suit the variant Hebrew *Vorlage* of Chronicles but some element of TJ nevertheless persisted in TC.

The Relationship of Targum Chronicles and the Pentateuchal Targums in Parallel Genealogical Lists

1   Opening

In his study of TC, Churgin described a general affinity between TC, on one hand, and TPJ and FT, on the other, drawing attention to translational choices common to these three Targums in the verses of Chronicles and their parallels in the Torah, and noting that these appear to attest to literary dependence between them.[1] Le Déaut and Robert argued that TC followed the tradition of the Palestinian Targums of the Torah, but did not distinguish between the various extant witnesses within this tradition.[2] McIvor, in a short paragraph in his introduction, argued that the presence of TPJ was felt especially powerfully in verses paralleled in the Torah.[3] Kalimi gives his blessing to Churgin's determination regarding TC's relationship with TPJ and FT, but adds in a footnote referencing Churgin's chapter,

It seems that further detailed research on this subject is desirable.[4]

I believe that Kalimi's brief comment is in order for two principal reasons. First, Churgin's study, which served as the basis of all succeeding studies, addressed only TPJ and FT. His study was written before the publication of the key MSS of TN (including both main text and glosses) and the various Genizah Targums, so that a need exists to examine whether the new information available to us today has altered the picture first formed seventy years ago. Second, though Churgin's study was the most comprehensive treatment of the subject at the time Kalimi's comments were made, it is not comprehensive enough. Churgin devoted four lines to the resemblance between parallel units in the

---

1   Churgin *Hagiographa*, p. 247 and especially pp. 263–266. It should be borne in mind that Churgin refers to TPJ as TJ and to FT as the Jerusalem Targum.

2   Le Déaut-Robert, vol. 1, p. 23.

3   McIvor, p. 16.

4   Kalimi *Journey*, p. 174, n. 88. While Kalimi's comment was made at the end of a sentence pertaining to the relationship between TC and TJ to the Prophets, it appears in the context of Churgin's study of the relationship between TC and TPJ to the Torah and of that between TC and TJ to the Prophets. Both topics are treated in the present study.

two Targums and one paragraph to their similarity in the remainder of the book. His account calls attention to several points of similarity between the two translations whose importance certainly must not be underestimated, but they alone cannot provide the whole picture.

Concurrently to the publication of Kalimi's comments, Hamiel published a study of TC containing a greater number of comparisons of the various translations and taking TN into account.[5] This paper brought attention to additional similarities between the Targums but neither considered all of the relevant material nor satisfactorily discussed textual and exegetical questions arising from comparisons drawn between the Targums. In point of fact, to this day no one has published an examination of the relationship between the various Targums that goes beyond pointing out the similarities present in a few verses, the sole exception being White's linguistic inquiry, which led him to historical conclusions that are difficult to accept.[6]

Therefore, we ourselves shall contrast the technique of TC in units paralleling the Torah with that of the various Pentateuchal Targums available today. The first chapter of Chronicles consists of a genealogical list based primarily on Chapters 10, 25, and 36 of Genesis. Many verses of these chapters are reiterated in Chronicles verbatim. How did the author of TC go about translating these units? Did he utilize preexisting translations, or did he embark on the task independently, without relying on his predecessors? We shall now examine these scriptures and their various Targums and consider whether TC to these verses was constructed under the influence of existing translations or generated as an independent, self-reliant work.

The sections to be examined are:

1) 1 Chr 1:5–23, paralleling many verses of the Table of Nations in Genesis 10, as detailed below.

2) 1 Chr 1:29–31, paralleling the account of the descendants of Ishmael, Gen 25:13–16.

3) 1 Chr 1:43–53, paralleling the list of the kings of Edom, Gen 36:31–43.

The order in which the Targums are given is based on the relationships between the targumic traditions that they represent. Whatever the origin of TO may be, it was accepted as an authoritative Targum of the Torah in the Babylonian tradition and, consequently, in most Jewish diasporas. The Targum of the Torah according to the Palestinian tradition has not been preserved to our day as a living document as has TO. FT, with its various witnesses, was the primary

---

5   Hamiel, pp. 367–371.
6   White, pp. 269–271.

remnant of this targumic tradition until the discovery of TN, which is the only surviving complete copy of a Pentateuchal Targum reflecting the Palestinian tradition. The marginal readings in this MS attest to parallel targumic texts that help provide a picture—however incomplete—of the Palestinian tradition of Pentateuchal Targum. A further, partial attestation of this tradition was discovered in various MSS of the Cairo Genizah. There is no witness in the Genizah remnants, however, of verses of the units here considered. TPJ integrates the tradition of TO and the Palestinian tradition of Pentateuchal Targum in its own way.[7] Accordingly, each verse will be presented as it appears in MT Genesis, followed by the following targumic texts: TO, TN, TNM, FT, TPJ, and finally TC.[8]

2   The Table of Nations (1 Chr 1:5–23 / Gen 10:2–4, 6–8, 13–18, 22–29)

1 Chronicles 1 partially recapitulates the list of the descendants of Japheth, Ham, and Shem that appears in the Table of Nations in Genesis 10. The purpose of our discussion is not to identify the nations and lands mentioned in the various Targums to these verses, but to identify links and common traditions linking the Pentateuchal Targums and TC.[9] We shall present below the parallel verses and their various Targums, and consider the noteworthy similarities and differences that they reflect between TC and the Targums of the Torah.

---

7 Many scholars view TPJ as consisting of a framework reflecting the Palestinian targumic tradition and additional elements inserted in that framework that have their origins in the tradition of TO; see Splansky, p. 117; Maher, pp. 1–2 (and sources cited ad loc., n. 5). Kuiper, however, offered an alternate description of the relationship between the various branches of the targumic tradition, arguing that TPJ was one of several branches belonging to the Palestinian tradition and TO a product of editing and further development within the same; see Kuiper, pp. 99–100. However, see also the powerful criticism of Kuiper in Kaufman *Review*. Flesher *Introduction*, pp. 87–89, provides a survey of scholarly views on the place of TPJ among the Pentateuchal Targums. However, based on recent studies by McDowell and myself, some important updates should be added to such a survey.

8 The verses of these units in Genesis and Chronicles are generally similar, such that there is no need to give the Hebrew verse twice. Where doing so is of specific utility, both verses will be given. We do not have documentation of the listed Targums for all of the verses presented here. For each verse, whatever material is available to us will be cited.

9 For a detailed discussion of the Table of Nations in targumic literature, see Alexander *Toponomy*; Goshen-Gottstein, vol. 2, pp. 99–106.

1 Chr 1:5 /

Gen 10:2	וְתִירָס:	וּמֶשֶׁךְ	וְתֻבָל	וְיָוָן	וּמָדַי	וּמָגֹוג	גֹּמֶר	בְּנֵי יֶפֶת
TO	ותירס:	ומשך	ותובל	ויון	ומדי	ומגוג	גמר	בני יפת
TN	ותירס	ומשך	ותובל	ויון	ומדי	ומגוג	גמר	בנוי דיפת
	ותרקא	ומוסיא	וביתניא	ומקדוניא	ומדי	אפריקי וגרמניה	אפרכייתהון	ושם
TNM	ותרקי	ומוסייא	ויטיניאה	ומקדוניאה			והמדאי	
FTV						גומר		בנוי דיפת
	ותרקי	ומוסקי	ויתניא	ומוקדוניא	ומדי	אפריקי וגרמניא	אפרכייתהון	ושם
TPJ	ותירס	ומשך	ותובל	ויון	ומדי	ומגוג	גמר	בנוי דיפת
	ותרקי	ואוסיא	ויתניא	ומקדינייא	והמדיי	אפריקי וגרמנא	אפרכייתהום	ושום
TC	ומשך	ותובל		ויון	ומדי	ומגוג	גמר	בנוי דיפת
	ותרקי:	ואוסיא	ויתניא	ומקדוניא	והמדאי	אפריקי וגרמנא	ארפכוייתהון	ושום
ל"א	ותרקי	ומוסיה	ויתניה	ואוביסוס	והמדן	גרמניה גיתיה		

NJPS Chr: The sons of Japheth: Gomer, Magog, Madai, Javan, Tubal, Meshech, and Tiras.

Dost: The sons of Japheth: Gomer, Magog, Madai, Javan, Tubal, Meshech, and Tiras. The name(s) of their provinces: Phrygia, Germania, the Medes, Macedonia, Bythinia, Usia, and Thrace. (Another Targum) Germania, Gethia, Hamdan, Ephesus, Bythinia, Musia, and Thrace.

On examining the Targums to Gen 10:2, we see that they fall into two groups On one hand is TO, which transcribes the names of the nations according to their Hebrew forms: in TO, even the construct phrase בני יפת is characteristically left in as in the Hebrew. On the other hand are TN and TPJ, which break apart the construct into the possessive phrase בנוי דיפת and add a series of seven names of regions, one for each of the names of nations in the verse, to the series of names transcribed from the Hebrew. All of these names are of late provenance and belong to the Greco-Roman world.[10] The great similarity between TN and TPJ in both form and content leaves no room for doubt: the two Targums are genetically related.[11] FT, too, is a member of this tradition, but the textual witness of FT that has reached our hands does not transcribe the Hebrew forms of all names that appear in the Hebrew verse, but does so only

---

10   As noted by Dray, p. 32, regarding the phenomenon of toponymic translations in general: "The Targumist's purpose appears to have been to produce a version of the Hebrew Bible that was easily accessible to his contemporaries. The result is that when a place name has changed in the course of time, the Targumist regularly identifies it by its 'modern' name."

11   The two Targums are not in agreement with regard to every detail, but the differences between them are explicable either as orthographic or as changes that arose during copying. As much is true not only of the present verse, but also of many verses of the Table of Nations here discussed.

for גּוֹמֶר, after which the Targum turns to the list of eparchies.[12] TNM provides a typically incomplete picture, but this picture is consistent with the names of five eparchies given in TN and TPJ. It is clear from a comparison of TC and the various Pentateuchal Targums that the former was influenced by a tradition that preceded it, and it is similarly clear that this tradition is precisely that represented by TN and TPJ. TC differs from all of the Pentateuchal Targums in a different line of its translation, which contains three names that occur exclusively within it (גרמניה, גיתיה and אוביסוס). This line is prefaced with the notation ל"א ("alternate version"), which also indicates that TC here quotes previously existent Targums.[13] The resulting impression is that two alternative, antecedent translations are set within TC: one belonging to the shared tradition of TN and TPJ (and related works, as noted), and another that is unknown to us from any other source. As for the precise source of the eparchical names in TC, it is not possible to reach any conclusions based solely on the present verse, but the fact is that the most similar Targum to it of those before us is TPJ, given their agreement on all listed eparchies and the handful of textual variants that distinguish them from several of the other translations where the names המדאי (except TNM) and אוסיא are concerned.

1 Chr 1:6 /

Gen 10:3	וְתֹגַרְמָה:	וְרִיפַת	אַשְׁכְּנַז		גֹּמֶר	וּבְנֵי	
TO	ותגרמה:	וריפת	אשכנז		גומר	ובני	
TN	ותוגרמה	וריפת	אשכנז		דגמר	ובנוי	
	וברבוי וברבריא	אסיה		אפרכיותההן		ושם	
TNM	ופרכוי	ועסייה					
FTV					דגומר	ובנוי	
	ופרכוי וברבריאה	אסיא		אפרכיותהון		ושם	
TPJ	ותורגמא	וריפת	אשכנז		דגומר	ובנוי	
TC	ותוגרמה	ודיפת	אשכנז		דגמר	ובנוי	
	ופרכוי וברבריא:	אסיא		ארפכויתהון		ושום	
	ל"א	ובנוי	דגמר		אסיה	ודריגת וגרמנקיה	

NJPS Chr: The sons of Gomer: Ashkenaz, Diphath, and Togarmah.
Dost: The sons of Gomer: Ashkenaz, Diphath, and Togarmah. The names of their provinces: Asia, Parkevi, and Barbaria. (Another Reading) The sons of Gomer: Asia, Darigath, and Germanicia.

---

12   In the following verse, as well, FT gives a list of names ending with גומר (the first name of the verse), then proceeds with a list of eparchies. Apparently FT goes only so far as this name and purposely omits the others that are identical to those in the Hebrew verse out of anticipation of the upcoming list of eparchic names.

13   Regarding alternate translations marked ל"א in the Targums, see p. 5, above.

As in the previous verse, the Targums here fall into two categories: on one side TO, which transcribes the Hebrew, and on the other TN and the Targums resembling it, which insert a series of eparchies. In this instance, TPJ begins as does TN (ובני דגומר) but lacks the anticipated series of eparchies. The source referenced by TC belongs to the tradition of TN, but here, too, TC adds an alternate translation marked ל״א containing names that do not occur in any other Targum (גרמנקיה, דריגת). If we were to judge the question of TC's relationship to the Pentateuchal Targums on the basis of this verse alone, we would not look at TPJ as one of its sources, due to its omission of the series of eparchies.

1 Chr 1:7 /

Gen 10:4	וְדֹדָנִים:	כִּתִּים	וְתַרְשִׁישׁ	אֱלִישָׁה	יָוָן	וּבְנֵי
TO	ודודנים:	כתים	ותרשיש	אלישה	יון	ובני
TN	ודודנים	כתים	ותרשיש	אלישא	דיון	ובנוי
	ודרדני	ואיטליא׳	וטרסס	אלס	אפרכיותהון	ושם
TNM			אלסטרסוס			
	ודרדרייא	אילטיאה		אלסו	ל״א	
FTV				אלישה	דיון	ובנוי
	ודרדניא	איטליא	אלסטרסוס		אפרכיותהון	ושם
FTP	ודודנים	כתים	תרשיש			
	ודרדניא	איטליא	טרסוס			
TPJ	ודרדניא	אכזיא	וטרסס	אלס		
TC	ודרדניא:	איטליון	וטרסוס	אלסו	דמקדון	ובנוי
				אלישה	ל״א	
	ודרדניה	אכזיה	טוסס	אלס		ובנוי

NJPS Chr: The sons of Javan: Elishah, Tarshish, Kittim, and Rodanim.
Dost: The sons of Mecodon: Hellas, Tarsus, Italy, and Dardania. (Another reading) Elishah, Hellas, Tusas, Achaia, and Dardania.

In this verse we find explicit reference to eparchies only in TN and FT (V). FT (P) does not translate the word אֱלִישָׁה, but the three names that it does include—טרסוס, איטליא, and דודניא—bear a similarity to the tradition of TN. The initial part of the verse in TC (ובנוי דמקדון) does not bear a resemblance to any other Targum, but the names of the children of מקדון are in fact quite similar to the eparchic names given in TN and FT. By substituting מקדון for יָוָן, TC preserves the identification of יָוָן with מקדוניה found in TN, TNM, FT, TPJ, and TC to verse 2, above. TC has an alternate line (marked ל״א) that in part resembles the tradition of TN, as well as the first alternative given in TC itself. It seems to me that the word אלישה given at the beginning of this line is intended not as a translation (or transcription) of the Hebrew אֱלִישָׁה, as in TO, but as an indication of the Hebrew word paralleled by the beginning of the alternate translation. Thus in this translation, as in all of the Palestinian Targums above, אלס corresponds to אֱלִישָׁה, טוסס to תַרְשִׁישׁ, and דרדניה to דֹדָנִים. How does the second translation in TC differ from the first? The most conspicuous difference is that it gives the word אכזיה for כִּתִּים, whereas the first version in TC and all of other Pentateuchal Targums aside from TO and TPJ give one form or another of the name אטליה, *Italy*. In TPJ we find אכזיא, which points to a relationship between it and TC. Le Déaut and Robert take the view that the original name is אכייה, i.e., ἀχαιά, and propose a corresponding emendation of the reading in TC.[14] If their argument is correct, this is further evidence of the relationship between TC and TPJ, with one preserving the textual corruption of the other and TPJ thus diverging from the Palestinian targumic tradition.

1 Chr 1:8 /

Gen 10:6	וּכְנָעַן:	וּפוּט	וּמִצְרַיִם	כּוּשׁ	חָם	וּבְנֵי
TO	וכנען:	ופוט	ומצרים	כוש	חם	ובני
TN	וכנען:	ופוט	ומצרים	כוש	דחם	ובנוי
TNM	וכנען	ואליהרק	ומצרים	ערביא	אפרכייותהון	ושום
TPJ	וכנען	ופוט	ומצרים	כוש	דחם	ובנוי
	וכנען:	ואליחרק	ומצרים	ערביא	אפרכיותהום	ושום
TC	וכנען:	אליחרק	ומצרים	ערב	דחם	ובנוי[15]

NJPS Chr: The sons of Ham: Cush, Mizraim, Put, and Canaan.
Dost: The sons of Ham: Arabia, Egypt, Allihrok, and Canaan.

In this verse we find a significant resemblance between TNM and TPJ. Both give names of eparchies that are identical save for minor scribal alterations, while TN neither gives eparchic names nor alters the Hebrew forms of the names that it does provide. TC resembles TN in that it appends no eparchic names, but bears a similarity to TNM and TPJ in its substitution of ערב for כּוּשׁ and אליחרק for פּוּט.[16]

---

14   Le Déaut-Robert, vol. 1, p. 39; vol. 2, p. 9; Goshen-Gottstein, vol. 2, p. 102, n. 8.

15   MT 1 Chr 1:8 has בְּנֵי חָם. The reading ובנוי of TC likely reflects the influence of the Book of Genesis and/or its Targums, but we cannot discount the possibility that the Hebrew *Vorlage* of TC read וּבְנֵי.

16   The former Targums, to be sure, have ערביא, as opposed to ערב in TC, but this discrepancy cannot disprove the notion that these Targums have a tradition in common and ultimately derive from the same source.

1 Chr 1:9 /

Gen 10:7	וְסַבְתְּכָא	וְרַעְמָה וְסַבְתָּה	וַחֲוִילָה	סְבָא	וּבְנֵי כּוּשׁ
TO	וסבתכא	וסבתא ורעמה	וחוילה	סבא	ובני כוש
TN	וסבתכא	וסבתא ורעמ'	וחוילה	סבא	ובנוי דכוש
TNM	וזינגאי	וסמראי ולובאי	סינירא ' והינדקאי		
TPJ	וסבתכא	וסבתה ורעמא	וחוילא	סבא	ובנוי דכוש
	וזינגאי	וסמראי ולובאי	סינירא והינדיקי	ושום אפרכיותהום	
TC	סינידאי והנדקאי וסמראי ולובאי ומווריאטינוס וזינגאי				ובנוי דערב

NJPS Chr: The sons of Cush: Seba, Havilah, Sabta, Raama, and Sabteca.
Dost: The sons of Arabia: the Sinidians, the Indians, the Semarians, the Lybians, Mauritanus, and the Zingites.

As in the previous verse, TPJ and TNM appear to share a common tradition regarding the eparchic names given in the verse, although the word אפרכיה does not expressly appear in TNM. The names in TC show that it, too, shares this tradition; the two pronounced differences in TC—ערב for כּוּשׁ and the appearance of the name מווריאטינוס—are not enough to blur the coincidence with the five names given in TNM and the list of eparchies in TPJ. The appearance of the name ערב in TC may be understood as intended to assure consistency of translation (whether on the part of the author of TC or that of his predecessor) with regard to the name כּוּשׁ found in the preceding verse, as evidenced by an examination of the next. The appearance of the name מווריאטינוס in TC should be seen as an example of a dual translation, with this word joining לובאי as an equivalent of רַעְמָה. As much seems clear from the continuation of the verse (see below), in which TNM and TPJ join TC in translating רַעְמָה as מוריטינוס. The end of the verse (see below) strengthens the links indicated by its beginning. TNM, TPJ, and TC all give the same names, representing a single, shared tradition.

1 Chr 1:9 (cont.) /

Gen 10:7 (cont.)	וּדְדָן: שְׁבָא	רַעְמָה	וּבְנֵי
TO	ודדן: שבא	רעמא	ובני
TN	ודדן: שבא	דרעמה	ובנוי
TNM	ומזג זמרגד	דמווריינוס	ובנוי
TPJ	ומזג: זמרגד	דמווריטינוס	ובנוי
TC	ומזג: זמרגד	דמווריאטינוס	ובני

NJPS Chr: The sons of Raama: Sheba and Dedan.
Dost: The sons of Mauritanus: Smaragdus and Mezag.

The name שְׁבָא is transcribed verbatim in TO and TN, while in TNM, TPJ, and
TC it is replaced with זמרגד, *Smaragdus*. The word זמרגד serves two functions
in targumic literature, either denoting a precious stone or serving as an equivalent of scriptural שְׁבָא. The first sense, derived from the Greek σμάραγδος,[17] appears (sometimes with the orthography אזמרגד; see below) to signify several
types of precious stones in TO, TN, FT, TJ, *Tg. Job*, TC, and *Tg. Esth II*.[18] The
word appears as an equivalent of scriptural שְׁבָא in TNM, TPJ, *Tg. Job*, and TC.[19]
Weiss considered the various possibilities suggested up to his day to explain
the identification of שְׁבָא with זמרגד and, correctly rejecting these proposals,
was left with no satisfactory explanation.[20] Alexander suggested that a tradition had taken shape that identified scriptural שְׁבָא with the location named
Mons Smaragdus (in southeastern Egypt), after the precious stones once quar-
ried there.[21]

Even if Alexander's analysis is found to be correct, it is unreasonable to
imagine that the author of TC had any part in constructing this identification.
Rather, he preserved it as a tradition he had received from earlier Targums,
transmitting it to generations to come in his own composition. In examining
how TC relates to this word, we see that the Targum substitutes זמרגד for שְׁבָא
five times in the book, aside from the occurrence in the present verse, while
on one other occasion (1 Chr 1:22) transcribing שבא from the Hebrew. This deviation on the part of TC appears to be a clear indication that in the only two
parallels in Chronicles to verses of the Torah containing the name שְׁבָא, the
targumist followed a Pentateuchal Targum of the brand of TPJ, given the resemblance between TC and TPJ in both verse 9 (זמרגד) and verse 22 (שבא). A
further sign that TC is a preserver rather than a creator is in the orthographic
forms preserved in TC for the two functions of this word. The term appears
in *Tg. Job* and in TC both as a toponym and as the name of a precious stone,
and the text of these two Targums records the toponym with the orthography
זמרגד and the precious stone as אזמרגד. What is the meaning of these disparate
spellings? Does it reflect some bygone differentiation between the word's two
functions? The answer appears to be that this distinction simply reflects two
orthographic forms used for the same word in different targumic traditions. If
we survey the orthographic forms used for the word where it signifies a precious stone, we see that it is written in TO and TJ with an *aleph*, and in TN and

17   Krauss *Lehnwörter*, pp. 28, 248; Sokoloff *JPA*, p. 179.

18   TO Exod 28:18; 39:11; TN Exod 28:19; 35:22; 39:12; FTV Exod 28:19; TJ Ezek 28:13 (thus in
      Peshiṭta, ad loc.); *Tg. Job* 42:14; *Tg. Esth II* 1:2; 8:15 (זמרגד); TC 1 Chr 29:2. The term also ap-
      pears once in *Tg. Prov* 25:12, under the influence of the Syriac.

19   TNM Gen 10:7; TPJ Gen 10:7; *Tg. Job* 1:15; 6:19; TC 1 Chr 1:9, 32; 2 Chr 9:1, 3, 9, 12.

20   See these proposals in Weiss, pp. 268–269, and the sources cited ad loc.

21   Alexander *Toponomy*, p. 139.

FT without.[22] It thus would seem that when *Tg. Job* and TC required an equivalent for the precious stone פּוּך,[23] they turned to a tradition of the category of TO or TJ, and the form אזמרגד was inscribed accordingly. When they required an equivalent for scriptural שְׁבָא, they turned to the tradition of TPJ, and thus used the form זמרגד. In the meantime, an artificial orthographic distinction came into being in TC and *Tg. Job* between the two functions of this word.

1 Chr 1:10 /

Gen 10:8	אֶת־נִמְרֹד	יָלַד	וְכוּשׁ
TO	ית נמרוד	אוליד	וכוש
TN	ית נמרוד	אוליד	וכוש
TPJ	ית נמרוד	אוליד	וכוש
TC	ית נמרוד	אוליד	וערב

Gen 10:8 (cont.)	בָּאָרֶץ:				לִהְיוֹת גִּבֹּר	הוּא הֵחֵל
TO	בארעא:				למהוי גיבר	הוא שרי
TN	באר':				למהוי גיבר	הוא שרי
TNM	בא'	ולמרדה קדם ה'		בחטאה		
TPJ	בארעא:	ולמרדא קדם ה'		בחיטאה	למיהוי גיבר	הוא שרי
TC		ומרוד קדם ה':	שדי אדם זכאי	בחטאה	למהוי גבר	הוא שרי

NJPS Chr: Cush begot Nimrod; he was the first mighty one on earth.

Dost: Arabia fathered Nimrod. He became a mighty man in sin. He shed innocent blood and was a rebel before the Lord.

In this verse, TO and TN transmit a literal translation of the Hebrew, while TPJ and TC insert similar but not identical additions within a literal translation. Both limit Nimrod's exploits to his being a great sinner who brought about a rebellion against God. They are joined in this tradition by TNM. The words קדם ה' in these three Targums deviate, of course, from the Hebrew *Vorlage* of the verse, but are suited to the following verse in Genesis, absent from Chronicles, where the Hebrew expression לפני ה' appears twice: הוּא־הָיָה גִבֹּר־צַיִד לִפְנֵי הְ׳ עַל־כֵּן יֵאָמַר כְּנִמְרֹד גִּבּוֹר צַיִד לִפְנֵי הְ׳. The natural place of the expression קדם ה' is in this verse, and it is here that the expression in fact appears in all Targums available to us. Due to the similarity between the two consecutive verses, both of which describe Nimrod's might, the expression קדם ה' slipped backward in a

---

22   It is well known that a Greek loanword beginning with a consonant cluster of which the first is a sibilant tends to be prefixed with an *aleph*, so as to avoid hiatus and thus ease pronunciation. In the dialect of TO and TJ, the word is prefixed with an *aleph*, while in that of TN and FT no *aleph* is added.

23   אזמרגד in TO and TJ serves to translate the word נֹפֶךְ, a close relation of פּוּך. As Weiss, p. 77, notes, "it may be that our targumist [i.e., the author of *Tg. Job*—L.G.] associated הפוך with נפך."

tradition common to TNM and TPJ. The appearance of the expression קדם ה' in
TC, whose Hebrew *Vorlage* in no way contained the expression לְפְנֵי ה', is hard
evidence that its translation reflects the Pentateuchal Targum that lay before
its author.

The Hebrew verse gives Nimrod the title גִּבּוֹר, *mighty man*, but gives no indication of what characterized his might beyond giving quite a general description of the venue of his exploits: בָּאָרֶץ, *on Earth*. TC, meanwhile, adds to this
appellation a continuum of negative characteristics and omits the description
of the place. The negative insertions concerning Nimrod made their way to
the targumist as the legacy of a tradition that we encounter in certain of the
Pentateuchal Targums to Gen 10:8, above. In order to gain an understanding of
the development of the targumic tradition regarding this verse, we must first
consider the Hebrew text and Targums of the following verse, Gen 10:9, which
is not paralleled in Chronicles:

Gen 10:9	עַל־כֵּן	לִפְנֵי הָ'	הוּא־הָיָה גִּבֹּר־צַיִד
TO	על כן	קדם ה'	הוא הוה גיבר תקיף
TN	בגין כן	קדם ה'	הוא הוה גיבר בחטאה
FTP[24]		בצידא	הוא הוה גיבר תקיף
	קדם ה' הוה צייד בני אינשא בלישנהון ואמר להון		וגיבר בחטאה
	רחוקו מן דיני דשם ואדביקו בדינוי דנמרוד בגין כדין		
TPJ	בגין כן	קדם ה'	הוא הוה גיבר מרודא

Gen 10:9 :	לִפְנֵי הָ'׃	גִּבֹּר צַיִד	כְּנִמְרֹד	יֵאָמַר
TO	קדם ה'׃	גיבר תקיף	כנמרוד	יתאמר
TN	קדם ה'׃	גיבר בחטאה	כנמרוד	יתאמר
FTP		גיברא	כנמרוד	יתאמר
		גיבר בצידא		
	קדם ה'׃	גיבר בחיטאה		
	ומרודה דה'׃	מן יומא דאתבּרי עלמא לא הוה גיבר בחטאה נמרוד		
TPJ	ומרודא קדם ה'׃	יתאמר מן יומא דאיתברי עלמא לא הוה כנמרוד בצידא		

NJPS Gen: He was a mighty hunter by the grace of the LORD; hence the saying,
"Like Nimrod a mighty hunter by the grace of the LORD."

Clem (TPJ): He was a mighty man of rebellion before the Lord; therefore it will
be said, "From the day that the world was created, there was none like Nimrod,
a mighty man of hunting and rebellion before the Lord.

---

24   For a similar but not identical reading, see FTV:
הוא הוה גיבר בצידה בחטאה קו' ה' הוה צאיד בני אינשא בלישניהון ואמר להון רחוקו מן דינוי
דשם ואדבקו בדינוי דנימרו' בגין כדין יתאמר כנמרוד גיברא גיבר בצידה בחטאה קו' ה'.

The chronology, apparently, was as follows: the tradition behind TNM[25] and TPJ Gen 10:8 anticipated several elements of the targum to the following verse. The word בחטאה, *in sin*, is one of the ways in which the word צָיִד, *hunting*, was translated in the various Targums. Formally speaking, the word מרודה, *rebellion*, functions in TNM and TPJ as an alternate translation of the word צָיִד, but it also serves as a midrashic exposition of the name נמרוד. These two elements, along with the expression קדם ה', were added to verse 8 in cooperation with a rabbinic exegetical agenda seeking to tarnish Nimrod's name.

As for the absence of the word בארעא in TC, let us again examine how elements of Gen 10:9 are anticipated in verse 8. The expression מרודא/ה קדם ה' appears twice in verse 9 in TPJ and once in TNM. The first appearance of מרודא in TPJ serves as an adjective accompanying גיבר. The second appearance in TPJ (and the first in TNM) serves as a verbal noun. In verse 8, the word is intended to form a natural part of the sentence: הוא שרי למיהוי גיבר בחיטאה, and the verbal noun/adjective therefore is exchanged for an infinitive into which the central verb of the sentence flows: הוא שרי למיהוי גיבר בחיטאה ו(הוא שרי) למרדא קדם ה'. The form preserved in TC is not an infinitive, but an abbreviated form of the verbal noun or adjective, מרוד. A logical explanation for this disparity, as well as for the absence of the word בארעא, is that TC (or else the Pentateuchal Targum that its author consulted) skipped from verse 8 to verse 9 due to the similar phrases they contain (verse 8: מרודא קדם ה' בארעא; verse 9: ולמרדא קדם ה'). The end result is that the end of the targum to 1 Chr 1:10 takes after the targum to the end of Gen 10:9 rather than Gen 10:8.

1 Chr 1:11 /

Gen 10:13	וּמִצְרַ֖יִם	יָלַ֑ד	אֶת־לוּדִ֧ים	וְאֶת־עֲנָמִ֛ים	וְאֶת־לְהָבִ֖ים	וְאֶת־נַפְתֻּחִֽים
TO	ומצרים	אוליד	ית לודאי	וית ענמאי	וית להבאי	וית נפתוחאי
TN	ומצרים	אוליד	ית לודיא	וית ענמיה	וית להבייא	וית נפתוחייא
TNM			לווקאי	וית מרטיוני[26]	וית פניפוליטיא	וית סכינאי
FTV	ומצרים	אוליד	ית לודאי	וית מריוטאי	וית באנטפוליטאי	וית לוסטאי
TPJ	ומצרים	אוליד	ית ניווטאי	וית מריוטאי	וית ליווקאי	וית פנטסכינאי
TC	ומצרי׳ אוליד	ית ניוטאי	וית מריוטאי	וית ליווקאי	וית פנטסכינאי	

NJPS Chr: Mizraim begot the Ludim, the Anamim, the Lehabim, the Naphtuhim,

Dost: Egypt fathered the Nabateans, the Mareotians, the Lybians, and the Pentaschianites,

---

25   The word order in TNM, גיבר בחטאה נמרוד ומרודה דה', is difficult, but that is how it appears in the MS.

26   Díez Macho reads מרטיונא. However, the word in the MS reads as מרטיX̄ני, followed by a stroke above the X.

In this verse, as in that above, the various Targums may be divided into two categories. The first includes TO and TN, which leave the nations' names as in the Hebrew source, making only the changes required to render them in their Aramaic forms. The second group consists of TNM, FT, TPJ, and TC, which generally replace the Hebrew names with names of a later vintage. Although the translations in the second category are not identical, the Targums' relationship is obvious from the pool of similar names that they share. A comparative textual analysis shows that, where these names are concerned, all of the Targums of the second category drew inspiration from a single targumic tradition.

לוויקai, substituted by TNM for לוּדִים, is similar to the name ליוקאי, which is the equivalent of לְהָבִים used in TPJ and TC. לוסטאי, which in FT corresponds to נַפְתֻּחִים, is dissimilar to the other names in the Targums to the verse, but resembles the name לוטסאי given by TPJ and TC (Gen 10:18 and 1 Chr 1:16, respectively) as an equivalent for הָאַרְוָדִי, as opposed to the name אנטרדיאי, given in FT. מרטיונא of TNM is simply a variant of מריוטאי, which appears in TPJ, FT, and TC. סבינאי, of TNM, resembles the final part of the name פנטסכינאי, found in TPJ and TC. פניפוליטא, the translation given in TNM for לְהָבִים, resembles the name given in TPJ for כַּסְלֻחִים and in TC for פַּתְרֻסִים (Gen 10:14 and 1 Chr 1:12, respectively), and the name באנטפולטאי, given in FT as the translation of לְהָבִים, is simply another variant of the same name.

Thus all of the Targums of the second group share a common pool of names, with the proviso that the various translations showcase the names as they undergo a number of changes in terms of both the order of their appearance in the verse and their precise forms. This is not the place to establish which of the various witnesses preserves the primary order of these names, and which a secondary sequence. For the purpose of this discussion, it suffices to note that of all of the Targums in this group, the rendering of the verse in TPJ and TC is identical in nearly all respects. Although all of the Targums in this group have a single tradition in common, TC is closer to TPJ than to any of the other Targums. Further, they are in agreement regarding the "updated" names (ניוטאי, פנטסכיינאי, ליווקאי, מריוטאי).

1 Chr 1:12 /

	וְאֶת־כַּפְתֹּרִים:	וְאֶת־פְּתֻסִים	אֲשֶׁר יָצְאוּ מִשָּׁם פְּלִשְׁתִּים	וְאֶת־כַּסְלֻחִים	וְאֶת־פַּתְרֻסִים
Gen 10:14					
TO	וית קפוטקאי:	פלשתאי	דנפקו מתמן	וית כסלוחאי	וית פתרוסאי
TN	וית קפודקייא:	פלישתייא	די נפקו מן תמן	וית כסלוחיא	וית פתרוסיא
TNM				וית פנטסבינאי	פילוסאי
FTV	וית קפדיקאי:	פלשתאי	די נפקו מתמן	וית פנטסבינאי	וית פילוסאי
TPJ	וית קפודאי:	פלישתאי	דנפקו מתמן	וית פנטפוליטי	וית נסיוטאי
TC	וית קפוטקאי:	פלשתאי	דנפקו מנהון	וית נסיוטאי	וית פנטפוליטאי

NJPS Chr: the Pathrusim, the Casluhim (whence the Philistines came forth), and the Caphtorim.

Dost: the Pentapolitans, the Nasiotites, from whom the Philistines descended, and the Capadocians.

TO and TN to this verse are similar in the names they select to represent those given in the Hebrew, although there are a handful of grammatical and dialectal differences between them. TNM and FT are similar in substituting the names פילוסאי and פנטסכינאי for the Hebrew כַּסְלֻחִים and פַּתְרֻסִים. We saw the latter of these in TPJ and TC to the previous verse, where it was given as an equivalent of נַפְתֻּחִים. TPJ and TC translate פַּתְרֻסִים and כַּסְלֻחִים as נסיוטאי and פנטפוליטאי, respectively, but differ with regard to the order of this pair. Thus despite the inversion of names within them, TPJ and TC share a common pool of names in their renderings of this verse

1 Chr 1:13 /

Gen 10:15	וְאֶת־חֵת:	בְּכֹרוֹ		אֶת־צִידֹן	יָלַד	וּכְנַעַן
TO	וית חת:	בוכריה		ית צידון	אוליד	וכנען
TN	וית חת:	בכורא		ית צידון	אול׳	וכנען
TPJ	וית חת:	בוכריה		ית צידון	אוליד	וכנען
TC				ית בותניאס	אוליד	וכנען
	וית חת:	בוכריה	הוא	ית צידון		הוא דבנא

NJPS Chr: Canaan begot Sidon his first-born, and Heth,

Dost: Canaan fathered Bothneas—It is he who build Sidon; he was Canaan's firstborn—and Heth,

The Pentateuchal Targums to this verse are quite similar (excepting the absence in TN of the pronominal suffix appended to בכורא), and TC here stands alone in its differentiation between the man צידון, whom it dubs בותניאס, and the city צידון that he constructed, whose name is given without change. It seems at first glance that with this TC deviates from all of the Pentateuchal Targums. However, a look at TPJ four verses later—a verse not included in the survey given in Chronicles—suffices to show that the author of that book also identified צידון as בותנייס:

Gen 10:19	עַד־עַזָּה	גְּרָרָה	בֹּאֲכָה	מִצִּידֹן	וַיְהִי גְּבוּל הַכְּנַעֲנִי
TPJ	עד עזה	לגרר	מעלך	מן בותנייס	והוה תחום כנענאי

NJPS: The [original] Canaanite territory extended from Sidon as far as Gerar, near Gaza

Clem: And the Canaanite border extended from Bothneas, in the direction of Gerar, as far as Gaza

Nowhere else in the targumic literature to which we are privy does the name
בותניים appear.[27] To be sure, in TPJ בותניים appears as the name of a city, rather than that of a person, but for our purposes the identification of these two
names in TPJ will suffice. In effect, it is the very divergence of TC from all of
the Pentateuchal Targums that associates it with a tradition known to us only
from TPJ. What is more, since there is no evident need for the expansion given
in TC, that Targum well may preserve the version of TPJ that its author had
before him.

1 Chr 1:14 /

Gen 10:16	הַגִּרְגָּשִׁי׃	וְאֵת	הָאֱמֹרִי	וְאֶת־	הַיְבוּסִי֙	וְאֶת־
TO	גרגשאי׃	וית	אמוראי	וית	יבוסאי	וית
TN	גרגשיא׃	וית	אמוראי	וית	יבוסיא	וית
TNM	גרגשאי		אמוראי		ייבוסאי	
TPJ	גירגשאי׃	וית	אמוראי	וית	יבוסאי	וית
TC	גרגשאי׃	וית	אמוראי	וית	יבוסאי	וית

NJPS Chr: and the Jebusites, the Amorites, the Girgashites,
Dost: the Jebusites, the Amorites, the Girgashites,

1 Chr 1:15 /

Gen 10:17	הַסִּינִי׃	וְאֶת־	הָעַרְקִי	וְאֶת־	הַחִוִּי	וְאֶת־
TO	אנתוסאי׃	וית	ערקאי	וית	חיואי	וית
TN	ארתוסיא׃	וית	ערקיא	וית	חוויא	וית
TNM	סינאי	וית	ערקאי		חיואי	
FTV	כפרוסאי׃	וית	ערקאי	וית	טריפוליטאי	וית
TPJ	אנתוסאי׃	וית	עירקאי	וית	חיואי	וית
TC	אנתוסאי׃	וית	ערקאי	וית	חואי	וית

NJPS Chr: the Hivites, the Arkites, the Sinites,
Dost: the Hivvites, the [Arkites], the Anthusians,

The bulk of the names in these two verses are left unaltered by the various
Targums. FT diverges from the others in substituting טריפוליטאי for הַחִוִּי. Three
different translations are offered for הַסִּינִי: סינאי (TNM); כפרוסאי (FT); and
אנתוסאי (TO, TN, TPJ, and TC).[28] Thus TC, as TPJ, conforms in this case to the
classical Targums.

---

27   Krauss *Lehnwörter*, p. 147, cites the possibility of an identification with βίθυνος, a
     Phoenician pioneer.
28   Both forms—אנתוסאי of TO, TPJ, and TC and ארתוסיא of TN—are variants of a single
     name. See McIvor, p. 39, n. 41.

1 Chr 1:16 /

Gen 10:18	וְאֶת־	הָאַרְוָדִ֛י	וְאֶת־	הַצְּמָרִ֖י	וְאֶת־	הַחֲמָתִֽי
TO	וית	ארודאי	וית	צמראי	וית	חמתאי
TN	וית	ארוודייא	וית	זימרייא	וית	אנטוכיא
TNM		ארודיי		צמר׳		אנטיוכאי
		לוטסאי	וית	חממצאי		אנטיובאי
FTV	וית	אנטרדייא	וית	חממצאי	וית	אנטוכייא
TPJ	וית	לוטסאי	וית	חומצאי	וית	אנטיוכי
TC	וית	לוטסאי	וית	חומצאי	וית	אנטיוכאי:
ל"א		רידוס		וחמץ		ואנטיוך

NJPS Chr: the Arvadites, the Zemarites, and the Hamathites.
Dost: the Arethusians, the Emesites, and the Antiochians. (Another reading) Ridus, Emesa, and Antioch.

TO, as usual, transcribes the Hebrew names in this verse, giving one Aramaic form for each of those appearing in the Hebrew. TN integrates a transcription (ארוודייא) with updated names of its own era (אנטוכיא). TNM, TPJ, and TC render the three names similarly. All prefer to give names of a later era rather than transcribe the Hebrew, and it is clear that behind them lies a single, shared tradition. To this tradition, TC adds an additional line containing an alternate translation, beginning with the heading ל"א. In its identification of the last two names (notwithstanding the different forms thereof), this alternative parallels the tradition common to TNM and TPJ, but in the first identification, רידוס, this tradition diverges from the others.

1 Chr 1:17 /

Gen 10:22	בְּנֵי	שֵׁם	עֵילָ֣ם	וְאַשּׁ֔וּר	וְאַרְפַּכְשַׁ֖ד	וְל֑וּד	וַאֲרָֽם׃
TO	בני	שם	עילם	ואשור	וארפכשד	ולוד	וארם׃
TN	בנוי	דשם	עלם	ואשור	וארפכשד	ולוד	וארם׃
TPJ	בנוי	דשם	עילם	ואתור	וארפכשד	ולוד	וארם׃
TC	בנוי	דשם	עילמאי	ואתוראי	וארפכסדאי	ולודאי	וארמאי

Gen 10:23	וּבְנֵ֖י	אֲרָ֑ם	ע֥וּץ	וְח֖וּל	וְגֶ֥תֶר	וָמַֽשׁ׃
TO	ובני	ארם	עוץ	וחול	וגתר	ומש׃
TN	ובנוי	דארם	עוץ	וחול	וגתר	ומש׃
TC		וארמניאי		וחולאי	וגתראי	ומשכאי׃

NJPS Chr: The sons of Shem: Elam, Asshur, Arpachshad, Lud, Aram, Uz, Hul, Gether, and Meshech.
Dost: The sons of Shem: the Elamites, the Assyrians, the Arphaxadites, the Ludites, the Arameans, the Armenians, the Hulites, the Githrites, and the Mashkites.

TC stands alone in its treatment of this verse, changing all of the nations' names from singular to plural. It resembles TPJ in giving the word אתור with a *taw*, but differs in the form of the word ארפכסד, which it gives a *samekh*. We have no witnesses of TPJ to Gen 10:23 and thus do not know how it translated the names עוּץ, חוּל, גֶתֶר, and מַשׁ, but of the Targums available to us, TC to this verse stands alone in identifying עוּץ as ארמניאי. This identification recurs later in the chapter, in verse 42, where TC translates עוּץ (son of Dishon) as ארמניוס. TPJ to the parallel verse, Gen 36:28, transcribes the name עוּץ, but this cannot serve as evidence of its author's view regarding the present verse, which concerns a different man of the name עוּץ. The term אֶרֶץ עוּץ in Job 1:1 is translated as ארעא דעוץ, but in TL 4:21 it is translated as ארע ארמוניא, based on which it appears that this identification was not an innovation of TC, but known from a pre-existing tradition. The form משכאי given in TC (at the end of the verse) is faithful to the Hebrew original מֶשֶׁךְ in Chronicles, while MT Genesis has מַשׁ.

1 Chr 1:18 /

Gen 10:24:	אֶת־עֵבֶר	יָלַד	וְשֶׁלַח	אֶת־שָׁלַח	יָלַד	וְאַרְפַּכְשַׁד
TO	ית עבר:	אוליד	ושלח	ית שלח	אוליד	וארפכשד
TN	ית עבר:	אולד	ושלח	ית שלח	אולד	וארפכשד
TPJ	ית עבר:	אוליד	ושלח	ית שלח	אוליד	וארפכשד
TC	ית עבר:	אוליד	ושלח	ית שלח	אוליד	וארפכסדיי

NJPS Chr: Arpachshad begot Shelah; and Shelah begot Eber.

Dost: The Arphaxadites fathered Shelah, and Shelah fathered Eber.

The tendency in TC to pluralize nations' names in these verses (see pp. 64–66) brought its author to pen a sentence whose subject and verb are in disagreement: וארפכסדיי אוליד.

1 Chr 1:19 /

Gen 10:25	הָאָרֶץ	נִפְלְגָה	בְיָמָיו	כִּי	פֶּלֶג	הָאֶחָד	שֵׁם	בָנִים	שְׁנֵי	יֻלַּד	וּלְעֵבֶר
TO	ארעא	אתפלגת	ביומוהי	ארי	פלג	חד	שום	בנין	תרין	איתילידו	ולעבר
TN	ארעא	דיירי	אתפלגו	ביומוי	ארום	פלג	מנהון דחד	שמה	בנין	תרין	אתילד	ולעבר
TNM	ארעא	אתפלגת									
TPJ	ארעא	איתפליגת	ביומוי	ארום	פלג	חד	שום	בנין	תרין	איתילידו	ולעבר
TC	ארעא	דיירי	אתפליגו	ביומוי	ארום	פלג	חד	שום	בנין	תרין	אתילידו	ולעבר

ללישנהון

NJPS Chr: Two sons were born to Eber: the name of the one was Peleg (for in his days the earth was divided)

Dost: To Eber were born two sons: The name of one was Peleg, for in his days the inhabitants of the earth were divided according to their language,

Here the Targums diverge in the degree of literalness with which they translate the expression נִפְלְגָה הָאָרֶץ. TO, TPJ, and TNM translated literally, while TN and TC interpreted הָאָרֶץ as signifying *the inhabitants of* the land, consequent to which they pluralize the verb.[29] הָאָרֶץ also is translated as דיירי ארעא in the account of the Tower of Babel (Gen 11:9; cf. verse 1 in TN, FTV), which is understood by rabbinic interpretations as detailing circumstances to which our verse and Gen 10:25 faintly allude and due to which this generation is dubbed the Generation of the Division:

Gen 11:9	הָאָרֶץ	כָּל־	שְׂפַת	ה׳	בָּלַל	כִּי־שָׁם
TN	ארעא דאירי	כל	לישני	ה׳	ערבב	ארו׳ כדן
TPJ	ארעא דיירי	כל	לישן	ה׳	ערביב	ארום תמן

NJPS Gen: because there the LORD confounded the speech of the whole earth
Clem TPJ: because there the Lord confounded the language of all the inhabitants of the earth

TC adds the detail that the division of the inhabitants of the land was ללישנהון, i.e., into different languages. This addition is unique to TC to the present verse, but accords with both the context indicated by Gen 11:9 and the Hebrew expression לְלִשֹׁנוֹ/לִלְשֹׁנֹתָם, which occurs three times in the Table of Nations in Genesis (10:5, 20, 31).

Gen 10:25		וְשֵׁם אָחִיו יָקְטָן׃
TO (cont.)		ושום אחוהי יקטן׃
TN		ושמה דאחוי יקטן׃
TPJ		ושום אחוי יקטן׃
TC	מטול דביומוי שריאו שניהון דבני נשא לאתקטעא מן בגלל חוביהון׃	ושם אחוי יקטן

NJPS Chr: and the name of his brother Joktan.
Dost: and the name of his brother was Joktan, for in his days the years of the children of men began to diminish on account of their sins.

---

29   This addition belongs to the class of targumic group markers, discussed above (pp. 33–38). Here, the targumists' agenda is to offer a text more specific than the literal continuum of the Hebrew verse by clarifying that God's action affected not the earth per se, but humanity.

This midrashic interpretation of the name יָקְטָן, which expounds that name as derived from the root קט״ע, does not appear in the various Pentateuchal Targums available to us, but only in TC.[30]

1 Chr 1:20 /

Gen 10:26	וְאֶת־שָׁלֶף	וְיָקְטָן יָלַד אֶת־אַלְמוֹדָד
TO	וית שלף	ויקטן אוליד ית אלמודד
TN	וית שלף	ויקטן אולד ית אלמודד
TPJ	ית ארעא באשלוון וית שלף דישלף מוי דנהרוותא	ויקטן אוליד ית אלמודד דמשח
TC	דמשח ופליג ית ארעא באושליא וית שלף דשלף ית נהרוותא לתחומיא	ויקטן אוליד ית אלמודד

NJPS Chr: Joktan begot Almodad, Sheleph,

Dost: Joktan fathered Almodad, who measured and divided the land with ropes, Sheleph, who diverted the rivers to (their) borders,

The import and implications of the lengthy midrashic rendering in TPJ and TC demand a discussion in their own right (see pp. 387–392), but for the purposes of the present discussion it will suffice to note the great similarity between the two Targums, which cannot have come about by happenstance and thus evidences a genetic relationship between the two.

Gen 10:26	וְאֶת־יָרַח:	וְאֶת־חֲצַרְמָוֶת
TO (cont.)	וית ירח:	וית חצרמות
TN	וית ירח:	וית חצר מות
TPJ	וית ירח:	וית חצרמות
TC	וית חצרמות דאתקן אתר כמניא לקטלא עדי אורחא וית ירח דאתקן פונדוקין	
	והוה כל דעליל למיכל ולמשתי הוה מוכיל ליה סמא דקטול ונסיב כל מה דהוה בידוי:	

NJPS Chr: Hazarmaveth, Jerah

Dost: Hazarmaveth, who set the place of the ambushes for the slaying of those who pass by on the road, Jerah, who established inns—and so it was, to each one who would enter to eat and to drink he would feed lethal poison and would take all that was in his hands—

---

30   In *Gen. Rab.* 6 (p. 43) we find a different kind of exegesis of the name יקטן: "Because he would make little of his endeavors. How was he rewarded? He was rewarded by establishing thirteen clans." *Sefer ha-Yashar, Noaḥ* (p. 13), records yet another midrashic interpretation of the name: "And the second he named יקטן", indicating that human lives decreased and diminished (הקטינו) in his day." Churgin *Hagiographa*, p. 247, suggested the last of these traditions as the source employed by TC, but I do not believe that there is any direct connection, given that the object of the exegesis in *Sefer ha-Yashar* is the root קט״ן.

Whereas the midrashic treatments given names in the first half of the verse are found in both TPJ and TC, the two homilies pertaining to the end of the verse appear only in TC: as of the present we have not found a parallel in any other work. It may be that the version of TPJ referenced by TC included the homilies concerning Hazarmaveth and Yarach. Conversely, the author of TC may have completed the end of the verse independently following the style of TPJ at its beginning.

1 Chr 1:21 /

Gen 10:27	וְאֶת־דִּקְלָה׃	וְאֶת־אוּזָל וְאֶת־הֲדוֹרָם	
TO	וית דקלה׃	וית אוזל	וית הדורם
TN	וית דקלה׃	וית אוזל	וית הדורם
TPJ	וית דיקלא׃	וית אוזל	וית הדורם
TC	וית דקלה׃	וית אוזל	וית הדורם

NJPS Chr: Hadoram, Uzal, Diklah
Dost: and Hadoram, Uzal, Diklah,

1 Chr 1:22 /

Gen 10:28	וְאֶת־שְׁבָא׃	וְאֶת־אֲבִימָאֵל	וְאֶת־עוֹבָל
TO	וית שבא׃	וית אבימאל	וית עיבל
TN	וית שבא׃	וית אבימאל	וית עיבל
TPJ	וית שבא׃	וית אבימאל	וית עיבל
TC	וית שבא׃	וית אבימאל	וית עיבל

NJPS Chr: Ebal, Abimael, Sheba
Dost: Ebal, Abimael, Sheba

1 Chr 1:23 /

Gen 10:29	וְאֶת־יוֹבָב כָּל־אֵלֶּה בְּנֵי יָקְטָן׃	וְאֶת־חֲוִילָה	וְאֶת־אוֹפִר
TO	וית יובב כל אלין בני יקטן׃	וית חוילה	וית אופיר
TN	וית יקטן[31] כל אלין בני דיקטן׃	וית חוילה	וית אופיר
TPJ	וית יובב כל אילין בנוי דיקטן׃	וית חווילא	וית אופיר
TC	אתר מפקנות מרגליתא וית יובב כל אלין בנוי דיקטן	וית אופיר אתר מפקנות דהבא וית חוילה

NJPS Chr: Ophir, Havilah, and Jobab; all these were the sons of Joktan.
Dost: Ophir, the place that is the source of gold, Havilah, the place that is the source of pearls, and Jobab. All these were the sons of Joktan.

---

31   Sic in MS.

The additions to אוֹפִיר and חֲוִילָה appear in TC alone, but are consistent with what is known from Scripture itself. אוֹפִיר is described many times in the Bible as a land abundant in gold: 1 Kgs 9:28; 10:11; 22:49; Isa 13:12; Ps 45:10; Job 28:16; 1 Chr 29:4; 2 Chr 8:18; 9:10, and the designation אתר מפקנות דהבא thus is fitting. חֲוִילָה, too, is mentioned, in Gen 2:11, as a land אֲשֶׁר־שָׁם הַזָּהָב (and is thus characterized in the ninth-century CE accounts of Eldad the Danite), but in the next verse the Torah adds to its description of חֲוִילָה that שָׁם הַבְּדֹלַח וְאֶבֶן הַשֹּׁהַם. חֲוִילָה thus is here called אתר מפקנות מרגליתא. Perhaps the commentary in TC was influenced by the targumic tradition evidenced by TN to חֲוִילָה in these two verses, which also contains the root נפ״ק and the word מרגליתא:

Gen 2:11–12	וְאֶבֶן הַשֹּׁהַם:	שָׁם הַבְּדֹלַח ...	אֲשֶׁר־שָׁם הַזָּהָב ...
TN	ואבניא טבתה ומרגליתא:	תמן בדלחא נפק	דמן תמן דהבא נפק ...

NJPS: where the gold is ... bdellium is there, and lapis lazuli.

Clem: from where gold comes out ... from there bdellium comes out, as well as fine stones and pearls.

3   Ishmael's Descendants (1 Chr 1:29–31 / Gen 25:13–16)

1 Chr 1:29 /

Gen 25:13	וְאַדְבְּאֵל וּמִבְשָׂם:	וְקֵדָר	נְבָיֹת	בְּכֹר	יִשְׁמָעֵאל	לְתוֹלְדֹתָם ...	וְאֵלֶּה ... בְּנֵי יִשְׁמָעֵאל ...
TO	ואדבאל ומבשם:	וקדר	נביות	בוכרא	דישמעאל	לתולדתהון ...	ואלין ... בני ישמעאל ...
TN	ומבשם	ואדבאל	וקדר	נביות	בכורה	דישמעאל	לתולדותהון ... ואלין ... בנוי דישמעאל ...
TPJ	ואדבאל ומבשם:	וערב	נבט	דישמעאל	בוכרא	לתולדתהון ...	ואילין ... בני ישמעאל ...
1 Chr 1:29	וְאַדְבְּאֵל וּמִבְשָׂם:	וְקֵדָר	נְבָיֹות	בְּכֹור	יִשְׁמָעֵאל	תֹּלְדֹותָם	אֵלֶּה
TC	ואדבאל ומבשם:	וערב	נבט	דישמעאל	בוכרא	תולדתהון	אלין

NJPS: This is their line: The first-born of Ishmael, Nebaioth; and Kedar, Abdeel, Mibsam

Dost: These are their genealogies. The firstborn of Ishmael is Nebat, then Arabia, Adbeel, Mibsam

The word תולדה does not appear in TC outside of this verse. In many other instances, the book contains the words גניסה and זרעי as equivalents of תולדות. Why does the present verse not conform to this pattern? Because TC to this verse is simply an echo of the Targum to Gen 25:13, where all targumic versions have תולדה. Of these Pentateuchal Targums, the only one known to us that translates נְבָיֹת as נבט and קֵדָר as ערב, as does TC, is TPJ.

1 Chr 1:30 /

Gen 25:14–15	וְתֵימָא	חֲדַד	15	וּמַשָּׂא׃	וְדוּמָה	וּמִשְׁמָע
TO	ותימא	חדד		ומשא׃	ודומה	ומשמע
TN	ותימא	חדד		ומשא׃	ודומה	ומשמע
TPJ	ותימא	חריפא		וסוברא׃	ושתוקא	וצאיתא
1 Chr 1:30	וְתֵימָא׃	חֲדַד		מַשָּׂא	וְדוּמָה	מִשְׁמָע
TC	ואדרומא׃	חריפא		ומסוברא	ושתוקא	ציתא

NJPS: Mishma, Dumah, Massa, Hadad, Tema
Dost: Listening, Silence, Endurance, [Sharp—L.G.], South

1 Chr 1:31 /

Gen 25:15 (cont.)–16	בְּנֵי יִשְׁמָעֵאל	הֵם	אֵלֶּה	16	וָקֵדְמָה׃	נָפִישׁ	יְטוּר
TO	בני ישמעאל	אנון	אלין		וקדמה׃	נפיש	יטור
TN	בנוי דישמעאל	הינון	אילין		ודומה	נפיש	יתור
TPJ	בנוי דישמעאל	אנון	אלין		וקדמה׃	נפיש	יטור
1 Chr 1:31	בְּנֵי יִשְׁמָעֵאל׃	הֵם	אֵלֶּה		וָקֵדְמָה	נָפִישׁ	יְטוּר
TC	בנוי דישמעאל׃	הנון	אלין		וקדומא	נפיש	יטור

NJPS: Jetur, Naphish, and Kedmah. These are the sons of Ishmael.
Dost: Jetur, Naphish, and [East—L.G.]. These were the sons of Ishmael.

Whereas all of the above names are transcribed verbatim in TO and TN,[32] the names מִשְׁמָע, דוּמָה, מַשָּׂא, and חֲדַד are given similar non-literal translations in TPJ and TC, which find homiletical meaning in the names, unlike all other known Targums of Genesis. Further, neither TPJ nor TC does the same with the other names appearing in the preceding and following verses (except אדרומא and קדומא in TC). The content and origins of the homilies expounding these names will be discussed below, pp. 392–395. At present, let it suffice to note the clear relationship between TC and the tradition represented by TPJ.

---

32   The names חדר and יתור appear thus (with a *reish* and a *taw*, respectively); see Díez Macho, vol. 1, p. 153.

4   The Kings of Edom (1 Chr 1:43–54 / Gen 36:31–43)

1 Chr 1:43 /

Gen 36:31	לִבְנֵי יִשְׂרָאֵל׃	מֶלֶךְ־מֶלֶךְ	לִפְנֵי	אֱדוֹם	בְּאֶרֶץ	מָלְכוּ אֲשֶׁר	וְאֵלֶּה הַמְּלָכִים
TO	לבני ישראל׃	דימלוך מלכא	קדם	דאדום	בארעא	דמלכו	ואלין מלכיא
TN	לבני ישראל׃	ימלך מלך	עד לא	דאדומיי קדם	בארעהון	די מלכו	ואלין מלכיא
TPJ	לבני ישראל׃	מלך מלכא	עד לא	קדם דאדום	בארעא	די מלכו	ואילין מלכייא
TC	לבני ישראל	מלך מלכא	עד לא	קדם דאדום	בארעא	די מלכו	ואלין מלכיא

NJPS: These are the kings who reigned in the land of Edom before any king reigned over the Israelites:

Dost: These are the kings who reigned in the land of Edom before a king reigned over the children of Israel:

Of the three Pentateuchal Targums to Gen 36:31, TC corresponds to the reading in TPJ in translating בארעא דאדום (as TO, contra TN) and קדם עד לא מלך. The latter of these two translations resembles but is different from TN (which has ימלך rather than מלך) and differs from that in TO. It bears note that the differences between the Targums to this verse are not great and thus could have developed in a brief period as a result of the textual transmission process. Thus no argument is advanced here that the Targums stem from different sources. Still, the greater textual affinity between TPJ and TC, viewed against the other Targums, is evidence of a closer linkage between the two.

1 Chr 1:43 (cont.) /

Gen 36:32	דִּנְהָבָה׃	בֶּלַע בֶּן־בְּעוֹר	לִפְנֵי	וַיִּמְלֹךְ בֶּאֱדוֹם
TO	דנהב׃	בלע בר בעור ושם קרתיה		ומלך באדום
TN	דנהבה׃	בלע בר בעור ושמיה דקרתא		ומלך באדום
TPJ	דבית מלכותיה דנהבא׃	בלעם בר בעור ושום קרתא		ומלך באדום

TC: בלעם בר בעור רשיעא הוא לבן ארמאה דאתחבר עם בני דעשו מטול למחבלא ית יעקב וית בנוי ובעא להובדא יתהון

ומלך על אדום   ושום קרתא   דבית מלכותיה דנהבה   ואיתיהיבת ליה מגן׃

NJPS: Bela son of Beor, and the name of his city was Dinhabah.

Dost: The wicked Balaam son of Beor, who is Laban the Aramean who allied himself with the children of Esau in order to destroy Jacob and his sons. He sought to annihilate them, and he reigned over Edom. Now the name of the city of his royal palace was Dinhabah, and it was given to him freely.

TC adds to the middle of this verse an aggadic tradition (colored red) identifying Balaam with Laban the Aramean, which is absent from the other Targums. The source of this insertion in TC, as well as its statement in the following verse that Phineas killed Balaam, will be discussed below, pp. 395–397. If we turn our attention to the more literal sections in TC, we find that it takes after TPJ in identifying בֶּלַע as בלעם, unlike the other Pentateuchal Targums.[33] The translation in TC of וְשֵׁם עִירוֹ as ושום קרתא דבית מלכותיה similarly bespeaks a clear resemblance to TPJ, as opposed to the other Targums. This translation, which inserts the phrase בית מלכו between the word עִיר and the pronominal suffix affixed to it in the Hebrew *Vorlage*, is found exclusively in TPJ Genesis 36 (verses 35, 39, and the above verse) and in TC 1 Chronicles 1 (verses 46, 50, and the above verse). All other known Targums rendered the word עִיר literally, adding nothing between it and the associated pronoun.[34] TC also contains a homiletical treatment of the city name דִּנְהָבָה, absent from TPJ, which will be briefly discussed below, p. 471.

1 Chr 1:44 /

Gen 36:33	וַיִּמְלֹךְ תַּחְתָּיו יוֹבָב בֶּן־זֶרַח מִבָּצְרָה׃			וַיָּמׇת בֶּלַע
TO	ומלך תחותוהי יובב בר זרח מבצרה׃			ומית בלע
TN	ומלך בתרה יובב			ומית בלע
TPJ	ומלך תחותויי יובב בר זרח מבצרה׃			ומית בלע
TC	ומית בלע דקטליה פינחס במדברא ומליך תחותוי יובב בר זרח דמן בוטרא׃			

NJPS: When Bela died, Jobab son of Zerah from Bozrah succeeded him as king.
Dost: And Bela, whom Phineas killed in the wilderness, died, and in his stead reigned Jobab son of Zerah, who was from Botra.

Only TC adds the words דקטליה פינחס במדברא (on which see pp. 395–397, below). The addition, of course, is predicated on the tradition we encountered in the previous verse identifying בֶּלַע as בלעם בן בעור. It stands to reason that when he arrived at the laconic account of Bela's death given in verse 44, having already accepted the identification of that figure with Balaam, the author of TC felt it necessary to add at the appropriate point in the text a brief description of what was known to him of Balaam's death.

---

33 Thus in Ginsburger and in Clarke. In Rieder's edition, however, he gives בלע as the preferred version and the reading בלעם as an alternative.

34 (תא)בית מלכו as such appears as a living Aramaic phrase in Dan 4:27 and, in the Palestinian targumic tradition, TN and FT (see especially Num 34:15). It appears once in TJ Amos 7:3, but there functions as a literal translation of וּבֵית מַמְלָכָה, rather than as an independent expression. (The expression also appears in the Targums of Esther, but there similarly serves as a literal translation of the Hebrew בֵּית הַמַּלְכוּת.) In the three verses in Gen 36, meanwhile, the expression appears as an addition to the Hebrew *Vorlage* עִירוֹ only in TPJ.

In this verse we see that TN chose the word בתר as a translation for תַּחַת, while TC, along with TO and TPJ, preferred תחות. This distinction is preserved in the various Targums throughout the unit discussing the kings of Edom. The name בוטרא appears only in TC.

1 Chr 1:45 /

Gen 36:34	הַתֵּימָנִי:	מֵאֶרֶץ	חֻשָׁם	תַּחְתָּיו	וַיִּמְלֹךְ	וַיָּמָת יוֹבָב
TO	דרומא:	מארע	חושם	תחותוהי	ומלך	ומית יובב
TN	דרומא:	מן ארעא	חשם	בתרה	ומלך	ומית יובב בר זרח
TPJ	דרומא:	מארע	חושם	תחותוי	ומלך	ומית יובב
TC	דרומא:	דמן ארע	חושם	תחותוי	ומליך	ומית יובב

NJPS: When Jobab died, Husham of the land of the Temanites succeeded him as king.

Dost: Then Jobab died, and in his stead reigned Husham, who was from the land of the south.

1 Chr 1:46 /

Gen 36:35	אֶת־מִדְיָן	הַמַּכֶּה	הֲדַד בֶּן־בְּדַד	תַּחְתָּיו	וַיִּמְלֹךְ	וַיָּמָת חֻשָׁם
TO	ית מדינאי	דקטיל	הדד בר בדד	תחותוהי	ומלך	ומית חושם
TN	ית מדיני	די קטל	הדד בן בדד	בתרה	ומלך	ומית חשם
TPJ	ית מדינאה	דקטל	הדד בר בדד	תחותווי	ומלך	ומית חושם
TC	ית מדיינאי	דקטל	הדד בר בדד	תחותוי	ומליך	ומית חושם

Gen 36:35	עֲוִית:		עִירוֹ	וְשֵׁם	מוֹאָב	בִּשְׂדֵה
TO (cont.)	עוית:		קרתיה	ושם	מואב	בחקלי
TN	עוית:	דקרתיה	ושמה	דמואבאי	בתחומייהון	
TPJ	עמהון קרבא	דבית מלכותיה עוית:	קרתא	ושום	מואב	בסדרותיה בחקלי
TC	בעדן דסדרו קרבא עמהון	דבית מלכותיה עוית:	קרתא	ושום	מואבאי	בחקלי

NJPS: When Husham died, Hadad son of Bedad, who defeated the Midianites in the country of Moab, succeeded him as king, and the name of his city was Avith.

Dost: Husham died, and in his stead reigned Hadad son of Bedad, who killed the Midianites in the fields of the Moabites at the time when they arrayed for battle with them. The name of the city of his royal palace was Avith.

TC resembles TO and TPJ in its selection of the word חקל as the translation of שדה, whereas TN preferred תחום. Notwithstanding, TC differs from TO and TPJ in using the plural form מואבאי (as in TN) instead of the singular. TC also shares another intriguing point of similarity with TPJ in the form of its addition of בעדן דסדרו קרבא עמהון. The wording of this addition is similar, albeit not identical, to that found in TPJ: בסדרותיה עמהון קרבא. In TPJ the insertion appears before the translation of the phrase בְּשְׂדֵה מוֹאָב, while in TC it appears afterward, but the similarity is sufficient to establish a connection between the two. Later in the verse, TPJ and TC have in common the expansive translation קרתא דבית מלכותיה, as noted in the discussion of verse 43, above.

1 Chr 1:47 /

Gen 36:36	מִמַּשְׂרֵקָה:	שַׂמְלָה	תַּחְתָּיו	וַיִּמְלֹךְ	וַיָּמָת הֲדָד
TO	ממשרקה:	שמלה	תחותוהי	ומלך	ומית הדד
TN	מן משרקה:	שמלה	בתרה	ומלך	ומית הדד
TPJ	ממשרקה:	שמלה	תחותיה	ומלך	ומית הדד
TC	דמן משרקה:	שמלה	תחותוי	ומליך	ומית הדד

NJPS: When Hadad died, Samlah of Masrekah succeeded him as king.
Dost: Hadad died, and in his stead reigned Samlah, who was from Masrekah.

1 Chr 1:48 /

Gen 36:37	הַנָּהָר:		מֵרְחֹבוֹת שָׁאוּל תַּחְתָּיו וַיִּמְלֹךְ שַׂמְלָה וַיָּמָת
TO	פרת:	דעל	מרחבות שאול תחותוהי ומלך שמלה ומית
TN	נהרייא:		שאול מן ביני בתרה ומלך שמלה ומית
TPJ	פרת:	דעל	רחובות דמן שאול תחותוי ומלך שמלה ומית
TC	פרת:	דמן פלייותא קרתא רבתא דמתבניא על כיף פרת: שאול תחותוי ומליך שמלה ומית

NJPS: When Samlah died, Saul of Rehoboth-on-the-River succeeded him as king.
Dost: Samlah died, and in his stead reigned Saul, who was from Paltyutha, the great city, which was built on the shore of the Euphrates.

TC differs from all of the other Targums in its translation of רְחֹבוֹת הַנָּהָר. The reading found in TC MS V, פלייותא, appears to be a corruption of the word פלטיותא, which appears in MS C.[35] פלטיותא, a Greek loanword (πλᾰτεῖα) signifying a broad, open place, is common in Palestinian Aramaic as well as Syriac.[36] The word occurs in TN, FT, TNM, and TPJ Gen 10:11 as the translation of רְחֹבֹת עִיר.[37] Churgin was of the view that פלטיותא had appeared in the original text

---

35   Le Déaut-Robert, vol. 2, p. 12.

36   Krauss *Lehnwörter*, p. 456; Sokoloff *JPA*, p. 493; Sokoloff *Syriac*, p. 1199.

37   פלטיותא serves as a targumic translation of רחוב or רחב in the following: TN Gen 10:11 (for רְחֹבֹת עִיר, as noted); TNM Gen 10:11; 19:2; Deut 13:17; TPJ Gen 10:11; 42:6 (in aggadic insertion, alongside סרטייתא); Num 13:21; 22:39; Deut 13:17; FT Gen 10:11; 19:2; *Tg. Ps* 55:12; 144:14; *Tg. Job* 29:7; 30:14; 37:10 (see Weiss, p. 83); *Tg. Cant* 3:2. In LXX, this is the most common equivalent of רְחֹב.

of TPJ in our verse, Gen 36:37, as well, but the text had since changed.[38] Such a thing is possible but does not go without saying, as the underlying rationale is that TPJ reflects the Palestinian targumic tradition. Churgin, we recall, did not benefit from familiarity with TN, whose translation here reads ביני נהרייא. It thus is more logical to say that the text of TPJ, whose translation דמן רחובות דעל פרת is similar to that in TO, did not change here in the least, contrary to Churgin's view. Still and all, I believe that there is some affinity between the various Targums in this case. TC differs from all of the other Targums here both in its choice of the word פלטיותא and in adding the words קרתא רבתא דמתבניא ... כיף. We already have identified the word פלטיותא in TPJ and the Palestinian Targums to the words רְחֹבֹת עִיר in Gen 10:11, as discussed above. We then come across the following verse, Gen 10:12, which reads וְאֶת־רֶסֶן בֵּין נִינְוֵה וּבֵין כָּלַח הִוא הָעִיר הַגְּדֹלָה. As expected, all of the Targums render the end of this verse as קרתא רבתא (in TPJ, קרתא רבתי). It seems to me that on reaching the words רְחֹבֹת הַנָּהָר, TC borrowed the word פלטיותא from TPJ or another of the Palestinian translations of רְחֹבֹת עִיר, then added קרתא רבתא under the influence of the targum to the next verse. He added the words דמתבניא ... כיף as an explanation to address the difficulty arising from the literal nature of the verse in the Targums that rendered דעל פרת, and thus explained that the city had been built on the *shore* of the Euphrates.

1 Chr 1:49 /

Gen 36:38:	בֵּעַל חָנָן בֶּן־עַכְבּוֹר	תַּחְתָּיו	וַיִּמְלֹךְ	וַיָּמָת שָׁאוּל	וַיָּמָת שַׂמְלָה וַיִּמְלֹךְ תַּחְתָּיו
TO	בעל חנן בר עכבור:	תחותוהי	ומלך	ומית שאול	ומית שמלה ומלך תחותוהי
TN	בעל חנן בן עכבור:	בתרה	ומלך	ומית שאול	ומית שמלה ומלך בתרה
TPJ	בעל חנן בר עכבור:	תחותוי	ומלך	ומית שאול	ומית שמלה ומלך תחותוי
TC	בעל חנן בר עכבור:	תחותוי	ומליך	ומית שאול	ומית שמלה ומליך תחותוי

NJPS: When Saul died, Baal-hanan son of Achbor succeeded him as king.
Dost: Saul died, and in his stead reigned Baal-hanan son of Achbor.

1 Chr 1:50 /

Gen 36:39	פָּעוּ		עִירוֹ	וְשֵׁם	הֲדַר	וַיִּמְלֹךְ תַּחְתָּיו	וַיָּמָת בַּעַל חָנָן בֶּן־עַכְבּוֹר
TO	פעו		קרתיה	ושם	הדר	ומלך תחותוהי	ומית בעל חנן בר עכבור
TN	פעו		דקרתא	ושמה	הדד	ומלך בתרה	ומית בעל חנן בר עכבור
FTP	פעו		דקרתיה	ושמא	הדר	ומלך מן בתריה	ומית בעל חנן בר עכבור
FTV	פעו		דקרתא	ושמה	הדד	ומלך בתרה	ומית בעל חנן בר עכבור
TPJ	פעו	דבית מלכותיה	קרתא	ושום	הדר	ומלך תחותוי	ומית בעל חנן בר עכבור
TC	פעי	דבית מלכותיה	קרתא	ושום	הדד	ומליך תחותוי	ומית בעל חנן בר עכבור

---

38   Churgin *Hagiographa*, pp. 265–266.

TC and TPJ to this verse resemble each other in proffering the expansive translation קרתא דבית מלכותיה, as discussed above concerning verses 43, 46.

Gen 36:39	וְשֵׁ֥ם אִשְׁתּ֛וֹ מְהֵֽיטַבְאֵ֖ל בַּת־ מַטְרֵ֑ד
TO (cont.)	ושום איתתיה מהיטבאל בת מטריד
TN	ושמה דאתתה מהיטבאל ברתיה דגברא סרדא דהווה לעי במטרדה כל יומי חיוי
FTP	ושמא דאינתתיה מהיטבאל בת ברתא דגברא סרדא דהוה לעי במטרדא וטדרותא כל יומי חיוי
FTV	ושמה דאיתתיה מהיטבאל בת ברתא דמצרף דהבא דהוא גברא דהוה לעי במאד כל יומי חיוהי
TPJ	ושום אינתתיה מהיטבאל ברת מטרד הוא גברא דהוה לעי במטרדא ובסרדיתא
TC	ושום אנתתי מהיטבאל ברת מטרד דהוה לעי במטרדותא ובסרדותא

Gen 36:39	בַּת־ מֵ֥י זָהָֽב׃
TO (cont.)	בת מצריף דהבא׃
TN	ועתר וקנה נכסין וידע מה הוא כספא ומה הוא דהבא׃
FTP	ובתר דאיעתר וקנא נכסין חזר למהוי אמר מא הוא דהבא ומה הוא כספא׃
FTV	מן בתר דאכל ושבע חזר ואמר מהו מהו דהבא ומהו כספא׃
TPJ	ומן דעתר וקנה נכסין הדר למהוי מתגאי בלבביה למימר מאן הוא כספא ומאן הוא דהבא׃
TC	ומן דעתר וקנא נכסין הוה מתגאה והדר למימר מה הוא כספא ומה הוא דהבא׃

NJPS: When Baal-hanan died, Hadad succeeded him as king; and the name of his city was Pai, and his wife's name Mehetabel daughter of Matred daughter of Me-zahab.

Dost: Baal-hanan son of Achbor died, and in his stead reigned Hadad. The name of the city of his royal palace was Pai, and the name of his wife was Mehetabel, the daughter of Matred, who worked with the hunter's spear and the hunter's net, on account of which he became rich and acquired possessions. He became proud and puffed up, saying, "What is silver, and what is gold?"

In this verse we find that the translations given in several Targums for the names הֲדַד (as it appears in the Torah) and בַּת־מַטְרֵד בַּת מֵי זָהָב are supplemented with homiletical commentary. With the exception of TO, which makes do with substituting מצריף for מֵי, all of the Targums above in fact stem from a single tradition. It is clear from a survey of the various versions that TC, too, shares this tradition, albeit its rendering is not identical to that in any other Targum. Still, the most similar source to TC clearly is TPJ, as suggested by expressions such as הדר ... למימר, מתגאה, ומן דעתר וקנא נכסין, and, which appear only in TC and TPJ. Based on a consideration of the similar elements in this verse in TC and TPJ, compared to the remainder of the Targums, we may conclude that these two documents are more intimately related to each other than to any of the other works.

1 Chr 1:51 /

				וַיָּמָת הֲדָד
1 Chr 1:51	אֱדוֹם	אַלּוּפֵי	וַיִּהְיוּ	
Gen 36:40	עֵשָׂו	אַלּוּפֵי	וְאֵלֶּה שְׁמוֹת	
TO	עשו	רברבי	ואלין שמהת	
TN	דעשו	רברבנוי	ואלין שמהת	
TPJ	עשו	רברבי	ואילין שמהת	
TC			ומית הדר ופסקת מנהון מלכותא ארום	
	אדומאי	רברבי	אתכבישת ארעא קדם בני דעשו והוו	
	דגבלא	בארעא	שליטין	

TC to this verse includes an insertion explaining Scripture's shift from a list of kings to one of chieftains, which it gives following the Chronicler's addition (relative to MT Genesis) of וַיָּמָת הֲדָד.

1 Chr 1:51	אַלּוּף תִּמְנָע אַלּוּף וַיִּהְיוּ אַלּוּף יְתֵת:
Gen 36:40	אַלּוּף תִּמְנָע אַלּוּף עַלְוָה אַלּוּף יְתֵת: בִּשְׁמֹתָם לְמִקֹמֹתָם לְמִשְׁפְּחֹתָם
TO	בשמהתהון רבא תמנע רבא עלוה רבא יתת: לזרעיתהון לאתריהון
TN	בשמתיהון רבה תמנע רבה עלוה רבה יתת: לזרעיתהון לאתריהון
TPJ	לאתר מדוריהון בשמהותהן רבא תמנע רבא עלוה רבא יתת: לייחוסיהון
TC	רבא תמנת רבא עלוה רבא יתת:

NJPS: And Hadad died. The clans of Edom were the clans of Timna, Alvah, Jetheth,

Dost: Hadar died, and kingship ceased from them because the land was subdued before the children of Esau. The chiefs of the Edomites were rulers in the land of Gebal: the chief Timnath, the chief Alvah, the chief Jetheth,

1 Chr 1:52–53 /

Gen 36:41–42: אַלּוּף אָהֳלִיבָמָה אַלּוּף אֵלָה אֵלָה אַלּוּף פִּינֹן 42 אַלּוּף קְנַז אַלּוּף תֵּימָן אַלּוּף מִבְצָר:

TO   רבא אהליבמה רבא אלה רבא פינן   רבא קנז רבא תימן רבא מבצר:

TN   רבה קנז רבה תימן רבה מבצר:

TPJ   רבא אהליבמה רבא אלה רבא פינן: רבא קנז רבא תימן רבא מבצר:

TC   רבא אהליבמה רבא אלה רבא פנון 53 רבא קנז רבא תימן רבא מבצר:

NJPS: Oholibamah, Elah, Pinon, Kenaz, Teman, Mibzar,

Dost: the chief Oholibamah, the chief Elah, the chief Pinon, the chief Kenaz, the chief Teman, the chief Mibzar,

1 Chr 1:54 /

Gen 36:43 ... אֱדֹום   אַלּוּף עִירָם אֵלֶּה | אַלּוּפֵי   אַלּוּף מַגְדִּיאֵל

TO   ... אדום   רברבי   אלין   רבא עירם   רבא אלה

TN   ... אדומי   רברבני   אלין   רבה עירם   רבה מגדיאל

TPJ   רבא מגדיאל

                     על שום קרתיה   מגדיאל   הוא הוה מתקרי

                 ... אדום   רברבי   אילין   עירם   רבא   מגדל תקיף היא רומי חייבתא

TC   רבא אדומאי: רברבני   תימן   קנז   רבא   רבא מגדיאל

NJPS: Magdiel, and Iram; these are the clans of Edom.

Dost: the chief Magdiel, the chief Iram. These are the chiefs of the Edomites.

TC to this verse, as TN, keeps to a literal translation. TPJ contains an expansion expounding the name of the city מגדיאל and identifying it with Rome.[39]

5   Summary of Findings

The above survey addressed the three major units in Chronicles that have textual parallels in the Torah. Each verse of TC was examined in comparison to all of the Pentateuchal Targums available to us. Having reached this point, we now will be able to identify links between the Targums not based on general impressions, but on the basis of a comprehensive examination of the entire picture known to us.

The findings of our examination are as follows:

1.   In both form and content, the Pentateuchal Targums to the Table of Nations in Genesis fall into two categories. On one side of the divide is TO, which generally transcribes the proper nouns in these verses in forms that hew close to the original Hebrew. On the other are TN, FT, TNM, and

---

39   See additional relevant sources cited by Maher, p. 124, n. 15.

TPJ, whose inclination is to update the ancient Hebrew names by substituting them with Greco-Roman designations. Within this second group there is a tendency to offer a kind of dual translation to the list of nations, giving first a series of names in the singular, corresponding to those in the Hebrew, and then a list of eparchies in plural form, corresponding to the same list of names. A word-by-word comparison evidences shifts and textual mutations within the Targums comprising the second group. No one translation is identical to another in all its details, but it is apparent that all stem from a single tradition. TC to the Table of Nations is similar in both content and style to the second group of Targums, and it follows that the author of TC did not embark on his translation of 1 Chronicles 1 in a vacuum, but availed himself of a Pentateuchal Targum that belonged to the tradition shared by the Targums of the second group.

2. In four verses (5, 6, 7, 16), TC offers two alternatives for the translation of certain words, prefacing the latter of these with the acronym ל״א. In one of the alternatives to each of these verses, we found one or more elements unparalleled in any of the Targums of the Torah that are known to us, which is cause to believe that the author of TC was privy to a tradition (or the echoes of a tradition) for the Aramaic translation of the Table of Nations in the Torah that did not survive to our day.[40]

3. In five verses we found a similarity between TC, on one hand, and TNM and TPJ, on the other: verse 5 (המדאי); verse 8 (ערב, אליחרק); verse 9 (מר״ד קדם ה׳, גיבר בחטאה); verse 10 (זינגאי, לובאי, סמראי, הינדיקאי, סיניראי); verse 16 (לוטסאי).

4. In eleven verses we found a similarity in diction, word order, or aggadic content exclusively between TC and TPJ: verse 5 (אוסיא); verse 7 (אבזיא); verse 11 (ניוטאי, מריוטאי); verse 12 (פנטסכינאי, ליווקאי, מריוטקאי, נסיוטאי, but inverted); verse 13 (identification of צידון as בותניאס, found in TPJ Gen 10:19); verse 20 (homiletical treatment of the names אלמודד and שלף); verse 29 (ערב, נבט); verse 30 (homiletical treatment of the names משמע, דומה, משא, and חדד); verse 43 (identification of בלע with בלעם, the term בית מלכותיה); verse 46 (addition of בעדן דסדרו קרבא עמהון, the term בית מלכותיה); verse 50 (the term בית מלכותיה).

5. Of the points of similarity particular to TPJ and TC, we identified two that date to the Islamic era (the sons of Joktan in verse 20; the sons of Ishmael in verse 30).

6. In fourteen verses we found elements unique to TC that are unparalleled in any of the other Targums we have before us: verse 7 (מקדון); verse 9

---

40   It is unlikely that the author of TC himself penned these words; see p. 5.

(מוורייאטינוס); verse 10 (addition of שדי דם זכאי, omission of equivalent for בארץ); verse 13 (בותניאס built צידון); verse 16 (רידוס); verse 17 (plural names rather than singular, ארפכסד spelled with *samekh*, ארמנייא); verse 19 (homiletical treatment of the name יקטן); verse 20 (homiletical treatment of the names חצרמות and ירח); verse 23 (חוילה and אופיר); verse 30 (אדרומא); verse 31 (קדומא); verse 43 (identification of בלעם with לבן, though this appears elsewhere in TPJ; homiletical treatment of the name דנהבה); verse 44 (פינחס killed בלעם, though this appears elsewhere in TPJ; בוטרא); verse 48 (translation of רחבות הנהר).

6   Conclusions

The reality arising from these findings is a complex one. However, weighing the data with due circumspection, we may arrive at the following conclusions:

1.   The author of TC did not produce his translation of Chronicles ex nihilo, but relied on a targumic tradition that he had received. This tradition consists first and foremost of that of the Targums grouped in the second category above, i.e., those comprising the Palestinian targumic tradition or privy to it.

2.   TC was familiar with more than one voice belonging to this tradition, and in several instances retained a variety of voices by giving two alternate translations to names of nations. It thus is reasonable to believe that the author of TC was familiar with a pentateuchal targumic tradition that is unavailable to us.

3.   The Pentateuchal Targum most similar to TC in its treatment of the units here discussed is TPJ. Many of the similarities shared by these two Targums in contrast to the other Targums known to us cannot have come about coincidentally, but indicate literary dependence of TC on TPJ.[41]

4.   There also are not insignificant disparities between TC 1 Chronicles 1 and the parallel portion of TPJ. One potential explanation of the relationship between the two Targums is that the author of TC had TPJ before him and copied it at times, while taking license at others. Where he deviated from TPJ, he either did so in accordance with another tradition that he had received or conceived the altered text independently. Another possible

---

41   It is unlikely that the resemblance between the two Targums resulted from common reliance on a single, earlier source, as among the comparable elements in the two works are such that necessarily post-dated the Islamic conquests. It thus is most logical to assess that TC used TPJ itself as a source, until otherwise proven.

explanation of the relationship between these two Targums is that the version of TPJ that lay before the author of TC was different from that with which we are familiar. Churgin advanced such an argument, citing from TC a number of examples that he believed reflected the original text of TPJ,[42] and the findings and conclusions presented here strengthen the argument that several sections of TC can serve as something of a textual witness of TPJ. This matter deserves a comprehensive textual investigation in the form of a study whose focus is the text of TPJ.

---

42   Churgin *Hagiographa*, p. 265.

The Relationship of Targum Chronicles and Targum Pseudo-Jonathan and Its Implications

1 Opening

The findings of the previous chapter indicate direct literary dependence of TC upon TPJ in the three isolated units of Chronicles parallel with Genesis. This includes the case of Ishmael's descendants, which even proponents of the opinion that TPJ was composed gradually over many centuries would regard as having been written after the rise of Islam. It therefore leads to reason that TC was also composed after the rise of Islam. In one fell swoop, then, the lion's share of the fourth to eighth centuries—regarded by Rosenberg and Kohler, upon whose study almost all subsequent descriptions of TC relied, to be the period in which TC was composed—has been eliminated from consideration as the date of TC's composition. Given that it is necessary to allow for ample time to pass from the rise of Islam in the mid-seventh century till the frustration of Moslem rule over the Jews fermented to the point that it generated midrash-style responses, which later found their way into TPJ, and then even later were mirrored in TC, continuing to maintain the eighth century as a *terminus ante quem* for the composition of TC requires compelling justification. The example of Ishmael's descendants, then, serves well to illustrate why our understanding of TPJ may prove to be of great importance for the dating of TC. For as late as TPJ is found to be, TC should be regarded as even later.

The date of TPJ was a focus of debate between scholars in the last part of the twentieth century, with some scholars arguing for a pre-Islamic date and others for a post-Islamic date, but even proponents of a post-Islamic date argued that the Targum was composed in the first millennium.[1] Recent studies, however, indicate a much later date of composition than that, pushing it into the second millennium. Two separate and independent studies—one by Gavin McDowell and one by this author—have arrived at virtually the same conclusion: that TPJ

---

[1] Supporters of a pre-Islamic date (ca. fourth-fifth centuries) include Robert Hayward, Paul Flesher and Beverly Mortensen (cf. Hayward *Transmission*, pp. 124–125, 258; Flesher *Introduction*, p. 166; Mortensen, pp. 445–449). Supporters of a post-Islamic date (ca. eighth-ninth centuries) include Moise Ohana, Avigdor Shinan and Donald Splansky (cf. Ohana; Shinan *Embroidered*, p. 198; Splansky, *TPJ*, p. 118).

displays literary dependence on works of twelfth century Italy.[2] These findings have major ramifications for Targum studies in general, but for the purpose of the present discussion, if the dependence of TC upon TPJ is shown to be genuine and applies to the entire work, and not merely an isolated case that may also be explained as a result of secondary transmission of the TC text, the necessary conclusion would be to dramatically push the terminus post quem of TC up to the twelfth century. It is for this reason that a more extensive study of the relationship between TPJ and TC is of vital importance. The current chapter of this study shall undertake this task from a linguistic perspective, by examining what can be ascertained from the vocabulary of both Targums.

The linguistic character of TPJ is neither clearly Western nor clearly Eastern: the Targum's dialect is comprised of a late blend of elements taken from various Aramaic sources. It is therefore classified by Kaufman as Late Jewish Literary Aramaic, and by Cook as an artificial literary language.[3] Earlier scholars noted a handful of similarities between the language of TPJ and that of TC and, pursuant to these, argued that the author of TC had been familiar with TPJ and made use of it.[4] Nevertheless, as Kalimi has argued, there is a need for a more comprehensive study to define more precisely the relationship between the two Targums.[5] Consequently, in this chapter we shall examine the breadth and length of TC and see if it is possible to establish the existence of a connection between the two Targums in the Book of Chronicles in general, i.e., the book's sixty-one other chapters, which lack direct literary parallels in the Torah.

From the first glance, a significant similarity is evident between the lexicon of TC and that of TPJ, a function of the group of common words that comprise something of a framework within both Targums. We have already seen that the author of TC made direct use of TJ to the parallel chapters in Samuel and Kings. Nevertheless, the targumist systematically replaced specific dialectal elements of TJ with elements commonly found in his translation of chapters that have no parallel. We cited examples of consistent substitutions such as those in a

---

2   At the time of the writing of this footnote, the publication of both studies is still forthcoming and they are expected to be published in the same platform simultaneously. The reader is encouraged to consult them in their published form. Though this hardly does justice to McDowell's study, or to mine, I will tersely state here that McDowell identified in TPJ material that may be tied to the longer recension of the *Chronicles of Moses*, while I provided examples in which TPJ apparently makes use of material written by Menaḥem ben Solomon in his *Even Bochan*—a medieval lexicon of biblical Hebrew (a dissertation about which is currently being written by my student, Nissim Mizrachi). Both works lead to Italy of the twelfth century.

3   Kaufman *TPJ*; Cook *TPJ*, pp. 277–278.

4   Churgin *Hagiographa*, p. 265; Hamiel, p. 367.

5   Kalimi *Journey*, p. 174, n. 88. Cf. p. 142 n. 4, above.

list of basic words in the body of the Targum, including חזור, כדין, כדון, ארום, שד״ר, חמ״י, אוף, מטול, היך, חזור, and others. An examination of the language of TPJ reveals that this Targum, too, uses each of the words listed here almost exclusively. The identical selection of so many words—and, at that, words so common—gives rise to a similar linguistic framework for both Targums.

In our discussion here, we shall survey various lexical similarities between TC and TPJ, notwithstanding the fact that some of these words appear in a handful of other targumic works, as well (just as the framework words enumerated above are not unique to TC and TPJ). Identification of phenomena found in a handful of targumic works including TC and TPJ permits the construction of a general reference group, while identification of phenomena limited to TPJ and TC establishes a close link between these two Targums specifically. I shall divide the words into different categories according to a succession of groups, from the largest, which may well be common to many Palestinian Targums (as well as works influenced by them), to a limited group demonstrating direct dependence of TC on TPJ. First I shall present a list of shared Greek loanwords—a phenomenon more prevalent in Western than in Eastern Aramaic—to be followed by additional words characteristic of Western Aramaic. The next list will contain words common to the two Targums that are characteristic of Eastern Aramaic—words that we would not have expected to find in a "pure" Western work composed in the Land of Israel. Afterward I shall present a number of particular dialectal features whose presence serves to buttress the apparent link between TC and TPJ. The more unusual the elements identified that are shared principally by these two Targums, the stronger the linguistic similarity that we will be able to identify between them. Following this, I shall present a number of instances where TC appears to exhibit direct literary dependence on TPJ. This final list is fundamentally different from those preceding it in this section: in the case of the others, a similarity may result in two independent works due to closely related linguistic environments, while a finding of literary dependence reveals a direct, linear relationship. Having already expressed my opinion that TPJ is a product of no earlier than twelfth century Italy, proving TC's dependence upon TPJ will indicate that forms of Aramaic continued to be used as a literary language well beyond the period in which scholars regard Aramaic to be the vernacular in much of the Jewish world. Therefore, this chapter will present the use of Aramaic Piyyutim in medieval Europe as another example of continued Aramaic composition of religious literature.

At the end of this discussion (p. 222), I shall present a *table* containing the majority of the words discussed and, for each of these, the *number of occurrences* in the various targumic works. This table will provide an overall view of the relationship between TC and TPJ, particularly against the backdrop of the distribution of the words discussed found in the Targums of the Torah and in TJ. Although it is not the main focus of this section, the table will in some cases allude to a linguistic affinity between TC and TPJ, on one hand, and *Tg. Ps* and *Tg. Job*, on the other, based on the findings of this discussion, which may prove valuable to a future study of the matter. When considering the numbers in the table, the reader is asked to bear in mind that the different texts quoted have differing total word counts, which means that the absolute numbers displayed do not convey their statistical frequency in each individual text. Nevertheless, I believe the linguistic picture that emerges from the table will be quite compelling.

2   Greek Loanwords Shared by TC and TPJ

2.1   *Opening*

A high frequency of Greek loanwords is an identifying feature of Jewish Palestinian Aramaic, whose exposure to the influence of the Greco-Roman world was greater than that in the East.[6] In our discussion of the units with parallels in the Torah, we saw that TC had received Greek toponyms and ethnic appellations as part of a Palestinian targumic tradition. Here we shall present loanwords other than proper nouns appearing in both TC and TPJ.

2.2   אטימוס (*2 Chr 28:3*)—ἕτοιμος

The word אטימוס appears twice in TC, both in the following verse:

> ושיזיב מימרא דה׳ מנהון ית חזקיה מן בגלל דגלי קדם ה׳ דמניה אטימוסין די יפקון
> תלתא צדיקיא חנניה מישאל ועזריה דאטימוסין דימסרון גרמיהן דיתרמון לגו אתון
> נורא יקידתא.

Dost: but the Memra of the Lord saved from among them Hezekiah because it was revealed before the Lord that from him three righteous ones were *destined* to come forth—Hananiah, Mishael, and Azariah—who were *destined* to surrender their bodies, which would be thrown into the burning furnace.

אטימוס is a Greek loanword in Aramaic and its general sense is *to be prepared*.[7] The word appears in midrashic literature on rare occasion, with the sense of *at the ready*. For example, in *Gen. Rab.* 48 we find: "'God stands erect amidst the divine congregation,' etc.—R. Ḥaggai [said] in the name of R. Yiẓḥaq, 'Written

---

6   See McNamara *TN*, pp. 16–21.

7   Krauss *Lehnwörter*, p. 29; Sokoloff *JPA*, p. 21.

here is not *stands* (עומד), but *stands erect* (ניצב)—at the ready (איטימוס), just as you would say [quoting a comparable usage], "You shall stand erect (ונצבת) on the rock.""[8] Similarly, in *Gen. Rab.* 100: "Rabbi Yirmeyah would instruct, saying, 'Clothe me in clean white garments and clothe me in white socks, place my cane in my hands and sandals on my feet, and set me on the road, so that if I am summoned, I shall be at the ready (אוטמוס).'"[9]

The word occurs once in TNM, four times in TPJ, five times in *Tg. Job*, twice in *Tg. Esth I*, and once in *Tg. Esth II*.[10]

In this instance, TC is associated with TPJ not only by the very occurrence of the word, but also by similar usage. In TC, the word אטימוסין has a particular shade of meaning with the sense of having completed preparations for a specific action.[11] Similarly, in TPJ Gen 24:22 the word has precisely the same sense and, as in TC, appears as an Aramaic plural morpheme:

ונסיב גברא קדשא דדהבא דרכמונא מתקליה קבל דרכמונא לגולגלתא דאיטימוסין
בנהא למיתב לעיבידת משכנא.

Clem: the man took a gold nose-ring whose weight was a drachma, corresponding to the drachma for each head that her sons *were ready* to give for the work of the tabernacle.

2.3   גניסה (*1 Chr 2:17, 53, 55; 4:8, 21, 27, 38; 5:7; 6:39, 45–48, 51, 55–56; 7:5, 9;*
8:28, 40; 16:28; 26:31; 2 Chr 5:12)—γένος

The Greek loanword גניסה has the sense of family or race.[12] The word appears 25 times in TC. The word זרעי, of similar denotation, appears in TC on 21 occasions. TO, TJ, TN, FT, and GT never use גניסה, always preferring זרעי for מִשְׁפָּחָה. TPJ, meanwhile, almost always uses גניסה for מִשְׁפָּחָה, only rarely using זרעי. Aside from TC, גניסה also appears a handful of times in other Targums of the

---

8   *Gen. Rab.* 48, p. 482. Parallels to this midrashic homily appear in *Pesiqta de-Rab Kahana*, *Ha-Ḥodesh ha-Zeh* 8, p. 91; *Cant. Rab.* 2, p. 33; *Num. Rab.* 11:2, pp. 82–83.

9   *Gen. Rab.* 100, pp. 1285–1286.

10   TNM Lev 14:53; TPJ Gen 24:22; Lev 14:7, 53; Num 11:26; Job 3:8; 7:12; 15:22, 24; 18:12; *Tg. Esth I* 2:5; 8:13; *Tg. Esth II* 3:14 (cf. LXX on these last two, thus resulting in an interesting coincidence in which the Targum and the Septuagint use the same word).
     See discussion in Goshen-Gottstein, vol. 2, pp. 33–34.

11   Thus at several points in LXX: עֲתֻדֹת, Deut 32:35, is translated ἕτοιμα; עֲתִידִים, Esth 3:14 (and 8:13) is translated ἑτοίμους; עֲתִידִין, Dan 3:15, is translated ἑτοίμως.

12   Krauss *Lehnwörter*, p. 180; Levy, vol. 1, p. 149.

Writings: Ps 22:28; 107:41 (both for מִשְׁפָּחָה); Job 31:34; 32:2 (both for מִשְׁפָּחָה); Eccl 4:14 (for בַּיִת); Esth 8:6 (in a phrase, for מוֹלַדְתִּי).[13]

2.4   טימי (1 Chr 20:2; 2 Chr 23:11)—τīμή

The Greek loanword טימי signifies value or price.[14] Various forms of the word are familiar from Rabbinic Hebrew and Aramaic in the Talmud Yerushalmi,[15] *Gen. Rab.*,[16] and other sources. The word appears twice in TC, with regard to the precious stone set in David's crown:

ונסיב דוד ית כליל מלכהון מעל רישיה ואשכחה מתקל קנטינר דדהבא 1 Chr 20:2[17]
סנינא ובה קביעא אבן טבא דהות טימין דידה קנטינר דדהבא סנינא

Dost: Then David took the crown of their king from off his head. He found its weight (to be) a centarius of pure gold, and in it was set a precious stone, whose *price* was a centarius of pure gold.

ואפיקו ית ברא דמלכא ויהבו עלוי ית כלילא דמלכותא די דבר דוד מעל 2 Chr 23:11
רישא דמלכא דבני עמון ובה אבן טבא שייבא דהוה חקיק ומפרש עלה שמא רבא
ויקירא דקבעה תמן דוד ברוח קודשא והוה טימין דידה מתקל קנטינר דדהבא

Dost: Then they brought out the king's son, and he put on him the royal crown that David took from upon the head of the king of the children of Ammon, in which was the lodestone, upon which was clearly engraved the great and

---

13   Weiss, p. 79, following Levy and Krauss, briefly remarks that the word is characteristic of the Palestinian Targums. White, p. 183, cites some of the data and wishes to conclude the word's absence in TN (p. 227, n. 75).

14   Krauss *Lehnwörter*, p. 264; Levy, vol. 1, p. 300; Sokoloff *JPA*, p. 234.

15   E.g., *y. Pe'ah* 1:1 (15d, p. 82): "Artaban sent our holy teacher [i.e., Rabbi Yehudah the Prince] a single priceless (טבא אטמיטון) pearl. He said to him, 'Send me something as good as this,' He sent him a single *mezuzah*. He said to him, 'What did I send you? Something priceless (דלית לה טימי)—but you have sent me something worth a single folleron!' He said to him, 'Your possessions and mine cannot equal it, and what is more, you sent me something that I guard, but I sent you something that, when you sleep, guards you.'"

16   *Gen. Rab.* 2 (p. 15): "... a king who bought himself two slaves, both at the same time and at the same price (ובטימי אחת). Concerning one he decreed that he be sustained from the treasury (מטימיון), and concerning the other, that he labor for his nourishment.... a king who bought himself two maidservants at the same time and at the same price (ובטימי אחת). Concerning one he decreed that she not budge from the palace, and concerning the other he decreed expulsion ...

17   Excerpt is per MS C. The continuum ובה קביעא אבן טבא דהות טימין דידה קנטינר דדהבא סנינא is absent from MS V, apparently omitted as a result of its similarity to the phrase קנטינר דדהבא סנינא.

glorious name, where David placed it by the spirit of holiness. Its *price* was the weight of a centenarius of gold

The word טימי appears in TPJ four times, and in the example below takes precisely the same form of the occurrences in TC (טימין דידה):

TPJ Gen 23:15 ריבוני קביל מיני ארע דטימין דידה ארבע מאה סילעין דכסף בינא ובינך מה היא

Dost: My lord, receive from me: land, whose *price* is four hundred selas of silver, what is that between me and you?

2.5 טריגון (*1 Chr 9:24*)—τρίγωνος

The Greek loanword טריגון, which has the literal sense of *triangle*, appears once in TC:

1 Chr 9:24

MT		יָמָּה	לְאַרְבַּע רוּחוֹת הַשְּׁעָרִים יִהְיוּ מִזְרָח
TC	מדינחא אשתה מטרתא מערבא אשתה מטרתא...		לארבעתי טריגונין

NJPS: The gatekeepers were on the four sides, east, west

Dost: For the four *corners* there were six guards for the east side, six guards for the west side ...

The literal meaning of the word is not appropriate here. It stands to reason that the four cardinal directions were designated as triangles in reference to the four triangles that may be obtained by dividing a square into four.[18] The word's only other appearances in targumic literature are in TPJ, in which it has the same meaning, as indicated by the examples below. It bears note that all of the word's appearances in TPJ are in expansions:[19]

Ex 28:17

MT		אַרְבָּעָה טוּרִים אָבֶן	וּמִלֵּאתָ בֹ...
TPJ	ותשלים ביה... ארבעא סידרין דמרגליין טבאן כל קבל ארבעא טריגונין דעלמא		

NJPS: Set in it ... in four rows of stones

Clem: And you shall inlay it ... four rows of fine stones corresponding to the four *corners* of the world.

---

18 See Beck *I*, p. 120, for an explanatory illustration of the word. Le Déaut and Robert, as well as McIvor, explained in their commentaries ad loc. that the targumist had used the word in the sense of *angle* or *corner*.

19 See White, p. 214.

Ex 39:10

MT וַיְמַלְאוּ־בֹ֗ו אַרְבָּעָ֖ה טֻ֣וּרֵי אָ֑בֶן

TPJ ואשלימו ביה ארבעא סידרין מרגליין טבן כל קבל ארבעת טריגונין דעלמא

NJPS: They set in it four rows of stones.

Clem: And they filled it with four rows of fine jewels corresponding to the four *corners* of the world

Num 31:7

MT וַיִּצְבְּאוּ֙ עַל־מִדְיָ֔ן כַּאֲשֶׁ֛ר צִוָּ֥ה ה' אֶת־מֹשֶׁ֑ה

TPJ ואתחיילון על מדין אקפוהא מתלת טריגונהא היכמא דפקיד ה' ית משה

NJPS: They took the field against Midian, as the LORD had commanded Moses

Clem: Then they prevailed over Midian; they surrounded her from three *sides*, just as the Lord had commanded Moses,

Deut 21:2

MT וְיָצְא֖וּ... וּמָדְד֔וּ אֶל־הֶ֣עָרִ֔ים אֲשֶׁ֖ר סְבִיבֹ֣ת הֶחָלָֽל׃

TPJ ויפקון... וימשחון מארבע טריגונין ית קירויא די בחזרנות קטילא:

NJPS: ... shall go out and measure the distances from the corpse to the nearby towns.

Clem: ... shall come out and measure from the four *corners* of the cities that are in the area around the slain man,

2.6 מרגלית (*1 Chr 29:2, 8; 2 Chr 9:1, 9–10; 32:27*)[20] *for* אָ֫בֶן—μάργηλις, μαργᾰρίτης

The Greek loanword word מרגלית is a familiar one in rabbinic parlance as well as in Palestinian Aramaic.[21] A particular relationship between TC and TPJ is evidenced not by the word's appearance per se, but by its usage. מרגלית appears a handful of times in the Palestinian Targums of the Torah, both in text that corresponds to Hebrew words and in expansions, as part of the phrase אבנין טבן ומרגליין, *precious stones and gems*. The Hebrew words that correspond to מרגלית in this group are שֹׁהַם, קְשִׂיטָה, and יָשְׁפֵה, so that מרגלית seems to have been used to indicate a specific type of stone. TJ uses this word rarely, and not once as an equivalent for אָ֫בֶן. In parallel verses to those in which the word appears in Chronicles, TJ renders ואבנין טבן.

---

20 מרגלית also appears once in an expansion in TC 1 Chr 1:23, but our purpose here is to note the equivalent מרגלית ‖ אבן.

21 Krauss *Lehnwörter*, p. 350; Sokoloff *JPA*, p. 362. The word also is common in Babylonian Aramaic, but Sokoloff estimates that the Babylonian Aramaic form is a corruption of מרגנית under the influence of rabbinic parlance; see Sokoloff *JBA*, p. 704.

TPJ sets itself apart from the other Pentateuchal Targums where the Torah uses אֶבֶן to denote precious stones:

Ex 31:5

MT	וּבַחֲרֹשֶׁת אֶבֶן לְמַלֹּאת וּבַחֲרֹשֶׁת עֵץ לַעֲשׂוֹת בְּכָל־מְלָאכָה:
TO	ובאומנות אבן טבא לאשלמא ובנגרות אעא למעבד בכל עבידא:
TN	ובאומנות אבנא טבתא לאשלמתה ובנגרות קיסא למעבד בכל עבידא:
TPJ	ובאגלפות מרגליתא לאשלמא ובנגרות קיסא למעבד כל עיבידתא:

NJPS: to cut stones for setting and to carve wood—to work in every kind of craft.

Clem TPJ: and in craftsmanship of *fine stone* for inlaying, and in carpentry of wood, to work in all service.

TPJ and TC use the word מרגלית as a translation of the Hebrew אֶבֶן (in the sense of a precious stone) whether it is given with no description (1 Chr 29:8) or accompanied by a modifier, such as יְקָרָה. TC translates thus at several points, while in 1 Chr 29:2 and 2 Chr 32:27 the word is accompanied by the adjective יקיר.

2.7   פטק (*2 Chr 21:12; 30:1, 6; 32:17*)—πιττάκιον

פטק (פיטק), a loanword from the Greek, denotes a note or written memorandum.[22] Aside from TC, the word appears once in an expansion in TPJ, twice in *Tg. Job*, and eight times in *Tg. Esth 1*.[23]

2.8   פלטיוותא (*1 Chr 1:48*)—πλᾰτεῖα

As noted above (see discussion and distribution, pp. 167–168), this loanword appears in the Palestinian targumic tradition as well as five times in TPJ.

2.9   פלקה (*1 Chr 1:32; 2:46, 48; 3:9; 7:14; 2 Chr 11:21*)—παλλακᾰ

פלקה is a Greek loanword denoting a concubine, as opposed to a lawful wife.[24] פלקה appears in TC seven times, corresponding to the seven appearances of the Hebrew word פִּילֶגֶשׁ. In this, TC resembles TPJ, FT, and TNM, and differs from TO, TN, and TJ, which use לחנה. The word ܠܚܡܐ also is familiar in Syriac as signifying a concubine.[25]

---

22   Krauss *Lehnwörter*, p. 441; Sokoloff *JPA*, p. 486.

23   TPJ Num 11:26; Job 19:23; 31:35; Esth 1:22; 3:13; 8:5, 8, 10; 9:20, 30, 32.

24   Krauss *Lehnwörter*, p. 462; Sokoloff *JPA*, p. 495. See *LSJ*, p. 1293, for shades of meaning separating פילגש and נערה.

25   Sokoloff *Syriac*, p. 1203.

2.10　　　קנטינר (*1 Chr 19:6; 20:2; 22:14; 29:4, 7; 2 Chr 3:8; 8:18; 9:9, 13; 23:11; 25:6, 9,*
　　　　18; 27:5; 36:3)—κεντηνάριον

קנטינר, which appears in TC in translation of כִּכָּר, is a Greek loanword denoting
a unit of weight.[26] The word appears in TN as an equivalent of כִּכָּר, but only
twice (and in the form קנטר, Exod 25:39; 37:24). The equivalent is expressly
written thus once in FT (Exod 25:39, כבר קנטינר) and six times in TNM (Exod
25:39; 37:24; 38:24, 27, 29). It appears in TPJ in each of the eight instances in
which the word כִּכָּר appears in the Torah in the sense of a unit of weight.

2.11　　　אויר (שמיא) (*1 Chr 29:15*)—ἀήρ

The Greek loanword אויר, quite common in a variety of Aramaic dialects,[27] appears three times in TC (1 Chr 20:2; 21:16; 29:15) with no parallel Hebrew word
in the Masoretic *Vorlage*. In the last of these it occurs as part of the construct
phrase אויר שמיא:

כַּצֵל |　　　　　　　יָמֵינוּ עַל־הָאָרֶץ וְאֵין מִקְוֶה:
הי־כטולא דעופא דפרח באויר שמיא הכדין יומנא על ארעא ולית סיבור לבר־נשא דייחי עד עלם:
NJPS: our days on earth are like a shadow, with nothing in prospect.
Dost: As the shadow of the bird that flies in *the air of the sky*, so also are our
days on the earth, and there is no hope for a son of man that he should live
forever.

　　　The construct phrase אויר שמיא is very common (used with the verb פר״ח
or טו״ס) in TN, GT, TPJ, *Tg. Ps*, and *Tg. Eccl.* Its usage in its sole occurrence in
TC and the verb accompanying it are reminiscent of its usage in the Targums
of this group.

2.12　　　קורטור (*1 Chr 28:11; 29:8*)—κουρατορία

Aside from TC, the word קורטור appears in TPJ and *Tg. Job*, in all cases signifying a storage facility or repository.[28] There has been some speculation as to the
precise meaning of the word. The difficulty is that the Greek κουράτωρ (Latin:
curator) signifies the person in charge of the storage facility—not the facility
itself.[29] To my mind it is reasonable enough to surmise that the term for the
storage facility—κουρατορία—was abbreviated in LJLA to קורטור.

26　　Sokoloff *JPA*, p. 560.
27　　Krauss *Lehnwörter*, p. 17; Sokoloff *JPA*, p. 9; Sokoloff *JBA*, pp. 87–88; Sokoloff *Syriac*, p. 1.
28　　TPJ Num 22:18; 24:13; Job 3:15; 38:22.
29　　Sperber, vol. 4a, pp. 30–31. Weiss, p. 328, notes that Krauss cited no source for the word in
　　　his dictionary. A similar loanword exists in Syriac, ܩܘܪܛܘܪܐ, on which see Sokoloff *Syriac*,
　　　p. 1344, but like its Greek and Latin counterparts it too refers to a person rather than to a
　　　storage facility.

3 Other Words Shared by TC and TPJ Reflecting Western Aramaic

3.1 *Opening*

Many of the words noted above as comprising the linguistic framework of
TPJ and TC (שד״ר, חמ״י, אוף, היך, חזור חזור, כדין, כדון, ארום, etc.) are identifying features of the Western Aramaic that were common in Jewish Palestinian
Aramaic texts. Now we shall lend our attention to a number of Aramaic words
less common than these that are found in both TC and TPJ and strengthen the
impression of linguistic affinity between the two.

3.2 פירוג (*1 Chr 4:11*)

1 Chr 4:11

MT   וּכְלוּב אֲחִי־שׁוּחָה הוֹלִיד אֶת־מְחִיר הוּא אֲבִי אֶשְׁתּוֹן׃

TC   וכלוב אחוי דשוחא אוליד ית פירוג הוא אבא דאשתון׃

NJPS: Chelub the brother of Shuhah begot Mehir, who was the father of Eshton.
Dost: Chelub, the brother of Shuhah, fathered *Perug*, who was the father of
Eshton.

פירוג is a Palestinian Aramaic word signifying *exchange* or *price*;[30] thus TC
translates, rather than transcribes, the name מְחִיר. The noun פירוג appears in
TN, FT, TPJ Lev 27:10, as well, taking the place of the word תְּמוּרָה, and Deut
23:19 for the word מְחִיר (of מְחִיר כֶּלֶב; for this instance we also have GT, which
translates thus). The word also occurs in *Tg. Ps* 44:13 as an equivalent of מְחִיר;
Tg. Job 15:31; 17:2; 20:18; 28:17 for תְּמוּרָה ("substitution"); 28:15 for מְחִיר. The verb
פר״ג appears in TN, FT, TPJ Lev 27:10, 33 for מו״ר. It further appears in FT Gen
31:7 for וְהֶחֱלִף (there also in GT); 48:14 for שִׂכֵּל; Deut 20:6 for חִלְּלוֹ. It also appears
in TPJ Gen 48:14 for שִׂכֵּל (as in FT); Exod 32:5 in an expansion.

3.3 פסוגיא (*1 Chr 7:21*)

Within an aggadic expansion in the Targum on the premature Ephraimite exodus from Egypt, the phrase ביני פסוגיא appears twice in reference to the Torah's
account of the Covenant Between the Parts:

> ומנו ית קצא מן שעתא דהות דבירא דמרי עלמא מתמללא עם אברהם ביני פסוגיא
> וטעו דהוה חמי להון לממני מן יומא דאתיליד יצחק ונפקו ממצרים תלתי׳ שנין קדם
> קיצא ארום תלתין שנין מן־קדם דאתיליד יצחק הות דבירא דמרי עלמא מתמללא עם
> אברהם ביני פסוגי׳

---

30   Levy, vol. 2, p. 286; Sokoloff *JPA*, p. 489; Weiss, p. 100, classified the word as a Western form.

Dost: and they calculated the appointed time from the hour when the Divine Speech of the Lord of the World was conversing with Abraham between the pieces. They erred because they should have calculated from the day when Isaac was born, and (thus) they left Egypt thirty years before the end. For thirty years before Isaac was born the Divine Speech of the Lord of the World conversed with Abraham between the *pieces*.

TN, TNM, FT, and TPJ all employ this word to describe the animal parts prepared by Abraham in Genesis 15 (as well as sections of sacrifices in Exodus and Leviticus):

Gen 15:10

MT	וְאֶת־הַצִּפֹּר . לֹא בָתָר	רֵעֵהוּ	לִקְרַאת	אִישׁ־בִּתְרוֹ	וַיִּתֵּן	בַּתָּ֫וֶךְ	אֹתָם	וַיְבַתֵּר
TO	וית עופא	לא פליג	חבריה	לקביל	פלגיא פלג	ויהב	בשוי	ופליג יתהון
TN	וית עופה	לא פסג	חבריה	לקבל	כל חד פסגה	ושוי	במציעה	ופסג יתהון
TNM		[חב[ריה	לקדמות	גבר פסגייה	ושווי		לפסגין	
FT	וית עופא	לא פליג	חבריה	לקדמות	גבר פסגיה	ושווי	לפסגין	ופסג יתהון
TPJ	וית עופא	לא פסג	חבריה	כל קבל	פסגא דחד	וסדר	במציעא	ופסג יתהון

NJPS: He brought Him all these and cut them in two, placing each half opposite the other; but he did not cut up the bird.

Clem TPJ:

Both the verb פס״ג and the noun פסג are characteristic of Palestinian Aramaic.[31] The author of TC did not encounter any need for the expression due to his Hebrew *Vorlage*—the word occurs in an expansion—but sought to invoke the Covenant Between the Parts with an Aramaic expression familiar to him. The fact that the word he chose was פסוגיא associates him with the group described above, among whose members is TPJ.

For the purposes of the present study, this finding would suffice here, establishing that the word chosen by TC were the same as that appearing in the Palestinian Targums and TPJ and that this choice doubtless stemmed from their commonly shared tradition. Yet a more specific link may be proposed. In point of fact, none of the verses presented above contains the expression בין פסגיא. Aside from TC, we find this expression in available targumic literature only in the following locations:

---

31 Sokoloff *JPA*, pp. 496–497; Sokoloff *JBA*, p. 915, entertains doubts with regard to the textual reliability of the appearance of the verb פס״ג in a single MS of the Babylonian Talmud.

Gen 15:17

MT	אֲשֶׁר עָבַר בֵּין הַגְּזָרִים הָאֵלֶּה
TNM	בזמן דעבר בן פסגיא האילין
TPJ	והא עבר בין פסוגיא האילין

NJPS: which passed between those pieces.

Clem TPJ: And behold, it passed between these pieces.

TPJ Exod 12:40:[32] ומניין ארבע מאה ותלתין שנין מן דמליל ה׳ לאברהם מן שעתא דמליל
עמיה בחמיסר בניסן ביני פסוגיא עד יומא דנפקו ממצרים

Clem: But the number was four hundred thirty years from when the Lord spoke
to Abraham from the moment when he spoke with him between the pieces on
the fifteenth of Nisan until the day when they came out of Egypt.

Lev 26:42

MT	וְאַף אֶת־בְּרִיתִי אַבְרָהָם אֶזְכֹּר
TPJ	ואוף ית קיימא דקיימית עם אברהם ביני פסגיא אדכור

NJPS: and also My covenant with Abraham [shall I remember]

Clem: and also the covenant that I made with Abraham between the pieces
[shall I] remember

The use in TC of an expression found once in TNM and thrice in TPJ strongly
corroborates the links between these Targums. In the case of TPJ Exod 12:40,
the similarity between TPJ and TC goes beyond use of the expression ביני פסוגיא
and extends to the very similar manner in which the word is incorporated in its
sentence in the two Targums:

TPJ			לאברהם ה׳ · דמליל			מן		ומניין...
	ביני פסוגיא	עמיה...	דמליל		שעתא	מן		
TC	...פסוגיא ביני עם אברהם		דהות דבירא דמרי עלמא מתמללא	שעתא מן		ית קצא	ומנו
	ביני פסוגי׳ עם אברהם		הות דבירא דמרי עלמא מתמללא					

Clem: And the days ... from when the Lord spoke to Abraham from the moment when he spoke with him between the pieces

Dost: and they calculated the appointed time from the hour when the Divine
Speech of the Lord of the World was conversing with Abraham between the
pieces.... the Divine Speech of the Lord of the World conversed with Abraham
between the pieces

---

32   This excerpt from TPJ is an expansion of the Hebrew verse in Exod 12:40 and, therefore,
      appears here without a Hebrew counterpart.

This similarity may be evidence of a literary tradition common to the two Targums, or even of a direct link between the two.

3.4   טל"ק (2 Chr 15:16; 25:12; 28:3; 30:14; 33:15)

Use of the verb טל"ק, meaning *to throw*, is characteristic of the Palestinian Targums. It appears not once in TO or TJ, but is common in TN, FT, TPJ, GT, *Tg. Ps*, and *Tg. Job*. The word's various appearances in TC have no parallel verses in Kings.[33] The verb טל"ק appears in TC in 2 Chr 15:16, where there is no corresponding word in the Hebrew verse:

2 Chr 15:16 / 1 Kg 15:13

MT Chr	בְּנַחַל קִדְרוֹן:	וַיִּשְׂרֹף	וַיָּדֶק	מִפְלַצְתָּהּ	אֶת־	אָסָא	וַיִּכְרֹת
TC	וטליק בנחלא :דקדרון	ואוקיד	ואדיק	גיחוכה	טעוות	ית אסא	וקציץ
MT Kg	בְּנַחַל קִדְרוֹן:	וַיִּשְׂרֹף		מִפְלַצְתָּהּ	אֶת־	אָסָא	וַיִּכְרֹת
TJ	בנחלא :דקדרון	ואוקיד		טעותה	ית אסא		וקץ

NJPS Chr: Asa cut down her abominable thing, reduced it to dust, and burned it in the Wadi Kidron.
Dost: Asa cut down the idols of derision and he crushed, burned, and threw (them) into Wadi Kidron.
NJPS Kg: Asa cut down her abominable thing and burnt it in the Wadi Kidron.
Clem: and Asa cut down her idol and burned it in the Wadi Kidron.

It seems that in adding the word וטליק, the targumist had no concern with his altering the scriptural story, but believed that he was presenting it with utmost accuracy: in a similar incident in 2 Chr 30:14, where idolatrous objects are taken to Kidron Brook, these items are not burnt but thrown (טל"ק) into the brook. Inasmuch as the present verse gives Kidron Brook as a burning site, it may be assumed that the items in questions were not only burnt, but also cast into the brook. Given the need to choose a verb denoting *to throw* that would correspond to nothing in either the Hebrew *Vorlage* or TJ, TC chose the verb טל"ק. Moses took much the same course of action with the Golden Calf, as described in Deut 9:21—וָאֶשְׂרֹף אֹתוֹ | בָּאֵשׁ וָאֶכֹּת אֹתוֹ טָחוֹן הֵיטֵב עַד אֲשֶׁר־דַּק לְעָפָר וָאַשְׁלִךְ אֶת־עֲפָרוֹ אֶל־הַנַּחַל—*I took it and put it to the fire; I broke it to bits and ground it thoroughly until it was fine as dust, and I threw its dust into the brook*—and there TPJ, too, chose טל"ק, rather than the root רמ"י, preferred by TO and TN.

---

33   White, pp. 189, 217, comments briefly on the word's distribution. Sokoloff *JPA*, pp. 236–237, notes that the correct reading in *y. Ḥag.* 2:2 (77d, p. 787), following the MS published by Assis, is יטלק, rather than יטלון.

4   Words Shared by TC and TPJ Reflecting Eastern Aramaic

4.1   *Opening*

The Aramaic of the Palestinian Pentateuchal Targums is, naturally, Western Aramaic. This is the language of TN, FT, and the Genizah Targums. As noted above, many of the words comprising the linguistic framework of TC also are characteristic of Western Aramaic. It thus is surprising to find many words throughout TC that are characteristic not of Western Aramaic, but of that language's Eastern dialect. These words occur both in the continuum of the literal translation and in many expansions. The same phenomenon—that of a Western linguistic framework garnished throughout with numerous Eastern words—is characteristic of TPJ, as well. What is more, a not insignificant number of those Eastern words found in one Targum also occur in the other. We now shall turn our attention to words characteristic of Eastern Aramaic that appears in both TC and TPJ.

4.2   אֲ־ *(prefix, signifying on)*:

The particle אֲ־ appears as a prefix in three words in TC: אמטול (10 occurrences), אגב (2 occurrences), and אלביה (1 occurrence):

2 Chr 30:18[34]

MT	כִּי הִתְפַּלֵּל יְחִזְקִיָּהוּ עֲלֵיהֶם	
TC	ארום צלי חזקיהו אמטולהון	

NJPS: Hezekiah prayed for them
Dost: For Hezekiah prayed for them

1 Chr 11:21

MT   מִן־הַשְּׁלוֹשָׁה בַשְּׁנַיִם נִכְבָּד וַיְהִי לָהֶם לְשָׂר וְעַד־הַשְּׁלוֹשָׁה לֹא־בָא:
TC   מן תלתה אגב תרין הוה יקיר והוה להון לרבנא ולתלת גבורן לא מטא:

NJPS: among the three he was more highly regarded than the other two, and so he became their commander. However, he did not attain to the other three.
Dost: Of the three he was more revered than the (other) two, and he became their leader, but he did not perform three mighty acts.

1 Chr 11:25   מִן־הַשְּׁלוֹשִׁים הִנּוֹ נִכְבָּד הוּא וְאֶל־הַשְּׁלֹשָׁה לֹא־בָא
TC   מן גבריא תלתא הא הוא יקיר אגב תרין ולתלת גבורן לא מטא

NJPS: He was highly regarded among the thirty, but he did not attain to the three.

---

34   The nine further occurrences are in 1 Chr 4:18, 23; 12:19; 16:21; 2 Chr 13:2; 33:13; 34:21.

Dost: Behold, of the three mighty men he was more honored than the (other) two, but he did not perform three mighty acts.

TC 1 Chr 11:11[35] כד הוה נפיק לקרבא הוה מסתייע מעילא ובמתביה לאולפן אוריתא הות סלקה שמעתה אלביה

Dost: When he went out to war he was helped from above, and when he sat for Torah instruction in the Torah the legal tradition come to his mind.

The word אמטול is comprised of the prefix א־ (which is typical of Babylonian Aramaic and uncommon in PA) and the word מטול.[36] The word אגב is a Babylonian Aramaic compound[37] comprised of the elements א־גב, literally, *on the back [of]*. The word אלביה, meaning *on his heart*, appears alongside a further indicator of Babylonian Aramaic, viz., the phrase סלקה שמעתה. The entire sentence is absent from the parallel verse in TJ, 2 Sam 23:8. Notably, the instances cited here where the particle א־ is used are an exceptional minority in TC, which typically uses the word על, but the same is true of the other translations noted here that contain this prefix. We find the form על גב in one place in TC (2 Chr 21:3, ואקניאונון על גב קרקעא, *and on the basis of land they were given possession*), where the Targum's diction is directly influenced by that of the Talmud: אין לו תקנה עד שיקנם על גבי קרקע.[38]

Two of the three forms in which we find the prefix א־ in TC appear in TNM, TPJ, *Tg. Ps*, and *Tg. Job*, as well.[39]

---

35 This segment of the Targum is given without the Hebrew original because although the lengthy expansion it contains bears a connection to the Hebrew, the connection is easily discernible and cause for discussion in its own right; see pp. 292–294, below.

36 Sokoloff *JBA*, p. 140. Weiss, p. 307, did not distinguish between מטול and אמטול. The difference between them, however, is a significant one. מטול (along with the subordinating particle ד־/די) is a conjunctive particle, often the equivalent of Hebrew כִּי; see my discussion of this phrase above, pp. 46–47. The prefix of אמטול changes the word's meaning to *in behalf of*, *as a result of*, or *because of* whatever follows. In some cases the word is declined with a *taw*, as אמטולת; see Dan, p. 349.

37 White, p. 259.

38 Based on *b. Qidd.* 26a–27b. See discussion below, pp. 340–342.

39 See also the expansion given in *Tg. Ps*:

Ps 110:1 שֵׁב לִימִינִי עַד־...

TP תוב ואוריך לשאול דמן שבט בנימן עד דימות ארום לית מלכותא דמקרבא אחברתה

NJPS: Sit at My right hand while ...

Cook: Wait still for Saul of the tribe of Benjamin to die, for one reign must not encroach on another

The text above is that of Ashkenazi MSS of *Tg. Ps*, while Sephardic MSS lack the form אחברתה; see Dan, p. 14.

אמטול: TNM Lev 21:4.

TPJ Gen 12:13; Lev 9:7, 16; 17:11; 28:11; Deut 2:25; 28:15; 30:9.

Tg. Ps 7:8; 40:8; 52:8; 57:3; 58:8; 68:15; 69:8; 83:6; 86:17; 99:6, 8; 138:8; 139:11; 142:8.

Tg. Job 1:10; 3:23; 6:22; 9:7; 18:4, 6; 29:24; 42:8.

אגב: TNM Lev 27:18.

TPJ Num 35:8.

Tg. Job 13:12; 30:18.

In these Targums, the prefix א־ serves as a translation of words such as ל, על, בעד, and ב, sometimes in targumic expansions.

4.3   דיוקן (*2 Chr 33:7*)

2 Chr 33:7

| MT | הָאֱלֹהִים | בְּבֵית | עָשָׂה | אֲשֶׁר | הַסֶּמֶל | אֶת־פֶּסֶל | וַיָּשֶׂם |
| TC | דה' | מקדשא | בבית | בדיוקניה | עבד | די | צורתא | פסל | ית | ושוי |

NJPS: He placed a sculptured image that he made in the House of God

Dost: He put the idol of the figure that he had made in his own likeness in the house of the sanctuary of the Lord

Aside from its solitary appearance in TC, where there is no parallel word in the Hebrew, the word דיוקן appears six times in TPJ, corresponding to צֶלֶם or דְּמוּת, or else in the absence of a corresponding word in the Hebrew *Vorlage* (Gen 1:26–27; 5:1; 9:6; Lev 26:1; Deut 21:23) and once in *Tg. Ps* (39:7), corresponding to צֶלֶם. דיוקן is a Greek loanword, familiar in Rabbinic Hebrew, that signifies human semblance or form.[40] The word is documented in Hebrew mainly in the Babylonian Talmud and later midrashic works, though it also appears twice in *Mek. RSbY*, and its few appearances in Aramaic may be assumed to be owed to the influence of Hebrew.[41] This word thus directs us eastward despite its Hellenic origins.

Several MSS and editions of *Tg. Ruth* 3:18 read אבית דינא, but this appears to be a corruption; see Beattie, p. 29.

Also worthy of note is FTV Num 21:20, where וְנִשְׁקָפָה עַל־פְּנֵי הַיְשִׁימֹן, *overlooking the wasteland*, is translated as דמצטייפא כל קביל אבית ישימון, *that looks out over on Beth Jeshimon*. This version is problematic, as there is no need for the two consecutive prepositions כל קביל א־. The alternate version given in FTP is more convincing: דמצטפיא כל קבל בית ישימון, *that looks out over Beth Jeshimon*.

40   Levy, vol. 1, p. 170; Krauss *Lehnwörter*, vol. 1, p. 202; Jastrow, p. 297.

41   The more common word in Palestinian sources is איקונין, as demonstrated by the following comparison:

4.4   הד"ר (*1 Chr 1:50; 9:40; 2 Chr 15:16; 33:12*)

Use of הד"ר as signifying *to return* is characteristic of Babylonian Aramaic.[42]
TPJ uses this root heavily. Aside from that work, the root is found in targumic
literature only in TNM, *Tg. Eccl*, and *Tg. Job*.

4.5   כוורא (*2 Chr 33:14*)

שַׁעַר הַדָּגִים, *Fish Gate*, is translated in TC as תרע מזבני כווריא, i.e., the Fishmongers'
Gate. The word כוורא is characteristic of Eastern Aramaic.[43] It is common in
Babylonian Aramaic[44] and appears once in each of *Tg. Ps, Tg. Job*, and TC. In
TPJ the word appears twice (Gen 1:28; 48:16).

4.6   סרה"ב (*2 Chr 18:8; 24:5; 26:20; 35:21*)

The verb סרה"ב, signifying *to hasten* (in the transitive sense) or *to implore*, is familiar in both Syriac and Babylonian Aramaic.[45] The same meaning is a familiar one in Rabbinic Hebrew, though in this dialect it typically appears without
the letter *heh*: סר"ב.[46] Verbs and nouns of the root סרה"ב with this meaning
appear often in *Tg. Ps*, as well as in *Tg. Job*, in *Tg. Esth II*, and six times in TPJ.[47]

4.7   פיצתא (*1 Chr 6:39, 46, 48, 50*)

This word occurs in TC four times, in conjunction with the common word עדב,
in a kind of pleonastic construct phrase corresponding to גּוֹרָל in the Hebrew
Vorlage:

---

b. *Šabb.* 149a   כתב המהלך תחת הצורה ותחת הדיוקנאות אסור לקרותו   בשבת
y. *'Abod. Zar.*   כתב המהלך תחת הצורות או תחת האיקוניות אין מסתכלין בהן בשבת
3:1 (42b, pp. 1393–1394).
See Kohut *'arukh*, "דיוקן," vol. 3, pp. 49–50, who noted the appearance of the word דיוקן
principally in later midrashic works.

42   Though Lieberman *Studies*, p. 55, n. 12, argued that this stem was available for use in
      Palestinian Aramaic, his comments are unconvincing in light of the wealth of texts indi-
      cating a dialectal distinction between east and west in use of the root הד"ר.

43   Kaufman, *Akkadian*, p. 62.

44   Sokoloff *JBA*, p. 556.

45   Sokoloff *Syriac*, p. 1043; Sokoloff *JBA*, p. 830. Another meaning of the root is *to rebel*, but
      this sense is not relevant to the present discussion.

46   See discussion in Moreshet, p. 285, of the two forms of the root.

47   Weiss, p. 95; Cook *TPJ*, pp. 257–258.

1 Chr 6:39			:הַגּוֹרָל	הָיָה	לָהֶם	כִּי		הַקְּהָתִי	לְמִשְׁפַּחַת	לִבְנֵי אַהֲרֹן
TC		:פיצתא	עדב	הוה	להון	ארום		קהת	לגניסת	לבני אהר'
Josh 21:10	:רִאשֹׁנָה	הַגּוֹרָל	הָיָה	לָהֶם	כִּי	מִבְּנֵי לֵוִי	הַקְּהָתִי	מִמִּשְׁפְּחוֹת	מִבְּנֵי אַהֲרֹן	וַיְהִי לִבְנֵי אַהֲרֹן
TJ	:קדמותא	עדבא	הוה	להון	ארי	מבני לוי	קהת	מזרעית	לבני אהרן	והוה

NJPS Chr: to the sons of Aaron of the families of Kohathites, for theirs was the [first] lot

Dost: To the sons of Aaron of the lineage of Kohath, for the first lot was theirs

NJPS Josh: they went to the descendants of Aaron among the Kohathite clans of the Levites, for the first lot had fallen to them.

Clem: they went to the descendants of Aaron among the Kohathite clans of the Levites, for the first lot had fallen to them.

The word pair עדב פיצתא is not familiar from other targumic works (including the parallel verses in TJ Joshua 21, above, which use the term עדב). Even in TC, the term is not used consistently: in all occurrences of the word גּוֹרָל other than the four discussed here, TC translates the term as עדב, as was the practice of most other targumists (1 Chr 24:5, 7, 31; 25:8–9; 26:13–14). It may be that its appearance alongside עדב is to be understood as a gloss incorporated within the body of the Targum.[48] ܦ̈ܨܬܐ is the typical Syriac translation of גּוֹרָל, as seen in the following verse, which contains both the singular form ܦܨܬܐ and the plural form ܦ̈ܨܬܐ:[49]

Lev 16:8		וְגוֹרָל	לַה'	אֶחָד	גּוֹרָל	גֹּרָלוֹת הַשְּׂעִירִם	עַל־שְׁנֵי	אַהֲרֹן	וְנָתַן

:לַעֲזָאזֵל אֶחָד

Pesh. ܘܢܪܡܐ ܐܗܪܘܢ ܦ̈ܨܬܐ ܥܠ ܬܪܝܢ ܨ̈ܦܝܐ ܦܨܬܐ ܚܕܐ ܠܡܪܝܐ ܘܦܨܬܐ ܚܕܐ ܠܥܙܐܙܝܠ

NJPS: and he shall place lots upon the two goats, one marked for the LORD and the other marked for Azazel.

Gottlieb: and Aharon shall cast lots upon two goats, one lot for the LORD and one lot for Azaz-il.

פיצתא appears once in *Tg. Ps*, corresponding to גּוֹרָל:

Ps 125:3

MT	הַצַּדִּיקִים	גּוֹרַל	עַל	הָרֶשַׁע	שֵׁבֶט	יָנוּחַ	לֹא	כִּי
TP	דצדיקיא	פיצתא	על	דעשו	רישעא	שבט	ינוח	לא	ארום

NJPS: The scepter of the wicked shall never rest upon the land allotted to the righteous

---

48   White, p. 178.
49   See Peshiṭta Lev 16:8–10; Num 26:55–56; 33:54; 34:13; 36:2–3. Sokoloff *Syriac*, p. 1220.

Dost: For the scepter of wickedness will not rest on the lot of the righteous

פיצתא appears three times in TPJ, all in targumic expansions:[50]

TPJ Deut 4:34 או היך ניסא דעבד ה' לאתגלאה למיפרשא ליה אומא בפיצתא מיגו עם אוחרי...

Clem: Or has the Lord done signs to reveal Himself in order to set aside for Himself a people by lot from the midst of another people

TPJ Deut 32:8 ...רמא פיצתא עם שובעין מלאכיא רברבי עממין

Clem: He cast lots with the seventy angels, the princes of the nations ...

TPJ Deut 32:9 ...וכיון דנפל עמא קדישא בפיצתיה דמרי עלמא

Clem: And since the holy people fell by lot to the Lord of the World ...

Though in these three occurrences it is clear that the meaning of פיצתא in TPJ is in fact *lottery*, wherever the word גּוֹרָל appears in the text of the Torah, TPJ, as the other Targums, chooses to employ the term עדב.[51] The manner in which פיצתא is employed in TC thus is dissimilar to that in TPJ (as well as all other targumic works), and one cannot argue that TC was directly influenced by the rendering of the word גּוֹרָל that its author found in TPJ. Still, the very fact of the word's use and incorporation within the continuum of the Targum in 1 Chronicles 6 is evidence of a linguistic environment akin to that of TPJ and *Tg. Ps.*

4.8 פת״ק (*2 Chr 10:18; 26:15*)

The root פת״ק occurs once in TC as the translation of רג״ם, and a second time corresponding to יר״ה:

2 Chr 10:18	וַיִּרְגְּמוּ־	בֹו		בְנֵי־	יִשְׂרָאֵל		אֶבֶן	וַיָּמֹת
TC	ופתקו	ביה		בני	ישראל		אבניא	ומית
1 Kg 12:18	וַיִּרְגְּמוּ	כָל־		יִשְׂרָאֵל	בֹּו	אֶבֶן	וַיָּמֹת	
TJ	ורגמו	כל		ישראל	יתיה	באבנא	ומית	

NJPS Chr: but the Israelites pelted him to death with stones
Dost: and all Israel hurled stones at him, and he died
NJPS Kg: but all Israel pelted him to death with stones
Clem: and all Israel stoned him with stones, and he died

---

50 Cook *TPJ*, p. 258.
51 At the end of Deut 32:9 (excerpted here) we find the phrase עדב אחסנתיה in all Targums of the Torah, including TPJ, as the translation of the Hebrew phrase חֶבֶל נַחֲלָתֹו.

In this verse, the author of TC chose to use the verb פת״ק despite the use of רג״ם in TJ to the parallel verse in Kings and despite his use of אט״ל for the only other occurrence of רג״ם in Chronicles (2 Chr 24:21; see discussion of this novel verb, p. 197).

2 Chr 26:15

| MT | וּבָאֲבָנִים גְּדֹלוֹת | בַּחִצִּים | לִירוֹא | חִשְׁבֹנוֹת... | בִּירוּשָׁלַ͏ם | וַיַּעַשׂ |
| TC | ועבד | בירושלם | אומנותא... | למפתק בגירריןר ולמשדי | באבנין רברבן |

NJPS: He made clever devices in Jerusalem ... for shooting arrows and large stones

Dost: By the work of the artisan's craftsmanship he made in Jerusalem clever inventions ... for the shooting of arrows and for the hurling of large stones

The verb פת״ק is familiar in Babylonian Aramaic,[52] as well, but appears elsewhere in targumic literature only in two expansions in TPJ: למפתק גירין להון (Gen 49:8); מצראי דפתקין גירין ואבנין לישראל (Exod 14:19). Both occurrences in TPJ appear in expansions, rather than in correspondence to the Hebrew *Vorlage*, so that פת״ק is not to be viewed as a formal equivalent of the Hebrew רג״ם in TPJ. Further, the root רג״ם appears ten times in the Torah, and TPJ preferred to render these using not פת״ק, but the root אט״ל.

4.9   צנא (1 Chr 2:54)

צנא, meaning *basket*, is a hapax legomenon in TC, appearing as part of an aggadic expansion in a translation depicting the bringing of the first fruits to the Jerusalem Temple:

1 Chr 2:54   והוון בנוי דשלמא מעטרין פירי בכוריא בצנייא ומובלין בצנעא לירושלם

The word appears in no other Targum save TPJ (Deut 23:25; 26:3), and Cook identifies it with Babylonian Aramaic.[53]

Deut 23:25

MT	לֹא תִתֵּן:	וְאֶל־כֶּלְיְךָ	שָׂבְעֶךָ	כְּנַפְשְׁךָ	עֲנָבִים	וְאָכַלְתָּ
TO	לא תתין:	ולמנך	סבעך	כנפשך	ענבין	ותיכול
TPJ	לא תתן:	ולות צנך	עד דתיסבע	כרעוות נפשך		ותיכול

NJPS: you may eat as many grapes as you want, until you are full, but you must not put any in your vessel.

---

52   Sokoloff *JBA*, pp. 948–949.
53   Cook *TPJ*, p. 258; Sokoloff *JBA*, pp. 967–968.

Clem TO: you may eat grapes according to your appetite for satiety, but you shall not use a vessel.

Clem TPJ: you may eat grapes according to the desire of your appetite until you are sated, but you shall not use a basket.

Deut 26:3

MT   בַּיָּמִים הָהֵם   אֲשֶׁר יִהְיֶה אֶל־הַכֹּהֵן   וּבָאתָ

TPJ   ותעטרון בסליא וצניא ופיפייריא ותיעלון לות כהנא די יהוי ממני לכהין רב ביומיא האינון

NJPS: You shall go to the priest in charge at that time

Clem: and you shall decorate the baskets, and the palm-leaf baskets, and the papyrus baskets, and you shall bring them to the priest who will be appointed as high priest in those days

It may be that the appearance of the word צנא in TC in a context and with diction so similar to those in TPJ Deut 26:3 is indicative, at the least, of a kindred linguistic environment.

4.10   שבה״ר (1 Chr 2:18)

Among the compliments given Caleb's wife Azuba in a targumic expansion in praise of her is ואשתבהרת בחכמתא. The root בה״ר is declined in the various *shin*-stems to form the quadriliteral root שבה״ר. It is not to be found in most targumic works, but appears three times in TPJ,[54] corresponding to the root קר״ן (Exod 34:29, 30, 35), and once in *Tg. Job* (26:13, אפי שמיא אשתבהרו). The root צבה is a familiar Syriac term signifying *to beautify* or *to become beautiful*.[55]

4.11   שבהורא (1 Chr 16:27, 29; 29:11, 25; 2 Chr 20:21)

שבהורא is a noun with the root שבה״ר (see above) that appears in TC as an equivalent of הדר. It is quite common in *Tg. Ps* as well as present in *Tg. Job*, where it parallels words belonging to the semantic field of הוד, הדר, and תפארת. It appears in TPJ Deut 26:19 as an equivalent of תפארת and ibid. 33:17 in a targumic expansion. The word is familiar in Syriac and, along with the verb derived from the same root, to be regarded as Eastern Aramaic.[56]

---

54   Cook *TPJ*, p. 259, also describes this root as belonging to Eastern Aramaic.

55   Sokoloff *Syriac*, p. 1499. Cf. Peshiṭta Prov 25:6 (for תִּתְהַדַּר), 14 (for מִתְהַלֵּל); 27:1 (for אַל־תִּתְהַלֵּל), as well as *Tg. Prov* (which is based on the Syriac) to the above verses.

56   Sokoloff *Syriac*, p. 1517.

5   Unusual Dialectal Features and Other Indicators of Kindred Linguistic Environments

5.1   *Opening*

The Aramaic language served a variety of ethnic groups over the course of lengthy periods and in quite a few lands. It consequently developed into a wide variety of different dialects that left their own particular signs, which today assist us in identifying the origins of Aramaic texts. Below we shall present dialectal anomalies found in both TC and TPJ that serve to associate the particular linguistic strata of the two works.

5.2   אט״ל (אֶבֶן וַיִּרְגְּמֻהוּ || ואטלו יתיה באבנין; *2 Chr 24:21*)

The verb אט״ל is a hapax legomenon in TC, as well as uncommon generally. Were we familiar only with the verse under discussion, we would regard the verb as a derivative of the root נט״ל in the *aph'el* (as indeed is construed by Jastrow and Levy), but the verb appears in TC in a similar context 14 times, among them *Yiqtol* forms that preserve the *aleph* and thus are not in the *aph'el*.[57] These forms led Cook to conclude that late literary Aramaic had derived an erroneous, artificial form (Cook uses the term malapropism) based on the root נט״ל in the *aph'el*, giving rise to the root אט״ל in the *pa'el*.[58] The verb also occurs once in *Tg. Eccl* (3:2), in an expansion based on the deuteronomic passage of the rebellious son: ועידן בחיר לקטלא בנין מסרבין ומרגזין לאטולותהון באבניא, *and a time chosen for slaying rebellious and contemptible sons, for stoning them according to the edict of the judges.* In TPJ, too, we find the phrase אטלות אבנין, which occurs there 13 times. This root serves in TPJ as the translation of both רג״ם (in all of that verb's occurrences in the Torah) and the root סק״ל, with the object אבן appearing even when it is absent in the Hebrew source, so that it should be viewed as a required object for the purposes of the verb in question. The verb רג״ם appears twice in TC: 2 Chr 10:18; 24:21. At the first occurrence, TC translates the verb with the root פת״ק (see discussion of this verb, pp. 194–195); at the second, the root אט״ל is employed.

5.3   דר״ק (*2 Chr 29:22; 30:16; 34:4; 35:11*)

The consonant *zayin* of the Hebrew root זר״ק is an original, proto-Semitic *zayin* and not the result of a consonantal shift, as evidenced by its existence in the same form in other Semitic languages.[59] In TC we find a root whose meaning

---

57   TPJ Lev 20:27; 24:14, 16; Deut 13:11; 17:5; 21:21; 22:21, 24.

58   Cook *TPJ*, p. 261.

59   BDB, p. 284; HALOT, vol. 1, p. 283. HALOT describes the root דר״ק as a "false Aramaism."

and context are identical, but that contains a *dalet* instead of the *zayin*. This root is absent in other targumic works, which all employ ז‏ר"ק, with the exception of TPJ. Cook classified this root in TPJ as a pseudo-correction, while Kaufman identified it as a hypercorrection.[60] Unlike the verbal root, the noun מִזְרָק is translated by both TPJ and TC as מזרק, with a *zayin*.

5.4   נת"ב (*2 Chr 33:13*)

In a homiletic section of the translation discussing the prayer of Manasseh, we find the verb נת"ב in its sole appearance in TC:

2 Chr 33:13

MT	יְרוּשָׁלַ͏ִם לְמַלְכוּתוֹ	וַיְשִׁיבֵהוּ
TC	ונתביה בגזירת מימרא דה' וחזר לירושלים למלכותיה	ונפקת רוחא מביני כנפי כרוביא

NJPS: and returned him to Jerusalem to his kingdom

Dost: A wind went forth from between the wings of the cherubim, and it blew him by the decree of the Memra of the Lord, and he returned to Jerusalem to his kingdom

According to the plain sense of the verse, the verb וַיְשִׁיבֵהוּ is derived from the root שׁו"ב. The Targum, however, in an exegetical turn, derives the verb from the root נש"ב and gives a verb of equivalent meaning as its translation. The root of the Aramaic verb, however, is not the expected נש"ב, but נת"ב. The appearance of a *taw* is surprising because the same root exists with *shin* in various other dialects of Aramaic.[61] The root נת"ב is used elsewhere only in TPJ[62] and *Tg. Ps.*[63] Cook classifies the root found in TPJ as a pseudo-correction.[64]

5.5   יע"ט (*1 Chr 13:1*) / עטה (*1 Chr 4:15; 12:20*)

The parallel root in Hebrew is יע"צ; in Arabic, وعظ. One thus might expect, in accordance with the principles of consonantal shift, that the Aramaic would have the root יע"ט and the noun עטה, as in fact is the case in Biblical Aramaic and elsewhere.[65] The trend in Jewish-Aramaic, however, is to prefer יע"צ and עצה, presumably due to the influence of Hebrew, and it is these forms that we find in TO, TJ, TN, and others. Notwithstanding, in TPJ and TC we find the root יע"ט used for verbs and both the forms עטה and עצה as nouns.[66]

---

60   Cook *TPJ*, p. 262; Kaufman *TPJ*, p. 25, list 6, n. 214; see also comment by HALOT above.

61   Sokoloff *JPA*, pp. 402–403; Sokoloff *JBA*, p. 778; Sokoloff *Syriac*, pp. 951–952.

62   Gen 1:2; Num 11:31; Deut 32:2.

63   Ps 103:16; 129:6; 147:18.

64   Cook *TPJ*, p. 265 (following Blau; see ibid.).

65   BDB, pp. 1095–1096. HALOT, vol. 5, pp. 1891–1892, 1945.

66   Cook *TPJ*, p. 263.

5.6   צטר (2 Chr 31:15)

The word צטר is a secondary form of סטר, whose meaning is *a side*. The common form סטר appears twice in TC (1 Chr 23:28; 2 Chr 20:20), while the secondary form appears once, spelled with a *ẓadi* (2 Chr 31:15). Aside from its sole appearance in TC, this orthography is known to us only from TPJ. Of the 101 occurrences in TPJ, the word is spelled with a *ẓadi* in 48.

5.7   *Non-Peʿal Infinitive Forms with Preformative Mem*

One of the many morphological features that distinguish the language of TN and FT from that of TO is the preformative *mem* in infinitive forms.[67] In infinitive forms in TN and FT that lack a personal pronoun, a preformative *mem* precedes the initial letter of the root in all constructions other than a few exceptional ones, whereas in the Aramaic of TO this is the case only in *peʿal*. There are approximately 430 infinitive forms in TO that are not in *peʿal* and lack personal pronouns, and not one contains a preformative *mem*. When we examine the infinitive forms in TC, we find that the bulk of the roughly 250 non-*peʿal* infinitive forms in the document are declined without a preformative *mem*. In this respect, they have the appearance of the infinitive forms familiar to us from TO. Yet a preformative *mem* does appear in 11 of the infinitive forms found in TC, viz.:

למבשרא (2:55); במשבחיהון (2:17); למרחקא, למסייעא, למחבלא (1 Chr 1:43); למסדרא (2 Chr 11:1); למתבנייה (22:1); למשייל (18:10);[68] למשבחא (15:21); (10:9); למתגניה (15:16); למדחלון (32:18).[69]

In effect, nearly five percent of the non-*peʿal* infinitive forms in TC contain a preformative *mem*.[70] How does TPJ compare? In TPJ there are approximately 720 non-*peʿal* infinitive forms that lack personal pronouns. Of these forms, a

---

67   See distinction concerning this feature between Eastern Aramaic (until 700 CE, as defined by the author) and Late Western Aramaic in Fassberg *Infinitive*, pp. 246–247; Tal, p. 165.

68   The form in the parallel verse, TJ 2 Sam 8:10, is למשאל, in *peʿal*. It thus may be that this was the intention of TC, as well. Notwithstanding, the form appearing in the MSS, which reflects the *paʿel*, also is a possibility. Cf. 1 Chr 14:14; 2 Chr 1:11, as well as the use of *piʿel* in rabbinic parlance, e.g., *b. Yebam.* 76b: "While you are asking (משאיל) concerning him whether he is fit for kingship or is not, ask concerning him whether he is fit to enter the congregation or is not."

69   It may be in order to include 1 Chr 16:2, מן למסק (for מֵהַעֲלוֹת), in this list. The form למסק is a surprising one, as we would expect the Targum to use an infinitive of the *aphʿel*, rather than the *peʿal*, construct. There thus is due cause to consider whether this version reflects the original reading מן למסקא, with the *aleph* omitted.

70   Notably, two infinitive forms sometimes occur in TC even for the same root. Of those forms in TC that have a *mem* prefix, we find an infinitive for חב"ל, סי"ע, שב"ח, and סד"ר.

preformative *mem* appears in approximately 245, i.e., 34 percent of these instances. The frequency with which the preformative *mem* appears in infinitive forms in TPJ is seven times that in TC. Notwithstanding, the two Targums are similar in that most of the infinitive forms that they contain are of the type found in TO, with only a minority containing a preformative *mem*. A similar state of affairs is reflected by Barak Dan's examination of *Tg. Ps.*[71] We might presume that this inconsistency is due to the fact that these Targums were written not in a living tongue, but in literary language influenced to varying extents by the two competing dialects.

5.8   טפ״ז (*1 Chr 15:29*)

The verb טפ״ז appears on only one occasion in TC, as well as twice in expansions in TPJ (Exod 32:19; Num 21:35) and three times in *Tg. Ps* and *Tg. Job* (corresponding to רץ״ד, רק״ד, קפ״ץ, and נת״ר).[72] In TC, the verb serves to translate the Hebrew word מְרַקֵּד, a word choice by the author of Chronicles that deviates from that of the author of Samuel:

These stems appear throughout the work in additional infinitive forms lacking a prefixal *mem*.

71   See Dan, p. 40.

72   Appearances of the verb in *Tg. Ps* and *Tg. Job*:

Ps 68:17

MT		תֶּרַצְּדוּן הָרִים	לָמָּה
TP		למה אתון טפזין טוריא מאתריכון	

NJPS: why so hostile, O jagged mountains
Cook: Why do you leap, O mountains [from your spot]?

Ps 114:4,6

MT		הֶהָרִים רָקְדוּ כְאֵילִים... הֶהָרִים תִּרְקְדוּ כְאֵילִים
TP		טוריא טפזו היך דיכרין... טוריא מטפזין היך דיכרין

NJPS: mountains skipped like rams ... mountains, that you skipped like rams
Cook: the mountains leapt like rams ... O mountains, leaping about like rams?

Job 5:16

MT		קָפְצָה פִּיהָ:	וְעֹלָתָה
Tg. Job		ונכלתא דרשיעי טפזת פומה:	

NJPS: The mouth of wrongdoing is stopped.
Clem: and the deception of the wicked shuts its mouth.

1 Chr 15:29	בְּלִבָּהּ:	לוֹ	וַתִּבֶז	מְרַקֵּד וּמְשַׂחֵק	דָּוִיד	אֶת־הַמֶּלֶךְ	וַתֵּרֶא
TC	בלבבה:	עלוי	ובסרת	מטפז ומשבח		ית מלכא	וחמת
2 Sam 6:16	בְּלִבָּהּ:	לוֹ	וַתִּבֶז	מְפַזֵּז וּמְכַרְכֵּר לִפְנֵי ה'	דָּוִד	אֶת־הַמֶּלֶךְ	וַתֵּרֶא
TJ	בלבה:	עלוהי	ובסרת	מרקיד ומשבח קדם ה'	דויד	ית מלכא	וחזת

NJPS Chr: and saw King David leaping and dancing, and she despised him for it.

Dost: and saw the king leaping and praising, and she despised him in her heart.

NJPS Sam: and saw King David leaping and whirling before the LORD; and she despised him for it.

Clem: and saw King David dancing and praising before the Lord. And she despised him in her heart.

The rare Hebrew verb מְפַזֵּז of 2 Samuel was replaced by the author of Chronicles with the more familiar מְרַקֵּד; the translation of 2 Samuel in TJ reflects a similar dynamic. TC could have left the root unchanged and translated מרקיד, as in both his Hebrew *Vorlage* and TJ. The targumist's choice of the root טפ"ז shows that it was only natural for him to view טפ"ז as an equivalent of רק"ד, as in *Tg. Ps* and *Tg. Job* above. The root טפ"ז is similarly used in TPJ Exod 32:19, although within the context of an aggadic expansion:

והוה כד קריב משה למשריתא וחמא ית עיגלא וחינגין בידיהון דרשיעיא מחנגין ומג־
חנין קדמוי וסטנא הוה בגויה מטפז ומשוור קדם עמא...

Clem: And it came about when Moses came near to the camp and saw the calf and the musical instruments in the hands of the wicked, dancing and bowing down before it, *and Satan was in the midst of it leaping and jumping before the people* ...

Job 21:11

MT	יְרַקֵּדוּן:	וְיַלְדֵיהֶם	עֲוִילֵיהֶם	כַצֹּאן	יְשַׁלְּחוּ
Tg. Job	יטפזון:	ורוביהון	טליהון	היך ענא	ישדרון

NJPS: They let their infants run loose like sheep, and their children skip about.

Clem: They send their children like sheep, and their youths leap about.

Job 37:1

MT	מִמְּקוֹמוֹ:	וְיִתַּר	לִבִּי	יֶחֱרַד	אַף־לְזֹאת
Tg. Job	מן אתריה:	ויטפי	לבי יתווה		ברם לדא

NJPS: Because of this, too, my heart quakes, and leaps from its place.

Clem: But at this my heart is greatly surprised, and it leaps from its place.

TPJ's choice of מטפז ...סטנא was made against the backdrop of the Hebrew phrase מרקד ...השטן, recalling similar depictions found in Talmudic Hebrew.[73] Weiss correlates the root with the verb טפ״ס found in rabbinic parlance.[74]

5.9   יומא אחרן (1 Chr 10:8; 2 Chr 20:16)

The expression יומא אחרן appears twice in TC, corresponding to מָחָר and to מָחֳרָת, and diverging from the rendering given by TJ to the parallel verses:

1 Chr 10:8	פְּלִשְׁתִּים	וַיָּבֹאוּ	מִמָּחֳרָת	וַיְהִי
TC	פלשתאי	ואתו	ביומא אחרן	והוה
1 Sam 31:8	פְּלִשְׁתִּים	וַיָּבֹאוּ	מִמָּחֳרָת	וַיְהִי
TJ	פלשתאי	ואתו	ביומא דבתרוהי	והוה

NJPS Chr: The next day the Philistines came
Dost: Now on the following day, when the Philistines came
NJPS Sam: The next day the Philistines came
Clem: Then on the day afterwards the Philistines came

The common translation of מָחָר, *tomorrow*, both in TO and TJ and in TN is יומא דבתרוהי. TPJ, meanwhile, uses יומא חרן for eight appearances (out of 14) of מָחֳרָת and twice (of 17) for מָחָר. TC translates thus in one instance (of two) where the word מָחֳרָת appears, and at one occurrence (of two) of מָחָר.[75] Thus although both Targums are inconsistent, TC and TPJ have in common selective use of this phrase, which leads me to believe that the trend they exhibit reflects Late Jewish Literary Aramaic or, at the very least, the kindred linguistic environments of TPJ and TC.

---

73   *B. Pesaḥ.* 112b:

ואל תעמוד בפני השור בשעה שעולה מן האגם מפני שהשטן מרקיד לו בין קרניו.

And don't stand in the way of an ox when it comes up from the pasture, since Satan is dancing between its horns.

B. Meg. 11b:

בא שטן וריקד ביניהן והרג את ושתי.

Along came Satan and danced between them and killed Vashti.

Tanḥ. Balaq 7 (p. 186):

שבשעה שהולך אדם לחטוא השטן מרקד לפניו עד שהוא עומד לגמור את העבירה.

for at such time as a man goes to sin, Satan dances before him until he is about to consummate the sin.

74   See Weiss, p. 317. Weiss diffidently suggests a link between this root and the translation of the word שפן in TO Lev 11:5 (טפזא/טבזא; see also TO Deut 14:7; *Tg. Ps* 104:18). I believe that such a link is in fact likely. See also TN Deut 14:7 (טפסה).

75   TC 2 Chr 20:16 renders יומא אחרן, and in the next verse מחר. The word מָחֳרָת appears in 1 Chr 29:21 (לְמָחֳרַת הַיּוֹם הַהוּא), where TC translates לבתר יומא ההוא, but there יומא אחרן would not be a valid translation. See White, p. 51.

Notably, this is not to argue that either the use as such of יומא אחרן or its association with the Hebrew מָחָר was of late origin. To the contrary: there are strong indications that the Hebrew word מָחָר is in fact an abbreviation and blend of the words יוֹם־אַחֵר.[76] Yet irrespective of its origins, to our knowledge this expression occurs in targumic literature only in TPJ and TC.

5.10   קינום (2 Chr 15:15; 23:1; 34:24)

The word קינומה/קינום is found nowhere in targumic literature other than three occurrences in TC, corresponding to שְׁבוּעָה, בְּרִית, and אָלָה (translated קינום לוט) and once in TPJ, where it serves as an equivalent of אָלָה (Num 5:21, קיים קינומתא for שְׁבֻעַת הָאָלָה).

5.11   שרג"ג בתולתא (1 Chr 2:21; 2 Chr 18:19)

This verb is a *shaph'el* form of the root רג"ג (meaning *to lust* or *to desire*; see TO Gen 3:6 ומרגג אילנא לאסתכלא ביה, *and that the tree was desirable to look at*). שרג"ג serves as a translation of the root פת"ה, *to entice*, in *Tg. Ps*, *Tg. Prov*, *Tg. Job*, and TC.[77] It also appears in FTV, GT (MS A), and TPJ Exod 22:15 (for פת"ה) and TPJ Num 20:17 (also FTV); 21:22 (also FTP); Deut 23:1, where though in the context of an aggadic expansion, it is clear that the root פת"ה is present in the background. It also appears in TC 2 Chr 18:19 (מן ישרגג ית אחאב, *who will entice Ahab?*), where TJ uses טע"י, which serves in TO and TJ alongside שד"ל as a common translation of פת"ה. Meanwhile, in the two verses below, TC follows TJ in translating פת"י as טע"י.

Let us consider 1 Chr 2:21, where the verb שרג"ג first appears in TC:

1 Chr 2:21

MT   וְאַחַר   בָּא   חֶצְרוֹן   אֶל־בַּת־מָכִיר   אֲבִי גִלְעָד   וְהוּא לְקָחָהּ

TC   ומן בתר כדין שרגיג חצרון בתולתא ית ברת מכיר אבא דגלעד והוא נסבה לאנתו

NJPS: Afterward Hezron had relations with the daughter of Machir father of Gilead—he had married her

Dost: Later, Hezron seduced the virgin of Machir, the father of Gilead, and he married her.

In this verse the word בתולתא, *virgin*, is added in translation, reflecting no word present in the Hebrew text. What is the reason for this insertion? We find the word pair שרג"ג בתולתא, *to seduce a virgin*, in several instances in FT, GT, and

---

TPJ, in the context of a man's purpose of having sexual relations.[78] The verb
שרג״ג in this verse establishes a distinction between the first action described
(corresponding to Hebrew בָּא), viz., one of sexual seduction, and the second
(corresponding to לְקָחָהּ), defined with the words והוא נסבה לאנתו, describing
the act of marriage.[79] Thus in its use of the phrase שרג״ג בתולתא, TC is linguistically similar to a limited number of Targums, among them TPJ.

---

78   FT and TPJ Exod 22:15 (also GT to the same verse); Num 20:17; 21:22 coalesce the two words
      (see examples below), so that this terminology seems appropriate. It is not, however, in-
      escapable, as demonstrated by TPJ Deut 23:1 (see below), but there, too, the context in
      which we find the verb שרג״ג shows that the woman associated with the verb is at the
      time an unmarried virgin, contrasted as she is with איתת אבוי, *his father's wife*.

      Exod 22:15

MT	וְכִי־יְפַתֶּה	אִישׁ	בְּתוּלָה	אֲשֶׁר	לֹא־אֹרָשָׂה	וְשָׁכַב	עִמָּהּ
FT	ואֲרי ישרגג	גבר	בתולא	די	לא ארסת	וישמש	עימה
GT	ו[ארום] ישרגג	גבר	בתולה	די	לא מארסה	וישמש	עמה
TPJ	וארום ישרגג	גבר	בתולתא	די	לא מארסא	וישמש	עמה

      NJPS: If a man seduces a virgin for whom the bride-price has not been paid, and lies with
      her
      Clem TPJ: If a man should seduce a virgin who is unengaged and should lie with her

      Num 20:17

MT	לֹא	נַעֲבֹר	בְּשָׂדֶה	וּבְכֶרֶם	וְלֹא	נִשְׁתֶּה	מֵי	בְאֵר
FT	לא	נינוס	אניסין	ולא	נשרגגה	בתולן	ולא	נבעי	נשי	גוברין
TPJ	לא	נשרגגה	בתולן	ולא	נאנוס	אריסן	ולא	נבעול	נשי	גוברין

      NJPS: We will not pass through fields or vineyards, and we will not drink water from wells.
      Clem TPJ: We will not seduce virgins, and we will not rape betrothed women, and we will
      not have sexual intercourse with married women.

      Num 21:22

MT	לֹא	נֵטֶה	בְּשָׂדֶה	וּבְכֶרֶם	לֹא	נִשְׁתֶּה	מֵי	בְאֵר
FT	לא	נאנס	אנוסין	ולא	נשרגנה	בתולן	לא	נבעי	נשי	גוברין
TPJ	לא	נאנוס	אריסן	ולא	נשרגג	בתולן	לא	נבעול	נשי	גוברין

      NJPS: We will not turn off into fields or vineyards, and we will not drink water from wells.
      Clem TPJ: We will not rape betrothed women, and we will not seduce virgins, and we will
      not have relations with married women.

      Deut 23:1

MT	לֹא־יִקַּח	אִישׁ	אֶת־	אֵשֶׁת	אָבִיו
TPJ	לא יסב	גבר	ית	איתתא דאניס אבוי או דשרגיג אבוי כל דכן איתת אבוי

      NJPS: No man shall marry his father's former wife
      Clem: A man shall not take the wife who was raped or seduced by his father, all the more
      so the wife of his father

79   See Kister *Poetry*, p. 178, for further discussion of the stem שרג״ג.

5.12   תמהא (*1 Chr 16:12; 2 Chr 32:24, 31; 33:13*)

Though the verb תמ״ה is familiar in both Eastern and Western Aramaic, the noun תמהא is absent from the literature of the latter, occurring only in Babylonian Aramaic and as the Syriac ܬܡܗܐ.[80] In its first three occurrences in TC, תמהא corresponds to מוֹפֵת in the Hebrew *Vorlage*. Though the fourth occurrence (2 Chr 33:13) is part of an aggadic expansion, the fact that it, too, corresponds to the Hebrew מוֹפֵת is clear from the context, דעבד עמיה אתיא ותמהיא serving as an equivalent of אשר עשה עמו אותות ומופתים. TPJ translates the Hebrew מוֹפֵת as תמהא in all of the word's 14 appearances in the Torah (Exod 4:21; 7:3, 9; 11:9, 10; Deut 4:34; 6:22; 7:19; 13:2, 3; 26:8; 28:46; 29:2; 34:11), as well as three additional instances (two corresponding to צח״ק in Gen 19:14; 21:6; and one in an aggadic expansion but signifying מוֹפֵת, Exod 2:21).

The practice of TO and TJ is to translate מוֹפֵת, *sign, wonder*, as either את or מופת, rather than תמהא:

Exod 7:9

MT		תְּנוּ לָכֶם מוֹפֵת	
TO		הבו לכון אתא	
TN		הבו לכון סימן	
TPJ		הבו לכון תימהא	

NJPS: Give a sign
Clem TPJ: Give a miracle

1 Kgs 13:3

MT		וְנָתַן בַּיּוֹם הַהוּא מוֹפֵת		
TJ		ויתין ביומא ההוא אתא		

NJPS: He gave a portent on that day
Clem: And in that day he will give a sign

Joel 3:3

MT		וְנָתַתִּי מוֹפְתִים בַּשָּׁמַיִם וּבָאָרֶץ	
TJ		ואתין אתין בשמיא ובארעא	

NJPS: I will set portents in the sky and on earth
Lund: And I will give signs in the heavens, and on the earth

---

80   Sokoloff *JBA*, p. 1205; Sokoloff *Syriac*, p. 1651.

2 Chr 32:24

MT   וּמוֹפֵת נָתַן לוֹ:

TC   ותימהא יהב ליה:

NJPS: and gave him a sign

Dost: Thus He granted to him a miracle

The word does in fact appear twice in TJ (Jer 5:30; Ezek 32:10). However, it serves there not as an equivalent of מוֹפֵת, but as a translation of שַׁמָּה and שע"ר, and its meaning is accordingly different:

Jer 5:30

MT   שַׁמָּה וְשַׁעֲרוּרָה נִהְיְתָה בָּאָרֶץ:

TJ   תימה ושנו הוה בארעא:

NJPS: An appalling, horrible thing has happened in the land

Clem: Astonishment and change have come upon the land

Ezek 32:10

MT   וּמַלְכֵיהֶם יִשְׂעֲרוּ עָלֶיךָ שַׂעַר

TJ   ומלכיהון יתמהון עלך תימה

NJPS: And their kings shall be aghast over you

Gottlieb: And their kings will ponder over you in astonishment

We are privy to two additional translations where the word תמהא is used as an equivalent of מוֹפֵת:

1.   The expression תימה דה' appears interlinearly in MS Neophyti 1, Exod 7:3, apparently corresponding to the word מוֹפְתַי of the clause וְהִרְבֵּיתִי אֶת־אֹתֹתַי וְאֶת־מוֹפְתַי בְּאֶרֶץ מִצְרָיִם, *that I may multiply My signs and marvels in the land of Egypt.*

2.   *Tg. Ps* renders מוֹפֵת as תמהא in all of the appearances of the word מוֹפֵת in Psalms: 71:7; 78:43; 105:5, 27; 135:9. One of these verses, in fact, is paralleled in 1 Chr 16:12, and here the targumic renderings are quite similar:

1 Chr 16:12	וּמִשְׁפְּטֵי־פִיהוּ:	מֹפְתָיו	עָשָׂה	אֲשֶׁר	נִפְלְאֹתָיו	זִכְרוּ
TC	תמהוהי ודיני פומיה:		דעבד	פרישוותיה		אדכרו
Tg. Ps 105:5	ודיני פומיה:	תמהוי	עבד	די	פרישותיה	אדכרו

It seems to me that the identical word choice came about because TC and *Tg. Ps* shared a common targumic tradition, similar to that of TPJ, in which תמהא functioned as an equivalent of מוֹפֵת.

6   Direct Literary Dependence

6.1   *Opening*

Up to this point, our investigation has revealed similarities between the language of TC and TPJ on numerous planes. The two Targums contain similar linguistic blends that mix Western Aramaic, complete with its particular loanwords, with Eastern Aramaic. Further, the two exhibit a number of unexpected linguistic features familiar to us solely or principally from them. Within the context of our examination, we raised the possibility that several words had made the journey from one Targum to the other not only due to the existence of similar linguistic environments, but perhaps even due to direct literary dependence. Such dependence has already been fairly proven with regard to the units of 1 Chronicles 1 that have parallels in the Torah. Now I shall seek to point out instances in which TC exhibits direct dependence on TPJ in units that parallel no part of the Torah, i.e., those comprising the bulk of the Book Chronicles.

6.2   קסטרה (*1 Chr 4:32–33*) *and* כופרן (*1 Chr 6:39*)

קסטרה is a Latin loanword denoting a fortress.[81] The word appears twice in TC, as an equivalent of חָצֵר:

1 Chr 4:32–33

MT   וְחַצְרֵיהֶם֙   עֵיטָ֣ם וָעַ֔יִן ...33 וְכָל־חַצְרֵיהֶ֗ם   אֲשֶׁ֧ר סְבִיב֛וֹת הֶעָרִ֥ים הָאֵ֖לֶּה עַד־בָּ֑עַל

TC   וקסטרוותהון עיטם ועין... וכל קסטרוותהון די בחוזרניהון קרויא האלין עד בעל

NJPS: together with their villages, Etam, Ain ... along with all their villages that were around these towns as far as Baal

Dost: Their camps: Etam, Ain ... and all their camps, which are in the environs (of) these cities as far as Baal

The Hebrew word חָצֵר has two principal meanings: 1) an uncovered space enclosed by a building;[82] 2) a village or settlement not enclosed by a wall.[83] The word חָצֵר in the present verse should be understood in the latter sense, i.e., that of small villages associated with an urban hub.[84] This sense of חָצֵר is variously

---

81   Sokoloff *JPA*, p. 570.

82   BDB, pp. 346–347; Kaddari, pp. 338–339.

83   BDB, p. 347; Kaddari, p. 339. The word also serves as nomen regens within toponyms, e.g., חצר עינן, חצר שועל.

84   Cf., e.g., Knoppers, p. 359; Klein *1 Chronicles*, p. 143, who translate חָצֵר as *village*.

translated in the various Aramaic Targums. TO uses פצח, as does TJ; TN and FT, as TPJ, use כופרן.[85] Aside from the two appearances in 1 Chronicles 4 discussed here (rendered in Peshiṭta as ܚܰܩ̈ܠܳܐ), the word חָצֵר appears with this sense four additional times in Chronicles: 1 Chr 6:41, where it is translated פצח, as is the practice of TO and TJ;[86] 1 Chr 9:16, 22, 25, where it is translated as קריה. Translation of the Hebrew word חָצֵר as קסטרה is surprising, and unparalleled in targumic literature. Thus TC to 1 Chr 4:32–33, which uses קסטרה for חָצֵר, appears both to fail to give the sense of the Hebrew חָצֵר and to establish an equivalence that is indicated nowhere else even within TC itself. How, then, is this phenomenon to be explained? Before we offer an answer to this question, let us consider an additional surprise contained in TC.

The word טִירָה appears once in MT Chr:

1 Chr 6:39

MT וְאֵלֶּה מוֹשְׁבוֹתָם לְטִירוֹתָם בִּגְבוּלָם לִבְנֵי אַהֲרֹן לְמִשְׁפַּחַת הַקְּהָתִי
TC ואליין מותבניהון לכופרניהון בתחומיהון לבני אהר׳ לגניסת קהת

NJPS: These are their dwelling-places according to their settlements within their borders: to the sons of Aaron of the families of Kohathites
Dost: These are the dwelling places of their villages within their borders. To the sons of Aaron of the lineage of Kohath

The author of TC rendered טִירָה as כופרן, and here, too, the equivalent given is unparalleled anywhere else in targumic literature. Further, the word כופרן appears another seventeen times in TC, but in all other cases its usage follows that of TO and TJ, denoting suburbs of an urban hub; taking the place of the word חַוָּה; or, on one occasion, substituting for the Hebrew word כְּפָר. Thus the targumist's choice in translating חָצֵר in 1 Chr 4:32–33 leaves us surprised much as does his choice of the word טִירָה in 1 Chr 6:39.

The key to solving this double riddle appears to lie in Gen 25:16:

---

85   Cf. TO, TN, FT, and TPJ Gen 25:16; Lev 25:31 (FT is unavailable for the latter). It should be noted that TO uses the word כפרן in a similar sense, though not as an equivalent of חָצֵר, but for the suburbs of an urban hub (TO Num 21:25, 32; 32:42) or for חַוָּה (Num 32:41; Deut 3:14). TJ follows in the footsteps of TO: the former contains verses in which both כפרן and פצח appear, corresponding respectively to בנות and חָצֵר (see Josh 15:45, 47).

86   The verse parallels Josh 21:12, where TJ renders פצח, as expected.

Gen 25:16

MT	וּבְטִירֹתָם	בְּחַצְרֵיהֶם	שְׁמֹתָם	וְאֵלֶּה	יִשְׁמָעֵאל֙	בְנֵי	אֵלֶּה
TO	ובכרכיהון	בפצחיהון	שמהתהון	ואלין	ישמעאל	בני	אלין
TN	ובטירתהון	בכופרניהון	שמהתהון	ואלין	דישמעאל	בנוי	אלין
FT	[ובקסטרוותהון]	בכופרניהון	שמהתהון	ואלין	דישמעאל	בנוי	אילין
TNM	ובקסטרוותהון
TPJ	ובקסטרוותהון	בכופרניהון	שומהון	ואילין	דישמעאל	בנוי	אילין

NJPS: These are the sons of Ishmael and these are their names by their villages and by their encampments

Clem TPJ: These are the sons of Ishmael, and these are their names, by their villages and their fortresses

The Hebrew word טִירָה is translated by TO as כרך, i.e., a walled city, and as קסטרה by FT, TNM, and TPJ. The verse also contains the word חָצֵר, which is translated in TO and TJ as כופרן and פצח, respectively, as is characteristic for these two Targums (in this respect TPJ also resembles Peshiṭta the verses in Chronicles).

In this verse we find both the Hebrew word pair טִירָה/חָצֵר and (in TPJ) the Aramaic word pair קסטרה/כופרן—but in TC the relationship between the two pairs is the mirror image of that in TPJ. We can resolve the two quandaries we have encountered by hypothesizing that the author of TC used TPJ or a similar Targum to Gen 25:16 as the source for his translations of חָצֵר and טִירָה in 1 Ch 4:32–33 and 1 Chr 6:39 but the words כופרן and קסטרה were inverted. This inversion may already have been presented in the source used by the author of TC. This is to say, the two words may have been inverted in the targumic tradition to which he was a party. Alternately, it may be that the author of TC himself inverted קסטרה and כופרן as a result of injudicious reference to his source document. Also possible is that the example discussed here reflects TC's lack of real-world familiarity with these Aramaic words. Even if this phenomenon in fact resulted from a mere slip of his pen, this example is particularly enlightening for the author of TC cannot have produced such an error independently. The inversion can have come about only by virtue of reliance on a previously existing literary source.

6.3   טור מסרי פירוי (1 Chr 5:23)

Literally, the phrase טור מסרי פירוי denotes a mountain [that] causes its fruits to stink. The term is used in TC for שְׂנִיר, adjacent in its context to חֶרְמוֹן:

1 Chr 5:23

MT	וְהַר־חֶרְמוֹן	עַד־בַּעַל חֶרְמוֹן וּשְׂנִיר		מִבָּשָׁן
TC	מן בותנן עד מישר חרמון וטור מסרי פירו וטור חרמון			

NJPS: from Bashan to Baal-hermon, Senir, and Mount Hermon

Dost: [from] Buthnan unto the plain of Hermon, the mountain of insipid fruit, and Mt. Hermon

Jastrow suggested emending the term to משיר פרוי, *that drops its fruits*, from the root נש״ר,[87] but I find such a correction implausible, mainly due to the appearance of the phrase טור (ד)מסרי פירוי elsewhere in targumic literature. It occurs in several of the Targums of the Torah as well as once in *Tg. Ps*, as follows:

Deut 3:9

MT	שְׂרְיֹן	לְחֶרְמוֹן	יִקְרְאוּ	צִידֹנִים
TO	סריון	לחרמון	קרן	צידונאי
TN	טורא דמסרי פירוי	לטור תלגה	הוון קריין	צידוניי
FTV	ארע מסרי פירוהי	לחרמון	קרן	[צידונאי
GT	[....] טברא דסגי	לחרמון		
TNM	סיריון			צייידנאי
TPJ	טוורא דמסרי פירוי	לחרמון	הוון קרן	צידנאי

NJPS: Sidonians called Hermon Sirion

Clem TPJ: The Sidonians used to call Hermon "the mountain whose fruit stinks,"

Deut 3:9 (cont.)

MT	שְׂנִיר	יִקְרְאוּ־לוֹ	וְהָאֱמֹרִי
TO	טור תלגא:	קרן ליה	ואמוראי
TN	שניר:	הוון קריין יתיה	ואמוריי
FTV	ארעא מרבי פירי אילנא]	קרן ליה	ואימוראי
TNM	ה'		ואימוראיה
TPJ	טוור תלגא	קרן ליה	ואימוראי

דלא פסיק מיניה תלגא לא בקייטא ולא בסתווא:

NJPS: and the Amorites call it Senir

Clem TPJ: and the Amorites call it Mt. Snow, because snow never ceases from it, neither in summer nor in winter

---

87   Jastrow, p. 1026. He bases his argument on a marginal reading in Rahmer's edition, p. 14: פרזי. The reading מישר פרזי apparently was that in MS E, judging by its appearance in de Lagarde and Sperber's editions, but the reading in MS V is preferable in light of the Palestinian Pentateuchal Targums' rendering of Deut 3:9 and *Tg. Ps* 29:6.

Deut 4:48

MT	וְעַד־הַר	שִׂיאֹן	הוּא	חֶרְמוֹן׃
TO	ועד טורא	דסאון	הוא	חרמון׃
TN	ועד טורה	דסיאון	הוא	טור תלגה׃
FTV	עד טורא	דמסרי פירוי	הוא	טור תלגא׃
TNM		דמסרי פירוי	[הוא]	טור [תלגא]
TPJ	ועד טוורא	דסיאון	הוא	טוור תלגא׃

NJPS: as far as Mount Sion, that is, Hermon

Clem FTV: as far as the mountain that makes its fruit stink, which is Mount Snow

Ps 29:6

MT	וַיַּרְקִידֵם כְּמוֹ־עֵגֶל לְבָנוֹן וְשִׂרְיֹן	כְּמוֹ בֶן־רְאֵמִים׃
TP	ושוורינון היך עגלא לבנן וטור מסרי פרוי	היך בר רמיא׃

NJPS: He makes Lebanon skip like a calf, Sirion, like a young wild ox.

Cook: And he made them jump like a calf—Lebanon, and the Mount of Noisome Fruit, like the young of oxen.

Why is שְׂנִיר thus translated in TC? Le Déaut and Robert suggested that the targumist had assigned שְׂנִיר the translation given שִׂרְיֹן in the Palestinian Targums, as they put it.[88] If we take a closer look, we find that the phrase טור מסרי פירוי appears in TN and TPJ Deut 3:9 as an equivalent of the toponym שִׂרְיֹן, as is the case in *Tg. Ps* 29:6.[89] In FT and TNM Deut 4:48 it corresponds to the name שִׂיאֹן, while TPJ and TN transcribe סיאון.[90] Thus if the Targums of the Torah influenced TC, the logical point of departure to search for TC's source would be TN or TPJ. It may be, as suggested by Le Déaut and Robert, that the author of TC searched for the translation of שְׂנִיר given by one of these Targums in its

---

88   Le Déaut-Robert, vol. 1, p. 54, n. 17, followed by McIvor, p. 67, n. 37.

89   No phrase consisting of סר״י and פרי appears elsewhere in targumic literature (שְׂנִיר is translated in *Tg. Cant* 4:8 as טור תלגא, as in TO).

    See further *Yalquṭ Šimʿoni*, Deut 810 (p. 46): "'The Sidonians call Hermon Sirion'—because its fruits drop off (שפירותיו משירין); 'Senir'—because it detests plowing; 'Hermon'—because it belongs to desolation. Alternately, 'Hermon'—because it sits as a pomegranate."

90   The reading in FT and TNM seems to treat שִׂיאֹן as שִׂרְיֹן; Peshitta, too, has ܣܪܝܘܢ (LXX transcribes Σηων). Why do some Targums treat שִׂיאֹן as שִׂרְיֹן? It may be that the Hebrew *Vorlage* consulted by these targumists read שִׂרְיֹן, a result of the graphic similarity of the two forms. Also possible is that the targumists purposely rendered the hapax legomenon שִׂיאֹן in the same manner as the more common שִׂרְיֹן.

treatment of Deut 3:9 and mistakenly substituted that of שִׂרְיֹן.[91] If indeed this is what happened, in my view, the more likely source for the translation found in TC is TPJ, because its translations for both שִׂרְיֹן and שְׂנִיר begin with the word טור, while in TN the word טור appears not once in the vicinity of a translation of the word שְׂנִיר. The common word טור in TPJ very well may have been the cause of confusion between the translation of שְׂנִיר and that of שִׂרְיֹן. The present example is rather reminiscent of the confusion that we earlier argued is evidenced by TC 4:32–33 between the words חָצֵר and טִירָה in TPJ Gen 25:16 (see preceding discussion of the word קסטרה, pp. 165–167).

6.4   מנטר (1 Chr 15:27)

The word מנטר appears only once in TC—as the equivalent of Hebrew מְעִיל. Although 1 Chr 15:27 finds its parallel in 2 Sam 6:14, the textual variants between these two verses are of such nature that the meaning of the first half of the verse is different in both books.

1 Chr 15:27	:בָּד אֵפֹוד		דָּוִיד וְעַל־	...	בּוּץ בִּמְעִיל	מְכָרְבָּל	וְדָוִיד
TC	:דבוץ כרדוט		דוד ועל	...	דבוין במנטר מתעטף	הוה	ודוד
2 Sam 6:14	:בָּד אֵפֹוד חָגוּר	וְדָוִד	ה' לִפְנֵי	עֹז	בְּכָל־ מְכַרְכֵּר		וְדָוִד
TJ	:דבוץ כרדוט אסיר ודויד		ה' קדם תקוף	בכל משבח			ודויד

NJPS Chr: Now David ... [was] wrapped in robes of fine linen, and David wore a linen ephod.

Dost: Now David was covered with a tunic of fine-linen ... and upon David was a linen tunic.

NJPS Sam: David whirled with all his might before the LORD; David was girt with a linen ephod.

Clem: Then David was praising with all his might before the Lord, and David was girded with a linen tunic.

Since מְעִיל does not appear in the parallel verse in Samuel, it leads TC to render it independently, i.e. without relying on the corresponding verse in TJ. That in itself is of no surprise, but the Aramaic equivalent of מְעִיל provided by TC— מנטר—most certainly is. Hebrew מְעִיל is almost always rendered מעיל also in Aramaic. This is true for TJ on Samuel too, which the author of TC was entirely familiar with. In fact, the translation of אֵפֹוד בָּד as כרדוט דבוץ (and not as איפודא

---

91   Le Déaut-Robert, vol. 1, p. 54, n. 17. The two Hebrew words consist of similar groups of letters, and this similarity may have contributed to a transposition at the hands of TC. See below, however, for another potential reason for the mutual interchange of the two words' translations.

דבוץ, which would have been expected in light of the Pentateuchal Targums treatment of Hebrew אֵפוֹד) is based on the end of the parallel verse in TJ. It is therefore striking that TC chose מנטר for Hebrew מְעִיל. He did not do so based on TJ, nor on TO and TN in all ten appearances of מְעִיל in the Torah. In fact there is only one Aramaic text I am aware of outside TC in which the word מנטר is found and that text is TPJ. Apart from its first appearance (Ex 28:4, where TPJ uses מעיל like the other Targums), מְעִיל is rendered in TPJ by the double translation: מנטר מעיל. For example, see Exod 28:31 and its Targums:

MT	תְּכֵלֶת:	כְּלִיל	הָאֵפוֹד	אֶת־ מְעִיל	וְעָשִׂיתָ
TO	תכלא:	גמיר	איפודא	מעיל	ית	ותעביד
TN	דתכלה:	גמיר	דאפודה	מעילה	ית	ותעבד
TPJ	מנטר מעילא דאיפודא שזיר חוטא דתיכלא:	ית	ותעבד

NJPS Exod: You shall make the robe of the ephod of pure blue.
Clem TO: And you shall make the robe of the ephod completely of blue purple.
Clem TN: And you shall make the robe of the ephod completely of blue purple.
Clem TPJ: And you shall make the tunic of the robe of the ephod of twisted thread of blue purple.

Why TPJ employs two words for מְעִיל (here, and in the eight subsequent appearances in the Torah) is unclear to me. The decisive point, though, is that מנטר is presently not found in any earlier Aramaic text. Levy ties the word to German *Mantel* (which itself is related to Latin *mantellum*).[92] For TC to use such an idiosyncratic translation for מְעִיל suggests that he borrowed it directly from TPJ—the only known source for this word.

6.5   פרגודא (*2 Chr 3:14; 5:9*)

The word פרגודא serves as the translation of the single appearance of the word פָּרֹכֶת in Chronicles, and appears once more in TC in an aggadic expansion.[93] Let us consider the first of these verses:

---

92   Levy, vol. 2, p. 47. He entertains the notion of German Mantel being "viell. von unsern W. enstanden".

93

2 Chr 5:9   עַל־ מִן־הָאָרוֹן רָאשֵׁי הַבַּדִּים וַיֵּרָאוּ   הַחוּצָה וְלֹא יֵרָאוּ   פְּנֵי הַדְּבִיר

TC   ומתחזן רישי נגריא הי כתרתין תדיין על על (sic in V) אפי בית כפורי ולא מתחזן לברא מן פרגודא

2 Chr 3:14

MT   וַיַּעַשׂ אֶת־הַפָּרֹכֶת תְּכֵלֶת וְאַרְגָּמָן

TC   ועבד ית פרגודא תכלא וארגונא

NJPS: He made the curtain of blue, purple

Dost: He made the curtain of blue-purple, red-purple

Now let us compare this verse to a similar verse in the Torah:

Exod 36:35

MT   וְאַרְגָּמָן תְּכֵלֶת וַיַּעַשׂ אֶת־הַפָּרֹכֶת

TO   וארגונא דתכלא פרוכתא ית ועבד

TN   וארגוון תכלה פרוכתה ית ועבד

TPJ   וארגוונא דתיכלא פרגודא ית ועבד

NJPS: They made the curtain of blue, purple

Clem TPJ: And he made the veil of blue-purple, and red-purple

In their treatment of the verse, TO and TN alike choose to employ the Aramaic
form פרוכת, which is akin to the Hebrew. They maintain this practice across all
appearances of the Hebrew word פָּרֹכֶת.[94] TN, FT, and GT are aware of the word
פרגוד, but choose to use it only with regard to Joseph's tunic.[95] Though TPJ, too,
translates Joseph's tunic as פרגוד, it is the sole Pentateuchal Targum known
to us that also uses the word פרגוד for פָּרֹכֶת, which it does on 23 occasions.[96]

---

94   TPJ as we know it follows this practice in one instance, Exod 40:3, joining TO and TN in
     translating פרוכתא.

95   A midrashic methodology for these word choices is put forward in Gen. Rab. 84 (p. 1019):
     "'They stripped Joseph'—referring to his cloak; 'of his tunic'—referring to his shirt; 'the
     woolen tunic'—referring to his surcoat (הפרגוד)."

96   TPJ also once uses the talmudic expression שמעית מבתר פרגודא (Gen 37:17), i.e., "I heard
     from behind the curtain." Following is a list of all locations in TPJ where פרגוד occurs as
     a translation of פָּרֹכֶת: Exod 26:31, 33 (פָּרֹכֶת appears thrice in this verse, for the second
     occurrence of which TPJ MS Add. 27031 has ברוגדא, but this word apparently originated
     from פרגודא, as noted by Clarke in his concordance, p. 485), 35; 27:21; 30:6; 35:12; 36:35;
     38:27; 39:34; 40:21, 22, 26; Lev 4:6, 17; 16:2, 12, 15; 21:23; 24:3; Num 4:5; 18:7.
     The word appears once in Tg. Job, in a short textual expansion:

Job 26:9   מְאַחֵז פְּנֵי־ כִסֵּה פַּרְשֵׁז עָלָיו עֲנָנוֹ: עָלָיו

Tg. Job   ואחד באמיטתא דמן כורסיא מן בגלל דלא יחמוניה מלאכיא פריס היך פרגודא עלוהי ענני יקריה:

     NJPS: He shuts off the view of His throne, spreading His cloud over it.

     Clem: (who) grasps the dark cloud that is about the throne so that the angels do not see
     Him, spreads the clouds of His glory over it as a curtain.

     This occurrence may have a meaning similar to that of Hebrew פָּרֹכֶת, but the word פָּרֹכֶת
     does not appear in the verse, and this occurrence ought not be viewed as TC's source.

פרגוד, in the sense of a tunic, is to be viewed as a Greek loanword, defined as *a garment with an embroidered hem*.[97] In addition to this derivation, the word פרגוד, in the sense of a screen, may have arrived from the Persian.[98] In any event, it stands to reason that the decision by the author of TC to use פרגוד as the equivalent of פָּרֹכֶת was based on TPJ.

6.6   טוור פולחנא (*1 Chr 21:15*)

The phrase טוור פולחנא, which serves as an honorific term for Mount Moriah in Jerusalem, appears only once in TC, in an aggadic expansion:

TC 1 Chr 21:15 ...ואדכר קיימיה דעם אברהם דקיים ליה בטוור פולחנא...
Dost: and He remembered His covenant that was with Abraham, which was established with him on the mountain of worship

The expression טוור פולחנא is not common in the sources, and the use of this particular rare expression in TC associates that Targum exclusively with TPJ, because this is the only other work of all targumic literature in which we find the term used, in the following four verses:

TPJ Gen 2:15 ודבר ה' אלקים ית אדם מן טוור פולחנא אתר דאיתבריא מתמן
Clem: And the Lord God took Adam from the mountain of worship, the place where he had been created

TPJ Gen 23:2 ואתא אברהם מן טוור פולחנא ואשכחה דמיתת ויתיב למיספד לשרה ולמבכייה

Clem: and Abraham came from the mountain of worship and found her that she had died, so he sat to mourn for Sarah and to weep for her

TPJ Gen 25:21 ואזל יצחק לטוור פולחנא אתר דכפתיה אבוי
Clem: Then Isaac went to the mountain of worship, the place where his father had bound him

TPJ Lev 9:2 דכר לעלתא תיסב מן בגלל די ידכר לך זכותא דיצחק דכפתיה אבוי כדיכרא בטוור פולחנא
Clem: take also a ram for a burnt offering so that he might remember in your favor the merit of Isaac, whose father tied him like a ram on the mountain of worship

---

97   Krauss *Lehnwörter*, p. 477; Sokoloff *JPA*, p. 502.
98   Kohut *Tosaphot*, entry "גוד," p. 126.

It would seem that the origin of this term is TO Gen 22:2, which renders אֶל־אֶרֶץ הַמֹּרִיָּה as לארע פלחנא. TPJ ad loc. also rendered לארע פולחנא, following the received tradition of TO.[99] From here onward, TPJ viewed the word פולחנא as an equivalent of מוריה, and טוור פולחנא thus emerged as a term for Mount Moriah.

None of the verses of TPJ cited above associates טוור פולחנא with God's promise to Abraham,[100] so that the formulation in TC is not a direct quote from any of them. However, it is reasonable to believe that TC's decision to refer to Mount Moriah as טוור פולחנא came about under the influence of the targumist's familiarity with the expression as it appears in the only other source known to us that uses it: TPJ.

6.7   צבחר *as equivalent of* מִצְעָר (*2 Chr 24:24*)

2 Chr 24:24

MT   כִּי בְמִצְעַר אֲנָשִׁים בָּאוּ ׀ חֵיל אֲרָם וַה' נָתַן בְּיָדָם חַיִל לָרֹב מְאֹד
TC   ארום בצבחר גוברין אתו חילוות ארמאי וה' מסר ביידיהון חילא לסוגי לחדא
NJPS: The invading army of Aram had come with but a few men, but the LORD delivered a very large army into their hands
Dost: For with a few men the armies of the Arameans came, but the Lord delivered up a very great army into their hands

In translating the verse before us, the author of TC uses צבחר for the Hebrew word מִצְעָר, a hapax legomenon in Chronicles as well as a rare word in Scripture generally.[101] צבחר, or ציבחד, with a *dalet*, has the sense of *a small quantity* or *a small piece*.[102] The word appears five times in TJ in the context of the phrase ציב כזעיר חד, which serves to translate the Hebrew phrase מְעַט מִזְעָר (Isa 10:25; 16:14; 29:17) or the word מְעָט alone (Jer 51:33; Hos 1:4), as well as once in TJ where it appears within an exegetical expansion (Isa 5:18). *Tg. Job* uses צבחד once, for זְעֵיר (Job 36:2); *Tg. Ruth* once translates מְעָט as ציבחר (Ruth 2:7); and *Tg. Cant*

---

99   Cf. TC 2 Chr 3:1.

100   On the connection between the Abrahamic promise and Mount Moriah, see pp. 318–323, below.

101   Aside from its sole appearance in Chronicles, the word מִצְעָר appear in four other verses in Scripture: Gen 19:20 (twice, as discussed below); Isa 63:18; Ps 42:7; Job 8:7. In TO, TJ, *Tg. Ps*, and *Tg. Job*, the word is translated as זְעֵיר(א). TN, which translates the second occurrence of the word in the verse as זעירא, as in TO, uses קריבא for the first; even this deviation is "corrected" to זעירא in the MS's marginalia.

102   The word form spelled with a *reish* is a corruption with its source in the *dalet* form, which itself is a compound composed of two words: ציבחד > ציב חד; Sokoloff *JPA*, p. 526.

translates the Hebrew word כִּמְעַט with the phrase כזעיר ציב חד (Cant 3:4). With reference to TPJ, below, it becomes clear that TC is not the only Targum that uses ציבחר for תמורת:

Gen 19:20

MT	הָעִיר הַזֹּאת קְרֹבָה	לָנוּס שָׁמָּה וְהִוא מִצְעָר... הֲלֹא מִצְעָר הִוא
TO	קרתא הדא קריבא	למיעירק לתמן והיא זעירא... הלא זעירא היא
TN	קרתא הדה קריבה	למערק לתמן והיא קריבה... הלא זעירא היא
TPJ	קרתא הדא קריבא מותבהא וחמי למיעירוק לתמן והיא ציבחר... הלא ציבחר היא

NJPS: that town there is near enough to flee to; it is such a little place! ... it is such a little place
Clem TPJ: this city whose dwellings are near is suitable to flee there, and it is small ... Indeed, it is small

The fact that the word ציבחר appears as an equivalent of the Hebrew מִצְעָר only in TPJ and TC, coupled with the word's rarity in targumic literature in general, constitutes a significant point of contact between the two Targums and weighs in favor of identifying a relationship between them.[103] Possibly, on encountering the rare word מִצְעָר, the author of TC sought to find its translation in a familiar Aramaic translation of the only verse in the Torah that contains this word.[104]

7   Aramaic Piyyutim in the Liturgical Custom of Medieval Ashkenaz

In the context of the linguistic mosaic that has emerged from our comparison of TC and TPJ, I wish to make note of a very interesting collection of Aramaic poems that are found in the liturgy of Pesach (Passover) and Shavu'ot (Weeks, Pentecost) in medieval Ashkenaz. These Piyyutim introduce and accompany the Hebrew reading and Aramaic translation of the Torah and Haftarah (lection from the Prophets) on Pesach and Shavu'ot. Supplementing the Torah readings on these holidays with Targum was, apparently, the last remnant of

---

103   It may be that the corrupted form with a *reish* instead of a *dalet*—found, among those transmissions available to us, only in TPJ, *Tg. Ruth*, and TC—also constitutes a link between the two Targums. This similarity, however, is not a particularly weighty one, because such a substitution may be the product of nothing more than a shared common scribal error.

104   It should also be noted that both Targums employ the corrupt form of the word (that with a *reish*).

Targum being read in public regularly in Ashkenazi practice.[105] The addition
of Aramaic Piyyutim to the Targum added a degree of significance to these
readings. In current practice all that remains of this age-old collection in wide-
spread Ashkenazi custom is the recitation of the poem אקדמות מלין before the
reading of the Ten Commandments on Shavuʿot and to a lesser degree the insertion of יציב פתגם after the first verse of Haftarah on the additional Shavuʿot
day in the diaspora. But in Machzor manuscripts of medieval Europe a great
abundance of Aramaic Piyyutim appear in accompaniment to the scriptural
readings of these two festivals. This is true for the Jewish-Ashkenaz communities in Italy, Germany and northern France. These poems were discussed by
Zunz, Fleischer, Heinemann and Fraenkel, but I think their relevance to the
field of Targum studies has not yet been fully appreciated.[106]

That the Targum legacy of Ashkenazi Europe made use not just of Onqelos
and the Babylonian Talmud but also of much Palestinian material is indicative of the sources of influence on this part of the Jewish diaspora. How much
more so when considering that this legacy also included Aramaic poetry—
some of which was composed in Europe of the second millennium. The linguistic makeup of this Aramaic collection is comprised of words from both
great centers of Jewish scholarship. It is this striking phenomenon that I wish
to highlight here.

Aramaic was obviously not the spoken language of the Jews of Ashkenazi
Europe, but it was important enough to be used in the public readings of
Pesach and Shavuʿot. The Aramaic of these communities, therefore, could not
be expected to reflect a living language, but rather the literary legacy of the
Jewish texts that they were the beneficiaries thereof. The poems were not writ-
ten originally as a collection. They are disparate in all aspects of origin (time,

---

105   There are two instances of Targum preserved to this day in Jewish daily prayer service—
       including that of Ashkenaz custom. Exodus 15:18 is translated with Targum Onqelos at the
       end of the daily recitation of the Song of the Sea, and verses of קדושה דסידרא (Isa 6:3;
       Ezek 3:12 and Exod 15:18) are accompanied by Targums Jonathan and Onqelos, respec-
       tively. These, however, are not recited by a designated Meturgeman, nor is the Hebrew
       text read from a scroll publicly. In some Sephardi communities Targum Onqelos is recited
       when reading the first part of Gen 24 for a ceremonial lection in honor of a bridegroom
       on the Sabbath following his wedding. In Jewish-Yemenite practice public readings of
       Scripture are still accompanied by a Meturgeman who reads Onqelos (and Jonathan on
       the Prophets) on Sabbaths and festivals to this day.

106   A collection of these Piyyutim with introduction, previous studies, translation to Hebrew
       and textual apparatus may be found in Fraenkel Shavuʿot, pp. כח-לה, 402–564, 573–593;
       Fraenkel Pesach, pp. כ-כא, 608–611, 616–658. Five of the Piyyutim (חנניה, ארבין ה׳ שמיא
       יוסף תקיף, איתגבר בחיליה, אמר יצחק, מישאל ועזריה) are included in Sokoloff-Yahalom.
       See also Kaufman-Maori for the use of this material in the reconstruction of the
       Palestinian Targum to the Ten Commandments. More secondary literature can be found
       in all the above.

location, author). However, generally speaking, when reading these poems it is clear that the texts whose language left the greatest mark upon them were the chapters of Biblical Aramaic (Daniel in particular), the Babylonian Talmud and Targums Onqelos and Jonathan.

It is, therefore, of significance that, even so, the linguistic character of the Aramaic texts of Ashkenaz were not only Babylonian in nature, but they contained many elements of the western dialect, found in Palestinian Targum, Midrash and Talmud. The Aramaic Piyyutim read in these communities—some of which were composed in second millennium Europe—contained western words, or other words that were used frequently in LJLA, of the like discussed in this chapter, shared by TPJ and TC. Among words found in this collection are: שבהורא, פסג, פירוג, מטול, טלק, טימי, חמי, אוף, היך, ארום, אמטול.[107] There is frequent use of the verb צוח.[108] Also found are an abundance of loanwords from Greek or Latin: טימיקא, הוגניסי, דליס, דינמיס, דימוט, דיוקן, גנימוס, אפילגוס, איקון, אינדרטי, תיאורון, קיריס, קייסטרא, קוזמוז, פרנין, פרוז דוגמא, פטרון, ננס, כיריס.[109] The Piyyutim

---

107   אמטול: Fraenkel *Shavu'ot*, p. 419, 557; ארום: Fraenkel *Shavu'ot*, p. 459, 466, 470, 483, 503, 522, 541, 561; היך: Fraenkel *Pesach*, p. 657; Fraenkel *Shavu'ot*, p. 421, 436, 467, 469, 485, 571; אוף: Fraenkel *Shavu'ot*, p. 388; חמי: Fraenkel *Pesach*, p. 608, 647, 651, 656; Fraenkel *Shavu'ot*, p. 393, 398, 399, 433, 436, 443, 448–453, 469, 472, 482, 483, 490, 503, 522, 524, 525, 528–530, 541, 550, 559, 560, 583, 590; טימי: Fraenkel *Pesach*, p. 609; Fraenkel *Shavu'ot*, p. 482, 500, 510, 575; טלק: Fraenkel *Shavu'ot*, p. 426; מטול: Fraenkel *Pesach*, p. 608, 609, 628, 654; פירוג: Fraenkel *Shavu'ot*, p. 419; פסג: Fraenkel *Shavu'ot*, p. 503; שבהורא: Fraenkel *Shavu'ot*, p. 559.

108   Fraenkel *Shavu'ot*, p. 399, 416, 421, 423, 430, 440, 452, 459, 471, 472, 474.

109   This and adjacent lists are not intended to be comprehensive. They serve as illustrations of the linguistic makeup found in the various Aramaic Piyyutim in the Machzor manuscripts of Ashkenaz.

    אינדרטי: Fraenkel *Shavu'ot*, p. 424, 427.

    איקון: Fraenkel *Shavu'ot*, p. 398.

    אפילגוס: Fraenkel *Shavu'ot*, p. 399.

    גנימוס: Fraenkel *Shavu'ot*, p. 484.

    דיוקן: Fraenkel *Shavu'ot*, p. 435.

    דימוט: Fraenkel *Shavu'ot*, p. 458.

    דינמיס: Fraenkel *Shavu'ot*, p. 424.

    דליס: Fraenkel *Shavu'ot*, p. 484.

    הוגניסי: Fraenkel *Shavu'ot*, p. 433.

    טימיקא: Fraenkel *Shavu'ot*, p. 496.

    כיריס: Fraenkel *Shavu'ot*, p. 427.

    ננס: Fraenkel *Shavu'ot*, p. 422, 426, 433, 446.

    פטרון: Fraenkel *Shavu'ot*, p. 423, 425.

    פרוז דוגמא: Fraenkel *Shavu'ot*, p. 430 (see Fraenkel's comment on the word, ad loc.).

    פרנין: Fraenkel *Pesach*, p. 609.

    קוזמוז: Fraenkel *Shavu'ot*, p. 468.

    קייסטרא: Fraenkel *Pesach*, p. 625.

    קיריס: Fraenkel *Shavu'ot*, p. 399, 407, 423, 426, 446, 468, 525.

    תיאורון: Fraenkel *Shavu'ot*, p. 424, 426.

also display an uneven use of the 3rd masculine singular pronominal suffix following a *waw*. In many places one finds ‑והי, but ‑וי is very common as well.[110] Babylonian קמי is used often, but so is the western קומי.[111] What appears to be a direct influence from TPJ is the expression שזיר ותכלא.[112] Usage of the verb כאר (by-form of כער) is found in two poems.[113] As mentioned above, the Piyyutim in this collection are by no means uniform in dialect and style, but the resultant picture of the collection as a whole—some of which was composed in second-millennium medieval Europe—is that the Jews of Ashkenaz were the recipients of—and at times the authors of—an Aramaic that resembles in many ways the Aramaic of TPJ and TC. Its continued use in Jewish liturgical life in Europe is an example of Aramaic literature being used and, moreover, being composed by Jewish communities that no longer spoke the language, but preserved it as a scholarly language for religious purposes. This may prove to be of great importance for understanding the origin of Targum Chronicles.

8   Conclusions

The data that arise from our discussion allow us to answer affirmatively the question of the existence of a close relationship between TC and TPJ. Throughout the book—not only in the three units paralleling the Torah in 1 Chronicles 1—there are indications linking the two Targums. Both are characterized by a linguistic blend combining a Western linguistic framework with numerous Eastern elements arrayed within it. This blend is comprised of a long list of words from both sides of the Aramaic map that are common to the two Targums as well as unexpected dialectal features, such as the unusual consonantal shifts in the stems דר״ק, נת״ב, and יע״ט found in both, and the use of the apparently artificial root אט״ל. All of the above demonstrate an affinity between the two compositions, which is explicable by the fact that they were written in similar Aramaic idioms—specifically, idioms belonging to Late Jewish Literary Aramaic, as described by Kaufman.

---

110   Occurrences of ‑וי: Fraenkel *Pesach*, בנוי p. 608; קמוי p. 624; מעוי p. 626; קדמוי p. 642; Fraenkel *Shavu'ot*, בלחמוי p. 405; לבנוי p. 420 (despite Fraenkel's comment ad loc.); גוזלוי p. 426, 446; קדמוי p. 426, 451; נצחנוי p. 433; ברכוי p. 437; ורגלוי p. 437; וידוי p. 437; ידויי p. 437; ידוי p. 470; אבוי ואמוי p. 469; רחמוי p. 456, 532; עינוי p. 437; לויי p. 437; עובדווי p. 437; סודוי p. 437; נכסוי p. 555; אפוי p. 555–556; עובדוי p. 559. מילוי p. 486; p. 480;

111   Occurrences of קומי: Fraenkel *Pesach*, p. 609; Fraenkel *Shavu'ot*, p. 430, 506, 520. The form appears six times in TC (1 Chr 28:9; 29:25; 2 Chr 9:7; 20:21; 34:4, 30) and twenty-two times in TPJ (Gen 1:26; 3:22; 11:7; 15:1, 10; 17:18; 18:2–3, 21; 19:8; 24:12, 33, 40, 51; 27:29, 37; 28:10; 32:4; Num 21:28; Deut 7:24; 30:19).

112   Fraenkel *Shavu'ot*, p. 410; cf. TPJ Exod 28:28.

113   Fraenkel *Shavu'ot*, p. 444; p. 537. Cf. the discussion of this verb in TC, below, pp. 358–360

This general conclusion, viz., that both Targums were written in the same dialect of Aramaic, is indeed correct. This, however, is not the extent of the conclusion to be made with regard to the relation between TC and TPJ. Rather, an abundance of evidence has demonstrated that the relation between TC and TPJ is one of literary dependence—i.e. that TC relies directly on TPJ. This is clear from the few units in Chronicles that are parallel to the Torah as seen above, in Chapter 4, pp. 142–174. Of greater significance, however, is that it is clear from the findings presented that TC relies on TPJ not only in units paralleled in the Torah, but throughout the entire Book of Chronicles. The argument that tips the balance in favor of TPJ as a source upon which TC relied throughout is that arising from instances of what appears to be direct literary dependence by TC specifically on TPJ in usage of the expressions קסטרה, טוור פולחנא, פרגודא, מנטר, טור מסרי פירוי, כופרן, and צבחר. Included in this group are translations by TC that appear to result from errors dependent on TPJ.

This is not to suggest that TPJ was the only Targum of the Torah that was known to the author of TC. We have already seen in our discussion of the three parallel units in the Torah and 1 Chronicles 1 that the author of TC by all appearances was familiar with other targumic traditions concerning the Table of Nations. It is thus fair to say that he was privy to more than one Pentateuchal targumic tradition. This being said, the data surveyed here, regarding both the parallel units and the remainder of the book, paint a clear picture: TC was written wholly in the shadow of the Targum that would in the distant future be dubbed TPJ. The author of TC composed his Targum in language highly similar to that of TPJ, wrote in a similar style, and—most telling of all—used TPJ as a source for lexical equivalents in many instances. Surprisingly, although the quantity of words and verses in TC that are taken from TJ is far greater than the quantity of those taken directly from TPJ (due to the numerous parallel units in Samuel and Kings), given similar techniques and linguistic frameworks, TPJ is the Targum that most closely resembles TC in its present form.

Similarities between TC and TPJ have been mentioned in previous studies, as mentioned in the openings of this and the preceding chapter, but the scope of these similarities has not been realized and detailed in earlier works. This laborious effort, however, has proven to be of great importance, for its ramifications are far-reaching and even revolutionary in terms of the conclusions that are to be made with regard to the date of TC's composition. Direct dependence upon TPJ necessarily means a later date of composition than TPJ. As indicated in this chapter's opening discussion, the evidence available today suggests that TPJ is a product of the twelfth century. The necessary conclusion is that TC, in turn, can have been authored no earlier than that. This radical determination shall be discussed in this book's final conclusions, where it shall be weighed together with other pieces of evidence regarding the origins of TC.

Distribution of Most Words Discussed in Chapter 5 (Alphabetical)

	TC	TPJ	*Tg. Ps*	*Tg. Job*	TO	TJ	TN	TNM	FT	GT
א-	13	10	14	13	0	0	0	2	0	0
אויר שמיא	1	6	1	0	0	0	5	0	0	2
אטימוס	2	4	0	5	0	0	0	1	0	0
אט"ל	1	14	0	0	0	0	0	0	0	0
גניסה	25	179	2	3	0	0	0	0	0	0
דיוקן	1	6	1	0	0	0	0	0	0	0
דר"ק	6	18	0	0	0	0	0	0	0	0
הד"ר	4	32	0	2	0	0	0	2	0	0
טוור פולחנא	1	4	0	0	0	0	0	0	0	0
טימי	2	4	0	0	0	0	0	1	2	0
טל"ק	7	32	11	6	0	0	24	12	13	11
טפ"ז	1	2	3	3	0	0	0	0	0	0
טריגון	1	4	0	0	0	0	0	0	0	0
יומא אחרן	2	10	0	0	0	0	0	0	0	0
כוורא	1	2	1	1	0	0	0	0	0	0
מנטר	1	9	0	0	0	0	0	0	0	0
מרגלית[a]	6	18	0	0	0	0	0	0	0	0
נת"ב	1	3	3	0	0	0	0	0	0	0
סרה"ב	5	6	13	1	0	0	0	0	0	0
פטק	4	1	0	2	0	0	0	0	0	0
פירוג	1	3	1	7	0	0	3	3	3	1
פלטיותא	1	5	2	3	0	0	2	3	2	0
פלקה	7	6	0	0	0	0	0	1	2	0
פסוגיא	2	3	0	0	0	0	0	1	0	0
פרגודא[b]	2	23	0	1	0	0	0	0	0	0
פת"ק	2	2	0	0	0	0	0	0	0	0
קינום	3	1	0	0	0	0	0	0	0	0
קנטינר	24	8	0	0	0	0	2	6	1	0
קסטרה	2	1	0	0	0	0	0	1	1	0
שבה"ר	1	3	0	1	0	0	0	0	0	0
שבהורא	5	2	18	3	0	0	0	0	0	0
שרג"ג	2	4	1	2	0	0	0	3	3	1
תמהא[c]	4	17	5	0	0	0	0	1	0	0

a   Data shown for מרגלית as translation of אֶבֶן in Hebrew *Vorlage*.
b   Data limited to use of פרגוד in sense of פָּרֹכֶת.
c   Data for use of word in context of or as equivalent of מוֹפֵת.

CHAPTER 6

The Relationship of Targum Chronicles and Targum Psalms

1   Opening

Having set our sights on formulating a description of the relationship between TC and *Tg. Ps*, we encounter the challenge of establishing what text of *Tg. Ps* should be the object of our comparison. Though various editions of the work have been published, *Tg. Ps* has not seen a comprehensive, scientific effort at textual clarification, and no critical edition has yet been produced. The number of MSS of *Tg. Ps* is by far greater than is the case with TC, and the textual variants between these MSS are more profound. Faced with the unavailability of any living tradition for the reading of the Targum and lacking a tradition of preservation of the targumic text (as is the case with TO), scholars working with *Tg. Ps* over the past generation have tended to choose one MS that they deemed to be of greater quality than another and establish the targumic text accordingly.[1] For the purpose of the present comparison we have followed the *Mikra'ot Gedolot 'Haketer'* edition, which chose MS Paris 110 and thus bases its text of *Tg. Ps* on that MS, while referring to others for the correction of local errors. The same MS was chosen by Barak Dan for use in his linguistic study of *Tg. Ps* We compared the text of MS Paris 110 (a Sephardic MS) to that of MS Paris 17 (an Ashkenazi MS) for control purposes, and found that all statements made below regarding the text of *Tg. Ps* are generally true with regard to both MSS, which represent two transmissional branches of the text of *Tg. Ps*[2] The similarity of the two transmissions of *Tg. Ps* accentuates the disparities—where such exist—between *Tg. Ps* and TC.

---

1   In contrast with TC, the manuscripts of *Tg. Ps* display different textual traditions. A detailed discussion and classification of the wealth of this material is beyond the scope of this book. The reader is referred, for this purpose, to Stec *Psalms, pp. 21–24;* Dan, pp. 5–23.

2   There are several textual variants separating MS Paris 110 (S 4120/P 4814 in the JNL manuscript institute) and MS Paris 17 (S 2928), but what differences there are typically appear to stem from a single textual archetype, unlike the disparities between *Tg. Ps* and TC, which our discussion below will show are best attributed to the efforts of independent translators.

Tg. Ps belongs to the group of Targums classified by Kaufman as Late Jewish Literary Aramaic and by Cook as artificial Aramaic.[3] In our earlier consideration of the relationship between TC and TPJ, we came across many similarities between TC and *Tg. Ps* We identified numerous words exclusive to these Targums as well as other Targums of the Writings, such as the late-dated *Tg. Job*. The linguistic similarity of *Tg. Job* and *Tg. Ps* was briefly surveyed by Weiss, who isolated expressions common to the two Targums.[4] No comprehensive linguistic survey of all those Targums identified as Late Jewish Literary Aramaic has yet been produced, and I do not presume to offer any such thing with the present study. However, in considering the degree of the Targums' mutual influence on each other, I can draw attention to common elements of the Targums that have what to offer in painting a clearer picture of the language of Targums that followed. The bulk of the discussion I present here will concern parallel verses found in TC and *Tg. Ps* First, however, I will address myself to a unique and significant link between the vocabulary of the two works that is not evident from the parallel verses but has import ramifications for dating these documents.

2   The Word הונגראי and Its Significance for Dating TC and Targum Psalms

The gentilic noun הונגראי is known to appear four times in all of targumic literature, viz., once in *Tg. Ps* and three times in one chapter of TC, corresponding to the Hebrew word הַגְרִי:

Ps 83:7

MT   אָהֳלֵי אֱדוֹם וְיִשְׁמְעֵאלִים מוֹאָב וְהַגְרִים:

TP   משכני אדומאי וערבאי   מואבאי והונגראי:

NJPS: the clans of Edom and the Ishmaelites, Moab and the Hagrites
Cook: The tents of the Edomites and Arabs, the Moabites and Hungarites

---

3   Kaufman *TPJ*, p. 368; Cook *TPJ*, p. 277.
4   Weiss, pp. 93–98. Some have gone so far as to argue that a single targumist authored *Tg. Ps* and *Tg. Job* (see Weiss, pp. 73–74, for a brief synopsis of the various views), but this assumption seems unduly exaggerative. No scholar would argue that the two Targums have naught in common, but the commonalities are insufficient to point convincingly to common authorship, rather than a shared tradition.

1 Chr 5:10

MT   וּבִימֵי שָׁאוּל עָשׂוּ מִלְחָמָה עִם־הַהַגְרִאִים ... וַיֵּשְׁבוּ בְּאָהֳלֵיהֶם עַל־כָּל־פְּנֵי מִזְרָח לַגִּלְעָד:

TC   וביומי שאול עבדו קרבא עם הונגראיי ... ויתיבו במשכניהון על כל אפי מדנח גלעד:

NJPS: And in the days of Saul they made war on the Hagrites ... and they occupied their tents throughout all the region east of Gilead.

Dost: Now in the days of Saul they made war with the Hungarites ... Then they
dwelt in their tents over all the face of the east of Gilead.

1 Chr 5:19

MT   וַיַּעֲשׂוּ מִלְחָמָה עִם־הַהַגְרִיאִים וִיטוּר וְנָפִישׁ וְנוֹדָב:

TC   ועבדו קרבא עם הונגראיי ויטור ונפיש ונודב:

NJPS: They made war on the Hagrites—Jetur, Naphish, and Nodab.

Dost: They made war with the Hungarites, Jetur, Naphish, and Nodab.

1 Chr 5:20

MT   וַיֵּעָזְרוּ עֲלֵיהֶם וַיִּנָּתְנוּ בְיָדָם הַהַגְרִיאִים וְכֹל שֶׁעִמָּהֶם

TC   וסייעו עליהום אחיהון בית ישראל ואתמסרן בידיהון הונגראיי וכל דעמהון

NJPS: They prevailed against them; the Hagrites and all who were with them
were delivered into their hands

Dost: They assisted their brothers, the house of Israel, against them, and the
Hungarites and all who were with them were delivered into their hands.

As noted, in these four verses Scripture discusses the Hagrites (from Hagar),
kinsmen of the Ishmaelites placed by 1 Chr 5:10 to the east of the Jordan.
Because the Hagrite people are mentioned elsewhere in Scripture only in
1 Chr 27:31, it is impossible to compare the word choice of *Tg. Ps* and TC to that
appearing in the Targums to other books, but we would tend to imagine that
such other works would prefer an Aramaic form such as הגראי, rather than הונ־
גראי.[5] Indeed, this is the form given by TC itself in the final appearance of the
word noted above:

1 Chr 27:31

MT   וְעַל־הַצֹּאן יָזִיז הַהַגְרִי כָּל־אֵלֶּה שָׂרֵי הָרְכוּשׁ אֲשֶׁר לַמֶּלֶךְ דָּוִיד:

TC   ועל ענא יזיז הגראה כל אלין רבני קנינא די למלכא דוד:

---

5   The name הַגְרִי appears once more, in 1 Chr 11:38. There, however, it appears as a personal
    name rather than an ethnonym, so that we need expect no translation. In actuality, however,
    TC there translates גדא, reflecting the reading הַגָּדִי, as in MT 2 Sam 23:36, rather than הַגְרִי
    (cf. p. 12, above). In any event, that verse is of no consequence for the purposes of the present
    discussion.

NJPS: Over the flocks: Jaziz the Hagrite. All these were stewards of the property of King David.

Dost: Over the sheep was Jaziz the Hagrite. All of these were leaders of the property of King David.

Why in the other instances are the Hagrites translated as הונגראי? Are we witnesses here to a phonetic phenomenon in which a *nun* precedes the *gimel* as in Greek? If so, how is this word different from so many other Aramaic words where no *nun* is added? The question is only stronger for the fact that the *gimel* in question is soft, *raphe*. Equally unexplained is the unexpected presence of a *shuruq* in the Aramaic form, taking the place of the *pattaḥ* of the Hebrew.

Both Cook and Dost rendered Hungarites. Is it only coincidence that another English ending arrives at the name of a people known even today? Might it be that *Tg. Ps* and TC intend here to name the Hungarian people of Europe? Schorr mulled this question in a note to the list of textual variants that he compiled. I shall translate his note here verbatim from the original Hebrew, due to the difficulty of accessing it in the original:[6]

> Yet concerning the time when this Targum was written, the distinguished scholar Zunz, may he live, has not disclosed to us his view (*Die Gottesdienstlichen Vorträge der Juden Historisch Entwickelt*, p. 65 and p. 80) and I am flummoxed by his failure to remark on its translation in reference to the scripture עשו מלחמה עם ההגראים (1 Chr 5:10), הוּנְגְרָאֵיי (!), which seemingly refers to the people of Hungary, and if this is so, we truly are compelled to assign it a most late date at which it was written … I suspect, however, that this reading came from the publishers, something of a proof of which is that below יזיז ההגרי (27:31) is translated as הגראה, not הונגראה.

We have no need to concern ourselves with Schorr's doubts regarding the text of the Targum, as we have the benefit of reference to the text of MSS, all of which—whether of TC or of *Tg. Ps*, the latter of which Schorr did not discuss—read הונגראיי/הונגראי. Having no doubts concerning the text, we are left with Schorr's conclusion that the appearance of the Hungarians in TC dictates quite a late dating of that Targum. Levy took the view that the nation in question was indeed the Hungarians, but did not arrive at such a far-reaching conclusion for the dating of these Targums due to reliance on a historical source erroneously

---

6 Schorr, p. 135.

dating the appearance of the Hungarians as such to the end of the fourth century CE.[7] Jastrow interpreted הונגראי as denoting residents of the Hagrah district in the Arabian Peninsula. He did not, however, offer any explanation of
why the Targum might dub them הונגראי rather than הגראי.[8] Churgin rejected the very possibility that the authors of *Tg. Ps* and TC had referred to the
Hungarians with the word הונגראי, due to the great distance in both time and
space between David's reign and the Hungarians. He therefore believed that
the text had become corrupted over the course of transmission and the original form had been הגראי.[9] Dan, who deliberated over the question of the form
הונגראי in his linguistic study of *Tg. Ps*, argued that agreement on the form of
the word by all of the many textual witnesses of *Tg. Ps* made Churgin's conjecture less plausible. Dan evidently was aware of the historical ramifications of
the conclusion that the form indeed refers to the Hungarian people of Europe.
Notwithstanding, because this was not the purpose of his study, he did not discuss this question at length.[10] In the interest of buttressing Dan's reservations
concerning Churgin's view, I would add that it is extremely difficult to believe
that this presumed corruption took hold in every textual witness not of a single
work, but of two. It thus appears that the present text must be retained despite
the far-reaching historical consequences of the conclusion to be drawn.

The appellation Ungarian, or Hungarian, is familiar in European literature beginning in the mid-ninth century CE.[11] The Hungarians are known in
Hebrew literature from the mid-tenth century onward.[12] A converse identification, viz., of Hungary as the land of הגר/הגרא, is indicated in the writings of the
medieval Judaic scholars of France and Germany, demonstrated by Kohn in
the writings of Rashi, Rabbi Isaac b. Moses of Vienna, and others.[13] Over the
former half of the tenth century, the Hungarians made their way westward to
Central Europe, conducting a series of some fifty raids against various peoples

---

7   Levy, vol. 1, p. 203.

8   Jastrow, p. 339, in conjunction with p. 332.

9   Churgin *Hagiographa*, pp. 59–60. Churgin was aware that the reading הונגראי was documented in the MSS and therefore could not join Schorr in attributing the word's appearance to the publishers. He therefore pointed to copyists as the source of the presumed
corruption.

10   Dan, pp. 2–3 (on p. 2 he remarks [transl. from Hebrew], "There also would appear to be
in *Tg. Ps* a proof of the profoundly late date of the Targum or, at the minimum, of the late
date of its final redaction"), p. 365.

11   Lendvai, p. 14.

12   The author of *Jossipon* makes note of the sons of Ugar/Ungar as dwelling on the Danube;
see Flusser, pp. 4–5, n. 12, 14.

13   For the writings of the medievals, see discussion in Kohn, pp. 151, 159–160.

throughout the continent and sowing death and destruction wherever they turned. Over the course of this period they reached Spain to the west; Italy to the south; and the gates of Byzantium/Constantinople, the capital of the Byzantine Empire, to the southeast, and came to be perceived throughout the continent as marauding barbarians, as indicated by historical depictions penned by various peoples during the period.[14] The term *Hungarians* was commonly used during this period by European nations, while in Byzantium they were dubbed *Turks*.[15]

If indeed the ethnonym הונגראי appearing in TC and *Tg. Ps* refers to the Hungarians of Europe, we must ask why this particular name was associated with a nation of such recent origin while TC and *Tg. Ps* chose names of earlier provenance in rendering other ethnonyms. Most likely this phenomenon is due to the fact that the word הַגְרִי appears in Scripture only in Psalms and Chronicles, so that the targumists who translated these books had no tradition specifying how the name of this nation was to be translated, as opposed to the tradition, for instance, on which the author of TC was able to draw in translating all of the ethnonyms appearing in the Table of Nations in 1 Chronicles 1. In the absence of such a tradition and being familiar with a nation known as Hungarian—and perhaps also with the Hebrew term ארץ הגר, the land of Hagar, as an appellation for its land—the targumists may have produced an anachronistic ethnic identification that dovetailed with the world they knew, despite the sharp divergence from the plain sense of the verses. If this is so, the inescapable historical conclusion is that these verses were translated only after the Hungarians had earned a reputation as marauders, i.e., no earlier than the mid-tenth century, and perhaps even slightly later, once ארץ הגר had gained currency as the Hebrew term for Hungary. TC as we know it (as well as *Tg. Ps*) thus was written significantly later than previously believed.[16] The appearance of the term הונגראי may be an indication that the writer resided in Europe, as to the best of our knowledge it was there—rather than under Byzantine rule, as noted above—that this name was in use.

14   Lendvai, pp. 7, 30.

15   Via oral correspondence with Professor Constantine Zuckerman, to whom I offer my thanks.

16   At the conclusion of this study, p. 494, we shall return to this finding in the context of additional clues encountered over the course of the study and continue our consideration of how to date TC.

3   Similarities between TC and Targum Psalms in Parallel Verses

1 Chr 16:36–38 gives an account of the thanksgiving hymn that David and the Levites sang on the occasion of transferring the Ark of the Covenant to Jerusalem. Various psalms contain segments that parallel the song: Ps 105:1–15; 96:1–13; 106:1 (or 107:1); 106:47–48.[17] There are, to be sure, several textual disparities between the Hebrew in Chronicles and in Psalms,[18] but it cannot be doubted that any person well-versed in Psalms who reads the chapter will quite easily identify the two books' parallel units. Thanks to this circumstance, we have an additional opportunity to examine the character of TC in comparison to another Targum's treatment of a similar unit. We already have seen that the author of TC used TJ in his translation of chapters with parallels in Samuel and Kings, as well as TPJ for sections with parallels in the Torah. Now we shall consider whether there are any indications that TC used *Tg. Ps* as we know it in composing a translation of this thanksgiving hymn. A comparison of the translations given the parallel verses in Chronicles and Psalms yields not only many expressions but in fact whole verses where the treatment found in the two Targums is totally identical or nearly so. Below are the seven verses where a significant similarity exists between TC and *Tg. Ps*[19] A glance at the following examples suffices to reveal the degree of similarity between the two Targums.

1 Chr 16:8   הוֹדוּ לַה' קִרְאוּ בִשְׁמוֹ הוֹדִיעוּ בָעַמִּים עֲלִילֹתָיו:

TC   שבחו קדם ה' קרו בשמיה הודעו בעמיא עובדוי:

Ps 105:1   הוֹדוּ לַה' קִרְאוּ בִשְׁמוֹ הוֹדִיעוּ בָעַמִּים עֲלִילוֹתָיו:

Tg. Ps   שבחו קדם ה' קרון בשמיה הודעון בעמיא עובדוי:

NJPS Chr: Praise the LORD; call on His name; proclaim His deeds among the peoples.

Dost: Sing praise in the presence of the Lord; call on His name; tell of His deeds among the Gentiles.

NJPS Ps: Praise the LORD; call on His name; proclaim His deeds among the peoples.

Cook: Sing praise in the presence of the LORD, call on his name; tell of his deeds among the Gentiles.

---

17   See Curtis-Madsen, p. 221; Japhet *Ideology*, pp. 298–299; Japhet *OTL*, pp. 316–318; Klein *1 Chronicles*, pp. 361–368.

18   See comparison of the texts in Bendavid, pp. 41–42.

19   To be examined are the parallel verses of the two longest pastiches in Psalms, viz., Psalms 105 and 96. The concluding verse of the hymn in Chronicles, paralleling a verse in Psalm 106 (or 107) is not excerpted here, but this verse, too, is indicative of the dynamic described below.

1 Chr 16:9	בְּכָל־נִפְלְאֹתָיו׃	שִׂיחוּ	זַמְּרוּ־לֹו	שִׁירוּ לֹו
TC	כולהון פרישוותיה׃	מלילו	זמרו קדמוי	שבחו קדמוי
Ps 105:2	בְּכָל־נִפְלְאוֹתָיו׃	שִׂיחוּ	זַמְּרוּ־לֹו	שִׁירוּ־לֹו
Tg. Ps	בכל פרישוותיה׃	מלילו	זמרו קומוי	שבחו קומוי[20]

NJPS Chr: Sing praises unto Him; speak of all His wondrous acts.

Dost: Sing praise in His presence, make music in His presence; speak of all His wonders.

NJPS Ps: Sing praise in the presence of the LORD, call on his name; tell of his deeds among the Gentiles.

Cook: Sing praise in his presence, make music in his presence; speak of all his wonders.

1 Chr 16:12	וּמִשְׁפְּטֵי־פִיהוּ׃	מֹפְתָיו	אֲשֶׁר עָשָׂה	נִפְלְאֹתָיו	זִכְרוּ
TC	ודיני פומיה׃	תמהוהי	דעבד	פרישוותיה	אדכרו
Ps 105:5	וּמִשְׁפְּטֵי־פִיו׃	מֹפְתָיו	אֲשֶׁר־עָשָׂה	נִפְלְאוֹתָיו	זִכְרוּ
Tg. Ps	ודיני פמיה׃	תמהוי	דעבד	פרישוותיה	אדכרו

NJPS Chr: Remember the wonders He has done; His portents and the judgments He has pronounced

Dost: Call to mind the wonders that He has done; His miracles, and the judgments of His mouth.

NJPS Ps: Remember the wonders He has done, His portents and the judgments He has pronounced

Cook: Call to mind the wonders that he has done; his miracles, and the judgments of his mouth.

1 Chr 16:15	דֹּור׃	לְאֶלֶף	צִוָּה	דָּבָר	בְּרִיתֹו	לְעֹולָם	זִכְרוּ
TC	דרין׃	לאלפין	דפקיד	פתגמא	קיימיה	לעלם	אדכרו
Ps 105:8	דֹּור׃	לְאֶלֶף	צִוָּה	דָּבָר	בְּרִיתֹו	לְעֹולָם	זָכַר
Tg. Ps	דרין׃	לאלפי	דפקיד	פתגם	קיימיה	לעלם	דכיר

NJPS Chr: Be ever mindful of His covenant, the promise He gave for a thousand generations

Dost: He remembered His covenant forever, the word that He commanded for thousands of generations

NJPS Ps: He is ever mindful of His covenant, the promise He gave for a thousand generations

Cook: He remembered his covenant forever; he commanded a word for a thousand generations.

---

20 MS Paris 110 has the Palestinian form קומוי, while other MSS of *Tg. Ps* here read קדמוי, as does TC. I, therefore, do not view this word pair as exhibiting a disparity that can serve as the basis for any conclusions concerning the composition of the two Targums.

1 Chr 16:16   אֲשֶׁר כָּרַת אֶת־אַבְרָהָם וּשְׁבוּעָתוֹ לְיִצְחָק׃

TC   די גזר עם אברהם וקיימיה ליצחק׃

Ps 105:9   אֲשֶׁר כָּרַת אֶת־אַבְרָהָם וּשְׁבוּעָתוֹ לְיִשְׂחָק׃

Tg. Ps   די גזר עם אברהם וקיימיה ליצחק׃

NJPS Chr: that He made with Abraham, swore to Isaac

Dost: which He made with Abraham, and His covenant with Isaac

NJPS Ps: that He made with Abraham, swore to Isaac

Cook: That which he made with Abraham, and his covenant with Isaac.

1 Chr 16:17   וַיַּעֲמִידֶהָ לְיַעֲקֹב לְחֹק לְיִשְׂרָאֵל בְּרִית עוֹלָם׃

TC   ואוקמה ליעק׳ לגזירא ולישראל קיים עלם׃

Ps 105:10   וַיַּעֲמִידֶהָ לְיַעֲקֹב לְחֹק לְיִשְׂרָאֵל בְּרִית עוֹלָם׃

Tg. Ps   וקיימינה ליעקב לגזירא ולישראל קיים עלם׃

NJPS Chr: and confirmed in a decree for Jacob, for Israel, as an eternal covenant

Dost: And He established it for Jacob as a decree, and for Israel as a perpetual covenant

NJPS Ps: and confirmed in a decree for Jacob, for Israel, as an eternal covenant

Cook: And he established it for Jacob as a decree, for Israel as a perpetual covenant.

1 Chr 16:18   לֵאמֹר לְךָ אֶתֵּן אֶרֶץ־כְּנָעַן חֶבֶל נַחֲלַתְכֶם׃

TC   למימר לך אתן ית ארעא דכנען עדב אחסנתכון׃

Ps 105:11   לֵאמֹר לְךָ אֶתֵּן אֶת־אֶרֶץ־כְּנָעַן חֶבֶל נַחֲלַתְכֶם׃

Tg. Ps   למימר לך אתן ית ארעא דכנען עדב אחסנתכון׃

NJPS Chr: saying, 'To you I will give the land of Canaan as your allotted heritage.'

Dost: saying, 'To you I will give the land of Canaan as the lot of your inheritance,'

NJPS Ps: saying, "To you I will give the land of Canaan as your allotted heritage."

Cook: Saying, "To you I will give the land of Canaan as the lot of your inheritance."

4   Significant Disparities between Parallel Verses in TC and Targum Psalms

We saw above how great a similarity exists between many of the parallel verses in TC and *Tg. Ps* Are we to infer from this finding that the author of TC copied his translation from *Tg. Ps*? Even in the examples cited above the translations are not totally identical, but we cannot discount such a possibility merely because one Targum is not an exact duplicate of the other. Even if *Tg. Ps* did indeed serve the author of TC as a literary source, we would expect to find textual differences owing to the copying processes that every Targum underwent independently, just as there are textual differences even among the very MSS that comprise the *Tg. Ps* family. Theoretically, if the source on which TC drew differed from it in dialect, we might find a series of substitutions in the Aramaic linguistic stratum pointing in the direction of the dialect that generally characterizes TC, as we in fact saw in our comparison of TC and TJ. Although we might also find other differences in TC, perhaps resulting from its author's different interpretive tendencies or additions made to the targumic continuum, there is no certainty that such changes would be in evidence.

Below we shall present verses where disparities exist between the two Targums. Before proceeding, we shall exclude from this discussion differences resulting from disparities in the Hebrew *Vorlage*, as differences between the two Targums reflecting differences in the Hebrew *Vorlage* cannot inform us of whether the Targum at hand is an independent, unreliant work.[21] We also shall exclude from this discussion differences in orthography that are as likely to reflect copyists' tendencies as those of the targumist. We shall seek to ascertain what there is to learn from the significant disparities that remain: can we explain them as alterations resulting from copying processes, local additions made by TC, or perhaps evidence of independent translational work on his part, bearing no reliance on *Tg. Ps*?

1 Chr 16:10	:ה'		מְבַקְשֵׁי	לֵב	יִשְׂמַ֖ח
TC	דה':	מימרא	דתבעי	לבהון	יחדי
Ps 105:3	:ה'		מְבַקְשֵׁי	לֵ֣ב ׀	יִשְׂמַ֗ח
Tg. Ps	:מן קדם ה'	אולפן	דתבעי	ליבהון	יחדי

NJPS Chr: let all who seek the LORD rejoice
Dost: may the heart of those who seek the Memra of the Lord be glad.
NJPS Ps: let all who seek the LORD rejoice.
Cook: let all who seek the LORD rejoice.

1 Chr 16:11	:תָּמִֽיד	פָּנָ֥יו	בַּקְּשׁ֖וּ	וְעֻזּ֑וֹ	ה'		דִּרְשׁ֤וּ
TC	:תדירא	אפוהי	קבילו	ותוקפיה	דה'	מימרא	תבעו
Ps 105:4	:תָּמִֽיד	פָּנָ֥יו	בַּקְּשׁ֖וּ	וְעֻזּ֑וֹ	ה'		דִּרְשׁ֣וּ
Tg. Ps	:תדירא	אפוי	אקבלו	ואוריתיה	דה'	אולפנא	תבעו

NJPS Chr: Turn to the LORD, to His might; seek His presence constantly.

---

21   We should briefly note that although each of the Targums generally corresponds to the Masoretic version of its respective book, the degree of correlation between MT and the Targum is greater in TC than in *Tg. Ps* Interestingly, cases have been identified where *Tg. Ps* (across MSS) in fact is in agreement specifically with our Hebrew text of the Book of Chronicles. This intriguing fact is not consequential for the purpose of the present examination, but does call for a separate discussion of the nature of *Tg. Ps*.

Dost: Seek the Memra of the Lord and His strength; welcome His face continually.

NJPS Ps: Turn to the LORD, to His might; seek His presence constantly.

Cook: Seek the teaching of the LORD, and his Torah; welcome his face continually.

In TC the object of seeking in both verse 10 and verse 11 is מימרא דה', while in the parallel verses of *Tg. Ps* the object is אולפן received מן קדם ה'. The term תב"ע אולפן serves in TO, TJ, and *Tg. Ps* as a common (though not exclusive) equivalent both for דר"ש ה' and for בק"ש ה', and is a common phrase in TC itself.[22] The only place in all known targumic literature where we find the phrase תב"ע מימרא דה' is in these two verses of TC. The expression appears not even where it approaches the literal meaning of the Hebrew *Vorlage*, e.g., לְבַקֵּשׁ אֶת־דְּבַר־יְהֹוָה (Amos 8:12), which similarly is rendered by TJ as למתבע אולפן מן קדם ה'.

The second object of seeking (עֻזּוֹ), too, is differentially translated in the two Targums (אוריתיה, תוקפיה). Each Targum has its own internal logic, as reflected by the agreement of each pair of objects. TC, which gives the translation מימרא דה', replaced the mention of God with a standard honorific substitute. The phrase מימרא דה' serves as an honorific substitute for ה' in many hundreds of Hebrew verses in TO, TN, TPJ, FT, GT, TJ, and many Targums of the Writings, as well as throughout TC. In point of fact, it is a conspicuous identifying mark of the entire targumic enterprise. Among other functions of this important expression, we find it used to indicate physical feats of מימרא דה'. It therefore is fitting for TC to use the expression מימרא דה' jointly with the word תוקפיה, signifying His (i.e., God's) might, as the second of the verse's synonymous objects. Also worthy of note is that תקוף is the common equivalent of the word עֹז in TC.[23]

Tg. Ps, which renders אולפנא דה', i.e., the teaching of God, carries on with its own internal trend with the addition of אוריתיה, i.e., the instruction (or Torah) of God. The two terms appear jointly in dozens of instances across the various Targums, among them *Tg. Ps* The word עֹז typically is translated in *Tg. Ps* as עושן, but in several cases is rendered as אוריתא.[24] It thus is only natural that one seeking אולפנא דה' also would seek His instruction, and the two expressions are well-suited as synonymous members in this verse.

---

22   1 Chr 10:14; 2 Chr 11:16; 12:14; 14:6; 15:4; 16:12; 20:3, 4; 26:5; 34:21, 26. On this topic, see p. 91, above.

23   In five of six occurrences in the book; see discussion of verse 27, below.

24   Ps 29:11; 78:61; 105:4 (the case at hand); 132:8. The word is once (68:34) translated as נבואה.

TC and *Tg. Ps* here cannot be classified as representing two different versions of a single targumic tradition: they reflect two different targumic approaches to the Hebrew verse. Each approach has its own internal logic, and they thus do not lend themselves to reconciliation. It is clear from this circumstance that neither of the Targums is to be viewed as the source of the other. Rather, each is self-sufficient.

1 Chr 16:13		בְּחִירָיו׃	יַעֲקֹב	בְּנֵי	עַבְדּוֹ	יִשְׂרָאֵל	זֶרַע
TC	דאתרעי בהון׃		יעקב	בני	עבדיה	דיִשׂר׳	זרעא
Ps 105:6		בְּחִירָיו׃	יַעֲקֹב	בְּנֵי	עַבְדּוֹ	אַבְרָהָם	זֶרַע
Tg. Ps		בחירוי׃	יעקב	בני	עבדיה	דאברהם	זרעא

NJPS Chr: O offspring of Israel, His servant, O descendants of Jacob, His chosen ones.

Dost: O seed of Israel, His servant, O sons of Jacob, with whom He is pleased

NJPS Ps: O offspring of Abraham, His servant, O descendants of Jacob, His chosen ones.

Cook: O seed of Abraham his servant, O sons of Jacob, his chosen ones

1 Chr 16:14	מִשְׁפָּטָיו׃		בְּכָל־הָאָרֶץ	אֱלֹהֵינוּ	ה׳	הוּא
TC	דינוהי׃		בכולא ארע׳	אלהנא	ה׳	הוא
Ps 105:7	מִשְׁפָּטָיו׃		בְּכָל־הָאָרֶץ	אֱלֹהֵינוּ	ה׳	הוּא
Tg. Ps	דינוי׃	מתיחין	בכל ארעא	אלהנא	ה׳	הוא

NJPS Chr: He is the LORD our God; His judgments are throughout the earth.

Dost: He is the Lord, our God; His judgments are over all the earth.

NJPS Ps: He is the LORD our God; His judgments are throughout the earth.

Cook: He is the LORD our God; his judgments are extended over all the earth.

The Targums to these two verses differ on two significant points (aside from the difference in the Hebrew *Vorlage*, ישראל/אברהם). In the first verse, *Tg. Ps* substitutes a similar Aramaic form for the Hebrew word בְּחִירָיו, whereas TC prefers the root רע״י as well as changes the form of the text to a verbal relative clause ("whom He desired"). Substitution of the Aramaic root רע״י for the Hebrew בח״ר is not surprising as such, because the equivalent is a common one in targumic works. In the second verse, TC translates the sentence literally, while *Tg. Ps* supplements the literal continuum with the word מתיחין for the sake of explanation.

1 Chr 16:19	בָּהּ׃	וְגָרִים	כִּמְעַט	מִסְפָּר	מְתֵי	בִּהְיוֹתְכֶם
TC	ויתבין בה׃		קלילין	דמנין	עם	כד הויתון
Ps 105:12	בָּהּ׃	וְגָרִים	כִּמְעַט	מִסְפָּר	מְתֵי	בִּהְיוֹתָם
Tg. Ps	ויתבין בה׃		כזעירין	דמנין	עם	כד הויתון

NJPS Chr: You were then few in number, a handful, merely sojourning there
Dost: when you were a people few in number and dwelling in it
NJPS Ps: They were then few in number, a mere handful, sojourning there
Cook: When you were a people few in number, like little ones, and dwelling
in it

כִּמְעַט is here translated by *Tg. Ps* in accordance with the two elements comprising that Hebrew word (מעט + כ), while TC translates the term more freely. The
translation given in *Tg. Ps*, כזעירין, corresponds to the approach taken by most
of the targumists to the word כִּמְעַט throughout Scripture, as well as by TC to
the second occurrence of the word in Chronicles (2 Chr 12:7). The word preferred here by TC, קלילין, is familiar from earlier Targums, albeit less common
than the rendering found in *Tg. Ps* TN and FT translate כִּמְעַט in Gen 26:10 with
the two words קליל זעיר.

Tg. Ps reads כד הויתון (second person plural) for MT's בִּהְיוֹתָם (third person
plural) and by doing so resembles TC. However, the reading of בִּהְיוֹתְכֶם is found
in many Hebrew textual witnesses of Psalms.[25] Therefore, it is more likely that
Tg. Ps כד הויתון represents an internal reading within Psalms than it does dependence of *Tg. Ps* on TC.

1 Chr 16:21	לֹא־הִנִּיחַ לְאִישׁ לְעָשְׁקָם וַיּוֹכַח עֲלֵיהֶם מְלָכִים:
TC	לא ארשי גבר לטלמא להון ואוכח אמטולהון מלכיא:
Ps 105:14	לֹא־הִנִּיחַ אָדָם לְעָשְׁקָם וַיּוֹכַח עֲלֵיהֶם מְלָכִים:
Tg. Ps	לא שבק איניש לטלומהון ואוכח בגינהון מלכיא:

NJPS Chr: He allowed no one to oppress them; He reproved kings on their
account
Dost: He did not allow anyone to oppress them, and He rebuked kings on their
account
NJPS Ps: He allowed no one to oppress them; He reproved kings on their
account
Cook: He did not allow anyone to oppress them, and he rebuked kings on their
account

Both ארשי (i.e., permitted) of TC and שבק (i.e., left) of *Tg. Ps* correspond directly to the meaning of the verb הִנִּיחַ in the Hebrew verse; the choice of one or
the other is a matter of the targumist's personal preference. ארשי, in the *aph'el*,
is not common in most Targums but is characteristic of TC, which employs
this translation on five occasions.[26] By the same token, גבר and אמטולהון of TC,

---

25   Cf. BHS' comment on Ps 105:12.
26   Other than the present verse, 2 Chr 20:10; 23:8; 25:10; 32:31.

and אנש and בגינהון of *Tg. Ps*, reflect not a difference in meaning, but personal choices made by the targumists.

1 Chr 16:22   וּבִנְבִיאַי אַל־תָּרֵעוּ׃   בִּמְשִׁיחָי אַל־תִּגְּעוּ
TC   לא תנזקון בקדישי דרביתנון בשום טב ובנביי לא תבאשון׃
Ps 105:15   וְלִנְבִיאַי אַל־תָּרֵעוּ׃   בִּמְשִׁיחָי אַל־תִּגְּעוּ
Tg. Ps   לא תקרבון במשיחיי   ולנביאיי לא תבאשון׃

NJPS Chr: Do not touch My anointed ones; do not harm My prophets
Dost: Do not harm My holy ones, whom I have anointed with a good name, and do no harm to My prophets
NJPS Ps: Do not touch My anointed ones; do not harm My prophets
Cook: Do not come near my anointed ones, and do no harm to my prophets

Here *Tg. Ps* retained the Hebrew form מְשִׁיחָי, while TC preferred the word קדיש and thereafter inserted a verbal relative clause based on מְשִׁיחָי but employing a different, Aramaic root. As noted above (p. 130), TC commonly translates verbs whose root is מש״ח (though not the form משיח; cf. 2 Chr 6:42) using the Aramaic root רב״י, and the same practice is apparent in the short expansion found here. *Tg. Ps*, too, substitutes the root רבי for words of the stem מש״ח (cf. Ps 45:8; 89:21), but this practice is not reflected in the present instance because the Hebrew verse uses the word משיח, rather than a declined verb as in the expansion found in TC. The verb תִּגְּעוּ, too, is given different translations by the two Targums. The two roots נז״ק and קר״ב commonly appear in translation of the Hebrew root נג״ע in the various Targums; here, each targumist followed his own preference.

1 Chr 16:23   הָאָרֶץ כָּל־   לַה׳ שִׁירוּ
TC   ארעא יתבי כל ה׳ קדם שבחו
Ps 96:1   הָאָרֶץ׃ כָּל־ לַה׳ שִׁירוּ   חָדָשׁ שִׁיר לַה׳ שִׁירוּ
Tg. Ps   ארעא צדיקי כל ה׳ קדם שבחו מרומא אנגלי שבחו חדתא תושבחתא ה׳ קדם שבחו

NJPS Chr: Sing to the LORD, all the earth.
Dost: Sing in the presence of the Lord, all inhabitants of the earth
NJPS Ps: Sing to the LORD a new song, sing to the LORD, all the earth
Cook: Sing in the presence of the LORD a new psalm; sing praise, angels of the height, sing praise in the presence of the LORD, all righteous of the earth

We need not refer to the opening clause of the verse in Psalms, which is absent from Chronicles, to see that the rendering given in *Tg. Ps* here differs fundamentally from that in TC. The verb שבחו occurs twice in *Tg. Ps*, but appears only once in TC (as in the Hebrew). In *Tg. Ps* the first appearance is accompanied by addressees in the vocative, identified as אנגלי מרומא, i.e., the angels on high, while TC includes no such addition.[27] The structure of the verse that results in *Tg. Ps* differs from the verse in TC in that both the terrestrial and the heavenly realm are called upon to sing to God, whereas in TC (as in the Hebrew *Vorlage* of both books) nothing is said of heavenly beings. The two Targums have in common a preference to specify the identity of those singing on the earth more precisely than the Hebrew verses. Whereas the Hebrew employs the general, ambiguous term כָּל־הָאָרֶץ, each Targum gives a construct phrase in which הָאָרֶץ is the nomen rectum describing a nomen regens that is called upon to sing to God. The Targums are not in agreement, however, with regard to the identity of those singing. Where TC calls on all the inhabitants of the earth to sing a hymn of praise to God, *Tg. Ps* thus addresses only the righteous among them.[28] All the differences enumerated did not descend from a single original translation that branched into disparate versions over the course of the process of transmission. On the contrary, the differences described have the distinct appearance of embodying exegetical decisions made by two different authors.

1 Chr 16:25	כִּי גָדוֹל ה' וּמְהֻלָּל מְאֹד וְנוֹרָא הוּא עַל־כָּל־אֱלֹהִים:
TC	מטול דרב ה' ומשבח לחדא ודחיל הוא על כולהון מלאכייה:
Ps 96:4	כִּי גָדוֹל ה' וּמְהֻלָּל מְאֹד נוֹרָא הוּא עַל־כָּל־אֱלֹהִים:
Tg. Ps	ארום רב ה' ומשבח לחדא ודחיל הוא על כל אלהיא:

NJPS Chr: For the LORD is great and much acclaimed, He is held in awe by all divine beings

Dost: For great is the Lord and greatly to be praised; and He is more to be feared than all the angels

NJPS Ps: For the LORD is great and much acclaimed, He is held in awe by all divine beings

Cook: For great is the LORD and greatly to be praised; and he is more to be feared than any god

The word כִּי is rendered in TC as מטול ד- and in *Tg. Ps* as ארום. The two terms differ only in that they represent disparate linguistic tendencies—and for this reason the choice of these two different words in the Targums is a reflection of two different authors at work. Meanwhile, upon arriving at the disparity at the

---

27   Cf. אנגלי מרומא in TC v. 31, as opposed to חיילי שמיא in the parallel verse of *Tg. Ps* The specialized phrase אנגלי מרומא will be discussed ad loc., pp. 241–242.

28   Cf. 1 Chr 16:31 and parallel verse in *Tg. Ps*, below, and discussion ad loc.

close of the verse, we can discern a theological difference. TC and *Tg. Ps* agree that אֱלֹהִים of the Hebrew verse is used as a plural noun, but are at odds over how the word is to be translated. In *Tg. Ps* these powerful beings retain their designation, adjusted only so that the form is an Aramaic one, whereas TC, in a show of theological sensitivity to the idea that other gods might exist, prefers a different word entirely to indicate that the verse, far from acknowledging the potential existence of other gods, means simply to refer to the angels.

1 Chr 16:26	וַה׳ שָׁמַ֫יִם עָשָׂה׃		אֱלִילִ֑ים	הָעַמִּים֙	כִּ֤י כָּל־אֱלֹהֵ֣י
TC	וה׳ שמיא עבד׃	דלית בהון צרוך	דחלן	עממי[א] טעות	מטול דכלהון
Ps 96:5	וַ֝ה׳ שָׁמַ֥יִם עָשָֽׂה׃		אֱלִילִ֑ים	הָעַמִּים֮	כִּ֤י כָּל־אֱלֹהֵ֣י
Tg. Ps	וה׳ שמיא עבד׃		טעוותא	דעמיא	ארום כל דחלן

NJPS Chr: All the gods of the peoples are mere idols, but the LORD made the heavens.

Dost: For all of the idols of the Gentiles are (mere) objects of reverence, for whom there is no need; but the Lord made the heavens.

NJPS Ps: All the gods of the peoples are mere idols, but the LORD made the heavens.

Cook: For all the things feared by the Gentiles are idols; but the LORD made the heavens.

Aside from the disparate use of מטול ד- or ארום, as in the preceding example, the two Targums differ in their respective translations of אֱלֹהֵי and אֱלִילִים. טעוון of TC becomes דחלן in *Tg. Ps*, and vice versa. Even were it proposed that this interchange were the mere result of a copyist's error, TC would be set apart by the additional verbiage qualifying דחלן, viz., דלית בהון צרוך, which serves to deny that these entities might have any value justifying their being objects of reverence. The phrase used here is a familiar one used in similar contexts in other targums (e.g., TO Deut 32:17; TJ 1 Kgs 18:24, etc.), as well as in TC itself in 2 Chr 32:12.

1 Chr 16:27	בִּמְקֹמֽוֹ׃	וְחֶדְוָ֑ה	עֹ֭ז	לְפָנָ֑יו	ה֣וֹד וְהָדָר֮
TC	באתריה׃	ודיצותא	תוקפא	קדמוי	זיוא ושבהורא
Ps 96:6	בְּמִקְדָּשֽׁוֹ׃	וְתִפְאֶ֗רֶת	עֹ֭ז	לְפָנָ֑יו	הוֹד־וְהָדָ֥ר
Tg. Ps	בבית מקדשיה׃	ואודיצותא	עושנא	קומוי	שבחא ושיבהורא

NJPS Chr: Glory and majesty are before Him; strength and joy are in His place.

Dost: Splendor and glory are in His presence; strength and joy are in His place.

NJPS Ps: Glory and majesty are before Him; strength and splendor are in His temple.

Cook: Praise and splendor are in his presence; strength and praise are in his sanctuary.

In these parallel verses we find that the Targums differ in their translations of הוֹד (viz., שבחא or זיוא) and עֹז (viz., תוקפא or עושנא). All three appearances of the common noun הוֹד in Chronicles (aside from this verse, 1 Chr 29:11, 25) are rendered by TC as זיו, as was the single appearance of same word in the Torah (Num 27:20) in TO and TPJ and as is the standard practice of TJ. This equivalent does, to be sure, appear in *Tg. Ps*, but only in two of the eight appearances of הוֹד in the Book of Psalms.[29] The disparity in the translation of the word עֹז is characteristic of TC and *Tg. Ps* throughout these works. עושן functions as the translation of עֹז, מָעוֹז, and עזוז dozens of times in *Tg. Ps*; in TC, תקוף serves as the translation of עֹז in five of the six cases in which the word appears in Chronicles.[30]

1 Chr 16:28	וָעֹז:	כָּבוֹד	לַה'	הָבוּ	עַמִּים	מִשְׁפְּחוֹת	לַה'	הָבוּ
TC	ותוקפא:	יקרא	קדם ה'	הבו	עממי'	גניסת	קדם ה'	הבו
Ps 96:7	וָעֹז:	כָּבוֹד	לַה'	הָבוּ	עַמִּים	מִשְׁפְּחוֹת	לַה'	הָבוּ
Tg. Ps	ועושנא:	איקר	קדם ה'	איהבו	עמיא	ייחוסי	קדם ה' זמר	איהבו

NJPS Chr: Ascribe to the LORD, O families of the peoples, ascribe to the LORD glory and strength
Dost: Ascribe in the presence of the Lord, O families of the Gentiles; ascribe glory and strength in the presence of the Lord
NJPS Ps: Ascribe to the LORD, O families of the peoples, ascribe to the LORD glory and strength
Cook: Make music in the presence of the LORD, O races of peoples; ascribe glory and strength in the presence of the LORD

The two Targums to the present verse differ on three points of significance: *Tg. Ps*, but not TC, adds the object זמר to the continuum of the verse; the word מִשְׁפְּחוֹת is translated in *Tg. Ps* as ייחוסי but in TC as גניסת; and, as in the previous verse, עֹז is rendered in *Tg. Ps* as עושנא and in TC as תוקפא.

---

29 Occurrences of הוֹד in Psalms and their translations: Ps 96:6; 104:1; 111:3: שבחא; Ps 21:6; 148:13: תושבחתא; Ps 8:2; 145:5: זיו; Ps 45:4: הוד (i.e., a transcription of the Hebrew).

30 1 Chr 13:8; 16:11, 27, 28; 2 Chr 6:41. The exception is 2 Chr 30:21, where כלי עז is translated as זיני תושבחתא.

1 Chr 16:29	וּבֹ֣אוּ לְפָנָ֑יו	שְׂא֤וּ מִנְחָה֙	שְׁמ֑וֹ	כְּב֣וֹד	לַֽה'	לְה'	הָב֤וּ		
TC	ובאו קדמוהי	טולו תקרובתא	שמיה	איקר	קדם ה'		הבו		
Ps 96:8	לְחַצְרוֹתָֽיו׃	כְּב֣וֹד	שְׂאֽוּ־מִנְחָ֑ה	שְׁמ֑וֹ	כְּב֣וֹד	לַֽה'	לְה'	הָב֤וּ	
Tg. Ps	ועולו לדרתוי׃	סוברו תקרובתא	שמיה	ורוממו	איקר	קדם ה'	הבו	זמר	

NJPS Chr: Ascribe to the LORD the glory of His name, bring tribute and enter before Him, bow down to the LORD majestic in holiness

Dost: Ascribe in the presence of the Lord the glory of His name; carry an offering and enter His presence, and bow before the Lord in the splendor of (His) holiness

NJPS Ps: Ascribe to the LORD the glory of His name, bring tribute and enter His courts

Cook: Ascribe glory in the presence of the LORD, and exalt his name; carry and bring an offering and enter his presence in his courts

The present verses contain two significant disparities. *Tg. Ps* separates the elements of the construct phrase כְּב֣וֹד שְׁמ֑וֹ and inserts a verb between them, whereas TC retains the genitive as in the original. *Tg. Ps* chooses to translate the imperative verb שְׂא֤וּ as סובר, while TC prefers נטל. The meaning remains the same in either case, signifying that the different choices of diction reflect the independent work of two different translators. The fact of the selection of תקרובתא by both targumists for מִנְחָה does not evidence direct reliance by one on the other, as this Aramaic word is used as an equivalent of מִנְחָה in TO, TJ, and other targumic works, as well as elsewhere in *Tg. Ps* (45:13; 72:10) and TC (2 Chr 26:8).

1 Chr 16:30	אַף־תִּכּ֥וֹן תֵּבֵ֗ל בַּל־תִּמּֽוֹט׃		חִ֭ילוּ מִלְּפָנָיו֙ כָּל־ הָאָ֔רֶץ						
TC	ברם אתקין ארעא דלא תזדעזע׃		אזדעזעו מן קדמוהי כל יתבי ארעא						
Ps 96:9	הָאָ֑רֶץ׃ אִמְר֤וּ בַגּוֹיִ֙ם ה' מָלָ֗ךְ אַף־תִּכּ֣וֹן תֵּבֵ֭ל בַּל־תִּמּֽוֹט		חִ֭ילוּ מִפָּנָ֑יו כָּל־						
Tg. Ps	רתיתו מקומיה כל יתבי ארעא: אימרו בעמיא ה' מלך לחוד תקין תבל דלא תיתמוטט								

NJPS Chr: Tremble in His presence, all the earth! The world stands firm; it cannot be shaken

Dost: Tremble from before Him, all inhabitants of the earth; indeed, the world is fixed so that it shall never be moved

NJPS Ps: Bow down to the LORD majestic in holiness; tremble in His presence, all the earth!

Cook: Bow down before him in the splendor of holiness; tremble in his presence, all inhabitants of the earth

TC translates both חי"ל and מו"ט in these two verses as זעזע. *Tg. Ps*, however, uses the roots רת"ת and מו"ט. Here, too, the meaning of the text changes little, and the choice of different verbs is a sign of independent work by two different translators.[31]

1 Chr 16:31	יִשְׂמְחוּ הַשָּׁמַיִם וְתָגֵל הָאָרֶץ וְיֹאמְרוּ בַגּוֹיִם ה' מָלָךְ:			
TC	יחדון אנגלי מרומא ויבועון יתבי ארעא יימרון בעמיא ה' מלך:			
Ps 96:11	יִשְׂמְחוּ הַשָּׁמַיִם וְתָגֵל הָאָרֶץ			
Tg. Ps	יחדון חיילי דשמיא וידוצון צדיקי ארעא			

NJPS Chr: Let the heavens rejoice and the earth exult; let them declare among the nations, "The LORD is King!"

Dost: The angels of the height will rejoice, and the inhabitants of the earth will exult. they will say among the Gentiles, 'The Lord reigns.'

NJPS Ps: Let the heavens rejoice and the earth exult

Cook: The forces of heaven will rejoice and the righteous of the earth will exult

To both Targums, the references in the Hebrew to the heavens and the earth denote heavenly and terrestrial beings, respectively, but the targumists differ in their choice of words and, in the case of the earth, with regard to the identity of those beings under discussion. Both Targums interpret the word הַשָּׁמַיִם in these parallel verses as signifying heavenly beings, but they express this meaning in two disparate ways. In the Aramaic translation of *Tg. Ps*, הַשָּׁמַיִם becomes צְבָא הַשָּׁמַיִם (a phrase translated by TO and TJ as חילי שמיא), while TC uses the word מרומא for הַשָּׁמַיִם and prefaces it with the nomen regens אנגלי, from the Greek ἄγγελοι, i.e., angels (see discussion of this phrase just below). The two Targums' choice of disparate verbs (יבועון or ידוצון) of similar meaning for וְתָגֵל would appear to attest to the work of two different targumists.

The terrestrial beings addressed in TC are יתבי ארעא, i.e., all inhabitants of the earth, while in *Tg. Ps* only the righteous among them merit mention. We saw a similar case earlier, in 1 Chr 16:23 and its parallel in Psalms, where TC had יתבי ארעא and *Tg. Ps* has צדיקי ארעא. Meanwhile, in 1 Chr 16:30 and its counterpart, above, both Targums have יתבי ארעא. It may be that this discrepancy is evidence of different exegetical approaches on the part of the two Targums. The phrase צדיקי ארעא is used exclusively in *Tg. Ps*, where it appears in Ps 35:20; 50:4, aside from the two instances already noted. In 50:4, as in 96:1, the expression is a substitute for אנגלי מרומא, and in 96:11 for חיילי דשמיא, both of which serve as amplifications of the word השמים. Perhaps *Tg. Ps*, taking cognizance of the verses' meaning, sought to stress the impropriety of equating all the

---

31   See my discussion of the following verse concerning a possible exegetical distinction by *Tg. Ps* between יתבי ארעא and צדיקי ארעא.

inhabitants of the earth to the angels, instead indicating that the reference is solely to the righteous among them, and it is they who are described as singing to God and rejoicing before Him. In 96:9, however, the action in question is not song, but trembling. *Tg. Ps*, then, limits rejoicing and song to the righteous, but ascribes fear to all inhabitants of the earth. No such distinction is made in TC.

The phrase אנגלי מרומא appears in *Tg. Ps*, *Tg. Job*, *Tg. Esth I*, and TC, where it functions as an equivalent of שמים, בני עליון, אלהים, or מרומים, or occurs within an expansion in the text.[32] The common denominator of the various uses of the phrase is that in no cases does it ever function as an equivalent of the Hebrew מַלְאָךְ.[33] As noted above (pp. 103–104), when the word מַלְאָךְ appears in Scripture in the sense of a mortal emissary, the Targums conventionally translate it as אזגד, while mention of a heavenly emissary typically is rendered by the targumists as מלאך in the Aramaic, as well. The authors of those Targums discussed here translated similarly, following in the footsteps of the targumic traditions that had preceded them. However, in verses where the word מַלְאָךְ does not appear—where these targumists were not beholden to tradition—there appeared a form of expression that by all appearances seems to have served in the dialect of Aramaic to which they were personally accustomed.

אנגלי מרומא appears in liturgical Palestinian Aramaic of the Byzantine Era. Yahalom and Sokoloff included the phrase in a select set of words that they dubbed "words in vogue in the Aramaeophone world of the Hellenized East."[34] The appearance of אנגלי מרומא in the aforementioned Targums demonstrates the existence of a linguistic link amongst them as well as between them and the Palestinian Aramaic of the Byzantine Era.

5   Conclusion

We have before us two parallel units, viz., TC and *Tg. Ps* On one hand, we have seen numerous verses where a significant similarity—sometimes to the point of identity—exists between the two Targums, tantalizing us with the notion that TC used *Tg. Ps* as a source for its translation of 1 Chr 16, rendering only local adjustments to the text as required. On the other hand, we have taken note of many elements in these units that differ to the point that such discrepancy

---

32   *Tg. Ps* 50:4, 6; 82:6; 86:8; 96:1; 97:6; 148:1; *Tg. Job* 15:15; 20:27; 35:10; *Tg. Esth I* 6:1 (an occurrence incorrectly attributed by several studies to *Tg. Esth II*); TC 1 Chr 16:31. The word אנגליא, independent of the nomen rectum מרומא, appears once in *Tg. Ps* 68:18.

33   Weiss, pp. 77–78, remarked thus concerning *Tg. Ps* and *Tg. Job*, but the same is true of *Tg. Esth I* and TC.

34   Sokoloff-Yahalom, pp. 44–45; See also Kister *Poetry*, pp. 109–110.

cannot be attributed to the textual transmission process alone, indicating that the two Targums were composed by two different authors. In what way can we reconcile these contradictory signals? We have two options. We may say either that *Tg. Ps* is the literary source of TC, thus compelling ourselves to find various and sundry explanations for the many discrepancies between them, or that TC did not copy the translation of this chapter's hymn from *Tg. Ps*, thus compelling ourselves to account for the many similarities in the two Targums.

Many of the discrepancies between these Targums are extraordinarily difficult to explain as resulting from purposeful adjustment of the text of a source document; we already have discounted the possibility that these are changes that crept in over the course of the two texts' transmission. As for the existence of such a great similarity between the two Targums, it seems that this phenomenon is best explained by the fact of the two translators' having worked within quite similar targumic traditions and—more important still—within the same general linguistic environment, characterized by the dialect described by Kaufman as Late Jewish Literary Aramaic, in which TPJ, TC, and *Tg. Ps* all were written.[35] Two translators well-versed in their predecessors' modes of expressions and writing in similar Aramaic dialects very well could yield a great number of similarities in their efforts to translate the short, measured lyrical verses of 1 Chronicles 16. If we reconsider the similar elements of the two translations, we see that the translational choices made are very much of a boilerplate type. The similar equivalents in TC and *Tg. Ps* are not surprising, but constitute a continuation of the tradition put in motion by previous targumists. All of the similarities between the two Targums are of the same provenance. Put otherwise, in the similarly translated sections there is not one example of a word or phrase that is not attested or paralleled in previous Targums, and there is nothing that associates TC specifically with *Tg. Ps* rather than with another Targum. The two translators embarked on their work with reference to similar targumic traditions and with kindred dialects of Aramaic, and therefore composed works bearing numerous similarities.

Nevertheless, two artists do not create identical handiwork, and the paths taken by the two targumists in their treatment of several of the hymn's expressions thus diverged. It bears emphasis that not all of these disparities are illustrative of independent work by the targumists in question. On the contrary, many of the examples discussed above appear in some form in other targumic works, and these elements mark the work of our targumists as a continuation of a long tradition preceding them. Yet sometimes, upon finding themselves at

---

35   Kaufman *TPJ*, p. 368.

a crossroads with several options available within targumic tradition, TC took one road and *Tg. Ps* took the other. The independence of the two targumists' work is amply evidenced not by their creativity or innovations, but by their disparate decisions within the bounds of targumic tradition.

Thus we must conclude that TC is closely related to *Tg. Ps* in dialect, and thus, perhaps, also in time and place, but neither targumist referred to the other's work in translating the text of the parallel units here surveyed.

Targum Chronicles and the Babylonian Talmud

1   Opening

We have seen thus far in our examination that TC tends to adhere closely to the Hebrew *Vorlage* of Chronicles. On those occasions when it deviated from a strictly literal translation,[1] the divergence typically stemmed from the reasons described in chapter two on translation technique, and these reasons indeed explain the presence of much of the nonliteral material to be found in TC— but not all. There are cases where the targumist departed from literal translation by inserting nonliteral expansions into the translation's continuum. These additions, generally of an aggadic homiletical character, are characterized by a style and role in the text rather reminiscent of the Palestinian Targums of the Torah, and more so of TPJ.[2]

All of the scholars who have published studies of TC have taken different approaches to the treatment of these aggadic expansions. Rosenberg and Kohler cited a few sources in rabbinic literature for a small part of the additions.[3] Churgin allotted this topic an entire section of his discussion, in which he listed the expansions in order and listed sources for the aggadic traditions.[4] Churgin's compilation is an important and helpful contribution, but it lacks a discussion of the relationship between the Targum and the sources that served the targumist. In some instances he devoted a sentence or two to the matter, but in others he included no discussion at all. In many cases, in my view, Churgin cited sources to which the targumist had not in fact referred, or at least sources whose text is not reflected by TC, and a number of expansions are entirely absent from his list. Le Déaut and Robert's French translation contains footnotes discussing some insertions and sometimes suggesting sources, but for the most part these do not venture substantially beyond Churgin's proposals. McIvor, who was greatly influenced by Le Déaut and Robert, accepted the bulk of their citations. He discussed the expansions on a broader scale than had they as well as put forward a few novel comments in his notes, but did

---

1   Per the five criteria for evaluating a literal translation in Tov *LXX*, pp. 22–26.

2   This is contra to *Tg. Cant*, *Tg. Eccl*, and others, in which nonliteral matter and aggadic expansions figure much more prominently than in TPJ and TC.

3   Rosenberg-Kohler, pp. 146–151.

4   Churgin *Hagiographa*, pp. 247–263.

© KONINKLIJKE BRILL NV, LEIDEN, 2020 | DOI:10.1163/9789004417632_008

not proffer new information on a sufficient scale. Hamiel dedicated a unit of his discussion to TC's insertions while attempting to offer a rabbinic source for each. While he did identify sources for several insertions that had escaped Churgin, he declined to engage in a systematic discussion that would bring much-needed clarification to TC's aggadic expansions, and his citations are, in my view, sometimes imprecise.

Thus, in effect, the aggadic insertions of TC have not yet been subjected to an examination that satisfactorily identified their sources and described the manner of these homilies' emplacement within the Targum. That such a discussion transpire is important for a number of reasons. First, it would form a critical stage toward the creation of a comprehensive commentary on TC—and despite the existence of a number of commentaries that seek this distinction, no satisfactorily thorough discussion of the work has yet been published. Second, such a discussion would tend to teach us a substantial amount about the historical background of TC and its author. To the extent that we attain a precise understanding of the targumist's sources, we also will acquire a fuller appreciation of the world in which he lived; the books that influenced him; and, perhaps, consequently, the environment in which he authored his Targum. Third, so much as a translator adheres strictly to the literal meaning in the continuum of his translation, it is correspondingly difficult to learn anything about him other than whatever is indicated by the linguistic stratum. Yet where the translator deviates from literal translation with the addition of material that goes beyond the content of the *Vorlage*, he is likely to divulge information that says something about him, the era in which he lived, and the environment in which he functioned. Within TC we find hints of this sort testifying (if not always in the fullest way) to the targumist's origins and the time in which he lived that have not been analyzed by any of the scholars who examined TC to date. I therefore will seek here to provide what information my predecessors left unreported. I will locate in the next two chapters, to the best of my ability, the sources of the aggadic expansions found throughout TC and the bits of information hidden within them that may shed new light on the targumist's background.

This present chapter contains two sections. The first section deals with various aggadic expansions found in TC that are likely based upon the Babylonian Talmud. These expansions will be discussed and I will attempt to identify the particular BT passage upon which the targumist formed his expansion. The second section contains aggadic expansions that may have been written based on the BT, but for which it is more difficult to make this determination.

Each expansion will be cited synoptically in the context of the book's Hebrew *Vorlage*, with every Hebrew word set above the Aramaic word that corresponds to it. Any words contained in the Targum that serve as an expansion relative to the Hebrew continuum of MT will generally be marked in one of two ways: 1) no Hebrew or Aramaic text will appear above them; 2) the words will appear beneath Hebrew or Aramaic text but will be colored red, meaning that the placement of the text does not indicate any correspondence whatsoever between the red word and that above it. Where TC contains dual translations, both will be set underneath the appropriate part of the Hebrew *Vorlage*, one line beneath the other. The manner in which verses and their targum are cited will serve as a foundational stage of each of the discussions to follow, and the reader therefore is encouraged to examine the textual alignments carefully and note how the Hebrew and Aramaic texts correspond to each other before proceeding to the ensuing analysis and discussion.

In each discussion, I shall seek to explain how the aggadic expansion corresponds to the Hebrew verse and, to the extent possible, from what source the targumist obtained the aggadic tradition referenced. In a few cases, the expansion discussed will not fit the definition "aggadic". Nevertheless, as will be shown, they, too, clearly were written under the direct influence of a rabbinic literary source (thus, e.g., 1 Chr 26:18, pp. 324–325, below; 2 Chr 21:3, pp. 340–342, below) and will, therefore, find their place in these two chapters.

2 Probable Usage of the Babylonian Talmud

2.1 *Jether the Ishmaelite/Israelite (1 Chr 2:17)*

1 Chr 2:17

MT   וַאֲבִיגַ֙יִל֙ יָלְדָ֣ה אֶת־עֲמָשָׂ֔א וַאֲבִ֖י עֲמָשָׂ֑א יֶ֖תֶר הַיִּשְׁמְעֵאלִֽי׃

TC   והוו צווחין ליה   יתר ישראלא   ואבא דעמשא יתר עמשא   ואביגיל ילידת ית עמשא
    יתר ישמעאלא

מטול דזריז ית חרצוי בסיפא למסייעא ית דויד הי־כערבאה כד בעא אבנר למרחקא

ית דויד וכל גניסת ישי דלא ידכון למיעל בקהלא דה' על־עיסק רות מואביתא:

NJPS: Abigail bore Amasa, and the father of Amasa was Jether the Ishmaelite.
Dost: Abigail bore Amasa, and the father of Amasa was Jether the Israelite, but they would call him Jether the Ishmaelite because he girded his loins with a sword to help David like an Arab, when Abner sought to banish David and the entire lineage of Jesse, which was not allowed to enter into the congregation of the Lord on account of the matter of Ruth the Moabitess.

This verse contains a well-known variant separating Samuel and Chronicles, the former of which gives the name of Amasa's father as Jether the Israelite *Amasa*, וַעֲמָשָׂ֣א בֶן־אִ֗ישׁ וּשְׁמוֹ֙ יִתְרָ֣א הַיִּשְׂרְאֵלִ֔י אֲשֶׁר־בָּ֛א אֶל־אֲבִיגַ֥ל בַּת־נָחָ֖שׁ (2 Sam 17:25,

*was the son of a man named Ithra the Israelite, who had married Abigal, daugh-
ter of Nahash*).[5] The lengthy expansion in TC is a proposal intended to do away
with the contradiction between the two books by arguing that both are in
the right. Jether is dubbed ישראלא, *the Israelite*, for his heredity (though the
Targum does not explicate as much, this appears to be the intent) as well as
called ישמעאלא in recognition of an unusual action of his that redounded to
David's benefit.

This explanation appears in numerous rabbinic sources, and the connection between these and the description in TC indicates that the targumist was
a recipient of the tradition that included this.[6] Churgin opined that TC's source
was *y. Yebam.* 8:3 (9c, p. 870):[7]

ורבנין אמרין: ישראלי היה, ואת אומ[ר] 'ישמעאלי'? אלא שחגר מתניו כ[יש]מעאלי
ונעץ את החרב בבית הדין: או נהרוג או נהרג או נקיים דברי ר[בי], כל מי שהוא עובר
על הלכה זו בחרב זו אני הורגו. 'עמוני' ולא עמונית. 'מואב[י]' ולא מואבית.

The Rabbis say: he was an Israelite, yet you call him an 'Ishmaelite'?
Because he girded his waist like an Ishmaelite and thrust the sword at
court: kill or be killed or uphold my master's words, whosoever goes
against this law I shall kill him with this sword. 'Amonite' and not
Amonitess. 'Moabite' and not Moabitess.

Churgin, associating the expression חגר מתניו with זריז ית חרצוי in TC, considered this parallel to pose a similarity that set these sources apart from all others
in which such exegesis appears. Churgin went on to note that "there is no mention in the sources of Abner's desire to disqualify David and Jesse's family. The

---

5   The text of Samuel should be regarded as secondary in this instance. See Japhet *OTL*,
    pp. 77–78.
6   The sources are varied but share the halakhic question regarding the ethnic status of Ruth
    and whether the novel halakhic distinction limiting the Torah's exclusion to male Ammonites
    and Moabites was applied. See *y. Yebam.* 8:3 (9c, p. 870); *b. Yebam.* 76b–77a; *Ruth Rab.* 4, p. 98;
    Midr. Ps 9:11 (p. 87); *Midr. Sam* 22 (p. 71).
7   Churgin *Hagiographa*, p. 248 (where the source given is *Yebam.* 6:3, apparently a print-
    ing error). McIvor, p. 49, n. 13, diffidently suggested that TC's source might have been *Gen.
    Rab.* 82:4 (p. 981), as Abner is there depicted as opposing David's kingship and crowning
    Ish-bosheth. That source, however, does not suffice to explain TC, as it lacks a discussion
    of David's lineage, and its portrayal of Abner's opposition to David is taken from Scripture,
    rather than derived midrashically. Hamiel, pp. 372–373, entertains doubts arising from the
    degree of agreement between TC and BT but finds no satisfactory solution, because he found
    no source other than TC in which Abner was the figure who threw aspersions on David's
    lineage.

Babylonian [Talmud] ... indicates that Abner stood staunchly at his side and it is Doeg who denounced David." Churgin thus appears to have preferred to look to the *yerushalmi* for TC's source not only due to the textual similarity he noted, but also because the *yerushalmi* does not detail the entire halakhic deliberation that preceded Jether's dramatic declaration, and thus does not state expressly that Doeg worked against David while Abner unsuccessfully tried to protect him. I would note that the *yerushalmi*, too, does not support TC's contention that Abner was the antagonist in the story, but merely indicates that he did not expressly object.

I believe that a fresh reading of the text of Talmud Bavli will suffice to show that it, rather than the Yerushalmi passage indicated by Churgin, is the source to which TC in fact looked. Let us first consider and discuss the text of the Vilna edition of the Talmud:[8]

מתני': 'עמוני ומואבי אסורים ואיסורם איסור עולם, אבל נקבותיהם מותרות מיד'...
גמ': מנא הני מילי? אמר רבי יוחנן: דאמר קרא, 'וכראות שאול את דוד יוצא לקראת הפלשתי אמר אל אבנר שר הצבא בן מי זה הנער אבנר ויאמר אבנר חי נפשך המלך אם ידעתי'... אמר ליה דואג האדומי: עד שאתה משאיל עליו אם הגון הוא למלכות אם לאו, שאל עליו אם ראוי לבא בקהל אם לאו. מאי טעמא? דקאתי מרות המואביה. אמר ליה אבנר: תנינא, 'עמוני' ולא עמונית, 'מואבי' ולא מואבית. אלא מעתה 'ממזר' ולא ממזרת? 'ממזר' כתיב—מום זה. 'מצרי' ולא מצרית? שאני הכא דמפרש טעמא דקרא: 'על אשר לא קדמו אתכם בלחם ובמים'—דרכו של איש לקדם ואין דרכה של אשה לקדם. היה להם לקדם אנשים לקראת אנשים ונשים לקראת נשים! אישתיק! מיד, 'ויאמר המלך שאל אתה בן מי זה העלם'. התם קרי ליה 'נער' הכא קרי ליה 'עלם'? הכי קא אמר ליה: הלכה נתעלמה ממך, צא ושאל בבית המדרש. שאל. אמרו ליה: 'עמוני' ולא עמונית, 'מואבי' ולא מואבית. אקשי להו דואג כל הני קושייתא. אישתיקו! בעי לאכרוזי עליה. מיד, 'ועמשא בן איש ושמו יתרא הישראלי אשר בא אל אביגיל בת נחש', וכתיב 'יתר הישמעאלי'? אמר רבא: מלמד שחגר חרבו כישמעאל ואמר: כל מי שאינו שומע הלכה זו ידקר בחרב. כך מקובלני מבית דינו של שמואל הרמתי: 'עמוני' ולא עמונית, 'מואבי' ולא מואבית.

Mishnah: The male Ammonite and Moabite are prohibited [from entering the congregation of the Lord (Deut 23:4)], and the prohibition concerning them is forever. But their women are permitted forthwith ...

Gemara: *What is the scriptural basis for these rules?* Said R. Yohanan, "Said Scripture, 'And when Saul saw David go forth against the Philistine, he said to Abner, captain of the host: Abner, whose son is this youth?

---

8 *B. Yebam.* 76b–77a. As noted, the text of BT quoted here is that of the Vilna edition, with acronyms expanded and punctuation added.

And Abner said, As your soul lives, o King, I cannot tell' (1 Sam 17:55)." *But didn't Saul know him? Surely it is written,* "And he loved him greatly and he became his armor bearer' (1 Sam 16:21). *Rather, he was asking about the father. But didn't he know the father? 'And is it not written:* "And the man was an old man in the days of Saul, stricken in years among them'"(1 Sam 17:12), and said Rab, or some say, R. Abba, said, "This referred to the father of David, who came in with an army and went out with an army." *So this is what Saul meant:* "*Whether he derives from Peretz, or whether he derives from Zerah. If he derives from Peretz, he will be king, for* a king may exercise the right of eminent domain and none can stop him [M. San. 2:4B]. *Whether he derives from Zerah, he will be will be only an eminent authority.*" *How come he said to him,* "*Make inquiries concerning him*"? *Because it is written,* "And Saul dressed David with his clothing" (1 Sam 17:38), because he was the same size, *and concerning Saul it is written,* "From his shoulders upward he was taller than any of the people" (1 Sam 9:2). Said Doeg the Edomite to Saul, "Rather than asking concerning him whether or not he is worthy of the throne, ask whether he is worthy even of entering the community of Israel or not." *"How come?"* *"Because he comes from Ruth the Moabite."* *Said Abner to Doeg,* "*We have learned as a Tannaite statement:* [Invalid are] 'An Ammonite'? (Deut 23:4, and not a female Ammonite, 'a Moabite' and not a female Moabite.'" *"Well, in that case [since women are not covered by the prohibition],* how about accepting the offspring of not a mamzer but at least of a female mamzer?" *"What is written is* mamzer, meaning, any objectionable person [without regard to gender]." "So does the reference to Egyptian [at Deut 23:8) exclude Egyptian women?" *"That case is different, for Scripture spells out the consideration involved:* 'Because they did not meet you with bread and water' (Deut 23:5)—it is customary for men to go out and meet travels, not for women." "Well, the men should have met the men, but the women should have met the women." *He shut up.* "Thereupon the king said [to Doeg], Ask whose son this boy is" (1 Sam 17:56). *Elsewhere he calls him a youth but here he calls him a boy? This is what he said to him,* "There is a law that you have missed. Go and ask in the school house." He asked. They said to him, "[Invalid are] 'An Ammonite'? (Deut 23:4, and not a female Ammonite, 'a Moabite' and not a female Moabite.'" *But when Doeg laid before him all of these objections [that we have now spelled out], they fell silent. He wanted to make a public declaration against David [as the son of a Moabite woman, unfit in line with Deut 23:4]. Forthwith:* "now Amasa was the son of a man named Ithra the Israelite who went in to Abigal, daughter of Nahash" (2 Sam 17:25). But elsewhere: "Jether the Ishmaelite" (1 Chr 2:17). Said Raba, "This teaches that he strapped on his sword like Ishmael and said, 'Whoever will not obey this law will be stabbed with this sword: 'so have I received as a tradition from the court of Samuel of Ramah: "[Invalid are] 'An Ammonite'? (Deut 23:4), and not a female Ammonite, 'a Moabite' and not a female Moabite.'

While the Talmud recounts this aggadic tradition at considerable length, the part that is represented in TC is limited to the final scene, in which Jether resorts to threatening the scholars in the study hall with a sword in order to coerce them to accept the halakhic tradition favoring David. According to the text of the Talmud as it appears above, the scene's dramatis personae are Doeg, the scholars of the study hall, and Jether. Though it may be that Abner, too, is present in the study hall, this is nowhere acknowledged. Doeg voices the challenges to David's lineage, and all the scholars in the study hall are consequently silenced. TC, meanwhile, points to Abner as personally seeking to prevent David from entering the congregation, for which reason Churgin opined that all of the other sources, including BT, described the character of Abner positively, unlike TC. Yet it is evident from the textual witnesses of BT that the Vilna edition is alone in reading אקשי להו דואג כל הני קושייתא: the word דואג appears in no MS and in none of the early printed editions.[9] If we read the account without the word דואג, the source of all of the challenges posed in the study hall obviously must have been not Doeg, but Abner: Saul's instruction, צא ושאל בבית המדרש, based on the verse in which Saul asks Abner בן שאל אתה מי זה העלם, follows Saul's statement הלכה נתעלמה ממך. Abner is the one whom the answer to the halakhic quandary escaped, and it therefore is he who is sent to the study hall to seek clarification. True, in the first stage of the story Abner opposed Doeg and attempted to defend the halakhic ruling emphasizing that only an Ammonite, and not an Ammonitess, is to be barred, but in the final stage, upon arriving at the study hall, he assumed a position opposing all of the scholars and challenged them with all of the points he had learned from Doeg. Following the reading in the MSS and early printed editions that omits Doeg's name, one may say that just as the presumed subject of אקשי in the Talmud is Abner, so is that of the next sentence's predicate: בעי לאכרוזי עליה.[10] Thus BT in

---

9   See apparatus in *Diqduqei Soferim ha-Shalem* to *Yebam.*, vol. 3, p. 149.

10   The MSS are in disagreement as to whether this verb is in the third-person singular, as above, or plural, בעו (see apparatus in *Diqduqei Soferim ha-Shalem*, ibid.), a matter made no simpler by the fact that there is, of course, only a tiny graphical difference separating the two forms. If the verb is in the plural, then its subject is all of those present, especially the scholars in the study hall. Most likely TC was familiar with the reading בעי.

fact is the only source that correlates with TC's contention that it was Abner who sought (בעא) to bar David from entering the congregation.

The expression זריז ית חרצוי בסיפא ... הי־כערבאה also correlates with the text of BT no less than that of the *yerushalmi*, as the version in TC is fuller than that in either Talmud:

Yerushalmi	כישמעאלי	מתניו	חגר
Bavli	כישמעאל	חרבו	חגר
TC	זריז ית חרצוי בסיפא ... הי־כערבאה		

In effect, the most likely source for TC's aggadic expansion is *b. Yebamot*, based on which the targumist described Abner as the character who labeled David's pedigree illegitimate.

2.2 *Shallum's Name as an Allusion to the Time of His Reign (1 Chr 3:15)*

1 Chr 3:15

MT וּבְנֵי יֹאשִׁיָּהוּ הַבְּכוֹר יוֹחָנָן הַשֵּׁנִי יְהוֹיָקִים הַשְּׁלִשִׁי צִדְקִיָּהוּ הָרְבִיעִי שַׁלּוּם׃

TC ובני יאשיהו בוכרא יוחנן תנינא יהויקים תליתאה צדקיהו רביעאה שלום
דשלימת מלכותא דבית דוד ביומי׃

NJPS: The sons of Josiah: Johanan the first-born, the second Jehoiakim, the third Zedekiah, the fourth Shallum.

Dost: The sons of Josiah: the firstborn Johanan, the second Jehoiakim, the third Zedekiah, the fourth Shallum, in whose days the kingdom of the House of David came to an end.

This homiletic understanding of the name *Shallum* also appears in the *yerushalmi* (thrice) and BT. One of the three Yerushalmi sources is *y. Hor.* 3:4 (47c, p. 1424):[11]

אמר ר' יוחנן הוא יהואחז והוא יוחנן. והכת[יב] 'הבכור יוחנן'? הבכור למלכות.
והכת[יב] 'השלישי צדקיהו הרביעי שלום'? שלישי למלכות, רביעי לתולדת. 'צד־
קיהו'—שצידק עליו את הדין. 'שלום'—שבימיו שלמה מלכות בית דוד. לא שלום
הוה שמיה ולא צדקיה הוה שמיה אלא שמיה מתנייה, הדא היא דכת[יב], 'וימלך מלך בבל
את מתניה דודו תחתיו'.

R. Johanan says: Jehoahaz is the same as Johanan. But it is written, 'Johanan the first-born'? [This means he was] first in line to the throne. But it is written, 'the third Zedekiah, the fourth Shallum'? [This means]

---

11   Appears also in *y. Soṭah* 8:1 (22c, p. 939); *Šeqal.* 6:2 (49d, p. 624).

third in line to the throne, fourth [in order] of birth. 'Zedekiah'—[means] he accepted his fate/judgement. 'Shallum'—[means] in his days the Davidic monarchy reached its end. His name was neither Shallum nor Zedekiah, but Mattaniah, as is written, 'And the king of Babylon appointed Mattaniah, Jehoiachin's uncle, king in his place [, changing his name to Zedekiah]' (2 Kgs 24:17).

B. Ker. 5b:[12]

הוא שלום הוא צדקיהו. ולמה נקרא שמו שלום? שהיה משולם במעשיו. דבר אח[ר], שלום—ששלמה מלכות בית דויד בימיו. ומה שמו? מתניה שמו, שנ[אמר] 'וימלך את מתניה תחתיו ויסב את שמו צדקיהו'.

Zedekiah is the same as Shallum, and why is he called Shallum? Because he was whole and complete in all his deeds. Another explanation: he was called Shallum, because the kingdom of the house of David came to its completion and conclusion in his days. But what was his real name? It was Mattaniah, as it is written, "And the king of Babylonian made Mattaniah, his father's brother, king in his stead, and he changed his name to Zedekiah" (2 Kgs 24:17).

The wording of the Targum—דשלימת מלכותא דבית דוד ביזמוי—may have been influenced by either of the Talmuds, given the great similarity between them. Nevertheless, it should be noted that the wording of TC corresponds more fully to BT as we know it, since the word order matches that in *b. Ker.*, albeit TC contains no hint of the first exegetical possibility raised by the Talmud.

2.3 *Jabez, Man of Torah and Prayer (1 Chr 2:55; 4:9–10, 13)*

יַעְבֵּץ of the Hebrew verse 1 Chr 2:55 is a toponym, but the fact of the name's being identical to that of one of the lead figures of Chronicles as the book traditionally is interpreted rendered this appearance of the word an additional opportunity to do honor to the personage of that man. That no place called יַעְבֵּץ is known from another source only made it easier for the targumist to treat this occurrence as a person, rather than a place.[13]

---

12 Another parallel appears in *b. Hor.* 11b:
הוא שלום הוא צדקיה. למה נקרא שמו שלום? שהיה מושלם במעשיו. דבר אחר, ששלמה מלכות בית דוד בחייו.

13 Regarding the Hebrew text and the meaning of the verse, see Knights *Rechabites*. Klein *1 Chronicles*, p. 107, and Knoppers *vol. 1*, p. 316, note that this settlement has yet to be identified.

Jabez the man appears in 1 Chr 4:9–10, where his name already is expounded in the book's Hebrew *Vorlage*, once explicitly—וַיְהִי יַעְבֵּץ נִכְבָּד מֵאֶחָיו וְאִמּוֹ קָרְאָה שְׁמוֹ יַעְבֵּץ לֵאמֹר כִּי יָלַדְתִּי בְּעֹצֶב, *Jabez was more esteemed than his brothers; and his mother named him Jabez, "Because," she said, "I bore him in pain."*—and a second time by implication—וְעָשִׂיתָ מֵרָעָה לְבִלְתִּי עָצְבִּי, *and make me not suffer pain from misfortune.*[14] TC identifies Jabez with Othniel son of Kenaz in three instances (1 Chr 2:55; 4:9, 13) and, where his name first appears in the Targum, expounds it even beyond the exegesis given in the Hebrew. Let us now consider the statements made by TC about Jabez and search for their sources.

1 Chr 2:55

MT	וּמִשְׁפְּחוֹת	סֹפְרִים יֹשְׁבֵי (קרי)	יַעְבֵּץ

TC   וגניסת   רחביה בר אליעזר בר משה   תלמידיא   דיעבץ הוא עתניאל בר קנז

יעבץ הוון צווחין ליה דאוקים בעיצתיה תרביצא לתלמידיא

NJPS: The families of the scribes that dwelt at Jabez

Dost: The lineage of Rechabiah son of Eliezer, son of Moses: the disciples of Jabez, who was Othniel son of Kenaz. They called him Jabez because he established by his counsel the study halls for the disciples.

1 Chr 4:9

MT	מֵאֶחָיו	נִכְבָּד	יַעְבֵּץ	וַיְהִי

TC   והוה יעבץ הוא עתניאל יקיר וחכים באוריתא יתיר מן אחוהי

MT (cont.)	בְּעֹצֶב יָלַדְתִּי כִּי לֵאמֹר יַעְבֵּץ שְׁמוֹ קָרְאָה וְאִמּוֹ

TC   ואמיה קרת שמיה יעבץ למימר ארום בצערא ילדתיה:

NJPS: Jabez was more esteemed than his brothers; and his mother named him Jabez, "Because," she said, "I bore him in pain."

Dost: Now it happened that Jabez, who was Othniel, was more honorable and versed in the Torah than his brothers. His mother called his name Jabez, saying, "Because in pain I bore him."

1 Chr 4:10

MT	תְּבָרֲכֵנִי אִם־בָּרֵךְ לֵאמֹר יִשְׂרָאֵל לֵאלֹהֵי יַעְבֵּץ וַיִּקְרָא

TC   וצלי יעבץ לאלהא דישראל למימר אין ברכא תברכנני בבניא

MT (cont.)	וְעָשִׂיתָ	וְהָיְתָה יָדְךָ עִמִּי	וְהִרְבִּיתָ אֶת־גְּבוּלִי

TC   ותסגי ית תחומי בתלמידיא ותהי ידך עמי במשקל ומכרא ותעביד לי

——————
14   Japhet *OTL*, pp. 109–110, views the allusion to his name in verse 10 as a means of mitigating the name's unhappy meaning.

(cont.) :אֲשֶׁר־שָׁאָל   אֵת   אֱלֹהִים   וַיָּבֵא   עָצְבִּי   לְבִלְתִּי   מֵרָעָה

TC   :חבריא דיכמתי מן בגלל דלא ירגזינני יצרא בישא ואייתי ה׳   ית מה דשאיל

NJPS: Jabez invoked the God of Israel, saying, "Oh, bless me, enlarge my territory, stand by me, and make me not suffer pain from misfortune!" And God granted what he asked.

Dost: Jabez prayed to the God of Israel, saying, "O that You would bless me with sons and increase my borders with disciples, and that Your hand would be with me in buying and selling, and that You would make for me companions who are like me so that the evil impulse would not provoke me!" So the Lord granted what he requested.

1 Chr 4:13

MT   :וּבְנֵי קְנַז עָתְנִיאֵל   וּשְׂרָיָה וּבְנֵי עָתְנִיאֵל חֲתַת

TC   :ובני קנז עתניאל הוא יעבץ ושריה ובני עתניאל חתת

NJPS: The sons of Kenaz: Othniel and Seraiah; and the sons of Othniel: Hathath

Dost: The sons of Kenaz: Othniel, who was Jabez, and Seraiah. The son of Othniel: Hathath.

Jabez is idealized in the Targum as a rabbinic saint. He establishes institutions of Torah education, trains many disciples, prays to God for both physical and spiritual success, and is granted what he requests. Jabez's identification with Othniel, who appears in many rabbinic sources, adds to his character the traits of Othniel as described in midrashic sources, including the ability to reconstruct the entire Torah by his great deductive powers.[15]

Midrashic Exegesis of the Name Jabez in the Targum: 1 Chr 2:55

יעבץ הוון צווחין ליה דאוקים בעיצתיה תרביצא לתלמידיא: The two key words of the Targum's midrashic homily on the name are בעיצתיה and תרביצא,[16] both playing

---

15   Among the various sources identifying Jabez with Othniel are *Sifre Deut.* 352 (p. 412); *b. Tem.* 16a; *Eccl. Rab.* 1:250 (p. 49); *Cant. Rab.* 4:7 (p. 52).

16   The word תרבץ has its source in the Akkadian *tarbāṣu*, i.e., yard. It is a familiar term in the Aramaic of BT, Geonic works, and later literature (Shelomoh the Babylonian, Abitur). The word also exists in Syriac, ܬܪܒܨܐ (Kutscher, p. 41; Sokoloff *JBA*, p. 1231; Sokoloff *Syriac*, p. 1664). Following is an excerpt from *Tanḥuma, Tazriaʿ* 9 (p. 123):

אלא שצדקה עשה עמנו שהקדים גלות יכניה לגלות צדקיה. ואי זו צדקה? שהקדים והגלה גלות יכניה לבבל עם החרש והמסגר ועם כל גבורי החיל וירדו לבבל ועשו תרבץ לתורה, שאילמלא היה כן לא היתה התורה משתכחת בגלות צדקיה ...

He did us a favor by preceding the exile of Jechoniah to that of Zedekiah. What is the favor? That He first exiled Jechoniah to Babylon with the [scholars and spiritual leaders] and they prepared a Tarbetz for the Torah, for if not for this the Torah would have been forgotten during the exile of Zedekiah ...

on the word יַעְבֵּץ. This exegesis is no innovation on the part of the targumist, but a further development of a tradition reported in *b. Tem.* 16a:

> תנא: הוא קנז הוא ענתיאל (sic) הוא יעבץ. ומה שמו? יהוד[ה] אחי שמע[ון] שמו.
> ענתיאל—שענאו אל. יעבץ—[ש]יעץ וריבץ תורה בישר[אל].

The two words יעץ and ריבץ,[17] which function talmudically to provide an etymology for the name *Jabez*, are replaced in TC by a pair of nouns: עיצה and תרביצא. It may be that the targumist saw תרביצא as a name derived from the verb רב״ץ. One way or the other, the exclusively Babylonian Aramaic noun here won out over the verb רב״ץ—a phenomenon with implications for the era of TC and influences on its author.

No Glory other than Torah: 1 Chr 4:9

In 1 Chr 4:9, TC expansively translates the Hebrew נִכְבָּד as יקיר וחכים באוריתא, *honorable and wise in the Torah*, thus explaining in what Jabez's glory lay: his Torah scholarship. The commentary should not be deemed as an innovation of the targumist: the verse serves in rabbinic literature as a source for the contention that glory is synonymous with greatness in Torah scholarship, as described in *Tanḥuma, Teẓavveh* 9 (p. 89):[18]

> 'וזה הדבר אשר תעשה להם'—ז[הו] ש[אמר] ה[כתוב]: 'כבוד חכמים ינחלו'. נאה
> הכבוד לחכמים היגיעין בתור[ה]. אמרה תורה: 'עושר וכבוד אתי הון עושר (sic)
> וצדקה'—את מוצא שלשים וששה דורות מאדם ועד יעבץ ולא כתיב באחד מהן כבוד
> אלא ביעבץ, שנ[אמר] 'ויהי יעבץ נכבד מאחיו'. ולמה כתיב בו כבוד? שהיה תלמיד
> חכם מקהיל קהילות ודורש טעמי תור[ה] ברבים, שנ[אמר] 'ומשפחות סופרי[ם]
> יושבי יעבץ' ...

---

17   Verbs of the root רב״ץ with the sense of disseminating Torah appear throughout rabbinic literature, e.g., *y. Kil.* 9:4 (32b, p. 175):

> אמ', מה הוה לעי באוריתא סגין מיני? אמ[ר] ליה, ריבץ תורה ביש[ראל] יותר ממך, ולא עוד
> אלא דהוה גלי.

He said, 'In what way did he tire himself in the Torah more than me?' He answered, 'He *spread* Torah throughout Israel more than you, and what's more he went into exile.'
B. Meg. 29a:

> והלא דברים קל וחומר: ומה תבור וכרמל שלא באו ללמד תורה אלא לפי שעה נקבעו בארץ
> ישראל, בתי כנסיות ובתי מדרשות שקורין בהן ושונין בהן ומרבצין בהן את התורה—על אחת
> כמה וכמה.

And the matter is an inference from minor to major. Just as Tabor and Carmel, which came only for a while to learn Torah, are fixed in Israel, how much more so [should this apply to] synagogues and academies, in which they read the Bible and *spread* Torah.

18   A parallel homily appears in *Exod. Rab.* 38:5 (p. 132).

'This is what you shall do to them to cleanse them' (Num 8:7)—of this Scripture has said: 'The wise shall obtain honor,' (Prov 3:35). Honor is fitting for the wise who toil in Torah. The Torah states: 'Riches and honor belong to me, enduring wealth and success.' (Prov 8:18)—one finds thirty six generations from Adam to Jabez and not of one is honor mentioned but of Jabez, as stated, 'Jabez was more esteemed (נכבד) than his brothers' (1 Chr 4:9). Why is he [worthy of] honor? He was a Torah scholar, he assembled crowds and explicated Torah to the masses, as stated, 'The families of the scribes that dwelt at Jabez' (1 Chr 2:55).

This addition in the Targum, inspired by this type of midrashic literature, is a part of the targumist's cultural agenda, in which scriptural heroes are depicted as Torah scholars.

The Prayer of Jabez: 1 Chr 4:10

In both content and style, the Targum to 1 Chr 4:10 interprets the elements of the prayer of Jabez in direct correspondence to the continuation of *b. Tem.* 16a, quoted in part above.[19] The Talmud there notes two different approaches for expounding the parts of the verse. Let us compare the two talmudic homilies to TC (an English translation of both homilies appears below the chart:

Verse	Homily 1 (*b. Temurah*)	Rabbi Yehudah's Homily (*b. Temurah*)	TC
אִם־בָּרֵךְ תְּבָרֲכֵנִי	בתורה	בפרייה ורבייה	בבניא
וְהִרְבֵּיתָ אֶת־גְּבוּלִי	בתלמידים	בבנים ובבנות	בתלמידיא
וְהָיְתָה יָדְךָ עִמִּי	שלא ישתכח תלמודי מלבי	במשא ובמתן	במשקל ומכרא
וְעָשִׂיתָ מֵרָעָה	שיזדמנו לי ריעים כמותי	שלא יהא מחוש ראש מחוש אזנים ומחוש עינים	ותעביד לי חבריא דיכמתי
לְבִלְתִּי עָצְבִּי	שלא ישגבני יצר הרע מלשנות	שלא ישגבני יצר הרע מלשנות	מן בגלל דלא ירגזינני יצרא בישא
לְבִלְתִּי עָצְבִּי	אם אתה עושה בי מוטב, ואם לאו הריני הולך כרסי־ סי [ל]שאול	אם אתה עוש[ה] כן מוטב, אם לאו הריני הולך ברסיסי לשאול	

---

19 A parallel to the two talmudic homilies appears in *Mek. RY, Yitro* 2 (p. 201). The argument made by Churgin *Hagiographa*, p. 250, to the effect that the author of TC used both BT and *Mekilta* is imprecise. All elements informing TC (interpretation of the name *Jabez*, first homily on the verse, homily on the verse by Rabbi Yehudah the Patriarch) are found in BT. *Mekilta*, meanwhile, contains the two homilies on the verse but lacks the interpretation of the name. The logical conclusion thus is that the author of TC here used specifically the Talmud.

b. Tem. 16a

How do we know that God had answered him? "Jabez called on the God
of Israel, saying, 'Oh that you would bless me and enlarge my border and
that your hand might be with me, and that you would keep me from harm
so that it might not hurt me!' And God granted what he asked" (1 Chr 4:10).
"that you would bless me:" in Torah-learning. "and enlarge my border:" in
disciples. "and that your hand might be with me:" that my learning should
not be forgotten from my heart. "and that you would keep me from harm:"
so that companions of my sort may be provided for me. "so that it might
not hurt me:" that the inclination to do evil not have power over me so as
to keep me from repeating my traditions. "If you do so, well and good,
but if not, lo, I shall go to the grave with my grief." Forthwith: "And God
granted what he asked."...

R. Judah the Patriarch says, "'Oh that you would bless me and enlarge
my border and that your hand might be with me, and that you would
keep me from harm so that it might not hurt me!' And God granted what
he asked" (1 Chr 4:10)—"'Oh that you would bless me:' in procreation.
"'and enlarge my border:' with sons and daughters. "'and that your hand
might be with me:' in the give and take of business. "'and that you would
keep me from harm:' so that I not suffer head-aches, ear-aches, or eye-
aches. "'so that it might not hurt me:' that the inclination to do evil not
have power over me so as to keep me from repeating my traditions. "If
you do so, well and good, but if not, lo, I shall go to the grave with my
Grief." Forthwith: "And God granted what he asked."

The first homily in *b. Temurah* expounds the entire verse as relating to Torah
study, while the homily offered by Rabbi Yehudah the Patriarch refers the bulk
of the verse to physical accomplishment and growth, turning to scholarship
only at its end (שלא ישגבני יצר הרע מלשנות, *that the inclination to do evil not
have power over me so as to keep me from studying*). Unlike the two talmudic
homilies, it appears that the text of the homily that lay before the targumist did
not have a single overriding focus, so that the targumist repeatedly moves back
and forth between matters personal and academic.

The first subject described in TC—children—occupies this place in neither
of the talmudic homilies, while the second subject given in TC, viz., disciples,
corresponds to that in the first talmudic homily. The result in TC is an equilib-
rium between blessings within the family—children—and blessings through
"children" in the study hall, i.e., disciples. Neither talmudic version offers such
a way to incorporate the two fields of endeavor.

In the homily quoted in the name of Rabbi Yehudah the Patriarch, reproduction is given as the first area in need of blessing, and children (sons and daughters) as the second. We may assume that he thus distinguished between reproduction—the birth of children per se—and children's maturation and emergence into the wide world, paralleling "and you expand my border" in the prayer. The targumist, choosing to dedicate the second part of the homily to students, may have chosen sons for the first area as something of a compromise including both of the initial subjects of the homily of Rabbi Yehudah the Patriarch, i.e., both children's birth and their maturation and development.

The third area to be blessed given by TC, following the reading of MS V, is משקל ומכרא. MSS C and E here read משקל ומטרא. The pair found in MS V, משקל ומכרא, is unfamiliar in Aramaic (the stem מכ״ר is one used in Hebrew rather than Aramaic), but corresponds to the common and ancient Hebrew expression מִקָּח וממכר.[20] The reading in C and E, which brings together verbal nouns for the roots שק״ל and טר״י, is the Aramaic equivalent of the Hebrew expression משא ומתן. The Aramaic expression, characteristic of Babylonian Aramaic, may be understood as denoting either the give-and-take of a commercial transaction or the give-and-take in a discussion of Torah.[21] It seems that the intention of the targumist here was to pen an expression reflecting the homily of Rabbi Yehudah the Patriarch, במשא ובמתן, and he thus gave the translation משקל ומטרא, as witnessed by MSS C and E. The reading found in V, במשקל ומכרא, may have arisen due to a scribal error resulting from the rare form מטרא.

---

20   It may appear in the *Damascus Document*, but the reading there is a dubious one (CD 13:15–16): ואל יעש איש דבר למקח ולממכר למבקר כי אם הודיע אשר במחנה, *No one should do any buying or selling unless he has informed the Overseer who is in the camp.* The expression is highly common in rabbinic parlance.

21   The idiomatic pairing of שק״ל and טר״י appears in BT in two contexts. Following is one example of usage in a business context (*B. Meṣiʿa'* 64a):

הגוזל את חברו והבליע לו בחשבון יצא. ואי איניש דאתי מעלמ[א] דלא שקיל וטרי בהדיה, מאי?

In the sense of a discussion of Torah matters (*B. Mak.* 11b):

לא הוה קא ידע מישקל ומיטרא בהדי רבנן;

לא הוה קא מסתייעא מלתיה למשקל ולמיטרא בהדי רבנן (*B. Qam.* 92a).

Aside from the present instance in TC, the verb pair of שק״ל and טר״י appears in two places in targumic literature: *Tg. Ruth* 4:7 וכהדא מנהגא ... בזמן דשקלין וטרן ופרקן ומחלפן; *Tg. Cant* 3:8 חד עם חבריה; וכהניא וליואי וכל שבטיא דישראל כולהון אחידין בפתגמי אוריתא דמתילן לחרבא ושקלן וטרן בהון כגברין מאלפי קרבא. Here, too, the expression belongs both to the business world and to that of Torah: in *Tg. Ruth* the context is financial, while in *Tg. Cant* it is religious. On the pairing of שק״ל and טר״י, see Levy, vol. 2, pp. 511–512; Sokoloff *JBA*, p. 1175.

The next request voiced by Jabez in the Targum is ־ותעביד לי חבריא דיכמ
תי. It is distinctly clear that this is an Aramaic version of the first homily in
b. Temurah: שיזדמנו לי ריעים כמותי. Up to this point, the structure of the homily consisted of the quotation of a request from the verse and description of
the area of endeavor in which the request's fulfillment was sought, with the
preposition ב indicating this area (ב + area). Now the structure of the homily
changes, and the area no longer is indicated by the preposition ב. The words of
the homily become more closely tied to those of the verse (ריעים—מֵרָעָה). The
targumist, who wanted not only to incorporate the homily in his work, but also
to provide an Aramaic sentence paralleling the Hebrew continuum, replaced
the homily's Hebrew verb שיזדמנו with the Aramaic verb ותעביד, aiming to position the latter word parallel to וְעָשִׂיתָ, its equivalent in the verse. The word
ריעים, appearing in the talmudic homily, corresponds to מֵרָעָה in the verse, and
the targumist translated the talmudic ריעים with the Aramaic word חבר, the
common equivalent of the biblical word רֵעַ in the various Targums, including
TC (2 Chr 6:22; 20:23).[22]

The homilies in BT are in agreement with regard to the final request: שלא
ישגבני יצר הרע מלשנות. In the Talmud the request is presented as an exegetical interpretation of the words לְבִלְתִּי עָצְבִּי and followed by another homily on
the same words: ואם לאו הריני הולך כרסיסי לשאול, אם אתה עושה בי מוטב.[23] TC
included the final request, מן בגלל דלא ירגזינני יצרא בישא, but not the additional
exegetical unit. It may be that this final unit is absent from TC because it did
not appear in the original text of the homily, a possibility suggested by the
double treatment of the words לְבִלְתִּי עָצְבִּי, which deviates from the homily's
expected structure. In any event, by substituting the verb רג״ז for שג״ב, TC referred this part of the homily to the word עָצְבִּי, as well. Here, too, the targumist
clearly made a point of associating his expansions with the language of the
Hebrew *Vorlage*, for which reason he added the words מן בגלל, thus connecting the homily's fourth and fifth requests. This linkage produces a deviation
from the structure of the homily in BT, but this deviation puts it more in
line with the Hebrew verse, which the targumist understood as a continuum

---

22   In MS Vatican 119, the version in the Talmud has three occurrences of מרעים rather than
     מרעה.

23   The form כרסיסי apparently is a corruption of בנסיסי, the word found in the textual wit-
     nesses to the parallel in *Mek. RY, Yitro* 2 (p. 202; see variant readings ibid.). The sense of
     the word is *to be sad* or *angry* (cf. TO Gen 40:6: וַיַּרְא אֹתָם וְהִנָּם זֹעֲפִים || וחזא יתהון והא
     אינון נסיסין, [*he*] *saw them, and behold, they were **downcast***). In the sentence in the Talmud
     and *Mekilta*, the meaning of בנסיסי thus is that the speaker will descend to Sheol in sad-
     ness, as in Gen 37:35: כִּי־אֵרֵד אֶל־בְּנִי אָבֵל שְׁאֹלָה, *I will go down mourning to my son in Sheol.*

comprised of a series of requests, each juxtaposed to an appropriate explanation: לְבִלְתֵּי עָצְבֵּי ←וְעָשִׂיתָ מֵרָעָה.

In conclusion, the targumist here created an eclectic homily combining
both competing talmudic homilies, while remaining mindful of the link between his composition and his *Vorlage*, viz., the Hebrew text of Chronicles.

2.4 Why Caleb Was Dubbed Son of Jephunneh (*1 Chr 4:15*)

1 Chr 4:15

MT	וּבְנֵי כָּלֵב בֶּן־יְפֻנֶּה עִירוּ אֵלָה וָנָעַם וּבְנֵי אֵלָה וּקְנַז:
TC	הוא חצרון והון צווחין ליה ובני כלב בר יפנה
	מטול דפני לביה מן עיטת מאלייא כלב בר יפנה
	ואלין בנוי עירו אלה ונעם ובני אלה קנז:

NJPS: The sons of Caleb son of Jephunneh: Iru, Elah, and Naam; and the sons
of Elah: Kenaz.

Dost: The sons of Caleb son of Jephunneh, who was Hezron. They called him
Caleb son of Jephunneh, because he turned his heart from the counsel of the
spies. These were his sons: Iru, Elah, and Naam. The son of Elah: Kenaz.

The motivation for identifying Jephunneh with Hezron lies in the appearance
of Caleb son of Hezron in 1 Chr 2:18. Those identifying Hezron with Jephunneh
sought to unify Caleb of 1 Chr 2 and Caleb son of Jephunneh, the familiar figure
from the story of the spies, who appears in the present verse. In order to establish that the two characters are the same, the targumist added to this verse
a homiletic treatment of the name *Jephunneh*. A similar homily appears in a
passage of BT that we already have seen was familiar to TC: in our discussion of
the prayer of Jabez, we found that the targumist had included in his composition midrashic material taken from two homilies found in *b. Temurah* 16a. In
their talmudic context, these homilies are preceded by a question concerning
the name of Caleb's father, as follows:[24]

וכלב בן קנז? והא כלב בן יפנה הוא! מאי יפנה? שפנה מעצת מרגלים. ואכתי בן קנז
הוא? בן חצרון הוא, דכת[יב] 'וכלב בן חצרון הוליד את עזובה אשה'. א[מר] רבא:
חורגיה דקנז הוא.

---

24   Another parallel appears in *b. Soṭah* 11b:

בן חצרון? בן יפנה הוא! א"ר יוח[נן], שפנה מעצת מרגלים.

Son of Hezron? He was the son of Jephunneh?! R. Johanan said, he turned away from the
advice of the spies.

Now was Caleb the son of Kenaz? Was Caleb not the son of Jephunneh?
The meaning of the word Jephunneh is that he turned away from the
advice of the spies. Still, was Caleb the son of Kenaz? He was the son of
Hezron: "And Caleb the son of Hezron begat Azubah" (1 Chr 2:18). *Said
Raba, "He was the step-son of Kenaz".*

The Talmud's comment שפנה מעצת המרגלים is reflected by TC in the words
דפני לביה²⁵ מן עיטה²⁶ מאלייא, while the talmudic assertion that he was the son
of Hezron is reflected in TC by כלב בר יפנה הוא חצרון. Significantly, the identification here established between Jephunneh and Hezron is only a formal one.
In effect, the name יפנה serves in the Talmud, and subsequently in TC, not as a
reference to the name of Caleb's father, but as a description of Caleb himself,
based on his actions during the saga of the spies.

2.5   *The Many Names of Moses, and Bithiah's Marriage to Caleb
(1 Chr 4:18)*

1 Chr 4:18 challenges the reader with a Hebrew sentence that is semantically
complex and exegetically enigmatic. The nature of the relationship between
the first woman who appears in the verse, who in MT is presented not by name
but by title, and the second, designated Bithiah daughter of Pharaoh, is not entirely clear.²⁷ Even if we reach the conclusion that the verse is concerned with
just a single woman, her name is highly surprising: if indeed she is a daughter
of the Egyptian pharaoh, how could it be that she married an undistinguished
native Israelite, even if he was the head of a clan?²⁸ Further, why does she have
a theophoric Israelite name? These very questions that trouble students of the
plain sense of Scripture serve midrashic exegetes as an opportunity to present

---

25   It may be that the targumist added the word לביה, *his heart*, in order to clarify the Talmud's
       comments. Also possible is that the targumist referred to a variant version of the Talmud;
       MS Vatican 119 indeed gives the text of BT as שפנה עצמו מעצת מרגלים. Finally, the word
       לביה may have been intended to include Caleb's name in the homily: כלב בן יפנה—שפנה
       לבו מעצת המרגלים.
26   On the form עיטה (with *ṭeit* rather than *ẓadi*) see p. 198.
27   Cf. deliberation in Knoppers *vol. 1*, p. 341.
28   Cf. comments by Japhet *OTL*, pp. 114–115:
       The name and title of this Egyptian wife, the unique 'Bithiah the daughter of Pharaoh',
       are both extraordinary ... That an undistinguished member of the tribe of Judah would
       marry a 'daughter of Pharaoh' is extremely unlikely, not only in the context of biblical
       tradition but for historical reasons as well.
           Due to this difficulty, Demsky, p. 433, proposed that the version in MT is secondary and
       the original form of the name of Bithiah's father was עפר, brother of Mered, who appears
       in verse 17.

the verse as well illustrating Chronicles' place as a treasure whose very purpose is exegesis. Let us now consider the verse and its targum, which includes ex-egetical insertions concerning all of the names found within it:

1 Chr 4:18

MT   יֶ֫רֶד   אֶת־ יָלְדָ֣ה הַיְהֻדִיָּ֗ה וְאִשְׁתּ֣וֹ

TC   דאוחית   ירד שמיה וקרת מיא מן שחלתיה כד משה   ית רביאת יהודיתא ואנתתיה

MT (cont.)   וְאֶת־חֶ֫בֶר   אֲבִ֣י גְדֹ֔ר

TC   לאבוהון ישראל דחבר   חבר וית   דישר' חורבנהון דבנא דגדור רבא לישראל מנא

(cont.)   וְאֶת־יְקוּתִיאֵ֖ל   אֲבִ֥י שׂוֹכ֑וֹ

TC   לאלהא ישראל דאמתינו   יקותיאל וית   בזכותיה ישר' בית על דטליל דסוכו רבא דבשמיא

(cont.)   אֲבִ֣י זָנֽוֹחַ

TC   אמטולתיה ישראל חובי על אלהא דשבק   זנוח רבא במדברא שנין ארבעין ביומי דבשמי'

(cont.) מֶ֑רֶד   לָקַ֖ח אֲשֶׁר   בַּת־פַּרְעֹ֔ה בִתְיָ֣ה   בְּנֵ֣י וְאֵ֨לֶּה

TC   מרד ליה   מרד ונסבה ואתגירת נבואה ברוח פרעה ברת בתיה   ליה קרת שמהן אליין

לאתו הוא כלב דמרד במלכת מאלליא:

NJPS: And his Judahite wife bore Jered father of Gedor, Heber father of Soco, and Jekuthiel father of Zanoah. These were the sons of Bithiah daughter of Pharaoh, whom Mered married.

Dost: Jehuditha his wife raised Moses after drawing him from the water, and she called his name Jered because he brought manna to Israel; Prince of Gedor because he rebuilt the ruins of Israel; Heber because he bound Israel to their Father who is in heaven; Prince of Soco because he covered the house of Israel by his merit; Jekuthiel because in his days Israel waited forty years in the wil-derness for their God, who is in heaven; Prince Zanoah because God forgave the sins of Israel on his account. These are the names that Bithia daughter of Pharaoh named him through the spirit of prophecy. She converted to Judaism and married Mered, who is Caleb, who opposed the counsel of the spies.

The targumist here mediated between his task of transmitting a complete Aramaic verse and his desire to preserve the homiletic traditions he had re-ceived concerning each of the figures mentioned in the verse. Despite the verse's complexity and length, the targumist successfully generated a synthesis between a typical targum, in which all words of the Hebrew verse are sequen-tially treated, and a rabbinic homily, in which an expression is isolated from the surrounding sentence and intensively analyzed. Each name in the verse functions as a heading of sorts for the homily attached to it, but the Targum nevertheless preserves the structure of a complete sentence, whose constituent parts connect like links in a chain.

The parts comprising this intricate structure come together to express a complete idea: all of the homilies that the Targum attaches to the names in the verse concern Moses not as a private individual, but in terms of the good he did for the people of Israel in various areas: he supplied them with manna, he rebuilt their ruins, he forged a connection between them and God, his merit protected them, Israel hoped to God in his day, God forgave the sins of Israel on his account.[29] The common thread is particularly evident in the treatment of the name שׂוֹכוֹ, viz., דטליל על בית ישראל בזכותיה, *he covered (i.e. protected) the house of Israel by his merit*. The name very well could have been expounded as meaning שהיה סוכה ברוח נבואה, *he gazed through the spirit of prophecy*, but the general homiletical theme of the verse—the benefits that accrued to Israel due to Moses—dictated the content of the exegesis given to the name in TC.[30]

This framework, however, is no innovation of the targumist: he found it ready for the taking in an exegetical tradition in *b. Meg.* 13a.[31] The author of

---

29 Additional names are attributed to Moses in TC 1 Chr 24:6.

30 Cf. the following homily on the name in *Lev. Rab.* (excerpted in full in the following note): אבי סוכו—זה היה אבי שלכל הנביאים שהיו סוכין ברוח הקו[דש]. Cf. discussion of the name שׂוֹכָתִים in context of 1 Chr 2:55 (pp. 368–369).

31 The present verse also is treated in the following homily (*Lev. Rab.* 1:3, vol. 1, pp. 7–11), many of whose details differ from those in BT:

ר' סימון בש[ם] ר' יהושע בן לוי ור' חמא אבוה דרב הושעיה בש[ם] ר[בי]: לא ניתן ספר
דברי הימים אלא לידרש. 'ואשתו היהודיה ילדה את ירד אבי גדור ואת חבר אבי סוכו ואת
יקותיאל אבי זנוח אלה בני בתיה בת פרעה אשר לקח מרד'. 'ואשתו היהודיה'—זו יוכבד.
וכי משבטו שליהודה היתה? והלא מלוי היתה! ולמה נקרא שמה היהודיה? על שום שהעמי־
דה יהודים בעולם. 'ילדה את ירד'—זה משה. ר' חננא בר פפא ור' סימון. ר' חננא אמ[ר]:
'ירד'—שהוריד את התורה מלמעלה למטה. ד[בר] א[חר]: 'ירד'—שהוריד את השכינה מל־
מעלה למטה. אמ[ר] ר' סימון: אין לשון 'ירד' אלא לשון מלוכה. היך מה דא[ת] אמ[ר], 'ויֵרד
מים עד ים ומנהר עד אפסי ארץ'. וכת[יב]: 'כי הוא רודה בכל עבר הנהר'. 'אבי גדור'—ר'
חונא בש[ם] ר' אחא אמ[ר]: הרבה גודרים עמדו להן לישראל וזה היה אביהן שלכולן. 'ואת
חבר'—שהחיבר את הבנים לאביהם שבשמים. ד[בר] א[חר]: 'חבר'—שהעביר את הפורענות
מלבוא לעולם. 'אבי סוכו'—זה היה אבי שלכל הנביאים שהיו סוכין ברוח הקודש. ר' לוי
אמ[ר]: לשון ערבי הוא, בערביה צוחין לנביא סכייא. 'יקותיאל'—ר' לוי ור' סימון. ר' לוי
אמ[ר]: שעשה את הבנים מקוין לאביהן שבשמים. אמ[ר] ר' סימון: בשעה שהקהו בנים לאל
במעשה העגל. 'אבי זנוח'—בא משה והזניחן מאותה עבירה. ה[דא] ה[וא] ד[כתיב]: 'ויֵזר על
פני המים' וגו'. 'אלה בני בתיה בת פרעה'—ר' יהושע דסיכנין בש[ם] ר' לוי. אמ[ר] לה הקב"ה
לבתיה בת פרעה: משה לא היה בנך וקראת אותו בנך. אף את לא את בתי ואני קורא אותך
בתי: 'אלה בני בתיה'. 'אשר לקח מרד'—זה כלב. ר' אבא בר כהנא ור' יהודה בר סימון. ר'
אבא בר כהנא אמ[ר]: זה מרד בעצת מרגלים וזו מרדה בעצת אביה. יבוא מורד ויקח את
המורדת. ר' יהודה בר' סימון אמ[ר]: זה הציל את הצאן וזו הצילה את הרועה. יבוא מי שהציל
את הצאן ויקח מי שהצילה את הרועה.

that tradition, R. Shimʿon b. Pazi, introduces his comments with a declaration preparing his audience for a homily that reveals an underlying theme that lies latent in what at first glance appears to be a series of a great many disparate details. A look at his homily will make clear that its framework is quite similar to that in TC:

ר' שמעון בר פזי, כד הוה פתח בדברי הימים, אמר הכי: כל דבריך אחד הם ואנו
יודעים לדרשם ...

'היהודייה'—והלא בתיה שמה! ואמאי קרי לה יהודייה? על שם שכפרה בע[בודה]
ז[רה], שנ[אמר] 'ותרד בת פרעה לרחוץ על היאור'. אמ[ר] ר' יוחנן משום ר'
שמעון בן יוחאי: שירדה לרחוץ מגילולי בית אביה.

'ילדה את ירד'—ירד זה משה. ולמה נקרא שמו ירד? שירד להם לישראל מן בימיו.
'ילדה'—והא רבויי רביתיה? אלא לומר לך שכל המגדל יתום בתוך ביתו מעלה עליו
הכת[וב] כאלו ילדו.

'גדור'—שגדר פרצותיהן שלישראל.

'חבר'—שחיבר את ישראל לאביהן שבשמים.

'סוכו'—שנעשה להן לישראל כסוכה.

'יקותיאל'—שקוו ישראל לאל בימיו.

'זנוח'—שהזניח עונותיהן שלישראל.

'אבי' 'אבי' 'אבי'—אב בתורה, אב בחכמה, אב בנביאות.

'ואלה בני בתיה בת פרעה אשר לקח מרד'—וכי מרד לקחה? והלא כלב לקחה! ולמה
נקרא מרד? שמרד בעצת המרגלים. אמ[ר] הקב"ה: יבוא מרד, שמרד מיעצת
המרגלים, וישא בתיה בת פרעה, שמרדה בגלולי בית אביה.

*When R. Shimon ben Pazi began to expound Chronicles, he said as follows:
All your words are one, and we know how to explain them:... Why was she
called "Jewish"?* Because she rejected idolatry, as is written, "and Pharaoh's
daughter went down to wash on [the shore of] the Nile" (Exod 2:5). And
said R. Yohanan: Because she went down to wash [i.e., to purify] herself
from the abominations of her father's house. "Bore" (1 Chr 1:14)? Actually
she raised him. [But Scripture considers her like a parent,] to tell you

---

The midrashic tradition concerning the many names of Moses came down through the
generations as far as an anonymous liturgical poem, beginning with the words מי גבר
יחיה ולא יראה מות, that serves as a *qedushtaʾ* for the Sabbath on which the final Torah
portion of the annual cycle is read in the synagogue. The poem, dated by the Historical
Dictionary Project to 300–600 CE, has the following to say about Moses' names (lines
102–111):

אני ירד אשר הורדתיה, אני חבר אשר חברתיה, אני יקותיאל אשר הקויתיה, אני אביגדור
אשר גדרתיה, אני אבי סוכו אשר סככתיה, אני אבי זנוח אשר לא זנחתיה, אני טוביה אשר
הטיבותיה, אני נתנאל אשר נתתיה, אני שמעיה אשר שמעתיה, אני משה אשר שמתיה.

that anyone who raises an orphan or orphaness in his house, Scripture considers it as if he bore him. "Yered" is Moses; and why was he called Yered? Because Manna came down (*yarad*) for Israel in his days; "Gedor," because he forced in (*gadar*) the breaches of Israel; "Heber," because he caused Israel to draw near (*hibber*) to their father in heaven; "Sokho," because it was made for Israel like a tabernacle (*sukkah*); "Yequtiel," because Israel hoped in God (*qavu yisra'el la-'el*) in his days; "Zenoah," because he disregarded (*hizniah*) the sins of Israel; "Father of …, father of …, father of …," [meaning] father in Torah, father in wisdom, father in prophecy. "And these are the sons of Bityah whom Mered married" (ibid.). And is his name Mered? His name is Caleb. Said The Holy One, Blessed Be He: Let Caleb, who rebelled against the advice of the spies [and gave a good report about Canaan (Num 14:30)], come and marry the daughter of Pharaoh, who rebelled against the abominations of her father's house.

Now let us consider the wording in TC in comparison to the talmudic homily:

ואנתתיה יהודיתא רביאת ית משה: Because the targumist considered the woman in question to be Pharaoh's daughter, rather than Moses' biological mother, he replaced the Hebrew verb יָלְדָה with the Aramaic root רב״י, thus changing the meaning from birth to rearing. This approach is in accordance with the comments on the word יָלְדָה found in the above talmudic passage: והא רבויי רביתיה? אלא לומר לך שכל המגדל יתום בתוך ביתו מעלה עליו הכת׳ כאלו ילדו.[32]

כד שחלתיה מן מיא: This insertion is not reflected by the sources containing exegesis of the present verse, but corresponds to the wording of Exod 2:10 (כִּי מִן־הַמַּיִם מְשִׁיתִהוּ, *I drew him out of the water*) as translated by TO (ארי מן מיא) and TPJ (ארום אמרת מן מוי דנהרא שחילתיה).[33] Nowhere else in targumic literature is the root שח״ל used, so that its appearance in TC in the same context as TO and TPJ presumably reflects TC's decision to borrow the term from the Targum of the Torah. Surely nothing could be more appropriate than to incorporate that verse, which tells of Moses' adoption by Pharaoh's daughter, in the present one, with its exegesis regarding the man.

---

32 See also *b. Sanh.* 19b:
וכי בתיה בת פרעה ילדה? והלא יוכבד ילדה! אלא יוכבד ילדה ובתיה גידלה, לפיכך נקראו על שמה.
And did Bithia give birth [to Moses], and did not Jochebed do so? But while Jochebed gave birth to him, Bithia raised him, therefore he bore her name.

33 Cf. other verbs in TN (ארום מן מיא דלית); FTP (שליבתיה); FTV (ארום מן מיא שזבת יתיה); יתיה).

ירד זה משה. ולמה נקרא שמו :In keeping with BT above ירד דאוחית מנא לישראל
ירד? שירד להם לישראל מן בימיו.

רבא דגדור דבנא חורבנהון דישׂר[אל] :The Targum's choice of words (בנא חורבן)
does not correspond to that of BT, which uses the root גד"ר (in the expression
גדר פרצה) to reflect גְדוֹר of the verse. Still, TC seems to have had the same homily in mind, as in 1 Chr 4:23 (i.e., later in the chapter; see discussion, p. 275) the
word וּגְדֵרָה is given an expansive translation based on the word pair בנ"י חורבן,
to (re-)build a ruin. The word pair בנ"ה חורבה appears in Hebrew alongside גד"ר
פרץ in Isa 58:12: ... וּבָנוּ מִמְּךָ חָרְבוֹת עוֹלָם ... וְקֹרָא לְךָ גֹּדֵר פֶּרֶץ, *Men from your midst
shall rebuild ancient ruins ... and you shall be called "Repairer of fallen walls"*....
The title גֹּדֵר פֶּרֶץ in the verse is associated in rabbinic literature with Moses,
in accordance with a comparison with another verse linking Moses with the
word פרץ: לוּלֵי מֹשֶׁה בְחִירוֹ עָמַד בַּפֶּרֶץ לְפָנָיו, *he would have destroyed them had
not Moses His chosen one confronted Him in the breach* (Ps 106:23).[34] It may be
presumed that the exegetical baggage of Isaiah 58 and Psalm 106 had a part in
the framework of the wording of BT, but the baggage's footprints grow faint
in the Aramaic text of TC. This faintness results from the semantic difference
between the Hebrew גד"ר פרצה and the Aramaic בנ"י חורבן. When BT used the
term גד"ר פרצה in its homily, it apparently did so in reference to Moses' distancing Israel from sin and taking a firm stand for ethical behavior.[35] When
TC replaced this word pair from BT with the Aramaic equivalent בנ"י חורבן,
the change came at the expense of the strong ethical meaning of the original
expression.

שחיבר את ישראל :In keeping with BT above וית חבר דחבר ישׂראל לאבוהון דבשׁמיא
לאביהן שׁבשׁמים.

---

34   *Lev. Rab.* 34:16 (vol. 2, pp. 813–814):

     'וקורא לך גודר פרץ'—ר' אבין בש[ם] ר' ברכיה סבא: אמ[ר] הקב"ה, הפרצה הזאת שלי
היתה לגודרה ועמדתה וגדרתה. מעלה אני עליך כאותו שׁעמד בפרץ, דכת[יב]: 'לולי משׁה
בחירו עמד בפרץ לפניו'.

     you shall be called "Repairer of fallen walls"—R. Abin in the name of R. Berekhia the elder:
The Holy One blessed be He said, it was My breach to repair, but you arose and repaired
it. I shall consider you the one who arose (and repaired) the breach, as is written: *'had not
Moses His chosen one confronted Him in the breach'.*

35   In addition to the literal meaning of גד"ר פרצה, the expression serves as a metaphor for
rectification of moral failings and action against lawlessness; see Jastrow, p. 214. Isa 58:12,
גֹּדֵר פֶּרֶץ מְשׁוֹבֵב נְתִיבוֹת לָשָׁבֶת, is rendered by the Targum according to the metaphoric
sense: מקיים אורחא דתקנא מתיב רשׁיעיא לאוריתא, *the establisher of the proper way who
restores the wicked to the Torah.*

שנעשה להן [רבא דסוכו דטליל על בית ישר[אל] בזכותיה: The comment by BT above, לישראל כסוכה, does not explain how it is that Moses resembled a hut. TC speci-fies that he would shelter, i.e., protect, the House of Israel with his merit. The version of the talmudic homily found in *Yalquṭ Šimʿoni*, שזכו שנעשה לישראל כסוכה, *they were fortunate that he became for Israel like a booth*, brings the version in TC closer to that of the Talmud, though there the verb זכו refers to the Israelites, rather than to Moses.[36] The word זכותיה refers to Moses in 1 Chr 2:55, as well: דטב להון זכותיה מפרשין וארתיכין (regarding which see pp. 370–371).

וית יקותיאל דאמתינו ישראל לאלהא דבשמי׳ ביומו׳ ארבעין שנין במדברא: The Hebrew homily in BT, שקוו ישראל לאל בימיו, interprets the name יקותיאל as derived from the stem קו״ה.[37] The common targumic translation of קו״ה is סב״ר, based on which we would have expected TC to use a form such as דסברו. The root מת״ן does, however, function as an equivalent of קו״ה in five instances in *Tg. Ps*, and the root's sense of anticipation exists in Syriac, as well.[38] We therefore may say that the targumist had in mind the Hebrew root קו״ה, as in BT, when he wrote the Aramaic root מת״ן. The word בימיו in the talmudic homily finds its expres-sion in TC in the word ביומו׳, but rather than make do with this, the targumist clarified the Talmud's comments with the addition ארבעין שנין במדברא. Perhaps the targumist felt a need to explain that the Israelites did not hope to God all of Moses' days from the time of his birth: the purpose of the homily is to teach that the Israelites' good behavior was a result of Moses' character, and the tar-gumist therefore limited this behavior to the period during which Moses led the Israelites in the wilderness.

רבא זנוח דשבק אלהא על חובי ישראל אמטולתיה: The targumist's comments cor-respond to and expound those of the Talmud. חובי ישראל of the Targum are עונותיהן שלישראל of the Talmud. BT expounded the word זנוח with reference to the verb הזניח, the subject of the verb being Moses. For the targumist, though, it was easier to change the structure of the sentence wholesale than to translate the challenging form הזניח. God thus became the subject of the sentence, with the accustomed form שבק serving as predicate. However, because the homily

---

36   *Yalquṭ Šimʿoni* 1 Chr 1074 (p. 1033), the reading in which is not supported by MSS of BT.

37   Contrary to the view of R. Simon in *Lev. Rab.*, who interpreted יקותיאל as derived from the root קה״ה.

38   Ps 52:11; 56:7; 69:21; 119:95; 130:5. The various MSS of *Tg. Ps* are not in agreement regarding usage of the verb מת״ן. Data presented here are based on the text of MS Paris 110. See comment by Dan, pp. 20–21, that מת״ן appears as a marginal version secondary to אר״ך in this MS as a translation of וְהִתְחוֹלֵל in Ps 37:7.
     Sokoloff *Syriac*, p. 1327.

is concerned with Moses, the targumist added אמטולתיה: God forgave the sins of Israel on account of Moses.

אליין שמהן קרת ליה בתיה ברת פרעה ברוח נבואה: This statement concluding the exegesis of the preceding names does not parallel the language of the original homily. Having interpreted all of the names in the verse as alluding to Moses' life, the targumist was compelled to alter the meaning of the Hebrew ending, וְאֵלֶּה בְּנֵי בִתְיָה בַת־פַּרְעֹה, as the verse now contains not multiple sons, but multiple names of Bithiah's sole son, Moses. The targumist therefore changed the text of the Aramaic verse accordingly. What is left is for the targumist to explain how Pharaoh's daughter could have provided so many names—and names so detailed—referring to events that would not transpire for decades. He answered this question with an addition consisting of the words ברוח נבואה, *in the spirit of prophecy.*

ואתגירת ונסבה ליה מרד לאתו הוא כלב דמרד במלכת מאלליא: The conversion of Pharaoh's daughter is alluded to in the beginning of the homily recorded in BT:

'היהודייה'—והלא בתיה שמה! ואמאי קרי לה יהודייה? על שם שכפרה בע[בודה] ז[רה], שנ[אמר] 'ותרד בת פרעה לרחוץ על היאור'. אמ[ר] ר' יוחנן משום ר' שמעון בן יוחאי: שירדה לרחוץ מגילולי בית אביה.

This detail was not relevant to the targumist when he set about his literal translation of the verse's beginning: אנתתיה יהודיתא. Now that it becomes clear that Pharaoh's daughter married Caleb, though, the targumist clarifies that she converted prior to her marriage. The end of the verse also is translated in accordance with the talmudic homily: וכי מרד לקחה? והלא כלב לקחה! ולמה נקרא מרד? שמרד בעצת המרגלים.[39]

2.6   *A Homily Praising Those Who Study Torah (1 Chr 4:22–23)*
1 Chr 4:22

MT	וְיוֹקִים וְאַנְשֵׁי כֹזֵבָא
TC	ונבייא וספרי' דנפקו מזרעא דיהוש' וגבעונאי דמתיהבין לעבדין בבית־מקדשא מטול דכדיבו לרברביא דישראל

---

39   Cf. *b. Sanh.* 19b: מרד—זה כלב. ולמה נקרא שמו מרד? שמרד בעצת מרגלים; *Lev. Rab.* 1:3 (excerpted above).

TC translated the Hebrew expression עצת מרגלים as מלכת מאלליא, but three verses prior, 1 Chr 4:15, we find מאלליא עיטה. והוון צוווחין ליה כלב בר יפנה מטול דפני לביה מן עיטת מאלליא. I have no explanation for why the targumist used עיטה above but מלכה here.

MT (cont.) לְמוֹאָב   אֲשֶׁר־בָּעֲלוּ   וְשָׂרָף   וְיוֹאָשׁ

TC   ויואש הוא מחלון ושרף הוא כליון די נסיבו נשין מבנת מואב

(cont.)   וְהַדְּבָרִים עַתִּיקִים: לֶחֶם   וְיָשֻׁבִי

TC   ובועז רב חכימיא דמתיבת בית־לחם דמתעסקין בפתגמי עתיק יומין:

NJPS: and Jokim, and the men of Cozeba and Joash, and Saraph, who married
into Moab and Jashubi Lehem (the records are ancient).

Dost: and the prophets and the scribes who were born of the seed of Joshua,
and the Gibeonites, who were appointed as servants in the temple because
they deceived the leaders of Israel, and Joash, who was Mahlon, and Saraph,
who was Chilion, who took wives from the daughters of Moab, and Boaz, the
chief of the sages of the Academy of Bethlehem, who were occupied with the
words of the Ancient of Days.

1 Chr 4:23

MT   הֵמָּה   הַיּוֹצְרִים   וְיֹשְׁבֵי   נְטָעִים

TC   הנון תלמידי אוריתא דאמטילהון עלמא אתברי דיתבין על דינא ומיצבי עלמא

MT (cont.) בִּמְלַאכְתּוֹ   הַמֶּלֶךְ   עִם־   וּגְדֵרָה

TC   ובנן ומשכללין ית חורבני בית ישראל עם שכינת מלכא דעלמא בפולחן אוריתא
     ובעבור ירחיא
ובקביעות רישי שניא ומועדיא

(cont.)   שָׁם: יָשְׁבוּ

TC   אתיתבו תמן וסכמין מן שמיא על דעתהון ביומי רות אמא דמלכותא
     עד יומי שלמה   מלכא:

NJPS: These were the potters who dwelt at Netaim and Gederah; they dwelt
there in the king's service.

Dost: They were the disciples of the Torah for whom the world was created,
who preside in judgment and make the world stand sure, and (who) rebuild
and bring to an end the desolations of the house of Israel with the Shekhinah
of the King of the World, by the service of the Torah, by the intercalation of
months, and by the establishing of the beginnings of the years and appointed
times. They sat there and determined from heaven by their knowledge in the
days of Ruth, the mother of the kingdom, until the days of King Solomon.

Both of the above verses undergo dramatic enlargement in their translation
to Aramaic. The names in the first verse are identified with familiar scriptural
characters: Joshua, the Gibeonites, Mahlon, Chilion, Boaz. The words of the
second verse, understood as areas of activity, are interpreted as referring to

scholars who study the Torah diligently and set the calendar. These pursuits, according to their context in the Targum, occupied the figures noted in the preceding verse. TC thus partially follows the homilies to these two verses in *b. B. Bat.* 91b.[40] Let us first refer to the homily as it appears in the Talmud. Afterward we shall consider the various elements of the Aramaic verse in terms of their relationship both with the Hebrew *Vorlage* and with rabbinic exegeses:

'ויויקים'—זה יהושע שהקים שבועה לגבעונים. 'אנשי כזיבה'—אלו הגבעונים שכיזבו ליהושע ואמרו לו: 'מארץ רחוקה באנו', והם באו מארץ קרובה. 'יואש ושרף'—אלו מחלון וכליון. ולמה נקרא שמן יואש ושרף? 'יואש'—שנתיאשו מן הגאולה; 'שרף'—שנתחייב שריפה למקום. 'אשר בעלו למואב'—שנשאו נשים מואביות. 'וישובי לחם'—זו רות ששבה ודבקה בבית לחם יהודה. 'והדברים עתיקים'—דברים אלו עתיק יומיא אמרן ... 'היוצרים'—אלו בני יונדב בן רכב שנצרו שבועת אביהם, לא אכלו בשר ולא שתי יין ולא בנו בתים ולא נטעו כרמים. 'יושבי נטעים'—זה שלמה המלך שדומה לנטע במלכותו. 'ישבו שם'—זו רות שזכתה וראתה במלכות שלמה בן בנו של בן בנה. 'וגדרה'—אלו סנהדרין שגדרו פרצותיהן של ישראל. 'וישם כסא לאם המלך'—א"ר אלעזר: לאימה של מלכות.

"Jokim": this refers to Joshua, who kept his oath to the men of Gibeon (Josh 9:15, 26). "And the men of Cozeba": these are the men of Gibeon who lied to Joshua (Josh 9:4). "And Joash and Saraph": Their names really were Mahlon and Chilion, and why were they called Joash? Because they despaired hope of redemption, and Saraph? Because they become liable by the decree of the Omnipresent to be burned. "Who had dominion in Moab": they married wives of the women of Moab. "And Jashubilehem": this refers to Ruth of Moab, who had returned and remained in Bethlehem of Judah. "And the things are ancient": these things were stated by the Ancient of Days ... "These were the potters": this refers to the sons of

---

40   TC here is most similar to BT, but interpretations of this verse also appear in *Sifre Num* 78 and variously in *Ruth Rab.* 2:1–4 (pp. 42–54). Following is the homily in *Sifre* (p. 74):

'ויוקים'—שקיים להם יהושע ברית. 'כוזיבא'—שכזיבו ליהושע ואמרו 'מארץ רחוקה מאד באו עבדיך'... 'יואש ושרף'—זה מחלון וכליון'. 'יואש'—שנתיאשו מן הגאולה. 'יואש'—שנ־ תיאשו מדברי תורה. 'שרף'—ששרפו בניהם לעבודה זרה. 'אשר בעלו למואב'—שנשאו נשים מואביות. 'אשר בעלו למואב'—שהניחו ארץ ישראל ונהפכו בשדה מואב. 'והדברים עתיקים'—כל אחד ואחד מפורש במקומו. 'ויושבי נטעים'—זה שלמה שהיה דומה לנטיעה במלכותו. 'וגדרה'—זו סנהדרין שהיתה יושבת וגודרת בדברי תורה. 'עם המלך במלאכתו ישבו שם'—מנין אתה אומר שלא מתה רות המואביה עד שראתה שלמה בן בנה שהיה יושב ודן דינן של זונות? שנא[מר], 'עם המלך במלאכתו ישבו שם'. והרי דברים ק[ל] ו[חומר]: ומה אם מי שהיתה מן העם שנ[אמר] בו 'לא תבואו בהם והם לא יבואו בכם', על שקירבה את עצמה כך קירבה המקום—ישראל שעושים את התורה על[ל] א[חת] כ[מה] ו[כמה].

Jonadab, son of Rahab, who kept the oath of their father (Jer 35:6). "And those that dwelt among plantations": this speaks of Solomon, who in his rule was like a fecund plant. "And hedges": this refers to the Sanhedrin, who hedged in the breaches in Israel. "There they dwelt occupied in the kings work": this speaks of Ruth of Moab, who lived to see the rule of Solomon, her grandson's grandson: "And Solomon caused a throne to be set up for the king's mother" (1 Kgs 2:19), in which connection R. Eleazar said, "For the mother of the dynasty."

[ע]דיהוש מזרעא דנפקו [א]וספרי ונבייא: The Talmud identifies יוקים with Joshua, who is thus named in reference to the covenant he established with the Gibeonites. The targumist explained that the verse refers not to Joshua himself, but to his descendants, who had careers as prophets and scribes. Prophets and scribes together comprise a hendiadys, as targumic works commonly use the word ספר (or ספרייא) as an equivalent of נביא (or נביאים). As noted by Levita, s.v. סָפָר:[41]

> The expression *prophet* in the Prophets generally is translated as ספר or ספריא, other than those [occurrences concerning individuals] known to be prophets: Nathan the Prophet, Jeremiah the Prophet, Habakkuk the Prophet, and others such as they all are translated נבייא, and others are translated ספר, e.g., "by the hand of any prophet" (ביד כל נביא—ביד כל) ספר ...

This explanation by the targumist, viz., that the verse is concerned with Joshua's descendants rather than with Joshua himself, is not explicit in any rabbinic homily, but the targumist understood that the verse sought to describe not merely Joshua's generation, but the transmitters of the Torah over the course of multiple generations following the Israelites' arrival in the Land of Israel. He therefore interpreted the reference to Joshua as merely indicating the beginning of the chain. In the targumist's view, the terms that he selected, viz., *prophets* and *scribes* (as well as *sages*, further along in the verse), span the entire period from Joshua to the Rabbis, and these figures function as a pathway through which the Torah is transmitted from the time of its giving until the exile.

---

41   *Meturgeman* 103a. See also Goshen-Gottstein, vol. 1, p. 152. For a study of equivalents of the word נביא in TJ, see Saldarini. See also summary of various studies in Dray, pp. 119–120, 129–133.

וגבעונאי דמתיהבין לעבדין בבית־מקדשא מטול דכדיבו לרברביא דישראל: The words אַנְשֵׁי כֹזֵבָא are understood not as referring to the men of a place called Cozeba, but as alluding people who lied regarding their origins, viz., the Gibeonites. The Talmud and other sources of exegesis to this verse describe the Gibeonites as having lied to *Joshua*. TC, however, names רברביא דישראל, *the leaders of Israel*. It may be that the targumist was influenced by the relevant verses of Joshua and TJ, where several verses state that the oath to the Gibeonites was made by the princes of the congregation, who appear in TJ as רברביא (Josh 9:15, 18, 19, 21). The Gibeonites' punishment, servitude to the Temple, also is absent in the sources of this exegesis, and appears only in the Targum.

ויואש הוא מחלון ושרף הוא כליון די נסיבו נשין מבנת מואב: The various exegetical sources are in agreement that Joash is Mahlon and Saraph is Chilion, but differ regarding the meaning of the names *Joash* and *Saraph*. The identification itself stems not from any particular feature of the names themselves, but from the statement in the Hebrew that they בָּעֲלוּ לְמוֹאָב, an expression understood as appropriate for the sons of Elimelech and Naomi, who married Moabite women.[42] The author of TC, who received the identification as a tradition, is beyond the point of needing to justify it with a homily on the meaning of the names *Joash* and *Saraph* and instead cites the identification without comment as a *fait accompli*: Joash is Mahlon, Saraph is Chilion.

ובועז רב חכימיא דמתיבת בית־לחם: An exegetical take on the Hebrew וְיֹשְׁבִי לָחֶם. The word ישבי is interpreted as indicating a yeshiva, and לחם as referring to the city of Bethlehem.[43] Due to the presence of both of these elements, Boaz's name is mentioned—not because the words as such allude to his name, but because the targumist was familiar with the rabbinic tradition that Boaz headed a rabbinical court in Bethlehem. We are aware of no source other than TC that interprets יֹשְׁבִי לָחֶם as referring to a yeshiva in Bethlehem or mentions Boaz in connection with the phrase.[44] Some interpreted the Hebrew phrase positively and some negatively, but even those in the first camp did not give it

---

42 Notably, although the version in the Talmud is שנשאו נשים מואביות (not שנשאו נשים), following Ruth 1:4, וַיִּשְׂאוּ לָהֶם נָשִׁים מֹאֲבִיֹּת, TC here has די נסיבו נשין מבנת מואב. This terminology adds to the negativity of the homily by recalling Num 25:1: וַיָּחֶל הָעָם לִזְנוֹת אֶל־בְּנוֹת מוֹאָב.

43 מתיבה, in the sense of an academic institution, is a loan translation of the Hebrew ישיבה. This sense of the word is not documented in Aramaic prior to the Geonic Period; see Sokoloff *JBA*, p. 720, and sources cited ibid.

44 *Ruth Rab.* 2:2 (p. 50) interprets a different expression—הֵמָּה הַיּוֹצְרִים of the following verse—as an allusion to Boaz and Ruth.

a meaning associated with Torah study.[45] Regardless of whether the targumist received this homily from a source now unknown or conceived it independently, he selected it instead of other extant interpretations for its description of Torah scholars and study in the institution of the yeshiva. The word חכימיא is a complement to נבייא וספריא at the start of the translated verse. In the eyes of the targumist, these three words span the tradition of Torah from the days of Joshua to the era of the Rabbis.

דמתעסקין בפתגמי עתיק יומין: Here the Targum bases its translation on the Talmud's exegesis (דברים אלו עתיק יומיא אמרן), but adds the verb מתעסקין so as to associate this part of the verse and the sentence in general with Torah study, using a turn of phrase reminiscent of the familiar liturgical expression לעסוק בדברי תורה.

הנון תלמידי אוריתא דאמטילהון אתברי עלמא: Now that the targumist has established that these verses are concerned with the tradition of Torah and its students, he proceeds with a homily in praise of those who study Torah. I believe it is for this reason that he here ignored BT's homily to the verse concerning Jonadab son of Rechab. Although even in the targumist's view the verse describes only specific Torah scholars, he adds words of praise in order to glorify and encourage Torah study in his own generation. The word on which the expansion here hinges is הַיּוֹצְרִים, which is interpreted as referring to the creation of the world (אתברי עלמא).

דיתבין על דינא ומיצבי עלמא: The targumist continues with his autonomous homily concerning Torah scholars, making no mention of the Talmud's association of the text here with King Solomon. The word יֹשְׁבֵי is interpreted with reference to those who sit in judgment, and נְטָעִים (according to the simple sense of the verse, the name of a settlement) is taken to portray halakhic guides as planting the world—a figure that, in combination with דאמטילהון אתברי עלמא, above, is reminiscent of a homily on the present verse reported by *Gen. Rab.* 8 (p. 61):

עם המלך במלאכתו ישבו שם—עם מלך מלכי המלכים הקב״ה ישבו נפשותן שלצדיקים שבהן נמלך וברא העולם.

The homily in *b. B. Bat.* interprets the phrase in praise of Ruth. The homily in *Sifre Num*, which scathingly describes Mahlon and Chilion as having left the Land of Israel only to be overturned in the Land of Moab, may read וישובו להם; see interpretation by M. Kister cited in Kahana, vol. 3, p. 542.

'they dwelt there in the king's service'—with the King of all kings' kings, the Holy One blessed be He, did the souls of the righteous dwell, with whom He consulted and created the world.

The present form מיצבי is an enigmatic one. On one hand, it appears to have the stem יצ״ב, which is why Le Déaut and Robert translated it as *"affermissent,"* McIvor as "establish" and Dost as "stand sure".[46] On the other hand, the Hebrew word נְטָעִים has the stem נט״ע, whose typical Aramaic translation is the Aramaic root נצ״ב,[47] which is the term we would expect to find used in the text of TC. Levy derived the present form from the root יצ״ב, but argued that it was synonymous with נצ״ב, while considering whether the text of TC might perhaps require emendation to read מנצבין.[48] Adding to the conundrum is that Aramaic verbal forms from the root יצ״ב are extremely rare. To say the least, they are uncommon in Jewish Aramaic literature from the talmudic period onward.[49]

וּבנן ומשכללין ית חורבני בית ישראל: These words express a homily on וּגְדֵרָה. In the homily on the names of Moses, the phrase אבי גדור was interpreted as דבנא [בנ״ה חורבה]/חורבנהון דישר[אל] (1 Chr 4:18; see discussion ibid., p. 267). The pair appears in Hebrew alongside גד״ר פרץ in Isa 58:12: וְקֹרָא ... וּבָנוּ מִמְּךָ חָרְבוֹת עוֹלָם. In Amos 9:11, as well, גד״ר פרץ is part and linguistic parcel with לְךָ גֹּדֵר פֶּרֶץ. construction and rehabilitation of something that has been ruined: בַּיּוֹם הַהוּא אָקִים אֶת־סֻכַּת דָּוִיד הַנֹּפֶלֶת וְגָדַרְתִּי אֶת־פִּרְצֵיהֶן וַהֲרִסֹתָיו אָקִים וּבְנִיתִיהָ כִּימֵי עוֹלָם, *in that day, I will set up again the fallen booth of David: I will mend its breaches and set up its ruins anew. I will build it firm as in the days of old.* For this reason, the targumist used the translation בני חורבן for the toponym גְּדֵרָה. Such treatment is consistent with BT's interpretation of this verse: אלו סנהדרין שגדרו פרצותיהן של ישראל, *these are the Sanhedrin who mended the breaches of Israel.* The targumist, however, had no need to mention the Sanhedrin, because unlike the talmudic context, the homily in TC already is in the midst of a discussion of Israel's Torah scholars.

---

46 MS C reads מייצבין; MS E has מיצבן. See Le Déaut-Robert, vol. 1, p. 50; McIvor, p. 61.

47 E.g. Gen 2:8:

MT	וַיִּטַּע ה׳ אֱלֹהִים גַּן־ בְּעֵדֶן מִקֶּדֶם
TO	ונצב ה׳ אלהים גנתא בעדן מלקדמין

NJPS: The LORD God planted a garden in Eden, in the east

Clem: And the Lord God planted a garden in Eden, from the beginning

48 Levy, vol. 1, p. 341.

49 Twice in Elephantine papyri (TAD B3 10:22; 11:17), on which see relevant comment by Kutscher, p. 41; once in Dan 7:19; once in *Tibat Markeh*, p. 289.

הַמֶּלֶךְ עם שכינת מלכא דעלמא: of the Hebrew verse is construed by the Targum as referring to God, whose title מלך העולם, *King of the world*, is used here in agreement with the homily on these words in *Genesis Rabbah*, noted above.[50] The word *Shekhinah* is added in the interest of avoiding a formulation that might seem to describe God as a physical being (see pp. 84–87, above), since the scholars of the Torah are described as sitting with Him.

בפולחן אוריתא ובעבור ירחיא ובקביעות רישי שניא ומועדיא: The Hebrew word בִּמְלַאכְתּוֹ caused the use of the word פולחן in the Aramaic translation. Now the targumist goes on to establish what labor is intended. It already has been ascertained that the king in the verse is the king of the world and the verses have been interpreted as a discussion of Torah scholars. What work do the Creator and Torah scholars have in common? The work of Torah, פולחן אוריתא. The targumist proceeds to specify the tasks for which these sages bore responsibility, listing a series of calendric activities, including intercalation of months and calculation of new years and holidays. All of these depended on decisions of the Sanhedrin in Jerusalem, which received visual testimony of the appearance of the new moon. Later, following the transition to a fixed calendar, dates were set in advance by mathematic calculation. The targumist's lengthy expansion on this topic, including God's endorsement of the Torah scholars' actions, suggests that the task of setting the calendar was one of special importance in the eyes of the targumist. A possible reason for this will be considered in the discussion of 1 Chr 12:33, pp. 478–481.

אתיתבו תמן: Corresponding to יָשְׁבוּ שָׁם of the Hebrew verse.

וסככמין מן שמיא על דעתהון: This expansion gives a heavenly imprimatur to actions taken by Israelite scholars to set the calendar and gives expression to the commonality of this task to God and the sages. The verb סכ״ם found here is a hapax legomenon in TC. The word appears nowhere in TO or TJ, but does appear in TN and TPJ, as well as a in a few isolated occurrences in *Tg. Ps*, *Tg. Job*, and *Tg. Cant.*

ביומי רות אמא דמלכותא עד יומי שלמה מלכא: After taking his leave of the Talmud's homily and other midrashic sources to glorify and praise Torah scholars, the targumist now returns to the Talmud's homily, associating the people in the

---

50   The expression מלכא דעלמא is rare in targumic literature, as in Aramaic literature generally. Aside from the present verse, it appears once in *Tg. Ps* 45:15. The similar phrase מלכיה דעלמא appears in *Pesiqta Rabbati*; see Goshen-Gottstein, vol. 2, p. 30.

verse with Ruth and Solomon. The decision is a natural one within the context of the homily recorded in BT, where Solomon has been associated with the words יֹשְׁבֵי נְטָעִים. Based on that identification, another verse already has been quoted and interpreted: וישם כסא לאם המלך—א"ר אלעזר: לאימה של מלכות, this woman being Ruth. In TC, however, the statement is somewhat removed from its context, and included solely due to the targumist's familiarity with the talmudic homily. The expression אמא דמלכותא is a translation of אימה של מלכות of BT.[51]

As we have seen, large parts of TC 1 Chr 4:22–23 bear the mark of *b. Bava Batra*, while others interpret the verses differently from the Talmud. Based on this finding, Churgin believed that the targumist had worked two different sources into his composition.[52] This proposal explains the departure of many of the targumist's words from the Talmud, but fails to grant due weight to two circumstances: 1) TC's second source is unknown, differing even from other known sources of these homilies to the verses. 2) The translation that results from combining the two sources generally keeps to a consistent topic.

It thus seems unjustified to assume that the targumist here must have relied on another midrashic source. Instead, it must be taken into account that the targumist himself may have been the source of changes made to the talmudic homily. The point of departure for the targumist's translation to 1 Chr 4:22–23 was a homily recorded in *b. Bava Batra*, but he wanted the topic of the homily to be a series of praises heaped upon Torah scholars. Where the talmudic homily agreed with this topic, he adopted the talmudic text and set it within the Targum. Where the talmudic homily went too far afield of this subject, the targumist did without the Talmud's comments and found his own way to interpret the verses in reference to Torah scholars. It is not impossible that the targumist here employed an unknown source, but at least equally likely is that this second source was the targumist himself.

2.7 *The Ephraimites' Tragic Error (1 Chr 7:21)*
1 Chr 7:21

MT	וְזָבָד בְּנוֹ וְשׁוּתֶלַח בְּנוֹ וְעֵזֶר וְאֶלְעָד
TC	וזבד בריה ושותלח בריה ועזר ואלעד הנון הוו אמרכליא לבית אפרי' ומנו ית קצא

---

51 Other sources identify אֵם הַמֶּלֶךְ of 1 Kgs 2:19 as Ruth, but the phrase אמה של מלכות appears only in BT and *Ruth Zuṭa'* 1:1 (p. 39), the latter of which appears in any event to have obtained the expression from the former.

52 Churgin *Hagiographa*, pp. 251–252.

מן שעתא דהות דבירא דמרי עלמא מתמללא עם אברהם ביני פסוגיא וטעו דהוה
חמי להון לממני מן יומא דאתיליד יצחק ונפקו ממצרים תלתי׳ שנין קדם קיצא ארום
תלתין שנין מן־קדם דאתיליד יצחק הות דבירא דמרי עלמא מתמללא עם אברהם ביני
פסוגי׳ ובמפקהון ממצרים הוון עמהון מאתן אלפין גברין במאני זינא משבטא דאפרי׳

| MT (cont.) | וַהֲרָגוּם אַנְשֵׁי־גַת הַנּוֹלָדִים בָּאָרֶץ כִּי יָרְדוּ לָקַחַת אֶת־מִקְנֵיהֶם: |
| TC | וקטלונן אנשי גת דאתילידו בארע פלישתאי ארום נחתו למבוז גיתיהון: |

NJPS: his son Zabad, his son Shuthelah, also Ezer and Elead. The men of Gath,
born in the land, killed them because they had gone down to take their cattle.
Dost: Zabad his son, Shuthelah his son, and Ezer and Elead. They were officers of the house of Ephraim, and they calculated the appointed time from the
hour when the Divine Speech of the Lord of the World was conversing with
Abraham between the pieces. They erred because they should have calculated
from the day when Isaac was born, and (thus) they left Egypt thirty years before the end. For thirty years before Isaac was born the Divine Speech of the
Lord of the World conversed with Abraham between the pieces. When they
left Egypt there were with them 200,000 men from the tribe of Ephraim with
weapons, but the men of Gath, who were born in the land of the Philistines,
killed them, because they went down to plunder their herds.

A variety of versions of this aggadic tradition appear in a range of sources, incorporating exegesis of Exod 13:17; Ps 78:9; and the present verse.[53] The details
of the different versions of the tradition are not wholly in agreement, but the
source most similar to TC is TPJ. Therefore, for the purposes of the discussion
at hand, we shall focus on the similarities between the story of the Ephraimites
as recorded in TC and in TPJ relative to the other sources in which the tradition
appears. TPJ Exod 13:17 reads:

והוה כד פטר פרעה ית עמא ולא דברינון ה׳ אורח ארע פלישתאי ארום קריב הוא
ארום אמר ה׳ דילמא יתהון עמא במחמיהון אחוהון דמיתו בקרבא מאתן אלפין גוברין
בני חילא משבטא דאפרים מאחדין בתריסין ורומחין ומני זיינין ונחתו לגת למיבוז
גיתי פלישתאי ובגין דעברו על גזירת מימרא דה׳ ונפקו ממצרים תלתין שנין קדם קיצא

---

53   List of rabbinic and targumic sources containing this tradition: *b. Sanh.* 92b; *Mek. RY,
      Be-Shallaḥ* (pp. 76–77); *Exod. Rab.* 20:11 (p. 77); *Cant. Rab.* 2:7 (p. 32); *Pesiqta de-Rab
      Kahana, Be-Shallaḥ* 10 (p. 186); FTP Exod 13:17; GT X Exod 13:17; TPJ Exod 13:17; TC 1 Chr 7:21;
      Tg. Ps 78:9–10; *Tg. Cant* 2:7; TT Ezek 37 (Kasher *TT*, p. 199 [fragment 131a]; Kasher *TT*,
      p. 201 [fragment 131b]. McIvor, p. 74, n. 17, cites *Pirqe Rabbi Eliezer* 48 (in Higger edition,
      47, p. 237), where indeed there is a legend concerning the death of the Ephraimites, but in
      this source they are killed not by the Philistines, but by the Egyptians.

איתמסרו בידא דפלשתאי וקטלונון הינון הוו גרמיא יבישיא דאחי יתהון מימרא דה'
על ידא דיחזקאל נביא בבקעת דורא ואין יחמון כדין ידחלון ויתובון למצרים

And it came about when Pharaoh released the people, that the Lord did not lead them by the way of the land of the Philistines, since it was near, because the Lord said, "Perhaps the people will regret when they see their brothers who died in battle, two hundred thousand men, men of valor from the tribe of Ephraim, clutching shields and lances and weapons (now they had gone down to Gath to plunder the herds of the Philistines, and since they had transgressed the decree of the Memra of the Lord and had gone out of Egypt thirty years before the time, they had been handed over into the hand of the Philistines, and they had killed them. They were the dry bones that the Memra of the Lord had made to live by the hand of Ezekiel the prophet in the plane of Dura). For if they see them like this, they will fear and return to Egypt."

Each of the Targums contains elements absent from the other, but there is an identifiable resemblance between the two that may even be understood as evidencing literary dependence. The words selected by TC for the translation of לָקַחַת אֶת־מִקְנֵיהֶם, *to take their cattle*, in the present verse are למבוז גיתיהון. The choice is a somewhat surprising one, because this is the only instance in which TC translates the root לק״ח as בז״ז, *to loot*, despite the existence of other cases where the sense of the verb is *to take property by military force* (1 Chr 20:2; 2 Chr 12:9). In the other five instances in TC where the root בז״ז corresponds to a Hebrew word in MT (2 Chr 14:13; 20:25; 25:13; 28:8), the Hebrew word, too, has the root בז״ז. I therefore view as significant the fact that the surprising word choice in TC is similar to that in the above excerpt from TPJ referencing the account in Chronicles (גיתי פלישתאי ונחתו לגת למיבוז). Since the author of TC was well acquainted with TPJ, as proven above, I assume that the choice of a translation from the root בז״ז was influenced by the text of TPJ.[54]

The numbers in TC—both the number of years by which the Ephraimite exodus was premature (thirty) and the number of Ephraimites killed (200,000)—are similar to those in the Palestinian targumic tradition and in TPJ, and I presume that TPJ received them from the Palestinian Targums, and TC from TPJ.

Amid TC's lengthy comments here we find the phrase ומנו ... קצא ... טעו .... The selection of these words may indicate that the targumist had reference

---

As noted above (pp. 185–188), the word פסוגיא found here in TC is indicative of a link to another verse in TPJ.

to another source, as well, viz., *b. Sanh.* 92b–the only place where BT cites
this verse:

ומאן אינון מתים שהחיה יחזקאל? אמ[ר] רב: אלו בני אפרים שמנו לקץ וטעו,
שנ[אמר] 'בני אפרים שותלח ... והרגום אנשי גת הנולדים בארץ כי ירדו לקחת את
מקניהם'.

And who were the dead whom Ezekiel resurrected? Said Rab, "They were
the Ephraimites who reckoned the end of time and erred, as it is said,
'And the sons of Ephraim, Shuthelah ... whom the men of Gath that were
born in the land slew' (1 Chr 7:20–21).

The lengthy text of TC appears to be an expansion of the Talmud's brief comments, which do not give any explanation of the error made in counting the
years. TC provides something of an explanation of when the Ephraimites
began counting and the nature of their error.[55]

2.8 *Villages Destroyed during the Israelite Campaign against Benjamin (1 Chr 8:12)*

1 Chr 8:12

MT   וּבְנֵי אֶלְפַּעַל עֵבֶר וּמִשְׁעָם וָשָׁמֶד הוּא   בָּנָה   אֶת־אֹונֹו וְאֶת־לֹד וּבְנֹתֶיהָ:

TC   ובני אלפעל עבר ומשעם ושמר הוא אלפעל דבנא ית אונו וית לוד וכופרנהא
דצדיאו בני ישראל ואוקדנון בנורא כד אגחו קרבא בגבעתא עם שיבט בנימן:

NJPS: The sons of Elpaal: Eber, Misham, and Shemed, who built Ono and Lod
with its dependencies.

Dost: The sons of Elpaal: Eber, Misham, and Shamer. It was Elpaal who built
Ono as well as Lod and its villages, which the children of Israel desolated and
burned with fire when they waged war against Gibeatha with the tribe of
Benjamin.

The targumist adds to the Hebrew verse that the cities it lists were rebuilt after
they were incinerated in the wake of the incident of the concubine at Gibeah
and the ensuing war with the Benjaminites. TC here refers to Judg 20:48: וְאִישׁ

---

55   Cf. *Tg. Ps* 78:9, which is similar to BT: מנו קיצא וטעו. Churgin *Hagiographa*, p. 253, distin-
      guishes between TPJ, according to which their exodus from Egypt was a sinful action, and
      BT, according to which it was in error, and argues that TC's source was BT. My sense is that
      the targumists were not open to this distinction between sin and innocent error, given the
      presentation in *Tg. Ps* (ibid., vv. 9–10) of the very attempt to calculate the time of the end
      as undesirable and even sinful:
      כד הוון יתבין במצרים איתרברבו בני אפרים מנו קיצא וטעו ונפקו ... ואיתקטלו ... מטול דלא
      נטרו קים אלהא ובאורייתיה סריבו להלכא.

יִשְׂרָאֵל שָׁבוּ אֶל־בְּנֵי בִנְיָמִן וַיַּכּוּם לְפִי־חֶרֶב מֵעִיר מְתֹם עַד־בְּהֵמָה עַד כָּל־הַנִּמְצָא גַּם כָּל־הֶעָרִים הַנִּמְצָאוֹת שִׁלְּחוּ בָאֵשׁ, *the men of Israel, meanwhile, turned back to the rest of the Benjaminites and put them to the sword—towns, people, cattle—everything that remained. Finally, they set fire to all the towns that were left.* The interpretation given by TC is not based on any allusion contained in the Hebrew verse, but follows *b. Megillah* 3b–4a,[56] which quotes the verse from Chronicles and establishes a link with the incident at Gibeah.

ואמ[ר] ר' יהושע בן לוי לוד ואונו גאי חרשים מוקפות חומה מימות יהושע בן נון. והני יהושע בננהי? והלא אלפעל בננהי, דכת[יב]: 'ובני אלפעל עבר ומשעם ושמד הוא בנה את אונו ואת לוד ובנתיה'?... אלא אמר ר' אלעזר הני מוקפות חומה מימות יהושע בן נון הוו ואיחרוב בימי פילגש בגבעה ואתא אלפעל ובננהי ...

And said R. Joshua ben Levi: Lod, and Ono, and Gei HaHarashim have been surrounded by a wall since the time of Joshua bin Nun. *Did Joshua [really] build them? Elpaal build them, for it is written,* "The sons of Elpaal were Eber, and Misham, and Shemer. He built Ono, and Lod, and its suburbs" (1 Chr 8:12)... *Said R. Eleazar: They were* surrounded by a wall at the time of Joshua bin Nun. They destroyed them in the time of the concubine in Gibeah [cf. Judg 20], *and along came Elpaal and built them.*

2.9 *The Ulamites' Reward for Subduing Their Urges (1 Chr 8:40)*

1 Chr 8:40

MT			דַּרְכֵי קֶשֶׁת	אֲנָשִׁים גִּבּוֹרֵי־חַיִל	בְּנֵי־אוּלָם	וַיִּהְיוּ
TC			בקשתא בחוכמתא	דנגיד	גברי חילא כבשין יצריהון הי־כגברא	והוו בני אולם גברין

MT (cont.)	מֵאָה וַחֲמִשִּׁים כָּל־אֵלֶּה	וּבְנֵי בָנִים	בָּנִים	וּמַרְבִּים
TC	גניסתהון מאה וחמשין כל אליין	ובני בנין	בנין	בגין כן הוו מסגין

(cont.)	בִנְיָמִן:	מִבְּנֵי
TC	בנימן:	מבני שיבט

---

56 Cf. *y. Meg.* 1:1 (70a, p. 740):

והכת[יב] 'ובני אלפעל עבר ומשעם ושמד הוא בנה את אונו ואת לוד ובנותיה'? אמ[ר] ר' לעזר ביר' יוסה: בימי פילגש בגבעה חרבה ועמד אלפעל ובנייה. הדא היא דכת[יב]: 'גם כל הערים הנמצאות שלחו באש'.

Is it not written, 'The sons of Elpaal: Eber, Misham, and Shemed, who built Ono and Lod with its dependencies'? R. Lazar son of R. Josa said: it was destroyed at the time of the Gibeanite concubine and Elpaal arose and rebuilt it. Thus is written, *'finally, they set fire to all the towns that were left'* (Judg 20:48).

NJPS: The descendants of Ulam—men of substance, who drew the bow, had many children and grandchildren—one hundred and fifty; all these were Benjaminites.

Dost: The sons of Ulam were men (who were) valiant warriors, (who) mastered their desires just as the man who skillfully draws the bow. Therefore, they grew numerous in sons and grandsons. Their family was 150. Also these were sons of the sons of the tribe of Benjamin.

The Hebrew verse states two unrelated facts regarding the sons of Ulam: they were expert archers, and they had many children. TC offers a midrashic proposal for linking the two parts of the verse: they were not in fact archers, but men whose ability to control their sexual urges was comparable to that of an expert archer, and they were blessed with many sons as reward for their conduct. The unexpected association established by TC between the two parts of the verse was explained by Le Déaut and Robert as stemming from the metaphoric sexual meaning given the word קשת, *bow*, in rabbinic parlance.[57]

I believe that Le Déaut and Robert were right to understand the Targum here as having a sexual connotation, but this alone does not suffice to reveal the targumist's intent here. *B. Nid.* 31a–b interprets the verse specifically with regard to the conception of boys:

תנו רבנן: בראשנה היו או[מרים], אש[ה] מזר[עת] תחלה—יולד[ת] זכר, איש
מזריע תחלה—יולד[ת] נקבה. ולא פירשו חכמ[ים] את הדבר, עד שבא ר' צדוק
ופירשו: שנ[אמר] 'אלה בני לאה אשר [י]לדה ליעקב בפדן ארם ואת דינה בתו'—
תלה הכת[וב] את הזכר[ים] בנקבות ואת הנקבות בזכרים. ואו[מר] 'ויהיו בני אולם
אנשים גבורי חיל דורכי קשת מרבים בנים ובני בנים'. וכי בידו של אדם להרבות בנים
ובני בנים? שמתוך שמשהין עצמן בבטן כדי שיזריעו נשותיהם תחלה שיהו בניהם
זכרים, מעלה עליהן הכת[וב] כאילו מרבים בנים ובני בנים.

Our rabbis have taught on Tannaite authority: Earlier people would say, "If the woman reaches orgasm first, she will bear a male child, and if the male reaches orgasm first, she bears a female child." But sages did not articulate the basis for saying so, until R. Sadoq came along and spelled it out: "'These are the sons of Leah, whom she bore to Jacob in Paddan-aram with his daughter Dinah' (Gen 46:15). In this way Scripture makes the males depend upon the females, and the females upon the males." "And the sons of Ulam were mighty men of valor, archers; and they had many sons and sons of sons" (1 Chr 8:40)—but does a person

---

57   Le Déaut-Robert, vol. 1, p. 61, n. 9.

have the power to increase the number of sons and sons of sons? Rather, since in having sexual relations, they held themselves back in the womb so that their wives would reach orgasm first so that their children would be male, Scripture credits them as though they were the ones to increase the number of sons and sons of sons.

The Talmud's comments contain no explicit statement of a causal relationship between the two parts of the verse, so that an exegete inclined to view them as causally related must identify a connection between גִּבּוֹרֵי־חַיִל דֹּרְכֵי קֶשֶׁת, *men of substance, who drew the bow*, of the verse and the act described in the Talmud of holding oneself in the womb, and I believe that this is what the targumist did in turning the verse's description from a concrete to a metaphoric one. The traditional equivalence drawn between a mighty person and a person who subdues his urges is entirely familiar to any novice from *m. 'Abot* 4:1. The act described in the Talmud of holding oneself in the womb was understood by the targumist as an act of self-control suitable for the expression כבשין יצריהון הי־כגברא דנגיד בקשתא בחוכמתא, (*who*) *mastered their desires just as the man who skillfully draws the bow*: just as an archer well-versed in his art (בחוכמתא) knows how to land his arrow precisely, so did the sons of Ulam know how to exert control over their bodies and execute the act of insemination with precision that brought about the birth of many boys. In this case it would be difficult fully to understand the intent of the targumist without knowledge of the above talmudic passage, since the Targum's vague comments do not specify how the sons of Ulam subdued their urges. The targumist may have felt that such a matter, with its sexual implications, was best left to an allusion, and thus purposely left it ambiguous.

2.10 *Merib-baal as Mephibosheth (1 Chr 9:40)*

1 Chr 9:40

MT	וּבֶן־יְהוֹנָתָן	מְרִיב בָּעַל	וּמְרִיב־בַּעַל הוֹלִיד אֶת־מִיכָה׃
TC	וברִיה דיהונתן	מריב־בעל	ומריב־בעל אוליד ית מיכה׃

{ל"א} וברִיה דיהונתן מריב־בעל הוא מפיבשת

ואתקרי מריב־בעל מן־בגלל דעבד פלוגתא עם מרי עלמא על דהדר דוד בשלם ולא פרע גומלא טבא ליה היכמא דקיים ליהונתן אבוי:

NJPS: and the son of Jonathan was Merib-baal; and Merib-baal begot Micah. Dost: Jonathan's son was Meribaal, and Meribaal fathered Micah. ANOTHER READING: Jonathan's son was Meribaal, who was Mephibosheth, but he was called Meribaal because he disputed with the Lord of the World because David returned safely and was not repaid the good deed to him as he had sworn to Jonathan his father.

TC gives two alternate translations of 1 Chr 9:40, the first literal, and the second a homiletical and expansive version paralleling only the beginning of the verse.

MS V is the only MS known to us containing the expansion, which thus did not receive the attention of Rosenberg and Kohler or of Churgin.[58] McIvor referred readers to *b. Yoma* 22b to understand the background behind TC's expansive translation.[59] The Talmud there indeed portrays David negatively for his treatment of Mephibosheth after returning to Jerusalem, but the various elements of the translation in TC cannot be derived from this source.[60] The precise source of the expansive translation, which identifies Merib-baal of Chronicles with Mephibosheth of Samuel and contains an exegesis of the name *Merib-baal*, is *b. Šabb.* 56b.

The Talmud there discusses at length how David related to the two contradictory versions of Mephibosheth's behavior when the former fled Jerusalem to escape his son Absalom, namely, the version of events he was given by Ziva, Mephibosheth's slave, and that of Mephibosheth himself. After citing the various versions, the Talmud places in Mephibosheth's mouth the following reaction to David's verdict, portraying Mephibosheth's behavior in a somewhat negative light:

אמ[ר] לו: אני אמרתי, מתי תבוא בשלום, ואתה עושה בי כך? לא עליך יש לי תרעו־
מת אלא על מי שהביאך בשלום! והינו דכתיב 'ובן יהונתן מריבעל'. וכי מריבעל שמו?
והלא מפיבשת שמו! אלא מתוך שעשה מריבה עם בעליו, יצתה בת קול ואמרה לו:
נצא בר נצא ...

He said to him, 'I said, when will you come back in peace? Yet you treat me so! Not against you do I have resentment, but against Him who restored you in peace.' So it is written, 'And the son of Jonathan was Meribbaal' (1 Chr 8:34, 9:40). Now was his name really Meribbaal? Surely it was Mephibosheth. But because he brought about a quarrel [meribah]

---

58   Hamiel, published in 2009, used Sperber's edition and therefore he made no mention of this targumic expansion.

59   McIvor, p. 82, n. 43.

60   I present below the text of *b. Yoma* 22b to clarify that it was not the primary source for the present targumic expansion:
ולרב דאמ[ר], קבל דוד לשון הרע, איפרעו מיניה, דאמ[ר] רב יהודה אמ[ר] רב: בשעה
שאמ[ר] לו דוד למפיבשת, 'אמרתי אתה וציבא תחלקו את השדה', יצאה בת קול ואמרה לו:
רחבעם וירבעם יחלקו את המלכות.
And from the perspective of Rab, who has said, "David did listen to gossip," *wasn't he punished on that account anyhow? For* said R. Judah said Rab, "When David said to Mephibosheth, 'I say, you and Ziba divide the land' (2 Sam 19:30), an echo came forth and said to him, 'Rehoboam and Jeroboam will divide the monarchy.'"

with his master, an echo came forth and rebuked him: 'You man of strife son of a man of strife!'...

The targumist enmeshed the Talmud's comments within the Aramaic verse. First, he acknowledged the talmudic position that *Merib-baal* was not the man's true name, but a term used for Mephibosheth in reference to a particular event. Then he interpreted the name מריב־בעל in accordance with the exegesis given by the Talmud. The basic explanation of the name found in TC runs very much parallel to the talmudic version:

Talmud	שעשה מריבה עם בעליו
TC	דעבד פלוגתא עם מרי עלמא

Though the Talmud uses the word בעליו, *his master*, the targumist did not want to write מריה alone. Instead, preferring to clarify that God is the master of the entire world, he wrote מרי עלמא. The targumist explained Mephibosheth's anger at God as reflecting Mephibosheth's belief that He should not have brought David back to Jerusalem safely:

Talmud	(... יש לי תרעומת ... על מי) שהביאך בשלום
TC	(דעבד פלוגתא עם מרי עלמא) דהדר דוד בשלם

The ingratitude with which Mephibosheth faults David in the Talmud also is reflected in TC—if not stylistically, then at least in terms of the meaning of the text:

Talmud	אני אמרתי, מתי תבוא בשלום, ואתה עושה בי כך?
TC	ולא פרע גומלא טבא ליה

2.11 *David Depicted as a Rabbi and a King (2 Sam 23:8)*

2 Sam 23:8	אֵלֶּה שְׁמוֹת הַגִּבֹּרִים אֲשֶׁר לְדָוִד יֹשֵׁב בַּשֶּׁבֶת תַּחְכְּמֹנִי‖ רֹאשׁ הַשָּׁלִשִׁי
1 Chr 11:11	וְאֵלֶּה מִסְפַּר הַגִּבֹּרִים אֲשֶׁר לְדָוִיד יָשָׁבְעָם בֶּן־חַכְמוֹנִי רֹאשׁ הַשָּׁלִישִׁים (קרי)

2 Sam 23:8 (cont.)	הוּא עֲדִינוֹ הָעֶצְנוֹ (קרי) עַל־שְׁמֹנֶה מֵאוֹת חָלָל בְּפַעַם אֶחָת (קרי):
1 Chr 11:11 (cont.)	הוּא־עוֹרֵר אֶת־חֲנִיתוֹ עַל־שְׁלֹשׁ־מֵאוֹת חָלָל בְּפַעַם אֶחָת:

NJPS Sam: These are the names of David's warriors: Josheb-basshebeth, a Tahchemonite, the chief officer—he is Adino the Eznite; [he wielded his spear] against eight hundred and slew them on one occasion.

NJPS Chr: This is the list of David's warriors: Jashobeam son of Hachmoni, the chief officer; he wielded his spear against three hundred and slew them all on one occasion.

Above are two parallel verses that introduce a list of David's warriors. The verse in Samuel poses a number of exegetical challenges, two of which we shall note here. At the beginning of the list, instead of the name of one of David's warriors, as we would expect, we find the word pair יֹשֵׁב בַּשֶּׁבֶת, which appears to be not the name of a person, but some kind of a description beginning with a participle. Another difficulty is how to understand the word pair עֲדִינוֹ הָעֶצְנִי, which appears where we would expect to find a verb describing what happened to the eight hundred corpses noted at the end of the verse (cf. the addition of the missing verbal clause in the NJPS translation above). The verse in Chronicles, meanwhile, is clear and easy to read: the first of David's warriors was יָשָׁבְעָם בֶּן־חַכְמוֹנִי, who attained the rank of chief officer. His battlefield prowess was so great that he managed independently to strike down the corpses of three hundred enemies with his spear in a single battle.[61]

Corresponding to the well-defined text of the verse in Chronicles, we might have expected to find an Aramaic translation that were similarly short and to the point, e.g., ואלין סכומי גבריא דהוו לדויד ישבעם בן חכמוני ריש גבריא הוא מתביב על ידא דמורניתיה על תלת מאה קטילין בזמנא חדא. In actuality, however, the verse in TC contains quite a lengthy expansion that does not correspond to any part of its Hebrew *Vorlage*. To understand the expansion in its proper context, one must compare it to TJ to the parallel verse, 2 Sam 23:8, which contains a similar expansion, albeit one shorter than that in TC. Following is a synoptic presentation of the two Targums, with expansions that appear in TC but not TJ colored red:

TJ אלין שמהת גבריא דהוו עם דויד גברא ריש משריתא

TC ואליין סכומי גבריא דהוו עם דוד גברא ריש משריתא

Clem: These are the names of the mighty men who were with David the mighty, the head of the armies.

---

61   The text of the Hebrew verse has, with reason, been the subject of expansive discussions. Instead of the three words יֹשֵׁב בַּשֶּׁבֶת תַּחְכְּמֹנִי, LXX B to this verse has the name Ιεβοσθε ὁ Χαναναῖος, i.e. יש־בשת הכנעני (this may be a corruption that developed within the internal transmission of LXX), while Lucian LXX has Ιεσβάαλ υἱὸς Θεκεμανεί, i.e., בן ישבעל תכמני. The parallel verse in 1 Chr 11:11 has another name: ישבעם בן חכמוני. The original form apparently was ישבעל, which in the text that preceded MT Samuel was emended to יש־בשת, just as all of the baalistic names in 2 Samuel were emended; see Japhet *OTL*, p. 244. This presumed name was corrupted under the influence of the similar word in 2 Sam 23:7 (שָׂרֹף יִשָּׂרְפוּ בַשֶּׁבֶת), resulting in יֹשֵׁב בַּשֶּׁבֶת. Baalistic names in Chronicles were not emended, but somehow the *lamed* of ישבעל became exchanged with a *mem*. For further discussion, see notes and citations in McCarter *II Samuel*, pp. 489–490; Knoppers *vol. II*, p. 537.

Dost: Now these are the tallies of the warriors who were with David the warrior, the head of the camp,

TJ יתיב על כרסי   דינא וכל נבייא וסבייא   מקפין ליה

TC יתיב על כורסי   דינא וכל נבייא וחכימיא   מקפין ליה

Clem: Enthroned on the throne of judgment, and all the prophets and elders surround him,

Dost: enthroned on the throne of judgment, and all the prophets and sages surrounding him,

TJ משיח   במשח   קדשא   בחיר ומפנק שפיר ברויה   ויאי בחזויה

TC מרבי   במשח   קודשא

כד הוה נפיק לקרבא הוה מסתייע מלעילא ובמתביה לאולפן אוריתא הות סלקה שמעתה אליביה

בחיר ומפנק שפיר ברויה   ויאה בחזוה

Clem: anointed with holy anointing, chosen and pampered, beautiful in his presence, and comely in his appearance,

Dost: anointed with holy oil. When he went out to war he was helped from above, and when he sat for Torah instruction in the Torah the legal tradition come to his mind. (He was) distinguished and erudite, handsome in his appearance, comely in his looks,

TJ חכים בחכמתא וסכלתן בעיצא   גבר בגברותא ריש גבריא

TC בקי   בחכמתא וסוכלתן בעצתא גבר בגבורתה ריש

מתיבתה בסים בקלא ורבן בשירתה וסרכן על כל   גברייה

Clem: wise in wisdom and intelligent in counsel, mighty in strength, the head of the mighty men.

Dost: an expert in wisdom and intelligent in counsel, mighty in strength, the head of the academy, sweet of voice, a teacher of song, and an officer over all the warriors.

TJ הוא מתקן במני   זינא נפיק בפום קלא   ונצח בקרבא

TC והוא מתקן במאני זינא   ונטיל מורניתה דביה תלי אתא דטיקס משרית יהודה

ונפיק על פס קל רוחא דקודשא ונצח בקרבא

Clem: He was equipped with weapons, going out with a loud shout and victorious in battle,

Dost: He was equipped with weapons, carrying a spear on which was hung a sign of the battle standard of the camp of Judah, going forth according to the voice of the holy spirit, victorious in battle,

TJ   ומתביב על ידי מורניתיה תמני מאה קטילין בזמן חדא:

TC   ומתביב על ידא דמורניתא תלת מאה קטילין בזמנא חדא:

Clem: and bringing back with his spear eight hundred slain at one time.

Dost: and executing with the spear 300 slain at one time.

A brief glance at the two translations is sufficient to see that TC used the text of TJ as he knew it as a foundation for his translation of this verse. If we filter out disparities that stem from copying or from linguistic or writing tendencies, we see that TC deviated from the text of TJ in two places where there are disparities between the *Vorlage* of the two Hebrew books. TC has סכומי, instead of שמהת of TJ, because Chronicles reads מִסְפַּר, rather than שְׁמוֹת as in 2 Samuel. TC reads תלת מאה, rather than תמני מאה, as in TJ, because the version given in Chronicles is not שְׁמֹנֶה מֵאוֹת, as in 2 Samuel, but שְׁלֹשׁ־מֵאוֹת.

A few other differences between the two Targums are the result of different lexical choices with no effect on the structure of the verse, such as TC's חכי־מיא, which hews closer to the scriptural תַּחְכְּמֹנִי/חַכְמוֹנִי, instead of TJ's סבייא; the substitution of מרבי for משיח;[62] and the choice of בקי rather than חכים. Having addressed those variants, we are left with four expansions in TC relative to TJ (colored red above, as noted).

Van Staalduine-Sulman explained the disparity between TJ and TC as the difference between a description of the Davidic messiah sitting in judgment at the End of Days in continuation of the eschatological account in TJ 2 Sam 23:1–7 and a description of David as a rabbi and scholar corresponding to the Jewish ideal in the period following the destruction of the Second Temple—that of the Rabbis.[63] I believe that van Staalduine-Sulman was right in her insight that the image of David in TC adds many elements that lend him the contours of a talmudic sage, but her description of TJ as depicting the Day of Judgment in the End of Days goes far beyond what the targumist had in mind. The first

---

62   It seems to me that van Staalduine-Sulman *TJ Samuel*, p. 684, ascribes more meaning to the lexical exchange of משיח with מרבי than is warranted. In her view, this disparity between TJ and TC is the most important of all changes in TC. She opines that the entire verse in TJ describes the messiah of the future and that the exchange of the root משׁ״ח for רב״י is part of a programmatic alteration of the verse by TC to turn it from an eschatological description to a portrayal of David as the chief rabbi of Jerusalem (to use van Staalduine-Sulman's terminology ibid.). In truth, this exchange reflects no attempt to change the character of the verse: the replacement of all verbs from the root משׁ״ח with the root רב״י in TC is part of a systematic dialectal change that applies to the entirety of TC, as demonstrated above, p. 130. The attempt to find משׁ״ח in acronym form in TJ (van Staalduine-Sulman, ibid., p. 683) is similarly unconvincing.

63   Van Staalduine-Sulman *TJ Samuel*, pp. 664–685. The author, p. 664, views verses 1–8 as a single literary unit.

seven verses of TJ 2 Samuel 23 do indeed have a clear, manifest eschatological character, but there is no justification for linking those first seven verses, which in the Hebrew *Vorlage* appear as a separate paragraph containing David's final words, and verse 8, which as in the Hebrew introduces a separate literary section with the Aramaic words אלין שמהת גבריא דהוו עם דויד, after which a description of David himself appears prior to the description of his various warriors that comes in the following verses. Verse 8, unlike the seven preceding it, contains no eschatological expressions, and in neither Hebrew nor Aramaic may be seen as a part of the same literary unit.[64]

Still and all, we are left to explain how it is that a Hebrew literary unit that announces itself as a list of David's warriors, becomes, in the Aramaic translation, a poem in praise of David himself.[65] The answer is first and foremost a matter of the textual and exegetical difficulties of the Hebrew verse in Samuel excerpted above, which the Rabbis addressed midrashically. To these exegetes, the expressions in the verse became descriptions of a wise king enthroned on the throne of Torah justice. Thus we find the following interpretation in *b. Moʻed Qaṭ.* 16b:

מאי אמ[ר]? ר' אבהו אמ[ר], הכי קאמ[ר]: אלה שמות גבורותיו שלדוד. 'יושב
בשבת תחכמוני'—בשעה שהיה יושב בישיבה לא היה יושב לא על גבי כרים ולא
על גבי כסתות אלא על גבי קרקע, דכל כמה דהוה עירא היאירי קיים הוה מתני להו
לרבנן. כי נח נפשיה דעירא היאירי הוה דוד מתני להו איהו לרבנן.

"And these are the names of the mighty of David: Joseb-basshebeth a Tachkemonite" (2 Sam 23:8): *What is the meaning of this statement? Said R. Abbahu, "This is the meaning of this statement:* These are the mighty deeds of David: Joseb-basshebeth, meaning, sitting at the session.

---

64 The expression כרסי דינא appears in TJ in both verse 7 and verse 8. In verse 7, the expression has clear eschatological import: באתגלאה בית דינא רבא למתב על כרסי דינא למדן ית עלמא. In verse 8, however, there is no cause for understanding the expression יתיב על כרסי דינא as referring to the final Day of Judgment: it is simply a description of David sitting on the throne of judgment due to being the king of Israel in his day. These two adjacent verses, in both the Hebrew and the Aramaic, belong to two different literary units. The outward similarity of sitting על כרסי דינא stems from an outward similarity between the Hebrew *Vorlage* of the two verses: the word בשבת, which was the motivation for invoking the throne of judgment in the Aramaic translation of both verses.

65 Le Déaut-Robert, vol. 1, p. 66, suggest that the two Hebrew names ישבעם (denoting one who sits at the head of the people) and חכמוני (one who is wise) are what stirred the targumist to compose the panegyric, but I do not believe that this suggestion can provide a complete explanation of the phenomenon that we encounter here, much less of TJ, in whose text the word ישבעם is entirely absent.

"When he would go into session, he would not take his seat on a pillow or coverlet but sat on the ground." *For so long as his master, Ira the Jairite, was alive, he taught the rabbis while seated on pillows and coverlets, but when he died, David would teach the rabbis seated on the ground.*

TJ's description focuses on David's role as a king, while the talmudic homily gives precedence to his role as dean of a yeshiva—a depiction very much in keeping with TC—but the basic motivation for both the homily in TJ and that in the Talmud is one and the same. The translation in TJ constitutes a kind of brief paean extolling the personage of King David. The source of several of the expressions in the poem is the challenging Hebrew *Vorlage* of 2 Sam 23:8: for יֹשֵׁב בַּשֶּׁבֶת, TC writes יתיב על כרסי דינא; for תַּחְכְּמֹנִי, the words חכים בחכמתא; and for רֹאשׁ הַשָּׁלִשִׁי, the translation ריש גבריא, all of which refer to David.

Alongside these interpretive translations with their basis in the Hebrew verse itself, it is evident that TJ took advantage of the opportunity to supplement the description of David with additional expressions inspired by other verses: since the king is seated on his throne, it is in order to describe the dignitaries around him—וכל נבייא וסבייא מקפין ליה—reminiscent of 1 Kgs 22:10: וּמֶלֶךְ יִשְׂרָאֵל וִיהוֹשָׁפָט מֶלֶךְ־יְהוּדָה יֹשְׁבִים אִישׁ עַל־כִּסְאוֹ ... וְכָל־הַנְּבִיאִים מִתְנַבְּאִים לִפְנֵיהֶם *The king of Israel and King Jehoshaphat of Judah were seated on their thrones ... and all the prophets were prophesying before them.*[66] The description of David as משיח במשח קדשא, *anointed with sacred oil*, brings to mind Ps 89:21: מָצָאתִי דָּוִד עַבְדִּי בְּשֶׁמֶן קָדְשִׁי מְשַׁחְתִּיו, *I have found David, My servant; anointed him with My sacred oil.* The expression בחיר is used of David in Ps 89:4, כָּרַתִּי בְרִית לִבְחִירִי,

---

66 Saul is portrayed in 1 Sam 22:6 as sitting while surrounded by his servants: וְשָׁאוּל יוֹשֵׁב בַּגִּבְעָה תַּחַת־הָאֶשֶׁל בָּרָמָה וַחֲנִיתוֹ בְיָדוֹ וְכָל־עֲבָדָיו נִצָּבִים עָלָיו, *Saul was then in Gibeah, sitting under the tamarisk tree on the height, spear in hand, with all his courtiers in attendance upon him.* We find a similar description to TJ 2 Sam 23:8 in the description of Solomon in *Tg. Esth II* 1:2: וכד אתי כהנא למשאל שלמה דמלכא שלמה וכל סביא הוו יתבין מן ימיניה ומן שמאליה ודנין דינא דעמא ..., *when the High Priest would come to inquire (of) Solomon, and all the elders were seated on his right and on his left and making legal decisions of the people ...* This is to argue not that TJ was directly influenced by these sources, but that the context of David's sitting on the throne as a king inspires the description of the dignitaries standing around him, because it is appropriate for a distinguished king to be surrounded by distinguished attendants. The same applies to various descriptions of God enthroned as a king. Thus in 1 Kgs 22:19, רָאִיתִי אֶת־ה' יֹשֵׁב עַל־כִּסְאוֹ וְכָל־צְבָא הַשָּׁמַיִם עֹמֵד עָלָיו מִימִינוֹ וּמִשְּׂמֹאלוֹ, *I saw the LORD seated upon His throne, with all the host of heaven standing in attendance to the right and to the left of Him;* Isa 6:1–2, ...

שְׂרָפִים עֹמְדִים | מִמַּעַל לוֹ, *I beheld my Lord seated on a high and lofty throne ... Seraphs stood in attendance on Him;* the same is suggested in Job 1:6; 2:1, וַיָּבֹאוּ בְּנֵי הָאֱלֹהִים לְהִתְיַצֵּב עַל־ה', *the divine beings presented themselves before the LORD.* See also *Tg. Cant* 7:3, where the dean of a yeshiva is portrayed in similar terms.

I have made a covenant with My chosen one, as well as ibid., v. 20: שַׁוִּיתִי עֵזֶר עַל־גִּבּוֹר, הֲרִימוֹתִי בָחוּר מֵעָם, *I have conferred power upon a warrior; I have exalted one cho-sen out of the people*. The word מפנק, *pampered*, reminds us of 2 Sam 3:39: וְאָנֹכִי הַיּוֹם רַךְ וּמָשׁוּחַ מֶלֶךְ, *and today I am weak, even though anointed king*, (which goes hand-in-hand with the description משיח במשח קדשא, *above*); שפיר בריויה ויאי בחזויה corresponds to the scriptural depiction of David's handsomeness, as in the story of his anointment in 1 Sam 16:12, וְהוּא אַדְמוֹנִי עִם־יְפֵה עֵינַיִם וְטוֹב רֹאִי, *He was ruddy cheeked, bright eyed, and handsome*, and the story of his being brought to Saul's court, ibid., v. 18: הִנֵּה רָאִיתִי בֵּן לְיִשַׁי בֵּית הַלַּחְמִי יֹדֵעַ נַגֵּן וְגִבּוֹר חַיִל וְאִישׁ מִלְחָמָה וּנְבוֹן דָּבָר וְאִישׁ תֹּאַר וַה' עִמּוֹ, *I have observed a son of Jesse the Bethlehemite who is skilled in music; he is a stalwart fellow and a warrior, sensible in speech, and handsome in appearance, and the LORD is with him*. TJ translates both טוֹב רֹאִי (ibid., v. 12) and תֹּאַר (v. 18) with the phrase שפיר בריויה, while נְבוֹן דָּבָר (v. 18) is translated as סכלתן בעיצא, which also appears in the present verse.[67] If we separate out the first and the last word of the continuum ומפנק שפיר בריויה ויאי בחזויה חכים בחכמתא וסכלתן בעיצא, the result is the expression מפנק בעיצא, which is a suitable translation for the problematic Hebrew phrase עֲדִינוֹ הָעֶצְנִי (קרי).[68]

The resulting Aramaic verse TJ 2 Sam 23:8 thus incorporates exegetical elements based on the Hebrew verse itself as well as a series of praises that, though they do not reflect the words of the Hebrew verse, were produced under the influence of various scriptural verses and their targumic renderings, with their positive descriptions of David. What we see in the Targum here is a carefully formed compilation of praises of David gathered from various sources and brought together as a panegyric to the ideal Israelite king.

Had the author of TC embarked on his task uninfluenced by the Book of Samuel or its Targum, he would have produced a succinct, literal translation along the lines of the theoretical targum given at the beginning of this discussion. In actuality, TC is highly influenced by TJ, as is clear from our analysis of the relationship between these two Targums (pp. 108–141). Though TJ to that verse is far from the literal meaning of the verse in Chronicles, the author of

---

67   Goshen-Gottstein, vol. 1, pp. 157–158, notes that the noun סכלתנו serves as the almost exclusive equivalent of Hebrew nouns from the stem בו"ן.

68   The word עֲדִינָה in Isa 47:8 is translated in TJ as מפנקתא. One possible indication of the circumstance that the beginning and end of the noted continuum come together as a translation of עֲדִינוֹ הָעֶצְנִי is that the text of TJ 2 Sam 23:8 is the result of a number of stages of composition and editing, which is a matter deserving of discussion in its own right. The determining datum for the purposes of the present discussion is the final form of TJ, because this is the form that was received by the author of TC and served as a foundation for his Targum.

TC preferred not to do without the special poem of praise that he had received ready for use and decided to employ it as a foundation for his translation of the verse in Chronicles. To the praises of TJ, TC added further descriptions of David, principally such that paint him as not only an ideal king, but also the impeccable dean of a yeshiva. Now let us examine the expansions added by TC relative to TJ.

Expansion 1

כד הוה נפיק לקרבא הוה מסתייע מלעילא ובמתביה לאולפן אוריתא הות סלקה שמעתה אלביה

The targumist describes David as enjoying enormous successes both on the battlefield and in the study hall. The depiction of David as the synthesis of a military leader and a scholar is reminiscent of the continuation of the talmudic discussion cited above, in *b. Mo'ed Qaṭ.* 16b, where the various elements of 2 Sam 23:8 are scrutinized homiletically:

'הוא עדינו העצני'—כשהיה יושב ועוסק בתורה, היה מעדן עצמו כתולעת, ובשעה שיוצא למלחמה, היה מקשה עצמו כעץ.

"He is Adino the Eznite": When he was sitting and engaged in Torah-study, he made himself as pliable as a worm, but when he went marching out to war, he made himself as hard as a lance.

TC continues along the path forged by the Talmud in the translation of both verse 2 and verse 11.

ובמתביה לאולפן אוריתא ... נפיק לקרבא: The juxtaposition of going out to battle and Torah study previously appeared in TC to verse 2 of the present chapter. Let us look at the verse and its translation in the context of the parallel verse in Samuel and its targum:

2 Sam 5:2	אֶת־ יִשְׂרָאֵל	וְהַמֵּבִי	אַתָּה הָיִיתָ הַמּוֹצִיא
TJ	בריש ישראל	ועליל	את הויתא נפיק
1 Chr 11:2	אֶת־ יִשְׂרָאֵל	וְהַמֵּבִיא	אַתָּה הַמּוֹצִיא
TC	ומליף ית ישראל	יתנא לבית מדרשא	יתנא לקרבא ומעיל	את הויתא מפיק

NJPS Sam: it was you who led Israel in war

Clem: you were going out and coming in as head of Israel

NJPS Chr: you were the leader of Israel

Dost: you were the one who led us out to war, brought us into the academy, and taught Israel

The influence of TJ on TC is clear from the addition of the word הוִיתָא, which has no equivalent in the Hebrew *Vorlage* of TC, but the author of the latter expanded the translation of the verse and gave it a different meaning from that in TJ: David הוֹציא, *led out*, the Israelites to war and הבִיא, *brought* them *in* to the study hall, where he taught them Torah.

Several forms of expression in this expansion of TC are terms that belong to the vocabulary of Late Jewish Aramaic:

מסתייע מלעילא: Nowhere else in targumic or talmudic literature have I found a phrase combining סי"ע with the preposition מלעיל. It appears to me that this expression, which the author of TC did not inherit from TJ or from the Talmud, is characteristic of the late date of his linguistic stratum.

ובמחתביה לאולפן אוריתא: The form במתב corresponds to the Hebrew verse's form בשבת. TJ described David as sitting on the royal throne. To this TC adds a description of David as sitting down to study Torah. Aside from the many aggadic sources containing general descriptions of David's Torah study, the expression used in TC is reminiscent of *Tg. Ps* 110:1, which has David say אמר ה' במימריה למתן לי רבנותא חולף דיתיבית לאולפן אורית ימיניה, *the LORD spoke by his decree to give me the dominion in exchange for sitting in study of Torah.* David's rule over Israel, according to *Tg. Ps*, was strictly a reward for his sitting and studying Torah. The phrase ית"ב לאולפן אוריתא is not known from Talmudic Aramaic, and the expansion's appearance in TC, like that of the preceding phrase, מסתייעא מלעילא, is an indicator of the late date of the document's dialect.

הות סלקה שמעתה אליביה: The form שמעתה, as opposed to שמועתה, is characteristic of Eastern Aramaic.[69] Combination of the verb סל"ק סל"ק with שמעתה is documented in BT and became common in the Geonic Period.[70] The present verse marks its only appearance in known targumic literature, and the term שמעתה

---

69 Sokoloff establishes a clear dialectal distinction between the two orthographic forms. Sokoloff *JPA*, pp. 641–642, "שמועה": "Occasional spellings as שמעתא... are due to the influence of JBA שְׁמַעְתָּא."

In the entry on שמעתא in his Babylonian Aramaic dictionary (Sokoloff *JBA*, p. 1156): "Since the form שמעתא is much more common in JBA, it is likely that the sporadic occurrence of the present form is due to the influence of the other JA dialects."

70 The combination appears in the Talmud as part of a fuller phrase: סל"ק שמעתא אליבא דהילכתא. See *b. Yoma* 26a; *Soṭah* 7b; 21a; *B. Qam.* 92a; *Sanh.* 106b; *Halakhot Gedolot* 36 (*Halakhot Ketuvot*, p. 372); *Responsa of Rav Naṭronai Ga'on, 'Oraḥ Ḥayyim* 62; 168; *Yoreh De'ah* 216–218, 251; *Teshuvot Parshaniyyot* 455; *Responsa of the Ge'onim* (ed. Miller) 227, 234; *Early Ge'onim* 23, 79, 80; *Responsa of the Ge'onim* (ed. Harkavy) 79, 82, 247; *Responsa of the Ge'onim* (ed. Musafia) 59; *Sha'arei Teshuvah* 52.

(or שמועתה) in the sense of a halakhic decision and the context of Torah study appears in targumic literature only twice in TC and once in *Tg. Cant.*[71] The word אלביה, too, clearly was extracted from the Aramaic of BT (see pp. 189–190).

Thus throughout the first expansion that sets the present verse apart from TJ, a sharp-eyed reader can deduce that the text was written by a different hand, later than TJ.

Expansion 2

ריש מתיבתה בסים בקלא ורבן בשירתה וסרכן על כל גברייה

As indicated by the red color above, TC separated out the expression ריש גברייה found in TJ and inserted within it a series of words further amplifying the praise of David.

ריש מתיבתה: Like the term שמעתה above, the term ריש מתיבתה appears in targumic literature only in TC and *Tg. Cant.*[72] *Tg. Cant* 4:4 describes the dean of a yeshiva as a person who is חסין בזכותא ורב בעובדין טבין כדויד מלכא דישראל, *is strong in merit and great in good deeds like David the king of Israel. Tg. Cant* 7:3 describes the dean of a yeshiva in terms suiting the chief justice of the Sanhedrin and in context very similar to that of David in the present verse: ושבעין חכימין מסחרין יתיה כאידר סגלגל, *and seventy sages surround him, like a round threshing floor.* Thus, in the final analysis, David's metamorphosis in the aggadic world into the dean of a yeshiva was so successful that he became the ultimate point of comparison for the holder of such an office.

בסים בקלא ורבן בשירתה: David's renowned musical ability is conspicuously absent from the fine traits attributed to him in the list of praises given by TJ. Was it not due to his virtuosity as a musician that he was first brought to Saul's court and the Book of Psalms was attributed to him? It may be that TJ did not include musical capability in its list of praises because of a conscious decision

---

71   The phrase סלקה שמעתה appears only in the present verse. The phrase מסברין אפין בשמעתתא appears in TC 1 Chr 2:55. In *Tg. Cant* 5:10, in an expansion praising God as He studies Torah, we find the following line: וזיו יקרא דאפוהי זהירין כנורא מסגיאת חוכמתא וסברא דהוא מחדת שמעתן חדתין בכל יומא, *and the splendor of the glory of whose face shines like fire because of the abundance of wisdom and insight (concerning) which He offers new meanings every morning.*

72   Aside from the present verse, ריש מתיבתה appears in TC in verse 25 of the present chapter, with regard to Benaiah son of Jehoiada, appointed by David as ריש מתיבתא על תל־ מידוי. This verse parallels 2 Sam 23:23, which does not in any way reflect the term in TJ. Appearances of the term in *Tg. Cant*: 4:4; 7:3; 8:13.

to focus on the abilities for which David stood out as an impressive ruler. In any event, TC added what was missing with the words בסים בקלא ורבן בשירתה, *sweet of voice, maestro of song*. It seems to me that this pair of terms was conceived under the influence of the scriptural expression נְעִים זְמִרוֹת יִשְׂרָאֵל, which appears in the first verse of David's final words (2 Sam 23:1), adjacent to the list of David's warriors in the Book of Samuel.[73] The expression is translated in TJ as תקין למְמני בחיך בסים תשבחתיה דישראל, *fit to recount the praises of Israel with a sweet palate*. The word נְעִים is translated as בסים elsewhere, as well, so that a person who is בסים בקלא is one who possesses a pleasant voice.[74] The phrase יְפֵה קוֹל, *with sweet voice*, in Ezek 33:32 is translated by TJ as דבסים קליה. The word רבן in this verse has the sense of a master craftsman or maestro, as in TN Exod 31:2, חמי משה דמנית וקראת בשם טב דרבן בצלאל, *see, Moses, I have appointed and called by the good name of master Bezalel*, and the parallel verse, Exod 35:30, חמו דמני ה׳ בשם דרבן בצלאל, *see that the Lord has appointed by name as a master Bezalel*.

וסרכן על כל כל גברייה: The word סרכן is comprised of סרך, which functions as an equivalent of שׁוֹטֵר in TO, TN, TPJ, and TJ (also once of נוֹגֵשׂ, Isa 3:12), as well as in TC,[75] and the morpheme ן־.[76] It appears seven times in TC, thrice in TPJ, and thrice in *Tg. Esth I*, denoting an appointed leader, head, or authority figure.[77] We find סרכן used with רב and רבן in both *Tg. Esth* (8:2, ושויאת אסתר ית מרדכי רבן וסרכן על גניזיה דהמן ארום אפטרופוס ורב סרכן מרדכי בבית מלכא) and TC (2 Chr 32:21, ושיצי כל גבר חילא וסרכן ורבן במשרית מלכא דאתור), and thus may say that in the context of the present verse, the word serves as a synonym of the term רבן (בשירתה) that precedes it in the series of David's titles that set him at the helm of various areas of endeavor. In terms of the sentence's structure, it also is a synonym of ריש (מתיבתה). As noted above, the author of TC broke apart the original phrase, ריש גברייה, and framed within it more titles describing David. Having used ריש for the phrase ריש מתיבתה, the targumist was in

---

73   The original meaning of this expression most probably has nothing to do with song or music; cf. McCarter *II Samuel*, p. 480. However, rabbinic Jewish sources did understand זמירות as pertaining to song, and the targumists belong to this group.

74   *Tg. Ps* 16:6, 11; 81:3; 133:1; 135:3; 147:1; *Tg. Job* 36:11; *Tg. Prov* 22:18; 23:8; 24:4.

75   The word סרך appears eight times in TC: five times as an equivalent of שׁוֹטֵר (1 Chr 23:4; 26:29; 27:1; 2 Chr 19:11; 26:11); twice for נָגִיד (2 Chr 31:13; 35:8); and once for שָׂר (1 Chr 22:17).

76   Levy, vol. 2, p. 191, took the view that the word is a corruption of the Greek loanword ארכון. White, p. 235, opines that the two words are exchanged in 1 Chr 11:2 due to corruption. Sokoloff *JPA*, p. 436, presumes that the word is derived from סרך.

77   TC 1 Chr 9:11, 20; 11:2, 11; 13:1; 2 Chr 31:12; 32:21; TPJ Gen 41:41, 43; Exod 24:1; *Tg. Esth I* 2:13; 8:2; 9:4.

need of a word of similar meaning to couple with גיברייה at the end of the
series, and so he turned to סרכן, which indeed is suitable for such a function.

Expansion 3

ונטיל מורניתה דביה תלי אתא דטיקס משריית יהודה

The Hebrew expression describing the warrior's activity on the battlefield, עוֹרֵר
אֶת־חֲנִיתוֹ, does not appear in the problematic version of 2 Sam 23:8 (the parallel text there is read עֲדִינוֹ הָעֶצְנִי), but is present in 1 Chr 11:11. TC therefore chose
not to make do with the translation of TJ, which for the text of Chronicles is
not a satisfactorily literal one, and added נטיל מורניתה, *carrying a spear*, which
can serve as a literal translation of עוֹרֵר אֶת־חֲנִיתוֹ (but see below). The relative
clause referring to מורנית, viz., דביה תלי אתא דטיקס משריית יהודה, *on which was
hung a sign of the battle standard of the camp of Judah*, at first glance seems
an almost arbitrary insertion on the part of TC. Surprisingly, however, these
words, too, are based on the Hebrew text of Chronicles. Having translated
אֶת־חֲנִיתוֹ literally, the targumist found that, with a change of vocalization, they
alluded to two other words: אֹת חֲנִיָתוֹ, *sign of his encampment*. The relationship
between the continuum of Hebrew letters and the expansion may be demonstrated thus:

MT		את	חניתו	את
TC	דביה תלי אתא דטיקס משריית יהודה			

The targumist viewed these words as signifying the insignia that were emblazoned on the tribal banners, as appears in the context of the Israelite tribes'
encampment around the Tabernacle, Num 2:2:

Num 2:2	לְבֵית אֲבֹתָם יַחֲנוּ בְּנֵי יִשְׂרָאֵל	בְּאֹתֹת	אִישׁ עַל־דִּגְלוֹ
TO	לבית אבהתהון ישרון בני ישראל	באתון	גבר על טקסיה
TN	לבית אבהתהון ישרון בני ישראל	באתין	גבר על טכסיה
TPJ	ישרון בני ישראל	גבר על טיקסיה באתון דמסתמנין על טיקסיהון לבית אבהתן

NJPS: The Israelites shall camp each with his standard, under the banners of
their ancestral house

Clem TPJ: The Israelites should camp each by their order, according to the
standards that are indicated for their order, according to their father's houses

Each of the Targums to this verse contains a combination of טקס, the word
את, and the verb שר״י. TN writes טכס, while TNM has טק׳, with a *qof*, but all

refer to the Greek word τάξις, signifying a standard or banner.[78] The translation in TPJ is supplemented by additional clarification specifying that the insignia were illustrations appearing on the banners. It is possible that TC was directly influenced by TPJ, as we have observed in other places as well. Here, too, TPJ is the closest known Targum to TC, both in terms of the shared spelling טיקס and in view of TPJ's expansive translation describing the relationship between the insignia and the banner, which corresponds to nothing in the Hebrew *Vorlage* and is absent from the other Targums.

The possessive pronoun forming the end of the word חניתו, in the context of the Aramaic sentence in TC, refers to David. What banner is this? It is the banner of David's encampment or camp, i.e., the banner of David's tribe, Judah.

The author of TC thus represented the Hebrew continuum of letters את חניתו twice in this verse.[79] Now, in light of the targumist's need to form a sentence referring to both a spear and a tribal banner, we will try to link together the parts of the sentence. How did the targumist link the two representations of the Hebrew continuum? The spear (מורניתא) in question, with which David would go out to battle, was used to fly the banner on which the insignia of the camp (משריתא) of Judah were emblazoned. The resulting image fits well in the list of David's praises, because it is only fitting that the king of Israel, who also is the leader of the tribe of Judah, fly his tribal insignia on the way out to battle.

This expansion was inserted in a sentence of TJ that is cause for discussion in its own right. As noted, the words עוֹרֵר אֶת־חֲנִיתוֹ do not appear in MT 2 Sam 23:8. Their place is taken by the variant עֲדִינוֹ הָעֶצְנִי. However, TJ here reads ומתביב על ידי מורניתיה, a translation of עוֹרֵר אֶת־חֲנִיתוֹ.[80] TC had no justification for omitting these words of TJ, because their presence in the sentence is required for the three or eight hundred casualties killed at once appearing at the end of the verse to be connected to the preceding words, and TC therefore translated the continuum את חניתו a third time, as well.

---

78 Sokoloff *JPA*, pp. 234–235, 242.
79 We well may wonder whether this dual representation is a witness to the existence of another reading tradition of this verse, or else the dual translation given by TC is simply a midrashic rendering of the traditional reading. I shall not discuss the matter here, because for the purposes of the present discussion it suffices that we have successfully explained the surprising expansion in TC by demonstrating dual representation of a single Hebrew continuum.
80 The indication is that TJ read the Hebrew verse with the words עוֹרֵר אֶת־חֲנִיתוֹ. On rabbinic and targumic approaches to variant readings, see Lieberman, pp. 185–212; Rosenthal *Text*.

Expansion 4

(ונפיק על פס קל) רוחא דקודשא

Bacher understood the briefer text of TJ, נפיק בפום קלא, to be a corruption of the Latin loanword *fasciculus*, i.e., as part of a band, a group,[81] while van Staalduine-Sulman suggested that the word stemmed from the Akkadian *pungullu*, i.e., extremely powerful.[82] In any event, the changes undergone by the expression by the time of its appearance in TC seem to show that the author did not understand its meaning. He changes the preposition ב of TJ to על, which in conjunction with פם (thus MS C; MS V has פס) forms the Aramaic expression על־פם, meaning *according to*.[83] Because the text of TJ does not clearly indicate what voice or sound is intended, he adds an explanation to the expression, with the resulting continuum reading על פם קל רוחא דקודשא, i.e., *according to the voice of the holy spirit*: David would go out to war only after receiving heavenly approval. This idea is in agreement with the many verses that describe David as consulting God before deciding to go out to battle or to a given city (1 Sam 23:2; 30:8; 2 Sam 2:1; 5:19; 1 Chr 14:10), as well as the statement in TC (1 Chr 27:34) that David would consult the Urim and Tummim prior to going out to war. This is not, however, the original intent of TJ.[84]

The Aramaic expression קל רוחא דקודשא appears elsewhere in *Tg. Cant* 2:12; 5:2, in expansions, as in TC.[85] Witnesses to *Tg. Ps* 137:5 include the variants ברת

---

81 Bacher *Zwei Corruptelen*, p. 240; Krauss *Lehnwörter*, vol. 2, p. 432.

82 Van Staalduine-Sulman *Lamb*, p. 281. According to her proposal, the phrase entered Aramaic from the Akkadian as the single word פומקלא, which brings her to surmise that the original reading in TJ was נפיק בפומקלא, i.e., emerging mightily. She also published a TT to 1 Sam 17:8 that places the expression פום קלא in the mouth of Goliath of Gath (ibid., p. 280).

ואל כל קרב וקרב דהוה להון לפלשתאי אנא נפקנא לפום קלא ונצחנא בקרבא ורמינא קטילין כעפרא דארעא.

Van Staalduine-Sulman presented the two words לפום קלא as one in her article despite the appearance of the expression as two words in the MS, the better to clarify her interpretation of the expression. Kasher *TT*, pp. 107–108 [fragment 53c], preferred for this TT a MS with the reading לחקלא, but on p. 231 reports two MSS with the reading לפום קלא (and possibly a third reading לפומקלא).

83 De Lagarde and Sperber read פום in their editions. The form פם is characteristic of Palestinian Aramaic; see Sokoloff *JPA*, p. 495.

84 Much the same dynamic is reflected in *b. Ber.* 3b; *b. Sanh.* 16a.

85 The phrase רוחא דקודשא also appears in the following Targums: TPJ Gen 35:22: ... מתיבא רוחא דקודשא וכן אמר ליה; *Tg. Esth II* 1:2 (but not in all recensions): ומרדכי צדיקא; *Tg. Esth II* 4:1: שבישת רוחא דקדשא ואובילת יתיה לארע בנימן; TT Ezek 1:1 [Kasher *TT*, fragment 125(a), line 18 = הוה ידע מה דאתעביד ברוחא דקודשא

קלא מן שמיא and קל רוחא דקודשא, and it appears that such interchangeability is in keeping with the meaning of the expression everywhere it appears: קל רוחא דקודשא, like a divine echo (בת קול), signifies the act of consulting with God.

2.12   Half Lentils, Half Barley (1 Chr 11:13)

1 Chr 11:13	שְׂעוֹרִים	חֶלְקַת הַשָּׂדֶה מְלֵאָה	וַתְּהִי
TC	אחסנת חקלה מליא עללתה פלגה טלופחין ופלגה סערין		והות
2 Sam 23:11	עֲדָשִׁים	חֶלְקַת הַשָּׂדֶה מְלֵאָה	וַתְּהִי־ שָׁם
TJ	טלופחין	אחסנת חקלא מליא	והות תמן

NJPS Chr: There was a plot of ground full of barley there

Dost: There was a plot of land full of produce, half of which was lentils and half of which was barley

NJPS Sam: there was a plot of ground full of lentils

Clem: there was an inheritance of a field full of lentils

Chronicles states that the field was full of barley, but according to the version transmitted in Samuel, it was full of lentils. TJ says nothing of the contradiction, instead simply giving the version in Samuel. TC, however, reconciles the contradiction between the two scriptural sources by indicating that both are correct. The entire field was full of produce, but not all that grew in it was of the same species: half was lentils, and half barley. The contradiction between the two sources is discussed in both TY and BT. TC does not incorporate the language of either Talmud in the body of the Aramaic verse,[86] but it nevertheless may be proposed that the content of the interpretation given by TC corresponds to b. B. Qam. 60b:

---

fragment 125(c), line 8 = fragment 125(d), line 13: ... מתיבא (יתיה) רוחא דקודשא]; TT Hab 3:1 [Kasher TT, fragment 142(a), line 5: מתיבא רוחא דקודשא וכן אמרת ליה].

86   Y. Sanh. 2:4 (20b–c, pp. 1277–1278); cf. parallels in Ruth Rab. 5:1 (p. 118); Midr. Sam 20 (pp. 66–67). Following is the passage in the yerushalmi:

"ופלשת' נאספים" וגו'. ר' יעקב דכפר חנן אמ': עדשין היו אלא שהיתה ענבה שלהן יפה כשלשעורין. אמ' ר' לוי: אילו הן הפלשתים שהיו באין זקופין כשעורין והולכין להן נמוכין כעדשין. כתוב אחד או' "ותהי שם חלקת השדה מליאה שעורים". וכת' "מליאה עדשים". ר' שמואל בר נחמן אמ': שנה אחת היתה ושתי שדות היו, אחת שעורים ואחת עדשים.... ורבנין אמרין: שדה אחת אחת ושתי שנים היו ...

It is difficult to view this passage as the source of the exegesis given in TC. The yerushalmi here cites four approaches to reconciling the two contradictory verses (R. Ya'akov of Kefar Ḥanan, R. Levi, R. Shemu'el b. Naḥman, and the sages). Of these, the only opinion explaining that the barley and lentils grew at once is that of R. Shemu'el b. Naḥman, but his view is that they were grown in two separate fields, rather than in two halves of a single tract.

'ויתאוה דוד ויאמר מי ישקני מים מבור בית לחם אשר בשער ויבקעו שלשת הגבורים
במחנה פלשתים וישאבו מים מבית לחם אשר בשער'. מאי [קא מ]בעיא לה? ... רב
הונא בר יהודה אמ[ר] רב ששת: גדיש[י]ן דשעורין] דישראל הוו דהוו מטמרי בהו
פלשתים, וקא מבעיא ליה, מהו למיקלינהו להציל עצמו בממון חברו ... רבנן ואיתימא
רבה בר מרי אמרי: גדיש[י]ן דשעורי[ן] דישראל הו[ו] וגדיש[י]ן דפלשת[י]ם דעדשים
הוו, וקא מבעיא ליה, מהו [לחלופי] גדיש[י]ן דשעורי[ן] דישראל] ליתן לפני בהמתן
על מנת לשלם גדיש[י]ן של עדשי[ן] דפלישתאי]... בשלמ[א] למאן דאמ[ר] לחלו-
פי—הינו דכת[יב] תרי קרא[י]': 'ותהי שם חלקת השדה מלאה עדשים' וכת[יב]:
'ותהי חלקת השדה מלא[ה] שעורי[ם]',' אלא למאן דאמ[ר] למקלא—מאי א[בעי]
להו להני [תרי] קראי? אמ[ר] לך דהוו נמי גדיש[י]ן ד[עדשין] דישראל דהוו מיטמרי
בהו פלשת[אי]...

And David longed and said, Oh that one would give me water to drink of
the well of Bethlehem which is by the gate. And the three mighty men
broke through the host of the Philistines and drew water out of the well
that was by the gate" (2 Sam 23:15–16): *What was the problem?... R. Huna
said, "Well, this is the problem: there were near the battlefield stacks of barley that belonged to Israelites, and Philistines had concealed themselves in
them, and he wanted to know the law as follows:* Is it permitted to save one's
own life at the cost of the property of someone else?"... *Rabbis, and some
say, Rabbah bar Mari, said, "There were near the battlefield stacks of barley
that belonged to Israelites and stacks of lentils that belonged to Philistines.
And this is the question that required an answer:* What is the law on taking
the stacks of barley belonging to the Israelites to feed the beasts of the
army on the stipulation that later on they would pay for them with the
stacks of lentils that belonged to the Philistines?... *Now from the viewpoint
of him who has said that he wanted to make an exchange of barley and
lentils, that is in line with the verse,* "Where was a plot of ground full of
lentils" (2 Sam 23:11) and also "where there was a plot of ground full of
barley" (1 Chr 11:13). *But from the perspective of him who says that at issue
was whether or not he could burn them down, what need is there for these
two verses? He may say to you,* "There were also stacks of lentils there that
belonged to Israelites, in which Philistines were concealed" [*and had to be
burned down*]...

The translation given by TC can conform to either of the competing views cited
in the talmudic passage (viz., that of R. Sheshet or that of the sages), as the
conclusion reached there is that lentils and barley were planted concurrently.
The Talmud makes no explicit statement that half of the field contained barley and half lentils, but it is quite possible that the targumist thus understood

the Talmud's comments when he read the verses.[87] The harmonization proposed here by TC thus appears to have been proposed under the influence of *b. B. Qam.*

2.13 *Benaiah, Valiant in Torah* (1 Chr 11:22)

Benaiah son of Jehoiada features in quite extended aggadic accounts relative to other characters in TC. The point of departure for his description is a somewhat enigmatic Hebrew verse in the list of David's warriors in 1 Chronicles 11 (and the parallel list in 2 Samuel 23). The description of Benaiah, like other verses in the chapter, describes his personal exploits. The verse's language, though, appears to conceal more than it reveals. It is evident that out of a desire to be brief, the scriptural author gave some indication of relevant occurrences and alluded to unusually great military feats while leaving some of these events shrouded and difficult to comprehend.[88] This nebulousness, along with Benaiah's position in King Solomon's court, encouraged aggadists to expand on his exploits in both breadth and depth. TC adds only a limited degree of material within the targumic matrix obtained from TJ, but includes far more at the verse's end. Below are the Hebrew verses and their Aramaic translations, followed by the targumic expansion at the end of the verse, displayed independently.

1 Chr 11:22	בְּנָיָה בֶן־יְהוֹיָדָע בֶּן־אִישׁ־חַיִל רַב־פְּעָלִים מִן־קַבְצְאֵל
TC	בניה בר יהודע בר גבר דחיל חטאין וליה עובדין טבין מן קבצא'
2 Sam 23:20	וּבְנָיָהוּ בֶן־יְהוֹיָדָע בֶּן־אִישׁ־חַיִל (קרי) רַב־פְּעָלִים מִקַּבְצְאֵל
TJ	ובניה בר יהודע בר גבר דחיל חטאין דליה עובדין מקבצאל

1 Chr 11:22 (cont.)	הוּא הִכָּה אֵת שְׁנֵי אֲרִיאֵל מוֹאָב
TC	הוא קטל ית תרין רברבי מואב דהוון דמין לתרין אריון תקיפין
2 Sam 23:20 (cont.)	הוּא הִכָּה אֵת שְׁנֵי אֲרִאֵל מוֹאָב
TJ	הוא קטל ית תרין רברבי מואב

1 Chr 11:22 (cont.)	וְהוּא יָרַד וְהִכָּה אֶת־הָאֲרִי בְּתוֹךְ הַבּוֹר בְּיוֹם הַשָּׁלֶג׃
TC	והוא נחת וקטל ית אריוא במצע גובא ביומא דתלגא
2 Sam 23:20 (cont.)	וְהוּא יָרַד וְהִכָּה אֶת־הָאֲרִי (קרי) בְּתוֹךְ הַבְּאֵר בְּיוֹם הַשָּׁלֶג׃
TJ	והוא נחת וקטל ית אריא בגו גובא ביומא דתלגא׃

---

87   It is also possible that the word פלגה in TC, which refers once to lentils and once to barley, reflects an independent interpretation of the Hebrew word (הַשָּׂדֶה) חֶלְקַת by the targumist, under whose harmonistic reading the two scriptural books describe two different sections of a single field.

88   For a contextual explanation of the Hebrew verses, see McCarter *II Samuel*, pp. 489–490, 494; Klein *1 Chronicles*, pp. 292–293, 303.

1 Chr (cont.)   הוא הוה צדיקא רבא דלא הוה היכמיה לא במקדשא קדמאה ולא במקדשא
תניינא יומא חדא דחקת רגליה בחרדונא דמית ונחת לשלוח ותבר גזיזא
דברדא וטבל וסליק ותנא ספרא דבי רב הוא ספרא דאוריית כהניא ביומא
זוטא דסתווה בעשר[ה] יומין בירחא דטבת:

NJPS Chr: Benaiah son of Jehoiada from Kabzeel was a brave soldier who
performed great deeds. He killed the two [sons] of Ariel of Moab. Once, on a
snowy day, he went down into a pit and killed a lion.

Dost: Benaiah son of Jehoiada was the son of a warrior who feared sins and had
(many) good deeds to his (credit). He was from Kabzeel. He killed two leaders
of Moab, who were like two strong lions, and he went down and killed a lion
in a pit on a snowy day. He was righteous, with none greater than him in either
the First Temple or in the Second Temple. One day, his foot kicked a large lizard, which died, and he went down to Siloam and broke a chink of ice, and he
immersed himself. Then he went up and expounded the Sifra debe Rab, which
is the book of the instruction of the priests, on the shortest day of winter on the
tenth day of the month of Tebet.

NJPS Sam: Benaiah son of Jehoiada, from Kabzeel, was a brave soldier who
performed great deeds. He killed the two [sons] of Ariel of Moab. Once, on a
snowy day, he went down into a pit and killed a lion.

Clem: And Benaiah son of Jehoiada, the son of a man fearing sins, who had
(good) deeds, from Kabzeel, killed two chiefs of Moab. And he went down and
killed a lion in a pit on a snowy day.

TC preserved the general framework of the translation taken from TJ, with the
exception of two significant additions to the literal continuum of the verse. TC
inserted the word טבין, thus forming the expression עובדין טבין, and added the
clause describing רברבי מואב, viz., דהוון דמיין לתרין אריוון תקיפין.

The word עובדין in TJ serves as a translation of the Hebrew word פְּעָלִים. The
translation is a literal one, and in the Aramaic as in the Hebrew, the word is
not supplemented with any further verbiage. The addition of טבין in TC had
two causes. First, one who reads the Hebrew is compelled to decide for himself what sort of feats Benaiah performed, and the targumist wished to give a
very clear answer to this question. The second reason for the insertion is that
the word עובדין already was part of the Jewish Aramaic expression עובדין טבין,
younger sibling of the Hebrew מעשים טובים, *good deeds*.[89] Both the Hebrew
and the Aramaic expression have religious associations in talmudic and

---

89   The Hebrew expression appears as early as *m. 'Abot* 3:11 and is found throughout rabbinic
literature. The Aramaic expression is not common in the Talmuds. It does, however, occur
in *Eccl. Rab.* 3:60 (p. 227): מן בגין דאתון רחיצין על עובדיכון טביא, *for you rely on your good
deeds*, and is an obvious loan translation of the Hebrew.

post-talmudic Judaism. As part of TC's general tendency to portray scriptural heroes in rabbinic regalia, the targumist added the word טבין, thus creating an association with the world of Torah and good deeds familiar from rabbinic literature. It may be that TC did not in fact independently conceive this wording, given Sperber's report of two MSS of TJ that also have the reading עובדין טבין,[90] and there is no reason to assume that the text of TJ that lay before TC did not already contain such a reading, which was simply copied into the later Targum. Whoever it was who made the addition, though, his motivations are clear: the result is that Benaiah is positioned at the heart of the world of the Sages.

The second addition, דהוון דמיין לתרין אריוון תקיפין, was intended to link the short translation in TJ, רברבי מואב, to the challenging Hebrew *Vorlage*, אֲרִיאֵל מוֹאָב. Why are the princes of Moab given the distinction of the title אֲרִיאֵל? Because they resembled two powerful lions (אריות).

Now we arrive at the lengthy addition made by TC to the end of the verse. Many of the expressions in this section are taken directly from the passage in *b. Ber.* 18a–b, which contains interpretations of the verse:[91]

'כי החיים יודעים שימותו'—אילו צדיקים שאפילו במיתתן קרויים חיים, שנ[אמר]
'ובניהו בן יהוידע בן איש חי'. אטו כולי עלמא בני מיתי נינהו? אלא 'בן איש חי'—
שאפילו במיתתו קרוי חי. 'רב פעלים מקבצאל'—[בן] שריבה וקבץ פועלים לתורה.
'והוא הכה את שנ[י]' אריאל מוא[ב]'—'שלא הניח כמותו לא במקדש ראשון ולא
במקדש שיני. 'והוא ירד והכה את הארי בתוך הבו[ר] ביום השלג'—איכ[א] דאמרי
דתבר גזיזי דברדא ונחת וטבל. ואיכ[א] דאמ[רי] דתנא סיפרא דבי רב ביומא זוטא
דסיתוא.

'For the living know that they shall die' (Qoh 9:5) refers to the righteous, for, when they have died, they still are called the living. "For it is said, 'And Benaiah, son of Jehoiada, son of a living man from Kabzeel, who had done mighty deeds, smote the two altar-hearths of Moab; he went down and also slew a lion in the midst of a pit in the time of snow' (2 Sam 23:20). "'The son of a living man:' *Then were all other people sons of corpses? Rather, the sense of* 'son of a living man' is that, even after he had died, he was called 'living.' "From Kabzeel, who had done mighty deeds:' for he did much in collecting works for the Torah. "'He smote two altar-hearths of Moab:' He did not leave behind anyone like himself, either in the time of the first sanctuary or in the time of the second sanctuary. "'He went down and also slew a lion in the midst of a pit in the time of snow:' *some*

---

90   MS Or. 1471 (British Museum); MS Reuchlin; Sperber, vol. 2, p. 208.
91   The talmudic text here follows MS Firenze II-1-7.

*say he broke through blocks of ice and went down and immersed, and some
say that he repeated the Sifra of the house of Rab in a single winter day.*

הוא הוה צדיקא רבא: The Talmud's point of departure above is that the righteous are described as alive even after death. Proof that this is true is adduced
from Benaiah son of Jehoiada, whom the Talmud presents as an archetyp-
ally righteous person. The Talmud interprets the *ketiv* form in the verse, חי,
as indicating that the man's status as a living being continued to apply even
after the time of his death. This may suffice to explain the title given Benaiah,
צדיקא רבא, but the title is an extremely rare one in both Aramaic and Hebrew
(צדיק גדול). Aside from the present verse, the expression appears once in *Tg.
Job* 34:17, and there, too, it serves in an attempt at a literal translation and does
not reflect living usage.[92]

דלא הוה היכמיה לא במקדשא קדמאה ולא במקדשא תניינא: These words are an unmistakable translation to Aramaic of the above talmudic interpretation of the
words הוא הכה את שני אריאל מואב: "who left none resembling him in either
[the period of] the First Temple or [the period of] the Second Temple." The
Talmud found an allusion to the Temple in the word אריאל. Since the verse
reads שני אריאל, it may be understood as referring to both the First Temple and
the Second.[93]

יומא חדא דחקת רגליה בחרדונא דמית ונחת לשלוח ותבר גזיזא[94] דברדא וטבל וסליק:
With the translation of this exploit, TC continues shadowing BT, incorporating into the Targum the first homily on the words והוא ירד והכה את־הארי בתוך
הבור ביום השלג. The Talmud relates that Benaiah descended and immersed

---

92 The words ואין צדיק רב תחייב in *Tg. Job* translate the Hebrew ואם־צדיק כביר תרשיע; the
   Targum here is not in keeping with the verse's plain sense.
93 The word אריאל commonly is understood in rabbinic literature and liturgical poetry as
   referring to the Temple, owing to the influence of the following two verses: Isa 29:1: הוי
   אריאל אריאל קרית חנה דוד והראל, *Ah, Ariel, Ariel, city where David camped!*; Ezek 43:15: וההראל
   ארבע אמות ומהאריאל (קרי) ולמעלה הקרנות ארבע, *and the height of the altar hearth shall
   be 4 cubits, with 4 horns projecting upward from the hearth: 4 cubits*. The first verse serves as
   the basis of a formal analogy between the Temple and the body of a lion in *m. Mid.* 4:7:
   ההיכל צר מאחריו ורחב מלפניו, דומה לארי, שנ' 'הוי אריאל אריאל קרית חנה דוד'. מה הארי
   צר מאחריו ורחב מלפניו, אף ההיכל צר מאחריו ורחב מלפניו.
   The sanctuary was narrow behind and wide in front, and like a lion—since it is said, Ho,
   Ariel, Ariel, the city where David encamped (Is. 29:1) just as the lion is narrow behind and
   broad in front, so the sanctuary is narrow behind and broad in front.
94 Le Déaut-Robert in their edition, vol. 2, p. 40, read גזיגא, but MS V clearly has גזיזא.

himself, but does not explain why this immersion was necessary.[95] TC specifies that he had become impure due to contact with a creeping creature. It is likely that the name of the creature in TC—חרדון—was taken from TPJ to the list of creeping creatures, Lev 11:29.[96] Benaiah's breaking through the layer of ice and immersing himself in the freezing water are meant to illustrate the immense care that he took to observe the commandments of the Torah.

ותנא ספרא דבי רב הוא ספרא דאוריית כהניא: The work ספרא דבי רב, referenced in BT, is given an additional title in TC: הוא ספרא דאוריית כהניא. This last term in Hebrew, תורת כהנים, is used in rabbinic parlance and in the Talmuds to denote the scriptural book of Leviticus, for which reason the major halakhic midrashic collection on that book with time came to be designated with the same name. Epstein argued that the Babylonians had been accustomed to calling the midrashic collection ספרא דבי רב (or simply ספר or ספרא), while the Palestinian Jews used תורת כהנים,[97] but this distinction between east and west no longer existed by the time of the Ge'onim, who also took to using the name תורת כהנים on occasion.[98] Seder Rav 'Amram Ga'on quotes b. Ber. 11b as containing testimony that רב חייא בר אשי זמנין סגיאין הוה קאימנא קמיה דרב ודקא מסהיד ר' לתנויי בספרא דבי רב, then adds in explanation of the term, ... דהוא תורת כהנים.[99] That TC felt it necessary to add a clarification (הוא אוריית כהניא) to material taken from BT (ספרא דבי רב)[100] thus points to a late historical period, certainly no earlier than that of the Ge'onim. Use of the Aramaic name אוריית כהניא, rather than the Hebrew תורת כהנים, is known to occur only in TC. My impression is that the targumist did not use a living Aramaic term, but gave a literal

---

95 Rashi ad loc. opined that Benaiah had immersed due to seminal impurity so that he might study Torah.

96 The Hebrew and Aramaic word חרדון is not particularly common, but it appears in TN and TPJ for צָב of Lev 11:29 (as in Peshitta, ܐܪܕܘܢ). TN reads חרוונה in the MS, but this reading should be emended, as proposed by Díez Macho (Lev., p. 69), to חרדונה. Talshir, pp. 75–80, demonstrates that the Jews identified צב as the large Libyan lizard from the talmudic period to the Middle Ages. He does not discuss the appearance of the lizard in TC. The word further appears in y. Ber. 1:4 (3d, p. 11); 8:5 (12b, p. 62); Gen. Rab. 82 (p. 995). See also Sokoloff JPA, p. 221; Sokoloff Syriac, p. 487.

97 Epstein, p. 645; see excerpts from rabbinic sources cited ibid. to buttress his argument.

98 Finkelstein Sifra, vol. 1, p. 4.

99 Seder Rav 'Amram Ga'on 8:10–11 (p. 7).

100 Rashi, feeling a similar need, wrote in his commentary ad loc. בסיפרא דבי רב—תורת כהנים. Rashi employs this work heavily in his commentaries, referring to it by its Hebrew name, תורת כהנים. Finkelstein, ibid., argued that this tradition had arrived in Italy, France, and Germany under the influence of the Palestinian tradition.

translation of the Hebrew name that was the common and accepted term for the midrashic work.

[ה] יומין בירחא דטבת ביומא זוטא דסתווה בעשר: Taking his cue from BT's second interpretation of וְהוּא יָרַד וְהִכָּה אֶת־הָאֲרִי בְּתוֹךְ הַבּוֹר בְּיוֹם הַשָּׁלֶג, the targumist credits Benaiah with an exploit of another sort. His prowess in Torah study was so great that he succeeded in reciting all of *Sifra'* in a single day none other than the tenth of Ṭevet, when daylight hours are near their annual nadir.[101] Beyond the general description יומא זוטא דסיתוא, most textual witnesses to the Talmud do not specify a date on which the feat of immersion was accomplished. MS Paris 671, however, states that it occurred during the period of Ṭevet, i.e., the winter. Based on this evidence, I believe it likely that the text of the Talmud that lay before the targumist specified the tenth of Ṭevet. The specification of this date may have been intended further to aggrandize Benaiah, who not only recited all of *Sifra'* on a single day, but did so without benefit of food or drink, the tenth of Ṭevet being a public fast day.[102] The form זוטא, which is characteristic of Eastern Aramaic, appears in no Targum other than TC (here and 1 Chr 18:17), and here, too, it is simply transcribed from BT.[103]

Since the entire insertion was composed in accordance with BT's interpretation of the verse, it effectively serves as the latter part of a dual translation of the entire verse. Churgin was right to note that the author of TC did not distinguish between competing opinions in BT, but collected them and integrated them as a single narrative.[104]

2.14 *The Blessing of Obed-edom (1 Chr 13:14; 26:4–5; 2 Chr 25:24)*
1 Chr 13:14

MT	וַיֵּשֶׁב	אֲרוֹן	הָאֱלֹהִים	עִם־בֵּית	עֹבֵד אֱדֹם	בְּבֵיתוֹ	שְׁלֹשָׁה	חֳדָשִׁים
TC	ואשתהי ארונא דה'		לות	עבד־אדום	בביתיה	תלתא	ירחין	

---

101 Regarding possible exegetical motivations for the link between Benaiah and *Sifra'*, rather than another book, see *Tosafot* ad loc., s.v. Sifra debe Rab; Epstein, p. 646. In any event, the mention of *Sifra'* in TC does not indicate the targumist's view, as for purposes of this matter he acted merely as a copyist.

102 TC nowhere states explicitly that he was fasting, but this may be understood from the date. The glaring anachronism placing the fast of Ṭevet in Benaiah's period does not compel us to discount this possibility any more than the anachronism of positing the existence of *Sifra'* in his time poses a problem for exegetes.

103 Several MSS of BT read ביומא דסיתוא, *on a winter day*, omitting the word זוטא, but the text of TC shows that its author used a Talmud whose text resembled that described here. On זוטא as an Eastern Aramaic word, see Sokoloff *JBA*, p. 403; Sokoloff *Syriac*, p. 372; White, p. 257.

104 Churgin *Hagiographa*, p. 254.

MT (cont.) ‏וַיְבָרֶךְ ה׳ אֶת־בֵּית עֹבֵד־אֱדֹם וְאֶת־כָּל־אֲשֶׁר־לֽוֹ:

TC ‏ובריך מימרא דה׳ ית עבד־אדום בבנין ובני בנין

‏דאתעברת אתתיה ותמניא כלתיה ויֿלֿידן תמניא תמניא בכריסא חד

‏עד דאשתכחו ביני אבהן ובנין ביום חד תמנין וחד ית כל די־ליה בריך ואסגי עד לחדא:

NJPS: The Ark of God remained in the house of Obed-edom, in its own abode, three months, and the LORD blessed the house of Obed-edom and all he had.

Dost: So the ark of the Lord stayed with Obed-edom in his house for three months. The Memra of the Lord blessed Obed-edom with children and grandchildren, for his wife and his eight daughters-in-law became pregnant. (Each of) the eight bore eight in one pregnancy until they were found one day between fathers and sons to be eighty-one. All that were his He blessed, and He multiplied (him) exceedingly.

1 Chr 26:4–5

MT ‏וּלְעֹבֵד אֱדֹם בָּנִים שְׁמַעְיָה הַבְּכוֹר ... פְּעֻלְּתַי הַשְּׁמִינִי כִּי בֵרֲכוֹ אֱלֹהִים:

TC ‏ולעבד אדום בנין שמעיה בוכרא ... פולתי תמניאה ארום בריך יתיה ה׳

‏על עיסק ארונא דה׳ דהוה בביתיה כד איתיוהי ואצניעוהי בביתיה ופליג ליה

‏איקרא וחמא מבנוי מבני בנוי תמניין וחד רבני ליואי:

NJPS: Sons of Obed-edom: Shemaiah the first-born ... Peullethai the eighth—for God had blessed him.

Dost: Obed-edom had sons: Shemaiah the firstborn ... Peulethai the eighth, for the Lord blessed him because of the matter of the ark of the Lord, which was in his house when they brought it. They left it in his house, so He distinguished him honorably, and he saw from his sons and from his grandsons eighty-one leaders of the Levites.

2 Chr 25:24

MT ‏וְכָל־הַזָּהָב וְהַכֶּסֶף וְאֵת כָּל־הַכֵּלִים הַנִּמְצְאִים בְּבֵית־ הָאֱלֹהִים עִם־

TC ‏וכל דהבא וכספא וית כל מניא דאשתכחו בבית־ מקדשא דה׳ דאקדיש

MT (cont.) ‏עֹבֵד אֱדֹם

TC ‏עבד־אדום בעדן די נסיב דוד מן ביתיה ית ארונא דה׳ כד אתיבו יתיה פלשתאי וברכיה ה׳

NJPS: Then, with all the gold and silver and all the utensils that were to be found in the House of God in the custody of Obed-edom

Dost: And (he took) all of the gold, the silver, all of the vessels that were found in the temple of the Lord that Obed-edom sanctified—when David took from his house the ark of the Lord, when the Philistines returned it and the Lord blessed (him)

At three points, TC states that Obed-edom was blessed due to the presence of the Ark of the Covenant in his household. The first two verses, whose Hebrew

Vorlage explicates the blessing, appear in *b. Ber.* 63b–64a as the basis of a homily concerning hospitality for Torah scholars:

ועוד פתח ר' אליעזר, בנו של ר' יוסי הגלילי בכבוד אכסניא ודרש: 'ויברך אלהים את
בית עובד-אדום ואת כל ביתו'. והלא דברים ק[ל] ו[חומר]: ומה ארון שלא אכל ולא
שתה אלא כבדו ורבצו לפניו—המארח תלמיד חכם בתוך ביתו ומאכילו ומשקהו
ומהנהו מנכסיו, על אחת כמה וכמה. מה ברכה שברכו? אמ[ר] רב יהודה בר' חנינא:
זו חמות ושמנה כלתיה שילדו לו שש[ה] ששה בנים בכרס אחת, שנא[מר] 'פעלתי
השמיני כי ברכו אלהים', וכתי[ב] 'כל אלה ששים ושנים לעובד-אדום'.

R. Eliezer, son of R. Yosé the Galilean, commenced discourse, speaking on the honor owing to hospitality. He gave this exposition: "'And the Lord blessed Obed Edom and all his house … because of the ark of God' (2 Sam 6:12). "Now is it not an argument a fortiori? Now if the ark, which ate and drank nothing, but required only that one sweep and lay the dust, [produced such a reward], he who makes a disciple of a sage a guest in his home and feeds him and gives him drink and supports him from his property—how much the more so [will such a one be blessed]!" What was the blessing with which [God] blessed [Obed Edom]? Said R. Judah bar Zabida, "This refers to Hamoth and her eight daughters-in-law, each of whom produced six children at a birth, as it is said, 'Peullethai, the eighth son for God blessed him' (1 Chr 26:5), and it is written, 'All these were of the sons of Obed-Edom, they and their sons and their brethren, able men in the strength for the service, threescore and two of Obed Edom' (1 Chr 26:5).

The talmudic homily explains how sixty-two children were born in the home of Obed-edom. Initially he had eight sons. After these sons married, his daughters-in-law and his wife each gave birth to sextuplets. In mathematical terms: $8 + (9 \times 6) = 62$. As much is indicated not only in the Talmud, but also in several parallel rabbinic sources.[105]

The general framework of the expansions in TC concerning the blessing of Obed-edom is in keeping with BT, but the numbers are different. The first of the verses in TC states that the women gave birth to octuplets, and according to both verses the number of members of the household reached eighty-one (Obed-edom himself, his first eight sons, his grandchildren, and his eight latter sons): $1 + 8 + (9 \times 8) = 81$. TC thus differs from the talmudic tradition with regard to the number of sons to whom each woman gave birth as well as the total, the

---

105   See list of parallels in Ginzberg, vol. 6, p. 275.

latter of which also is at odds with 1 Chr 26:8, שִׁשִּׁים וּשְׁנַיִם לְעֹבֵד אֱדֹם, *sixty-two of Obededom*, which is the basis of the talmudic homily. I would conjecture that the numbers in TC reflect an error based on BT. According to BT, as noted, Obed-edom's wife and eight daughters-in-law each gave birth to sextuplets. I believe that the juxtaposition of the numbers six and eight caused the latter to take the place of the former, and the total number of men in Obed-edom's household changed accordingly. Since to the best of my knowledge there is no other source that records this tradition as does TC, it is probable that the targumist himself was responsible for the error.[106]

2.15 Interpretation of אשפר and אשישה (1 Chr 16:3)

1 Chr 16:3	וַיְחַלֵּק לְכָל-אִישׁ שְׂמַעְיָה יִשְׂרָאֵל מֵאִישׁ וְעַד-אִשָּׁה לְאִישׁ כִּכַּר-לֶחֶם
TC	ופליג לכל אנש שמעיה ישר׳ מגבר ועד אתתא לכל חד חד טולמא דלחמא
2 Sam 6:19	וַיְחַלֵּק לְכָל-הָעָם לְכָל-הֲמוֹן יִשְׂרָאֵל לְמֵאִישׁ וְעַד-אִשָּׁה לְאִישׁ חַלַּת לֶחֶם
TJ	ופליג לכל עמא לכל המונא דישראל למגבר ועד אתא לגבר גריצתא דלחים

1 Chr (cont.)	וְאֶשְׁפָּר וַאֲשִׁישָׁה:
TC	חדא ופלוג חד מן אשתה בתורא ומנא חד מן אשתא בהינא דחמרא:
2 Sam (cont.)	אַחַת וְאֶשְׁפָּר אֶחָד וַאֲשִׁישָׁה אֶחָת
TJ	חדא ופלוג חד ומנתא חדא

NJPS Chr: And he distributed to every person in Israel—man and woman alike—to each a loaf of bread, a cake made in a pan, and a raisin cake.

Dost: Then he distributed to all the people of Israel, from man to woman, to everyone, one loaf of bread, and a one-sixth share of a bull, and a one-sixth portion of a hin of wine.

NJPS Sam: And he distributed among all the people—the entire multitude of Israel, man and woman alike—to each a loaf of bread, a cake made in a pan, and a raisin cake

Clem: Then he distributed for all the people, for all the multitude of Israel, from man to woman, to each a cake of bread, one portion and one share

In his translation of the unusual words אשפר and אשישה, TJ substituted for each a single Aramaic word, viz., פלוג and מנה, respectively. TC thereafter did not transcribe the text of TJ verbatim, but added clarifications explaining that אשפר is one-sixth of a bull and אשישה is one-sixth of a hin of wine.[107] These

---

106 The targumist's description of the sons of Obed-edom as רבני ליואי at the end of 1 Chr 26:5 is based on 1 Chr 15:16, 24.

107 Regarding the relationship between TC and TJ, see p. 134, above.

interpretations are not an original conception of the targumist, but based on
b. Pesaḥ. 36b:

מאי משמע דהאי אשישה לישנא דחשיבותא הוא? דכת[יב] 'ויחלק לכל העם לכל
המון ישראל למאיש ועד אשה לאיש חלת לחם אחת ואשפר אחד ואשישה אחת.'
ואמ[ר] רב חנן בר רבא: אשפר—אחד מששה בפר; אשישה—אחת מששה באפה.
ופליגא דשמואל, דאמ[ר] שמואל: אשישה—גרבא דחמרא, דכת[יב] 'ואוהבי
אשישי ענבים.'

*And on what basis do we maintain that the word for pancakes denotes some-
thing of considerable value? Because it is written, "And he dealt among all
the people, even among the whole multitude of Israel, both to men and
women, to every one a cake of bread and a good piece of meat and a
pancake" (2 Sam 6:19), on which R. Ḥanan bar Abba said, "A piece of meat
refers to a sixth of a bullock, and a pancake refers to one made with a
sixth of an ephah of flour." And he differs from Samuel, for said Samuel,
"The word under discussion here as pancake refers to a cask of wine: 'And
love casks of grapes' (Hos 3:1)."*

The view of R. Ḥanan b. Rava' traces both terms' etymology to common usage,
and this interpretation is incorporated by the author of TC within the targumic
matrix of TJ that he had before him: פלוג חד ומנתא חדא. Though the words אֶחָד
and אֶחָת of 2 Samuel do not appear in Chronicles, TC made use of the words'
translations while turning פלוג חד and מנתא חדא into פלוג חד מן אשתה בתורא
into מנא חד מן אשתה בהינא דחמרא. The expansions in TC relative to TJ are
simply an Aramaic translation of R. Ḥanan b. Rava's comments in the Talmud.

An obvious disparity between TC and the Talmud is the substitution of a
hin of wine for an ephah. The ephah is a unit of volume used for grain and
grain products, while the hin is one used for liquid measurements, in Scripture
generally used for oil or wine.[108] All of the known textual witnesses to BT are
in agreement that the reading is אפה/איפה, rather than הין, so it would be difficult to argue that the alteration reflected in TC stems from the version of BT
used by the targumist. Apparently the place of the ephah was taken by a hin
because אֲשִׁישָׁה was understood as denoting wine in deference to the view of
Shemu'el in the Talmud, and perhaps because the verse previously described
David's distribution of bread and meat but made no mention of anything
to drink. Also possible is that the substitution of a hin for the ephah has its

---

108   BDB, pp. 35, 228–229.

origins in a different exegetical source, as suggested by a similar interpretation in Pseudo-Rashi ad loc.[109]

2.16   *Benaiah, Chief Justice of the Sanhedrin (1 Chr 18:17)*

In the preceding discussion of 1 Chr 11:22 (pp. 301–306), we saw how the depiction of Benaiah son of Jehoiada as a glorified warrior had given way to that of a sage expert in Torah matters. TC (ibid., v. 26) goes so far as to describe Benaiah as the dean of a yeshiva.[110] In TC 1 Chr 18:17, Benaiah's portrayal as a man of Torah develops further with his depiction as a chief justice of the Sanhedrin who consults the Urim and Tummim.

1 Chr 18:17		וְהַפְּלֵתִי	עַל־הַכְּרֵתִי	וּבְנָיָהוּ בֶּן־יְהוֹיָדָע
TC		ממנא על סנדרי רבתא ועל סנדרי זוטא והוא שאיל באוריא ותומי'		ובניהו בר יהוידע
	נחתין לקרבא	וקלעיה	קשתייה	ועל מימר פומיה הוון
2 Sam 8:18		וְהַפְּלֵתִי	וְהַכְּרֵתִי	וּבְנָיָהוּ בֶּן־יְהוֹיָדָע
TJ		ועל קלעיא	ממנא על קשתיא	ובניה בר יהוידע

NJPS Chr: Benaiah son of Jehoiada was commander of the Cherethites and the Pelethites

Dost: Benaiah son of Jehoiada was appointed over the great Sanhedrin and the small Sanhedrin. He would enquire by the Urim and the Thummim, and by the word of his mouth the archers and the slingers would descend to battle.

NJPS Sam: Benaiah son of Jehoiada (was commander of) the Cherethites and the Pelethites

Clem: and Benaiah son of Jehoiada was appointed over the archers and over the slingers

If we assume that TJ viewed the word pair הַכְּרֵתִי וְהַפְּלֵתִי as referring literally to marksmen equipped respectively with bows and arrows and with slingshots (which indeed is how TJ renders these words wherever they appear), then that Targum's rendering strays only slightly from a literal translation of its *Vorlage*. Those changes that TJ did introduce clarify that Benaiah's relationship to הַכְּרֵתִי וְהַפְּלֵתִי was that of a commander (ממנא על) to those under his command,

---

109   His precise words are: ואשפר—אחד משישה בפר; ואשישה—אחד משישה בהין, *Eshpar* is one-sixth of a bull; *Ashisha* is one-sixth of a *Hin*.

110   1 Chr 11:25

MT	עַל־מִשְׁמַעְתּוֹ:	דָּוִיד		וַיְשִׂימֵהוּ
TC	על תלמידוי:	מתיבתא	ריש	ומני יתיה דוד

NJPS: David put him in charge of his bodyguard
Dost: David appointed him as head of the academy over his disciples

which is not clear from MT.[111] TJ essentially transmitted here the translation of a very similar verse, 2 Sam 20:23, וּבְנָיָ֗ה בֶּן־יְהֽוֹיָדָ֖ע עַל־הַכְּרֵתִ֥י (קרי) וְעַל־הַפְּלֵתִ֑י, *Benaiah son of Jehoiada was commander of the Cherethites and the Pelethites*, where the relationship of commander and commanded is clear from the Hebrew verse.

As we shall see below, TC was familiar with TJ's interpretation of the words הַכְּרֵתִי וְהַפְּלֵתִי. However, in a lengthy translation of the few words in MT, TC added an additional exegetical stratum based on an aggadic tradition in *b. Ber.* 3b–4a:

וכיון שעלה עמוד השחר, נכנסו חכמי ישראל אצלו ואומ[רין] לו: אדוננו המלך, עמך ישראל צריכין פרנסה! אמ[ר] להם: ... לכו ופשטו ידיכם בגדוד. מיד יועצין באחיתו־ פל ונמלכין בסנהדרין ושואלים באורים ותומים. אמ[ר] רב יוסף מאי קראה? 'ואחרי אחיתופל יהוידע בן בניהו ואביתר ושר צבא למלך יואב'. אחיתופל—זה יועץ, וכן הוא אומ[ר] 'ואחיתופל יועץ למלד'. יהוידע בן בניהו—זה סנהדרי, וכן הוא אומ[ר] באביו 'ובניהו בן יהוידע על הכרתי ועל הפלתי'. ולמה נקרא שמם כרתי ופלתי? כרתי—שכו־ רתים דבריהם; פלתי—שמופלאים בדבריהם.

"When it was dawn, the sages of Israel came into him. They said to him, 'Our lord, O king, your people Israel needs sustenance.' "He said to them,... 'Go and organize marauders.' "They forthwith took counsel with Ahitophel and sought the advice of the sanhedrin and addressed a question to the Urim and Thumim." *Said R. Joseph, "What verse indicates this?* 'And after Ahithofel was Jehoiada, son of Benaiah, and Abiathar, and the captain of the king's host was Joab' (1 Chr 27:34). "Ahithofel was counsellor,' and so it is said, 'Now the counsel of Ahithofel, which he counselled in those days, was as if a man inquired of the word of God' (2 Sam 16:23). "'[Jehoiada, son of Benaiah]' refers to the sanhedrin. And so it says [concerning his father], 'And Benaiah, son of Jehoiada, was in charge of the Kerethi and Pelethi' (2 Sam 20:23). *"Why were the [Kerethi and Pelethi] so called? They were called 'Kerethi' because their words are decisive [korethim], and 'Pelethi' because they are distinguished (muflaim) through what they say.*

The verse adduced by R. Yosef as a source for the order of events when David's army went out to battle is 1 Chr 27:34. The Talmud derives from 2 Sam 20:23 that the consultation with Benaiah was tantamount to consultation with the Sanhedrin. The Talmud has no need to say הכרתי והפלתי—אלו הסנהדרין, but

---

111   See discussion of MT and parallels in McCarter *II Samuel*, p. 254.

assumes that this is the case, and merely offers a homily explaining why the sages of the Sanhedrin were thus designated.

TC to the present verse incorporates elements of both of the above verses (2 Sam 20:23 and 1 Chr 27:34) as interpreted by the Talmud, and thus portrays Benaiah as the leader of the Sanhedrin and then describes him as consulting the Urim and Tummim.[112] Naturally, though, exegetes will innovate, and surely enough TC adds to the Talmud's comments a distinction between the כְּרֵתִי and the פְּלֵתִי. No longer are these two descriptions of a single entity. Instead, כְּרֵתִי indicates the Great Sanhedrin, and פְּלֵתִי the Lesser Sanhedrin. Alongside this aggadic tradition, TC to the verse contains material that its author obtained from TJ: the description of the marksmen going down to battle is simply an echo of TJ's accustomed translation of הַכְּרֵתִי וְהַפְּלֵתִי. TC writes similarly in 1 Chr 27:34, as discussed below (pp. 325–327).

2.17 David's Magnetic Crown (1 Chr 20:2)[113]

1 Chr 20:2	וַיִּקַּח דָּוִיד אֶת־עֲטֶרֶת־מַלְכָּם ׀ מֵעַל רֹאשׁוֹ וַיִּמְצָאָהּ ׀ מִשְׁקַל כִּכַּר־זָהָב
TC	ונסיב דוד ית כליל מלכהון מעל רישיה ואשכחה מתקל קנטינר דדהבא סנינא
2 Sam 12:30	וַיִּקַּח אֶת־עֲטֶרֶת־מַלְכָּם מֵעַל רֹאשׁוֹ וּמִשְׁקָלָהּ כִּכַּר זָהָב
TJ	ונסיב ית כלילא דמלכהון מעל רישיה ומתקלה ככרא דדהבא

1 Chr (cont.)	וּבָהּ אֶבֶן יְקָרָה וַתְּהִי עַל־רֹאשׁ דָּוִיד וּשְׁלַל הָעִיר הוֹצִיא הַרְבֵּה מְאֹד:
TC	[ובה קביעא אבן טבא דהוה טימין דידה קנטינר דדהבא סנינא
	היא הות אבנא שאיבתא דסוברא ית רימון דהבא באוירא
	והות על ריש דוד ועדי קרתא אפיק סגי לחדא:
2 Sam (cont.)	וְאֶבֶן יְקָרָה וַתְּהִי עַל־רֹאשׁ דָּוִד וּשְׁלַל הָעִיר הוֹצִיא הַרְבֵּה מְאֹד:
TJ	ובֵיה אבן טבא והוה על רישא דדויד ועדי קרתא אפיק סגי לחדא:

NJPS Chr: David took the crown from the head of their king; he found that it weighed a talent of gold, and in it were precious stones. It was placed on David's head. He also carried off a vast amount of booty from the city.

Dost: Then David took the crown of their king from off his head. He found its weight (to be) a centarius of pure gold, and in it was set a precious stone, whose price was a centarius of pure gold. It was a lodestone, which held the setting of gold in the air. It was (placed) on the head of David, and the plunder of the city (that) he had brought out was very great.

---

112 See discussion of the reason for attribution of responsibility for the Urim and Tummim to Benaiah son of Jehoiada in context of 1 Chr 27:34, pp. 325–327, below.

113 In TC MS V occurred an omission due to the two appearances of the phrase קנטינר דדהבא סנינא. The text of TC cited here within brackets is restored with MS C, as proposed by Le Déaut-Robert, vol. 2, p. 58.

NJPS Sam: The crown was taken from the head of their king and it was placed on David's head—it weighed a talent of gold, and [on it] were precious stones. He also carried off a vast amount of booty from the city.

Clem: Then he took the crown of their king from off his head. And its weight was a talent of gold, and a precious stone was in it. And it was on the head of David. Now the plunder of the city he had brought out was very great.

Absent the textual variants that separate the Hebrew *Vorlage* of 2 Sam 12:30 and 1 Chr 20:2, which are reflected by a number of differences between the two verses' respective targums, the most conspicuous difference between TJ and TC is an expansion in TC describing the crown that David plundered from the head of the king of Ammon. The purpose of the Hebrew description of the crown is to aggrandize its beauty and uniqueness, which in turn are intended to reflect on David, its new owner. The nonliteral insertion in TC is meant to address the physical problem arising from the Hebrew verse, which states that the weight of the gold in the crown was one talent—far greater than the anticipated weight of a crown worn on a person's head.[114] The solution offered in the expansion, that the weighty crown was suspended by a magnet, is taken from *b. ʿAvod. Zar.* 44a:[115]

---

114 This problem is discussed as early as the Talmud; see below. Exegetes with a preference for the simple sense of Scripture found various means of contending with the challenge. Yosef Qaraʾ on 2 Samuel ad loc. took the verse's statement at face value, understanding it as an indication of David's unusual physical strength:

ואל תתמה על אדם אשר נחתו קשת נחושה זרועותיו אם היה סובל עטרה שמשקלה ככר זהב. ואף הכתוב בא ללמדך שבחו של דוד, שממה שהיה יכול לסבול על ראשו עטרת שמשקלה ככר זהב, את למד גבורתו.

Qimḥi to 2 Samuel ad loc. proposed two ways of understanding the verb and preposition in question:

'ותהי על': ותהי על ראש דוד—תלויה היתה למעלה מראשו בשעה שהיה יושב על הכסא, כי איך היה סובל אותה ומשקלה ככר זהב?... ויש לפרש עוד כי לא היתה על ראשו תמיד, אלא פעמים היתה על ראשו, ויכול לסבלה זמן מועט שהיתה על ראשו.

Pseudo-Rashi to Chronicles gave a similar explanation, based on what he had heard regarding Arab kings while in Narbonne (regarding which see Viezel *Pseudo-Rashi*, pp. 46–47, who raises the possibility that the source of the interpretation that he heard in Narbonne was the commentary to Chronicles attributed to a student of Saadyah Gaʾon). Klein *1 Chronicles*, p. 408, questioned the verse's testimony:

"*it weighed a talent of gold*: This would be an extremely heavy crown, wearing nearly seventy pounds. The weight may be exaggerated ..."

115 Rosenberg-Kohler, p. 149, cited this talmudic passage as a source; they were subsequently followed by Churgin *Hagiographa*, p. 255.

'ומשקלה ככר זהב'—מי מנח לה? אמ[ר] רב: ראויה היתה לנוח בראש דוד. ר' יוסי

בר' חנינא אמ[ר]: אבן שואב[ת] היתה בה דהוה דארי לה. ר' אלע[זר] אמ[ר]: אבן

יקרה היתה בה שהיה שוה ככר זהב.

*[But if the crown] weighed a talent of gold, how could [David] have put it
[on his head]? Said Rab, "It was worthy of resting on the head of David."
R. Yosé b. R. Ḥanina said, "There was a lodestone in it, that raised it up."*
R. Eleazar said, "There was a precious stone in it, that was worth a talent
of gold."

Rab's explanation seeks to solve the problem with an alternate understanding of the words וַתְּהִי עַל־רֹאשׁ דָּוִד: David could not have held such a heavy object on his head, but the circumference of David's head was suited by that of
the crown, and it thus fit David's head in size even though he was unable to
wear it on a regular basis due to its weight. R. Yosei b. R. Ḥanina, for his part,
states that the crown was in fact perched on David's head, and explains that
although the gold of the crown was one talent in weight, its mass was suspended above David's head by a magnetic field. Finally, according to R. 'Il'ai,
the words וּמִשְׁקָלָהּ כִּכַּר זָהָב in the verse do not refer to the weight of the gold
in the crown, but give the monetary value of a gem that was set in it, and the
weight of the crown was not in fact unusually great. The expansion in TC integrates the two latter talmudic views as a single explanation: according to the
Targum, the magnet described by R. Yosei b. R. Ḥanina and the gem worth one
talent of gold described by R. 'Il'ai were one and the same. This synthesis is one
example of TC's tendency to integrate different talmudic opinions and present
them jointly.[116] David's crown would yet find a place in aggadic lore as a means
of identifying the legitimate Davidic king; see discussion of the coronation of
Joash, pp. 409–412, below.

2.18   *David, the Pious Poet, Called Elhanan (1 Chr 20:5)*

1 Chr 20:5			אֶת־לַחְמִי	אֲחִי	גָּלְיָת הַגִּתִּי	בֶּן־יָעִיר (קרי)	אֶלְחָנָן	וַיַּךְ
TC			בר ישי			דוד	וקטל	

הוא גברא חסידא ההוא   מתער   משנתיה בפלגות ליליא לשבחא קדם ה'

ית   לחמי   אחוהי דגלית

ביומא דקטל

דמן גת   גלית   ית   אחוהי דגלית

2 Sam 21:19	גָּלְיָת הַגִּתִּי	אֵת	בֵּית הַלַּחְמִי	בֶּן־יַעְרֵי אֹרְגִים		אֶלְחָנָן	וַיַּךְ	
TJ	גלית גתאה	ית	פרוכית בית מקדשא	בר ישי מחי		דויד	וקטל	

---

116   This example was noted as early as Rosenberg-Kohler, p. 150. Regarding the phenomenon,
        see also p. 78, above.

NJPS Chr: ... and Elhanan son of Jair killed Lahmi, the brother of Goliath the Gittite; his spear had a shaft like a weaver's beam.

Dost: ... and David son of Jesse, the pious man who would arise from his sleep in the middle of the night to sing praise before the Lord, he killed Lahmi, the brother of Goliath, on the day that he killed Goliath, who was from Gath, the wood of whose spear was like a weaver's beam.

NJPS Sam: ... and Elhanan son of Jaareoregim the Bethlehemite killed Goliath the Gittite, whose spear had a shaft like a weaver's bar.

Clem: ... and David son of Jesse, the weaver of the curtain of the sanctuary, killed Goliath the Gittite. Now the wood of his spear was like a weaver's beam.

The present verse confronts us with quite an interesting exegetical challenge tackled as early as the scriptural text itself. 2 Sam 21:19 states that one of David's warriors, whose name is given by MT as Jaare-oregim, killed a Philistine warrior named Goliath of Gath, which is complicated by the well-known previous attribution (1 Samuel 17) to David of the slaying of a Philistine warrior named Goliath of Gath. No such contradiction is posed by the text of the parallel Hebrew verse in Chronicles, according to which the warrior killed by Elhanan was not Goliath, but his brother Lahmi.[117] A further stratum of exegesis to this event appears in TJ 2 Samuel, which resolves the contradiction within the Book of Samuel by identifying the Hebrew verse's Elhanan with David son of Jesse.[118] The Chronicler and TJ offered different solutions that never were intended to meet. Yet the author of TC, who worked with the Hebrew text of Chronicles and the Aramaic text of TJ Samuel, brought together these two traditions in his own effort at harmonization.

The approach taken by TC to the verse is to integrate two different traditions. Elhanan of the Hebrew verse appears in TC as David, despite the absence of any contradiction between the Hebrew verse in Chronicles and the text of Samuel. I do not believe that TC viewed this rendering as materially diverging from the *Vorlage* of Chronicles, as TC follows TJ in treating *Elhanan* as a true alternate name for David. The solution, as understood by TC, is that David killed both Goliath and his brother Lahmi. That David killed Goliath was known to TC from the event's two appearances in the Samuel (1 Sam 17; 2 Sam 21:19); David's slaying of Lahmi was known to him from the present verse in

117   For a discussion of MT to these two parallel verses and the changes that arose in them, see McCarter *II Samuel*, p. 449; Klein *1 Chronicles*, pp. 411–412.

118   His description in the Hebrew verse as בֶּן יַעְרֵי אֹרְגִים is translated as containing not a proper noun, but a participle: מחי פרוכית, and the Hebrew words בֵּית הַלַּחְמִי similarly become בית מקדשא; see van Staalduine-Sulman *TJ Samuel*, p. 630. Elhanan also is identified as David in *Ruth Rab.* 2:2 (p. 48).

Chronicles. Aside from the preceding, there are two expansions in the Aramaic text of TC to the verse.

That discussing David's midnight hymns is based on a long talmudic discussion in *b. Ber.* 3b–4a, which contains all of the elements found in the targumic expansion. The Talmud derives David's practice of rising at midnight from Ps 119:62, חֲצוֹת־לַיְלָה אָקוּם לְהוֹדוֹת לָךְ, *I arise at midnight to praise You.* R. Ashi describes David as occupying himself with Torah study until midnight, after which he offered songs and praises (מכאן ואילך בשירות ותשבחות). The expansion in TC echoes the verse in Psalms as understood by the Talmud. The words חֲצוֹת־לַיְלָה אָקוּם, in their targumic representation, describe David as מתער משנתיה בפלגות ליליא, *rising from his sleep at midnight.* The purpose of rising at midnight is לְהוֹדוֹת לָךְ, expressed in the Targum with the words לשבחא קדם ה׳, *to sing praise before the Lord.*

The Targum defines David as גברא חסידא, which also has its origins in the talmudic discussion of David. In any event, both the Talmud and TC assume that David described himself as worthy of the title חסיד. The Talmud (*b. Ber.* 4a) cites two opinions in explanation of Ps 86:2, שָׁמְרָה נַפְשִׁי כִּי־חָסִיד אָנִי, *preserve my life, for I am steadfast*:

> ר׳ לוי ור׳ יצחק. חד אמ[ר], לאו חסיד אני, שכל מלכי מזרח ומערב ישנים עד שלש
> שעות ואני 'חצות לילה אקום להודות לך'? ואידך אמ[ר], לאו חסיד אני, שכל מלכי
> מזרח ומערב יושבין אגודות אגודות בכבודן ואני ידי מלוכלכות בדם שפיר ובשליא
> כדי לטהר אשה לבעלה?[119]

Levi and R. Isaac. One of them said, "am I not pious? For all kings, east and west, sleep to the third hour, but as for me: "At midnight, I rise to give thanks to you" (Ps 119:62)."" The other said, "am I not pious? For all kings, east and west, sit in all their glory with their retinues, but as for me, my hands are sloppy with menstrual blood and the blood of the foetus and placenta, which I examine so as to declare a woman clean for sexual relations with her husband.

In sum, we have found that all of the elements of this expansion—David's description as חסיד and his practice of rising at midnight to sing hymns to God—are taken directly from *b. Ber.* 3b–4a. Because the targumist views the verse as describing David son of Jesse, he seeks to explain why Elhanan/David is called

---

119   Later in this passage, the Talmud wonders: ודוד היכי קרי לנפשי[ה] חסיד?, how could David call himself pious?

בֶּן־יָעוּר (כתיב), and accordingly pins the entire talmudic description of David's midnight hymns on the word יָעוּר/יָעִיר of the Hebrew verse.

2.19 *God's Mercy at the Temple Mount due to the Patriarchs (1 Chr 21:15)*

1 Chr 21:15

MT וַיִּשְׁלַח֩ הָאֱלֹהִ֨ים ׀ מַלְאָ֥ךְ ׀ לִירוּשָׁלִַ֘ם֮ לְהַשְׁחִיתָהּ֒ וּכְהַשְׁחִ֗ית רָאָ֤ה ה'

TC ושדר מימרא דה' מלאכא דמותנא לירושלם לחבלותה ובחבלותיה אסתכל

באפרא דעקדתא דיצחק די ביסודא דמדבחא ואדכר קיימיה דעם אברהם דקיים ליה בטוור

פולחנא ובית־מוקדשא דלעיל דתמן נפשת דתמן צדיקיא ואיקונין דיעקב דקביע בכורסי יקרא

MT (cont.)		עַל־הָֽרָעָ֔ה	וַיִּנָּ֣חֶם
TC	ותב במימריה על בשתא דאמר למעבד

(cont.)				הֶ֥רֶף יָדֶֽךָ	עַתָּ֖ה	רַ֚ב הַמַּשְׁחִ֔ית	לַמַּלְאָ֣ךְ	וַיֹּ֨אמֶר
TC				מסתייד כדון	מחבלא	למלאכא	ואמר

| | מן שייר עמא | מחתך | ופסוק | מביניהון | רבהון | אבישי | טול |

(cont.)	הַיְבוּסִֽי׃	אָרְנָ֖ן	עִם־גֹּ֔רֶן	עֹמֵד֙	ה'	וּמַלְאַ֨ךְ
TC	יבוסאה:	דארון אדרי בבית קאים הוה ה' מן־קדם שליח ומלאך

NJPS: God sent an angel to Jerusalem to destroy it, but as he was about to wreak destruction, the LORD saw and renounced further punishment and said to the destroying angel, "Enough! Stay your hand!" The angel of the LORD was then standing by the threshing floor of Ornan the Jebusite.

Dost: Then the Memra of the Lord sent the angel of death to Jerusalem to destroy it, but when He was about to begin destroying, He looked at the ash from the binding of Isaac, which was at the base of the altar, and He remembered His covenant that was with Abraham, which was established with him on the mountain of worship, and the temple, which is above, where are the souls of the righteous and the image of Jacob, which is affixed on the throne of glory, and He repented in His Memra against the evil that He had declared to do. So He said to the destroying angel, "You have done enough! Now take up Abishai their leader from among them, but restrain your smiting of the rest of the people." So the angel sent from before the Lord was standing at the threshing floor of Arwan the Jebusite.

The Hebrew verse describes the tension as it reaches a climax. God's wrath reaches Jerusalem—but, in a twist of fate, is suspended. The verse intimates that this act of mercy is associated with a certain geographic location: the threshing floor of Ornan the Jebusite, later the site of the Temple. The Targum liberally expands the content of the verse, detailing what God saw (in the verse's terminology) that caused Him to reverse his decision and have mercy on the city. The change stemmed from three sights: Isaac's ashes, God's promise to Abraham on Mount Moriah, and the likeness of Jacob on God's throne. The Targum further states that although the bulk of the people were spared from the disaster, the plague came at a price: the angel, following the order of God, singled out Abishai son of Zeruiah from the other inhabitants of the city and slew him.

Both elements of TC's insertion—the specific things seen by God and Abishai's being singled out to die—appear together in a series of homilies on the verse in *b. Ber.* 62b:

'ויאמר למלאך המשחית בעם רב'—מאי 'רב'? אמ[ר] ר' יהודה אמ[ר] רב: אמ[ר]
לו הב״ה למלאך, טול לי הרב שבהם שיש לפרוע מהם כמה כמה חובות. באותה שעה מת
אבישי בן צרויה, שהוא שקול כרובן של סנהדרין. 'ובהשחית ראה ה' וינחם'—מה
ראה? דמותו של יעקב ראה, דכת[יב] 'ויאמר יעקב כאשר ראם'. ושמואל אמ[ר]:
אפרו של יצחק ראה, שנא[מר] 'אלהים יראה לו השה לעולה בני'. ר' יצחק נפחא
אמ[ר]: כסף כפורים ראה, שנא[מר] 'ולקחת את כסף הכפורים' וג'. ר' יוחנן אמ[ר]:
בית המקדש ראה, שנ[אמר] 'אשר יאמר היום בהר ה' יראה'. פליגי בה ר' יעקב בר
אידי ור' שמואל בר נחמני. חד אמ[ר]: בית המקדש ראה. וחד אמ[ר]: כסף כפורים
ראה. ומסתבר כמ[אן] ד[אמר] בית המקדש ראה, שנא[מר] 'אשר יאמר היום בהר
ה' יראה'.

"And he said to the angel that destroyed the people, it is great" (2 Sam 24:16): Said R. Eleazar, "Said the Holy One, blessed be he, to the angel, 'Take for me the great man among them, from whom may be exacted the penalty for many sins for [all of] them. At that moment Abishai, son of Zeruiah, died, who was in himself worth the better part of the sanhedrin." "And as he was about to destroy, the Lord saw and changed his mind" (1 Chr 21:15): *What did he see?* Said Rab, "He saw Jacob, our father. "For it is written, 'And Jacob said when he beheld them' (Gen 32:3)." Samuel said, "He saw the ashes of [the ram of] Isaac, as it says, 'God will see to the lamb for himself' (Gen 22:8)." R. Isaac Nappaha said, "He saw the atonement-money, as it is said, 'And you shall take the atonement money from the children of Israel and it shall be a memorial' (Exod 30:16)." R. Yohanan said, "He saw the house of the sanctuary, as it is said, 'In the mount where the Lord will see' (Gen 22:14)." R. Jacob bar Idi and R. Samuel bar Nahmani debated the matter. One of them said, "He saw the atonement money." The other said, "He saw the house of the sanctuary." *And the more reasonable position accords with the view of him who said that he saw the house of the sanctuary, for it is said,* "As it will be said on that day in the mountain where the Lord sees" (Gen 22:14).

Where Abishai son of Zeruiah is concerned, the expansion in TC appears to be modeled on the tradition as it appears in the Talmud:

BT   שבהם   הרב   לי טול

TC   מביניהון רבהון אבישי   טול

The Talmud interprets the word רַב as denoting the greatest member of the people, i.e., Abishai, who was as great as a majority of the Sanhedrin. TC followed the Talmud, but took a step further and, by appending a suffixed pronoun in the third-person plural to the word רב, gave it the meaning of a leader or a Torah sage.[120] The word רַב is translated previously in the literal continuum of TC in its simple sense, as מסתייך, a term comparable to the rabbinic דיך, so that by incorporating BT's exegesis, as well, TC effectively produced a dual translation of the word רַב, which now has equivalents in both מסתייך and רבהון.

How the objects of the action of seeing in the Targum found their place there is less clear. The homilies cited in BT contain different views regarding the object seen. Rosenberg and Kohler took this verse as an example of the targumist's tendency to incorporate various competing views in his work, apparently out of his belief that each reflects a valid truth.[121] Churgin similarly noted that TC combined opposing opinions into one homily.[122] Yet though the fingerprints of BT are clearly visible on this verse of TC, the comments made by Rosenberg and Kohler and by Churgin do not suffice to explain all of the elements of the nonliteral expansion found in the Targum here. BT says nothing of the covenant with Abraham, does not indicate that the Temple in question is a heavenly one, and does not explicitly associate it with the likeness of Jacob. Also of note is that TC says nothing of the view that God saw the money of atonement. Given all of the above, the treatment of this verse in TC does not appear to be a haphazard collection of various opinions from the talmudic passage that the targumist wished to include indiscriminately in his composition.

---

120   We might consider whether the word רבהון in TC ought to be translated as *their rabbi,* or, as proposed by Le Déaut-Robert, vol. 1, p. 87, *leur chef* (followed by McIvor, p. 116: *their leader*). In any event, the sense of the word in TC is altered from that in the homily in the Talmud.

121   Rosenberg-Kohler, p. 150.

122   Churgin *Hagiographa*, p. 256.

To understand the nonliteral insertion in fuller context, we must first of all satisfy ourselves that the targumist referred to additional sources in writing these words. TC's comments on the covenant with Abraham are reminiscent of the content of two homilies to the present verse found in the late midrashic collection 'Aggadat Genesis.[123]

וכן את מוצא בימי דוד, כשמנה את ישראל, הלך המלאך להשחיתן ... מיד הלך לו המלאך וישב לו בהר המוריה. ואמר לפניו: רבש"ע, זכור מה שהתנית ברית עם מי שהעלה את בנו על ההר הזה, שנאמר 'ויקרא אברהם שם המקום [ההוא ה' יראה]'. ה[דא] ה[וא] ד[כתיב] 'וכהשחית ראה ה' וינחם על הרעה'. מה ראה? ראה מה שאמר לאברהם ...

Thus one finds in the time of David, when he counted Israel, the angel went to destroy them ... Then the angel went and stopped at Mt. Moriah and said before him: Master of the world, remember the covenant you made with he who offered his son on this mountain ... This is why it was written, 'but as he was about to wreak destruction, the LORD saw and renounced further punishment' (1 Chr 21:15). What did He see? He saw what He promised to Abraham ...

ור' נחמיה אומר: מה הוא ראה ה' וינחם על הרעה? אלא הלך לו המלאך וישב לו בהר המוריה ואמר לפניו: רבש"ע, כן התנית ברית עם אברהם אביהם, שכבש רחמיו לעשות רצונך בעולם הזה. לא כך אמר לפניך 'ויקרא אברהם שם המקום ההוא ה' יראה'? ... היה לי זכות להשיב לפניך ולא אמרתי כלום, אלא עשיתי עצמי כאלם ועשיתי רצונך, כך כל זמן שיהיו בני חוטאין לפניך ויש לך זכות על שחטאו לך, שתהא מכבש את חמתך ולא תפרע מהם, אלא שתהא זוכר עקדתו של יצחק ומרחם עליהם ... מה ראה? עקדתו של יצחק ראה ונתרחם עליהם.

R. Nehemiah said: What did the Lord see that He renounced the punishment? Rather, the angel went and stopped at Mt. Moriah and said before him: Master of the world, so did you make a covenant with Abraham their father, who subdued his mercy to do your will in this world. Did he not say before you, 'And Abraham named that site Lord yireh' (Gen 22:14)? ... I had a claim I could have presented before you but I said nothing, feigned dumbness and did your will. Similarly, whenever my children sin before You and You have a claim (against them) because they sinned, You shall subdue Your rage and not punish them, but rather recall Isaac's binding and pity them ... What did He see? Isaac's binding He saw and pitied them.

---

123   First selection: 'Aggadat Gen. 30 (p. 61); second selection: ibid. 38 (pp. 77–78).

These traditions link the present verse not only to the Binding of Isaac, but also to God's covenant and oath to Abraham on Mount Moriah. The covenant is one whose existence is derived by *'Aggadat Genesis* from the words ה׳ יִרְאֶה in Gen 22:14, which appear adjacent to the explicit oath, בִּי נִשְׁבַּעְתִּי נְאֻם־הֹ׳, *by Myself I swear, the LORD declares*, in verse 16 of that chapter. The expansion in TC refers to קיימיה דעם אברהם דקיים ליה בטוור פולחנא, *His covenant that was with Abraham, which was established with him on the mountain of worship*, whose final two words are a rare alternative name for Mount Moriah (on this name, see pp. 215–216). The link between TC and *'Aggadat Genesis* here appears to be one of content and not necessarily to extend to specific diction, and thus the relationship between the documents apparently is not direct, but a function of a common tradition.

We saw the likeness of Jacob mentioned in the passage in BT as one possible answer to the question of what God saw. Another proposal was that the object of the action of seeing had been the Temple. In the expansion in TC, the two are integrated along with other elements: the likeness of Jacob on God's throne in the heavenly Temple, where the souls of the righteous are found. Apparently, because he already had made mention of the sanctuary where the divine throne is located, the targumist decided also to refer to the souls of the righteous because they, too, are associated with the throne. This tradition is found in various rabbinic sources, among them *b. Šabb.* 152b:[124]

ר׳ אליעזר אומ[ר]: נשמתן של צדיקים גנוזות תחת כסא הכבוד, שנא[מר] 'והיתה נפש אדוני' וגו'.

> R. Eliezer says, "The souls of the righteous are hidden away under the throne of glory" 'Yet the soul of my lord shall be bound up in the bundle of life with the Lord your God' (1 Sam 25:29).

The likeness of Jacob appears independently in the talmudic homily, with no indication of where God saw it and no association with the divine throne. The words describing the likeness of Jacob in TC, meanwhile, resemble those in TN, FT, and TPJ to the story of Jacob's dream, Gen 28:12:

TC	יקרא	בכורסי	דקביע	דיעקב	ואיקונין			
TN	איקרא	בכורסיה	קביעא	דידיה	דאיקונין	חסידא	לגברא	חמון	אתון
FTP	יקרא	בכורסי	קביע	דידיה	די איקונין	חסידא	גוברא	חמין	אתון
FTV	יקריה	בכורסי		דידיה	דאיקונין	חסידא	גברא ליעקב	חמון	אתון
TPJ	יקרא	בכורסי	קביעא	דיליה	דאיקונין	חסידא		יעקב חמון	איתון

124   Cf. *'Abot de Rabbi Nathan* A 12 (p. 50); idem B 25 (p. 51).

The revelation that Jacob experienced and his vow, described in Gen 28:10–22, are said by Scripture to have taken place in Bethel. Rabbinic tradition and the Targums, however, view the episode as having occurred on Mount Moriah, in Jerusalem.[125] As much is explicit in TC 2 Chr 3:1: ושרי שלמה למבני ית בית מקדשא דה' בירושלם בטוור מוריה ... תמן צלי יעקב במעירקיה מן קדם עשו אחוי, *so Solomon began to build the temple of the Lord in Jerusalem on Mt. Moriah ... there Jacob prayed when he was fleeing from before his brother Esau.* The tradition also appears in TPJ 28:11, whose opening words identify the "place" described by the verse: וצלי באתר בית מוקדשא, *he prayed at the site of the Temple.* Jacob (ibid., v. 17) describes the place with the words לית דין אתר חול ארום אלהן בית מקדש לשמיה דה' ודין כשר לצלן מכוון כל קבל תרע שמייא משכלל תחות כורסי יקרא, .The language with which TC refers to the likeness of Jacob on the divine throne thus dovetails with the tradition concerning Jacob's dream on Mount Moriah.

Possibly the targumist wanted to limit his homily to a single, unified topic: the place where God relented is linked with each of the three Patriarchs, and it is specifically the merit of these Patriarchs in this place that tips the balance toward divine grace and brings about the voidance of the fatal decree.[126] With this in mind, we can understand why TC makes no mention of the talmudic opinion that God saw the money of atonement: that view is inconsistent with what the targumist believes to be the subject of the verse, viz., Mount Moriah.

2.20   *Rehabiah's Fertility through Moses (1 Chr 23:17)*

1 Chr 23:17

MT	וַיִּהְיוּ בְנֵי־אֱלִיעֶזֶר רְחַבְיָה	הָרֹאשׁ	וְלֹא־הָיָה לֶאֱלִיעֶזֶר	בָּנִים אֲחֵרִים		
TC	והוו בני אליעזר רחביה	ממנא לרישא	ולא הוה לאליעזר	בנין חורנין		

MT (cont.)		וּבְנֵי רְחַבְיָה רָבוּ לְמָעְלָה:		
TC	ובגין זכותיה דמשה	רבו		
	בני רחביה וסגיעו לעיל	מן שתין ריבבן:		

NJPS: And the sons of Eliezer were: Rehabiah the chief. Eliezer had no other sons, but the sons of Rehabiah were very numerous.

Dost: The sons of Eliezer were Rahabiah, who was appointed as head, but Eliezer did not have other sons, yet because of the merit of Moses, the sons of Rehabiah grew and increased to more than 600,000.

---

125   For a compilation of sources, see Ginzberg, vol. 5, pp. 289–290, nn. 130–131.

126   TC also associates Mount Moriah with the three Patriarchs in 2 Chr 3:1 (see pp. 452–454, below), but there describes Abraham's acts of prayer and worship on the mount and says nothing of a covenant or promise.

The Hebrew verse states that Eliezer son of Moses had only one son, Rehabiah, but this son had many descendants. To this the targumist adds two things. First, the blessing of fertility was due to Moses' merit. Second, Rehabiah's descendants ultimately numbered more than 600,000. The source of both additions is a homily in *b. Ber.* 7a that cites the present verse:[127]

אמ[ר] ר' יוחנן משום ר' שמעון בן יוחאי: כל דיבו[ר] ודיבו[ר] שיצא מפי הקב"ה
לטובה—אפי[לו] על תנאי—לא חזר. מנא לן? ממשה רבנו, דכתי[ב] 'הרף ממני
ואשמידם' וגו' [...]ואעשה אותך לגוי עצום ורב ממנו—ל"ג]. ואע"ג דבעא משה רחמי
עלה דמילתא ובטלה—ואפי[לו] הכי אוקמה בזרעו, דכתי[ב] 'ובני משה גרשום ואלי-
עזר', 'ובני אליעזר רחביה הראש', 'ובני רחביה רבו למעלה'. תנא משמיה דר' אלי-
עזר: למעלה מששים רבוא. אתיא רביה רביה: כתי[ב] הכא 'רבו למעלה', וכתי[ב]
התם 'ובני ישראל פרו וישרצו וירבו ויעצמו'.

And R. Yohanan said in the name of R. Yosé, "Every word containing a blessing that came forth from the Mouth of the Holy One, blessed be he, even if stated conditionally, was never retracted. *"How do we know it?* It is from Moses, our master. "For it is said, 'Let me alone, that I may destroy them and blot out their name from under heaven, and I will make of you a nation mightier and greater than they' (Deut 9:14). *"Even though Moses prayed for mercy, so that the matter was nullified, even so,* [*the blessing*] *was carried out in his seed.* "For it is said, 'The sons of Moses, Gershom and Eliezer … and the sons of Eliezer were Rehabia the chief … and the sons of Rehabia were very many' (1 Chr 23:15–17). *And in this regard R. Joseph stated on Tannaite authority,* "They were more than sixty myriads." "This is to be derived from an analogy between two uses of the word 'many.' "Here it is written, 'They were very many' (1 Chr 23:17). "And elsewhere it is written, 'And the children of Israel were very fruitful and increased abundantly and became very many' (Exod 1:7).

2.21 *Translation of* פַּרְבָּר *(1 Chr 26:18)*

1 Chr 26:18

MT	לַפַּרְבָּר לַמַּעֲרָב אַרְבָּעָה לַמְסִלָּה שְׁנַיִם לַפַּרְבָּר:
TC	כלפי ברא למערבא ארבעא לכיבשא תרין כלפי ברא:

NJPS: at the colonnade on the west—four at the causeway and two at the colonnade.

Dost: Facing outward to the west were four on the street, two facing outward.

---

127 Churgin *Hagiographa*, p. 256.

The word פַּרְבָּר appears in Scripture only in this verse. Churgin identified the source of the targumist's translation of the word, כלפי ברא, as *b. Tamid* 27a:[128]

מאי 'לפרברי'? א[מר] רבה בר ר' שילא: כמאן דא[מר] כלפי בר.

What is the meaning of parbar? *Said Rabbah bar R. Shila, "It is in line with the expression for 'outside'* [bar standing for 'outwards'].*"*

The unique word is similarly interpreted elsewhere in the Talmud, in *b. Zebaḥ.* 55b.[129] Whether the targumist obtained his translation from *b. Tamid* or *b. Zebaḥim* is not ascertainable, but in any event his source was a report in BT of an exegetical tradition of the Babylonian Amora'im, which he quoted in his work.

2.22 *Protocol for Initiation of War (1 Chr 27:34)*
1 Chr 27:34

MT:	וְאַחֲרֵי אֲחִיתֹפֶל יְהוֹיָדָע בֶּן־בְּנָיָהוּ וְאֶבְיָתָר וְשַׂר־צָבָא לַמֶּלֶךְ יוֹאָב:

TC
וכד הוון צריכין למפק בקרבא מתמלכין באחיתפל
ומן בתר מלכת אחיתפל
הוו שאלין באוריא ותומיא מן(יהוידע בר בניהו ריש סנהדרין אמרכלא דכהניא
ומן אביתר כהנא רבא
ומן דשאלין באוריא ותומיא נפקין לקרבא מזרזי חילא קשתיא וקלעיא
ועליהון רב חילא די למלכא יואב:

NJPS: After Ahitophel were Jehoiada son of Benaiah and Abiathar. The commander of the king's army was Joab.

Dost: Now when they needed to go out into battle, counsel was taken with Ahithophel, and after the counsel of Ahithophel they would inquire of the Urim and the Thummim by Jehoida son of Banaiah, the head of the Sanhedrin, the chief of the priests, and from Abiathar, the high priest. After they would ask the Urim and the Thummim, those girded for war, the archers, and the slingers would go out to battle, and over them was Joab, the commander of the king's army.

The expansive translation above is based on *b. Ber.* 3b–4a, other lines of which also served TC as a source for 1 Chr 18:17 (see pp. 311–313, above).

---

128   Churgin *Hagiographa*, p. 257.
129   Notwithstanding, there are MSS of *b. Zebaḥim* that testify to the reading אפייה לבר.

B. Ber. 3b–4a:[130]

וכיון שעלה עמוד השחר, נכנסו חכמי ישראל אצלו ואומ[רים] לו: אדוננו המלך, עמד
ישראל צריכין פרנסה. אמ[ר] להם: ילכו ויתפרנסו זה מזה. אמרו לו: אין הקומץ
משביע את הארי ואין הבור מתמלא מחוליתה. אמ[ר] להם: לכו ופשטו ידיכם בגדוד.
מיד יועצין באחיתופל ונמלכין בסנהדרין ושואלים באורים ותומים. אמ[ר] רב יוסף
מאי קראה? 'ואחרי אחיתופל יהוידע בן בניהו ואביתר ושר צבא למלך יואב'. אחיתו־
פל—זה יועץ, וכן הוא אומ[ר] 'ואחיתופל יועץ למלך'. יהוידע בן בניהו—זה סנהדרי,
וכן הוא אומ[ר] באביו 'ובניהו בן יהוידע על הכרתי ועל הפלתי'. ולמה נקרא שמם
כרתי ופלתי? כרתי—שכורתים דבריהם; פלתי—שמופלאים בדבריהם. 'ואביתר'—
אלו אורים ותומים. ואחר כך 'שר צבא למלך יואב'.

"When it was dawn, the sages of Israel came into him. They said to him,
'Our lord, O king, your people Israel needs sustenance.' "He said to them,
'Let them go and make a living from one another.' "They said to him,
'A handful [of food] cannot satisfy a lion, and a hole in the ground cannot be filled up from its own clods.' "He said to them, 'Go and organize
marauders.' "They forthwith took counsel with Ahitophel and sought
the advice of the sanhedrin and addressed a question to the Urim and
Thumim." *Said R. Joseph, "What verse indicates this?* 'And after Ahithofel
was Jehoiada, son of Benaiah, and Abiathar, and the captain of the king's
host was Joab' (1 Chr 27:34). "'Ahithofel was counsellor,' and so it is said,
'Now the counsel of Ahithofel, which he counselled in those days, was
as if a man inquired of the word of God' (2 Sam 16:23). "'Benaiah, son of
Jehoiada' refers to the sanhedrin. "'And Abiathar' refers to the Urim and
Thumim. And so it says, 'And Benaiah, son of Jehoiada, was in charge of
the Kerethi and Pelethi' (2 Sam 20:23). *"Why were the Urim and Thumim
so called?* They were called 'Kerethi' because their words are decisive [ko-
rethim], and 'Pelethi' because they are distinguished (muflaim) through
what they say. "And then comes 'the captain of the king's host, Joab.'"

R. Yosef quotes the present verse and interprets it in a manner that ensconces in
it the protocol for initiation of hostilities described in the aggadic portrayal of
King David's court. The author of TC incorporated R. Yosef's homily within his
translation, but it is evident from a comparison of the Targum and the Talmud
that the targumist made several changes. The homilist assumes that Jehoiada
son of Benaiah is a son of Benaiah son of Jehoiada, who is understood to be the
leader of the Sanhedrin, as noted above, and that the son Jehoiada inherited his

---

130   Paralleled in *b. Sanh.* 16a–b.

father's status as head of the Sanhedrin. The targumist bestowed two honorific titles on this Jehoiada: ריש סנהדרין, *head of the Sanhedrin*, and אמרכלא דכהניא, *chief of the priests*, representing dual responsibilities attached to Jehoiada by TC in an attempt to mediate between the aggadic tradition and the statement in 1 Chr 27:5 (in the same chapter as the present verse) שַׂר הַצָּבָא הַשְּׁלִישִׁי לַחֹדֶשׁ הַשְּׁלִישִׁי בְּנָיָהוּ בֶן־יְהוֹיָדָע הַכֹּהֵן רֹאשׁ, *the third army officer for the third month— Benaiah son of Jehoiada, the chief priest*.[131] The targumist assumed that just as leadership of the Sanhedrin had been passed from one generation to the next, so had Benaiah's priestly function described by the verse been inherited by his son, and the targumist therefore was left with two priestly figures: Jehoiada and Abiathar. To Abiathar he naturally assigned the high priesthood, while he described Jehoiada as administrator of the priests, which is one possible translation of הַכֹּהֵן רֹאשׁ in verse 5 (there translated as כהנא ממנא לרישא).[132]

Jehoiada having now been defined as the leader of the priests, the targumist decided that he must share responsibility for the Urim and Tummim with Abiathar. This interpretation not only deviates from the exegesis of BT, but also is not logically dictated by the approach that requires the information in verse 5 to be incorporated in verse 34. The targumist could have assigned Jehoiada responsibility only for the Sanhedrin, despite his role as leader of the priests, and left Abiathar alone with responsibility for the Urim and Tummim.

The expansion describing מזרזי חילא קשתיא וקלעיא, *those girded for war, the archers, and the slingers*, going out to battle brings together two different pairings. קשתיא וקלעיא (the translation of הכרתי והפלתי in TJ) are described in TC 1 Chr 18:17 as going out to battle as ordered by Benaiah son of Jehoiada, and their appearance here thus is in keeping with the context of the Aramaic verse. מזרזי חילא appears in TC as the equivalent of two terms: חלוץ (צבא) and גדוד. It may be that the targumist in this way sought to give expression to the word גדוד, which appears in the talmudic homily cited above.

2.23 God's Triumphant Acts throughout History (1 Chr 29:11)

1 Chr 29:11

MT					הַגְּדֻלָּה	ה׳	לְךָ
TC	רבתא	בגבורתא	עלמא	דבריתא	רבותא	ה׳	דילך

---

131 Ginzberg, vol. 6, p. 302, n. 95, notes the view of the author of *Maḥzor Vitry* that this Benaiah is not Benaiah son of Jehoiada described in 2 Sam 8:18, informed by that author's assumption that he cannot have been a priest. TC, however, clearly did not concur.

132 See syntactic note by Mizrahi, p. 691, n. 14, concerning the meaning of this expression in the plain sense of MT.

וְהַגְּבוּרָה   MT (cont.)

TC ית ימא   וגבורתא דאפיקתא אבהתנא דבריתא ממצרים בגבוח רברבן ואעברתנון

וְהַתִּפְאֶרֶת   (cont.)

TC   ואתגליתא על טוורא דסיני בשבהורא עם כתי מלאכיא למתן אוריתא לעמך

וְהַנֵּצַח   (cont.)

TC   ועבדתא נצחנין בעמלק ובסיחון ובעוג ובמלכי כנענאי

וְהַהוֹד   (cont.)

TC   ובזיו   יקרך אקימתא שמשא בגבעון וסיהרא במישר אילון עד דאתפרעו עמך
בית ישראל מן סנאיהון

(cont.) וּבָאָרֶץ   בַּשָּׁמַיִם   כִּי־ כֹל

TC ובארעא   בשמיא   ארום כלהון עובדי ידך

ואת שליט עליהון וסביל   כל   מה די בשמיא וכל מה די בארעא

(cont.)   לְרֹאשׁ:   וְהַמִּתְנַשֵּׂא לְכֹל | לְךָ ה׳ הַמַּמְלָכָה

TC   מלאכיא דבשמיא   על כלהון   דילך ה׳ מלכותא ברקיעא ומתנטל

בארעא: דמתמנן לרישין   ועל כל

NJPS: Yours, LORD, are greatness, might, splendor, triumph, and majesty—yes, all that is in heaven and on earth; to You, LORD, belong kingship and preeminence above all.

Dost: Yours, O Lord, is the greatness—for You created the world with great power—and the power—for You brought out our fathers from Egypt with many mighty deeds, and You made them pass through the sea, and You were revealed on Mt. Sinai in splendor with bands of angels to give the Torah to Your people, and You accomplished victories against Amalek, against Sihon, against Og, and against the kings of the Canaanites; and in the splendor of Your glory You stayed the sun and the moon in the plain of Aijalon until Your people, the house of Israel, were avenged of their enemies. For all of them are works of Your hand in the heavens and on earth, and You rule over them and sustain all that is in the heavens and all that is on the earth. Yours, O Lord, is the kingship in the firmament, and (You) are exalted over all of the angels who are in the heavens and over all who are appointed as leaders on the earth.

The Hebrew verse transmits David's praises of his God on the occasion of consigning the plans for the Temple to his son Solomon in the presence of the entire nation, whom the king assembled for the purpose of this special event. The verse, later incorporated in various parts of the Jewish liturgy due to it jubilant tone, belongs to the genre of psalmic praises of God.[133] David enumerates a number of lofty attributes identified with God, but does not provide any detail or argue the correctness of the list by referring to specific events. TC adds additional information to the work of the Chronicler, linking each of the listed attributes with historical deeds from what he views as the Golden Age of ancient Israel, then concludes the list by including other great beings under the absoluteness of God's supremacy.

Rosenberg and Kohler, followed by other scholars, identified the source of TC's treatment of the verse as *b. Ber.* 58a.[134] The Talmud there relates a story from the life of R. Shila in which he not only was saved from the king's wrath but also subsequently assumed high office. As a token of his gratitude, R. Shila conceived a homily on the present verse in which he detailed God's great acts over the course of history. Let us compare R. Shila's homily and its talmudic parallels to the expansion in TC:[135]

... אמ[ר] (ר' שילא—ל"ג): הואיל ואיתעביד לי ניסא בהאי פסוקא אפיק אדרשיה
בי מידרשא. אזל בי מדרשא ודרש: 'לך ה' הגדולה'—זה מעשה בראשית, וכן
הוא אומ[ר], 'עושה גדולות עד אין חקר'; 'והגבור[ה]'—זו יציאת מצרים, וכן הוא
אומ[ר], 'או הנסה אלהים' וגו'; 'והתפארת'—אלו חמה ולבנה שעמדו ליהושע,
דכתיב 'וידם השמש ירח עמד'; 'והנצח'—זו מפלתה של רומי, שנא[מר] 'ויז נצחם
על בגדי'; 'וההוד'—זו מלחמת עמלק, שנא[מר] 'ויאמר כי יד על כס יה'; 'כי כל
בשמים ובארץ'—זו מלחמת סיסרא, שנא[מר] 'מן שמים נלחמו'; 'לך ה' הממלכה'—
זו מלחמת נחלי ארנון, שנא[מר] 'על כן יאמר בספר מלחמות ה'' 'והמתנשא'—זו
מלחמת גוג ומגוג, שנא[מר] 'הנני אליך גוג נשיא' וגו'; 'לכל לראש'—א"ר חנינא בר
פפא אמ[ר] רב: אפי[לו] ריש גרגותא מן שמיא מוקמו ליה.
במתניתא] תנא משמיה דר' עקיבא: 'לך ה' הגדולה'—זו קריעת ים סוף, וכן הוא
אומ[ר], 'וירא ישראל את היד הגדולה'; 'והגבורה'—אלו מכת בכורות; 'והתפארת'—
זו מתן תורה; 'והנצח'—זו ירושלם; 'וההוד'—זה בנין בית המקדש, יהי רצון שיבנה
במהרה בימינו.

[*R. Shila saw that the man was going to go and report this to them, saying that he had called them asses. R. Shila said, "This man is a persecutor, and the Torah has said that if one comes to kill you, forestall matters by killing him first (cf. Exod 22:1)." He hit him with his sash and killed him. R. Shila*]

---

133 The direct address to God and enumeration of His qualities and mighty deeds mark a similarity to psalmic units such as Ps 89:5–14. For a more detailed discussion of the present verse's place in psalmic literature, see Klein *1 Chronicles*, p. 537, and sources cited ibid.

134 Rosenberg-Kohler, p. 149; Churgin *Hagiographa*, p. 257; Le Déaut-Robert, vol. 1, p. 102.

135 The talmudic text here follows MS Oxford 366. Several variants exist between the various MSS and printed editions, but these do not shed light on the specific source of TC.

said, "Since a miracle has been done for me through the particular verse of Scripture that I cited, I shall expound the whole of it: "'Yours O Lord is the greatness'—this refers to the works of creation, and so Scripture says, 'Who does great things past finding out' (Job 9:10). "'And the power'—this refers to the Exodus from Egypt, [as it is said, 'Or has any god ventured' (Deut 4:34)]. "'And the glory'—this refers to the sun and moon, standing still for Joshua, as it is said, 'And the sun stood still and the moon stayed' (Josh 10:13). "'And the victory'—this speaks of the fall of Rome, and so it says, 'And their life-blood is dashed against my garments' (Isa 63:3). "'And the majesty'—this [is the war against Amalek, as it says, 'Hand upon the throne of the Lord' (Exod 17:16). "'For all that is in heaven and earth'— this speaks of the war of Sisera, as it is said, 'They fought from heaven, the stars in their courses fought against Sisera' (Judg 5:20). "'Yours is the kingdom, O Lord'—this is the battle of the valleys of Arnon, as it is said, 'Wherefore it is said in the book of the Wars of the Lord: Vaheb in Supah and the valleys of Arnon' (Num 21:14). ['and preeminence'–] this refers to the war of Gog and Magog, and so it is said, 'Behold I am against you, Gog, chief prince of Meshech and Tubal' (Ezek 38:3)." "Head above all" (1 Chr 29:11): Said R. [Ḥanina bar Pappa, said Rab], "Even the designation of who will be in charge of the irrigation well is decided in heaven."

In a teaching on Tannaite authority it has been taught in the name of R. Aqiba, "'Yours, Lord, is the greatness' refers to the splitting of the sea of Reeds[, as it says, 'And when Israel saw the wondrous power']. "'And the power' refers to the blow against the first-born.' "'And the glory' refers to the giving of the Torah. "'And the victory' refers to Jerusalem. "'And the majesty' refers to [the building of] the Temple [—may it be built speedily in our days]."

Though there obviously is a great deal of overlap between the talmudic exegeses and that in TC, they are not in complete agreement, as demonstrated by the following table:

1 Chr 29:11	TC	R. Shila	R. Aqiva
לְךָ ה' הַגְּדֻלָּה	Creation of the World	Creation of the World	Splitting of the Sea
וְהַגְּבוּרָה	The Exodus and the Splitting of the Sea	The Exodus	Plague of the Firstborn
וְהַתִּפְאֶרֶת	Giving the Torah	Stopping the Sun and Moon	Giving the Torah

1 Chr 29:11	TC	R. Shila	R. Aqiva
וְהַגְּצַח	Victories over Amalek, Sihon, Og and the Canaanite kings	The Fall of Rome	Jerusalem
וְהַהוֹד	Stopping the Sun and Moon	Victory over Amalek	Construction of the Temple
כִּי־כֹל בַּשָּׁמַיִם וּבָאָרֶץ	You Control Everything	Victory over Sisera	
לְךָ ה' הַמַּמְלָכָה	In the Sky	Victory at the Arnon Streams	
וְהַמִּתְנַשֵּׂא	Over the Angels of Heaven	The War of Gog and Magog	
לְכֹל ׀ לְרֹאשׁ	Leaders on Earth		

The homily in TC initially takes after that of R. Shila, but diverges as early as the inclusion of the Splitting of the Sea (associated by R. Aqiva with the word הַגְּדֻלָה) with the exodus from Egypt in the interpretation of וְהַגְּבוּרָה. TC parallels R. Aqiva's homily in the association of the word וְהַתִּפְאֶרֶת with the giving of the Torah, while the object of R. Shila's exegesis of this word, viz., Joshua's stopping the movement of the sun and moon, is included by TC under the word וְהַהוֹד.[136] From this point onward, the three homilies go their separate ways. TC describes God's utter control of all things and R. Shila enumerates additional wars, while the Talmud preserves no representation of R. Aqiva's interpretation of the remainder of the verse.

These differences result from the different exegetical motives of the various homilies. R. Shila's homily appears in the Talmud in connection with the exegete's lack of liberty, a function of his living under the rule of non-Jews. R. Shila was saved in the Talmud's story from the dark fate that initially awaited him, and for this he thanks God with his homily, but even this improvement resulted from the mood of a human king, who could devastate or elevate his subjects at will. In his homily, R. Shila expresses his longing for both personal and national freedom from the yoke of foreign rule, and therefore every stage of the homily, with the exception of the introduction's treatment of the creation of the world, relates to wars waged by God against other nations, beginning in the distant past and concluding with the final victory against Gog and Magog.[137]

---

136 As briefly noted by Churgin *Hagiographa*, p. 257.

137 The Exodus also plays a part in this thematic trajectory: the verse informing the homily (Deut 4:34) stresses the afflictions brought by God against the Egyptians and the war He waged against them.

R. Shila's reserves a separate stage of the homily for the downfall of Rome, giving it place of its own outside the chronological order of listed events, because this is what he most desires and the essential point of the entire homily.[138]

R. Aqiva's homily does not come as the consequence of an event described in the Talmud, but is recorded as a self-contained tradition. We therefore cannot know what occasioned its conception. Notwithstanding, we can identify a central theme. The events that it invokes describe the junctures at which God revealed Himself to the Israelites (or in their behalf, as during the Plague of the Firstborn). The order of events proceeds from the Exodus to the days in which the Temple stood. From a chronological perspective, the Plague of the Firstborn should have appeared prior to the Splitting of the Sea, but it is given precedence due to the word הַגְּדֻלָּה, which naturally is interpreted as referring to the Splitting of the Sea (Exod 14:31: וַיַּרְא יִשְׂרָאֵל אֶת־הַיָּד הַגְּדֹלָה).

The targumist apparently did not fully follow either R. Shila or R. Aqiva because neither of their homilies suited the Targum's context. Unlike the talmudic homilies, the verbs in TC describing God's actions are addressed directly to God in the second person (עבדתא, אתגליתא, אעברתנון, אפיקתא, בריתא, אקימתא)—in accordance with the Hebrew verse—and are placed in David's mouth. Therefore, the events that appear in the Targum all preceded David's time. The targumist did employ elements of the different homilies cited by the Talmud, but even these elements underwent some alteration at his hand. The targumist wishes to present various divine actions to which the words of the verse allude that together testify to God's might. The creation of the world is depicted as evidence of the Creator's power. The Exodus is linked to the Splitting of the Sea to serve as an example of His might. We may assume that the targumist considered the Plague of the Firstborn, which is mentioned separately in R. Aqiva's homily, as part of the miracles and wonders (גבורן רברבן) that transpired when God took the Israelites out of Egypt. The targumist, in his detail of the word וְהַתִּפְאֶרֶת, added to the Giving of the Torah the revelational dimension of the descent of the divine presence, attended by the angels.[139] The word וְהַנֵּצַח, in his view, alludes to military victories, and the targumist thus included under this rubric all of the wars from the time of the Exodus until the Israelite conquest of Canaan. The battle of Aijalon Valley merits special

---

138   The interpretation of the words לְכֹל לְרֹאשׁ is not a part of R. Shila's homily, but a comment attributed to R. Ḥanina b. Pappa with a different subject of exegesis.

139   The angels' descent to the terrestrial realm with God at the Giving of the Torah appears in various rabbinic sources, e.g., *Midr. Tanna'im*, Deut 32:9 (p. 190): את מוצא בשעה שירד הקב"ה לסיני ירדו עמו מחנות מחנות של מלאכי השרת, *one discovers that when the Holy One blessed be He descended to Sinai descended with him many camps of attending angels*.

mention due to the immobilization of the sun and moon. At this point the targumist transitions to a summary of what all of the deeds listed have in common: God exercises absolute control of all things in the heavens and on the earth. The end of the homily in TC, ועל כל דמתמנן לרישין בארעא, functions in the context of the Targum as a supplement noting God's absolute dominion over the firmament and the angels, but seems also to give expression to a homily quoted by R. Ḥanina b. Pappa in the name of Rab: אפילו ריש גרגותא מן שמיא מוקמו ליה, *even the designation of who will be in charge of the irrigation well is decided in heaven.*

2.24 *The Danite Woman and Her Father (2 Chr 2:13)*

2 Chr 2:13		מִן־בְּנוֹת דָּן	בֶּן־אִשָּׁה
TC	נפתלי	מבנת דן ואבוהא דאתא משבט	בר אתתא
1 Kgs 7:14	נַפְתָּלִי מִמַּטֵּה	הוּא אַלְמָנָה בֶּן־אִשָּׁה	
TJ	משבטא דבית נפתלי	בר אתתא ארמלתא הוא	

2 Chr 2:13 (cont.) ... יֹדֵעַ לַעֲשׂוֹת	אִישׁ־צֹרִי		וְאָבִיו
TC	ואתנסיבת לגבר דמן צור		
... צוארה ידע למעבד	ואבוהי דחירם		
1 Kgs 7:14 (cont.) ... חֹרֵשׁ	אִישׁ־צֹרִי		וְאָבִיו
TJ ... אומן	גבר צורי		ואבוהי

NJPS Chr: the son of a Danite woman, his father a Tyrian. He is skilled at working ...

Dost: the son of a woman of the daughters of Dan, and the woman's father is of the tribe of Naphtali, and she is married to a man who is from Tyre, and the father of Hiram the Tyrian knows (how) to work ...

NJPS Kgs: He was the son of a widow of the tribe of Naphtali, and his father had been a Tyrian, a coppersmith ...

Clem: He was the son of a widow woman from the tribe of the house of Naphtali, and his father was a Tyrian man. He was a craftsman ...

The Book of Kings indicates that the mother of Hiram, the artisan assigned responsibility for tasks required for the construction of the Temple, was a member of the tribe of Naphtali. Chronicles, however, indicates that she was a Danite. TC harmonizes the information from the two books, stating that the woman was a Danite but her father belonged to the tribe of Naphtali. How could this be? Apparently the targumist was of the view that the woman had been born to a Naphtalite man but married a man of the tribe of Dan, on whose account she had been described in Chronicles as מִן־בְּנוֹת דָּן. This woman and the Danite man then had a son, following which she was widowed and married a man from Tyre. Thus Hiram was affiliated with the tribe of Dan, the tribe of Naphtali, and Tyre.

Where TC went to quite great lengths to reconcile Kings and Chronicles, other commentators proposed a simpler solution. The commentary attributed to a student of Saadyah Ga'on, Samuel Masnuth, Qimḥi, and Pseudo-Rashi ad loc. all explained that the two tribal affiliations are those of the two parents of the boy who became an artisan.[140] According to this interpretation, Hiram's mother was a Danite, his father was a Naphtalite, and his father's place of residence was Tyre. Given the solution put forward by these exegetes, we might ask what caused the targumist to go so far as the artisan's maternal grandfather to find an answer to his difficulty.[141] Perhaps the targumist did not independently conceive this solution to the contradiction between the books, but received it as a tradition. Let us refer to *b. 'Arak.* 16b as it appears in the Vilna edition:

אמר ר' יוחנן: מנין שלא ישנה אדם מאומנותו ומאומנות אבותיו? שנאמר, 'וישלח המלך שלמה ויקח את חירם מצר בן אשה אלמנה הוא ממטה נפתלי ואביו איש צרי חרש נחושת'. ואמר מר: אימיה מבית דן. וכתיב, 'אתו] [את] [אהליאב בן אחיסמך למטה דן'.

> Said R. Yohanan, "How do we know [on the basis of Scripture] that a person should not change his calling and that of his ancestors? As it is said, 'And King Solomon sent and called Hiram out of Tyre. He was the son of a widow of the tribe of Naphtali [on his father's side] and his father was a man of Tyre, a worker in brass' (1 Kgs 7:13–14)." A master has said, "His mother came from the house of Dan, and it is written, 'And I, behold, I have appointed him with Ohaliab, the son of Ahisamach, of the tribe of Dan' (Exod 31:6).

This talmudic dictum seeks to give Hiram Danite lineage in order to demonstrate that he pursued the same craft as his forebears (specifically, Oholiab of Dan, the artisan who was Bezalel's junior partner in the construction of the Tabernacle and its vessels). The standard edition of the Talmud does not explicitly seek to mediate between Kings and Chronicles. It quotes Kings, yet states that Hiram's mother was a Danite, without explaining how such a thing

---

140   Thus also in *Tanḥuma, Ki Tissa'* 13 (p. 96).

141   Authors of previous studies seem not to have considered the targumist's motivation for offering such a complicated solution; cf. Rosenberg-Kohler, p. 146; Le Déaut-Robert, vol. 1, p. 109; McIvor, p. 145; Hamiel, p. 433.

may be reconciled with the quoted verse. This incongruity is met by the *Tosafot* ad loc. with the comment:

הכי גרסינן: דאמר מר, אימיה מדן ואבוה מנפתלי, דבדברי הימים כתיב, 'ואמו מבני דן'.

Read thus: A master has said, "His mother is of Dan, and his father is of Naphtali, for it is written in Chronicles, 'and his mother was of Dan'".

According to the textual version preferred by the *Tosafot*, the verse quoted from Kings describes the boy's father and that in Chronicles describes his mother, as proposed by the various exegetes above. No known MS of the Talmud contains the text preferred by the *Tosafot*. Those MSS known to us contain a version similar to that in printed editions in that they contain a statement regarding only the mother's lineage—with the exception of MS Munich 95. We may refer to *b. ʿArak.* 16b as it appears in this MS for further insight into the matter at hand:

א״ר יוחנן: מניין שלא ישנה אדם מאומנותו ומאומנו[ת] אבותיו ומאומנות אביו? שנ[אמר], 'וישלח המלך שלמה ויקח את חירם מצור', וכתי[ב], 'בן אשה אלמנה הוא ממטה נפתלי ואביו איש צורי'. וא[מר] מר: אמו מדבית נפתלי ואבוה מדבית דן. וכתי[ב], 'ואתו אהליאב בן אחיסמך למטה דן חרש וחושב'.

Said R. Yohanan, "How do we know that a person should not change his calling and that of his ancestors? As it is said, 'And King Solomon sent and called Hiram out of Tyre.' And it is written, 'He was the son of a widow of the tribe of Naphtali [on his father's side] and his father was a man of Tyre.' A master has said, "His mother came from the house of Naphtali and his father from the house of Dan. And it is written, 'I have appointed him with Ohaliab, the son of Ahisamach, of the tribe of Dan, a skilled craftsmaster' (Exod 31:6).

The MS preserves a version that mentions both the mother and the father, but their tribal affiliations are the inverse of that given by the *Tosafot*: in MS Munich 95, the mother is a Naphtalite and the father a Danite. Nevertheless, the general structure of the MS is in keeping with that of the Tosafists' version, and well may reflect a transposition that took root in a version similar to that of the *Tosafot*. Also of note is the MS's reading of the Hebrew form אמו alongside the Babylonian Aramaic form אבוה, a circumstance that makes it quite easy to transpose Aramaic אבוה, *his father*, with the Hebrew form אביה, *her father*. Based on these two witnesses, we may suppose that:

1. The targumist was familiar with a version of *b. ʿArakin* that contained a statement regarding both the mother's and the father's lineage, such as that preserved in the *Tosafot*, i.e., that the mother was a Danite and the father a Naphtalite.

2. The targumist understood that the father in question was the mother's father, rather than that of her son. He read the Aramaic form אבוה as the Hebrew form אביה, whether due to the analogy with the Hebrew אמו, a corrupted MS, an error in comprehending the Babylonian Aramaic form (which differs from the common targumic אבוהי/אבוי), or some other reason. As understood by the targumist, the Talmud resolved the contradiction thus: אמו מדן ואביה מנפתלי, *his mother was of Dan and her father was of Naphtali*.

3. The targumist incorporated in his composition the talmudic solution with which he was familiar, following the erroneous understanding described above, while expressing the tradition in the continuum of the Targum using a new, unequivocal phrasing: אבוהא דאתתא.

The advantage of this hypothesis is that it explains what caused the targumist to reconcile the contradiction that he faced with a resolution more complicated than that offered by other exegetes. If this conjecture is correct, we have identified another example of the targumist's use of the Talmud in his work.

2.25 *The Capacity of Solomon's Sea (2 Chr 4:5)*

2 Chr 4:5	יָכִיל׃	מַחֲזִיק בַּתִּים שְׁלֹשֶׁת אֲלָפִים
TC	אלפין בתין ביובש תרין אלפין בתין רוטבא מחסיל׃	נקיט תלת
1 Kgs 7:26	יָכִיל׃	בַּת אַלְפַּיִם
TJ	ברטיבא מחסיל׃	תרין אלפין בתין

NJPS Chr: It was a handbreadth thick, and its brim was made like that of a cup, like the petals of a lily. It held 3,000 bath.

Dost: Its thickness was a handbreadth, and its rim was like the rim of a cup, shaped into the form of a lily, containing in total 3000 baths according to the dry measure, containing 2000 according to the liquid measure.

NJPS Kgs: It was a handbreadth thick, and its brim was made like that of a cup, like the petals of a lily. Its capacity was 2,000 baths.

Clem: Its thickness was a handbreadth and its rim was like the work of the rim of a cup, gathered in the shape of a lily, containing in total two thousand baths of liquid.

In the verses above we find a contradiction regarding the volume of the basin (יָם in Hebrew; literally sea) constructed by Solomon: the Book of Kings states that the Sea had a volume of two thousand baths, whereas according to Chronicles it had a capacity of three thousand baths. TC explains that both measurements are correct. The lesser of the two, in Kings, is the total liquid capacity of the basin, and the greater, that in Chronicles, gives the measure of the maximum quantity of dry matter that fit.[142] This is a quintessential example of harmonization, albeit the targumist was not the originator of the interpretation.

TJ Kings indicated only the quantity given by the Hebrew *Vorlage* of that book, but added that that quantity of two thousand was ברטיבא, i.e., a liquid measure, an indication that that targumist penned this translation while cognizant of the distinction between dry and liquid measures. The contradiction between the two verses and the distinction between dry and liquid content appears explicitly in *b. 'Erub.* 14b:

... 'אלפים בת יכיל' ... והכת[יב], 'שלשת אלפים בת יכיל'? ההוא לגודשא. ואמ[ר]
אביי: שמ[ע] מי[נה] האי גודשא תולתא הוי. ותנן נמי: שידה תיבה ומגדל, כוורת
הקש וכוורת הקנים ובור, ספינה אלכסנדרית [טהורים], אע"פ שיש להן שולים
מחזקת ארבעים סאה [בלח שהן כוריים ביבש].

"It held two thousand baths" (1 Kgs 7:26)... But isn't it written, "It held three thousand baths" (2 Chr 4:5)? *That covers the addition of the heap in dry measure. Said Abbayye, "That proves that a heap in dry measures is a third."* So, too, we have learned in the Mishnah: ... a straw hive, and a reed hive [basket], and a tank of an Alexandrian ship which have [flat] bottoms and hold forty seahs in liquid measure, which are the same as two kors in dry measure lo, these are clean.

The solution to the contradiction between the two books thus predated the composition of TC: the targumist simply preserved the solution he had received as a tradition in his composition. While in TJ the solution appears only implicitly, suggested by a single word, TC takes that translation, lengthens it, adds detail, and produces one that, though more convoluted, more clearly distinguishes between the information contained in the two verses.

---

142 Despite the fact that the basin was intended to contain not dry matter, but water.

2.26   *Maacah's Abomination (2 Chr 15:16)*

וְגַם־ מַעֲכָ֣ה אֵ֣ם ׀ אָסָ֣א הַמֶּ֗לֶךְ הֱסִירָהּ֙ מִגְּבִירָ֔ה אֲשֶׁר־עָשְׂתָ֥ה	2 Chr 15:16
ואף מעכה אמיה דאסא מלכא אעדייה מלמהוי מלכתא מטול דעבדת	TC
וְגַ֣ם ׀ אֶת־ מַעֲכָ֣ה אִמּ֗וֹ וַיְסִרֶ֙הָ֙ מִגְּבִירָ֔ה אֲשֶׁר־עָשְׂתָ֥ה	1 Kgs 15:13
ואף ית מעכה אמיה אעדיה ממלכותה דעבדת	TJ

לַאֲשֵׁרָ֖ה מִפְלָ֑צֶת וַיִּכְרֹ֤ת אָסָא֙ אֶת־מִפְלַצְתָּ֔הּ	2 Chr 15:16 (cont.)
טעוותא למגחך קדם אשרתא וקציץ אסא ית טעוות גיחוכה	TC
לַאֲשֵׁרָ֖ה מִפְלָ֑צֶת וַיִּכְרֹ֤ת אָסָא֙ אֶת־מִפְלַצְתָּ֔הּ	1 Kgs 15:13 (cont.)
טעוותא לאשירתא וקץ אסא ית טעותה	TJ

וַיָּ֙דֶק֙ וַיִּשְׂרֹ֔ף בְּנַ֖חַל קִדְרֽוֹן׃	2 Chr 15:16 (cont.)
ואדיק ואוקיד וטליק בנחלא דקדרון ומן־בתר דתבת מעכה אמיה למהוי	TC
וַיִּשְׂרֹ֖ף בְּנַ֥חַל קִדְרֽוֹן׃	1 Kgs 15:13 (cont.)
ואוקיד בנחלא דקדרון׃	TJ

כשירתא אהדר ית שמה מיכיהו בת אוריאל דמן גבעתא מן־בגלל דלא למדכר ית שמה (.cont) TC
קדמאי דלא למתגניה ביה׃

NJPS Chr: He also deposed Maacah mother of King Asa from the rank of queen mother, because she had made an abominable thing for [the goddess] Asherah. Asa cut down her abominable thing, reduced it to dust, and burned it in the Wadi Kidron.

Dost: Moreover, as for Maacah, King Asa's mother, he removed her from being the queen because she made idolatrous divinities for committing derisive practices before Asherah. Asa cut down the idols of derision and he crushed, burned, and threw (them) into Wadi Kidron. Once Maacah his mother returned to being righteous, he changed her name back to Micaiah daughter of Uriel, who was from Gibeatha, so that her former name would not be remembered so that he might not be shamed by it.

NJPS Kgs: He also deposed his mother Maacah from the rank of queen mother, because she had made an abominable thing for [the goddess] Asherah. Asa cut down her abominable thing and burnt it in the Wadi Kidron.

Clem: And also Maacah his mother, he removed her from her kingdom because she had made an idol to the Asherah, and Asa cut down her idol and burned it in the Wadi Kidron.

Twice in these parallel verses, the object produced by Maachah is called מִפְלֶצֶת. TJ translated the term simply as טעותא, meaning *a false god, an idol*, or *an object of worship*, while TC produced an expression combining that word with another from the root גח״ך. TC characteristically followed the text of Chronicles for the better part of the verse, but where the abomination first appears, the

Targum's words appear to be more in line with the text of 1 Kings. It seems to me that the motivation for changing the order of the words in this case was not a desire to transmit a translation that followed 1 Kings, but the targumist's interest in clarifying the relationship between the two words לַאֲשֵׁרָה מִפְלֶצֶת in the Hebrew verse. In TJ the relationship between the two words seems to be that the abomination is an idol that functions in pagan worship (טעותא), while Asherah is the entity represented by the idol or in whose honor the idol was designed. TC took the foundation of his translation, טעותא, from TJ, and to this added an infinitive form (למגחך) and preposition (קדם), thus expressing the idea that the idol not only was produced in honor of Asherah, but had a function for which it was used before Asherah (on which see below). The use of the stem גח"ך, which in this context serves to convey the derision of the targumist, indicates the negativity that he associated with this act.[143] Why did TC deviate from the simple translation of TJ by incorporating an action associated with גח"ך that does not appear in the Hebrew verse?

Maacah's abomination is discussed both in the Tosefta and in BT.[144] B. 'Avod. Zar. 44a reports:

מאי 'מפלצתה'? אמ[ר] רב יהודה אמ[ר] רב: דהות מפליא ליצנותא. תני רב יוסף: כמין זכרות עשתה לו והיתה נבעלת לו בכל יום.

What is the meaning of "abominable image"? *Said R. Judah, "An object that serves as an aphrodisiac, as it has been taught as a Tannaite formulation by R. Joseph, 'She had a kind of phallus with which she had sexual relations every day.'"*

The meaning of the expression מפליא has not yet been satisfactorily clarified; even Sokoloff does not wholly explain it.[145] The *Tosafot* to BT ad loc. associate מפליא with the root פל״י, which appears in *Genesis Rabbah* in the sense of derision. Whatever the meaning of the term, TC seems to have understood the

---

143   Similar usage of the root is reflected by the Targum to verses whose aggadic baggage associates pagan activity with various sorts of sexual licentiousness:
FTP Gen 21:9 (cf. TN and TPJ): וחמת שרה ית ברה דהגר מצריתא מא דילדת לאברהם עבד
עובדין בישין לא כשרין למתעבדא מגחך בפולחנא נוכריא:
Clem: Then Sarah saw the son of Hagar the Egyptian, whom she had borne to Abraham, doing evil deeds that are not proper to be done, bowing down in foreign worship.
TN Exod 32:6 (cf. FT and TPJ): ויתבו עמ[א] למיכל ולמישתי וקמו למגחכה בפלחנא נכריה
Clem: and the people sat around to eat and drink, and rose up to make sport in foreign worship.
144   *T. 'Avod. Zar.* 3:19 (p. 465); *b. 'Avod. Zar.* 44a.
145   Sokoloff *JBA*, p. 913.

word מְפְלֶצֶת as denoting frivolity rather than terror, and added this interpretation to TJ's existing translation, טעותא. It thus is likely that with the words טעותא
אשרתא קדם למגחך, TC referred to the object that served Maacah in her frivolity before Asherah, as described in b. ʿAvodah Zarah.[146] After once explaining
the nature of the abomination produced by Maacah, upon encountering it a
second time the targumist made do with the shorter designation טעוות גיחוכה,
declining recourse to a verbal form and preposition as in the initial translation.

Regarding the alteration of Maacah's name, as indicated by the expansion in
TC, see above, pp. 482–484.

2.27   *The Spirit of Naboth and the Price of Falsehood* (2 Chr 18:20–21)

This passage in TC is based upon b. Sanh. 102b. However, it is also based upon
a tradition similar to that found in MS Reuchlin. It is, therefore, discussed in
full, below, pp. 401–405.

2.28   *Jehoshaphat's Gifts to His Sons* (2 Chr 21:3)

2 Chr 21:3

MT	מְצֻרוֹת	עִם־עָרֵי	וּלְמִגְדָּנוֹת	וּלְזָהָב	לְכֶסֶף	רַבּוֹת מַתָּנוֹת	אֲבִיהֶם לָהֶם | וַיִּתֵּן
TC		דיקר וללבושין	ולדהבא לכספא סגיעין	מתנן	אבוהון	להון	ויהב
	כרכין קרוין בהדי		קרקעא על־גב ואקניאונון				

| MT (cont.) | הַבְּכוֹר: | כִּי־הוּא | לִיהוֹרָם | נָתַן הַמַּמְלָכָה וְאֶת־ | בִּיהוּדָה |
| TC | בוכרא: הוא ארום בריה ליהורם יהב מלכותא ית יהודה דבית בארעא |

NJPS: Their father gave them many gifts of silver, gold, and [other] presents, as
well as fortified towns in Judah, but he gave the kingdom to Jehoram because
he was the first-born.

Dost: Their father gave to them many gifts of silver, of gold, and of glorious
clothing, and on the basis of land they were given possession along with fortified cities in the land of the house of Judah; but the kingdom he gave to his son
Jehoram because he was the firstborn.

This verse of TC contains an unexpected insertion describing how Jehoshaphat
transferred possession of the gifts that he bestowed on his sons. The distinctly
halakhic diction of this insertion gives the translation the feel of a talmudic

---

146   Cf. translation by Le Déaut-Robert, vol. 1, p. 133: "parce qu'elle avait fait des idoles pour se
livrer à des pratiques obscènes devant Ashérah."
        Their lead is followed by McIvor, p. 179: "because she had made idols, so that she could
indulge in obscene practices before the Asherahs."

sentence, and Churgin indeed correctly located TC's source in *b. Qiddushin*.[147] *M. Qidd.* 1:5 states that:

נכסים שאין להן אחריות ניקנים עם הנכסים שיש להן אחריות בכסף ובשטר ובחזקה.

Property for which there is no security is acquired along with property for which there is security through money, writ, and usucaption.

The Babylonian Talmud (*Qidd.* 26a) seeks a source for the Mishnah's claim:

מנהני מילי? אמ[ר] חזקיה: אמ[ר] קרא, 'ויתן להן אביהם מתנות רבות לכסף ולזה[ב]
ולמגדנות עם ערים בצורות אשר ביהודה'.

How on the basis of Scripture do we know that fact? Said Hezekiah, "Said Scripture, 'And their father gave them gifts ... with walled cities in Judah' (2 Chr 21:3)."

The feasibility of secondary acquisition of chattel with real estate appears elsewhere in the Talmud, as well,[148] but the passage excerpted here not only notes the existence of such a possibility under the law, but buttresses its argument with reference to the present verse, which in the view of Hezekiah is a scriptural source of this principle. TC includes the expansion ואקניאונון על־גב קרקעא, *on the basis of land they were given possession*, not because, on reaching the verse, the targumist felt that it described a legal situation reminiscent of the rules of acquisition as laid down in the Talmud, but because he knew that the Talmud viewed the verse as a source of the above law, and therefore saw fit to include in the verse the information derived from it by the Talmud, which informed his work.

על־גב: The targumist could have chosen to employ the preposition אגב, used in Babylonian Aramaic. His familiarity with that word is illustrated by its use on two occasions in his composition: 1 Chr 11:21, 25. His use of על־גב, which appears nowhere else in TC, stems directly from the language of the Talmud in the continuation of the above passage, ibid., 26b:

147   Churgin *Hagiographa*, p. 259.
148   Thus, by way of example, Le Déaut-Robert, vol. 1, p. 143 (as well as McIvor, p. 194), refer to *b. B. Meṣi'a'* 11b and *B. Bat.* 156b. In my opinion, however, these passages are not what motivated the author of TC to compose the insertion in question.

מעשה במרוני שהיה בירושלים שהיה לו מטלט[לין] הרבה וביקש ליתנם במתנה.
אמרו לו: אין לו תקנה עד שיקנם על גבי קרקע ...

There was a case of a certain man of Meron who was in Jerusalem, who
had a large volume of movables that he wanted to give away. They told
him that he had no remedy except to transfer title along with a piece of
real estate ...

This informs us something about the talmudic text that appeared before our
targumist, for the reading אגב קרקע for this excerpt in the Talmud is found in
one of the printed versions and in a responsum by ibn Adret.[149] By employing
על גב קרקעא, then, TC is in accordance with the majority reading of textual
witnesses of the Talmud.

בהדי: A Babylonian word, found in TC only here.[150] It seems to me that the
word is employed in this context because the preceding words, too, bear the
influence of BT. True, בהדי does not appear as part of the passage discussing
acquisition of chattel, but the targumist included it here under the influence
of talmudic style.

2.29   *Joash Vindicated through David's Crown* (2 Chr 23:11)

This passage in TC is based upon *b. ʾAvodah Zarah* 44a. However, it is also based
upon a tradition similar to that found in MS Reuchlin. It is, therefore, discussed
in full, below, pp. 409–412.

2.30   *Why Did God Bring Sennacherib?* (2 Chr 32:1)

2 Chr 32:1

MT	בָּא	אַחֲרֵי הַדְּבָרִים וְהָאֱמֶת הָאֵלֶּה
TC	בתר פתגמיא וקושטא האלין דעבד יחזקיהו כד קיים ה' במימריה לאיתאה ית

MT (cont.)	סַנְחֵרִיב מֶלֶךְ־אַשּׁוּר
TC	סנחריב מלכא דאתור וית חילוותיה על ארעא דישראל מן־בגלל לתברא

ית אתוראי בארעא דבית יהודה ולדוששא ית אוכלוסיהון על טווריא דירושלם
ולממסר ית כל עדאה ובזתא בידא דחזקיה ועמיה דבירושלם

---

149   See apparatus in *Diqduqei Soferim ha-Shalem* to Qidd., vol. 1, p. 258.

150   Sokoloff *JPA*, p. 67, describes the word's use in *Gen. Rab.* as a "Corrupt form borrowed from
JBA." The word appears six times in *Tg. Job* (6:4; 9:35; 13:19; 15:10; 20:11; 31:13); five times in
TPJ (Gen 24:61; Exod 26:34; 37:9; 40:20; Deut 22:15); and once in FTP (Exod 20:3).

(cont.) וַיָּבֹא

TC הא בכין אתא סנחריב מלכא דאתור במשריין סגיעין דלית להון מניין ושרא בארע

(cont.) אֵלָיו: לְבִקְעָם וַיֹּאמֶר הַבְּצֻרוֹת עַל־הֶעָרִים וַיִּחַן בִּיהוּדָה

TC שיבט יהודה ואשרי אוכלוסוהי על קרוי כריכתא ואמר במימריה לשויותהון עמיה:

NJPS: After these faithful deeds, King Sennacherib of Assyria invaded Judah and encamped against its fortified towns with the aim of taking them over.

Dost: After these faithful deeds that Hezekiah did, when the Lord decided by His Memra to bring Sennacherib king of Assyria and his armies against the land of Israel in order to defeat the Assyrians in the land of the house of Judah and to crush their multitudes upon the hills of Jerusalem and to deliver over all of the booty and plunder into the hand of Hezekiah and his people who were in Jerusalem, behold, then Sennacherib king of Assyria came with many armies for which there was no number, and he dwelt in the land of the tribe of Judah, and he had his multitudes dwell by the fortified cities, and He commanded by himself to annex them.

The Hebrew verse conjures an air of tension and apprehension with its description of the Assyrian king as he comes to conquer Judea. The Targum, though, exempts the reader from such unpleasantness, explaining that the unfolding series of events will not endanger the Judeans, but bring about the fulfillment of the word of God through Sennacherib's downfall. McIvor proposed that the lengthy expansion in TC was based mainly on the description of Gog and Magog in Ezekiel 38–39, due to what he viewed as a thematic similarity to the nemesis in those prophecies on the part of Sennacherib, a mortal king brought by God to the Land of Israel to meet his downfall.[151] I believe that McIvor's proposal to cast Sennacherib as Gog and Magog is implausible and betrays a failure to note clear the dictional parallels between the Targum to the present verse and that to Isa 14:24–25. Hamiel correctly noted that an important part of the background of the Targum to the present verse is *b. Sanh.* 94b, where the Talmud seeks to account for the dissonance between the beginning of the verse, אַחֲרֵי הַדְּבָרִים וְהָאֱמֶת הָאֵלֶּה, *after these faithful deeds*, and its conclusion, which describes the arrival of King Sennacherib of Assyria:[152]

'אחרי הדברים והאמת האלה בא סנחריב מלך אשור ויבא ביהודה ויחן על הערים הבצרות ויאמר לבקעם אליו'—האי דשנא להאי פרדשנא?! מאי 'אחריי? אמ[ר] רבינא: אחר שקפץ הקב"ה ונשבע. אמ[ר]: אי אמינא ליה לחזקיה דמיתינא ליה

---

151 McIvor, p. 225, n. 1–1 (sic).

152 Hamiel, pp. 450–451.

לסנחריב וסיעתו ומסרנא ליה בידך? אמ[ר]: לא איהו בעינא ולא בעתתיה בעינא.
ואי נמי גזירנא גזירתא בעי רחמי ומבטיל לה. מיד קפץ הקב"ה ונשבע דמיתינא ל[י]
ה, שנאמ[ר] 'נשבע ה' צבאו' לאמר אם לא כאשר דמיתי כן היתה וכאשר יעצתי היא
תקום'. וכת[יב] 'לשבר אשור בארצי ועל הרי אבוסנו'.

"After these things, and the truth thereof, Sennacherib, king of Assyria,
came and entered Judea and encamped against the fortified cities and
thought to win them for himself" (2 Chr 32:1): *Such a recompense* [*to
Hezekiah*] *for such a gift? What is the sense of,* "After these things and the
truth thereof" (2 Chr 32:1)? Said Rabina, "After the Holy One, blessed be
he, went and took an oath, saying *'If I say to Hezekiah that I am going to
bring Sennacherib and hand him over to you, he will say to me, "I don't want
him and I don't want his terror either."'* "So the Holy One, blessed be he,
went ahead and took an oath ahead of time *that he would bring him,* as it
is said, 'The Lord of hosts has sworn, saying, Surely as I have thought, so
shall it come to pass, and as I have purposed, so shall it stand, that I will
break the Assyrian in my land and upon my mountains tread him under
foot' (Isa 14:24–25)."

The targumist, following the Talmud, described the divine vow to bring
Sennacherib to Judea, detailing God's intention with a periphrastic Aramaic
translation of Isa 14:25:

Isa 14:25	אֲבוּסֶ֑נּוּ	וְעַל־הָרַ֖י	בְּאַרְצִ֔י	אַשּׁוּר֙	לִשְׁבֹּ֤ר
TJ	אדושׁשׁיניה	ועל טורי עמי	בארעי	אתוראה	למתבר
TC	ולדושׁשׁא ית אוכלוסיהון	דבית יהודה	בארעא	ית אתוראי	לתברא
				על טווריא דירושלם	

NJPS: To break Assyria in My land, to crush him on My mountain.
Clem TJ: To break Assyria on My mountain. And I will trample him on the
mountain of my people.

TC's expansion proceeds to discuss the plunder of the Assyrian army to be
claimed by the people of Jerusalem: ולממסר ית כל עדאה ובזתא בידא דחזקיה
ועמיה דבירושלם. This depiction accords with the spirit of the continuation of
the above talmudic discussion:

'לשבר אשור בארצי ועל הרי אבוסנו'—א"ר חננא בר פפא, א"ר יוחנן: אמר הקב"ה,
יבא סנחריב וסיעתו ויעשה אבוס לחזקיה וסיעתו ... 'ואסף שללכם אסף החסיל
כמשק גבים שקק בו'—אמ[ר] להן נביא לישראל: אספו שללכם! אמרו לו: לחלוק
או לבזוז? אמ[ר] להן: כאוסף החסיל—מה אסיפת חסיל זה כל אחד ואחד לעצמו,

אף שללכם כל אחד ואחד לעצמו. אמרו לו: והלא ממון שלעשרת השבטים מעורב
בו? אמ[ר] להן: 'כמשק גבים שקק בו'—מה גבים הללו מעלין את האדם מטומאה
לטהרה, אף ממונם שלישראל כיון שנפל ביד גוי, נטהר.

I will break the Assyrian in my land and upon my mountains tread him
under foot—Said R. Yoḥanan, "Said the Holy One, blessed be he, 'Let
Sennacherib and his company come and serve as a crib for Hezekiah and
his company.' ... "And your spoil shall be gathered like the gathering of a
caterpillar" (Isa 33:4): Said the prophet to Israel, "Gather your spoil." They
said to him, "Is it for individual spoil or for sharing?" He said to them,
"'Like the gathering of a caterpillar' (Isa 33:4): Just as in the gathering of
a caterpillar it is each one for himself, so in your spoil it is each one for
himself." They said to him, "And is not the money of the ten tribes mixed
up with it?" He said to them, "'As the watering of pools does he water it'
(Isa 33:4): Just as pools of water serve to raise up a human being from a
state of uncleanness to a state of cleanness, so the money that has belonged to Israelites, once it has fallen into the hands of idolators, forthwith imparts cleanness.

R. Yoḥanan interprets the word אֲבוּסֶנּוּ as derived from the trough (אֵבוּס) of an
animal, understanding the verse to mean that God seeks to bring Sennacherib
to Jerusalem as sustenance for its inhabitants, and TC here interprets
R. Yoḥanan's homily and applies it to the text of Chronicles. The Talmud explains that the prophet encourages the people to loot the Assyrian camp, each
to the best of his ability. When the people express concern that they might thus
be in violation of stealing the property of the Ten Tribes, the prophet rouses
them to action with a halakhic allowance that resolves the issue.

The Targum then proceeds to describe the size of the Assyrian camp, whose
forces are so many as to be innumerable, a description meant to emphasize the
scale of Sennacherib's downfall and indicate the vast amount of plunder to ac-
crue to the people of Jerusalem. This part of the text, too, arrived in the hands
of the targumist in the form of pre-existing traditions. Most of the sources, as
compiled by Ginzberg,[153] in fact give different numbers of soldiers who arrived
with Sennacherib, but the numbers all are so impressive that TC reasonably
described them as coming במשריין סגיעין דלית להון מניין, *with many armies for
which there was no number.*

---

153   Ginzberg, vol. 6, p. 362, n. 52.

2.31 *Sennacherib's Downfall on Passover Eve (2 Chr 32:21)*

2 Chr 32:21

MT   וַיִּשְׁלַח   ה׳   מַלְאָךְ

TC   ושדר מימרא דה׳ גבריאל מלאכא ושיצי בלילי פסחא באשא מנתכא ואוקיד

MT (cont.)   וַיַּכְחֵד כָּל־גִּבּוֹר חַיִל וְנָגִיד וְשָׂר בְּמַחֲנֵה מֶלֶךְ אַשּׁוּר

TC   נשמתהון בגווהון ושיצי כל גבר חילא וסרכן ורבן במשרית מלכא דאתור

(cont.)   וַיָּשָׁב בְּבֹשֶׁת פָּנִים לְאַרְצוֹ

TC   ותב בביהות אפיא לארעיה

(cont.)   וַיָּבֹא בֵּית אֱלֹהָיו וּמִיצִיאֵי (קר׳) מֵעָיו שָׁם הִפִּילֻהוּ בֶּחָרֶב:

TC   ועל לבית טעותיה ובנוהי דאוליד תמן רמוהי קטיל בחרבא:

NJPS: The LORD sent an angel who annihilated every mighty warrior, commander, and officer in the army of the king of Assyria, and he returned in disgrace to his land. He entered the house of his god, and there some of his own offspring struck him down by the sword.

Dost: Then the Memra of the Lord sent the angel Gabriel, and on the night of Passover he destroyed with fire poured forth, and he burned up their breath within them, and he destroyed every valiant warrior, officer, and leader in the camp of the king of Assyria, and he returned in shame to his land. He entered the temple of his idol, and his sons whom he fathered struck him down there, slain by the sword.

The Targum adds to the Hebrew verse that:

1. The angel dispatched to strike the Assyrian army was Gabriel;
2. The event described occurred on Passover eve;
3. The death of the Assyrian soldiers was supernatural: their souls were incinerated from within while their bodies remained intact.

The angel's identity: The textual witnesses of TC itself are not in agreement with regard to the identity of the angel who struck the Assyrians. The version above is that of MS V, while MS C has מיכאל וגבריאל and de Lagarde and Sperber read מיכאל גבריאל (omitting the *waw*). Other sources, too, offer different views of the matter.[154] A TT to 2 Kgs 19:35 in MS Reuchlin reads: ונפק מיכאל מלאכא דה׳ וקטל במשיריית אתוראי מאה ותמנן וחמשה אלפין,[155] while a TT to Isa 10:32 in the same MS that describes the Assyrian king's arrival at Jerusalem with an

---

154   For additional sources, see Ginzberg, vol. 6, pp. 362–363, n. 55. Rofé, pp. 165–176, demonstrates that the primary story did not feature an angel, and that this part of the story is a secondary literary development.

155   Kasher *TT*, p. 148 (fragment 103, lines 3–4).

enormous military entourage and whose focus is the downfall of the Assyrians
states: מינין משרייתיה מאתן ושית ריבואן חסר חד מטול דעתידא משירייתיה למחסר על
ידוי דגבריאל חד סרכיא דמשמשין ק[דם] ה'.[156] The uncertainty within the text of
TC thus parallels that found in related sources.

The Assyrian downfall on Passover eve: A range of sources give Passover eve as
the date of the Assyrian defeat, among them the beginning of the above TT to
2 Kgs 19:35: והוה בליליא ההוא היא ליליא דפסחא שדר מימרא דה' שיגושא במשיריית
סנחריב מלכא דאתור, *that night, Passover night, the Memra of the Lord sent confusion in King Sennacherib's army*.[157] It is not unlikely in the least that the beginning of this aggadic tradition is of ancient origin. Kasher was of the view
that the identification with Passover was meant "to associate the salvation of
Hezekiah's day with the redemption from Egypt."[158] In my view, however, the
date arises not only from exegetical proclivities, but also from a particularly
fertile midrashic matrix characterized by verbiage in 2 Kgs 19:35 that is mark-
edly similar to Exod 11:4; 12:29:

Exod 11:4–5	מִצְרַיִם	בְּאֶרֶץ	כָּל־בְּכוֹר וּמֵת	אֲנִי יוֹצֵא ...	כַּחֲצֹת הַלַּיְלָה
Exod 12:29	מִצְרַיִם	בְּאֶרֶץ	כָּל־בְּכוֹר הִכָּה וַה'		וַיְהִי בַּחֲצִי הַלַּיְלָה
2 Kgs 19:35	אַשּׁוּר	בְּמַחֲנֵה	וַיַּךְ ה' מַלְאַךְ וַיֵּצֵא		וַיְהִי בַּלַּיְלָה הַהוּא

If this indeed is the basis of the midrashic identification with Passover eve,
then it supports what would in any event be a well-founded assumption: the
targumist did not give the identification with Passover eve due to elements of
the Hebrew *Vorlage* suggesting as much, but predicated his comments on a
midrashic tradition that had already developed around 2 Kings.

The supernatural demise of the Assyrian forces: A tradition found in various
sources states that the soldiers of the Assyrian army were incinerated from
within, such that their bodies appeared untouched from without. The tradition appears in hagiographic literature, Christian exegesis, the Talmud, midrashic sources, and targumic literature.[159] TC here contains elements found

---

156 Kasher *TT*, p. 151 (fragment 107a, lines 6–7).

157 Kasher *TT*, pp. 147–148 (fragment 103, lines 2–3). For additional sources, see Ginzberg,
vol. 6, p. 362, n. 54. Among the sources cited by Ginzberg, ibid., and subsequently others,
is *y. Pesaḥ.* 9:3. However, I do not believe that this source is a relevant one to the matter at
hand.

158 Kasher *TT*, p. 148.

159 For a detailed list of sources, see Ginzberg, vol. 6, pp. 363–364, n. 59; Kasher *TT*, p. 148.
Here we shall excerpt the text of a few of the sources listed:

in none of these sources, e.g., the verb שׁיצי, the participle אשא מנתכא, and the preposition נשמתהון בגווהון. The targumist may have had reference to an additional source that served as the source of his formulation, but in any event his work has a part in the well-documented aggadic tradition describing the supernatural demise of the soldiers of Assyria.

2.32   *Why Was Josiah So Stubborn?* (2 Chr 35:21–22)

Chronicles describes a series of messages exchanged between Pharaoh Necho and Josiah when the former sought to make his way to Carchemish via Judea.[160] Pharaoh Necho invokes God in comments intended to persuade Josiah not to interfere with his army's passage northward, but Josiah refuses to be moved by Pharaoh Necho and consequently meets his demise.

B. Šabb. 113b (parallels *b. Sanh.* 94a) associates the death of the soldiers of the Assyrian army with that of Aaron's sons:

'ותחת כבודו יקד יקוד כיקוד אש'—... ר' אליעזר אומ[ר]: 'תחת כבודו' ממש. ר' שמואל בר נחמני אמ[ר]: 'תחת כבודו' וכשריפת בני אהרן. מה להלן שריפת נשמ[ה] וגוף קיים, אף כאן שריפת נשמה וגוף קיים.

"And beneath his glory shall he light a burning like the burning of a fire" (Isa 10:16) ... R. Eleazar says, "'Under his glory' literally." R. Samuel bar Nahmani said, "'and beneath his glory' as in the burning of the sons of Aaron. Just as is the burning of the sons of Aaron. [Just as in that case it was a burning of the soul while the body endured, so here there is a burning of the soul while the body remained intact.]"

The above source may be read in conjunction with one of the many views cited in the continuation of the passage, *b. Sanh.* 95b:

במה הכם?... ויש אומרין: בחוטמו נפח בהן ומתו, שנ' 'וגם נשף בהם וייבשו ושערה כקש תשאם'.

How did [the angel] smite [the army]?... Others say, "He blew into their noses and they died, as it is said, 'And he shall also blow upon them, and they shall wither' (Isa 40:24)."

TPJ Lev 10:2:

ונפקת שלהובית אישתא מן קדם ה' ברגז ואיתפליגת לארבעתי חוטין ואעלת בגוא אפיהון ואוקידת ית נשמתהון ברם גופיהון לא איתחרכו ומיתו קדם ה'.

Clem: Then a flame of fire went forth from before the Lord in anger and was divided into four threads, and it entered into their noses and burned their souls, but their bodies were not scorched. And they died before the Lord.

TT 2 Kgs 19:35 (Kasher *TT*, p. 148, fragment 103, lines 4–5):

ומחנון מחת יקידת נשמתא וגושמא קיים ואקדימו סנחריב ותלתא בנוי ונבוכדנצר חתניה בצפרא וחמון והא כולהון שלדין מיתין מיתוקדין בנישמתהון.

Gottlieb: He smote them a blow of incinerating the soul while the body remained intact. Sennacherib, his three sons and his son-in-law, Nebuchadnezzar, arose early in the morning and observed and, lo, they were all dead corpses, burnt by their souls.

160   The Chronicler calls this figure נְכֹו, without the title פרעה. Where he first appears in the book (2 Chr 35:20), TC translates פרעה חגירא, in accordance with TJ Kings, while in the latter two appearances (2 Chr 35:22; 36:4) the targumist did without the title פרעה, simply translating חגירא.

2 Chr 35:21

MT וֵאלֹהִים אָמַר לְבַהֲלֵנִי חֲדַל־לְךָ מֵאֱלֹהִים אֲשֶׁר־עִמִּי וְאַל־יַשְׁחִיתֶךָ:

TC וטעווהי אמר לסרהבותי כדון פסוק לך מני ומן טעוותי דעמי ולא תחבל יתך:

NJPS: [Necho] sent messengers to him, saying, "What have I to do with you, king of Judah? I do not march against you this day but against the kingdom that wars with me, and it is God's will that I hurry. Refrain, then, from interfering with God who is with me, that He not destroy you."

Dost: And he sent messengers to him, saying, "What do I have to do with you, king of the tribe of the house of Judah? I have not come up to wage war against you—for you are provoking me this day!—but against the dynasty with which I am at war. My idols said to hasten myself. Now leave off from me and from my idols who are with me, and do not destroy yourself."

2 Chr 35:22

MT וְלֹא־הֵסֵב יֹאשִׁיָּהוּ פָּנָיו מִמֶּנּוּ

TC וכד שמע ית מה דאדכר ית טעותיה לא אסתחר לאחורא ולא אחזר יאשיה ית אפוהי מניה

MT (cont.) כִּי לְהִלָּחֶם־בּוֹ הִתְחַפֵּשׂ וְלֹא שָׁמַע

TC ארום לאגחא קרבא ביה אשתני ואטקס בזיני קרבא ולא קביל

(cont.) אֶל־דִּבְרֵי נְכוֹ מִפִּי וַיָּבֹא לְהִלָּחֵם בְּבִקְעַת מְגִדּוֹ:

TC לפתגמי חגירא דמליל על־עיסק טעותיה ואתא לאגחא קרבא במישר מגדו:

NJPS: But Josiah would not let him alone; instead, he donned [his armor] to fight him, heedless of Necho's words from the mouth of God; and he came to fight in the plain of Megiddo.

Dost: But when he heard how he mentioned his idol, he did not turn back, and Josiah did not turn his face from him. For he had decided to wage war against him, and he prepared for battle with weapons of war and did not hearken to the words of the lame one, who spoke concerning his idol, and he came to wage war in the valley of Megiddo.

The targumist adds to the verse Josiah's rationale for refusing to heed the warnings of Pharaoh Necho. Josiah was certain of his ability to emerge victorious against Pharaoh Necho because the latter put his faith in gods other than the God of Israel, as indicated by his message to Josiah. This interpretation is in keeping with a tradition regarding the present verse that is cited and expanded on by the Talmud. We shall see the original oral tradition and then the Talmud's discussion of it. *Tosefta Taʿan.* 2:10 (p. 333):

חרב העוברת ממקום למקום—אפי[לו] חרב של שלום—מתריעין עליה, ואין צריך
לומ[ר] חרב של פורענות. ואין לך חרב של שלום יותר משל פרעה נכה, ושטפה את
הצדיק ההוא—זה יאשיהו—שנ[אמר] 'וישלח אליו מלאכים מה לי לך ואלים אמר
לבהלני'—מפי הקודש אני עולה. 'חדל לך מאלהים אשר עמדי'—זה לשון ע״ז. 'ולא
הסב יאשיהו פניו ממנו כי להלחם בו התחפס' וגו'.

When a sword goes en route through the area—even a sword of peace—
the alarm is sounded, which goes without saying for a sword of destruction. There was no sword of peace more than that of Pharaoh Necho, yet
it still swept away that righteous one—i.e. Josiah—as stated, '[Necho]
sent messengers to him, saying, "What have I to do with you ... God's will
that I hurry'—I am ascending on orders of the Holy One. 'Refrain, then,
from interfering with the gods who are with me'—this is idolatrous language. 'But Josiah would not let him alone; for he sought to fight him etc.'.

B. Ta'an. 22b:

מאן 'אלהים'? אמ[ר] רב: ע״ז. אמ[ר]: הואיל וקא בטח בע״ז, יכילנא ליה.

What is meant by "God who is with me"? *Said R. Judah said Rab,* "Idols." *He
said,* "Since he trusts in idols, I will overcome him."

The Tosefta quotes 2 Chr 35:21, where the word אלהים appears twice, and establishes that the first refers to the God of Israel and the second to a foreign
god. Rab's comment in the Talmud that the term אלהים in the verse refers to a
foreign god is problematic in that it either makes the Tosefta's treatment of the
second occurrence of אלהים in the verse superfluous or contradicts what is said
of the first. Lieberman, discussing the meaning of קודש in the Tosefta, showed
that it had been understood by Edels (i.e. מהרש״א) as referring to the God of
Israel. *Minḥat Bikkurim*, however, understood the word differently: פרעה נכה
אמר שעולה מפי הקדש, והיא הע״ז אשר עמו, *Pharaoh Necho said he is ascending at
the orders of the* קדש, *and this is the idolatry he had.*[161] As support for this latter
view, Lieberman cited TC's translation of אלהים in its first appearance, too, as
טעוותי, the targumist's usual translation for a false god.

Regardless of which explanation best fits the context of the Talmud, it seems
that—like Lieberman—TC understood the first occurrence of אלהים also to be
within the purview of Rab's comments in the Talmud. The sentence placed by
the Talmud in the mouth of Josiah, *since he trusts in idols, I will overcome him,*

---

161 Lieberman *Tosefta*, part 5, *Mo'ed*, p. 1095.

is interpreted in TC's expansion as וכד שמע ית מה דאדכר ית טעותיה לא אסתחר
לאחורא, *but when he heard how he mentioned his idol, he did not turn back.*[162]
These words add to TC a depiction of Josiah as a righteous king, unwavering
in his loyalty to the God of Israel, who ironically met his end as a result of an
excess of faith in God.

2.33 *Josiah's Great Righteousness (2 Chr 35:27)*
2 Chr 35:27

MT	וְהָאַחֲרֹנִ֑ים הָרִֽאשֹׁנִ֖ים וּדְבָרָ֛יו
TC	ופתגמוהי קדמאין מא דעבד בינקותיה ובתראי מא דעבד בעולימותיה

וכל דיניא דדאן מן יומא דמלך בר תמניא שנין דהוה טלי עד שנת תמניסרי דהוה
עולים כד שרי לתקפא ית בית־מוקדשא דה׳ כולהון אתיב למארי דינא מן ממוניה
והיך דכי ית בית ישראל ויהודה מן כל סואבותא

MT (cont.)	וִיהוּדָֽה׃ יִשְׂרָאֵ֖ל מַלְכֵי־ עַל־סֵ֥פֶר כְּתוּבִ֕ים הִנָּ֛ם
TC	האנון כתיבין על ספר מלכיא דבית ישראל ודבית יהודה׃

NJPS: and his acts, early and late, are recorded in the book of the kings of Israel
and Judah.

Dost: his affairs, (both) former—what he did in his childhood—and latter—
what he did in his youth, and all the judgments that he judged from the day
he began to rule at eight years old, while he was (still) a boy, until the eighteenth year, when he was a young man, when he began to restore the temple
of the Lord—all of these he restored for the Master of Judgment from his own
money—and how he purified the house of Israel and Judah from all uncleanness, they are written in the scroll of the kings of the house of Israel and of the
house of Judah.

The lengthy expansion in TC is comprised of two parts. The first describes
Josiah's absolute guiltlessness in his role as a judge. The Targum states that
Josiah compensated litigants from his own private funds for all amounts that
he had awarded from the time he was eight years old until he became eighteen.
In the second part of the expansion, the targumist underscores Josiah's efforts
to cleanse the land of anything impure, i.e., any foreign worship and any illegitimate forms of worship of the God of Israel.

---

162   As indicated in the synoptic presentation of the Hebrew verse and the Targum above, TC
       appears here to give a dual translation of the Hebrew expression וְלֹא־הֵסֵב. Both סח״ר (as
       in ולא אסתחר) and חז״ר (of ולא אחזר) can serve to translate the root סב״ב. The former
       translation serves to indicate an outcome of the targumic expansion concerning Josiah's
       considerations in his decision to ignore Necho's warning.

Josiah as judge: The expansion concerning Josiah's great righteousness in no way corresponds to either the Hebrew *Vorlage* or midrashic exegesis of the verse, but is based on an interpretation of 2 Kgs 23:25 that appears in *b. Šabb.* 56b:[163]

ואמ[ר ר׳] שמואל בר נחמני א״ר יונתן: כל האומ[ר] יאשיהו חטא אינו אלא טועה, שנא[מר] 'ויעש הישר בעיני ה׳ וילך בכל דרך דוד אביו ולא סר ימין ושמאל'. ואלא מה אני מקיים 'וכמוהו לא היה לפניו מלך אשר שב אל ה׳ בכל לבבו ובכל נפשו ובכל מאדו כל כל תורת משה ואחריו לא קם כמהו'? מלמד שכל דין מבן שמונה ועד שמונה עשרה החזירן להן. ושמא תאמר, נטל [מזה] ונתן לזה? ת״ל 'ובכל מאדו'—שהחזירן להם משלו.

Said R. Samuel bar Nahmani said R. Jonathan, "Whoever says that Josiah ever sinned errs, as it is said, 'And he did that which was right in the eyes of the Lord and walked in all the ways of David his father' (2 Kgs 22:2). Then how do I read, 'and like unto him there was no king before him, who returned to the Lord with all his heart' (2 Kgs 23:25)? [If he returned to the Lord, it means he had sinned and so had to repent.] It means, ever judgment he made between the age of eight and eighteen he reviewed. [He wanted to see whether he had made any mistakes.] Might you suppose he took from one and gave to another? Scripture says, 'He took from his own might,' meaning, he restored a judgment out of his own property."

The table below shows how TC corresponds to the solution offered by R. Jonathan in his homily, in both choice of words and the order of the constituent elements:

R. Jonathan's homily	TC
שכל דין שדן מבן שמונה	וכל דיניא דדאן מן יומא דמלך בר תמניא
	שנין דהוה טלי
ועד שמונה עשרה	עד שנת תמניסרי דהוה עולים כד שרי
	לתקפא ית בית מוקדשא דה׳
החזירן להן.	כולהון אתיב למארי דינא
ושמא תאמר, נטל [מזה] ונתן לזה? ת״ל 'ובכל	מן ממוניה
מאדו'—שהחזירן להם משלו.	

The foundation of the Targum here is based word-for-word on R. Jonathan's exegesis. There are points where the targumist adds to the talmudic homily to provide additional clarification, e.g., by referencing events related to Josiah's

---

163   As correctly identified by Hamiel, p. 457.

life from age eight to eighteen, and he sometimes replaces a general word in the homily with a more specific one, e.g. the substitution of specific references (למארי דינא and מן ממוניה, respectively) for the third-person plural pronoun (להן)[164] and the subordinating particle (משלו).[165] The targumist also made the natural choice to do without the initial question and adduction of the verse, instead including only the conclusion (מן ממוניה ... אתיב).

R. Jonathan himself derives from 2 Kgs 34:2 that Josiah never committed a sin, despite the statement in 2 Kgs 23:25 that Josiah returned to God, whose simple sense is that Josiah did sin but subsequently reformed himself. In R. Jonathan's exegesis of the verse, Josiah retroactively voided all of his financial rulings from age eight to age eighteen and drew on his own resources to reimburse all of the various litigants whom he had compelled to make payments under these rulings. The commentators of the Talmud differed as to why Josiah had pursued this course of action specifically with regard to rulings he had handed down in this particular age range. According to some, in the wake of the discovery of the Book of the Law during his renovation of the Temple, he understood that until that point he had ruled contrary to the law of the Torah and therefore came to view all of his previous rulings as defective.[166] According to others, Josiah's motivation was his age at the time, as a man who has not yet attained eighteen years of age is not qualified to serve as a judge.[167] The targumist here appears unwittingly to indicate his opinion on this matter by associating Josiah's being eighteen years old with the renovation of the Temple (עד שנת תמניסרי דהוה עולים כד שרי לתקפא ית בית־מוקדשא דה'), thus betraying his understanding that the reason for Josiah's compensation of litigants was one associated with this project, viz., the discovery of the Book of the Law.

---

164 The talmudic text of MS London BL Or. 5558 H/4 more closely resembles TC: מלמד שכל דין שדן מבן שמנה שנים ועד בן שמנה עשרה שנה החזיר לבעליהן. ושמא תאמר שנטל מזה ונתן לזה? תלמוד לומר: בכל מאורן (sic)—מלמד שנטל משלו והחזיר לבעלים.

165 By thus replacing משלו, derived in the Talmud from the words וּבְכָל־מְאֹדוֹ, with the words מן ממוניה, the targumist demonstrated his familiarity with another talmudic homily. *B. Ber.* 54a interprets: וּבְכָל־מְאֹדֶךָ—בכל ממונך.

166 Rashi, commentary to the Talmud ad loc.: עד בן שמונה עשרה—שמצא חלקיה את הספר, ועיין ודקדק בתורה ובדיניה בכתב ובעל פה, והבין שמא טעה בדינא.

Till he was eighteen—when Hilqiah found the scroll, he studied and searched in the Torah and its laws, both written and oral, and realized he may have erred in legal decisions.

167 *Shulḥan 'Arukh, Ḥoshen Mishpaṭ* 7:3: יש אומרים שאינו ראוי לדון אלא מבן י"ח ומעלה והביא שתי שערות, some opine that one may not preside as a judge till the age of eighteen and when he has grown [at least] two mature hairs. Kremer (i.e. the Vilna Ga'on) ad loc. cites *b. Šabb.* 56b as the source of this view.

Josiah the purifier: The brief expansion concerning Josiah's efforts to purify the land was not based on existing exegesis. The targumist summarizes in a few of his own words the campaign described at length in 2 Chr 34:1–8, where the Chronicler thrice employs the verb טה"ר in describing Josiah's actions:

2 Chr 34:3

MT   הֵחֵל לְטַהֵר אֶת־יְהוּדָה וִירוּשָׁלַ͏ִם מִן־הַבָּמוֹת וְהָאֲשֵׁרִים וְהַפְּסִלִים וְהַמַּסֵּכוֹת:

TC   שרי לדכאה ית יהודה וירושלם מן במסיא ואשירתא וצלמניא   ומתכיא:

NJPS: he began to purge Judah and Jerusalem of the shrines, the sacred posts, the idols, and the molten images.

2 Chr 34:5

MT   וַיְטַהֵר אֶת־יְהוּדָה וְאֶת־יְרוּשָׁלָ͏ִם:

TC   ודכי ית יהודה וית ירושלם:

NJPS: [he] purged Judah and Jerusalem.

2 Chr 34:8

MT   וּבִשְׁנַת שְׁמוֹנֶה עֶשְׂרֵה לְמָלְכוֹ לְטַהֵר   הָאָרֶץ וְהַבָּיִת

TC   ובשנת   תמניסרי כד מלך בדכאותיה ית ארעא ובית־מקדשא

NJPS: In the eighteenth year of his reign, after purging the land and the House

As expected, all of these verbs are translated by the targumist using the root דכ"י. The acts of purification described in the verses include long lists of varieties of pagan worship that Josiah destroyed, both in Judea and in *the towns of Manasseh and Ephraim and Simeon, as far as Naphtali* (v. 6). Here, having reached a point that calls for a synopsis of Josiah's deeds, the targumist gives a summary of the campaign characterized by three things:

1.   The targumist chose to use the root דכ"י, as in the above verses.
2.   The targumist used the single word סואבו to encapsulate all of the varieties of foreign worship targeted by Josiah. This word and its earlier but synonymous sibling סואבה, both equivalents of Hebrew טֻמְאָה, are the typical and expected objects of the verb דכ"י.
3.   The targumist briefly summarized the list of places where Josiah was active, given in the unit of verses noted above, as בית ישראל ויהודה.

Composite structure of the two sections: Having ascertained the meaning of the various part of the expansion, let us now consider the structure of the entire expansion and its relationship to the verse. Though the actions attributed to Josiah by the targumist were not derived from the present Hebrew verse, as noted above, the expansion in TC is patterned on the verse's structure. The verse describes Josiah's life as consisting of two periods, viz., his former deeds and his latter deeds, a formula unique to Chronicles that appears nine times in the book to summarize a king's life.[168] Six of these nine occurrences are rendered literally by the Targum, as קדמאי ובתראי [...]פתגמ,[169] but in the three remaining cases the targumist gave an expanded translation defining the former and the latter deeds of the given king. In the two verses with which we are not presently occupied we thus find:

2 Chr 25:26

MT		וְיֶ֨תֶר֙ דִּבְרֵ֣י אֲמַצְיָ֔הוּ הָרִאשֹׁנִ֖ים וְהָאַחֲרֹנִ֑ים
TC	דה׳	דהליך בדחלתא	ושאר פתגמי אמציה קדמאי
	די סטא מן אורחן דתקנן קדם ה׳	ובתראי

NJPS: The other events of Amaziah's reign, early and late
Dost: Now the rest of the deeds of Amaziah, how he first walked in the fear of the Lord, and how afterward he turned aside from upright ways before the Lord

2 Chr 26:22

MT		וְיֶ֨תֶר֙ דִּבְרֵ֤י עֻזִּיָּ֙הוּ֙ הָרִאשֹׁנִ֣ים וְהָאַחֲרֹנִ֔ים
TC	עד לא סרח ואסתגיר	ושאר פתגמי עזיהו קדמאי
	מן בתר דאסתגיר	ובתראי

NJPS: The other events of Uzziah's reign, early and late
Dost: Now the rest of the deeds of Uzziah, first before he sinned and was confined and later after he was confined

In both of these instances, the targumist understood the two parts of the king's life as the good part, in which he followed God, and the bad, in which he strayed from the right path. In Josiah's case, as interpreted by R. Yonatan in BT, there was no bad part, and the targumist therefore divided Josiah's life into two distinct periods based on chronology alone: וּדְבָרָיו הָרִאשֹׁנִים are מא דעבד בינקותיה, what he did in his childhood, while וְהָאַחֲרֹנִים refers to מא דעבד בעולימותיה, what he did in his youth. Next the targumist specifies what deeds these are. The initial period, from age eight to eighteen, is described in accordance with the talmudic homily. The targumist emphasizes that this period ends when Josiah attains the age דהוה עולים, when he was a youth, then proceeds to the second period of his life. This latter period, beginning after Josiah turned eighteen, is briefly recapitulated in accordance with 2 Chronicles 34, with a description of his purification of the House of Israel and Judea of all

---

168   1 Chr 29:29; 2 Chr 9:29; 12:15; 16:11; 20:34; 25:26; 26:22; 28:26; 35:27. Klein 1 Chronicles, pp. 543–544.

169   1 Chr 29:29 (David); 2 Chr 9:29 (Solomon, here with translation מלי rather than פתגמי); 12:15 (Rehoboam); 16:11 (Asa); 20:34 (Jehoshaphat); 28:26 (Ahaz).

things impure. That this final statement, too, is intended to fit logically within the structure of the Hebrew verse is clear from the targumist's careful ordering of the two geographic locations according to their sequence in the Hebrew verse, with Israel preceding Judea.

3   Possible Usage of the Babylonian Talmud

3.1   *Azubah: Talented, Wise, but Unattractive Wife of Caleb* (*1 Chr 2:18*)

1 Chr 2:18

MT   וְכָלֵב בֶּן־חֶצְרוֹן הוֹלִיד אֶת־עֲזוּבָה אִשָּׁה וְאֶת־יְרִיעוֹת וְאֵלֶּה בָנֶיהָ יֵשֶׁר וְשׁוֹבָב וְאַרְדּוֹן׃

TC   וכלב בר חצרו' אוליד מן עזובה אנתתיה

ומאי צווחין לה עזובה מן־בגלל דהות עקרה וכאיותא וגלי קדם ה' עולבנה ואתרווחת

ואשתבהרת בחכמתא והות עזלא בחכמתא ית מעזי על גויתהון דעזיא כדלא גזין

מטול יריעת משכנא

ואלין בנייהא ישר ושובב וארדון׃

NJPS: Caleb son of Hezron had children by his wife Azubah, and by Jerioth; these were her sons: Jesher, Shobab, and Ardon.

Dost: Caleb son of Hezron became a father by Azubah his wife. Why do they call her Azubah? Because she was infertile and despised. But her affliction was revealed before the Lord, and she was healed and was honored with wisdom. With skill she would spin the goat hair on the body of goats without sheering (them) because of the curtains of the tabernacle. These were her sons: Jesher, Shobab, and Ardon.

וכלב בר חצרו' אוליד מן עזובה אנתתיה: That Azubah was Caleb's daughter seems clear enough from the verse as it appears in MT (וְכָלֵב ... הוֹלִיד אֶת־עֲזוּבָה) but this notion is problematic, particularly in light of the following verse's indication that she was his wife: וַיִּקַּח־לוֹ כָלֵב אֶת־אֶפְרָת וַתֵּלֶד אֶת־עֲזוּבָה. The targumist resolves this challenge by describing her as Caleb's wife in the present verse, as well, using the translation מן עזובה. For the benefit of any reader who may still harbor doubts, he also adds the word אנתתיה. The targumist's reason for replacing the object marker את with the preposition מן is not entirely clear: it may be that he here treated את as a preposition with the sense of עם. In any event, the phrase יל"ד מן appears in Scripture in only two other instances, both in Chronicles and one in the same chapter: שְׁלוֹשָׁה נוֹלַד לוֹ מִבַּת־שׁוּעַ (1 Chr 2:3); וַיּוֹלֶד מִן־חֹדֶשׁ אִשְׁתּוֹ (1 Chr 8:9).[170]

---

170   We might consider including Ezra 10:3, לְהוֹצִיא כָל־נָשִׁים וְהַנּוֹלָד מֵהֶם, *to expel all these women and those who have been born to them*, in this list, but the two verses above are contextually closer to the present verse by virtue of belonging to a genealogy.

ומאי צווחין לה עזובה מן־בגלל דהות עקרה וכאיותא: Sic in MS V. The reading given for the last word in MS C is ובזיותא, while de Lagarde and Sperber (MS E) read ובזיתא. Le Déaut and Robert as well as McIvor view the version of MS V as corrupt and prefer that in C or E.[171] Their proposal does not explain what brought about the reading in MS V, which appears arbitrary in comparison to those in C and E. I believe that the reading found in V well may reflect some degree of corruption and that it is inadmissible in its present state, but this ought not necessarily be taken to mean that the reading found in C or E is preferable. Let us examine the data available to us from the Targum itself.

The agenda of TC in the present section is to transmit a homiletical interpretation of the name עֲזוּבָה. How did the originator of this homily understand the name's meaning? One possibility is that in *b. Soṭah* 12a:[172]

עזובה—זו מרים, ולמה נקרא שמה עזובה? שהכל עזבוה.

Azubah was the same as Miriam, and why was she called Azubah? Because at first she was abandoned by all men

She was abandoned because no person was willing to come near her, which the talmudic passage understands to have been a result of her outer appearance, and she was left alone. A different version of this homily, however, is given in *Tanḥuma* (ed. Buber) and *ʾAggadat Genesis*:[173]

ולמה נקראת עזובה? שהיתה עזובה וכעורה. אמר הקב״ה: הריני נותן לה בנים כדי
שתהא נאה בהם ...

Why was she called Azubah? For she was abandoned and ugly. The Holy One blessed be He said: I shall give her children so she will be appealing through them ...

Yalon authored a compilation of several Hebrew sources in which the stem עז״ב has the sense of ugliness, rather than the one of the more common senses of *to leave* and *to assist*. The compilation subsequently was supplemented by

---

171 Le Déaut-Robert, vol. 1, p. 44; McIvor, p. 49. McIvor, ibid., raises the possibility of explaining the version in MS V, כאיותא, as a metathesis of כאיתא, meaning *as a sign*, i.e., as a woman who is singled out (as an object of scorn). Such a thing appears improbable. McIvor himself declines to adopt this interpretation and instead prefers the reading in MS E.

172 The name also is thus interpreted in *Exod. Rab.* 1:17 (p. 65).

173 *Tanḥuma* (ed. Buber), *Vayyeẓeʾ* 10 (p. 152); *ʾAggadat Gen.* 49:2 (pp. 97–98). The version above is that in *Tanḥuma*.

Ben-Ḥayyim with a number of examples taken from Aramaic.[174] Following are a number of sources (not all of which are included in Ben-Ḥayyim's list) in which the root has this sense:

Liturgical Poems by Yannai 68:2 (p. 155):

מִיטַּמְאִים וּמְטַמְּאִים וְנֶעֱזָבִים / נִידוֹת וְיוֹלְדוֹת וְזָבוֹת וְזָבִים
סוֹדְר[ים] כָּרְאוּי בְּלֹא כְזָבִים / עִיטַּרְתָּם לָךְ כְּכִתְמֵי זְהָבִים

Tanḥuma, Va'etḥannan 1 (p. 201):

למלך שבקש לישא אשה. שלח שלוחיו לראותה אם נאה אם לאו. הלכו וראו אותה, ואמרו
לו: אין כעורה ועזובה הימנה. שמע שושבינו ואמר לו: לא כן מרי, אין נאה ממנה בעולם. בא
לישא אותה. אמר אבי הנערה לשלוחי המלך: נשבע אני שאין אחד מכם נכנס שעיזבתם
אותה לפני המלך.

Pesiqta Rabbati 31 (p. 143b):

ר' אליעזר אומר, מהו 'ושפח ה''? שהיו יושבות אצלם והיו רואים שורות שורות של כנים
יורדות משערם לתוך קדקד, והיו משתקצות ומתעזבות בפניהם. ומיד היו משליכין [אותן]
ארצה. הוא שציון אומרת 'עזבני ה''—עזבני ה''—'וה' פתחן יערה—אמר רבי ברכיה הכהן
ברבי: [שעירה] הנקבים [שלהן, וכולן] נתפתחו בדם, והיו משתקצות בפניהם ומתעזבות
בפניהם ומיד היו משליכים אותם.

It now is quite clear that in the above excerpts of *Tanḥuma* (ed. Buber) and *'Aggadat Genesis*, the name עֲזוּבָה is interpreted as signifying *ugly*. The corresponding root to עז״ב in *Tanḥuma* is כע״ר (specifically, כעורה ועזובה). In a poem by Yannai that employs עז״ב in the same sense, it is paralleled by a verb with the stem כא״ר:

Liturgical Poems by Yannai 120 (p. 296):

בִּימֵי מֹשֶׁה כְּכַלָּה כְּבוּדָה הָיוּ / וּבִימֵי יִרְמִיָהוּ כְּאִשָּׁה גְרוּשָׁה הָיוּ ...
בִּימֵי מֹשֶׁה מָה יָפוּ וּמָה נָעֵימוּ / וּבִימֵי יִרְמִיָהוּ מָה עֲזְבוּ וּמָה הֻכְאָרוּ

There is no denotational difference between the roots כא״ר and כע״ר. כא״ר is documented in the Dead Sea Scrolls and rabbinic literature, as well as used in

---

174 Ben-Ḥayyim, pp. 202–205 (where that author refers the reader to Yalon and additional literature).

Syriac.[175] Let us compare the text of Nah 3:6 as it appears in *Pesher Nahum*, MT, and TJ:[176]

Pesher Nahum	והשלכתי עליך שקוצים [ונ]בלתיך ושמתיך כאורה
MT Nah 3:6	וְהִשְׁלַכְתִּי עָלַיִךְ שִׁקֻּצִים וְנִבַּלְתִּיךְ וְשַׂמְתִּיךְ כְּרֹאִי׃
TJ	וארמי עלך שקוצין ואנבלינך ואשווינך מכערא לעיני כל חזך׃

NJPS: I will throw loathsome things over you and disfigure you and make a spectacle of you.

Clem: And I will cast abominations on you and defile you, and I will make you repulsive in the eyes of all who see you.

The reading of *Pesher Nahum* gives a passive participle form of the root כא״ר, while the corresponding word in MT combines the particle כ with the root רא״ה.[177] TJ gives a passive participle form of the root כע״ר (although a חז״י verb follows shortly thereafter).

Kutscher noted that כע״ר is the form typically found in BT, and this root effectively suppressed the root כא״ר over the course of the transmission and transcription of Palestinian rabbinic literature.[178] Nonetheless, many instances of כא״ר have survived in the best MSS of various rabbinic writings. We shall not list them all here, but by way of example let us briefly turn our attention to the Mishnah's use of the root כא״ר as an antonym of נא״ה:

M. Ned. 9:10:

קונס שני נישא לפלונית כאיורה (sic in MS Kaufmann), והרי היא נאוה; שחורה,
והרי היא לבנה; קצרה, והרי היא ארוכה—לא מפני שהיא כאורה ונעשת נאוה ...
אלא שהנדר טעות.

[If one said,] "Qonam if I marry that ugly Miss So-and-so," and lo, she is beautiful, "... dark ...," and lo, she is light, "... short ...," and lo, she is tall—not because she was ugly and turned beautiful ... but because the vow [to begin with] was based on erroneous facts.

---

175   Sokoloff *Syriac*, p. 594.
176   4Q169 f3_4iii:1–2; see DJD, vol. 5, p. 38. At line 4, the author continues with the explanation ורבים יבינו בעוונם ושנאום וכארום על זדון אשמתם ... (ibid., p. 39). He may have understood the root כא״ר in the sense of מא״ס or נא״ץ, as proposed by Kister *Style*, p. 141. כא״ר is also found in two Aramaic poems, found in the Machzor for Shavuʻot of Ashkenaz (and Rome); cf. Fraenkel *Shavuʻot*, p. 444, l. 13; p. 537, l. 52.
177   See discussion of possible explanations of MT in Cogan *Nahum*, p. 51.
178   Kutscher, p. 216.

We similarly find Qalir employing כא״ר as an antonym of יפ״ה:[179]

יופי פניהם שיחר והקדירם, "ישנו" פץ להכאירם ...

With that aside behind us, we now have the wherewithal to attempt a description of the textual relationship between the various MSS of TC. The original text read something like ומאי צווחין לה עזובה מן־בגלל דהות עקרה וכאירתא. The final two words are explanations of the name עֲזוּבָה. The word כאירתא (a feminine singular passive participle form) seeks to explain that no man took an interest in her due to her unattractiveness. The term, having ceased to be a familiar one, was exchanged over the course of the transcription process for a more accessible form, בזיתא, i.e., *scorned*, and the readings now found in MSS C and E thus came into being. An illustration of another such development, albeit not a proof as such, is an equivalent substitution that took root in printed editions of the selection of *Tanhuma* excerpted above. The first edition (p. 201) has נשבע אני שאין אחד מכם נכנס שעיזבתם אותה לפני המלך, while a later edition reads מפני שבזיתם אותה לפני, נשבע אני בחיי המלך שאין אחד מכם נכנס כאן המלך.[180] In MS V, rather than substitution of a more accessible form, we find a corruption of the original version, וכאיותא, whether because the word no longer was familiar to copyists or for some other reason. MS V predates the others by some 50 years, and Le Déaut and Robert were right to select it, rather than MS C or E, as the basis of their edition. In the present case the text it contains is closer to the original than is that given by the others, despite the fact that its version is corrupt. One way or another, the corruption preserved in this MS allows us to reconstruct the original text of TC.

ואשתבהרת בחכמתא: The root שבה״ר signifies the attribution of praise to Azubah (for a discussion of the root, see p. 196, above), so that the expression here reflects a Hebrew phrase along the lines of ותתהלל בחכמה, *she was praised in wisdom*. As we shall see below, Azubah here was identified as one of the women who participated in the work of spinning the panels of the Tabernacle, regarding which Scripture (Exod 35:26) states נָשָׂא לִבָּן אֹתָנָה בְּחָכְמָה, *who excelled in that skill*. In TNM the phrase is translated יתרברב לבהון עליהון בחכמה, *their heart became proud in wisdom* (a similar rendering is given in Exod 36:2). This sense comes close to that of TC here, and it seems that this verse—along with an interpretation akin to the sense of TNM, and perhaps a corresponding

---

179 *Qerovot* 18, אמתך וחסדך, for Purim, lines 92–93. Text is per Historical Dictionary Project.
180 'Eshkol edition, vol. 2, Jerusalem, 1971/1972, p. 851.

targumic tradition unavailable to us—served as a source of inspiration and an influence on TC for the expression ואשתבהרת בחכמתא.

והות עזלא בחכמתא ית מעזי על גויתהון דעזיא כדלא גזין מטול יריעת משכנא: The Targum describes Azubah as having the ability to spin goat hair prior to its removal from the animal's hide. According to *b. Šabb.* 74b, this ability is a sure sign of a person blessed with unusually great wisdom:

אמ[ר] רבה בר בר חנה אמ[ר] ר' יוחנן: הטווה את הצמר מעל גבי בהמה בשבת—
חייב שלש חטאות: משום גוזז, משום מנפץ, משום טווה. אמ[ר] רב כהנא: אין דרך
גזיזה בכך, ואין דרך ניפוץ בכך, ואין דרך טוויה בכך. ולא? והא תאנא משמיה דר'
נחמיה: שטוף בעזים וטווי מן העזים? חכמה יתירה שאני.

Said Rabbah bar bar Hannah said, R. Yohanan, "He who on the Sabbath spins wool from an animal's back is liable on three counts: One because of shearing, the second because of hackling, and the third because of spinning." R. Kahana said, "But this is not the ordinary manner of shearing, this is not the ordinary manner of hackling, and this is not the ordinary manner of spinning." So it isn't, is it? But hasn't it been taught on Tannaite authority in the name of R. Nehemiah, "It was washed directly on the goats and spun on the goats," which proves that spinning directly from the animal counts as spinning? An act that requires special skill is exceptional.

Thus as well in *b. Šabb.* 99a:

ת[נו] ר[בנן]: יריעות התחתונות של תכלת ושל ארגמן ושל תולעת השני ושל שש,
ועליונות של מעשה עזים. וגדולה חכמה שנאמרה בעליונות יותר ממה שנאמרה
בתחתונות. בתחתונות כתי[ב]: 'וכל אשה חכמת לב בידיה טוו את העזים', ואלו
בעליונות כתי[ב] 'וכל הנשים אשר נשא לבן אתנה בחכמה'. ותאנא משמיה דר'
נחמיה: שטוף בעזים וטווי מן העזים.

Our rabbis have taught on Tannaite authority: The lower curtains were made of blue wool, purple wool, crimson thread, and fine linen, and the upper ones were made of goats' hair. It took more skill to make the upper ones than the lower ones. For in respect to the lower ones it is written, "And all the women who were smart did spin with their hands" (Exod 35:25), and in reference to the upper ones, "And all the women whose heart stirred them up in wisdom spun the goats' hair" (Exod 35:26). And it has been taught on Tannaite authority in the name of R. Nehemiah: "It was washed directly on the goats and spun on the goats."

The talmudic discussion of the parameters of the ability to spin goat hair prior to its removal from the animal is based on a midrashic understanding of Exod 35:26 (as noted above in discussing the expression ואשתבהרת בחכמתא), which reads וְכָל־הַנָּשִׁים אֲשֶׁר נָשָׂא לִבָּן אֹתָנָה בְּחָכְמָה טָווּ אֶת־הָעִזִּים, *and all the women who excelled in that skill spun the goats' hair*. The words טוו את העזים are understood to indicate that the hair was spun while still connected to the goats, and Scripture testifies that the heart of those women who engaged in this work inspired them with wisdom. TPJ integrates a description of this unique spinning skill in its translation of the verse: וכל נשיא דאיתרעי לבהון עימהן בחכמתא הוון עזלו ית מעזיא על גווייתהון ומנפסן יתהין כד הינן חיין, *and all the women whose hearts were willing were skillfully spinning the goat's hair on their bodies and combing them when they were alive*. TPJ is the only known Pentateuchal Targum that describes the women as possessing the ability to spin the goats' hair prior to removal.

TC may have been familiar with this aggadic skill either from BT or from TPJ—but neither of the two mentions the name of Caleb's wife Azubah in the context of this fantastic spinning. Why, then, did TC include her here? The trigger in our verse is the word יְרִיעוֹת, which the targumist associated with the panels of the Tabernacle. Whereas other aggadic sources interpreted the word יְרִיעוֹת as a description of Azubah's external appearance,[181] the author of TC—or an aggadic tradition preceding him—was led by this word to the idea that Azubah had been one of the wise women with the knowledge to spin hair yet connected to a living animal who exploited this ability in helping to construct the Tabernacle.

3.2   *Ephrat is Miriam (1 Chr 2:19; 4:4, 17)*

The targumist identifies Ephrat with Miriam three times in TC, as follows:
1 Chr 2:19

| MT | וַתָּמָת עֲזוּבָה וַיִּקַּח־לוֹ כָלֵב אֶת־ אֶפְרָת וַתֵּלֶד לוֹ אֶת־חוּר |
| TC | ומיתת עזובה ונסיב ליה כלב ית מרים דמתקריא אפרת וילידת ליה ית חור: |

NJPS: When Azubah died, Caleb married Ephrath, who bore him Hur.
Dost: Azubah died, so Caleb married Miriam, who was called Ephrath, and she bore Hur to him

---

181   *B. Soṭah* 12a (cf. parallel in *Exod. Rab.* 1, p. 65):
          "יריעות—because her face resembled sheets of fabric."

1 Chr 4:4

MT אֵלֶּה בְנֵי־חוּר בְּכוֹר אֶפְרָתָה אֲבִי בֵית לָחֶם׃

TC אלין בני חור בוכרא דאפרת היא מרים ואתמנא רבא בבית־לחם׃

NJPS: and Penuel was the father of Gedor, and Ezer the father of Hushah. These were the sons of Hur, the first-born of Ephrathah, the father of Bethlehem.

Dost: Penuel was the father of Gedor, and Ezer was the father of Hushah. These were the sons of Hur, the firstborn of Ephrath, who was Miriam, who was appointed chief in Bethlehem.

1 Chr 4:17

MT וַתַּהַר אֶת־מִרְיָם וְאֶת־שַׁמַּי וְאֶת־יִשְׁבָּח אֲבִי אֶשְׁתְּמֹעַ׃

TC ואעדיאת מניה ית מרים היא אפרת ית שמי וית ישבח אבא דאשתמע׃

NJPS: She conceived and bore Miriam, Shammai, and Ishbah father of Eshtemoa.

Dost: and Miriam, who is Ephrath, bore from him Shammai and Ishbah, the father of Eshtemoa.

The identification of Ephrat with Miriam allows David's lineage to be traced to Miriam (a midrashic understanding of 1 Sam 17:12, וְדָוִד בֶּן־אִישׁ אֶפְרָתִי הַזֶּה, *David was the son of a certain Ephrathite*), who according to aggadic tradition was blessed with being a forebear of the Israelite monarchy as a reward for refusing when she worked as a midwife to kill male Israelite babies as demanded by Pharaoh. The identification is familiar from many sources, among them BT, *Sifre Numbers*, *Pirqe Rabbi Eliezer*, *Exodus Rabbah*, and *Tanḥuma*.[182] Here we will have reference to the comments on the matter found in *b. Soṭah* 11b:

'ויהי כי יראו המילדות את האלי״ם ויעש להם בתים'—רב ולוי: חד אמ[ר], בתי כהונה ולוייה. וחד אמ[ר], בתי מלכות. מאן דאמ[ר] בתי כהונה ולוייה: אהרן ומשה. ומאן דאמ[ר] בתי מלכות: דוד ממרים קא אתי, דכת[יב] 'ותמת עזובה ויקח לו כלב את אפרת ותלד לו את חור', וכת[יב] 'ודוד בן איש אפרתי'.

"And it came to pass, because the midwives feared God, he made them houses" (Exod 1:21): Rab and Samuel: one of them said, "Houses of the priestly and Levitical castes." And one of them said, "Houses of the monarchy." *As to the one who said,* "They are the houses of the priestly and Levitical castes," this refers to Aaron and Moses. *As to the one who said,*

---

182 *Sifre Num* 78 (p. 75); *Pirqe Rabbi Eliezer* 45 (p. 230); *Exod. Rab.* 1:17 (p. 66); 48:4 (p. 156); *Tanḥuma, Ki Tissa'* 13 (p. 96).

"This refers to the houses of kingship," *David also came forth from Miriam,*
For it is written, "And Azubah died, and Caleb took to him Ephrath, who
bore him Hur" (1 Chr 2:19), and it is written, "Now David was the son of
that Ephrathite (1 Sam 17:12).

The diction of TC here gives no indication of whether it is based on this source
or another.

3.3 *The Family of Moses' Progeny (1 Chr 2:55)*

1 Chr 2:55

MT		יַעְבֵּץ	יֹשְׁבֵי(קרי)	סֹפְרִים		וּמִשְׁפְּחוֹת
TC	ועתניאל בר קנז	דיעבץ הוא	תלמידיא בר משה	רחביה בר אליעזר		וגניסת

MT (cont.)	תִּרְעָתִים
TC	יעבץ הוון צווחין ליה דאוקים בעיצתיה תרביצא לתלמידיא תרעתים הוון צווחין להון

שׂוּכָתִים (cont.)		שִׁמְעָתִים
TC	דהוה קלהון במשבחיהון הי־כיבבא שמעתים דהוון מסברין אפין בשמעתתא סוכתים

הַבָּאִים (cont.)		הֵמָּה הַקִּינִים
TC	דהוון מטללין ברוח נבואה הנון שלמאי בני צפרה דמתיחסין עם גניסת ליואי דאתיין

(cont.)	בֵית־רֵכָב:	מֵחַמַּת אֲבִי
TC	וארתיכין:	מזרעית משה רבהון דישראל דטב להון זכותיה מפרשין

NJPS: The families of the scribes that dwelt at Jabez: the Tirathites, the
Shimeathites, the Sucathites; these are the Kenites who came from Hammath,
father of the house of Rechab.

Dost: The lineage of Rechabiah son of Eliezer, son of Moses: the disciples of
Jabez, who was Othniel son of Kenaz. They called him Jabez because he established by his counsel the study halls for the disciples. They were called
Terathites because when they were praising their voice was as a clamor.
Shimeathites, because they were hopeful while (studying) the legal tradition.
Sucathites, because they were overshadowed by the spirit of prophecy. These
were (the) Shalmites, the sons of Zipporah, who were registered with the lineage of the Levites, who came from the clan of Moses, the chief of Israel, whose
merit (was) better for them than horseman and chariots.

This verse is expounded at length in TC, as demonstrated in the synopsis
above. Some of the names in the verse (the series שׂוּכָתִים, שִׁמְעָתִים, תִּרְעָתִים) are

interpreted in various rabbinic sources,[183] but I do not believe that such exegesis exercised any direct influence on TC. Various rabbinic sources referred
their homilies in this vein to the descendants of Jonadab son of Rechab, taking
their cue from the words אֲבִי בֵית־רֵכָב at the end of the Hebrew verse, but TC
understood the verse as discussing the Mosaic family. Below we shall see the
exegetical methods employed by the Targum.

וגניסת רחביה בר אליעזר בר משה: The Hebrew verse begins with the words
וּמִשְׁפְּחוֹת סֹפְרִים. What scribes are these? Verse 53 made mention of a series of
families beginning with הַיִתְרִי, identified by the targumist as Levites descended
from Moses who were disciples of prophets. The conclusion of the present
verse mentions הַקִּינִים (who are identified with the family of Moses' father-in-
law). The title סוֹפֵר caused the targumist to identify the scribe Shemaiah son
of Nethanel with Moses in 1 Chr 24:6 (following the Rabbis; see below, pp. 375–
377). All the above brought the targumist to identify the family of scribes in
the present verse with descendants of Moses. But why Rehabiah? The targumist knows from 1 Chr 23:16–17 that the descendants of Moses branched into
two clans: the children of Shebuel son of Gershom, and those of Rehabiah son
of Eliezer. He identified Shebuel as Jonathan son of Gershom, whom rabbinic
tradition and the targumist both regard as having spent time as a pagan priest
(see pp. 371–375, below) until repenting of his sins after many generations.
TC thus was left with Rehabiah son of Eliezer, whose personal history is not
known to have been characterized by anything unsavory and whose descendants, Scripture attests, רָבוּ לְמָעְלָה, were very numerous (ibid., v. 17).

תלמידיא דיעבץ הוא עתניאל בר קנז יעבץ הוון צוווחין ליה דאוקים בעיצתיה תרביצא
לתלמידיא: The words יֹשְׁבֵי יַעְבֵּץ are interpreted as referring to disciples seated before their teacher Jabez, whose is identified with Othniel son of Kenaz. It
is only fitting in the eyes of an exegete for the teacher of the descendants
of Moses to have been Othniel, who served as judge, i.e., the greatest sage of
his generation, and who deductive powers were responsible for the restora-
tion of the entire Torah after it was forgotten during the days the nation spent

---

183   *Mek. RY, Yitro* 2 (p. 200); *Mek. RSbY* 18:27 (p. 135); *Sifre Num* 78 (p. 73); *Tanḥuma, Yitro* 4
       (p. 74). *Sifre* contains two homilies on these names, one as in *Mekilta* and one not; on the
       development of the version in *Sifre*, see Kahana, vol. 3, pp. 532–533. Most of these homi-
       lies, base their interpretations on the same stems as TC—רו"ע, שמ"ע, סכ"ך (*Sifre* also
       includes the Aramaic noun תרע)—but TC interprets these stems differently.

mourning Moses.[184] See discussion of the identification of Jabez with Othniel and exegesis of the name *Jabez*, pp. 253–256.

תרעתים הוון צווחין להון דהוה קלהון במשבחיהון הי־כיבבא: Trumpeting (תרועה) is associated with a sobbing or throbbing sound as early as the Mishnah (*Rosh ha-Sha.* 4:9), and it is in this sense that the name of the תרעתים, *Terathites*, is expounded in TC. They are described as singers (reciters of praise) because they are Levites, descendants of Moses.

שמעתים דהוון מסברין אפין בשמעתתא: The exegesis attached here to the name שמעתים, *Shimeathites*, is rooted in the word שמועה, which in talmudic literature has a halakhic sense, taking on the form שמעתא, or שמעתתא, in Babylonian Aramaic.[185] סב״ר אפין is the Aramaic equivalent of the rabbinic expression סב״ר פנים (e.g., והווי מקבל את כל האדם בסבר פנים יפות), *greet everybody cheerfully*, m. ʾAbot 1:15). The expression appears in TPJ twice in the story of Cain and Abel as a translation of שע״ה (Gen 4:4–5) and once in Gen 32:21 as a translation of נש״א פנים. The sense of the term as indicated by the context is that one party indicates to another that he is pleased with him.[186] The complete phrase found here, מסברין אפין בשמעתתא, is unique in rabbinic and targumic literature. Le Déaut-Robert (vol. 1, p. 46) translated it as "ils s'adonnaient avec joie (à l'étude) des traditions," while McIvor (p. 54) rendered, "they looked with favor on the traditional laws." That is to say, both understood that the disciples of Jabez adopted a positive affect toward the traditions that they studied.

In my opinion, this explanation does not conform to the mode of expression characteristic of the Rabbis and their successors, such as TC, and this was not the intent of the latter. I believe that there are two distinct possibilities for explaining the diction used by TC in accordance with accepted rabbinic tradition. One possibility is that the disciples showed a favorable expression not to

---

184 *B. Tem.* 16a:

אלף ושבע מאות קלין וחמורין וגזירות שוות ודיקדוקי סופרים נשתכחו בימי אבלו של משה.
א״ר אבהו :אעפ״כ, החזירן עתניאל (!) בן קנז מתוך פילפולו.

A thousand and seven hundred arguments a fortiori and arguments by analogy and scribal clarifications were forgotten in the time of the mourning for Moses. Said R. Abbahu, "Nonetheless, Othniel b. Kenaz restored them by means of his sharp wit: 'And Othniel son of Kenaz the brother of Caleb took it [the city of the book]' (Josh 15:17)."

185 See discussion of this word in context of 1 Chr 11:11, pp. 293–294, and sources cited ibid. See Sokoloff *JBA*, pp. 1161–1162.

186 Aside from these three occurrences, סב״ר אפן appears in *Tg. Job* 22: 8 (corresponding to נְשׂוּא פָנִים); 32:22 (the sense of the latter occurrence is similar to that of those in TPJ). The word pair also appears on rare occasion in rabbinic literature.

the traditions, but to those people to whom Jabez's disciples transmitted these traditions, in a sense similar to that of the homily in *b. Ber.* 63b:

'ודבר ה' אל משה פנים אל פנים'—א[מר] ר' יצחק: אמ[ר] לו הב"ה למשה: הסבור אתה שאין אתה מסביר להם פנים לישראל בהלכה? לא, אלא כשם שהסברתי לך פנים, כך אתה תסביר להם פנים לישראל באהל מועד והחזר אהל מועד למקומו.

"And the Lord spoke to Moses face to face" (Exod 33:11): Said R. Isaac, "Said the Holy One, blessed be he, to Moses, 'Moses, you and I will come face and face in discourse on the law.'" Some say, "This is what the Holy One, blessed be he, said to Moses, 'Just as I have shown favor to you, so you show favor to Israel, and bring the tent back to its place.'"

This usage would indicate that the sense of the expression in TC is to transmit a halakhic lesson to another person pleasantly and cheerfully.

Another potential means of understanding the phrase is that it says nothing of the manner in which a lesson is transmitted to the public, but rather speaks to the degree to which students immerse themselves in traditions they study, as indicated by *b. Sanh.* 106b:

ואמ[ר] ר' יצחק: מאי דכת[יב] 'איה ספר איה שקל איה ספר את המגדלים'? 'איה ספר'—זה דואג שהיה סופר כל אותיות שבתורה; 'איה שקל'—זה דואג שהיה שוקל כל קולין וחומרין שבתורה; 'איה ספר את המגדלים'—שהיה שונה שלש מאות הלכו[ת] פסוקות במגדל הפורח באויר, דאמ[ר] ר' אימי: ארבע מאה בעיי הוה בעו דואג ואחיתפל במגדל הפורח באויר ... אמ[ר] רב משרשיה: דואג ואחיתפל גמארא הוו גמיר, מסבר לא הוו סברי שמעתא. מתקיף ליה מר זוטרא: מאן דכתי[ב] ביה 'איה ספר איה שקל איה ספר את המגדלים', ואת אמרת לא הוו סברי שמעתא? אלא לא הוה סלקא להו שמעתא אליבא דהלכאתא, דכת[יב] 'סוד ה' ליראיו'.

And said R. Isaac, "What is the meaning of the verse of Scripture: 'Where is he who counted, where is he who weighed? Where is he who counted the towers' (Isa 33:18)? "'Where is he who counted all the letters in the Torah? Where is he who weighed all of the arguments a fortiori in the Torah?' "'Where is he who counted the towers'—who counted the three hundred decided laws that concern the 'tower that flies in the air' [that is, the laws governing the status of the contents of a closed cabinet not standing on the ground]." Said R. Ammi, "Four hundred questions did Doeg and Ahitophel raise concerning the 'tower flying in the air,' ... Said R. Mesharshayya, "Doeg and Ahitophel did not know how to reason concerning traditions." Objected Mar Zutra, "Can it be the case that one concerning whom it is written, 'Where is he who counted, where is he who weighed, where is he who counted the towers?' (Isa 33:18) should not be able to reason concerning traditions? But it never turned out that traditions [in their names] were stated in accord with the decided law, for it is written, 'The secret of the Lord is with those who fear him' (Ps 25:14)."

The verse (Isa 33:18) quoted in the question posed by Mar Zuṭra' serves in the excerpt above as a source indicating that Doeg and Ahithophel analyzed Torah matters in such a way that their reasoning placed them on the uppermost level of Torah study. The sense of סב"ר שמעתא in the talmudic excerpt above is *to arrive at the root of the rationale of a law*, illustrated by the enormous number of challenges that Doeg and Ahithophel would pose even on a topic as esoteric as a flying tower, and as opposed to mere broad familiarity with halakhic matters unaccompanied by any comprehension of relevant conceptual foundations.[187] True, neither אפין nor פנים appears in this expression in the Talmud here, but the word easily could have been incorporated. According to this explanation, TC praises the disciples of Jabez for immersing themselves in their scholarship and teasing out the roots of the laws they studied.

סוכתים דהוון מטללין ברוח נבואה: The root סכ"ך is reflected in Aramaic by the root טל"ל (a relation of the Hebrew root צל"ל) in both verbs and nouns—e.g., סֵכָה, מטלא. The targumist interprets the name סוכתים, *Sucathites*, as derived from this stem and describes the prophetic spirit that would rest upon the disciples of Jabez by comparing it to something spread over them and providing them with shade. The language of the homily, though, is surprising: the phrase ברוח בנבואה typically is accompanied by a verb such as אמ"ר or רא"ה (or a comparable verb): nowhere else do we find the phrase accompanied by a verb such as טל"ל, or similar. It would be natural, though, if סוכתים were derived from סכ"י and given an interpretation along the lines of שהיו סוכים ברוח נבואה, *they gazed with the spirit of prophecy*.[188]

---

187   Rashi ad loc. on the word סברי:

לא היו יודעין הלכה לפרשה כתקנה בטעמא.

They knew not how to sufficiently explain the rationale of a law.

188   Cf. *b. Meg.* 14a:

יסכה—זו שרה. ולמה נקרא שמה יסכה? שסוכה ברוח הקודש.

Yiskah is Sarah; and why was she named Yiskah? Because she saw through the holy spirit.

Lev. Rab. 1:3 (vol. 1, p. 9):

אבי סוכו—זה היה אבי שלכל הנביאים שהיו סוכין ברוח הקודש.

Father of Sokho—he was father of all the prophets who gazed through the holy spirit. The last name, סוכו, is also interpreted in TC as stemming from סכ"ך; see 268, below.

Further, the derivation of סוכתים from סכ״ך has a basis in other midrashic sources.[189] It may be that the language of TC blends together the two homiletical angles—both that of sheltering Israel and that of seeing with the prophetic spirit—thus secondarily forming the phrase מטללין ברוח נבואה.

In any event, we find that the names in the series שׂוּכָתִים, שִׁמְעָתִים, תִּרְעָתִים are interpreted by TC according to the three characteristics that the targumist associates with the descendants of Moses, including outside the present midrashic context: תִּרְעָתִים as signifying their being Levites (ליואי בני משה, 1 Chr 2:53); שִׁמְעָתִים for their outstanding Torah scholarship (תלמידיא דיעבץ, 1 Chr 2:55); שׂוּכָתִים as reflecting their prophetic status (תלמידי נביא, 1 Chr 2:53). There is no communication between the interpretive approach of TC and homilies authored by the Rabbis regarding this verse (noted above, p. 365, n. 183), as in rabbinic literature the people in the verse are not Levites descended from Moses.

הנון שלמאי בני צפרה דמתיחסין עם גניסת ליואי: McIvor argued that by replacing הַקֵּינִים with שלמאי, the targumist identified the people described in the verse with בני שלמא of verse 54.[190] With this he apparently followed the example of Le Déaut and Robert's French translation, which has "Shalma" in verse 54, and the equivalent indeed is given in his English translation. My assumption is that Le Déaut and Robert here were trying to remain faithful to MS V, which has the word שַׁלְמָא, thus vowelized, in both Hebrew and Aramaic. In truth, however, this diacritical tradition must be rejected with regard to the original text of TC, as not only does MT discuss them as Salma, but the text of TC itself contains a supplement expounding the name as related to both סולם and סלים, as we saw earlier.[191] In any event, despite the orthographic similarity, the targumic identification of הַקֵּינִים with שלמאי resulted not from the mention of בני שלמא in verse 54, but from the targumic tradition in the other places in Scripture where הַקֵּינִים appear.[192] The author of TC took his lead from his predecessors, not from verse 54.

---

189 *Mek. RY, Yitro* 2 (p. 200): "Sucathites (סוכתים)—because they dwelled in huts (בסוכות)."
   Mek. RSbY 18:27 (p. 135):

   סוכתים—... שהיו מסככין על ישראל ומגינין עליהן.

   Sukathites—... they would cover Israel and protect them.

190 McIvor, p. 54, n. 52, § c.

191 McIvor himself, for that matter, proceeds to give their name as *Salma* throughout n. 48 (pp. 53–54).

192 TO, TN, TPJ Gen 15:19; Num 24:21–22 (also FT in the preceding two verses; TPJ translates as יתרו in verse 21); TJ Judg 1:16; 4:11, 17; 5:24; 1 Sam 15:6; 27:10; 30:29.
   Thus also in *y. Qidd.* 1:9 (61d, p. 1159):

   'את הקיני ואת הקניזי ואת הקדמוני'—ר' יודה אמ[ר] שלמאה שכייה נבטייה.

בני צפרה דמתיחסין עם גניסת ליואי דאתיין מזרעית משה רבהון דישראל: The addition of the words בני צפרה creates an association with שלמאי, mentioned earlier, as well as the expansion in verse 53 (דילידת ליה צפרה) inspired by the appearance of היתרי there. In the plain sense of the Hebrew phrase הַבָּאִים מֵחַמַּת it appears that the word חַמַּת serves as a proper noun,[193] but this is not reflected in the Aramaic translation. In the Targum, instead, we find the words גניסה and זרעית, both of which signify *family* and correspond to nothing in the Hebrew *Vorlage*. In the context of a discussion of the meaning of the Hebrew text, Talmon suggested deriving the word חַמַּת from חָם, i.e., a groom's father, so that the word would be defined as signifying a family.[194] Regardless of whether this proposition holds true in Hebrew, it is not impossible that this meaning was at the root of the translation given by TC. The targumist may have believed that the word חַמַּת signified a familial relationship, and for this reason used גניסה and זרעית in his translation. Another possibility is that the targumist understood the word מחמת in its talmudic sense: *due to*.[195] According to this interpretation, the targumist believed that הַקֵּנִים of this verse enjoyed a pedigree that was theirs *due to* Moses, who according to the Targum is dubbed אֲבִי בֵית־רֵכָב. The fact of the targumist's association of the Kenites with Moses here is unsurprising as such, since this is stated explicitly by Scripture in Judg 1:16: וּבְנֵי קֵינִי חֹתֵן מֹשֶׁה, *the descendants of the Kenite, the father-in-law of Moses*. However, the targumist's decision to refer to them here as בני צפרה (along with naming Zipporah in verse 53, above) is unique and not familiar from other sources.

דטב להון זכותיה מפרשין וארתיכין: Literally, "for whom his merit was better than horsemen and chariots." It is the last word here that links this expansion with the Hebrew text אֲבִי בֵית־רֵכָב. The homily, which aggrandizes the personage of Moses, untellingly links the present verse with Elisha's scream when his master, Elijah, departed the world: אָבִי | אָבִי רֶכֶב יִשְׂרָאֵל וּפָרָשָׁיו, *Oh, father, father! Israel's chariots and horsemen!* (2 Kgs 2:12). The same words were uttered by King Joash of Israel over Elisha when the latter lay terminally ill in his sickbed (2 Kgs 13:14). Elisha's words serve in the Talmud as the source for a discussion of the laws pertaining to tearing one's garment on the death of a parent

---

There also is reason to believe that the Shalmaites appear previously in the Bible, in Song 1:5: שְׁחוֹרָה אֲנִי וְנָאוָה בְּנוֹת יְרוּשָׁלָ͏ִם כְּאָהֳלֵי קֵדָר כִּירִיעוֹת שְׁלֹמֹה—see Zakovitch, p. 50, according to whom שְׁלֹמֹה in this verse refers to the Shalmaites and not to Solomon.
See also Smolar-Aberbach, p. 117; van Staalduine-Sulman *TJ Samuel*, pp. 181–182.

193   Knoppers *vol. I*, p. 316.

194   Talmon, pp. 174–180. Talmon proposed the same uncommon meaning in Ps 76:11. Though Talmon did not discuss the Targum to the present verse, we may assume that he would find support for the same proposal here, as well.

195   Sokoloff *JBA*, pp. 656–657.

or a teacher. Within the talmudic passage, we find an Aramaic translation of Elisha's words, which TC uses as a source. *B. Moʿed Qaṭ.* 26a:

אביו ואמו ורבו שלימדו חכמה מנא לן? דכת[יב] 'ואלישע רואה והוא מצעק אבי אבי רכב ישראל ופרשיו ולא ראהו עוד ויחזק בבגדיו ויקרעם לשנים עשר קרעים'. 'אבי אבי'—זה אביו ואמו. 'רכב ישראל ופרשיו'—זה רבו שלימדו חכמה. מאי משמעא? כי דמתרגם רב יוסף: רבי דטב ליה לישראל בצלותיה מרתכין ומפרשין.

> "for his father or his mother, his master who taught him wisdom:" how on the basis of Scripture do we know this fact? As it is written, "And Elisha saw it and cried, My father, my father, the chariots of Israel and the horsemen thereof" (2 Kgs 2:12)—"My father, my father:" this means [his father and] mother. "the chariots of Israel and the horsemen thereof:" this means [his master] who taught him wisdom. *And what is the sense? It is in line with the Aramaic version given by R. Joseph, "My master, who protected Israel with his prayer better than chariots and horsemen could."*

TC drew inspiration from the translation given by R. Yosef on account of the appearance of the words אבי and רכב, and proceeded to apply this praise to Moses.[196] The targumist altered the order of the words to פרשין וארתכין in order to conclude the unit with the appropriate word for the Hebrew *Vorlage*, viz., רכב. I do not believe that any particular agenda of the targumist lies behind the interchange of the words בצלותיה and זכותיה. Such an exchange may reflect the targumist's recollection of the text of BT, or else a change that took place during the copying of TC—although with regard to the latter possibility it must be noted that all MSS of BT read צלותיה and all MSS of TC read זכותיה. Also worthy of note is that the reading of TC, זכותיה, conforms to the targumist's comments regarding Moses in 1 Chr 4:18: רבא דסוכו דטליל על בית ישר[אל] בזכותיה, *Prince of Soco because he covered the house of Israel by his merit* (regarding which see p. 268).

3.4   *Shebuel as Moses' Grandson Jonathan (1 Chr 23:15–16; 26:24)*
1 Chr 23:15–16

| MT | הָרֹאשׁ׃ | שְׁבוּאֵל גֵּרְשׁוֹם בְּנֵי אֱלִיעֶזֶר׃ וְגֵרְשׁוֹם גֵּרְשׁוֹם מֹשֶׁה בְּנֵי |
| TC | לרישא | בני משה גרשם ואליעזר: בני גרשם שבואל ממנא |

הוא יהונתן דאתמנא נבי שקרא ובסיבותיה עבד תתובא ומני יתיה דוד לרישא על אוצריא:

NJPS: The sons of Moses: Gershom and Eliezer. The sons of Gershom: Shebuel the chief.

---

196   R. Yosef's translation is the basis of TJ to these two verses; see ibid. McIvor, p. 55, n. 52, § c, correctly established a link between TC and TJ, but did not note the source in BT.

Dost: The sons of Moses: Gershom and Eliezer. The sons of Gershom: Sheboel was appointed as head. He is Jonathan, who was considered as a false prophet, but in his old age he repented, so David appointed him as head over his treasuries.

1 Chr 26:24

MT	עַל־הָאֹצָרֽוֹת׃	נָגִיד	בֶּן־מֹשֶׁה	בֶּן־גֵּרְשׁוֹם		וּשְׁבֻאֵל
TC		בר משה	בר גרשם	הוא יונתן		ושבואל

תב לדחלתא דה׳ וכד חמא דוד דהוה מתבהיל על ממונא מנייה נגידא על תסבריא׃

NJPS: Shebuel son of Gershom son of Moses was the chief officer over the treasuries.

Dost: Now Shebuel, who is Jonathan son of Gershom, the son of Moses, he returned to the fear of the Lord, and when David saw that he was acting carefully with regard to the money, he appointed him as the chief officer in charge over the treasuries.

Shebuel son of Gershom son of Moses appears twice in TC. The Hebrew *Vorlage* volunteers few details about this figure aside from his pedigree and position, but in the Targum the two verses that mention him become an epilogue to a story told elsewhere in Scripture. In both instances, TC identifies Shebuel with Jonathan son of Gershom son of Moses, who appears in Judges 17 in the story of Micah's idol. Both verses state that Jonathan returned to the worship of God, but do not state explicitly that he therefore is called Shebuel. The Targum's statements on the matter have parallels in rabbinic literature,[197] and it is clear that the targumist incorporates in his composition similar traditions to those of the Rabbis regarding Shebuel, but it is not possible to establish that his diction is based on one specific source rather than another.[198]

The structure of TC 1 Chr 23:16 contains two parallels to the main part of the Hebrew. TC first gives a brief Aramaic version of the verse very similar to many others that name a given person who is appointed as chief, or ממנא לרישא.[199] Thereafter, the targumist transmits the story behind the formal verse; here the word תתובא refers to the name שבואל. The Targum also recapitulates his

---

197 *Y. Ber.* 9:2 (13d, p. 71); *Sanh.* 11:5 (30b–c, p. 1330–1331); *b. B. Bat.* 109b–110a; *Cant. Rab.* 2:5 (p. 30).

198 Rosenberg-Kohler, p. 146, cited *b. B. Bat.* 110a, and were followed in this by Churgin *Hagiographa*, p. 256; Le Déaut-Robert, vol. 1, p. 91, n. 3. The argument is quite convincing, given the prolific use of BT throughout TC, but in this case there is no textual proof based on which we ought to prefer BT to other sources.

199 See pp. 31–33, above.

appointment in greater detail, adding that he was assigned to his post by David and was responsible for the treasury.

The second verse states that Jonathan returned to fearing God, an expression reflected by his new name, שבואל, which various rabbinic sources interpret to mean that he returned (שב) to God.[200] This Aramaic verse, like that preceding it, states that he was appointed over the treasury. Here, though, it is revealed that the reason for this appointment was David's insight that the man was obsessed with money. This datum also appears in the various rabbinic sources, although it is phrased differently here.[201] In the first verse the coffers are indicated by the word אוצריא, and in the second, תסבריא. The disparity between the terms may reveal a sliver of a difference between the targumist as a translator and the targumist as an exegete. תסבריא is a loanword, derived from the Greek θησαυρός, that appears frequently in Palestinian rabbinic literature in both Hebrew and Aramaic.[202] In TC it serves as the accustomed equivalent of אוצרות, so that it is the natural word to find in 1 Chr 26:24.[203] אוצריא of 1 Chr 23:16 does not correspond to a Hebrew word in its *Vorlage* and, perhaps for this reason, the targumist here uses a closer term to that found in *b. B. Bat.* 110a (וכיון שראה דוד ... שמו על האוצרות).[204]

---

200 Per sources cited above, n. 197:

y. Ber. 9:2 שבואל—ששב אל אל בכל לבו ובכל כחו; Shebuel—for he returned to God with all his heart and all his strength

y. Sanh. 11:5 שבואל—ששב לאל בכל כוחו; Shebuel—for he returned to God with all his strength

b. B. Bat. 110a וכי שבואל שמו? והלא יונתן שמו! א״ר יוחנן, ששב אל אל בכל לבו; Now was his name really Shebuel? Wasn't Jonathan his name? Said R. Yohanan, "It means that he returned to God with all his heart."

201 *Y. Ber.* 9:2 כיון שראה דוד כך שהוא אוהב ממון, מה עשה? העמידו קומוס על תיסבריות שלו; since David perceived how much he loved money, what did he? He appointed him in charge of his coffers.

y. Sanh. 11:5 כיון שראה דוד שהיה הממון חביב עליו, מינהו קומיס תיסוורין על בית המקדש; since David perceived that he was fond of money, he appointed him in chief treasurer of the Temple.

b. B. Bat. 110a וכיון שראה דוד שממון חביב עליו ביותר, שמו על האוצרות; since David perceived how much he was fond of money, he put him in charge of the treasury.

Cant. Rab. 2:5 כיון שראה דוד שהממון חביב עליו, עמד ומינה אותו קומיסטון תיסבריות שלו; since David saw that he was fond of money, he went and appointed him his chief treasurer.

202 Krauss *Lehnwörter*, p. 587; Sokoloff *JPA*, p. 671 (תיסוור).

203 Appearances of תסברא in TC: 1 Chr 9:26; 26:20, 24, 26; 27:25; 28:12; 2 Chr 8:15; 11:11; 12:9; 16:2; 25:24; 32:27; 36:18.

204 In contrast to aggadic sources in the *yerushalmi* and *Cant. Rab.* (n. 197, above), which read תסברא.

Judg 18:30 is the only place in the account of Micah's idol where Jonathan is mentioned by name: וַיָּקִימוּ לָהֶם בְּנֵי־דָן אֶת־הַפֶּסֶל וִיהוֹנָתָן בֶּן־גֵּרְשֹׁם בֶּן־מְנַשֶּׁה הוּא וּבָנָיו הָיוּ כֹהֲנִים לְשֵׁבֶט הַדָּנִי עַד־יוֹם גְּלוֹת הָאָרֶץ *the Danites set up the sculptured image for themselves; and Jonathan son of Gershom son of Manasseh, and his descendants, served as priests to the Danite tribe until the land went into exile.* Various rabbinic sources, taking their cue from the verse's wording (כהן, פסל), establish that Jonathan was an idolatrous priest.[205] TC does not describe him thus, but calls him a false prophet. This is not to say, though, that TC lumped idolatrous priests and false prophets together without distinction. It seems to me that the interchange of terms in TC also stems from a rabbinic tradition. TY and *Cant. Rab.* contain yet another epilogue to follow the epilogue about Jonathan/Shebuel. Below is the version found in *Cant. Rab.* (p. 30):[206]

נכנס רבי מאיר ודרש: 'ונביא אחד זקן יושב בבית אל'. ואיזה זה? זה אמציה כהן בית אל. אמר לו ר׳ יוסי: מאיר, פתבותי בצים יש כאן. איזה זה? זה יונתן בן גרשם בן משה ... אמרו, כיון שמת דוד חזר לסורו. ה[דא] ה[וא] ד[כתיב] 'ויאמר גם אני נביא כמוך' וגו׳ 'כחש לו'.

R. Meir came and expounded: 'There was an old prophet living in Bethel' (1 Kgs 13:11). Which one was he? He was Amaziah priest of Bethel. R. Josa said: Meir, this is worthless chattering. Which one was he? He was Jonathan son of Gershom son of Moses. They said, after David died he returned to his wayward ways. This is what was written, 'I am a prophet, too,'... He was lying to him.' (1 Kgs 13:18)

Thus, in the world of rabbinic lore, Jonathan lived the end of his life as a false prophet, and some part of this tradition found its way into TC. The tradition recorded by the targumist certainly is related to the aggadic sources discussed above, but the Targum's terminology is somewhat different from that of the other sources with which we are familiar.

If such expressions as עבד תתובא and מתבהיל על ממונא reflect the diction of TC's source, then apparently the precise work from which the tradition was transcribed has yet to be found.[207] Alternately, it is possible that the targumist

---

205 In addition to sources cited above, see also TJ Judg 18:30; *Mek. RSbY* 18:1.

206 The parallel aggadic text in *y. Sanh.* 11:5 (30b, p. 1330) is incomplete; the parallel in *Cant. Rab.* therefore is given here.

207 The expression מתבהיל על ממונא is a similar one to בהול על הממון, which appears in *b. Šabb.* 117b; 120b. The expression is related to the scriptural נִבְהָל לַהוֹן, Prov 28:22.

relied for this tradition on one of the sources noted above but chose, for one reason or another, to use expressions other than those in the original.

3.5 *Shemaiah as Moses (1 Chr 24:6)*

1 Chr 24:6

MT	הַלֵּוִ֔י	מִן־	הַסּוֹפֵ֜ר	בֶּן־נְתַנְאֵ֣ל	שְׁמַֽעְיָה֩		וַיִּכְתְּבֵ֡ם
TC		רבא	ספרא		משה		וכתבנון
	לוי	שיבט	מן		בר נתנאל	שמעי[ה]	דמתקרי

MT (cont.)	וְהַשָּׂרִים֙	הַמֶּ֗לֶךְ	לִפְנֵ֣י
TC	ורברביא	מלכא	קדם כתבא מתקרי והוה

NJPS: Shemaiah son of Nathanel, the scribe, who was of the Levites, registered them under the eye of the king, the officers ...

Dost: Moses the great scribe, who was called Shemaia son of Nethanel, from the tribe of Levi, recorded them, and the document was read before the king, the leaders ...

This chapter describes the division of the priests into twenty-four shifts, sixteen descended from Eleazar and eight from Ithamar. The division was executed by lottery, but the process was administered and recorded by a scribe named Shemaiah son of Nethanel. This scribe, whose name is unknown from any other verse, is identified by the Targum with none other than Moses. This identification by TC, which as we shall see accords with a rabbinic tradition, creates a chronological problem, as the verse states that the scribe recorded the proceedings in the presence of David and his ministers, who lived centuries after Moses' death. The Targum addressed this issue with the insertion of והוה מתקרי כתבא, *and the document was read*: Moses indeed was the scribe described by the verse and recorded the proceedings, but he did so during his own lifetime, and not in David's presence: the records merely were read before David and his ministers. This short expansion thus establishes a bridgeable gap between the recording performed by Moses in his day and the reading of those records in the days of David.

The identification of Shemaiah as Moses appears in *Lev. Rab.* 1:3 (vol. 1, pp. 11–12):

עשרה שמות נקראו לו למשה: ירד, חבר, יקותיאל, אבי גדור, אבי סוכו, אבי זנוח. ר' יהודה בר' אילעאי אמ[ר]: אף טוביה הוא שמו, ה[דא] ה[וא] ד[כתיב] 'ותרא אתו כי טוב הוא'—טוביה הוא. ר' ישמעאל בר אמי אמ[ר]: אף שמעיה היה שמו. אתא ר' יהושע בר' נחמיה ופריש ופריש הדין קריה: 'ויכתבם שמעיה בן נתנאל הסופר מן הלוי לפני המלך והשרים וצדוק הכהן ואחימלך בן אביתר'. 'שמעיה'—ששמע אל תפילתו.

'בן נתנאל'—בן שניתנה לו תורה מיד ליד. 'הסופר'—שהיה סופרן שלישראל. 'מן
הלוי'—שהיה משבטו שללוי. 'לפני המלך והשרים'—זה מלך מלכי המלכים הב"ה
ובית דינו. 'וצדוק הכהן'—זה אהרן הכהן.

Moses had ten names: Jared, Haber, Jekuthiel, Abigdor, Abisoko,
Abizanoah. R. Judah son of R. Il'ai says: He was also named Tobiah,
based on the verse, '*when she saw how beautiful he was*' (Exod 2:2)—he
was Tobiah. R. Ishmael son of Ami says: He was named Shemaiah too.
R. Joshua son of R. Nehemiah came and explained this verse: '*Shemaiah
son of Nathanel, the scribe, who was of the Levites, registered them under
the eye of the king, the officers, and Zadok the priest, and Ahimelech son
of Abiathar*' (1 Chr 24:6). '*Shemaiah*'—for God heard his prayer. '*son of
Nathanel*'—son who the Torah was given to with no intermediary. '*the
scribe*'—he was Israel's scribe. '*of the Levites*'—he was of the tribe of Levi.
'*under the eye of the king, the officers*'—this is the King of kings' kings,
the Holy One blessed be He and His court. '*and Zadok the priest*'—this is
Aaron the priest.

The homily also appears in other, later parallels. Churgin, Le Déaut and Robert,
and McIvor all gave *Lev. Rab.* as TC's source.[208] I do not believe that the targumist was directly influenced by *Lev. Rab.*, because the entirety of TC's treatment of the verse aside from the identification of Shemaiah with Moses differs
from that in the midrash, in which the chronological conundrum noted above
is solved in a wholly different manner: the king and his ministers are not David
and his dignitaries, but God and His angels, and Zadok is not Zadok, but Moses'
brother, Aaron. This being the case, I think it is most likely that once the identification of Shemaiah with Moses had gained currency in various circles, it
came to be accepted by various scholars separately from the lengthier original
homily' attributed in *Lev. Rab* to R. Yehoshua' b. R. Neḥemyah. The author of
TC accepted this identification that made its way to him (perhaps in writing
and perhaps by oral transmission, but apparently not directly from *Lev. Rab.*);
incorporated it in his work; and independently solved the chronological problem posed by it.

TC's expansion gives Moses the title ספרא רבא. Churgin (ibid.) located the
source of this title in *b. Soṭah* 13b:

---

208 Churgin *Hagiographa*, p. 257; Le Déaut-Robert, vol. 1, p. 92; McIvor, p. 124.

רב נחמ[יה] אמ[ר]: 'וימת שם משה עבד ה''. סמליון אמ[ר]: מית משה ספרא רבא
דישראל.

R. Nehemiah said, "'So Moses, servant of the Lord, died there' (Deut 34:5)."
Samilion said, "Moses, the great scribe of Israel, died."

Churgin (later followed by Le Déaut-Robert and by McIvor) also cited
Tg. Cant 1:2: בריך שמיה דה' דיהב לן אוריתא על ידוי דמשה ספרא רבא, *blessed be the*
name of the Lord, who gave us the Torah, by way of Moses, the great scribe.

Notwithstanding, the title appears as early as TO and also occurs in later
Targums. There therefore is no reason to prefer the targumic source indicated
above over any of the following:

TO Deut 33:21[209] ארי תמן באחסנתיה משה ספרא רבא דישראל קביר
Clem: for there in his inheritance, Moses the great scribe of Israel, is buried

Tg. Ps 62:12 אוריתא חדא מליל אלהא ותיניתא דנא שמענא מן פם משה ספרא רבא
Cook: God speaks one Torah, and now two times I have heard it, from the
mouth of Moses, the great scribe

Tg. Cant 2:4 אעיל יתי לבית מתיבת מדרשא דסיני למילף אוריתא מפום משה ספרא רבא
Dost: He brought me to the house of the school of study, which is Sinai, to learn
Torah from the mouth of Moses the great scribe

ibid. 3:3 … אתיב משה ספרא רבא דישראל וכין אמר
Dost: Moses the great scribe of Israel responded and said this

3.6 *David's Merit, Solomon's Prayer and the People's Sacrifices (2 Chr 7:10)*
2 Chr 7:10

MT	וּבְיוֹם עֶשְׂרִים וּשְׁלֹשָׁה לַחֹדֶשׁ הַשְּׁבִיעִי שִׁלַּח אֶת־הָעָם לְאָהֳלֵיהֶם
TC	וביום עשרין ותלתא לירחא שביעאה פטר ית עמא למשכניהון ואזלו לקרויהון

MT (cont.)	שְׂמֵחִים וְטוֹבֵי לֵב עַל־ הַטּוֹבָה אֲשֶׁר עָשָׂה ה' לְדָוִד
TC	חדן ושפירי לבא על כל טבתא דעבד ה' לדוד עבדיה
	דאתפתחן תרעי בית־מקדשא מטול זכותיה

---

209 In this verse, Targums paralleling TO (TN, FTP, FTV, TPJ) took a somewhat different line:
משה (נבייא) ס(ו)פריהון דישראל.

(cont.)   וְלִשְׁלֹמֹה

TC   ולשלמה   בריה דקביל ה׳ צלותיה ושרת שכנתא דה׳ בבית־מקדשא

(cont.)   עַמֹּוֹ:   וּלְיִשְׂרָאֵל

TC   דאתקבלן ברעוא קרבניהון   עמיה   ולישראל

וגמרת נכסיהון: ונחתת אשתא מן שמיא ואשתרבבת על מדבחא

NJPS: On the twenty-third day of the seventh month he dismissed the people
to their homes, rejoicing and in good spirits over the goodness that the LORD
had shown to David and Solomon and His people Israel.

Dost: On the twenty-third day of the seventh month, he sent away the people
to their tents, and they went to their cities rejoicing and glad-hearted over all
the good that the Lord had done for David His servant, on account of whose
merit the gates of the temple were opened, and for his son Solomon, whose
prayer the Lord received, (causing) the Shekhinah of the Lord to came to rest
in the temple, and for Israel His people, because their sacrifices were accepted
with favor and (because) the fire descended from the heavens, came down
upon the altar, and consumed their sacrifices.

In the first section of the verse, the targumist hewed close to the Hebrew
Vorlage, albeit with some signs of influence by TJ 1 Kgs 8:66 (see p. 124, above).
On reaching the end of the verse, the targumist began writing more expansively, providing additional detail for each of the entities listed: David, Solomon,
and the nation of Israel. The structure of the expansion is such that a description and an explanatory clause are attached to each of the three items:

> *for David His servant*—on account of whose merit the gates of the temple
>   were opened
> *and for his son Solomon*—whose prayer the Lord received, (causing) the
>   Shekhinah of the Lord to came to rest in the temple
> *and for Israel His people*—because their sacrifices were accepted with
>   favor and (because) the fire descended from the heavens, and con-
>   sumed their sacrifices.

David: The title given to David, עבדיה, *His servant*, reflects the influence of the
parallel verse, 1 Kgs 8:66, in addition to many other similar instances in the
Bible, rabbinic literature and Jewish liturgy. David's appearance at the beginning of the series in the Hebrew verse does not go without saying, as Solomon
and the people of Israel were present at the dedication of the Temple, but
David was not. Thus the question arises: what is the good thing described
by this verse that God did for David and is relevant to this occasion, which

postdates David's death? TC answered this question by invoking an aggadic tradition that appears in many rabbinic sources,[210] among them *b. Moʿed Qaṭ.* 9a, whose point of departure is 1 Kgs 8:66, the parallel to the present verse:

'ביום השמיני שלח את העם ויברכו את המלך וילכו לאהליהם שמחים וטובי לב על
כה הטובה אשר עשה ה' לדוד עבדו ולישראל עמו' ... בשלמא 'ישראל עמו'—לחיי,
אלא 'דויד עבדו' מאי היא? אמ[ר] רב יהודה אמ[ר] רב: בשעה שביקש שלמה
להכניס ארון לבית קדש הקדשים, דבקו שערי היכל זה בזה. אמר עשרים וארבע
רננות ולא נענה. הדר אמר 'שאו שערים ראשיכם והנשאו פתחי עולם' וכו', 'ה' גבור
מלחמה' ולא נענה. הדר אמ[ר] 'שאו שערים ראשיכם ושאו פתחי עולם' וכ', 'מי הוא
זה מלך הכבוד' וכו', ולא נענה. כיון שאמר 'ה' אלהים אל תשב פני משיחיך זכרה
לחסדי דויד עבדיך'—מיד נענה.

"'On the eighth day he sent the people home and they blessed the king and went to their own tents joyful and glad of heart for all the goodness that the Lord had shown to David his servant and to Israel his people' (1 Kgs 8:66)—*Now there is no problem understanding the reference to Israel, his people, since the sin of violating the Day of Atonement was forgiven them. But what is the meaning of the reference to David his servant?* Said R. Judah said Rab, "When Solomon had built the house of the sanctuary, he tried to bring the ark into the house of the Holy of Holies. The gates cleaved to one another. He recited twenty-four prayers, but was not answered. "He said, 'Lift up your head, O you gates, and be lifted up, you everlasting doors, and the King of glory shall come in. Who is this King of glory? The Lord strong and might, the Lord mighty in battle' (Ps 24:7ff.). "And it is further said, 'Lift up your heads, O you gates even lift them up, you everlasting doors. (Ps 24:7). "But he was not answered. "When he said, 'Lord God, turn not away the face of your anointed, remember the mercies of David, your servant' (2 Chr 6:42), forthwith he was answered.

Although David died longed before the dedication of the Temple, his presence is felt because the gates of the sanctuary opened only in his merit.[211] There is

---

210 The tradition appears in BT in three places: *Moʿed Qaṭ.* 9a; *Šabb.* 30a; *Sanh.* 107b. For a list of additional sources, see Ginzberg, vol. 6, p. 296, n. 65. The list contains an erroneous reference to *Tg. Ps* 76:17, which should instead refer to Ps 86:17. Churgin *Hagiographa*, p. 258, cites *b. Šabb.* 31a, which also is in error; the correct location of the parallel is *b. Šabb.* 30a.

211 The verse where the aggadists found an allusion to Solomon's request that the gates open in David's merit is 2 Chr 6:42: הֵ֣ אֱלֹהִ֗ים אַל־תָּשֵׁב֮ פְּנֵ֪י מְשִׁיחֶ֫ךָ זָכְרָ֖ה לְחַֽסְדֵ֥י דָּוִ֖יד עַבְדֶּֽךָ, O *LORD God, do not reject Your anointed one; remember the loyalty of Your servant David.* The Targum to the parallel verse Ps 132:10 refers to the same rabbinic legend: מטול זכותיה דדוד

nothing in the text of this tradition as it appears in the Targum to indicate what rabbinic source the targumist employed.

Solomon and Israel: The title assigned Solomon, בריה, *his son*, is not a reflection of another text, but a means used by the targumist to impose on this element of the verse stylistic consistency with the titles associated with David (under the influence of 1 Kgs 8:66) and Israel (which is explicit in the Hebrew verse here). The targumist's choice of this particular title is in keeping with the style of Chronicles, in which the phrase שלמה בנו appears nine times.[212] The two expansions concerned with the good that God did for Solomon and for His people, Israel, were formulated not under the influence of any particular aggadic tradition, but to be in keeping with the text of the beginning of the chapter and the translations given by TC there. Solomon requests twice in his prayer of 2 Chronicles 6 that God accept his prayer (קב״ל צלותא), and on five occasions asks God to accept the prayers of the entire nation of Israel.[213] The fire that descended from the heavens at the conclusion of his prayer thus is logically understood to have done so in answer to his prayer, as described at that point, 2 Chr 7:1–3:

וכד פסק שלמה מלצלאה ואשתא נחתת ואשתרבבת מן שמיא עלוי מדבחא וגמרת
עלתא ונכסת קודשיא ואיקר שכנתא דה׳ אתמלי ית ביתא: ולא יכילו כהניא למיעל
לבית מקדשא דה׳ ארום אתמלי איקר שכנתא דה׳ ית בית מקדשא דה׳: וכל בני
ישראל חמיין כד נחתת ואשתרבבת אשתא על ביתא ואיקר שכנתא דה׳ שרא על
ביתא וגחנו על אפיהון על ארעא על רובדא וסגדן ומודן קדם ה׳ ארום טב לעלם
טוביה:

Dost: When Solomon finished praying, fire descended and came down from the heavens upon the altar, and it consumed the burnt offering and holy sacrifices, and the glory of the Shekhinah of the Lord filled the temple: The priests were not able to enter the temple of the Lord because the

---

עבדך במיעל ארונא במצע תרעיה לא תתיב אפי שלמה משיחך, *because of the merit of David your servant; when the ark comes through the middle of the gates, do not turn back the face of Solomon your anointed.* Another reference to the tradition appears in *Tg. Ps* 86:17: עביד עימי את לטבא בזמן דיעיל שלמה ברי ית ארונא לבית מוקדשא יתפתחון תרעיא אמטולתי ויחמון סנאי ארום שבקתא לי ויבהתון ויודון ארום את ה׳ סייעתני ונחמתני, *perform for me a miracle for good; when my son Solomon shall bring the ark into the sanctuary, let the gates be opened on my account and my enemies will see that you have forgiven me, and they will be ashamed and confess; for you are the LORD, you have helped me and comforted me.*

212   1 Chr 22:6, 7 (thus *ketiv*, reflected by TC), 17; 23:1; 28:11, 20; 29:28; 2 Chr 33:7; 35:4.

213   קב״ל צלותא of Solomon: 2 Chr 6:19–20; קב״ל צלותא of Israel in Solomon's prayer: 2 Chr 6:21, 26, 35, 39–40.

glory of the Shekhinah of the Lord filled the temple of the Lord: All of the children of Israel were watching when the fire descended and came down upon the temple, and the glory of the Lord rested over the temple. And they bowed down on their faces upon the ground on the pavement, and they worshiped and gave thanks before the Lord because (He is) good, for His goodness is forever.

The expansion inserted by the targumist regarding the people of Israel also is borrowed from this unit in general, and verse 1 in particular.

דאתקבלן ברעוא קרבניהון ונחתת אשתא מן שמיא ואשתרבבת על מדבחא וגמרת
נכסיהון

Dost: because their sacrifices were accepted with favor and (because) the fire descended from the heavens, came down upon the altar, and consumed their sacrifices

In sum, due to the inclusion of the nonliteral continuum regarding David, the targumist felt that it was necessary to add verbiage about Solomon and Israel, and drew inspiration for these insertions from the beginning of the chapter, thus concluding the chapter as he had begun it.

3.7 *Zechariah's Outrage in the Temple on the Day of Atonement (2 Chr 24:20)*

2 Chr 24:20

MT אֱלֹהִים לָבְשָׁה אֶת־זְכַרְיָה בֶּן־יְהוֹיָדָע הַכֹּהֵן וַיַּעֲמֹד מֵעַל לָעָם וְרוּחַ

TC חמא ית כד סורחנות מלכא ועמא דמסקין קטרת לפסלא בבית־מקדשא דה׳ על מדבחא ביומא דכפוריא ומבטלין כהניא דה׳ מלמעבד עלוותא ונכסתא וקרבן יומא ומוספייה
הי־כמה דכתיב בספר אוריתא דמשה וקם מעל לעמא
ורוח נבואה מן־קדם ה׳ שרת על זכריה בר יהוידע כהנא

MT (cont.) וַיֹּאמֶר לָהֶם כֹּה | אָמַר הָאֱלֹהִים לָמָה אַתֶּם עֹבְרִים אֶת־מִצְוֹת ה׳

TC ואמר להון כדנן אמר ה׳ למא אתון עברין ית פקודיא דה׳

(cont.) וְלֹא תַצְלִיחוּ כִּי־עֲזַבְתֶּם אֶת־ ה׳ וַיַּעֲזֹב אֶתְכֶם:

TC ולא תצלחון ארום שבקתון ית פולחנא דה׳ וישבוק יתכון:

NJPS: Then the spirit of God enveloped Zechariah son of Jehoiada the priest; he stood above the people and said to them, "Thus God said: Why do you transgress the commandments of the LORD when you cannot succeed? Since you have forsaken the LORD, He has forsaken you."

Dost: Now the spirit of prophecy from before the Lord came to dwell upon
Zechariah son of Jehoiada the priest when he saw the sinfulness of the king
and the people, who were offering up incense to the image in the temple of
the Lord upon the altar on the day of atonement. And [they prevented] the
priests of the Lord [from] carrying out burnt offerings, sacrifices, the daily offering, and the additional commands, as is written in the scroll of the Torah
of Moses. So he stood above the people and said to them, "Thus says the Lord,
'Why are you transgressing the commandments of the Lord? You will not succeed. Because you have forsaken the worship of the Lord, He will forsake you.'"

TC gives a highly detailed expansion describing the death of Zechariah, only
some elements of which appear in parallel rabbinic sources. Churgin here
cited *y. Ta'an.* 4:6 (69a, p. 735), as well as parallels in other midrashic sources:[214]

אמ[ר] ר׳ יוחנן: שמונים אלף פירחי כהונה נהרגו על דמו שלזכריה. ר׳ יודן שאל
לר׳ אחא: איכן הרגו את זכריה—בעזרת הנשים או בעזרת ישראל? אמ[ר] לו: לא
בעזרת יש[ראל] ולא בעזרת הנשים, אלא בעזרת הכהנים ... שבע עבירות עברו
ישראל באותו היום: הרגו כהן ונביא ודיין, ושפכו דם נקי וטימאו את העזרה, ושבת
ויום הכיפורים היה ...

> R. Johanan said: Eighty thousand priestly trainees were killed over
> Zechariah's blood.R. Judan asked R. Acha: Where was Zechariah killed—
> in the women's section or in Israel's section? He said to him: Neither in
> Israel's section nor in the women's section, but rather in the priests' sec-
> tion ... Israel committed seven sins that day: they killed a priest, a prophet
> and a judge, they shed innocent blood, they defiled the courtyard, it was
> also on a Sabbath and on the Day of Atonement ...

The significant element shared by this talmudic passage, of course, is the fact
of Zechariah's being killed on the Day of Atonement. Nothing else, however,
evidences any particular link between TY and TC. If this is the extent of the
similarity between the two sources, there is no reason to give preference to
TY over any of the sources not discussed by the various studies of this verse.
B. Sanh. 96b also states that the murder of Zechariah occurred on the Day of
Atonement (which in the telling of BT, like that of TY, was on a Sabbath):[215]

---

214   Churgin *Hagiographa*, p. 260. The citation ibid. is of the *yerushalmi* 4:5, but is intended to
       refer to the source excerpted here. See also Ginzberg, vol. 6, p. 354, n. 14.
215   Note that most textual witnesses of this talmudic excerpt do not contain the mention of
       the Sabbath and Day of Atonement here. The text used here is taken from the Jerusalem,

נביא כהנא הוה לן דהוה מוכח לן לשום שמיא. קבולי לא קבילנא מניה אלא קומנא
עילויה וקטליניה ביום הכיפורים שחל להיות בשבת.

We had a prophet and priest that would reprove us for heaven's sake. We
did not accept [his words], but rather we rose against him and killed him
on the Day of Atonement that fell on a Sabbath day.

There is one word that can serve to establish a link between TC and some of
the sources paralleling TY, although not the tradition in TY as reflected in our
text, and that word is מבטלין. *Lam. Zuṭaʾ* (p. 28) preserves a list of seven sins that
differs slightly from that in TY:

[אמרו: ביום שהרגו את זכריה בן יהוידע] עברו שבע עבירות: הרגו כהן ונביא וחללו
שבת ויום הכפורים ועבדו ע״ז וטמאו את המקדש ובטלו את התמיד.

[They said: On the day they killed Zechariah son of Jehoiada] they committed seven sins: they killed a priest and prophet, they desecrated the
Sabbath and the Day of Atonement, they worshiped idols, they defiled
the Temple, and they did not offer the daily offering.

Perhaps the author of TC was familiar with a similar list that was the basis of
the expansive translation ומבטלין כהניא דה׳ מלמעבד עלוותא ונכסתא וקרבן יומא

Harav Herzog 1 MS, which was also chosen to represent the BT text in the Historical
Dictionary Project by the Academy for Hebrew Language. The parallel to this tradition
in *b. Giṭ.* 57b also does not indicate that the events described occurred on the Day of
Atonement. Another source according to which these events did transpire on the Day of
Atonement is *Tg. Eccl* 2:20 (cited in Le Déaut-Robert, vol. 1, p. 149, n. 6):

אם חזי למקטל כהנא ונבייא בבית מקדשא דה׳ כמא דקטלתון לזכריה בר עדוא כהנא רבא
ונביא מהימן בבית מוקדשא דין ביומא דכפוריא על דאוכח יתכון דלא תעבדון דין דביש
קדם ה׳.

Brady: Is it right to kill priest and prophet in the Temple of the Lord, as when you killed
Zechariah son of Iddo, the High Priest and faithful prophet in the Temple of the Lord on
the Day of Atonement because he told you not to do evil before the Lord?
Tg. Esth II 1:2 (not in all recensions), which refers to the prophet as זכריה בר עדו יהוידע
כהנא רבא, reprises the talmudic tradition with some changes. In the last two sources, the
name of Zechariah's father is different from that given in Scripture (עדוא in BT, עדו יהוידע
in *Tg. Esth II*, which combines the two names together). Another source that alters the
name of Zechariah's father (to Berechiah) is Matt 23:35, which also stresses that he was
killed in the very heart of the Temple:

ὅπως ἔλθῃ ἐφ᾽ ὑμᾶς πᾶν αἷμα δίκαιον ἐκχυννόμενον ἐπὶ τῆς γῆς ἀπὸ τοῦ αἵματος Ἄβελ τοῦ
δικαίου ἕως τοῦ αἵματος Ζαχαρίου υἱοῦ Βαραχίου, ὃν ἐφονεύσατε μεταξὺ τοῦ ναοῦ καὶ τοῦ
θυσιαστηρίου

ומוספייה הי־כמה דכתיב בספר אוריתא דמשה, *and they prevented the priests of the Lord from carrying out burnt offerings, sacrifices, the daily offering, and the additional commands, as is written in the scroll of the Torah of Moses.* TC's detailed list of types of sacrifices does not appear in the various other sources, but it is possible that the targumist, or his source, assumed that if the daily offering had not been offered that day, presumably the other sacrifices due then also had not been offered.

In TC's expansion, the king and the people are portrayed as separate from the priests. The priests wanted to fulfill the commandments associated with the Temple service, but the king and the people did not allow them to do so (ומבטלין כהניא דה׳ מלמעבד), as well as offered incense on the altar to an idol. The language of the expansion reflects Late Jewish Literary Aramaic. The form סורחנו—as opposed to סורחנא, which appears in many Targums—appears in targumic literature here and in verse 18 above, ten times in TPJ, and twice in *Tg. Ps*, and reflects a late stage of the language's development.[216] The word לפסלא is diacriticized in MS V as לְפַסָּלָא, indicating that the diacriticist viewed the term as a *pa'el* infinitive form. This understanding is linguistically and contextually problematic, and we may reasonably prefer the reading לפיסלא, *to an idol*, of MS C, a noun functioning as the indirect object of the incense offering. This noun, also characteristic of Late Jewish Literary Aramaic, appears in TPJ, *Tg. Ps*, and *Tg. Cant*, aside from the present verse.[217]

The list of sacrifices left unoffered reflects the Hebrew עולות וזבחים וקרבן היום והמוספים,[218] a list not known to exist in such a form in another source. Following these words the targumist concludes the sentence with words reflecting the Hebrew ככתוב בספר תורת משה, *as is written in the scroll of the Torah of Moses.* If the targumist wrote these words based on a written source that gave the list and conclusion in Hebrew, then it is one that we presently lack the ability to identify.

3.8   *Survivors of Fire (2 Chr 28:3)*

This passage in TC may possibly be based in part upon *b. Sanh.* 93a. However, it is also based upon a tradition similar to that found in MS Reuchlin. It is, therefore, discussed in full, below, 413–419.

---

216 TPJ Lev 10:17; 16:10, 30; Num 14:19; 15:24–25, 30; Deut 9:13, 21, 27; *Tg. Ps* 49:14; 69:6. A similar phenomenon pertains to the word סואבו (as opposed to the earlier form סואבה), which occurs only in TC, TPJ, and *Tg. Eccl.*

217 TPJ Gen 35:4; Num 11:1; *Tg. Ps* 53:6; 78:58; 97:7; *Tg. Cant* 2:15.

218 The typical translation of קרבן שלמים in targumic literature, including TC, is נכסת קודשא. The same term also serves in most cases as the translation of זבח, though at several points in TC זבח is translated simply as נכסה (1 Chr 29:21 [end of verse]; 2 Chr 29:31).

4   Closing Remarks

In the first part of this chapter we studied thirty-three expansions in Targum Chronicles found to be based on specific passages of BT. This dependence was demonstrated by noting linguistic and literary similarity between TC and the talmudic source. The sources employed are found in sixteen different tractates throughout BT, in all four orders (*Sedarim*) of that Talmud as well as tractates *Berakhot* and *Niddah*. In several of our discussions, by referring to various textual witnesses to BT, we also found it possible to ascertain what version of the talmudic text the targumist had before him. In these cases, TC may be considered a secondary textual witness of the Babylonian Talmud.

In the second part of this chapter we examined eight additional expansions in TC that may also be based on BT, but can be thus attributed only with lesser certainty due to the lack of a linguistic or literary resemblance that would associate them with the Talmud more closely than with other potential sources. Nonetheless, we may reasonably conclude that these expansions, too—or at least some of them—have their source in BT for two reasons. First, the degree of the targumist's reliance on BT in other cases is substantially greater than his reliance on any other rabbinic source. Second, in several cases the most likely talmudic source of the expansions is found in close proximity to a passage identified as the source of another expansion in TC.[219]

---

219   Expansion 2.14 (p. 306) may be dependent on *b. Ber.* 63. Expansion 2.19 (p. 319) was found to be dependent on *b. Ber.* 62.

Expansion 3.4 (p. 371) may be dependent on *b. B. Bat.* 110. *B. B. Bat.* 109 will be identified as a possible influence on expansion 5.10 (p. 482).

Expansion 3.7 (p. 381) may be dependent on *b. Sanh.* 96, and expansion 3.8 (p. 384) partially dependent on *Sanh.* 93. Expansion 2.7 (p. 277) was found to be dependent on *b. Sanh.* 92.

Expansion 3.2 (p. 362) may be dependent on *b. Soṭah* 11b, and expansion 3.5 (p. 375) on *Soṭah* 13b.

CHAPTER 8

Additional Expansions in Targum Chronicles and Their Sources

1 Opening

Having established the key role played by the Babylonian Talmud in the formation of many of Targum Chronicles' aggadic expansions, in this chapter we will examine the remaining expansions in TC—those that do not disclose a direct tie to the Bavli. I will attempt to identify the rest of the targumist's literary sources, where possible, and thereby add to our understanding of his library and environment. As in the previous chapter, the reader is urged to first use the graphic layout of the Hebrew and Aramaic texts as the first step in studying each example, before proceeding to read my ensuing discussion thereof.

2 Expansions Based upon Targum Pseudo-Jonathan

2.1 *Nimrod, Murderer of Innocents (1 Chr 1:10)*

1 Chr 1:10

MT	בָּאָרֶץ: וְכוּשׁ יָלַד אֶת־נִמְרֹד הוּא הֵחֵל לִהְיוֹת גִּבֹּר
TC	וערב אוליד ית נמרוד הוא שרי למהוי גבר בחטאה
	שדי אדם זכאי
	ומרוד קדם ה':

NJPS: Cush begot Nimrod; he was the first mighty one on earth.
Dost: Arabia fathered Nimrod. He became a mighty man in sin. He shed innocent blood and was a rebel before the Lord.

We already noted (pp. 151–153) that the end of this verse in TC evidences a mistranscription of Gen 10:9, instead of 10:8. This explains the lack of an Aramaic equivalent for בָּאָרֶץ, and the presence of ומרוד קדם ה'. It does not explain, however, why TC features the expression שדי אדם זכאי, *shedding innocent blood*.

McIvor believed that the targumist had independently conceived this expression, because neither the expression שופך דם נקי in Hebrew nor שדי אדם זכאי in Aramaic is known with regard to Nimrod outside of TC.[1] Such a proposal is, of course, plausible, but I see no local factor in Chronicles that would

---

1 McIvor, p. 38.

call for the addition of the expression שדי אדם זכאי. Based on this absence I find it reasonable to presume that these words in TC preserve a tradition received by the targumist regarding the personage of Nimrod whose source we have not been able to identify.

2.2 Late Midrashic Homilies on the Names of Joktan's Sons (1 Chr 1:20)

1 Chr 1:20

MT	וְיָקְטָ֣ן יָלַ֗ד אֶת־אַלְמוֹדָ֙ד וְאֶת־שָׁ֔לֶף וְאֶת־חֲצַרְמָ֖וֶת וְאֶת־יָֽרַח׃
TC	ויקטן אוליד ית אלמודד דמשח ופליג ית ארעא באושליא

```
                                   וית שלף     דשלף     ית נהרוותא    לתחומיא
עדי אורחא    כמניא לקטלא    דאתקן אתר    וית חצרמות
                          דאתקן פונדוקין
למיכל ולמשתי    והוה כל דעליל    וית ירח
סמא דקטול    הוה מוכיל ליה
ונסיב כל מה    דהוה בידוי׃
```

NJPS: Joktan begot Almodad, Sheleph, Hazarmaveth, Jerah

Dost: Joktan fathered Almodad, who measured and divided the land with ropes, Sheleph, who diverted the rivers to (their) borders, Hazarmaveth, who set the place of the ambushes for the slaying of those who pass by on the road, Jerah, who established inns—and so it was, to each one who would enter to eat and to drink he would feed lethal poison and would take all that was in his hands

Gen 10:26–29 enumerates thirteen sons of Joktan, who also appear in 1 Chr 1:20–23.[2] The list generally has been identified as one of tribes and places in the Arabian Peninsula, the most famous of which is חֲצַרְמָוֶת, identified as حضرموت of Yemen. The name יקטן itself also has served as a term for Arabia.[3]

The Targum includes a homiletical expansion for each of the sons of Joktan listed in verse 20: אלמודד, who measured and divided up the land with lengths of rope; שלף, who drew the rivers to within bounds; חצרמות, who prepared a place of ambush to slay passersby; ירח, who established inns and, when his guests sought what to eat and drink, poisoned them and took their belongings.

אלמודד and שלף: A tradition similar to that in TC appears in TPJ to the above verse's parallel, Gen 10:26:

---

2   LXX preserves a list of twelve names in both Genesis and Chronicles; see Liver.

3   As indicated in a liturgical poem cited by Lewis, p. 93, probably from the early stages of the Islamic conquest of Palestine: "And a king will go forth from the land of Yoqtan, And his armies will seize the Land, …"

ויקטן אוליד ית אלמודד דמשח ית ארעא באשלוון וית שלף דישלף מוי דנהרוותא וית
חצרמות וית ירח:

Clem TPJ: And Joktan begat Almodad, who measured the earth with cords, and
Sheleph, who drew off the water of the rivers, and Hazarmaveth, and Jerah.

The exegeses in TPJ and TC of the names *Almodad* and *Sheleph* are based on
a single tradition that is not known from any of the other Targums or rabbinic
literature. As for Almodad, though it is known that the ancients used ropes as
a means of measurement (see 2 Sam 8:2, וַיְמַדְּדֵם בַּחֶבֶל, where measurement by
rope separates prisoners of war into two groups), this does not explain either
what need there was for such a homily or the context in which it arose. Why
was land surveying selected as the appropriate basis for a homily on Almodad's
name? Is it only a coincidence that this homily appears nowhere else in targumic literature and is entirely absent from rabbinic literature?

In order to determine the answers to these questions, we must ascertain the
historical setting that is the background to this homily. The Hebrew expression
denoting measurement of land with lengths of rope is known to us from two
Hebrew texts, and the two date to a single historical setting: the Islamic conquests, as described from a thoughtful Jewish perspective.

Pirqe Rabbi Eliezer 29 (pp. 193–194):

ר׳ ישמעאל אומ[ר]: חמשה עשר דברים עתידין בני [ישמעאל] לעשות בארץ באח-
רית הימים, ואלו הן: ימודו הארץ בחבלים, ויעשו בית הקברות למרבץ צאן אשפתות
ומדדו בהן ומהן על ראשי ההרים וירבה השקר ויגנז האמת וירחק חק מישראל
ותרבה עונות בישראל שני תולעת כצמר ויקמל הנייר והקולמוס ויפסל סלע מלכות,
ויבנו ההרים הערים החרבות ויפנו הדרכים ויטעו גנות ופרדסים ויגדרו פרוצות חומות
בית המקדש ויבנו בניין בהיכל ושני אחים יעמדו אליהם נשיאים בגופן ובימיהן יעמד
צמח בן דוד, שנ[אמר] ביומיהון דמלכא אינון.

(translation by G. Friedlander) Rabbi Ishmael said: In the future the children of Ishmael will do fifteen things in the land (of Israel) in the latter days, and they are: They will measure the land with ropes; they will
change a cemetery into a resting-place for sheep (and) a dunghill; they
will measure with them and from them upon the tops of the mountains;
falsehood will multiply and truth will be hidden; the statutes will be removed far from Israel; sins will be multiplied in Israel; worm-crimson will
be in the wool, and he will cover with insects paper and pen; he will hew
down the rock of the kingdom, and they will rebuild the desolated cities

and sweep the ways; and they will plant gardens and parks, and fence in the broken walls of the Temple; and they will build a building in the Holy Place; and two brothers will arise over them,' princes at the end; and in their days the Branch, the Son of David, will arise, as it is said, "And in the days of those kings shall the God of heaven set up a kingdom, which shall never be destroyed"

Nistarot de-R. Shim'on b. Yohai:[4]

ועוד היה רבי שמעון אומר ששמע מרבי ישמעאל: כיון ששמע שמלכות ישמעאל בא
עתידין למוד הארץ בחבלים, שנאמר 'והארץ יחלק במחיר', ועושין בתי קברות מרעה
לצאן ...

(translation by J. Reeves) Moreover R. Šim'on reported that he learned from R. Ishmael at the time when the latter learned that the kingdom of Ishmael was coming that (the kingdom of Ishmael) will measure the land with ropes, as Scripture says: 'and the land will be apportioned for wages' (cf. Dan 11:39; also Joel 4:2). They will make cemeteries pastureland for (grazing) flocks ...

In both sources, one of the elements characterizing the Islamic conquest is the measurement of the land with lengths of rope by its new rulers. The sources do not clarify the purpose of this measurement, but it stands to reason that the procedure was an administrative one executed by the new authorities for purposes of regularizing the administrative borders of newly conquered lands as well as tax collection.[5] In any event, the Jewish sources employing the above expression for measuring the land with lengths of rope see it as characteristic of Arab rule. It transpires, then, that the occurrence of a precise Aramaic equivalent of this Hebrew expression in the two Targums here under discussion, in a list describing the Arabian Peninsula, is unlikely to be a coincidence. In their treatment of this verse, TPJ and TC preserve an echo of historical events that occurred in the era of the Islamic conquests.[6] This is the historical context that lies behind the homily, as well as the reason we find no mention of it in the other Pentateuchal Targums or in rabbinic literature: the homily is

---

4 Jellinek, vol. 3, pp. 78–79.

5 Dinur, p. 52, quotes *Pirqe Rabbi Eliezer*, as well as comments by Mujir al-Din (tenth century): "A time will come when people will measure the land of Nablus for each other with ropes." See additional sources cited in Kedar, pp. 2–4.

6 The ramifications for the dating of these two Targums are clear and will be considered below.

based on an event that happened at a very late date, the mid-seventh century at the very earliest.

The two Targums differ in that TC contains the additional verb ופליג, i.e., *and divided*, in addition to the verb משח. This additional element gives further meaning to the administrative significance of measuring the land with lengths of rope: the act of measurement is followed by precise division of the land. This explanation also permits us to draw another line connecting *Nistarot de-R. Shim'on* to our discussion, as that work found a scriptural basis for the Arabs' action in the quotation והארץ יחלק במחיר, a slight corruption of Dan 11:39: וַאֲדָמָה יְחַלֵּק בִּמְחִיר, *he will distribute land for a price*.

The name *Sheleph* is interpreted by TC as signifying דשלף ית נהרוותא לתחומיא and by TPJ, in slightly different form, דישלף מוי דנהרוותא.[7] The typical Jewish-Aramaic context of the verb של״ף is the unsheathing of a sword or removal of a shoe.[8] Based on these specific usages we may derive the general sense of *to pull*, which informed the understanding of this verse proposed by Le Déaut and Robert and by McIvor.[9] What exactly is indicated by the act of drawing rivers is unclear from the verse itself, but scholars in the past have understood it as referring to artificial alteration of a river's path. In any event, nowhere else have we found the verb של״ף with a river or water as its object, and on this basis I would say that the final word regarding the meaning of this word in TPJ and TC has yet to be said.

Perhaps the homily regarding שלף is to be understood within the context of a historical description of events that occurred in the early days of Islamic rule. In *Nistarot de-R. Shim'on b. Yohai*, in the paragraph following that quoted above with reference to measuring land with lengths of rope, we find (translation by J. Reeves):

> Then another king will arise who will seek to cut off the waters of the Jordan. He will bring far-away peoples from alien lands to excavate and build a canal to bring up the waters of the Jordan to irrigate the land. The excavated portion of the land will collapse upon them and kill them.

What we find recorded in TPJ and TC may correlate with a range of water supply projects, such as that described above, that were initiated following the Islamic conquests and the solidification of Islamic rule in conquered realms.

---

7   On the various opinions regarding the authenticity of the Aramaic form מוי and the history of its development, see Dan, pp. 214–215, and sources cited ibid.

8   Sokoloff *JPA*, p. 640; Sokoloff *JBA*, pp. 1152–1153.

9   Le Déaut-Robert, vol. 1, p. 40; McIvor, p. 40.

חצרמות and ירח: Unlike the two homilies regarding אלמודד and שלף, which
are known to us from TPJ, those concerning חצרמות and ירח are not known to
appear in any other source.[10] The homily in TC for the name חצרמות appar-
ently takes its cue from Ps 10:8: יֵשֵׁב בְּמַאְרַב חֲצֵרִים בַּמִּסְתָּרִים יַהֲרֹג נָקִי עֵינָיו לְחֵלְכָה
יִצְפֹּנוּ, *He lurks in outlying places; from a covert he slays the innocent; his eyes
spy out the hapless.* The source of this exegesis combined חצר, in the sense of
a hidden place or one used for purposes of an ambush (אתר כמניא), with the
death entailed in the slaying of an innocent passerby (לקטלא עדי אורחא).[11]
The homily does not appear in *Tg. Ps* or in any other midrashic treatment of
the verse I am aware of.

The homily on the name ירח describes an innkeeper whose true character is
concealed by his outer appearance. He receives his guests graciously, provides
them with food and drink—but all in the interest of poisoning them and taking their property for himself. The author of the homily seems to have interpreted ירח as from the root אר״ח. The name of the host is ירח; he establishes an
inn so that he will be prepared to welcome any guest in need of lodging for the
night. However, because the context requires a negative portrayal of the personage of ירח, coming as he does on the heels of חצרמות, the outwardly kindly
host becomes a nightmare awaiting whatever unfortunate guest might enter
the doors of the man's business.

Just as the homilies concerning Almodad and Sheleph were related, with
both describing alteration of the status quo by a new political authority, the
treatment of Hazarmaveth has a theme in common with that of Jerah. These
two figures represent the crime and dangers to which wayfarers were exposed.
There is nothing about the midrashic interpretations of the names חצרמות and
ירח that would require us to believe they reflect the reality of any given time
under Islamic rule, but at least in the case of ירח, the interpretation in TC well

---

10   Although an exegesis of Hazarmaveth's name appears in *Gen. Rab.* (see Le Déaut-Robert,
      vol. 1, p. 41, n. 15; McIvor, p. 40, n. 56), it is clear from that homily's content that the inter-
      pretation of the name in TC does not hark back to that tradition. *Gen. Rab.* 37 (p. 350):
      ר׳ חונא אמר: מקום שהיה שמו חצר מות, שהן אוכלין כרישים ולובשים כלי פפיר ומצפים
      למיתה בכל יום. שמואל א[מר]: אפילו כלי פפיר אין להם.
      R. Huna said: It refers to a place called Hazar Maweth, where people eat leeks, wear gar-
      ments of papyrus, and hope daily for death. Samuel said: They did not even have gar-
      ments of papyrus.
11   De Lagarde, whose edition is based on MS E, has עלי ארחא, *on the road*, a reading subse-
      quently adopted by Sperber. I judge as correct the version in MS V, עדי אורחא, *wayfarers*,
      based on other occurrences of the expression עדי אורחא in various Targums in this sense.
      The reading in MS E is simply a copyist's error, possibly produced under the influence of
      Gen 49:17: יְהִי־דָן נָחָשׁ עֲלֵי־דֶרֶךְ שְׁפִיפֹן עֲלֵי־אֹרַח, *Dan shall be a serpent by the road, a viper
      by the path.*

may reflect the establishment of a network of inns—*maḍāfa* and *manzil*—described in Arabic and Islamic literature as a development that commenced during the first generation subsequent to Muhammad's death.[12] If indeed this is the historical background of the homily, then we may assume that the original exegete sought to depict the institution of these inns, established for the benefit of travelers, as something preposterous.

2.3   *Enduring Oppression: the Names of Ishmael's Sons (1 Chr 29–31)*

Gen 25:13–15 and 1 Chr 1:29–31 record the names of Ishmael's twelve sons:[13]
1 Chr 1:29–30

MT	וְתֵימָא:	חֲדַד	מַשָּׂא	וְדוּמָה	30 מִשְׁמָע	וּמִבְשָׂם: וְאַדְבְּאֵל וְקֵדָר נְבָיֹ֔ת
TO	ותימא	חדד	ומשא:	ודומה	ומשמע	ומבשם: ואדבאל וקדר נביות
TN	ותימא	חדד	ומשא:	ודומה	ומשמע	ומבשם: ואדבאל וקדר נביות
TPJ	חריפא ותימא	וסוברא:	ושתוקא	וצאיתא	ומבשם: ואדבאל וערב נבט
TC	חריפא ואדרומא:	ומסוברא	ושתוקא ציתא	ומבשם: ואדבאל וערב נבט

1 Chr 1:31	וָקֵדְמָה	נָפִישׁ	יְטוּר
TO	וקדמה:	נפיש	יטור
TN	וקדמה:	נפיש	יתור
TPJ	וקדמה:	נפיש	יטור
TC	וקדומא	נפיש	יטור

NJPS: Nebaioth; and Kedar, Abdeel, Mibsam, 30 Mishma, Dumah, Massa, Hadad, Tema, 31 Jetur, Naphish, and Kedmah
Clem TPJ: Nebat, and Arabia, and Adbeel, and Mibsam, 14 and Listening, and Silence, and Endurance, 15 Sharp, and Tema, Jetur, Naphish, and Kedemah.
Dost: Nebat, then Arabia, Adbeel, Mibsam, 30 Listening, Silence, Endurance, Haripha, South, 31 Jetur, Naphish, and Kadoma.

TO and TN render all of these names in their Hebrew forms. TPJ and TC, meanwhile, employ three distinct techniques in translating the names. Some are identified with more current names taken from the biblical lexicon (נבט, ערב); others are given in their Hebrew forms (אדבאל, מבשם, יטור, נפיש in both Targums; קדמה, תימא in TPJ); and still others are translated as though they were common nouns (חריפא, סוברא, שתוקא, ציתא in both Targums; אדרומא, קדומא in TC). It is not typical targumic practice to translate proper nouns in such a way,

---

12   For detailed historical background regarding the establishment of these inns and for additional citations, see Elisséeff.

13   The Pentateuchal Targums are excerpted here without MT Genesis because the names are identical in the two scriptural books.

even where the context is a list of nations. Such an unusual translation is clear evidence of an exegete at work.

The similarity of the final group of names as rendered in TPJ and TC (despite the fact that the resemblance does not extend to all of the names) shows that the two have a targumic tradition in common. What, then, is the basis of the homilies attached to these names? A hint may be found in *Midrash Hagadol* to the verse in Genesis:[14]

וּמִשְׁמָע וְדוּמָה וּמַשָּׂא, שֶׁאָנוּ שׁוֹמְעִין חֶרְפָּתֵנוּ וְשׁוֹתְקִין וְנוֹשְׂאִין עוֹל וְדוֹמְמִין. וַעֲלֵיהֶם אָמְרָה תוֹרָה, אוֹי מִי יִחְיֶה מִשֻּׂמוֹ אֵל—אוֹי לְמִי שִׁחְיֶה בְּמַלְכוּת יִשְׁמָעֵאל.

Mishma, Duma and Massa, that we hear our disgrace, remain silent and bear their yoke and keep quiet. Of them the Torah says, "Woe, who can survive except God has willed it!" (Num 24:23)—woe to whom shall live under the rule of Ishmael.

It is self-evident that this homily post-dated the rise of Islam: "their yoke" (עוֹל) in this context is that placed by the Arabs on the necks of the Jews. Maimonides, in his Epistle to the Jews of Yemen, testifies to his familiarity with a similar interpretation:[15]

וְאַתֶּם, אַחֵינוּ, דְּעוּ, שֶׁה' יְרַטְנוּ בְּרֹב עֲווֹנֵינוּ עִם זֹאת הָאֻמָּה, רְצוֹנִי לוֹמַר אֻמַּת יִשְׁמָעֵאל, הַמַּרְבָּה לְצַעֲרֵנוּ, וּלְהוֹצִיא דִּינִים מִדָּתָם לְהָרַע לָנוּ וְלִמְאֹס אוֹתָנוּ ... וַאֲנַחְנוּ עִם הֱיוֹתֵנוּ סוֹבְלִים מֵהַכְנָעָתָם וְשִׁקְרוּתָם וּפְחִיזוּתָם מַה שֶׁאֵין בִּיכֹלֶת הָאָדָם לְסָבְלוֹ, וָשַׁבְנוּ כְּמוֹ שֶׁאָמַר הַנָּבִיא: וַאֲנִי כְחֵרֵשׁ לֹא אֶשְׁמָע וּכְאִלֵּם לֹא יִפְתַּח-פִּיו, וּכְמוֹ שֶׁיִסְּרוּנוּ הַחֲכָמִים ז"ל שֶׁנִּסְבֹּל שִׁקְרֵי הַיִּשְׁמָעֵאלִים וּכְזָבָם, וְנִשְׁמַע וְנִדֹּם, וְשָׂמוּ הֶעֱרַתְם עַל זֶה מִשְּׁמוֹת בָּנָיו: וּמִשְׁמָע וְדוּמָה וּמַשָּׂא—שְׁמַע וְדֹם וְשָׂא, וּכְבָר הֻרְגַּלְנוּ עַצְמֵנוּ, לִסְבֹּל הַכְנָעָתָם, כְּמוֹ שֶׁצִּוָּה יְשַׁעְיָהוּ וְאָמַר: גֵּוִי נָתַתִּי לְמַכִּים וּלְחָיַי לְמֹרְטִים פָּנַי לֹא הִסְתַּרְתִּי מִכְּלִמּוֹת וָרֹק ...

(translated by B. Cohen) Remember, my co-religionists, that on account of the vast number of our sins, God has hurled us in the midst of this people, the Arabs, who have persecuted us severely, and passed baneful and discriminatory legislation against us ... Although we were dishonored by

---

14 *Midrash Hagadol*, Gen 25:14 (vol. 1, p. 424). See Cashdan, pp. 38–39, who discusses the homiletical treatments of names in TPJ to the present verse and cited this homily and the Epistle to the Jews of Yemen. See also *Pirqe Rabbi Eliezer* 29 (p. 193): אוי מי יחיה בימיו, שנ' אוי מי יחיה משומו אל.

15 Translated to Hebrew by Shailat, p. 161.

them beyond human endurance, and had to put up with their fabrications, yet we behaved like him who is depicted by the inspired writer, "But I am as a deaf man, I hear not, and I am as a dumb man that openeth not his mouth." (Psalms 38:14). Similarly our sages instructed us to bear the prevarications and preposterousness of Ishmael in silence. They found a cryptic allusion for this attitude in the names of his sons "Mishma, Dumah, and Massa" (Gen 25:14), which was interpreted to mean, "Listen, be silent, and endure.". We have acquiesced, both old and young, to inure ourselves to humiliation, as Isaiah instructed us: "I offered my back to the floggers, And my cheeks to those who tore out my hair. I did not hide my face From insult and spittle." (50:6) ...

Maimonides, writing in the twelfth century, attributes this exegesis to "the Sages, of blessed memory," but does not specify who these sages might be. We have no way of identifying the source, but we can determine from the content of the tradition that it postdates the Muslim conquest—and it thus becomes apparent that TPJ to this verse contains a homily that cannot have been formulated before the mid-seventh century. The homily's appearance in TC attests to an affinity between the two Targums and points to a direct line of tradition leading from one to the other.

The comments of both Maimonides and *Midrash Hagadol* targeted the three names משמע, דומה, and משא. Yet TPJ and TC also expound the following name, חֲדַד, associating it with חד"ד in that root's sense of *sharp* or *biting* (חריפא). Had the original exegesis included this name, I believe, it would not have been omitted from the tradition recorded by Maimonides and *Midrash Hagadol*. Further, it is noteworthy that the treatment of the fourth name bears no natural connection to that of the three preceding it, all of which were intended to encourage the Jews of Islamic lands to comport themselves humbly in dealings with members of the dominant religion. For both reasons, it seems to me that the literal rendering of חֲדַד postdates the organic homilies on the three preceding names. Perhaps, after seeing a series of three names not transcribed verbatim from the Hebrew, but interpreted according to their respective roots, the author of TC followed suit and tried his hand at חֲדַד, as well.[16]

Despite the great similarity between TC and TPJ, which cannot be coincidental, we should note that TC differs from TPJ in expounding the name תֵּימָא, which in TPJ as we know it is transcribed as in the Hebrew. The homily given תֵּימָא in TC diverges from those associated with משמע, דומה, and משא in that

---

16   See also Kasher *Torah Shelemah*, Gen 25:14 (vol. 4, p. 1002), n. 51, who cites later interpretations cited by the Tosafists and others.

the word אדרומא ("the south") does not parallel the preceding behavioral descriptions (שתוקא, צייתא, etc.). Might the *taw* in תימא have been misconstrued as a *dalet* and *reish* and the word corrupted to דרומא, and that word then further corrupted to אדרומא? Most probably not, I think, because there is a relationship between the meaning of תֵּימָא and that of אדרומא. The translation אדרומא is used both for the word תֵּימָא and for תימן,[17] and, significantly, we find another of the four cardinal directions in the next verse of TC: קֵדְמָה of verse 31 is translated in TC as קדומא ("east"), as opposed to the transcription קדמה given in all of the Targums of the Torah. It may be that just as a targumist or copyist who had inherited the midrashic homilies involving the names משמע, דומה, and משא allowed himself to get caught up and render חֲדַד accordingly, TC (or else another copyist) tried his hand at two names that to him appeared to fit naturally with each other: the two cardinal directions אדרומא and קדומא. In any event, the original exegesis forming the core of the verse in TC is of relatively quite late provenance. Even if we do not assume the existence of a variety of targumic strata in these verses, it is clear that TC here is based on a source that itself postdated the rise of Islam.

2.4 *Balaam Was Laban and Was Killed by Phineas (1 Chr 1:43–44)*

1 Chr 1:43–44

MT	וְאֵלֶּה הַמְּלָכִים אֲשֶׁר מָלְכוּ בְּאֶרֶץ אֱדוֹם לִפְנֵי מְלָךְ־מֶלֶךְ לִבְנֵי יִשְׂרָאֵל
TC	ואלין מלכיא די מלכו בארעא דאדום קדם־עד־לא מלך מלכא לבני ישראל

MT (cont.)	בֶּלַע בֶּן־בְּעוֹר
TC	בלעם בר בעור רשיעא הוא לבן ארמאה דאתחבר עם בנוי דעשו
	מטול למחבלא ית יעקב וית בנוי ובעא להובדא יתהון ומלך על אדום ...

44 וַיָּמָת בֶּלַע וַיִּמְלֹךְ תַּחְתָּיו יוֹבָב בֶּן־זֶרַח מִבָּצְרָה: MT (cont.)

TC ומית בלע דקטליה פינחס במדברא ומליך תחותוי יובב בר זרח דמן בוטרא:

NJPS: These are the kings who reigned in the land of Edom before any king reigned over the Israelites: Bela son of Beor, and the name of his city was Dinhabah. 44 When Bela died, Jobab son of Zerah from Bozrah succeeded him as king.

Dost: These are the kings who reigned in the land of Edom before a king reigned over the children of Israel: The wicked Balaam son of Beor, who is Laban the Aramean who allied himself with the children of Esau in order to destroy Jacob

---

17 Treatment of תימא and תימן as similar words may be linguistically explicable by the phenomenon of nasalization familiar to us from words used in rabbinic parlance such as כאן, להלן, למטן, למעלן. See Kutscher, p. 55.

and his sons. He sought to annihilate them, and he reigned over Edom ... 44
And Bela, whom Phineas killed in the wilderness, died, and in his stead reigned
Jobab son of Zerah, who was from Botra.

The Targum identifies Bela with Balaam, and Balaam with Laban, and further
adds that Phineas killed Bela/Balaam in the wilderness. Statements of this sort
are scattered throughout generations of aggadic literature, but we find them
concentrated in one source easily accessible to TC, viz., TPJ.[18]

The identification of Bela with Balaam appears in TPJ ad loc., Gen 36:32: ומלך
באדום בלעם בר בעור. Balaam is identified with Laban twice in TPJ (Num 22:5;
31:8), and in the latter of these two sources TPJ gives a highly detailed description of how Phineas killed Balaam:

וית בלעם בר בעור קטלו בסייפא והוה כיון דחמא בלעם חייבא ית פנחס כהנא רדיף
מן־בתרוי עבד מילתא דקוסמין ופרח באויר שמיא מן־יד אדכר פנחס שמא רבא וקדי
שא ופרח בתרוי ואחדיה ברישיה ואחתיה שלף סייפא ובעא למקטליה פתח פומיה
במילי תחנונין ואמר לפנחס אין תקיים ית נפשי משתבענא לך דכל יומין דאנא קיים
לית אנא מלטיט ית עמך עני ואמר ליה הלא הלא אנת הוא לבן ארמאה דבעית למשיציא
ית יעקב אבונן ונחתתא למצרים בגין למובדא זרעיה ומן־בתר דנפקו ממצרים גריתא
בהון עמלק רשיעא וכדון איתגרתא איתגרא למילוט יתהון וכיוון דחמיתא דלא אהנין
עובדך ולא קביל מימרא דיי מינך אמליכת מילכא בישא ית בלק למוקמא ית בנתיה
בפרשת אורחתיה למטעיא יתהון ונפלו בגין כן מנהון עשרין וארבעא אלפין בגין כן
לית אפשר תוב למקיימא ית נפשך ומן־יד שלף סייפיה מן תיקה וקטליה

Clem: and they killed Balaam son of Beor by the sword. And it came about
when Balaam the sinner saw Phinehas the priest pursuing after him,
he used a magic word and flew in the air of the heavens. Immediately
Phinehas recited the great and holy name, and he flew after him and
caught him by his head and took him down. He drew the sword and was
about to slay him. He opened his mouth with words of supplication and
said to Phinehas, "If you preserve my life, I swear to you that I will not
curse your people all the days that I live." He answered and said to him,
"Indeed, you are Laban the Aramean who sought to destroy Jacob our
father. And you descended to Egypt to destroy his progeny, and after they

---

18   For numerous aggadic sources identifying Balaam with Laban, see Ginzberg, vol. 5, p. 303;
      vol. 6, pp. 123, 126, 128, 144. See also the short discussion by Churgin *Hagiographa*, p. 247.
      B. Sanh. 105a identifies Balaam as Laban; at 106b it is stated that Phineas killed Balaam. TC
      here may have been influenced by BT, but the latter contains no identification of Bela as
      Balaam. We also know that TPJ was an important literary source of TC. It thus is reason-
      able to identify it as TC's source concerning Balaam, as well.

came out of Egypt, you incited Amalek the wicked against them. And now you were indeed hired to curse them, but when you saw that your actions had no effect and that the Memra of the Lord did not hearken to you, you gave wicked counsel to Balak to set up his daughters at his crossroads to lead them astray, so that twenty four thousand of them fell. Therefore, it is not possible to preserve your life again." So immediately he drew his sword from its sheath and slew him.

TC does not give the entire lengthy account found in TPJ because this is not the place for it, but the later targumist does take advantage of the verse's reference to the death of Bela/Balaam as an opportunity to offer additional information known to him about Balaam's death, viz., that he was killed by Phineas in the wilderness.[19]

2.5 *Liberating a Slave for the Purpose of Marriage (1 Chr 2:34–35)*
1 Chr 2:34

MT וְלֹא־הָיָה לְשֵׁשָׁן בָּנִים כִּי אִם־בָּנוֹת וּלְשֵׁשָׁן עֶבֶד מִצְרִי וּשְׁמוֹ יַרְחָע:

TC ולא הוון לששן בנין אלא הן בנתא ולששן עבדא מצראה ושמיה ירחע:

NJPS: Sheshan had no sons, only daughters; Sheshan had an Egyptian slave, whose name was Jarha.

Dost: Now there were no sons to Sheshan, only daughters. But Sheshan had an Egyptian servant, and his name was Jarha.

1 Chr 2:35

MT וַיִּתֵּן שֵׁשָׁן אֶת־בִּתּוֹ לְיַרְחָע עַבְדּוֹ לְאִשָּׁה וַתֵּלֶד לוֹ אֶת־עַתָּי:

TC ושחרר יתיה ויהב ששן ית ברתיה לירחע עבדיה לאתו וילידת ליה ית עתי:

NJPS: So Sheshan gave his daughter in marriage to Jarha his slave; and she bore him Attai.

Dost: He freed him, and Sheshan gave his daughter to his servant Jarha for his wife, and she bore to him Attai.

TC found it necessary to specify that Sheshan liberated Jarha from slavery before giving him his daughter as a wife. Various commentators unfamiliar with TC similarly explained that Jarha was liberated prior to his marriage with

---

19   Another source that attributes the slaying of Balaam to Phineas is *b. Sanh.* 106b:

לדידי חזאי לי פינקסיה דבלעם והוה כתי[ב] ביה בר תלתין ותלת שנין הוה בלעם חגירא כד
קטל יתיה פנחס לסטאה.

I saw the notebook of Balaam, in which it is written, "Balaam, the lame, was thirty-three years old when Phineas, the brigand, killed him."

Sheshan's daughter. The commentary attributed to a student of Saadyah Ga'on
(ad loc.) explains:[20]

מכאן אמרו חכמים: בתך בגרה, שחרר עבדך ותנה לו. ירחע—הוא עצמו אחרי
למפרע, אלפין ועיינין מתחלפות כמו יאר יער ...

Based on this our sages said [b. Pes. 113a; Lev Rab. 21:8 (vol. 2, p. 487)]: If your
daughter is of age (and has not found a groom), release your slave and give her
to him. Jarha—spelled backwards is אחרי free) because alephs and ayins interchange, as in the words יאר and יער.

Qimḥi (ad loc.) comments:

ולשׁשן עבד מצרי ושׁמו ירחע—שגדל עמו והיה בן ביתו כמו אליעזר עבד אברהם,
ונתן לו את בתו אחר שׁשחררו. ודרך דרשׁ, כי מן השם למדו שעשאו בן חורין, כי
'ירחע'—'עבד חרי': העי"ן—'עבד', ו'ירח'—'חרי' בהפך. מכאן אמרו (שם): בתך
בגרה, שחרר עבדך ותנה לו.

Sheshan had an Egyptian slave, whose name was Jarha—that grew up
with him and was a house steward like Eliezer slave of Abraham, and
gave him his daughter upon releasing him. By method of derash, they derived from the name that he made him a free man, for ירחע—slave freed:
the Ayin for slave, and ירח is חרי backwards. From here they said: If your
daughter is of age (and has not found a groom), release your slave and
give her to him.

Pseudo-Rashi (ad loc.) also takes this approach:[21]

מכאן אמרו (שם): בתך בגרה, שחרר עבדך ותנהו לה.

From here they said: If your daughter is of age (and has not found a
groom), release your slave and give him to her.

The commentary attributed to a student of Saadyah and Qimḥi offer explanations of Jarha's name (though these differ from each other) and, along with
Pseudo-Rashi, base the quoted rabbinic advice on this verse. Berger justifiably
wondered at the commentators' interpretations, observing that no direct link

---

20   Commentary attributed to a student of Saadyah, p. 13.
21   Viezel Pseudo-Rashi, p. 27, n. 22, noted that later in his treatment of the present verse,
      Pseudo-Rashi cites an incorrect tractate of TY.

is found in rabbinic literature between the verse in question and the maxim on liberating a slave for one's daughter.[22] Whether the commentators found such an indication in the Talmud or independently assumed a link to 1 Chr 2:35, we have at our disposal no talmudic source that better fits the addition in TC. Le Déaut and Robert, as well as McIvor, therefore opined that the addition in TC concerning Jarha's liberation is based on *b. Pesaḥim*.[23] The three exegetes cited above state so similarly (מכאן אמרו) that the present verse is the source of the tradition in *b. Pesaḥim* that it is difficult to believe that each of them could have conceived of the idea autonomously. Nevertheless, the problem described by Berger remains.

Against this backdrop, we will be well-served by extending our attention to another verse as translated by TPJ. The root שחר״ר, typical in JBA, is quite rare in targumic literature.[24] Aside from its sole appearance in TC in this verse, it appears only in TPJ, where it occurs in only four places,[25] two of which describe a situation very similar to that in the present verse:

Gen 30:4

MT וַתִּתֶּן־לֹו אֶת־בִּלְהָה שִׁפְחָתָהּ לְאִשֶּׁה וַיָּבֹא אֵלֶיהָ יַעֲקֹב:

TPJ ושחררת ליה ית בלהה אמתה ומסרה ליה לאינתו ועל לוותה יעקב:

NJPS: So she gave him her maid Bilhah as concubine, and Jacob cohabited with her.

Clem: So she freed for him Bilhah her handmaid and handed her over to him for a wife, and Jacob went in to her.

Gen 30:9

MT וַתֵּרֶא לֵאָה כִּי עָמְדָה מִלֶּדֶת וַתִּקַּח אֶת־זִלְפָּה שִׁפְחָתָהּ וַתִּתֵּן אֹתָהּ לְיַעֲקֹב לְאִשֶּׁה:

TPJ וחמת לאה ארום קמת מלמילד ושחררת ית זלפה אמתא ויהבת יתה ליעקב לאינתו:

NJPS: When Leah saw that she had stopped bearing, she took her maid Zilpah and gave her to Jacob as concubine.

Clem: When Leah saw that she had stopped giving birth, she freed Zilpah her handmaid and gave her to Jacob in marriage.

In both verses, TPJ uses the verb שחר״ר as the formal equivalent of a verb for which it is not appropriate on the literal level. In verse 4 it corresponds to וַתִּתֶּן,

---

22 Berger, p. 48.

23 Le Déaut-Robert, vol. 1, p. 45, n. 15; McIvor, p. 51, n. 33. Rosenberg-Kohler, p. 144, also identified a halakhic motive for the addition in TC, but cited no source in rabbinic literature.

24 Levy, pp. 470–471; Sokoloff *JBA*, p. 1129.

25 The noun שחרור appears in TPJ once in Lev 19:29. The verb שחר״ר appears thrice: Gen 30: 4, 9; Exod 21:7.

whose literal translation, וּמְסָרָה, appears later in the verse. In verse 9 it substitutes for וַתִּקַּח, which serves as a prefatory verb to וַתִּתֵּן, found later in the verse. In both verses, the targumist sought to precede the giving of a maid to Jacob as a wife with the act of her liberation from her inferior legal standing. TPJ does the same with the giving of Hagar to Abraham in Gen 16:2, 3, 5, although there the verb used is חר״ר.[26]

We saw earlier, in chapter five, just how familiar the author of TC was with TPJ. Now let us compare TPJ Gen 30:9–10 to the present verse:

TPJ Gen 30:9: לאינתו   ליעקב   יתה   ושחררת ית זלפה אמתא ויהבת
TC 1 Chr 2:35   ויהב   ששן ית ברתיה לירחע עבדיה לאתו   ושחרר יתיה
Clem: she freed Zilpah her handmaid and gave her to Jacob in marriage.
Dost: He freed him, and Sheshan gave his daughter to his servant Jarha for his wife

TPJ Gen 30:10   וילידת זלפה אמתה דלאה ליעקב בר:
TC 1 Chr 2:35   וילידת   ליה   ית עתי:
Clem: Then Zilpah, the handmaid of Leah, bore to Jacob a son.
Dost: and she bore to him Attai.

Both books use similar sentence structure. The two Targums also have in common a willingness to continue referring to the liberated slave or maid according to his or her previous status. It may be, of course, that TC was aware of the Rabbis' advice to free a slave for the benefit of a grown daughter, but it does not seem to me that this was the direct source of TC's expansion. On reaching 1 Chr 2:34–35, the targumist determined that he had before him a parallel to Jacob's marriage to Zilpah (though the translation also is informed by Abraham's marriage to Hagar and Jacob's to Bilhah) and followed the lead of TPJ. It seems that TC's expansion concerning the liberation of Jarha prior to his marriage came about as a direct result of the above verses in TPJ. This is not to say that TC adopted the jurisprudential view that a slave may not marry a free woman based on these verses of TPJ, but only that the manner in which the act of the slave's liberation is integrated within the scriptural verse is based on TPJ Genesis.

---

26   Maher, p. 62, notes that it would have been unseemly for Abraham to have children from a maidservant.

3 Expansions Linked to Targum Toseftot in MS Reuchlin

3.1 *The Spirit of Naboth and the Price of Falsehood* (2 Chr 18:20–21)[27]

2 Chr 18:20

MT ‏וַיֵּצֵא הָרוּחַ וַיַּעֲמֹד לִפְנֵי ה' וַיֹּאמֶר אֲנִי אֲפַתֶּנּוּ וַיֹּאמֶר ה' אֵלָיו בַּמֶּה:‏

TC ‏דנבות דמן יזרעאל ממחיצת צדיקיא‏ ‏ונפק רוחא‏

‏וקם קדם ה' ואמר אנא אטעניה ואמר ה' ליה במה:‏

NJPS: until a certain spirit came forward and stood before the LORD and said, 'I will entice him.' 'How?' said the LORD to him.

Dost: Then the spirit of Naboth, who was from Jezreel, departed from the precincts of the righteous and stood before the Lord and said, 'I will lead him astray.' Then the Lord said to him, 'How?'

2 Chr 18:21

MT ‏וַיֹּאמֶר אֵצֵא וְהָיִיתִי לְרוּחַ שֶׁקֶר בְּפִי כָּל־נְבִיאָיו‏

TC ‏ואמר אפוק ואיהי לרוח שקר נבואת בפומהן דכלהון נביוהי‏

MT (cont.) ‏וַיֹּאמֶר תְּפַתֶּה וְגַם־ תּוּכָל צֵא וַעֲשֵׂה־כֵן:‏

TC ‏ואמר תטעי ואוף אית לך יוכלא למטעי יתהון ברם לית לך רשו‏

‏למתב ביני צדיקיא מטול דכל מן דממליל שקר לית איפשר ליה‏

‏דיהוי מדוריה ביני צדיקיא מבכין‏ ‏פוק מן לותי ועביד כן:‏

NJPS: And he replied, 'I will go forth and become a lying spirit in the mouth of all his prophets.' Then He said, 'You will entice with success. Go forth and do it.'

Dost: Then he said, 'I will go forth and will become a spirit of false prophecy in the mouth of all of his prophets.' Then He said, 'You may lead him astray, and you also have permission to lead them astray, but you do not have authority to return to dwell among the righteous, for everyone who speaks a lie may not have his dwelling among the righteous anymore. Go out from Me and do so.'

Both the identification of the anonymous spirit as that of Naboth and the spirit's expulsion from the abode of the righteous for falsehood are familiar from an aggadic tradition recorded in *b. Sanh.* 102b:[28]

---

27 This expansion is also based upon the BT and is, therefore, mentioned above, p. 340. However, its discussion appears only here.

28 The tradition also appears in two other places in BT: *Šabb.* 149b; *Sanh.* 89a. See Rosenberg-Kohler, p. 149; Churgin *Hagiographa*, p. 259; Le Déaut-Robert, vol. 1, p. 137; McIvor, p. 186.

'ויצא הרוח ... ויאמר אצא והייתי רוח שקר ... ויאמ[ר] תפתה וגם תוכל צא ועשה
כן'. מאי 'רוח'? א"ר יוחנן: זו רוחו שלנבות היזרעאלי. מאי 'צא'? אמ[ר] רב: אמ[ר]
לו הקב"ה, צא ממחיצתי, דכתי[ב] 'דבר שקרים לא יכון לנגד עיני'.

"And there came forth the spirit ... and said, I will persuade him ... And
he said, You shall persuade him and also prevail. Go forth and do so"
(1 Kgs 22:21–23): *What spirit was it?* Said R. Yohanan, "It was the spirit of
Naboth the Jezreelite." *What is meant by "go forth"?* Said Rabina, "Go forth
from my precincts, as it is written, 'He who lies will not tarry in my sight'
(Ps 101:7)."

Churgin further cites a TT that gives a similar but differently phrased
interpretation:[29]

ואעפ"כ אכתוב דרך הדרש כמו שכת[וב] גם כן בתרג[ום] שלתוספתא: 'ותצא
הרוח'—ונפק רוחא דנבות וקם קדם ה' ואמר: בבעו מינך יתקם לדמי על ידי דאנא
מצינא לאטעיותיה ולאובדא יתיה מן עלמא. ואמ[ר] ליה ה': במה את יכיל? ואמר:
אפוק ואהא רוח שקר בצדקיה בר כנענה ובשאר נביאי שקרא דיליה. ומשום דליתיה
רעותיה דקודשא בריך הוא בעבדי ליאות שקר ולא צבי בהון אמ[ר] ליה לנבות:
מדבשקרא אתרחצת פוק ממתיבתא דידי ועיבד לך רעותך משום דלא ניחא קמאי
למימר שיקרא.

Nevertheless I will record in homiletic manner in accordance with what
is written in a Tosefta of the Targum: 'And there came forth the spirit'—
The spirit of Naboth went out and stood before the Lord and said: "I
beseech you, allow my blood to be avenged by way of me finding the opportunity to deceive him and rid him from the world." The Lord said to
him: "How can you do so?" He said: "I shall go out and be a spirit of false-
ness in Zedekiah son of Canaana and the rest of his false prophets." Now
since the Holy One blessed be He takes no pleasure in liars and desires
them not, He said to Naboth: "Since you put your faith in a lie exit my
seating (yeshiva) and do as you wish, for it is unacceptable to tell a lie in
My presence.

---

29   Churgin *Hagiographa*, p. 259, quoted the TT per Bacher. The text here is that in Kasher *TT*,
      p. 136 (fragment 90b).

Also relevant to our purposes, though, is another TT, found in MS Reuchlin, whose similarity to TC not only includes exegesis, but extends to diction:[30]

ספ]ר] אח]ר]
ונפק רוחא דנבות מן מחיצת צדיק]יא]
ספ]ר] אח]ר]
ברם לית לך רשו לימתב בין צדיק]יא] דמן דמלל שקר]א] לית איפשר דיהי מדוריה
בין צדיקיא, פוק מלוותי ועביד כן

Alternate reading: Naboth's spirit exited the precinct of the righteous.
Alternate reading: However, no longer may you sit among the righteous, for he who tells a lie may not dwell among the righteous. Exit My presence and do so.

Kasher (ibid.) correctly noted that "the diction of the passage before us is quite close to the diction of *Targum Chronicles*." He also suggested that the appearance of the word מחיצה in BT, TC, and the TT above indicated that all shared a common basic tradition. In my view, the various sources do indeed have a shared basic tradition in common, but they should not be afforded equal status. TC does not parallel BT, but is dependent on it. The TT in MS Reuchlin, meanwhile, so clearly resembles TC as to justify the assumption that this TT and TC are two witnesses to a single text, with the logical consequence that either one copied from the other, or both copied from a common source.

Notably, while the Talmud refers to "My precinct," i.e., God's precinct, the term appearing in TC and the TT is "the precinct of the righteous."[31] This is the space described by the Talmud as occupied by the souls of the righteous who have passed away.[32] A similar concept appears in a talmudic tradition in *b. Ber.* 12b concerning the conversation between Saul and the spirit of Samuel:

ואמ]ר] רבה בר חנינא סבא משמיה דרב: כל העושה דבר ומתבייש בו, מוחלין לו על
כל עונותיו, שנא]מר]... 'ויאמר שמואל אל שאול למה הרגזתני להעלות אותי ויאמר
שאול צר לי מאד ופלשתים נלחמים בי וה׳ סר מעלי ולא ענני עוד גם ביד הנביאים
גם בחלומות'... ומנא לן דאחילו ליה? דכת]יב] 'ומחר אתה ובניך עמי'. מאי 'עמי'?
עמי במחיצתי.

---

30   MS Reuchlin 3 in Kasher *TT*, p. 135 (fragment 90a). According to its colophon, the MS was
      written in 1106.

31   Unlike the other TT we have seen (Kasher *TT*, fragment 90b), in which the space is called
      מתיבתא דידי, *My seating/yeshiva.*

32   McIvor, pp. 116, 186, identifies this space as the place of the righteous who are closest to
      the divine throne, as intimated in TC 1 Chr 21:15.

And Rab bar Hinena, the elder, said in the name of Rab, "Whoever commits a transgression but is ashamed on that account is forgiven all his transgressions. "For it is said, "And Samuel said to Saul, Why have you disturbed me to bring me up? And Saul answered, I am sore distressed, for the Philistines make war against me, and God has left me and does not answer me any more, neither by prophets nor by dreams; therefore I called you that you may tell me what I should do" (1 Sam 28:15). *And how do we know that he was forgiven by Heaven?* As it is said, 'And Samuel said, 'Tomorrow you and your sons will be with me" (1 Sam 28:16, 19)." And R. Yohanan said, "'With me' means 'in my [precinct; i.e. in Heaven].'"

The verse adduced by the Talmud in *b. Sanh.* 102b to justify the expulsion of Naboth's spirit from God's abode is Ps 101:7: דֹּבֵר שְׁקָרִים לֹא־יִכּוֹן לְנֶגֶד עֵינָי, *he who speaks untruth shall not stand before my eyes.* The term מחיצת צדיקים (in Aramaic, מחיצת צדיקיא) is not used frequently in rabbinic literature,[33] and appears in targumic literature in only two cases: the present verse (including the version in MS Reuchlin) and the verse preceding that adduced by the Talmud:

Ps 101:6

MT   עֵינַי ׀ בְּנֶאֶמְנֵי־אֶרֶץ לָשֶׁבֶת עִמָּדִי הֹלֵךְ בְּדֶרֶךְ תָּמִים הוּא יְשָׁרְתֵנִי:

Tg. Ps: עייני בקשיטי ארעא למתב במחיצת צדיקי דאזל באורח שלים הוא יקום עם שמשיי:

NJPS: My eyes are on the trusty men of the land, to have them at my side. He who follows the way of the blameless shall be in my service.

Cook: My eyes are on the honest of the land, to dwell in the precincts of the righteous; he who walks perfect on the way—he shall stand among my ministers.

---

33   *Midr. Sam* 19 (p. 65):

ויאמר שמואל אל ישי שלחה וקחנו' וגו'—אמר ר' שמואל בר נחמן: לפי שבעולם הזה לא ישבו שני גדולי עולם ישי ושמואל עד שישב דוד ביניהם, כך לעתיד לבא אין כל מחיצה ומחיצה של צדיקים שאין דוד עומד על גבה.

'And Samuel said to Jesse, "Send someone to bring him"' (1 Sam 16:11)—R. Samuel son of Nachman said: Just as in this world two giants such Jesse and Samuel did not congregate without David joining them, so in the world to come there will not be any *precinct of righteous* where David is not present.

The term also occurs in a late passage of *Tanḥuma, Ha'azinu* 1 (quoted from 'Eshkol edition, Jerusalem, 1971/1972, p. 934):

... כך הוא טובל בכל שעה בנהרי אפרסמון ובחלב ובדבש ובשמן ואוכל מעץ החיים תמיד הנטוע במחיצת הצדיקים ונופו נוטה על כל שלחן של צדיק וצדיק וחי לעולם.

... so he is always immersed in rivers of balsam, milk, oil and honey. He also always eats from the tree of life which is planted in the *precinct of the righteous* and its boughs bend over every righteous one's table and he lives forever.

Ps 101:6 is the positive counterpart of verse 7 mentioned above. The faithful of the earth, the best of humankind, are chosen to sit with God, and this convocation is designated in the Targum as מחיצת צדיקי. A dictional relationship thus binds not only TC and the homily in BT, but also the version in the TT. There still is a need to ascertain the precise relationship between these sources, but in any event the dictional resemblance is too great to be attributed to mere chance.[34]

3.2 *Naaman Kills Ahab with an Arrow* (2 Chr 18:33)

2 Chr 18:33

MT		מָשַׁ֤ךְ בַּקֶּ֙שֶׁת֙ לְתֻמּ֔וֹ		וְאִ֗ישׁ
TC		מלכא דארם נגד בקשתא לקבליה	ונעמן רב חילא דרב[35]	

לאשלמא נבואת אליה דמן תשוב
ונבואת מיכה בר ימלה

MT (cont.)	וּבֵ֖ין הַשִּׁרְיָ֑ן	הַדְּבָקִ֖ים	בֵּ֥ין	יִשְׂרָאֵ֖ל	אֶת־מֶ֣לֶךְ	וַיַּךְ֙
TC	ובֵיני חצר־כבדא	לבא	בֵיני	דישראל	ית מלכא	ומחא

מאתר מדבקייה דשריינא

NJPS: Then a man drew his bow at random and hit the king of Israel between the plates of the armor

Dost: But Naaman, the commander of the army of the king of Aram, drew a bow toward him in order to fulfill the prophecy of Elijah, who was from Teshub, and the prophecy of Micah son of Imlah, and struck the king of Israel between the heart and the lobe of the liver, where the armor connects.

ונעמן: The expansive translation to this verse identifies the anonymous soldier of MT with the most famous Aramean soldier in Scripture: Naaman. Churgin proposed that the identification was based on *Midr. Ps* 78:11 (p. 350): וחץ נעמן ...שהכה את אחאב ונכנס לתוך השריון והכהו, *and Naaman's arrow that struck Ahab and pierced his armor and killed him*.[36] However, the soldier's identification as

---

34 There are several possibilities for the precise nature of the influence exerted between the texts. *Tg. Ps* as we know it clearly postdates BT, so that the talmudic legend may have influenced not only TC, but also *Tg. Ps*. However, given the absence of any allusion in *Tg. Ps* to the tradition regarding the spirit of Naboth, it may be that the talmudic homily in fact is based on a targumic tradition concerning Ps 101 that already contained the word מחיצה and the authors of the Talmud applied this ancient tradition to the spirit of Naboth.

35 This word is undiacriticized in MS V. Apparently the word רב was subject to a dittography and the correct reading is that of MS E: רב חילא דמלכא דארם; Le Déaut-Robert, vol. 2, p. 121.

36 Churgin *Hagiographa*, p. 259. He is followed by McIvor, p. 187. The identification also appears in Rashi to 1 Kgs 22:34.

Naaman appears in earlier sources. In a midrashic collection to the book of Numbers discovered in the Genizah, we find:[37]

'ויאמר ה' [מי יפ[תה' וגו'. א[מר] הק[ב"ה]: [הרי יצא הדין] שיעלה לרמות גל[עד]
וימות שם, ואינו מבקש לצאת! א[מר] לו המלאך: אני עושה אותו שייצא שלא
בטובתו. 'ויאמר תפתה וגם' 'ועתה הנה נתן ה' רוח' וג'...' 'ויאמר מיכיהו אם שוב
ת[שוב] ב[שלום] לא ד[בר] ה' ב[י]'—עד כאן דיבר מיכה. מה עשה אחאב? עמד
והיכריז: 'ויאמר שמעו עמים ...'—אמר: אליהו, רבו שלזה, א[מר] לי: 'במקום אשר
לקקו' וגו', וזה או[מר] לי שאני הולך לרמת גל[עד] ומת שם. אין זה יודע דבר! מה
מוטב לקיים דברי הרב או שלתלמ[יד]? לא שלרב? אינו יודע זה דבר! א[מר] לו
הק[ב"ה]: חייך, אין דבר משלי בטל, אלא הרי אני עושה דבר שניהם. והוא עולה
ונעמן מקשט לו, והחץ ניכנס בו, ולא שלפו עד שהלך ליזרעאל. שלפו ביזרעל והוציא
דמו ומת ...

'The LORD asked, Who will entice etc.' (1 Kgs 22:20)—The Holy One blessed be He said: It has been decided that he ascend to Ramoth Gilead and die there, but he has no desire to go out! The angel said to Him: I will cause him to go out against his own interest. 'Then He said, 'You will entice and etc.' 'So the LORD has put a lying spirit etc....' 'To which Micaiah retorted, If you ever come home safe, the LORD has not spoken through me'—end of Micah's quote. What did Ahab? He arose and proclaimed: 'Listen, all you peoples'—He said: Elijah, this one's master, said to me: '', while this one tells me I will go to Ramoth Gilead and die there. He knows nothing! The Holy One blessed be He said to him: By your own life, My words are not void, rather I shall perform both of their statements. He ascended and Naaman wielded his bow, and the arrow pierced him, and it was not removed till he reached Jezreel. He pulled it out in Jezreel and then he bled and died ...

The version in the Targum bears two key resemblances to this midrashic tradition: the identification of the archer as Naaman, and the argument that the prophecies of both Elijah and Michaiah came true. The Targum differs from the midrash in that the latter stresses the contradiction between the two prophecies and suggests a resolution, while the Targum neither raises the difficulty nor offers a solution, but simply states that the predictions of both prophets came true. Kasher notes that the tradition describing both prophets as

37   Rabinowitz, p. 67.

having correctly predicted what would transpire appears as early as Josephus' *Antiquities of the Jews*.[38]

לאשלמא לקבליה: TJ to the parallel verse, 1 Kgs 22:34, does not diverge from the literal continuum of that verse's Hebrew *Vorlage*:

1 Kgs 22:34

MT וְאִישׁ מָשַׁךְ בַּקֶּשֶׁת לְתֻמּוֹ וַיַּכֶּה אֶת־מֶלֶךְ יִשְׂרָאֵל בֵּין הַדְּבָקִים וּבֵין הַשִּׁרְיָן

TJ וגברא נגד בקשתא לקבליה ומחא ית מלכא דישראל בין דבקיא ובין שרינא

NJPS: Then a man drew his bow at random and he hit the king of Israel between the plates of the armor

Clem: But a man drew the bow towards him and struck the king of Israel between the scales of the armor

TC uses TJ's existing translation as a foundation for his own, for which reason לְתֻמּוֹ is translated in TC as לקבליה. The insertion regarding the prophecies of Elijah and Michaiah has its source in *b. Sanh.* 39b:

'ואיש משך בקשת לתומו'—א"ר אלעזר: לפי תומו. רבא אמר: כדי לתמם שני חזיונות, אחת שלמיכיהו ואחת שלאליהו.

"And a certain man drew his bow innocently and smote the king of Israel' (1 Kgs 22:34): R. Eleazar said, "It was in all innocence." Rava' said, "It was to perfect two visions, the one of Micaiah, the other of Elijah.

The content and technique of the homily attributed to Rava' are similar to those of the parallel in TC. In effect, the word לְתֻמּוֹ is twice represented in TC: once as לקבליה, and again as לאשלמא, paralleling the word לתמם in the talmudic tradition ascribed to Rava'. TC's comments following those of the Talmud are paralleled almost precisely by a TT in MS Reuchlin to 1 Kgs 22:34:[39]

---

38   Kasher *TT*, p. 136. *Antiquities of the Jews* 8:417–418:
        "but when they had washed his chariot in the fountain of Jezreel, which was bloody with the dead body of the king, they acknowledged that the prophecy of Elijah was true ... but still he died at Ramoth, as Micaiah had foretold. And as what things were foretold should happen to Ahab by the two prophets came to pass, we ought thence to have high notions of God, and everywhere to honor and worship him ..."

39   Kasher *TT*, pp. 136–137 (fragment 91).

ספ[ר] אח[ר] ואיש משך
וגבר נגד בקשתא לאשלמא נבואת אליה דמן תשוב ונבואת מיכה בר ימלא ומחא
ית מלכא דישראל ביני ליבא וביני חצר כבדא מאתר מדבקייא דשירייגא

Alternate reading: 'and a man drew'
A man drew a bow in order to fulfill the prophecy of Elijah, who was from
Teshub, and the prophecy of Micah son of Imlah, and struck the king
of Israel between the heart and the lobe of the liver, where the armor
connects.

Although we do not find the archer identified as Naaman at the beginning of
the verse, this TT very much resembles TC, down to its use of the abbreviated
form of Michaiah's name and inclusion of his father's name (מיכה בר ימלא/ה).
The TT offers a complete translation of the verse containing only a single
equivalent of the word לְתֻמּוֹ, as opposed to the two words, לקבליה and לאשלמא,
in TC. The similarity between the Targums from the word לאשלמא to the end
of the verse makes the conclusion that they are linked by literary dependence
inescapable. The probable direction of this literary influence is from the TT to
TC, rather than the reverse, as the exertion of influence in this direction can
explain why TC contains dual translations of the word לְתֻמּוֹ.[40] In this verse
of TC we thus have been able to identify a variety of literary influences. Two
sources of direct influences on TC are the two alternative Aramaic translations
of the verse: TJ (from which TC borrowed the word לקבליה) and the text of the
TT (from which TC took the translation from לאשלמא to the conclusion of the
verse). *B. Sanh.* 39b apparently is one of the sources that informed the reading
contained in the TT (לאשלמא → לתמם → לְתֻמּוֹ). The identification of the archer
as Naaman may have reached TC due to the influence of the midrashic tradition contained in the Genizah document above, but there is no clear literary
indication to link the two sources, and it thus may be that the author of TC
received the identification from elsewhere.

This is the second instance in 2 Chronicles 18 where we find a substantive link between TC and the TT in MS Reuchlin (see regarding the spirit of

---

40   To remove all doubt, this is to say not that the author of TC possessed MS Reuchlin, but
      that he had in his possession some source whose text resembled that of the TT in MS
      Reuchlin, which cites works that predated it as the sources of the TT it contains. In this
      instance, TC was familiar with the same targumic tradition that was known to the author
      of MS Reuchlin.

Naboth, pp. 401–405).[41] This may say something about the text of TJ with which TC was familiar, which perhaps contained alternative nonliteral translations that TC sometimes incorporated within his own Targum. Also possible is that, aside from a text of TJ comparable to our own, the author of TC had in his possession another Targum of Kings that included additional expansions, and sometimes integrated the readings of the two Targums in his work.

3.3   *Joash Vindicated through David's Crown (2 Chr 23:11)*[42]

2 Chr 23:11   וַיּוֹצִיאוּ אֶת־בֶּן־הַמֶּלֶךְ וַיִּתְּנוּ עָלָיו אֶת־הַנֵּזֶר וְאֶת־הָעֵדוּת וַיַּמְלִיכוּ אֹתוֹ

TC   ואפיקו ית ברא דמלכא ויהבו עלוי ית כלילא דמלכותא די דבר דוד מעל רישא

דמלכא דבני עמון ובה אבן טבא שייבא דהוה חקיק ומפרש עלה שמא רבא

ויקירא דקבעה תמן דוד ברוח קודשא והוה טימין דידה מתקל קנטינר דדהבא

וסהדותא

היא לבית דוד דכל מלכא דלא הוה מזרעיה דדוד לא הות מתקבלא על רישיה

ולית איפשר דיסובר יתה וכד חמון עמא דאתקבלת על רישיה דיהואש וסובר

ית כלילא הימינו דמזרעיה דדוד הוא

ומן־יד אמליכו יתיה

2 Kgs 11:12   וַיּוֹצֵא אֶת־בֶּן־הַמֶּלֶךְ וַיִּתֵּן עָלָיו אֶת־הַנֵּזֶר וְאֶת־הָעֵדוּת וַיַּמְלִכוּ אֹתוֹ

TJ   ואפיק ית בר מלכא ויהב עלוהי ית כלילא וית סהדותא ואמליכו יתיה

2 Chr 23:11 (cont.)   וַיִּמְשָׁחֻהוּ יְהוֹיָדָע וּבָנָיו וַיֹּאמְרוּ יְחִי הַמֶּלֶךְ:

TC   ורביאו יתיה יהוידע ובנוהי ואמרו יצלח מלכא במלכותיה:

2 Kgs 11:12   וַיִּמְשָׁחֻהוּ וַיַּכּוּ־כָף וַיֹּאמְרוּ יְחִי הַמֶּלֶךְ:

TJ   ומשחוהי וטפחו יד ואמרו יצלח מלכא:

NJPS Chr: Then they brought out the king's son, and placed upon him the crown and the insignia. They proclaimed him king, and Jehoiada and his sons anointed him and shouted, "Long live the king!"

Dost: Then they brought out the king's son, and he put on him the royal crown that David took from upon the head of the king of the children of Ammon, in which was the lodestone, upon which was clearly engraved the great and glorious name, where David placed it by the spirit of holiness. Its price was the weight of a centenarius of gold, and it was a testimony to the house of David that every king that was not from the seed of David could not fit it on his head and it was impossible for him to wear it. And when the people saw that

---

41   According to its colophon, the MS was written in 1106.

42   This expansion is also based upon the BT and is, therefore, mentioned above, p. 342. However, its discussion appears only here.

it fit the head of Jehoash and (that) he was wearing the crown, they believed
that he was from the seed of David. So they immediately made him king, and
Jehoiada and his sons anointed him and said, "May the king prosper during his
reign."

NJPS Kgs: [Jehoiada] then brought out the king's son, and placed upon him
the crown and the insignia. They anointed him and proclaimed him king; they
clapped their hands and shouted, "Long live the king!"

Clem: Then he brought out the son of the king, and he put on him the crown
and the testimony, and made him king and anointed him and clapped hands
and said, "May the king prosper."

According to talmudic lore, David's crown described above (see pp. 313–315)
played an important role in the life of one of his descendants, Joash son of
Ahaziah. Joash was reared secretly from his infancy until he was seven years
old, out of fear that his grandmother Athaliah would kill him. When Jehoiada
the Priest decided that the time had come for him to emerge from hiding and
take his place as the legitimate heir of King Ahaziah, it was necessary to prove
that the boy's identity had not been fabricated, as the people were totally un-
aware that any child of Ahaziah had survived. The aggadists found an intriguing solution to this problem: David's crown, which he took from the king of
Ammon, fit only the head of the legitimate heir to David's throne. Therefore,
when the crown was placed on the head of seven-year-old Joash and all the
people saw that it fit, this was proof that the child truly was the rightful king
of Judah. In effect, this legend is a continuation of Rab's argument cited above
(p. 315) that the crown suited David's head (and in fact is quoted in Rab's name
by R. Yehudah). Below is the continuation of the passage from *b. 'Avod. Zar.* 44a
quoted above that discusses the question of David's ability to hold a crown of
such weight on his head:

'ויוציאו את בן המלך ויתן עליו את הנזר ואת העדו[ת].' 'נזר'—כלילא. 'עדות'—
אמ[ר] רב יהודה אמ[ר] רב: עדות היא לבית דוד, שכל הראוי למלכו[ת] בית דוד—
הולמתו; ושאינו ראוי למלכות בית דוד—אין הולמתו. 'ואדוניה בן חגית מתנשא
לאמר אני אמלוך'—אמ[ר] רב יהודה אמ[ר] רב: שבקש להלמו ולא הולמתו.

"Then he brought out the king's son and put on him the *neser* and the
testimony" (2 Kgs 11:12)—*"The neser" is the crown, and as to the testimony?*
Said R. Judah said Rab, "It was testimony concerning the house of David
that whoever was suitable for the throne would fit into the crown, and
whoever was not suitable for the throne would not fit into the crown."

Churgin gave the Talmud's discussion here as one of the sources of TC's expansion.[43] We should note, however, that the text of the Talmud differs from the targumic expansion in several significant details. In the Talmud, the crown attests to the identity of David's legitimate heir by virtue of its unusual size, as it fit only the rightful king.[44] According to TC, however, this testimony was obtained through the power of the ineffable name (שמא רבא ויקירא), which was engraved in a stone in the crown.[45] This stone had the power to distinguish the rightful heir from all other people, as only the former who could bear its great weight. Nevertheless, the insertion found in TC resembles the version in BT in that the stone was magnetic (שייבה) and in that the crown not only was too heavy for any person other than the rightful king (לית איפשר דיסובר יתה), but also did not fit any other person (לא הות מתקבלא על רישיה).

The expansion in TC thus includes both a few elements that are familiar from talmudic lore and others that are foreign to the talmudic version, so that TC's expansion appears to be based on both the Talmud and another aggadic tradition. As we shall see, this tradition served the targumist as a framework for the entire verse. In the TT in MS Reuchlin to 2 Kgs 11:12 we find the following passage:[46]

תרג[ום] ירוש[למי] ויוציא את בן המלך
ואפיק ית בר מלכא ויהב עלוהי ית כלילא דמלכא דדבר דוד מעל ריש מלכא
דבני עמון ובה אבן טבא חקיק ומפרש עלוהי שמא רבא ויקירא דשויה מתקל ככרא
דהבא וסהדותא היא לבית דוד דכל מלכא דליתוהי מזרעית דוד לית איפשר לסוברא

---

43   Churgin *Hagiographa*, pp. 259–260, cited the passage in *b. ʿAvodah Zarah* as a partial parallel of *b. Sanh.* 21b, as well as to the TT discussed below.

44   Rashi, in his comments to the parallel in *b. Sanh.* 21b, offered an intriguing interpretation of how the crown fit the legitimate heir to the throne:
      שבקש ... שתשב בראשו כתר מלכות ולא הולמתו, לפי שהיה שרביט של זהב בתוך חללה
      מדופן לדופן ואינה מתיישב בראשו אלא למי שיש לו חריץ בראשו, והיא עדות לבית דוד, שכל
      הראוי למלכות—הולמתו ומי שאינו ראוי למלכות—אינו הולמתו.
      He wished to place the crown on his head but it would not fit him, for there was a golden rod within it from one side to the other and it would not fit one's head unless they had a groove on their head, and this was a testimony for the Davidic dynasty. If one was worthy of kingship—it would fit him, and if one was not worthy of kingship—it would not fit him.

45   On the power of the ineffable name in rabbinic thought and its use for magical purposes, see Urbach, pp. 102–114. The words דהוה חקיק ומפרש עלה שמא רבא ויקירא in the Targum are taken from the TT cited below. The tradition may have developed as a homily on the words אֶבֶן יְקָרָה in 2 Sam 12:30 and 1 Chr 20:2, stating that the crown contained a stone on which was inscribed שמא רבא ויקירא.

46   Kasher *TT*, pp. 144–145, fragment 99.

 יתיה וכד חמון עמא דסובר יתה יואש ימינו דמזרעא דדוד הוא ואמליכו יתיה ומש־
חוהי וטפחו ידא לידא ואמר[ו] יחי מלכא

Yerushalmi Targum (for) '[Jehoiada] then brought out the king's son'
He brought out the king's son, and he put on him the royal crown that
David took from upon the head of the king of the children of Ammon, in
which was a gem, upon which was clearly engraved the great and glorious
name. Its price was the weight of a talent of gold, and it was a testimony
to the house of David that every king that was not from the lineage of
David could not carry it. And when the people saw that Joash carried it
they believed that he was from the seed of David and they made him king,
and anointed him, and clapped their hands, saying, "May the king live."

This TT contains the elements of TC's expansion that are absent from the
Talmud. It mentions the stone in which the ineffable name is engraved, as well
as the nature of the crown's test, i.e., no person who was not from the House of
David could bear its weight.[47] The TT also can explain why TC 1 Chr 20:2 reads
ונסיב דוד (following TJ to the parallel verse) but here the text reads די דבר דוד
(following the TT). Conversely, the TT does not describe the stone as magnetic (שייבה) as does TC and does not state that the crown did not fit the head
(לא הות מתקבלא על רישיה) of any person but the legitimate heir.

The targumist's goal in composing this verse thus seems to have been to integrate the two above interpretations, viz., that of the Talmud and the tradition
reflected in the TT. He used a text similar to that of MS Reuchlin as the verse's
framework, then supplemented it with a few elements from the Talmud. The
outcome was that the targumist produced an unwieldy, problematic translation: if the ineffable name was engraved in the stone, then there is no need to
describe it as magnetic, and if no unworthy person could wear the crown due
to its weight, then the story contains no practical requirement that the crown
not fit such a person. Be this as it may, the presence of these superfluous, even
contradictory elements in the Targum gives us a window into the targumist's
sources and technique.

---

47   The text of the TT is somewhat problematic. On one hand, it states that the value (TC:
טימין דידה) of the stone was that of a talent of gold, indicating that it was not heavy, but
of great value. On the other hand, it states that only a descendant of David could bear the
weight (לסוברא) of the crown, indicating that it was heavy. The text of the TT thus evinces
the influence of different traditions.

3.4 *Survivors of Fire (2 Chr 28:3)*[48]

2 Chr 28:3

MT   וְהוּא הִקְטִיר בְּגֵיא בֶן־הִנֹּם וַיַּבְעֵר אֶת־בָּנָיו בָּאֵשׁ

TC   והוא אסיק קטרתא בחילת בר הנם ואעבר ית בנוהי באשתא

ושיזיב מימרא דה' מנהון ית חזקיה מן־בגלל דגלי קדם ה' דמניה אטימוסין די יפקון תלתא

צדיקיא חנניה מישאל ועזריה דאטימוסין דימסרון גרמיהון דיתרמון לגו אתון נורא יקידתא

מן־בגלל שמא רבא ויקירא ואשתיזיבו מן יקידתא

בקדמיתא אשתיזב אברהם מן יקידת אתון נורא דכשדאי דטלקיה תמן נמרוד מן בגלל דלא

פלח לטעוותיה

ובתנייתא אשתיזיבת תמר מן יקידת נורא דבית דינא דיהודה כד אמר אפקוהא ותתוקד

בתליתיתא אשתיזב מן יקידת נורא חזקיהו בר יותם[49] בזמן דטלקיה אבוי בחילת[50] בר הנם

בבמסייה דתופת

ברביעיתא אשתיזיבו חנניה מישאל ועזריה מן אתון נורא יקידתא דנבוכד־נצר מלכא דבבל

בחמשיתא אשתיזב יהושע בר יהוצדק כהנא רבא כד טלקיה נבוכד־נצ[ר] רשיעא באתון

נורא יקידתא עם אחאב בר קוליה וצדקיה בר מעשיה נביאי שקרא והנון אתוקדו בנורא

ויהושע בר יהוצדק אשתיזב מטול זכוותיה

MT (cont.)   כְּתֹעֲבוֹת הַגּוֹיִם אֲשֶׁר הֹרִישׁ ה' מִפְּנֵי בְּנֵי יִשְׂרָאֵל:

TC   ברם אחז ארשע [ת]הי־כתועב עממיא דתריך ה' מן־קדם בני ישראל:

NJPS: He made offerings in the Valley of Ben-hinnom and burned his sons in fire, in the abhorrent fashion of the nations which the LORD had dispossessed before the Israelites.

Dost: He offered up incense in the Valley of the Son of Hinnom, and he caused his sons to pass over the fire, but the Memra of the Lord saved from among them Hezekiah because it was revealed before the Lord that from him three righteous ones were destined to come forth—Hananiah, Mishael, and Azariah—who were destined to surrender their bodies, which would be thrown into the burning furnace for the sake of the great and glorious name. Now (the following) were saved from burning. First, Abraham was saved from the burning by the fire of the furnace of the Chaldeans, where Nimrod threw him because he would not bow to his idols. Second, Tamar was saved from the burning by fire of the legal court of Judah when he said, "Bring her out and let her be burned." Third, Hezekiah son of Jotham was saved from burning by fire when his father threw him into the Valley of the Son of Hinnom on the elevated

---

48   This expansion is possibly based upon the BT and is, therefore, mentioned above, p. 384. However, its discussion appears only here.

49   Sic in MSS V, E. MS C and de Lagarde's and Sperber's editions have the reading אחז.

50   Le Déaut-Robert, vol. 2, p. 142, read בהילת, but MS V contains no justification for this reading. We therefore must prefer בחילת, which also fits the context.

stands of Topheth. Fourth, Hananiah, Mishael, and Azariah were saved from
the furnace of burning fire of Nebuchadnezzar king of Babylon. Fifth, Joshua
son of Jehozadak, the chief priest, when wicked Nebuchadnezzar threw him
into the furnace of burning fire with Ahab son of Kolaiah and Zedekiah son
of Measeiah, the false prophets. And they burned in the fire, but Joshua son
of Jehozadak was saved because of his merits. But Ahaz acted wickedly in accordance with the abomination of the gentiles whom the Lord drove out from
before the children of Israel.

This nonliteral expansion, the longest and most formally structured in all of
TC, is comprised of two parts. First it tells of Hezekiah's miraculous rescue
from the flames of the Valley of Ben Hinnom in the merit of his three descendants who in the future would cast themselves into a fiery furnace in sanctification of God's name and be saved. Once Hezekiah's rescue from the fire has
been linked to that of Hananiah, Mishael, and Azariah, the targumist begins
the second section of the expansion, in which he details (and even numbers)
the five scriptural events in which Jewish collective memory recalls that righteous individuals were saved from fire. Based on this structure, it appears that
the two parts were not jointly authored, but the incorporation of one led to the
inclusion of the other by way of association.

Let us examine the expansion's first section:

ושיזיב מימרא דה׳ מנהון ית חזקיה מן־בגלל דגלי קדם ה׳ דמניה אטימוסין די יפקון
תלתא צדיקיא חנניה מישאל ועזריה דאטימוסין דימסרון גרמיהון דיתרמון לגו אתון
נורא יקידתא מן־בגלל שמא רבא ויקירא ואשתיזיבו מן יקידתא

but the Memra of the Lord saved from among them Hezekiah because
it was revealed before the Lord that from him three righteous ones were
destined to come forth—Hananiah, Mishael, and Azariah—who were
destined to surrender their bodies, which would be thrown into the burning furnace for the sake of the great and glorious name. And they were
saved from burning.

The legend of Hezekiah's miraculous rescue from fire serves to solve an exegetical challenge posed by the verse. If Ahaz in fact burned his sons through
the fire, as attested by the Hebrew verse, then how did his son Hezekiah survive
the conflagration and live to reign over Israel? The Hebrew text of 2 Kgs 16:3,
וְגַם אֶת־בְּנוֹ הֶעֱבִיר בָּאֵשׁ, *he even consigned his son to the fire*, with its direct object
in the singular, does not make the quandary any less urgent, because in aggadic
eyes it focuses the question on Hezekiah himself. As much is indicated, by way

of example, in a TT to 2 Kgs 16:3 in MS Reuchlin.[51] The passage begins with a generally literal translation of the Hebrew verse, but specifies that the son passed through fire was Hezekiah:

2 Kgs 16:3

MT	הַגּוֹיִם	כְּתֹעֲבוֹת	בָּאֵשׁ	הֶעֱבִיר	בְּנוֹ	אֶת־	וְגַם
TT	עממיא	כריחוק	בנורא	אעבר	בריה	חזקיה	ית	ואף

MT (cont.)	אֲשֶׁר הוֹרִישׁ ה' אֹתָם מִפְּנֵי בְּנֵי יִשְׂרָאֵל:
TT	דתריך ה' מן־קדם בני ישראל

NJPS: He even consigned his son to the fire, in the abhorrent fashion of the nations which the LORD had dispossessed before the Israelites.

Gottlieb: He even consigned his son, Hezekiah, to the fire, in the abhorrent fashion of the nations which the Lord sent away before the children of Israel.

The translation of the verse in TT is followed by an aggadic tradition further detailing the preceding, which is unmistakably reminiscent of TC:

והוה כד איתגלי ק[דם] ה' ארום חזקיה הוה צדיקא שיזביה מן יקידתא ולא איתוקד מן בגלל דמיניה עתידין למפק חנניה מישאל ועזריה דנחתין לאתון נורא בבבל מן בגלל קדושת שמא רבא ויקירא

but when it was revealed before the Lord that Hezekiah was righteous He saved him from the fire and he was not burned because from him were destined to come forth Hananiah, Mishael, and Azariah, who were to descend into a furnace of fire in Babylon for the sanctity of the great and glorious name.

The diction of the expansion in TC is somewhat different from that in the TT, but the sentence's content and many unusual expressions within it resemble the TT,[52] indicating that these are two versions of a single aggadic tradition.

---

51   Kasher *TT*, p. 146, fragment 101.

52   The TT notes that Hezekiah was a righteous man, while TC says this of Hananiah, Mishael, and Azariah. The TT has the word עתידין, whereas TC twice has the different but synonymous Greek loanword אטימוסין (about which see pp. 178–179, above). Following is a partial comparison of the two texts highlighting structural and lexical similarities:

TC	דמיניה אטימוסין די יפקון תלתא צדיקיא חנניה מישאל ועזריה דאטימוסין דימסרון גרמיהון
TT	דמיניה עתידין למפק חנניה מישאל ועזריה

TC	שמא רבא ויקירא	מן־בגלל	יקידתא	דיתרמון לגו אתון נורא
TT	בבבל מן בגל קדושת שמא רבא ויקירא	נורא	דנחתין לאתון

TC probably was familiar with a TT whose text closely resembled that in MS Reuchlin and chose to incorporate it in his translation.

Now let us revisit the second part of the expansion, with its five sections:

בקדמיתא אשתיזב אברהם מן יקידת אתון נורא דכשׂדאי דטלקיה תמן נמרוד מן
בגלל דלא פלח לטעוותיה

ובתנייתא אשתיזיבת תמר מן יקידת נורא דבית דיניה דיהודה כד אמר אפקוהא
ותתוקד

בתליתיתא אשתיזב מן יקידת נורא חזקיהו בר יותם דטלקיה אבוי בחילת
בר הנם בבמסייה דתופת

ברביעיתא אשתיזבו חנניה מישאל ועזריה מן אתון נורא יקידתא דנבוכד־נצר
מלכא דבבל

בחמשׂיתא אשתיזב יהושע בר יהוצדק כהנא רבא כד טלקיה נבוכד־נצ[ר]
רשׂיעא באתון נורא יקידתא עם אחאב בר קוליה וצדקיה בר מעשׂיה נביאי שׂקרא
והנון אתוקדו בנורא ויהושע בר יהוצדק אשתיזב מטול זכוותיה

First, Abraham was saved from the burning by the fire of the furnace of the Chaldeans, where Nimrod threw him because he would not bow to his idols.

Second, Tamar was saved from the burning by fire of the legal court of Judah when he said, "Bring her out and let her be burned."

Third, Hezekiah son of Jotham was saved from burning by fire when his father threw him into the Valley of the Son of Hinnom on the elevated stands of Topheth.

Fourth, Hananiah, Mishael, and Azariah were saved from the furnace of burning fire of Nebuchadnezzar king of Babylon.

Fifth, Joshua son of Jehozadak, the chief priest, when wicked Nebuchadnezzar threw him into the furnace of burning fire with Ahab son of Kolaiah and Zedekiah son of Measeiah, the false prophets. And they burned in the fire, but Joshua son of Jehozadak was saved because of his merits.

The passage's structure, organized by ordinal numbers, is a familiar one in other Targums and midrashic works.[53] The five events described here appear

---

53   Cf. TN, FT, and TPJ Gen 28:10. Following is the relevant text of TPJ:

חמשא ניסין איתעבידו ליעקב בזמן דנפק מן בירא דשבע:
ניסא קמאה—איתקצרו שעוי דיומא וטמע שימשא בלא אשוניה מן בגלל דהוה דבירא
מתחמד למללא עימיה
ניסא תנינא—ארבעתי אבניא דשוי איסדוי אשכח יתהון בצפרא לאבנא חדא

in chronological order. We know of no source prior to TC that compiled the five stories together, but we may reasonably assume that the targumist had access to such a source and copied the list from it. The various components of the passage appear in a range of sources, as we shall see presently.

Abraham and the fiery furnace: This famous aggadic tradition appears in many sources.[54] We may reasonably link the version in TC with that in TPJ, which thrice mentions Nimrod's throwing Abraham into a fiery furnace.[55] TPJ did not use the same words in all three instances, but in two of them the diction used is similar to that in TC:

TPJ Gen 11:28   דלא פלח לטעותיה   נימרוד ית אברם לאתונא דנורא   כד רמא
TC 2 Chr 28:3   מן בגלל דלא פלח לטעותיה   דטלקיה תמן נמרוד
Clem TPJ: when Nimrod threw Abram into the fiery furnace because he did not worship his idols

TPJ Gen 16:5   לאתונא דנורא: נימרוד דטלקך
TC 2 Chr 28:3   נמרוד   תמן   דטלקיה
Clem TPJ: Nimrod who threw you into the furnace of fire

There are other Pentateuchal Targums that allude to this tradition, but the only one to state explicitly that it was Nimrod that cast Abraham into the fiery furnace is TPJ.[56] TC resembles TPJ Gen 11:28 in using the phrase דלא פלח לטעותיה, and is similar to TPJ Gen 16:5 in selecting the verb טל"ק instead of רמ"י, the latter of which (bearing the influence of Daniel 3) is characteristic of most of the other sources.[57] The text of TC may have been directly influenced by TPJ, although this does not go without saying. For the purposes of this discussion,

---

ניסא תליתאה—אבנא דהוו כל עדריא מתכנשין ומגלגלין לה מעילוי פם בירא גלגל יתא כחדא
מן דרעוי
ניסא רביעאה—דטפת בירא מיא וסליקו מיא לאנפוי והות טייפא כל יומין דהוה בחרן
ניסא חמישאה—קפצת ארעא קומוי ובההוא יומא דנפק אזל לחרן:

See also *Tg. Ruth* 1:1 (ten times of hunger); *Tg. Esth II* 1:1 (ten wealthy kings—reading עתיר, not עתיד).

54   See Ginzberg, vol. 5, pp. 212–213, nn. 33–34.

55   TPJ Gen 11:28; 14:1; 16:5.

56   There is no doubt that TN and FTV were familiar with the legend of Abraham and the fiery furnace, given their translation of אור כשדים in Genesis as אתון נורא (דכשדאי), but the actual elements of the tradition, e.g., Nimrod's name and the reason for casting Abraham into the furnace, are not incorporated in their Targum.

57   Another Targum whose reference to the legend, as in TPJ and TC, includes Nimrod's name and the phrase פל״ח לטעוותא, is *Tg. Eccl* 4:13, but there, too, we find the verb רמ״י:

let it suffice to say that the two targumists were recipients of similar aggadic traditions.

Tamar and the fiery furnace: With the words כד אמר אפקוהא ותתוקד, the targumist quotes Gen 38:24: וַיֹּאמֶר יְהוּדָה הוֹצִיאוּהָ וְתִשָּׂרֵף, *"bring her out," said Judah, "and let her be burned*. In this respect, the text of TC here is closer to that of TO, אפקוהא ותיתוקד, than to any other Targum to the verse in Genesis,[58] although in giving a legal description to the process of bringing Tamar to be burned, TC resembles the Palestinian Targums and TPJ. The aggadic tradition found in TC, as well as the TT cited above, links Hezekiah to Hananiah, Mishael, and Azariah, who one day would descend from him. The Palestinian Targums and TPJ similarly state that while being brought to the pyre, Tamar offered a prayer promising that these three righteous men who would sanctify God's name in the fiery furnace would descend from her.[59] The expansion in TC is a thematic extension of the tradition, in which a protagonist is saved from a fiery furnace in the merit of these three righteous descendants who in the future would be willing to sacrifice their lives in sanctification of God's name.

Hezekiah cast into the fire: Though the story in which Hezekiah is passed through a fire is the motivation for the inclusion of the expansion in TC, the diction used here by TC to describe the event is different from that at the beginning of the verse. The verb selected by the targumist here—טל״ק, meaning *to throw*—is similar to that used in the description of the parallel story involving Abraham, and unlike the verb עב״ר, which appears in the Targum's literal rendering of the verse. This disparity, in my view, supports the hypothesis that the second part of the expansion was not authored jointly with the first or with the verse's literal translation. TC took two different sources discussing Hezekiah's rescue from the fire and incorporated them within the existing translational continuum, ואעבר ית בנוהי באשתא.

Hananiah, Mishael, and Azariah and the fiery furnace: The story of these three figures is the lynchpin of the other stories in which biblical figures are saved from fire, because Scripture explicitly states only that these three individuals

---

טב הוא אברהם ... ולא צבא למפלח לטעוותא, יתיר מן נמרוד רשיעא ... ומן בגלל דלא צבא
אברהם למפלח לטעוותא, רמאהי לגו אתון נורא יקידתא ...

Dost: Better is Abraham ... who did not wish to worship idols, than wicked Nimrod ... because Abraham did not want to serve idols he threw him into a furnace of burning fire ...

58   Cf. TN: אפקו יתה ותתוקד; GT E: הנפקוהא ותיתוקד; TPJ: אפיקו יתה ותיתוקד.

59   This story appears in various versions in TN, FT, GT, and TPJ Gen 38:25.

were miraculously saved from a fiery furnace.[60] Abraham, like them, was cast into a fiery furnace for his refusal to prostrate himself to an idol. Tamar was sentenced to death by burning, and according to legend was saved in the merit of her descendants. Hezekiah was passed through fire and was saved when God saw that these three righteous men would descend from him in the future. Joshua son of Jehozadak was cast into a fiery furnace on the decree of King Nebuchadnezzar of Babylonia, who also sentenced Hananiah, Mishael, and Azariah. They also appear in the Targum (below) as archetypes for the casting of no fewer than three people into a furnace.

Joshua son of Jehozadak and the fiery furnace: The aggadic tradition concerning the rescue of Joshua son of Jehozadak is offered as an interpretation of הֲלוֹא זֶה אוּד מֻצָּל מֵאֵשׁ, *for this is a brand plucked from the fire*, in Zech 3:2, whose context is a revelation featuring Joshua. As with all of the other events described in the expansion in TC, the author does not give a complete story detailing the given event, but relies on his readers' knowledge of Jewish lore. The story of Joshua and the fiery furnace appears in fine detail in *b. Sanh.* 93a. At the end of that passage, his story is compared to those of Hananiah, Mishael, and Azariah and Abraham.[61]

4 Other Sources

4.1 *Er and Onan (1 Chr 2:3)*

1 Chr 2:3

| MT | בְּנֵי יְהוּדָה עֵר וְאוֹנָן וְשֵׁלָה שְׁלוֹשָׁה נוֹלַד לוֹ מִבַּת־שׁוּעַ הַכְּנַעֲנִית |
| TC | בני יהודה ער ואונן ושלה תלתיהון אתילידו ליה מן בת שוע פרקמטתא |

| MT (cont.) | וַיְהִי עֵר ׀ בְּכוֹר יְהוּדָה רַע בְּעֵינֵי הֹ׳ וַיְמִיתֵהוּ׃ |
| TC | והוון ער ואונן עבדין דביש קדם ה׳ וקטלנון על דהוון מחבלין ית אורחתהון: |

NJPS: The sons of Judah: Er, Onan, and Shelah; these three, Bath-shua the Canaanite woman bore to him. But Er, Judah's first-born, was displeasing to the LORD, and He took his life.

---

60   Dan 3:23–29. This story is the source of the Aramaic expression אתון נורא יקידתא (found eight times in Dan 3), which appears in various aggadic sources.

61   For additional sources containing the story of Joshua son of Jehozadak and the fiery furnace, see Ginzberg, p. 426, n. 106. To his list we would add a TT in Kasher *TT*, pp. 214–215 [fragment 144a: 36–44], lines 35–44, as well as TC.

Dost: The sons of Judah: Er, Onan, and Shelah. The three of them were born to him by Bath-shua the merchant. Now Er and Onan were doers of evil before the Lord, so He slew them because they corrupted their ways.

TC translates הַכְּנַעֲנִית not as an ethnonym, but as an occupation. Both meanings are known in Scripture,[62] but it is clear that the rendering in TC is not the simple sense of the present verse. Why, then, is this route taken by TC? Judah's wife is described in Gen 38:2 with the words בַּת־אִישׁ כְּנַעֲנִי, *the daughter of a certain Canaanite*. The modifier כְּנַעֲנִי in that verse is translated as an ethnonym in all Targums of the Torah except TPJ, which has ברת גבר תגר, i.e., the daughter of a man who was a merchant.[63] It stands to reason that the author of TC was influenced by this translation. He was unable to transcribe it verbatim, however, because in Genesis כְּנַעֲנִי describes the woman's father, while in Chronicles הַכְּנַעֲנִית describes the woman herself. He could have translated בת שוע תגרא, *Bath-shua the merchantess*, but preferred to adapt the word to the form פרקמטתא, whose meaning is similar. Possibly he also was influenced by TPJ to the chapter prior to the story recorded here, where אֲנָשִׁים מִדְיָנִים סֹחֲרִים, *Midianite traders*, (Gen 37:28) is translated as גברי מדינאי מרי פרקמטיא.

Later in verse 3, the translation in TC departs significantly from the Hebrew verse. The targumist does not translate Er's description, בְּכוֹר יְהוּדָה, *Judah's firstborn*. He has Onan join Er as a subject of the verse, inserts a comment describing both as "doing evil," and ultimately states that both died at the hand of God due to their wicked ways. The reason for including Onan in the verse is clear enough: any reader of the present verse who is familiar with Genesis 38 will be surprised by Onan's absence here.[64] The targumist therefore added

---

62   See BDB, p. 489. כְּנַעֲנִי of Zech 14:21 is translated by TJ as עביד תגרא.

63   Cf. the late midrashic work *Sekhel Tov* (ed. Buber) 38:2 (vol. 1, p. 226):
'בת איש כנעני'—תגר, ודומה לו, 'אשר סחריה שרים כנעניה נכבדי הארץ'.
'the daughter of a certain Canaanite'—a merchant, like (in the verse), 'whose merchants were nobles, whose traders [lit. Canaanites—L.G.] the world honored?' (Isa 23:8).

64   Gersonides ad loc. writes: קצר המאמר ולא זכר מות אונן, *he abridged the passage and did not mention Onan*. Rudolph, p. 15, argued that the original text had in fact included Onan: וגם אונן משנהו רע בעיני ה' וימיתהו, *Onan, his second son, too, was evil in the Lord's eyes*. In his view, an omission occurred in MT due to the words' similarity to others here (see similar comment in BHS ad loc.; Rudolph was the editor of Chronicles for this series). TC is presented there as something of a textual testimony to the secondary nature of MT. Klein *1 Chronicles*, p. 82, accepted this hypothesis, while Knoppers tends toward the view that the text of TC is intended to bring Chronicles closer to Genesis. In my view, Knoppers is right and we must reject the idea of TC as a witness to a reading different from MT, as a reverse translation of the text of the Targum yields a reading far removed from the presumed Hebrew text. Citation of TC here serves only to demonstrate that the targumist

Onan to the verse and equated him with his brother Er, in terms of both their actions and their punishment. Onan's addition to the verse brought with it the deletion of Er's expected title, בוכרא דיהודה, because its inclusion would have somewhat hurt the balance between the brothers, contrary to the targumist's efforts to equate the two.[65]

Er's deeds are not detailed in Gen 38:7, but Onan's sin is thus described in verse 9: וַיֵּדַע אוֹנָן כִּי לֹא לוֹ יִהְיֶה הַזָּרַע וְהָיָה אִם־בָּא אֶל־אֵשֶׁת אָחִיו וְשִׁחֵת אַרְצָה לְבִלְתִּי נְתָן־זֶרַע לְאָחִיו, *But Onan, knowing that the seed would not count as his, let it go to waste whenever he joined with his brother's wife, so as not to provide offspring for his brother*. TO ad loc. translates the phrase וְשִׁחֵת אַרְצָה as ומחביל אורחיה על ארעא, *he corrupted his way on the earth*. The addition of the word אורח, *way*, by TO reminds us of the description in Gen 6:12 of those who perished in the Flood: כִּי־הִשְׁחִית כָּל־בָּשָׂר אֶת־דַּרְכּוֹ עַל־הָאָרֶץ, *for all flesh had corrupted its ways on earth* (also translated by TO as אורחיה על ארעא+חב״ל). A direct link associating the deeds of those who perished in the Flood with those of Er and Onan appears in *Kallah Rab.* 2:7 (p. 200):

דור המבול כלן מוציאין שכבת זרע לבטלה היו ... מנא הני מילי? דכתיב באונן 'והיה אם בא אל אשת אחיו ושחת ארצה'—שהיה מחמם את עצמו ומוציא שכבת זרע לבטלה, וכתיב בדור המבול 'כי השחית כל בשר את דרכו על הארץ'. ער מאי עוב־דיה? כמעשה אונן, והיינו דכתיב 'וימת גם אותו'.

> The generation of the flood would all ejaculate semen in vain ... What is the source for this? Of Onan it is written, '[*He*] *let it go to waste whenever he joined with his brother's wife*'—he would excite himself and ejaculate semen in vain, and of the flood generation it is written, '*for all flesh had corrupted its ways on earth*'. What did Er's deed? Similar to Onan's, and that is what it means when it says, '*and He took his life **also***'.

Aside from the explicit association with Gen 6:12, this source equates the deeds of Er and Onan. The author of TC seems to have understood their sin similarly to the manner in which it is described in *Kallah Rab.* and intended to indicate as much in writing דהוון מחבלין ית אורחתהון, *because they corrupted their ways*, although no further information is provided. This is not to say that the author of TC had the above source before him—there is no literary or linguistic proof

---

was aware of Onan's absence and therefore added him to the verse, but this is an exegetical, rather than a textual, proof.

65 Cf. the proposal by Rudolph (prior note), who felt a need to dub Onan משנהו, *his second son*, in order to preserve this literary balance.

of such a thing—but this interpretation does appear to have been a well-known one at the time of TC's composition and so found its way into TC.[66]

4.2　　*The Five Prophetic Rulers (1 Chr 2:6)*

1 Chr 2:6

MT: זִמְרִי וְאֵיתָן וְהֵימָן וְכַלְכֹּל וָדָרַע כֻּלָּם חֲמִשָּׁה׃

TC: זמרי ואיתן והימן וכלכל ודרע כולהן אמרכולין דרוח נבואה שריית עליהון והנון חמשא׃

NJPS: The sons of Zerah: Zimri, Ethan, Heman, Calcol, and Dara, five in all.

Dost: The sons of Zerah: Zimri, Ethan, Heman, Calcol, and Dara. All of them were temple officials on whom rested the spirit of prophecy, and they were five.

The obvious question regarding the formulation of the Hebrew verse appears as early as *t. Sanh.* 9:5 (p. 429):[67]

וכי אין אנו יודעין שכולן חמשה? אלא מלמד שאף עכן הוא עמהם לעולם הבא.

> Wouldn't we know [by counting] that they were five altogether? This indicates that Achan, too, was included among them in the world to come.

It may be that the seemingly superfluous calculation is what gave rise to the need to insert an exegetical expansion in the verse, although no direct connection exists between the comment added by TC and *t. Sanhedrin* or parallel traditions.[68] With regard to all five, *Seder 'Olam* comments, "These prophesied in Egypt."[69] The expansion in TC appears to have such a tradition in common, although no direct linguistic influence is in evidence. The presentation of the five as not only prophets, but also princes (אמרכולין),[70] which is unexpected

---

66　Cf. additional sources on the shared sin of Er and Onan in Ginzberg, vol. 5, p. 333, n. 79.

67　Parallels to this question appear in *y. Sanh.* 6:2 (23b, p. 1292); *b. Sanh.* 44b; *Lev. Rab.* 9 (vol. 1, pp. 174–175); *Semaḥot* 2:9 (p. 21).

68　Another potential exegetical approach to the verse leads to the list of wise men in 1 Kgs 5:11: וַיֶּחְכַּם מִכָּל־הָאָדָם מֵאֵיתָן הָאֶזְרָחִי וְהֵימָן וְכַלְכֹּל וְדַרְדַּע בְּנֵי מָחוֹל, *He was the wisest of all men:* [wiser] *than Ethan the Ezrahite, and Heman, Chalkol, and Darda the sons of Mahol*, and this route indeed is that taken by Rashi to 2 Kings as well as Pseudo-Rashi to Chronicles; see Viezel *Pseudo-Rashi*, pp. 107–108. This understanding may have been shared by TJ, who translated the name אֵיתָן הָאֶזְרָחִי in 1 Kgs 5:11 as איתן בר זרח, *Ethan son of Zerah*, which accords with the present verse. TC, however, does not appear to have chosen this direction.

69　*Seder 'Olam* 20 (p. 345). A similar comment appears in *Yalquṭ Šim'oni* 1074 (p. 1032).

70　The word אמרכל is a typical equivalent of the word נשיא in TC (1 Chr 4:38; 5:6; 7:40). The translation, prince, is in keeping with TO Num 3:32 and many verses in TPJ. See also Dray,

and does not hinge on any element of the Hebrew that calls out for additional interpretation, presumably reflects a tradition unknown to us.

4.3   *Shem as High Priest (1 Chr 1:24)*

1 Chr 1:24

MT	אַרְפַּכְשַׁד שָׁלַח׃	אַרְפַּכְשַׁד	שֵׁם׀
TC	שלח׃	שם כהנא רבא ארפסדיי	שם

NJPS: Shem, Arpachshad, Shelah

Dost: Shem the high priest, Arphaxad, Shelah

The appearance of the name שם in the Hebrew verse is supplemented by TC with the remark that he was a high priest. The targumist apparently was influenced by the tradition identifying שם with מלכיצדק (who is described in Gen 14:18 as a high priest), on whose basis the Palestinian Targums of the Torah and Pseudo-Jonathan (as well as BT; see below) sometimes added to the name שם the honorific רבא or the capacity כהונתא רבתא:

Gen 14:18

MT	לֶחֶם וָיָיִן	הוֹצִיא		שָׁלֵם	מֶלֶךְ	וּמַלְכִּי־צֶדֶק
TN	לחם וחמר	אפק	הוא שם רובה	דירושלם	מלכא	ומלכי צדק
FTP	מזון וחמר	דהוא שם רבא הוה כהן עילאה אפיק		דירושלם	מלכא	ומלכי צדק
FTV	ואפיק ליה לחים וחמר	הוא שם רבא		דירושלם	מלכא	ומלכי צדק
TPJ		הוא שם בר נח	...	דירושלם מלכא	מלכא צדיקא	ומלכא

MT (cont.)	עֶלְיוֹן׃	לְאֵל	וְהוּא כֹהֵן
TN	קדם אלהא עלאה׃	בכהנת' רבתה	והוא הוה כהן משמש
FTP	עילאה׃	קדם אל	והוא קאים ומשמש בכהונתא רבתא
FTV	עילאה׃	לאל	הוה כהן
TPJ	קדם אלקא עילאה׃	הוה משמש	ובההיא זימנא

NJPS: And King Melchizedek of Salem brought out bread and wine; he was a priest of God Most High.

Clem TN: Then Melchizedek the king of Jerusalem, he was Shem the Great, brought out bread and wine, and he was a priest serving in the high priesthood before God Most High.

---

pp. 7–8. Dost, ad loc., translated אמרכל as Temple official, which fits the word's usage in rabbinic Hebrew; cf. Jastrow, p. 79.

Clem FTP: Then Melchizedek, the king of Jerusalem, who was Shem the Great, a priest of the Most High, brought out food and wine, standing and serving in the high priesthood before God Most High.

Clem FTV: Then Melchizedek, the king of Jerusalem, he was Shem the Great, a priest to God Most High.

Clem TPJ: Then the righteous king, who was Shem the son of Noah, king of Jerusalem, came out towards Abram, and he brought out for him bread and wine. Now at that time he was serving before God Most High.

TN, FT, and TPJ here identify מלכיצדק as שם, with the former two dubbing him שם רבא (/רובה) and specifying that he served as high priest. TPJ gives no such explicit title here, but the appellation שם רבא appears four times in TPJ to other verses (Gen 22:19; 24:62; 25:22; 38:6).[71] The same sobriquet also appears in an aggadic tradition recorded in b. Sanh. 108b. The terminology used by TC may be explained as an expansion of and commentary on the targumic and talmudic tradition pertaining to שם רבא. Why was he called רבא? In what way was he great? The identification of שם with מלכיצדק gives TC an appropriate opportunity to answer these questions by explaining that he was a high priest.[72]

It bears note that the title רבה is found as one indicating high priesthood in an inscription found in Givʿat ha-Mivtar (lines 1–2), which though from an earlier date than these Targums may be a helpful source of information regarding the linguistic conventions that gave rise to the appellation שם רבא:

אנה אבה בר כהנא אלעז בר אהרן רבה

Rosenthal interpreted the phrase אהרן רבה as "Aaron the Great, Doubtless Aaron the High Priest."[73] Rosenthal offered two possible cultural explanations for the title רבה that accompanies the name אהרן in the inscription. One is that the individual in question was a Samaritan high priest, as evidenced by the Samaritans' tendency to use this title for their leaders. Another possibility is that this high priest was a Jewish one, an explanation buttressed by the use in Sifre Zuṭaʾ of the Hebrew phrase בגדי גדול as a contraction referring to the garments of the high priest.[74] To the example given by Rosenthal of Hebrew

---

71   The title also appears in TN Gen 24:62; 25:22; TNM Gen 25:22; FT Gen 24:62; 25:22.

72   On the identification of Shem as Melchizedek, see also Ginzberg, vol. 5, pp. 225–226, n. 102.

73   Rosenthal Inscription, p. 345.

74   For a complete discussion of the term אהרן רבה, see Rosenthal Inscription, pp. 345–354.

usage, I would add the occurrences of the Aramaic שם רבא in the Palestinian Targums and TPJ, as noted.[75]

4.4 The Sons of Salma (1 Chr 2:54)

1 Chr 2:54

MT   וּנְטוֹפָתִ֥י   בֵּ֣ית לֶ֑חֶם   בְּנֵ֣י שַׂלְמָ֗א

TC   בנוי דשלמא דמן בית־לחם צדיקיא דשומהון טב הי־כנטופא דבטילו פרוזדואוון
דאותיב ירבעם באורחא דלא יעלון בכוריא לירושל' והון בנוי דשלמא

MT (cont.)   עַטְר֖וֹת

TC   מעטרין פירי בכוריא בצניא ומובלין בצנעא לירושלם וצלחין קיסיא ועבדין

(cont.)   בֵּ֣ית יוֹאָ֑ב

TC   סולמיא ומסקין לירושלם לסדור בית מוקדה לקרבניא הנון אתו מזרעית יואב בר צרויה

(cont.)   הַצַּרְעִֽי׃   הַמָּנַחְתִּ֖י   וַחֲצִ֥י

TC   ומנהון כהניא דמפלגין מותר קרבניא בירושלם ותלמידי נבייא דמן צרעה:

NJPS: The sons of Salma: Bethlehem, the Netophathites, Atroth-beth-joab, and half of the Manahathites, the Zorites.

Dost: The sons of Salma, who were from Bethlehem, the righteous ones, whose name was as good as balm, because they removed the guard posts that Jeroboam placed on the road so that the first-fruits would not enter Jerusalem. The sons of Salma would hide the first-fruits in baskets and would bring (them) secretly to Jerusalem, and they would split wood and make ladders, and would bring (them) to Jerusalem to arrange the place of the burning of sacrifices. They came from the clan of Joab son of Zeruiah, and some of them were priests who divide the remainder of the sacrifices in Jerusalem, as well as the disciples of the prophets who were from Zorah.

The great divide between the simple sense of the verse and its interpretive Targum, sufficient to surprise anyone unaccustomed to this phenomenon, results from the exegetical tradition attending the verse. The text of the verse is the foundation of an intricate aggadic tradition appearing in a great number of parallel rabbinic sources, some of them quite early.[76] Churgin argued that the targumist's source was y. Ta'an. 4:7, but I do not believe that the available

---

75   Goshen-Gottstein, vol. 1, p. 41, reports an additional example of the use of the phrase שם רבה in Gen. Zuṭaʾ.

76   T. Taʿan. 3:7–8 (pp. 339–340); scholium to Megillat Taʿanit, 15 Av (see Noam, pp. 81–84); y. Taʿan. 4:5 (68b, p. 730); b. Taʿan. 28a.

data support this conclusion.[77] The Aramaic verse praises the sons of Salma for continuing to bring first fruits and wood for the altar to Jerusalem, at great personal risk, when the roads were blocked to such activity by the soldiers of Jeroboam son of Nebat. Here let us refer to *t. Ta'aniyyot* 3:7–8:

מהו בני גונבי עלי ובני קוצעי קציעות? שבשעה שהושיבו מלכי יון פרדדיאות על הדרכי[ם] שלא לעלות לירושלם, כדרך שהושיב ירבעם בן נבט, כל מי שהוא כשר וירא חטא באותו הדור מה היה עושה? הוא מביא את הבכורים ועושין כמין סלים ומחפן בקציעות ונוטל את הסל ואת הבכורים ומחפן כמין קציעות ומניחן בסלים ונוטל את הסל ואת העלי על כתיפו ועולה. כשהגיע לאותו משמר אמרו לו: לאן אתה הולך? אמ[ר] להם: לעשות שתי קציעות הללו שני כפין של דבילה במכתש הלז שבפניו, בעלי זה שעל כתפי. כיון שעבר מאותו משמר, מעטרן ומעלן לירושלם. מהו או[מר] 'בני סלמאי הנטופתי'? שבשעה שהושיבו מלכי יון פרסדדיאות על הדרכים שלא לעלות לירושלם כדרך שהושיב ירבעם בן נבט, כל מי שהוא ירא חטא וכשר באותו הדור היה נוטל שני גזירי עצים כמין סולם ומניחן על כתיפו ועולה. כשהגיע לאותו משמר, אמרו לו: לאן אתה הולך? ליטול שני גוזלות משובך הלז שבפני, בסולם זה שעל כתפי. כיון שעבר מאותו משמר, מפרקן ומעלן לירושלם. לפי שמסרו עצמן על התורה ועל המצות, לפיכך נמצא להם שם טוב וזכר טוב בעולם, ועליהם הוא אומ[ר]: 'זכר צדיק לברכה'; ועל ירבעם בן נבט וחביריו הוא או[מר]: 'ושם רשעים ירקב'.

What is [the reason for the names] Pestle Smugglers and Fig Pressers? For when the Greek kings set guardposts on the highways to prevent [Jews] from making the ascent to Jerusalem, as did Jeroboam son of Nebat, what would all those who were proper and fearful of sin in that generation do? [He] would bring the first fruits and make types of baskets and cover them with pressed figs and would take the basket and the first fruits and cover them as if they were pressed figs and place them in the baskets. [He] would carry the basket and the pestle on their shoulder and go up [towards Jerusalem]. When he arrived at the guardpost, the guards would

---

77 Churgin *Hagiographa*, pp. 248–249; Hamiel, pp. 405–406. According to Hamiel, the *yerushalmi* should be taken as TC's source because it places the roadblocks in the days of Jeroboam son of Nebat, as does the Targum, whereas the *bavli* places them in the Hellenic Period. This conclusion, however, is not self-evident, as BT, too, describes the events of Jeroboam's day as a historical precedent for those of the Second Temple Period. Because the entire composition is devoted to events from the dawn of the Israelite nation to the final days of the Davidic monarchy, it is unreasonable to expect TC to place the events described by the verse in the Second Temple Period. Therefore, even had the targumist been familiar only with BT, we would expect him to place the actions of the sons of Salmai in the days of Jeroboam, rather than in the Hellenic Period.

ask: Where are you going? He would reply: To make these two fig-presses into two fig cakes in this mortar up ahead, by using this pestle that is on my shoulder. After [successfully] passing through the guardpost, he would decorate them and bring them up to Jerusalem.

What is [the meaning of] the family of Salmai the Netophathite? For when the Greek kings set guardposts on the highways to prevent [Jews] from making the ascent to Jerusalem, as did Jeroboam son of Nebat, what would all those who were fearful of and sin proper in that generation do? [He] would take two wooden logs and make them into a type of ladder and place them on his shoulder and go up [towards Jerusalem]. When he arrived at the guardpost, the guards would ask: Where are you going? To gather two chicks from this dovecote up ahead, with this ladder on my shoulder. After [successfully] passing through the guardpost, he would take them apart and bring them up to Jerusalem. Because they [were willing to] forfeit themselves for the Torah and the Commandments, therefore they had a good name and favorable mention in the world. Of them it is said [in Prov 10:7], "The name of the righteous is invoked in blessing"; and of Jeroboam son of Nebat and his ilk it is said, "But the fame of the wicked rots".

This tradition contains many of the same elements found in the passage in TC. *T. Taʿaniyyot* tells two similar tales of goods smuggled to Jerusalem for the Temple service. In the first story, produce is smuggled to Jerusalem as first fruits; in the second, firewood is smuggled there so that there will be sufficient wood for the altar. The former story explains the names of the sons of pestle smugglers and the sons of fig-pressers,[78] while the latter explains the name of the sons of Salmai the Netophathite. One might wonder why two such similar stories developed regarding names of different origin (the sons of Salmai the Netophathite appear in Scripture, while the sons of pestle smugglers and fig-pressers appear not in Scripture, but in the Mishnah), but we must grant that the tradition in *t. Taʿaniyyot* differentially ascribes the stratagem involving produce to the sons of pestle smugglers and fig-pressers, and the firewood-related

---

78   These names are analyzed in the *baraitaʾ* on account of their appearance in *m. Taʿan.* 4:5:
זמן עצי כהנים והעם ... בחמישה באב בני פרעוש בן יהודה ... בחמישה עשר בו בני זתואל בן
יהודה. ועמהם כהנים ולוים וכל מי שטעה שבטו, בני גנבי עלי ובני קוצעי קציעות.
The time of the wood offering of priests and people ... on the fifth of Ab [is the offering of] the family of Parosh b. Judah ... on the fifteenth of that month [is the offering of] the family of Zattuel b. Judah. And with them [comes the offering of] priests, Levites, and whoever is in error as to his tribe, and the families of Gonbe Eli, the pestle smugglers, and fig pressers.

exploit to the sons of Salmai.[79] The Targum, meanwhile, includes both the story of the produce and that of the firewood in its expansion regarding the sons of Salma.

בנוי דשלמא דמן בית־לחם צדיקיא דשומהון טב הי־כנטופא: The acclaimed reputations earned by these personages is detailed in *t. Ta'aniyyot*, above: לפיכך נמצא להם שם טוב וזכר טוב בעולם, and similarly in the scholium to *Megillat Ta'anit*.[80] The Targum goes further, likening their good name to stacte, i.e., נָטָף, one of the spices of the incense listed in Exod 30:4.

This analogy, based on exegesis of the word וּנְטוֹפָתִי in the verse, does not appear in the parallel sources, with the exception of *Tg. Ruth* 4:20:[81]

Ruth 4:20

MT   וְנַחְשׁוֹן הוֹלִיד אֶת־שַׂלְמָה:

Tg. Ruth   ונחשון אוליד ית סלמא   צדיקא הוא סלמא מבית לחם ונטופה דבטילו
פרוודאוון דאותיב ירבעם חייבא על אורחי והוו עובדי אב ובנין יאוון כנטופא:

NJPS: Amminadab begot Nahshon, Nahshon begot Salmon

Brady: Nahshon fathered Salma the Righteous, that is Salma from Bethlehem and Netophah, [whose sons] did away with the guardposts which Jeroboam the Wicked placed on the roads, and the deeds of the father and sons were beautiful as balm.

---

79   We well may wonder whether the two stories stem from a single source and the language used in the two stories reflects a homily on the present verse, albeit there is no explicit indication that this is the case. Both stories in effect are based on the name סלמאי, which they take as an allusion to commodities transported to Jerusalem. The derivation is clearer in the second story, in which the smugglers are called בני סלמאי for constructing ladders (סולמות) from pieces of wood in order to mislead the authorities. In the first story, the devices employed are baskets (סלים) carried in pestles on the shoulders of the smugglers. Each of the two stories contains the repetitious phrases על כתיפו and שעל כתפי. The emphasis on the word for *shoulder*, which is not intrinsically required by the story, may indicate that this word, too, arrived in these stories as a homily on a word in the verse, viz., נטופתי. (Possibly the homily associated this word with that for shoulder due to the two terms' juxtaposition in the Mishnah and other rabbinic sources concerning clusters of grapes; see *m. Pe'ah* 7:5: ... איזו היא עוללת? כל שאין לה כתף ולא נטף). Notably, it is the first story that uses the verb עט״ר, corresponding to עטרות in the verse.

80   See Noam, pp. 83–84, lines 94–107.

81   Cf. *Tg. Eccl* 3:11, which also refers to the roadblocks (פרוזדאוון) set up by Jeroboam but lacks the context of the sons of Salmai. This verse in *Tg. Eccl*, moreover, contains the epithet ירבעם חייבא, Jeroboam the sinner, (also in 4:16; 10:16; *Tg. Cant* 5:4), as in *Tg. Ruth*.

The insertion in *Tg. Ruth* identifies Salma son of Nahshon with Salma of our verse, and that expansion in fact has a great number of elements in common with TC:

					צדיקא		סלמא	
Tg. Ruth							הוא סלמא מבית לחם	
	ונטופה				...והוו עובדי אב ובנין יאוון כנטופא			
TC	הי־כנטופא	טב	צדיקא דשומהון		צדיקיא דשומהון	דמן בית־לחם	דשׁלמא	בנוי

Tg. Ruth	על אורחי	חייבא	דאותיב ירבעם	דאותיב	פרוודאוון	דבטילו
TC	באורחא		דאותיב ירבעם		פרוזדואון	דבטילו

It is clear that the foundation of the expansion in *Tg. Ruth* is 1 Chr 2:54, but the expansion also constitutes something of an alternative translation to TC, based on a similar aggadic tradition. At the close of the insertion, *Tg. Ruth* gives the word וּנְטוֹפָתִי a different interpretation from that in TC: it is not the name they earned themselves that is as good as stacte, but their deeds that are as seemly as that substance. Another point of contention between the two Targums is that while *Tg. Ruth* credits the sons of Salma with putting an end to the institution of the barricades, it says nothing of any smuggling activity pursued by them. Below we shall discuss the relationship between the two descriptions given in TC, but if we were to read *Tg. Ruth* alone, it would not occur to us that the sons of Salma smuggled goods through the checkpoints. Still and all, this omission does not demonstrate that the author of *Tg. Ruth* was unfamiliar with this smuggling: one may instead take the position that he simply chose to formulate a brief expansion, basing it on terminology that he had received as a tradition (... דבטילו פרוזדואון דאותיב ירבעם), and chose to make do with this rather than branch out further and give a detailed account of the entire exploit.[82]

All told, the comparison to stacte, absent from the early sources, appears solely in these two Targums of late date, and even in them it appears in two different forms. It thus appears that the targumists received the above traditions, known to us from Tosefta and *Megillat Taʿanit*, in a form including the positive mention of the sons of Salma, in contradistinction to the excoriation reserved for Jeroboam. TC integrated the tradition concerning the good repute of the sons of Salma within the continuum of the verse by expounding the word

---

82   The precise nature of the relationship between the tradition contained in *Tg. Ruth* and that in TC is worthy of a separate study.

וּנְטוֹפָתִי as derived from the Hebrew for stacte, while the author of *Tg. Ruth*, representing a later exegetical stage, is not directly dependent on the good name noted in the sources, but interprets the word וּנְטוֹפָתִי metaphorically.

דבטילו פרוזדואוון דאותיב ירבעם באורחא דלא יעלון בכוריא לירושל': The word פרוזדואוון, derived from Greek[83] or Latin,[84] has the general sense of a garrison. In the present context, it refers to roadblocks set up by the authorities. The word appears in many sources describing the decree issued by Jeroboam son of Nebat (as well, in some sources, as the Greek decree) and in a variety of corrupt forms.[85]

The Targum states that the sons of Salmai put an end to (דבטילו) Jeroboam's roadblocks, but then says that they simply pulled the wool over his soldiers' eyes. McIvor suggested a number of ways to bridge the gap between these two descriptions, preferring as most logical the explanation that ongoing trickery ultimately caused the barricades to be discontinued.[86] In my opinion, the contradiction within TC between the voidance of the roadblocks and the acts of smuggling reflects not the orderly recordation of a particular tradition, but a partial fusion of two competing traditions found in rabbinic sources. We noted earlier that the story of Jeroboam's roadblocks appears in numerous sources; some of these sources concern the smuggling exploits of the sons of Salmai and the sons of pestle swindlers and fig-driers, but others credit Hoshea son of Elah (or Abijah son of Jeroboam) with closing the roadblocks in his day:[87]

אלא חמשה עשר באב מאי היא? ... עולא אמ[ר]: יום שבטל הושע בן אלה אותן פרדסיות שהושיב ירבעם בן נבט על הדרכים שלא יעלו ישראל לרגל.

But why the fifteenth of Ab? ... Ulla said, "It was the day on which Hosea son of Elah removed the guards whom Jeroboam had put on the roads to keep the Israelites from making the pilgrimages to Jerusalem."

---

83 Thus Lieberman *t. Ta'an.*, p. 339 (πραισίδια).

84 Thus Levy, vol. 2, p. 288 (*praesidia*); Krauss *Lehnwörter*, vol. 2, p. 483.

85 *T. Ta'an.* 3:8 (pp. 339); *Y. Ta'an.* 4:7 (68b, p. 730); *b. Ta'an.* 28a; 30b; *Mo'ed Qaṭ.* 28b; *Giṭ.* 88a; *B. Bat.* 121b; *Lam. Rab.*, Introduction 33 (p. 35); *Seder 'Olam* 22 (p. 369); scholium to *Megillat Ta'anit* (Noam, pp. 81–82); *Tg. Ruth* 4:20; *Tg. Eccl* 3:11; TT 1 Kgs 14:13 (Kasher *TT*, p. 132, fragment 86, MS Montefiore 7).

For an investigation of the variants of the various sources and the precise sense of the word, see Milikowsky.

86 McIvor, p. 54, end of n. 48.

87 The excerpt is from *b. B. Bat.* 121b, but see also parallels in n. 85, above. *B. Mo'ed Qaṭ.* 28b credits Abijah son of Jeroboam with discontinuing the roadblocks.

TC's use of the root בט״ל (which we saw in the expansion in *Tg. Ruth*, as well) is explained by the use of this root in Hebrew regarding the rabbinic tradition concerning Hosea son of Elah. TC associatively blends the two aspects of the roadblocks that are addressed by the Rabbis: the acts of smuggling performed during the time of their operation, and their removal in the day of Hosea son of Elah. I do not believe that the author of TC was aware of the resulting contradiction in his composition.

והוון בנוי דשלמא מעטרין פירי בכוריא בצניא ומובלין בצנעא לירושלם: The smuggling of the first fruits, attributed in *t. Taʿanit* to the sons of pestle smugglers and fig-pressers, in TC is attributed to the sons of Salma. As we noted above, it may be that the name *Salma* was seen in the first place as alluding to the smuggling of firewood, which is explicitly attributed to them in rabbinic sources, as well as to that of first fruits, because the name *Salma* may be seen as an allusion to the ladders (סלם) that figured in the story of the firewood as well as to the baskets (סלים; in the Targum, צנייא) of the story of the first fruits. In any event, the word מעטרין is inspired by the present verse's עֲטָרוֹת, and the same root appears regarding the story of the sons of pestle smugglers, as well.

וצלחין קיסיא ועבדין סולמיא ומסקין לירושלם לסדור בית מוקדה לקרבניא: These words summarize the act of smuggling firewood for the altar. The name סלמא/שלמא was taken as an allusion to the ladders that were brought to Jerusalem and disassembled there to serve as firewood.

הנון אתו מזרעית יואב בר צרויה: From this point forward there is no connection between the Targum and the traditions about smuggling things past the roadblocks. The impression received here is that the exegesis reflected in TC to the verse's end is not the result of any direct inspiration from rabbinic sources known to us. The verse makes mention of בֵּית יוֹאָב, and the targumist characteristically identifies this Joab with Joab son of Zeruiah.

ומנהון כהניא דמפלגין מותר קרבניא בירושלם: This continuum corresponds to the words וַחֲצִי הַמְּנֻחֹתִי in the verse. In accordance with his earlier translation (verse 52), the author of TC interprets the toponym מְנָחַת as derived from מנחה, a type of sacrifice. חֲצִי is translated literally, with the root פל״ג, and converted to a verbal form, so that the verse refers to the distribution of sacrificial gifts as a part of the priests' due. This having already being said in the Targum, the author also inserts a reference to the priests and Jerusalem.

ותלמידי נבייא דמן צרעה: The targumist knows that there is no connection between the distribution of the sacrificial gifts and the residents of Zorah, who are known not to have been of priestly descent. Nevertheless, he has a homily ready to explain the appearance of the residents of Zorah here, having already established in verse 53, above, that Zorah was the home of disciples of prophets descended from Moses.

4.5 *Daniel is Chileab (1 Chr 3:1)*

1 Chr 3:1

MT וְאֵ֣לֶּה הָי֤וּ בְנֵֽי־דָוִיד֙ אֲשֶׁ֣ר נֽוֹלַד־ל֣וֹ | בְּחֶבְר֔וֹן הַבְּכ֣וֹר אַמְנֹ֗ן לַאֲחִינֹ֙עַם֙ הַיִּֽזְרְעֵאלִ֔ית

TC ואליין הוו בני דוד דאתילידו ליה בחברון בוכרא אמנן לאחינעם דמן יזראל

MT (cont.) שֵׁנִ֣י דָּנִיֵּ֔אל לַאֲבִיגַ֖יִל הַֽכַּרְמְלִֽית׃

TC תנינא דניאל הוא כלאב דדמי כוליה לאבא דיליה לאביגיל דמן כרמלא׃

NJPS: These are the sons of David who were born to him in Hebron: the first-born Amnon, by Ahinoam the Jezreelite; the second Daniel, by Abigail the Carmelite.

Dost: These were the sons of David who were born to him in Hebron. Amnon, the firstborn of Ahinoam, who was from Jezreel; the second Daniel, who was Chileab—who completely resembled his father—by Abigail, who was from Carmel.

In a list similar to that presented above, the Book of Samuel names Abigail's son as כִּלְאָב:

2 Sam 3:2–3

וַיִּוָּלְד֧וּ (קרי) לְדָוִ֛ד בָּנִ֖ים בְּחֶבְר֑וֹן וַיְהִ֤י בְכוֹרוֹ֙ אַמְנֹ֔ן לַאֲחִינֹ֖עַם הַיִּזְרְעֵאלִֽת׃ וּמִשְׁנֵ֣הוּ כִלְאָ֔ב לַאֲבִיגַ֕ל (קרי) אֵ֖שֶׁת נָבָ֥ל הַֽכַּרְמְלִ֑י

NJPS: Sons were born to David in Hebron: His first-born was Amnon, by Ahinoam of Jezreel; his second was Chileab, by Abigail wife of Nabal the Carmelite

TC inserts in the translational continuum a comment identifying the two figures with each other—דניאל הוא כלאב—as well as a homily playing on the name כִּלְאָב, viz., דדמי כוליה לאבא דיליה.[88] The exegetical solution found in the expansion added here by the targumist is not an original one: a similar

---

88 The targumist's usage of the form דיליה is somewhat surprising. It would have been expected to use a pronominal suffix, thus arriving at the form לאבוהי, a form found in TC more than thirty times.

Another homily that offers another solution for the appearance of both names is found in *b. ber.* 4a:

ולא כלאב שמו, אלא דניאל שמו, שנא[מר] 'והשני דניאל לאביגיל הכרמלית'. ולמה נקרא שמו כלאב? שמכלים פני מפיבושת בהלכה.

technique is used to resolve the difficulty in a number of rabbinic sources. In *Tanḥuma, Toledot* 6 (pp. 27–28), we find the following aggadic account:[89]

אמ[ר] ר' יצחק: אין לך דור שאין בו ליצנין. בשעה שגזז נבל את צאנו שלח דוד נעריו
אצלו ... 'ויהי כעשרת הימים ויגף ה' את נבל וימת'—מיד, 'וישלח דוד וידבר באביגיל
לקחתה לו לאשה'. כיון שבאה, פירש דוד ממנה של[שה] חדשים שלא תהא מעוב-
רת מן נבל. לאחר שלשה חדשים, בא עליה ונתעברה הימנו. והיו ליצני הדור מליזין
ואומר[ים] מן נבל היא מעוברת. מה עשה הקב"ה? צוה המלאך הממונה על צורת
הוולד ואמ[ר] לו: לך וצר אותו בדמות אביו, כדי שיעידו הכל שדוד הוא אביו. מנין?
שכן כתיב, 'ויהי אמנון בכורו לאחינועם היזרעאלית ומשנהו כלאב לאביגיל אשת נבל
הכרמלי'. מה תל[מוד] לו[מר] 'כלאב'? שהיה כלו אב. כל הרואהו אומר דוד אביו
של זה.

Let us note the language of the two sources we have before us. Both expound the name כְּלָאָב as denoting an absolute resemblance of its bearer to his father, but the language of *Tanḥuma* poses a certain difficulty. The form of the expression אב כלו שהיה is lacking in clarity, while the diction of TC is far clearer. According to the Targum, Chileab was in his entirety reminiscent of his father, i.e., his resemblance to David was not limited to certain parts of the body, but his entire body resembled his father's, as if he were his father's double. The language used by TC is easier to understand because the verb דמי is used to clarify the sentence's meaning. The need to elucidate the language of the foundational homily by adding this verb apparently arose as a result of an alteration that the tradition's text had undergone in the source to which the targumist had reference. Hyman, in his notes to *Yalquṭ Šimʿoni*, compiled various sources containing this exegesis.[90] A few of the sources read כולו אב, as in *Tanḥuma*, while others have כאלו אב, as with Hyman's foundation text:

His name was not Kileab but rather Daniel. Why, then, was he called Kileab? Because he shamed Mephibosheth in criticizing his legal decisions.

Interestingly enough, this solution did not find its way into TC, despite the targumist's using this same talmudic section elsewhere, cf. my discussion, p. 317.

89 This aggadic tradition is brought up in the context of a similar situation in the patriarchal narrative, in a homily on Gen 25:19, in which Isaac is described as looking just like Abraham. TPJ makes mention of this tradition ad loc:

ומן בגלל דהוה איקונין דיצחק מדמיין לאיקונין דאברהם הוון בני נשא אמרין בקושטא אברהם
אוליד ית יצחק

Clem: And because the image of Isaac resembled the image of Abraham, people said, "Truly, Abraham begat Isaac."

90 *Yalquṭ Šimʿoni*, 2 Sam, 141 (p. 201). We can add to Hyman's sources the commentary attributed to a student of R. Saadyah Gaʾon, p. 15, which cites Jeroam of Magdiel, based on R. Saadyah Gaʾon.

למה נקרא שמו כלאב? לפי שהיו ליצני הדור אומרים איפשר שמדוד היא מתעברת, אבל מנבל היא מתעברת. מה עשה הב״ה? צר צורתו כצורתו של אביו, וזהו כלאב— כאלו אב.

Why was he called by the name Kileab? Because the mockers of the day would say, 'is it possible that she conceived by David? She conceived by Nabal! What did the Holy One blessed be He? He gave him the form of his father, therefore [he was called] Kileab—'just like his father'.

כאלו אב is a clearer formulation than is כולו אב. The former conforms in its pronunciation to the name כְּלְאָב as traditionally diacriticized, and even is a more appropriate version to appear in *Tanḥuma*:

מה ת״ל כְּלְאָב? שהיה [כאלו] אב—כל הרואה אומר דוד אביו של זה.

What does the name Kileab signify? That it was as if he was his father—anyone who saw him would say, 'David is this one's father'.

Most probably the original exegesis related כְּלְאָב to the words כאלו אב, *as if [his] father*, and the term was written כילו, whether by the original author or by a later hand. The form כילו was corrupted to the familiar form כלו/כולו, *entirely*, and thence proceeded to the text of *Tanḥuma* as we know it.[91] It appeared thus in the source that lay before the author of TC, as well. The targumist integrated the homily in his Targum, but due to the linguistic oddness in which the corruption had resulted, he added to it the verb דמי, *resembled*, thus clarifying the words' meaning.

4.6 *Anani: Name of the Messiah (1 Chr 3:24)*

1 Chr 3:24

MT וּבְנֵי אֶלְיוֹעֵינַי הוֹדַוְיָהוּ (קרי) וְאֶלְיָשִׁיב וּפְלָיָה וְעַקּוּב וְיוֹחָנָן וּדְלָיָה וַעֲנָנִי שִׁבְעָה:

TC ובני אליועיני הודויהו ואלישיב ופליה ועקוב ויוחנן ודליה וענני הוא מלכא משיחא דעתיד לאתגלאה כולהון שבעה:

NJPS: And the sons of Elioenai: Hodaviah, and Eliashib, and Pelaiah, and Akkub, and Johanan, and Delaiah, and Anani—seven.

Dost: he sons of Elioenai: Hodaviah, Eliashib, Pelaiah, Akkub, Johanan, Delaiah, and Anani, who is King Messiah, who will be revealed. In all, seven.

---

91 On interchange of כאילו, כילו, כולו, and כולן as well as other terms in MSS of rabbinic sources, see Kister *ARN*, pp. 260–261, and sources cited ibid.

The identification of *Anani* as the name of the messiah is found as early as a liturgical poem by Qalir found in the Cairo Genizah:[92]

ויצמח צמח ממטה תפארה

בשם אום כחמה ברה

ועל שם דויד הורו נקרא

כי מלכות בית דויד בידו כתורה

ובשם ה' צדקנו הוקרא

על כי תצדק אום מאמנה שרה

ובשם ענני כנהו עונה עתירה

ושמו מנחם להניח אנחה וצרה

ונתכנה בשם נהירה

כי רכובו עם ענני נהורה

The tradition appears in *Tanḥuma* (ed. Buber), which quotes the verse under discussion and then adds:[93]

ועד כאן פרט [לך] הכתוב. מי הוא ענני? זה [מלך] המשיח, שנאמר, חזה הוית [בחזוי ליליא] וארו עם ענני שמיא וגו'

> Thus is listed by Scripture. Who is Anani? He is the Messiah King, as stated, "As I looked on, in the night vision, one like a human being came with the clouds (ענני) of heaven; he reached the Ancient of Days and was presented to Him." (Dan 7:13)

The author of TC was familiar with the exegetical tradition concerning Anani as a code name for the messiah, and included it in his expansion.[94] Based on a survey of the various sources where the tradition is mentioned, it would seem that the motivation for the homily is not Anani's name, despite the adduction of Dan 7:13 to bolster his identification as the messiah, but Anani's place as the final descendant of the Davidic house to be listed. It stands to reason that this was the understanding of the author of TC—such exegesis otherwise would appear arbitrary—but the targumist does not go out of his way to call attention

---

92 *Qedushtot* for Special Sabbaths, זכר חסדו ואמונתו, Sabbath 5, lines 103–112. Text of poem is per Bodleian Library Genizah MS Heb. d.41, pp. 54b–55a.

93 *Tanḥuma* (ed. Buber), *Toledot* 20 (p. 140). A similar but different version is cited in *Yalquṭ Šimʿoni* Zech 571 (p. 797). Another version appears in *ʾAggadat Gen.* 45:1 (p. 89):
הודויהו ואלישיב ופליה ועקוב ויוחנן ודליה וענני שבעה'. מהו שבעה? מה שכתוב במשיח ...

94 This tradition also appears in the commentary attributed to a student of Saadyah, p. 16, and Pseudo-Rashi.

to this in the formulation he chooses. The terminology used, דעתיד לאתגלאה, *who will be revealed*, appears to be an addition made by him personally, but it was made under the influence of the habitual linguistic convention when mentioning the messiah. We similarly find in TJ Zech 6:12: הא גברא משיחא שמיה עתיד דיתגלי, *Behold the man—Messiah is his name—will be revealed*; TPJ Gen 35:21: דהתמן עתיד דאיתגלי מלכא משיחא בסוף יומיא, *the place where King Messiah will be revealed at the end of days*.

4.7 *Saul as Zimri the Sinner (1 Chr 4:24)*

1 Chr 4:24

MT   בְּנֵי שִׁמְעוֹן נְמוּאֵל וְיָמִין יָרִיב זֶרַח שָׁאוּל:

TC   בני שמעון נמואל וימין יריב זרח   שאול   הוא זמרי דאשאיל גופיה לפורענותא:

NJPS: The sons of Simeon: Nemuel, Jamin, Jarib, Zerah, Shaul

Dost: The sons of Shimon: Nemuel, Jamin, Jarib, Zerah, Saul—who is Zimri, who lent his body to punishment

This list has two parallels in the Torah (Gen 46:10; Exod 6:15), in both of which Saul's name is accompanied by the sobriquet בן הכנענית, *son of the Canaanitess*. The identification of שאול בן הכנענית of the Torah with זמרי appears in rabbinic literature along with other names that are interpreted as referring to the same individual.[95] TPJ, like TC, includes a homily on Saul's name:

---

95   *B. Sanh.* 82b:

אמר רבי יוחנן: חמשה שמות יש לו. זמרי, ובן סלוא, ושאול, ובן הכנענית, ושלומיאל בן צורי שדי. זמרי—על שנעשה כביצה המוזרת, בן סלוא—על שהסליא עונות של משפחתו, שאול—על שהשאיל עצמו לדבר עבירה, בן הכנענית—על שעשה מעשה כנען. ומה שמו? שלומיאל בן צורי שדי שמו.

Said R. Yohanan, "Zimri had five names: Zimri, son of Salu; Saul, son of the Canaanite woman; and Shelumiel, son of Zurishaddai. '"Zimri,' because he became like an addled egg. '"Son of Salu,' because he outweighed the sins of his family; '"Saul,' because he lent himself to sin; '"Son of the Canaanite woman,' because he acted like a Canaanite. "But what was his real name? It was Shelumiel, son of Zurishaddai."

Num. Rab. 21:3 (p. 176):

ו' שמות יש לו לזמרי: זמרי, בן סלוא, בן כנענית, ושאול, ושלומיאל, בן צורי שדי. זמרי—שנעשה על אותה מדינית כביצה המוזרת. בן סלוא—בן שסילא עון משפחתו. שאול—שהשאיל עצמו לעבירה. בן הכנענית—שעשה מעשה כנען. ומה שמו? שלומיאל.

Zimri had six names: Zimri, son of Salu, and Saul, son of a Canaanite woman, and Shelumiel, son of Zurishaddai. "Zimri", because on account of that Midianite woman he became like an addled egg. "son of Salu", son that made his family's sin heavy. "Saul", because he lent himself to sin. "son of the Canaanite woman", because he acted like a Canaanite. And what was his name? Shelumiel.

Gen 46:10

| MT | הַכְּנַעֲנִית׃ | וְשָׁאוּל בֶּן־ | יְמוּאֵל ... | שִׁמְעוֹן | וּבְנֵי |

TPJ: ובנוי דשמעון ימואל ... ושאול הוא זמרי דעבד עובדא דכנענאי דשיטים׃

NJPS: Simeon's sons: Jemuel ... and Saul the son of a Canaanite woman

Clem: And the sons of Simeon: Jemuel ... and Shaul (he was Zimri who followed the practice of the Canaanites of Shittim)

Exod 6:15

| MT | הַכְּנַעֲנִית | וְשָׁאוּל בֶּן־ | יְמוּאֵל ... | שִׁמְעוֹן | וּבְנֵי |

TPJ: ובנוי דשמעון ימואל ... ושאול הוא זמרי דאשאיל נפשיה לזנותא הי ככנענאי ...

NJPS: The sons of Simeon: Jemuel ... and Saul the son of a Canaanite woman

Clem: And the sons of Simeon: Jemuel ... and Shaul (he is Zimri who lent his soul to fornication like the Canaanites)

No known Pentateuchal Targum other than TPJ adds any comment to the Hebrew name of שָׁאוּל בֶּן־הַכְּנַעֲנִית. TPJ in both cases begins with the identifying statement ושאול הוא זמרי, but the homily on each of the verses has a different focus. Gen 46:10 is chiefly concerned with the words בֶּן־הַכְּנַעֲנִית and contains no explicit discussion of the name שָׁאוּל. The term בֶּן־הַכְּנַעֲנִית is understood as denoting that this figure comported himself as a Canaanite, taking its cue from the diction of Lev 18:3 (וּכְמַעֲשֵׂה אֶרֶץ־כְּנַעַן ... לֹא תַעֲשׂוּ) as interpreted by the Rabbis in *b. Sanh.* 82b et al. In Exod 6:15, TPJ interprets the first part of the name (שָׁאוּל) as indicating that he lent (השאיל) himself (to promiscuous behavior) and the second (בֶּן־הַכְּנַעֲנִית) as indicating his resemblance to the Canaanites. The similarity between TC and TPJ lies in the first three words of the added verbiage in Exod 6:15, הוא זמרי דאשאיל. Beyond this point, their paths diverge.

TC, TPJ, and the rabbinic sources all appear to have essentially the same exegesis in mind, viz., that שָׁאוּל lent himself to *X*, with the proviso that TPJ and TC have different interpretations of the word *himself* and choose different words for *X*. Further, the author of TC chose to add to his Targum only the homily on the name שָׁאוּל and to omit that regarding בֶּן־הַכְּנַעֲנִית, because the latter words are absent in Chronicles.

4.8 Reuben's Disqualification as Firstborn (1 Chr 5:1)

1 Chr 5:1

| MT | וּבְנֵי רְאוּבֵן בְּכוֹר־יִשְׂרָאֵל כִּי הוּא הַבְּכוֹר וּבְחַלְּלוֹ |
| TC | ובני ראובן בוכרא דישראל ארום בוכרא הוא ובאפסותיה קדושתיה כד סליק |

| MT (cont.) | יְצוּעֵי אָבִיו בְּכֹרָתוֹ נִתְּנָה לִבְנֵי יוֹסֵף בֶּן־יִשְׂרָאֵל |
| TC | לדרגשא דאבוי אשתקלת מניה ואתיהיבת בכירותיה לבנוי דיוסף בר ישר׳ |

וְלֹא לְהִתְיַחֵשׂ לַבְּכֹרָה׃ (cont.)

TC דלא לאתיחסא בנוי דראובן לבכורותא׃

NJPS: The sons of Reuben the first-born of Israel. (He was the first-born; but when he defiled his father's bed, his birthright was given to the sons of Joseph son of Israel, so he is not reckoned as first-born in the genealogy.

Dost: The sons of Reuben, the firstborn of Israel. Indeed, he was the firstborn, but when he desecrated his holiness by going up to his father's bed his birthright was taken from him and it was given to the sons of Joseph son of Israel, so that the children of Reuben would not be registered with the status of firstborn.

1 Chr 5:2

MT	מִמֶּנּוּ	וּלְנָגִיד		גָּבַר בְּאֶחָיו		יְהוּדָה	כִּי
TC	מן ראובן	מלכותא ברם אשתקלת		אתגבר באחוי	דיהודה	מטול
	מניה ומלכותא		דהוא גברא	ליהודה	ואתיהבת
	כהונתא	ואשתקלת ולא חבו בעגלא	חסידא הוה	לוי	אוף
מבנוי דראובן רבתא					
מכלהון בוכריא ומטולתהון					

ואתיהיבת לאהרן ובנוי ומטרת קודשא ליואי

MT (cont.) וְהַבְּכֹרָה לְיוֹסֵף׃

TC ובכורותא ליוסף׃

NJPS: though Judah became more powerful than his brothers and a leader came from him, yet the birthright belonged to Joseph.)

Dost: Because Judah prevailed over his brothers, the kingdom was indeed taken from Reuben and was given to Judah, who was a warrior, and the kingdom is from him. Moreover, Levi was pious, and (his descendants) did not become guilty in (the matter of) the calf, so the high priesthood was taken from the sons of Reuben, and because of them, from all their firstborn, and it was given to Aaron and his sons, and the charge of the sacred service to the Levites, and the birthright to Joseph.

The Hebrew verse describes the transfer of the status of firstborn from Reuben to Joseph while clarifying that the monarchy is not an appurtenance of this status. This explanation is in keeping with the Chronicler's view that the crown belonged to Judah from time immemorial, and specifically was the possession of David and his line. In the words of S. Japhet:[96]

---

96   Japhet *Ideology*, pp. 349–350.

The book of Chronicles gives no reason for Judah's destiny; he was chosen *a priori*. In the course of history, Judah's chosenness is "put into practice": because the tribe was destined to govern Israel, David is selected as king ... Chronicles takes Jacob's blessing as an historical fact: Judah's destiny to govern was first foretold and then realized the course of history, and David's election is contingent upon the choice of Judah as ruling tribe ... Thus, the process of election is a gradual one. The choosing of David was no isolated phenomenon, a simple contrast to the election of Saul. It was the culmination of a process which began with the selection of Judah and which, by its very nature, could only result in the election of David.

The targumist, however, deviates from the line taken by the author of the Hebrew book. According to TC, Reuben originally was chosen to reign, but Judah was granted the monarchy due to later developments.

In a further deviation from the Hebrew, the targumist adds that Reuben originally was destined to receive another distinction in addition to the birthright and the monarchy, viz., the high priesthood. The Aramaic verse describes the loss of these three privileges, each under its own particular circumstances. Reuben was stripped of the birthright due to his affair with Bilhah. He lost the monarchy because Judah proved himself worthier of the position. The targumist reads the beginning of verse 2 as giving a reason for the transfer of the monarchy from Reuben to Judah: kingship was taken from Reuben because Judah waxed mightily among his brothers. Finally, Reuben lost the high priesthood for a reason that is not written explicitly but nevertheless is implied. The Levites did not sin with the Golden Calf, and therefore were granted priesthood, specifically awarded to Aaron and his sons, as well as the privilege of guarding the Temple, which went to the remainder of the tribe.[97] The children of Reuben thus lost this distinction because, unlike the Levites, they participated in the sin of the Golden Calf. The monarchy and high priesthood are depicted as naturally flowing from the birthright. Why Reuben originally was meant to reign is not written—the targumist assumes that it is only natural for the firstborn to be king. The dynamic concerning the status of the priests (and that of the other members of the tribe of Levi) is a clearer one, given the targumist's explanation that the initial selection of Reuben for this position was to be realized by the selection of the firstborn to serve as Temple functionaries,

---

97   The targumist states that Levi הוה חסידא, *was pious*, an expression influenced by Deut 33:8: וּלְלֵוִי אָמַר תֻּמֶּיךָ וְאוּרֶיךָ לְאִישׁ חֲסִידֶךָ, *and of Levi he said: let Your Thummim and Urim be with Your faithful (/pious) one.*

only to be voided when they were replaced by the Levites. The loss of the latter two privileges thus resulted from other brothers' or tribes' proving themselves better suited for the given position than Reuben.

The differentiation of the status that was to be Reuben's into the three distinct spheres noted above is not an original idea put forward by TC. Just as 1 Chr 5:1–2 is influenced by Gen 49:3–4 (וּבְחַלְּלוֹ || כִּי עָלִיתָ מִשְׁכְּבֵי אָבִיךָ אָז חִלַּלְתָּ יְצוּעִי יְצוּעִי אָבִיו; *for when you mounted your father's bed, you brought disgrace—my couch he mounted! || but when he defiled his father's bed*),[98] TC here bases itself on the midrashic and targumic tradition to those verses, many representatives of which describe the three privileges noted in TC as accruing to Reuben prior to his sin.[99] Given lexical choices made by TC in giving translations of several words of Genesis 49 that diverge from those in the Targums ibid., it seems that

---

98   Japhet *OTL*, pp. 132–133; Klein *1 Chronicles*, p. 159; Knoppers *vol. I*, p. 382.

99   See list of midrashic sources in Ginzberg, vol. 5, p. 367, n. 384. All known Targums of the Torah to Gen 49:3 also enumerate these three distinctions:

TO לך הוה חזי למסב תלתה חולקין בבירותא כהונתא ומלכותא

Clem: For you it would have been fitting to take three parts: the birthright, the priesthood, and the kingship.

TN חמי הויית מסב תלתא חולקין יתיר על אחך בכורותא דידך היא ומלכותא וכהנתא רבתא לך הוויין חמיין על דחטית ראובן ברי אתיהיבת בכורתא ליוסף ברי ומלכותא ליהודה וכהונתא רבתא לשבטוי דלוי

Clem: You were fit to take three parts more than your brothers: the birthright was yours, and the kingdom and the high priesthood were properly yours. Because you sinned, Reuben, my son, the birthright has been given to Joseph, my son, and the kingdom to Judah, and the high priesthood to the tribe of Levi.

FTP לך הויא חזיא למיסב תלתא חולקין יתירין על אחך בכירותא ומלכותא וכהונתא רבתא ועל דחבתא ראובן איתיהיבת בכירותא ליוסף ומלכותא ליהודה וכהונתא רבתא לבני שבטוי דלוי

Clem: You were fit to take three parts more than your brothers: the birthright, and the kingdom, and the high priesthood. Because you sinned, Reuben, the birthright has been given to Joseph, and the kingdom to Judah, and the high priesthood to the sons of the tribe of Levi.

FTV חמי הוה לך ראובן ברי למיסב תלתא חולקין יתיר על אחך בכורתא ומלכותא וכהונתא רבתה על דחטיית איתיהיבת בכורתא ליוסף ומלכותא ליהודה וכהונתא רבתה לשבטא דלוי

Clem: You were fit, Reuben my son, to take three parts more than your brothers: the birthright, and the kingdom, and the high priesthood. Because you sinned, the birthright has been given to Joseph, and the kingdom to Judah, and the high priesthood to the tribe of Levi.

GT MS Z [חמ]י הוה לך ראובן ברי למיסב תלתה חן[לקין ... ב]כורותה ומלכו[תה וכ]הנתה ... ברי אתי[ה][ב][ת] בכורו[תה....] וכהנת[ה ...]

Clem: It was fitting for you, Reuben my son, to take three parts [more than your brothers:] the birthright was yours, and the kingdom and the high priesthood [were properly yours. Because you sinned,] Reuben, my son, the birthright has been given [to Joseph, my son, and the kingdom] to Judah, and the high priesthood [to the tribe of Levi.]

TPJ חמי הוי לך בכורותא ורבות כהונתא ומלכותא ועל די חטית ברי איתיהיבת בכירותא ליוסף ומלכותא ליהודה וכהונתא ללוי

though TC relied on a tradition similar to those appearing in the Targums of the Torah, the author did not quote them directly. Thus the phrase חִלַּלְתָּ יְצוּעִי there is represented in TO as אֲחִילְתָּא לְשִׁוּוּיִי, *you defiled my bed*, in TPJ as בְּלִבִילְתָּא שִׁוּוּיִי, *you disarranged my bed*,[100] and in the Palestinian Targums in a nonliteral fashion. None of the Targums known to us translated the root חל״ל with the root פס״ס, and none adds Reuben's sanctity as the object of the act of desecration. דרגש, the word that functions in TC as the translation of יצוע, does not reflect the choices made by the Pentateuchal Targums, although the word דרגש does appear with the sense of *bed* in an expansion of the Palestinian Targums and TPJ in Gen 49:1, where it has no equivalent in the Hebrew verse.

Despite the multiplicity of both midrashic and targumic sources at our disposal, I cannot precisely identify the source used by TC. The targumist was familiar with the popular tradition of the three privileges that had been taken from Reuben, and included it within his Targum. It may be that TC's unique choices come from a source that is not known to us. Alternately, the targumist may simply have chosen to give expression to the popular tradition in his own way.

Yet even if this latter possibility is the case, we can identify an intriguing linguistic affinity between TC here and TPJ to a verse that does not directly touch on Reuben's sin. TC gave the word וּבְחַלְּלוֹ the expansive translation וּבְאַפְּסוּתֵיה קְדוּשְׁתֵיה,[101] a rare phrase found in targumic literature in only one other instance, TPJ Num 25:1:

| MT | וַיָּחֶל | הָעָם | לִזְנוֹת | אֶל־בְּנוֹת מוֹאָב: |
| TPJ | וְשָׁרִיאוּ | עַמָּא | | |

לְאוֹפָּסָא קְדוּשְׁתְּהוֹן וּלְמִפְעַר גַּרְמֵיהוֹן לְטוּפְסָא דִפְעוֹר וּלְמִטְעָיָא בָּתַר בְּנַת מוֹאֲבָאֵי דְמַפְּקָן יַת טוּפְסֵיה דִפְעוֹר מִתְּחוֹת פְּסִיקַיְיהוֹן:

NJPS: the people profaned themselves by whoring with the Moabite women
Clem: and the people began to desecrate their holiness, and to uncover themselves for the image of Peor, and to go astray after the daughters of the Moabites who were bringing out the image of Peor from under their girdles

---

Clem: The birthright, the high priesthood, and the kingship would have been fitting for you, but because you sinned, my son, the birthright was given to Joseph, and the kingship to Judah, and the priesthood to Levi.

100 On the use of the root בלב״ל with regard to the sin of Reuben, cf. *b. Šabb.* 55b.

101 These words not only are an expansion, but also alter the syntactic structure of the original sentence. In the Hebrew verse, יְצוּעֵי אָבִיו functions as the object of the verb וּבְחַלְּלוֹ, whereas in the Targum the object of וּבְאַפְּסוּתֵיה is קְדוּשְׁתֵיה (viz., that of Reuben), i.e., in Scripture Reuben desecrated his father's bed, while in the Targum he desecrated his own sanctity by mounting his father's couch.

TPJ offers two translations for the word וַיָּחֶל, the first rendering the word as a *hiph'il* form of the root חל"ל that signifies *commenced*, and the second in keeping with the meaning of that root in the *pi'el*, meaning *desecrated*, with the addition of the object קדושתהון, *their holiness*. The use of such an unusual expression in TC in the context of a sexual sin very well may signal the influence of the diction of TPJ.

4.9 The Two-and-a-Half Tribes Exiled to the Mountains of Darkness (1 Chr 5:26)

1 Chr 5:26

MT	וְאֶת־רוֹחַ	מֶלֶךְ־אַשּׁוּר	פּוּל	אֶת־רוּחַ	יִשְׂרָאֵל	אֱלֹהֵי	וַיָּעַר
TC	וית תגראת	דאתור	מלכא	פול	ית תגראת	דישראל	דאלהא	מימרא	וגרי

MT (cont.)	וְלַגָּדִי וְלַחֲצִי	לָראוּבֵנִי	אַשּׁוּר וַיַּגְלֵם	מֶלֶךְ	תִּלְּגַת פִּלְנֶסֶר
TC	ולפלגות	לשיבט גד	לשיבט ראובן	דאתור ואגלונון	מלכא	תלגת פלנסר

(cont.) עַד הַיּוֹם הַזֶּה:	וּנְהַר גּוֹזָן	לַחְלַח וְחָבוֹר וְהָרָא	שֵׁבֶט מְנַשֶּׁה וַיְבִיאֵם
TC	עד יומא הדין:	ונהר גוזן	קבלא טורי וחבור לחלח ואיתיאונון	שיבט מנשה

NJPS: So the God of Israel roused the spirit of King Pul of Assyria—the spirit of King Tillegath-pilneser of Assyria—and he carried them away, namely, the Reubenites, the Gadites, and the half-tribe of Manasseh, and brought them to Halah, Habor, Hara, and the river Gozan, to this day.

Dost: The Memra of the God of Israel incited the anger of Pul king of Assyria, the dispute of Tiglath-pilneser king of Assyria, and he exiled them, namely, the tribe of Reuben, the tribe of Gad, and the half-tribe of Manasseh. He brought them to Halah, Habor, the mountains of Kabla, and the river of Gozan, (where they are) to this day.

The Hebrew verse describes the exile of two-and-a-half of the tribes of Israel to four locations: חלח, חבור, הרא, and נהר גוזן. Three of the four are transcribed in TC as in the Hebrew, but הָרָא is rendered by the targumist as טורי קבלא, literally Mountains of Darkness (Dost's transcription of Kabla, as above, notwithstanding). Why is the toponym הָרָא translated differently from those accompanying it? Le Déaut and Robert, following the lead of Beck, suggested that this term might allude to הָרֵי נָשֶׁף of Jer 13:16, translated by TJ as טורי קבל.[102] I do not believe that there is any basis to this proposal, as the translation in TJ Jeremiah is simply a literal one, while that in TC unexpectedly diverges from the Hebrew *Vorlage*. Interpretations of the verse in Jeremiah appear in a

---

102 Beck *I*, pp. 93–95; Le Déaut-Robert, vol. 1, p. 54, n. 18; McIvor, p. 68, n. 45, opined similarly.

variety of midrashic sources, none of which associates the present verse with
that in Jeremiah, or הָרָא with הרי נשף. Following this line of reasoning further
in his comments to the verse, Beck associated טורי קבלא with an aggadic tradition he found in *Jossipon* stating that Alexander the Great made his way "to the
Mountains of Darkness, where the sun does not shine in daylight, and sought
to go to the place of the sons of Jonadab son of Rechab and those of the tribes
residing together beyond the Mountains of Darkness." Beck's text of *Jossipon*,
by all appearances, is a secondary one,[103] but it seems to me that the direction
he mapped out is consistent with the intention of TC.

The present verse serves as one of the sources based on which the various
traditions regarding the exile of the Ten Tribes took shape. Another verse that
had such a role in the traditions' development is Isa 49:9: לֵאמֹר לַאֲסוּרִים צֵאוּ
לַאֲשֶׁר בַּחֹשֶׁךְ הִגָּלוּ, *saying to the prisoners, "Go free," to those who are in darkness, "Show yourselves."*. This verse was interpreted in various sources as indicating that some of the Ten Tribes had been exiled to the Sambatyon River,[104]
while several versions of the homily state that they were exiled beyond the
Mountains of Darkness, which also appear in earlier sources unrelated to the
exile of the Ten Tribes. Thus, for instance, the Mountains of Darkness appear
in the context of a legend regarding Alexander the Great's journey to a place
populated exclusively by women (קרתגיני; literally, city of women).[105] The link
between the Mountains of Darkness and the Ten Tribes arises only in sources
of later date. One, by way of example, is the Midrash of the ten exiles:[106]

וגנזן הקב״ה מפניו ונתנן לאחר, והניח שבט יהודה ושמעון והלך לעשות מלחמה עמו
הרי חשך.

He left the tribes of Judah and Simeon and went to wage war against him,
while the Holy One blessed be He concealed them from him and placed
them behind the mountains of darkness.

---

103   The phrase הרי חשך is absent from the earlier version of the text. See Flusser, p. 472.

104   See list of aggadic sources regarding this exile and the Sambatyon River in Neubauer;
Ginzberg, vol. 6, pp 407–409.

105   This legend appears in various sources: *b. Tamid* 32a; *Gen. Rab.* 33:1 (pp. 301–302, see
variant readings ibid.); et al. See additional sources on the Mountains of Darkness in
Neubauer, p. 21; Ginzberg, vol. 6, p. 332.

106   Jellinek, vol. 4, pp. 133–134.

Similarly, in the liturgical poem אזור נא גבורות, lines 52–54:[107]

פרוק והביא במשך, גלות הרי חושך, בגשם נדבות.

Num. Rab. 16:25 (p. 141):

ולעתיד לבא הקב״ה מכנסן, שנאמר 'הנה אלה מרחוק יבאו והנה אלה אלה מצפון ומים
ואלה מארץ סינים', והגליות באים עמהם. והשבטים שהם נתונים לפנים מן סמבטיון
ושלפנים מן הרי חשך הם מתכנסין ובאין לירושלים.

In the future the Holy One blessed be He will assemble them, as stated,
'Look! These are coming from afar, these from the north and the west,
and these from the land of Sinim' (Isa 49:12), and the exiles shall come
with them. And the tribes placed in front of Sambatyon and in front of
the mountains of darkness—they shall assemble and come to Jerusalem.

Midrash Aggadah (ed. Buber) Num 24:22 (p. 145):

ד״א 'ושים בסלע קנך'—זה הקב״ה שנקרא סלע, ובא לחסות תחת כנפיו של הקב״ה,
שנא' 'ה' סלעי ומצודתי', שאלולי כן 'כי אם לבער קין', ומאימתי מתחייב לבער?
משגלו השבטים, אבל אותם שהיו בירושלם לא גלו, ואפילו בחרבן בית המקדש לא
גלו מבני יונדב בן רכב שהם היו מבני קני, שהקב״ה שלחם להרי חשך.

'And your nest be set among crags' (Num 24:21)—This is the Holy One
blessed be He who is called a crag, and he came to take refuge under the
Holy One blessed be He's wings, as stated, 'O LORD, my crag, my fast-
ness,' (2 Sam 22:2; Ps 18:3), if not for which 'yet shall Kain be consumed'
(Num 24:22). From when is he obliged to consume? From when the tribes
were exiled, but those that were in Jerusalem were not exiled, and even
when the Temple was destroyed the sons of Jonadab son of Rechab were
not exiled and they were Kainites, for the Holy One blessed be He sent
them to the mountains of darkness.

The tradition that grew up around the exile of parts of the Ten Tribes to the
Mountains of Darkness was a familiar one to the author of TC, who found הָרֵא
of the present verse an appropriate location to identify with that range because

---

107 An alphabetically arranged anonymous liturgical poem. Each stanza contains a plea for
the return of a diaspora as well as a plea for rain. Text is from Academy of the Hebrew
Language Historical Dictionary Project; the work dates to ca. eleventh century.

it reminded him of the word הר. He therefore translated the word using the literal translation of Mountains of Darkness: טורי קבלא.

4.10 *Saul's Kingship a Reward for Ner's Virtue (1 Chr 8:33)*

1 Chr 8:33

MT וְנֵר֙ הוֹלִ֣יד אֶת־קִ֔ישׁ

TC ונר דמתקרי אביאל אוליד ית קיש והוון צווחין ליה נר מטול דהוה מדליק שרגיא בבתי־מדרשיא ובבתי־כנישייתא והיא זכותא גרמת לשאול בר בריה למהוי מלכ׳ ארום מלכותא אמתילא לשרגא

NJPS: Ner begot Kish

Dost: Ner, who was called Abiel, fathered Kish, and they called him Ner because he would light the lamps in the academies and in the synagogues. That merit caused his grandson Saul to become king, for kingship was compared to the lamp.

The identification of Ner with Abiel does not stem from a literary need intrinsic to Chronicles, but is intended to allay a difficulty that arises from a comparison with Samuel. 1 Sam 9:1 states וַֽיְהִי־אִ֣ישׁ מִבִּנְיָמִ֗ין (קרי) וּשְׁמ֤וֹ קִישׁ֙ בֶּן־אֲבִיאֵ֔ל, *there was a man of Benjamin whose name was Kish son of Abiel*, while the verse in Chronicles reads וְנֵר֙ הוֹלִ֣יד אֶת־קִ֔ישׁ, *Ner begot Kish*, and the contradiction between the two verses leads to the conclusion that נֵר and אֲבִיאֵל are in fact two names of the same man. The Targum explains that נֵר is a sobriquet that Abiel earned for his practice of lighting candles in study halls and synagogues, thus serving the masses who came there to study and pray. The targumist further adds that it was due to this meritorious practice that his grandson Saul was chosen as king of Israel, as a candle is symbolic of the monarchy.

A similar tradition appears in three rabbinic sources: *y. Šeb.* 3:10 (34d, p. 189); *Lev. Rab.* 9:2 (vol. 1, p. 176); *Tanḥuma, Teẓavveh* 8 (p. 89). Scholars who previously published studies of TC identified its source here as *Leviticus Rabbah* and declined to discuss other sources in any depth.[108] Below is the text of that midrash:

---

108   The view that TC's source was *Lev. Rab.* is shared by Rosenberg-Kohler, p. 146; Churgin *Hagiographa*, p. 253; Le Déaut-Robert, vol. 1, p. 61, n. 8; and McIvor, p. 78, n. 18. The version in *Tanḥuma* will be presented below. Though I do not believe that TC here was influenced by the *yerushalmi*, the version found in the latter is provided here:

דאמ[ר] ר׳ שמעון בן לקיש: שאול לא זכה למלוכה אלא על ידי שהיה זקינו מדליק נר לרבים, נקרא שמו נר. כת[וב] אחד או[מר] 'ונר הוליד את קיש' וכת[וב] אחר או[מר] 'קיש בן אביאל'. והלא אביאל היה שמו? אלא על ידי שהיה זקינו מדליק נרו לרבים נקרא [שמו] נר.

R. Simon son of Laqish said: Saul did not attain kingship if not that his grandfather who would light lamps for the masses, he was called Ner. One verse says '*Ner begot Kish*' and

אמ[ר] ר' שמעון בן לקיש: אף שאול לא זכה למלכות אלא על ידי שהיה זקינו מדליק
נירות לרבים. אמרו, מבואות אפילין היה מביתו לבית הכנסת והיה מדליק בהן נירות
כדי שיאירו לרבים. כתוב אחד אומר 'ונר הוליד את קיש' וכתוב אחר אומר 'קיש בן
אביאל'. הכיצד? אביאל היה שמו ועל ידי שהיה מדליק נירות לרבים נקרא שמו נר.

R. Simon son of Laqish said: Saul did not attain kingship if not for his
grandfather who would light lamps for the masses. It was told that there
were dark alleyways from his house to the synagogue and he would light
lamps there to illuminate (the way) for the masses. One verse says 'Ner
begot Kish' and another verse says 'Kish son of Abiel'. How so? Abiel was
his name and for his lighting the lamps for the masses he was called Ner.

All three of the sources listed describe Abiel as lighting candles for public
benefit, but the placement of these candles in study halls and synagogues is
limited to TC. *Leviticus Rabbah* does make mention of a synagogue, but there
the candles serve not to provide light within the synagogue, but to illuminate
the way from his home to the synagogue. It seems to me, however, that previous scholars have ignored a textual similarity between TC and *Tanḥuma*, that
is sufficiently convincing to establish that TC's source was in fact *Tanḥuma*,
Teẓavveh 8 (p. 89):

אמר לו הקב"ה למשה: אמור להם לישראל: בני, בעולם הזה הייתם זקוקים לאור
בית המקדש ומדליקין נרות לתוכן [sic!]. אבל לעולם הבא בזכות אותו הנר אני
מביא לכם למלך המשיח שהוא משול כנר, שנ[אמר] 'שם אצמיח קרן לדוד ערכתי
נר למשיחי'. 'זובח תודה יכבדני ושם דרך אראנו בישע אלהים'—ר' מנחם בר' יוסי
או[מר]: אלו מדליקי נרות לרבים במבואות האפילין. אמר ר' שמעון בן לקיש: מפני
מה זכה שאול למלכו[ת]? מפני שהיה זקינו מדליק נרות לרבי[ם] במבואות אפילין.
כתוב אחד אומר 'ונר הוליד את קיש', וכתוב אחד או[מר] 'וקיש אבי שאול ונר אבי
אבנר בן אביאל'. הא כיצד? אביאל שמו, ועל שהדליק נרות לרבים נקרא שמו נר.

The Holy One blessed be He said to Moses: Tell Israel: My sons, in this
world you needed the light of the Temple and lit lamps in it. But in the
world to come, by the merit of that lamp, I will bring the Messiah King to
you, as he is akin to a lamp, as stated, 'there I will make a horn sprout for
David; I have prepared a lamp for My anointed one' (Ps 132:17). 'He who
sacrifices a thank offering honors Me, and to him who improves his way
I will show the salvation of God' (Ps 50:23)—R. Menaḥem son of R. Jose

---

another verse says '*Kish son of Abiel*'. Was not his name Abiel? Rather, on account of his
grandfather who would light lamps for the masses, he was called Ner.

says: These are those that light lamps for the masses in dark alleyways. R. Simon son of Laqish said: Why was Saul worthy of kingship? Because his grandfather would light lamps for the masses throughout dark alleyways. One verse says *'Ner begot Kish'*, and one verse says *'Kish, Saul's father, and Ner, Abner's father, were sons of Abiel'*. How so? Abiel is his name, and for his lighting of lamps for the masses he was called Ner.

A number of dicta found in rabbinic literature compare the human soul or the Torah to a candle, but TC's addition of the monarchy to the set of things represented by a candle is not known from other sources. This apparently is why Le Déaut and Robert took the view that the comparison of the monarchy to a candle in TC is based on 2 Sam 21:17 and the various verses that use the term נִיר to define the covenant between God and David.[109] Yet we saw above that before citing R. Shim'on b. Laqish regarding Abiel's practice of lighting candles, *Tanḥuma* notes that the messiah may be compared to a candle. The comparison, strictly speaking, is specific to the messiah who will come in the future, but TC easily could have taken this statement and applied it to the monarchy generally.

As noted, while the other sources discussing Abiel/Ner describe Abiel's meritorious actions as performed in dark alleyways, TC sets them in study halls and synagogues, while the description in *Leviticus Rabbah* is of candles lit in dark alleyways to illuminate the way to the synagogue. Now that we have taken note of the similarity between *Tanḥuma* and TC with regard to the things compared to a candle, we must ask on what basis the targumist determined that Abiel had illuminated places of study and prayer, and the most plausible answer is that the shift from dark alleyways to study halls and synagogues occurred by way of association. There are two instances in the Mishnah where illumination of dark alleyways is juxtaposed to synagogues and study halls:

M. Ter. 11:10:

[מדליקין] שמן שריפה בבתי כנסיות ובבתי מדרשות ובמבואות אפלים ועל גבי
החולין.

---

109   1 Kgs 11:36; 15:4; 2 Kgs 8:19 (this verse is not mentioned by Le Déaut and Robert but is as relevant as the others); 2 Chr 21:7. Le Déaut and Robert (and subsequently McIvor) correctly note that in each of these cases, as in 2 Sam 21:17, נִיר/נֵר, *lamp*, is translated as מלכו, *kingship*, and that the two phenomena presumably are linked. However, they failed to take into consideration the literary similarity between *Tanḥuma* and TC.

They kindle [unclean] oil which is fit for burning in synagogues, houses
of study, dark alleyways and for sick people.

M. Pesaḥ. 4:4:

מקום שנהגו להדליק את הנר בלילי יום הכיפורים מדליקים. מקום שנהגו שלא
להדליק את הנר אינן מדליקים. מדליקים בבתי כנסיות ובבתי מדרשות ובמבואות
האפלים ועל גבי החולים.

Where they are accustomed to light a candle on the night of the Day of
Atonement, they light it. Where they are accustomed not to light it, they
do not light it. But in any case they light it in synagogues, study houses,
dark alleys, and for the sick.

Either of these mishnaic passages alone could have been the source of the association drawn by the targumist, who was well-versed in talmudic literature,
between the dark alleyways of his source, on one hand, and synagogues and
study halls, on the other. Also clear is why he preferred to relate to these institutions rather than dark alleyways, as such a choice is consistent with his general
agenda of aggrandizing the world of Torah. The same agenda may also explain
why his translation, contrary to general usage, gives precedence to study halls
over synagogues. Also possible is that the targumist viewed Abiel's actions not
only as providing practical aid to members of the public spending time in the
synagogue, but also as related to the Temple service. A midrash found in the
Cairo Genizah interprets Lev 24:2 (צַ֞ו אֶת־בְּנֵ֣י יִשְׂרָאֵ֗ל וְיִקְח֨וּ אֵלֶ֜יךָ שֶׁ֣מֶן זַ֥יִת זָ֛ךְ כָּתִ֖ית
לַמָּא֑וֹר לְהַעֲלֹ֥ת נֵ֖ר תָּמִֽיד׃, *Command the Israelite people to bring you clear oil of
beaten olives for lighting, for kindling lamps regularly*) as having significance for
the provision of candles even following the destruction of the Temple:[110]

... [קבו]עות מיד ול[דו]רות, ואלו הן: פרשת נירות ... כך בין במקדש ובין ב[בתי]
כנסיות ובתי [מדרשות] ... הן כמעין [בית המקדש, שכ' כת' ואיהי להם למקדש [מעט
בארצות אשר באו שם] ... שאמ' הכת' צו את בני ישראל [ו]יקחו א[ליך שמן ... היא
קבועה מיד ול[ד]ורות.

... permanent from the onset and throughout the ages, these being: the
segment on lamps ... so, whether in the Temple and whether in synagogues and houses of study ... they are likened to the Temple, as is written, 'and I have become to them a diminished sanctity in the countries

---

110   Midrashic text is from Mann, p. 200.

whither they have gone' (Ezek 11:16) ... Scripture says, '*Command the Israelite people to bring you clear oil*' (Lev 24:2) ... this remains permanent from the onset throughout the ages.

This midrash further develops a homily found in *Sifra'*, *'Emor* 13 (p. 103a)— "Expressly, the meaning of צַו is to rouse with regard to the present and to [future] generations"—but while *Sifra'* is concerned only with future generations' lighting candles in the Temple, the Genizah midrash goes further, including the illumination of so-called lesser temples, i.e., synagogues and study halls, in the commandment.[111] It may be that the author of TC also was familiar with such an interpretation and sought to indicate that Abiel had been meticulous in his religious observance and fulfilled the commandment to light candles in synagogues and study halls.

4.11 *David Chooses Punishment by Elimination (1 Chr 21:13)*

1 Chr 21:13

MT וַיֹּ֧אמֶר דָּוִ֛יד אֶל־גָּ֖ד צַר־לִ֣י מְאֹ֑ד אֶפְּלָה־נָּ֣א בְיַד־ ה'

TC ואמר דויד לגד אין אנא בריר ית כפנא ימרון דבית ישראל אוריאיא דדויד
מליין עיבורא ולא אכפת ליה אין ימותון עמא בית ישר[אל] בכפנא
ואין אנא בריר ית קרבא ולמיפך מן־קדם דסנאיי ימרון דבית ישראל
דוד גברא גברא ומרי קרבא ולא אכפת ליה אין יפלון עמא בית ישראל
קטלין בחרבא הא עיק לי לחדא אתמסר כדון ביד מימרא דה'

MT (cont.) כִּֽי־רַבִּ֥ים רַחֲמָ֖יו מְאֹ֑ד וּבְיַד־אָדָ֖ם אַל־אֶפֹּֽל׃

TC ארום סגיעין רחמוהי וביד בני־נשא לא אתמסר:

NJPS: David said to Gad, "I am in great distress. Let me fall into the hands of the LORD, for His compassion is very great; and let me not fall into the hands of men."

Dost: Then David said to Gad, "If I choose famine, those of the house of Israel will say, 'The mangers of David are full of grain, so he does not care if the people the house of Israel die by famine.' But if I choose battle and fleeing from before my enemies, those of the house of Israel will say, 'David is a mighty warrior and master of war, but he does not care if the people, the house of Israel, fall slain by the sword.' Behold, I am greatly distressed. Let me be handed over now into the hand of the Memra of the Lord, for His mercies are great, but let me not be handed over into the hand of the children of man."

---

111 Some information regarding the spread of this interpretation may be gleaned from Mann, ibid., n. 3, who notes that the Karaites were opposed to the practice because they viewed it as defiling the Temple.

The Hebrew verse describes David's rationale for choosing the punishment of pestilence over famine or defeat on the battlefield. The Aramaic verse adds substantially to the account of David's various considerations, explains why he rejects two options, and only then finally returns to the Hebrew continuum and its description of the comparative advantage of being punished by pestilence: אתמסר כדון מימרא דה' ארום סגיען רחמוהי, *let me be handed over now into the hand of the Memra of the Lord, for His mercies are great*. The verse in Chronicles parallels 2 Sam 24:14, and TC clearly based his literal translation on his text of TJ. However, TJ lacks the extended insertion detailing David's thought process.

Churgin here cited parallels to the expansion in *Pesiqta Rabbati* 11 and *Seder Eliyahu Rab.* 8,[112] which indeed have elements in common with the expansion in TC, but it is evident from their diction as well as some of their content that they did not serve directly as sources of the material in TC. The aggadic tradition itself is an ancient one. A detailed version appears as early as Josephus' *Antiquities of the Jews:*[113]

> The king reasoned with himself, that in case he should ask for famine, he would appear to do it for others, and without danger to himself, since he had a great deal of corn hoarded up, but to the harm of others; that in case he should choose to be overcome [by his enemies] for three months, he would appear to have chosen war, because he had valiant men about him, and strongholds, and that therefore he feared nothing therefrom: so he chose that affliction which is common to kings and to their subjects, and in which the fear was equal on all sides; and said this beforehand, that it was much better to fall into the hands of God, than into those of his enemies.

---

112 Following are the relevant excerpts from the two sources:
Pesiqta Rabbati 11 (p. 44b):
אמר דוד: אם אני אומר רעב—ישראל אומרים מפני שהוא מלך ואוצרותיו מליאים. אם אומר אני 'נספה מפני צר'—ישראל אומרים מפני שיש לו גיבורים שיעמדו עליו. הריני שואל את המות שמשוה לגדולים ולקטנים.
Seder Eliyahu Rab. 8 (p. 39):
באותה שעה דוד המלך אמר בדעתו: אם אומר אני תבוא רעב—יהיו ישראל אומרים, בוטח באוצרותיו, לפיכך אמר יבא רעב. ואם אומר אני תבא חרב—יהיו ישראל אומרים, מפני שהוא בוטח על גיבוריו, לפיכך אמר תבא חרב. אשאל דבר שהכל שוין בו, עניים ועשירים ונערים וזקנים.

113 *Antiquities of the Jews* 7:322–323. The same passage is cited by Ginzberg, vol. 7, p. 270, alongside *Pesiqta Rabbati*, TC, *Seder Eliyahu Rabbah*, and *Midr. Ps.*

The structure of the version given by Josephus and the key elements of its content are the same as those in the later Hebrew sources and TC, based on which we may assume that the tradition appeared in a variety of versions over the course of many generations. One of these traditions, which bears a greater resemblance to TC than those above, appears in *Midr. Ps* 17:4 (p. 126):

בשעה שמנה דוד את ישראל היה כעס לפני הקב״ה, ושלח אליו גד החוזה, ואמר: 'שלש [אנכי] נוטל עליך' ... כיון שאמר לו כן ... היה דוד עומד וסוער ולא היה יודע מה להשיב. אמר ליה דוד: אם אומר רעב—יהו כל ישראל אומרים, עשיר היה דוד ואוצרותיו מלאים דגן, מה איכפת ליה? [ואם אומר מלחמה, יהו כל ישראל אומרים גבור היה דוד ואנשיו גבורין, מה איכפת ליה?] אלא הריני בורר דבר ששוה בעניים ובעשירים, בגבורים ובחלשים, בגדולים ובקטנים.

When David counted Israel there was anger before the Holy One blessed be He, and sent Gad the seer to him, and said: '*I hold three things over you; choose one of them*'... Since he told him so ... David stood in a frenzy and did not know how to respond. Said David to him: If I say hunger—all of Israel will say David was wealthy and his storehouses full of grain, what did he care? If I say war, all of Israel will say David was valiant and his men mighty, what did he care? Rather, I shall select something equal to the poor and the rich, to the mighty and the weak, to the adults and the children.

The greater similarity between the version in TC and that in *Midr. Ps* than between TC and *Pesiqta Rabbati* and *Seder Eliyahu Rabbah* is demonstrated by the following expressions:

TC	... אוריאיא דדויד מליין עיבורא ולא אכפת ליה ...					
Midr. Ps	... עשיר היה דוד ואוצרותיו מלאים דגן מה איכפת ליה					

TC	... דוד גברא גברא ומרי קרבא ... ולא אכפת ליה ...	
Midr. Ps	... גבור היה דוד ואנשיו גבורין מה איכפת ליה	

Mention of the grain (דגן, עיבורא) in David's stores also is common to the version given by Josephus (בר, σῖτον), but this similarity is not a sufficient basis to argue for direct contact between it and the other sources. The similarity between TC and *Midr. Ps* is no coincidence: it indicates that there were kindred traditions behind the two sources. Although no direct dependence may be proven, we may assume that each of these versions has more in common with the tradition or source of the other than with *Pesiqta Rabbati* and *Seder Eliyahu Rabbah*.

The conclusion of the legend as it appears in TC differs from all other trans- missions noted here in the absence of a sentence describing the punishment's egalitarian application to all parts of the population, but this omission need not indicate that TC's source had no such sentence. Whereas the calculations accompanying the options of famine and war constitute additions to the Hebrew text, the final sentence, which defines why pestilence is preferable, es- sentially parallels Scripture, albeit the sentence's content does not correspond to that of the verse. Upon arriving at this point, where the Targum reconverges with the wording of the scriptural verse, the targumist presumably preferred to return to the parallel text of TJ, which gives a literal translation of MT.

4.12 *Mount Moriah and the Patriarchs* (*2 Chr 3:1*)

2 Chr 3:1

MT	וַיָּ֣חֶל שְׁלֹמֹ֗ה לִבְנ֤וֹת אֶת־בֵּית־ ה' בִּירוּשָׁלַ֙͏ִם֙ בְּהַר֙ הַמּ֣וֹרִיָּ֔ה אֲשֶׁ֥ר נִרְאָ֖ה
TC	ושרי שלמה למבני ית בית־ מקדשא דה' בירושלם בטוור מוריה

באתר דפלח וצלי אברהם תמן בשמא דה'
הוא אתר ארע פולחנא דתמן פלחין קדם ה' ה' כל דריא
ותמן אסיק אברהם ית יצחק בריה לעלתא
ושיזביה מימרא דה' ואתמני דכרא חלופיה
תמן צלי יעקב במעירקיה מן־קדם עשו אחוי

תמן אתגלי מלאכא דה'

MT (cont.)	לְדָוִ֣יד אָבִ֑יהוּ אֲשֶׁ֣ר הֵכִ֔ין בַּמָּק֔וֹם דָּוִ֑יד
TC	לדוד בזמן דאתקין מדבחא באתרא דיזבן מן ארון

(cont.)	בְּגֹ֖רֶן אׇרְנָ֥ן הַיְבֻסִֽי׃
TC	בבית אדרי דארון יבוסאה׃

NJPS: Then Solomon began to build the House of the LORD in Jerusalem on Mount Moriah, where [the LORD] had appeared to his father David, at the place which David had designated, at the threshing floor of Ornan the Jebusite. Dost: So Solomon began to build the temple of the Lord in Jerusalem on Mt. Moriah on the place where Abraham worshiped and prayed in the name of the Lord. It is the place of the land of worship where all generations wor- shiped before the Lord. There Abraham offered up his son Isaac as a burnt offering, though the Memra of the Lord spared him, and a ram was appointed in exchange for him. There Jacob prayed when he was fleeing from before his brother Esau. There the angel of the Lord was revealed to David at the time when he prepared the altar in the place that he purchased from Orwan, on the threshing floor of Orwan the Jebusite.

The Hebrew verse, with its description of David's connection to the site where the Temple was constructed, is a majestic one. To this TC adds a description of the three Patriarchs' connection to the site: Abraham prayed and offered a sacrifice there; Isaac was brought there by Abraham as a burnt offering and his place taken by a ram; and Jacob prayed there while making good his escape from his brother, Esau. The reason for the lengthy expansion in the Targum is that this Hebrew verse is the only place in Scripture where the phrase הַר הַמּוֹרִיָּה occurs. This sole appearance—and, at that, one found in the context of the construction of the Temple—evokes an ideological and religious outburst that stimulates the targumist to associate the site of the Temple with the Patriarchs, i.e., with the very beginnings of the Israelite nation. The style of the expansion indicates that it is a product of the Pentateuchal Targums, as we shall see below, although the information as such is foundational to the Judaic ethos and by no means exclusive to targumic literature.

באתר דפלח וצלי אברהם תמן בשמא דה': All of the Targums of the Torah interpret וַיִּקְרָא אַבְרָהָם in Gen 22:14 as signifying prayer. The phrase פלח וצלי appears there in TO, TN, FTP, and FTV.

הוא אתר ארע פולחנא: TC follows the translation of the phrase אֶרֶץ הַמֹּרִיָּה given in TO and TPJ Gen 22:2: ארע פולחנא.[114]

דתמן פלחין קדם ה' כל דריא: Cf. TO Gen 22:14: הכא יהון פלחין דריא, *here generations will be worshipping*, and TPJ Gen 28:22 ואבנא הדא דשויתי קמא תהי מסדרא בבי־מוקדשא דה' ויהון דריא פלחין עלה לשמא דה', *and this stone that I have placed as a pillar shall be placed in the sanctuary of the Lord, and generations shall be worshipping on it to the name of the Lord.*

ותמן אסיק אברהם ית יצחק בריה לעלתא: This diction is drawn from the beginning of the story of the Binding of Isaac; cf. TO, TPJ Gen 22:2: ית ברך ... ית יצחק ... ואסיקהי ... תמן לעלתא.

---

114   A new name for Mount Moriah, טוור פולחנא, was coined under the influence of the expression ארע פולחנא; see pp. 215–216, above.

וְשֵׁיזִביה מימרא דה׳ ואתמני דכרא חלופיה: These words correspond to Gen 22:13; cf.
TPJ: וְהָא דיכרא חד דאיתברי ביני שימשתא דשכלול עלמא ... ואסיקהי לעלתא חולף בריה,
and behold, a certain ram, which had been created at the twilight of the founda-
tion of the world ... and offered it up as a burnt offering instead of his son.

תמן צלי יעקב במעירקיה מן־קדם עשו אחוי: Jacob's prayer at Mount Moriah is an
element that appears in the targumic tradition to Gen 28:11 in TN, FTP, and TPJ
(וְצלי באתר בית מוקדשא, *he prayed at the Temple site*). TC describes the circumstances of Jacob's prayer with a paraphrase of Gen 35:1, בְּבָרְחֲךָ מִפְּנֵי עֵשָׂו אָחִיךָ,
when you were fleeing from your brother Esau, which TPJ (quite similarly to TO
and TN) translates as במיערקך מן קדם עשו אחוך.

4.13   *The Ten Commandments and the Tablets (2 Chr 5:10)*

2 Chr 5:10

MT	בְּחֹרֵב	מֹשֶׁה		אֲשֶׁר־נָתַן	הַלֻּחוֹת	שְׁנֵי	רַק	בָּאָרוֹן		אֵין

TC: לית מדעם מיחת בארונא לחוד תרין לוחיא דיהב תמן משה

כד אתברו על־עיסק עגלא דעבדו בחרב

ותרין לוחיא חורניתא שריריא דעליהון חקיק

כתב מפרש עישרתי דביריא הנון לוחי קיימא

MT (cont.)	מִמִּצְרָיִם:	בְּצֵאתָם	יִשְׂרָאֵל	עִם־בְּנֵי	ה׳	כָּרַת	אֲשֶׁר

TC: ממצרים: במפקהון ישראל בני עם ה׳ גזר די

NJPS: There was nothing inside the Ark but the two tablets that Moses placed
[there] at Horeb, when the LORD made [a Covenant] with the Israelites after
their departure from Egypt.

Dost: There was nothing deposited in the ark except the two tablets that Moses
had put there when they were defeated because of the calf that they made at
Horeb, and the two other sound tablets on which were engraved with clear
writing the ten words, which are the tablets of the covenant, which the Lord
had cut with the children of Israel when they came out of the land of Egypt.

Let us compare this verse and its Aramaic translation to the parallel in Kings:

1 Kgs 8:9

MT	בְּחֹרֵב	מֹשֶׁה	שָׁם	הִנִּחַ	אֲשֶׁר	הָאֲבָנִים	לֻחוֹת	שְׁנֵי	רַק	בָּאָרוֹן	אֵין

TJ: בארונא מחתין תרין לוחי אבניא דאצנע תמן משה בחרב

דעליהון כתיבין עסרא פתגמי קימא

MT (cont.)	מִצְרָיִם:	מֵאֶרֶץ	בְּצֵאתָם	יִשְׂרָאֵל	עִם־בְּנֵי	ה׳	כָּרַת	אֲשֶׁר

TJ: דמצרים: מארעא במפקהון ישראל בני עם ה׳ דגזר

NJPS: There was nothing inside the Ark but the two tablets of stone which Moses placed there at Horeb, when the LORD made [a covenant] with the Israelites after their departure from the land of Egypt.

Clem: In the ark they placed the two stone tablets that Moses had set aside there at Horeb, on which were written the ten words of the covenant that the Lord had decreed with the children of Israel when they came out of the land of Egypt.

The foundation of TC's translation is a more literal one than TJ. Rather than translate them literally, TJ renders the words אֵין בָּאָרוֹן רַק as *in the ark they placed*, whereas the phrasing in TC is *there was nothing deposited in the ark except the two tablets*. TC characteristically gives a translation of the Hebrew *Vorlage* of Chronicles, both in the above phrase and by choosing the verb יה״ב as an equivalent of נָתַן (as opposed to הִנַּח and אצנע of 1 Kings). Nonetheless, some influence of Kings or of that book's Targum is felt in TC's addition of the words דיהב תמן despite the absence of any parallel in the Hebrew.

Both targumists added to the verse a description of the Tablets, i.e., those on which the Ten Commandments were inscribed, but the terminology and even the contents of the two Targums differ. TJ in no way intimates that there were multiple pairs of tablets, whereas TC details that both the original tablets, which had been broken in the wake of the sin of the Golden Calf, and the second, whole set, on which the Ten Commandments were inscribed, were placed in the Ark. TJ did not give any indication of his view as to where the shards of the original tablets were kept; if that targumist believed that they were not kept with the first set, support may be found for that view, as for the other, in various rabbinic sources.[115]

לוחיא חורניתא of TC appears to have been taken from TPJ Exod 34:28: וכתב על לוחיא חורניתא ית פיתגמי קיימא עישרתי דביריא דהוו כתיבין על לוחיא קדמאי, *and he wrote on the other tablets the words of the covenant, the ten words, that were written on the first tablets*.[116] The term added in TC to לוחיא to describe the whole tablets, שרירא, forms a unique phrase that I have yet to find paralleled in any other source.

TJ chose the passive participle form כתיבין to describe the text inscribed on the Tablets, while TC preferred the more detailed description חקיק כתב מפרש.

---

115   The view that the two pairs of tablets were kept in two different arks is reflected by, inter alia, *Sifre Num.* 82 (p. 78; see discussion and sources cited by Horovitz ad loc.). *B. B. Bat.* 14a–b, meanwhile, indicates that the whole tablets and the fragments were kept in a single ark. For additional sources, see Ginzberg, vol. 6, p. 65, n. 331.

116   Cf. *Tg. Esth I* 3:7: לוחין אוחרניתא.

TC's expansion is taken from the Palestinian targumic tradition attending the expression חָרוּת עַל־הַלֻּחֹת, as illustrated by the following comparison:

Exod 32:16

MT	עַל־הַלֻּחֹת:	חָרוּת	הוּא אֱלֹהִים		מִכְתַּב	וְהַמִּכְתָּב
TO	על לוחיא:	מפרש	הוא דה'		כתבא	וכתבא
TN	על לוחיה:	חקוק	הוא ה' מפרש מן קדם		כתב	וכתבא
TPJ	ומפרש על לוחיא:	חקיק	הוא דה'		כתבא	וכתבא

NJPS: and the writing was God's writing, incised upon the tablets.

Clem TPJ: and the writing was the writing of the Lord, clearly inscribed on the tablets.

Various permutations of the phrase כתב חקיק ומפרש are familiar from the treatment in TN and TPJ Deut 27:8 of the commandment to inscribe the words of the Torah in stone, as well as TPJ Exod 39:6, 14, 30 (and expansions in Num 2:3, 10, 18), regarding the stones of the high priest's breastplate and diadem, but only in Exod 32:16 is this phrase associated with the Tablets.

We are witnesses to a difference between the two Targums with regard to the expressions chosen by their authors to describe the text inscribed on the Tablets. The targumists fall into two distinct categories in their approaches to the matter. In one category are TO and TJ, which refer to the text as עסרא פתגמיא, *the ten things*,[117] while the Targums of the second category—TN, FT, GT, TPJ, *Tg. Cant*, and TC—refer to עשרתי[118] דבריא, *the ten communications*.[119] The approach taken by TO and TJ is to give a literal translation of the scriptural Hebrew expression עֲשֶׂרֶת הַדְּבָרִים (Exod 34:28; Deut 4:13; 10:4). The absolute state of the nomen rectum in this genitive is דָּבָר, which the targumists commonly translated as פתגם. All of the other Targums noted give a translation of the common Rabbinic Hebrew expression, עשרת הדברות, the absolute state of whose nomen rectum is דִּבֵּר,[120] which they accordingly translate as דביר.

---

117   TO Exod 34:28; Deut 4:13; 10:4; TJ 1 Kgs 8:9.

118   The Targums are not in agreement with regard to the orthography of the number that functions here as nomen regens. Most spell the word with *shin* (thus reflecting the Hebrew origin of the phrase), while others use *samekh*. The means of forming the genitive (with *yod* or without) also is not uniform.

119   TN Exod 19:25; 34:28; Deut 4:13; 10:4; 32:10; FTP,FTV Exod 19:25; Deut 32:10; GT F, BB Exod 19:25; TPJ Gen 24:22; Exod 19:25; 34:28; Num 7:86; Deut 10:4; *Tg. Cant* 1:11; TC 2 Chr 5:10.

120   See Greenberg, pp. 67–68. While דָּבָר has the sense of a divine law or commandment (BDB, p. 182), the sense of דִּבֵּר is the divine communication that delivers the command. Thus the first term denotes *the ten divine commandments*, and the second, *the ten divine statements*. Cf. *Mek. RY, Pisha'* 1 (p. 1):

TC uses the word קיימא as nomen rectum to לוחי, while in TJ it is the nomen rectum of פתגמי. With these two words, the targumists referred to two different pentateuchal phrases. In Exod 34:28 the Ten Commandments are designated דִּבְרֵי הַבְּרִית, *the terms of the covenant*, a term translated by TJ as פתגמי קימא (cf. TO, TN ad loc.). In Deut 9:9, 11, 15 the two tablets are described as לוּחֹת הַבְּרִית, *the tablets of the covenant*, a phrase that appears in TC as לוחי קיימא (cf. TO, TN, TPJ ad loc.).

4.14 *Joash Concealed in the Holy of Holies (2 Chr 22:11)*

2 Chr 22:11	אֹתוֹ וַתִּגְנֹב בֶּן־אֲחַזְיָהוּ אֶת־יוֹאָשׁ		בַּת־הַמֶּלֶךְ יְהוֹשַׁבְעַת וַתִּקַּח			
TC	ית יואש בר אחזיהו		ברת מלכא יהושבעת ונסיבת			
	וגניבת יתיה	דילידת ליה צביה מן באירא דשבע				
2 Kgs 11:2	אֹתוֹ וַתִּגְנֹב בֶּן־אֲחַזְיָה אֶת־יוֹאָשׁ אֲחַזְיָהוּ אֲחוֹת יוֹרָם בַּת־הַמֶּלֶךְ יְהוֹשֶׁבַע וַתִּקַּח					
TJ	וגנבת יתיה בר אחזיה ית יואש דאחזיה אחתיה יורם בת מלכא ונסיבת יהושבע					

2 Chr 22:11 (cont.)	הַמּוּמָתִים בְּנֵי־הַמֶּלֶךְ מִתּוֹךְ		
TC	דאתקטילו בני מלכא ממצע		
2 Kgs 11:2	הַמּוּמָתִים (קרי) בְּנֵי־הַמֶּלֶךְ מִתּוֹךְ		
TJ	דמתקטלין בני מלכא מגו		

2 Chr (cont.)	הַמִּטּוֹת בַּחֲדַר וְאֶת־מֵינִקְתּוֹ אֹתוֹ		וַתִּתֵּן	
TC	קודשיא בקדש תורבינתיה וית יתיה		ויהבת	
2 Kgs (cont.)	הַמִּטּוֹת בַּחֲדַר וְאֶת־מֵינִקְתּוֹ אֹתוֹ			
TJ	בית ערסתא באדרון מינקתיה וית יתיה ואטמרת			

NJPS Chr: But Jehoshabeath, daughter of the king, spirited away Ahaziah's son Joash from among the princes who were being slain, and put him and his nurse in a bedroom

---

ויאמר ה׳ אל משה ואל אהרן בארץ מצרים לאמר׳—שומע אני שהיה הדבר למשה ולאהרן. כשהוא אומר ׳ויהי ביום דבר ה׳ אל משה בארץ מצרים׳—למשה היה הדבר ולא היה הדבר לאהרן.

Ibid. (p. 6):

ר׳ שמעון בן יוחאי אומר: והלא כל הדברות שנדבר עם משה לא נדבר עמו אלא ביום. Ibid., *Ba-Ḥodesh* 4 (p. 218):

׳את (כל הדברים׳—מלמד שאמר עשרת הדברות) בדבור אחד, מה שאי אפשר לבשר ודם לומר כן, שנאמר ׳וידבר אלהים את כל הדברים האלה לאמר׳. אם כן מה ת״ל ׳אנכי ה׳ אלהיך׳, ׳לא יהיה לך׳? אלא מלמד שאמר הקב״ה עשרת הדברות בדיבור אחד וחזר ופרטן דיבור דיבור בפני עצמו.

Dost: But Jehoshabeath, the daughter of the king, took Joash son of Ahaziah, whom Zibiah of Beer-sheba bore to him, and stole him from among the sons of the king, who were being killed, and she put him and his nurse in the most holy place

NJPS Kgs: But Jehosheba, daughter of King Joram and sister of Ahaziah, secretly took Ahaziah's son Joash away from among the princes who were being slain, and [put] him and his nurse in a bedroom

Clem: Then Jehosheba daughter of king Joram, the sister of Ahaziah, took Joash son of Ahaziah and stole him from the midst of the sons of the king who were being killed, and she hid him and his nurse in a chamber of the bedrooms

Several differences separate TC from TJ in this parallel verse, but the most prominent one is found in the translation of the Hebrew expression חֲדַר הַמִּטּוֹת. TJ here gave the almost literal translation אדרון בית ערסתא, *bedroom chamber*, and TC the very much nonliteral translation קדש קודשיא, *most holy place*. What brought TC to pen such an unconventional, even brazen, translation? Churgin took the view that it had been written under the influence of *Midr. Ps* 18:23 (p. 151):

'כי אתה תאיר נרי'—ביהווידע. 'ה' אלהי יגיה חשכי'—ביהושבעת, אשתו של יהווידע. ר' אליעזר אומר: בעליית בית המקדש היה טמון. ר' שמואל [בר נחמן] אמר: בתאים היה טמון. אמר ר' סימון: נראין דברי ר' אליעזר שהיה בעליית בית המקדש בימות החמה, ודברי ר' שמואל [בר נחמן] נראין בימות הגשמים.

'It is You who light my lamp' (Ps 18:29)—with Jehoiada. 'the LORD, my God, lights up my darkness'—with Jehoshabeath, Jehoiada's wife. R. Eliezer says: he was concealed in the Temple attic. R. Samuel son of Nachman said: he was concealed in the cubicles. R. Simon said: it seems like R. Eliezer's opinion, that he was in the Temple attic during the sunny season, and it seems like R. Samuel son of Nachman's opinion during the rainy season.

I cannot accept that this midrashic tradition was TC's source, because it omits the main point: the Holy of Holies is neither the attic of the Temple nor the cubicles in its walls. Still, the general identification of the expression חֲדַר הַמִּטּוֹת with the Temple brings us closer to the sought-after tradition. A more precise parallel to this interpretation appears in *Cant. Rab.* 1 (p. 25), where the difference of opinions appears as a function of how the expression חֲדַר הַמִּטּוֹת of the present verse is to be understood:

'אַף עַרְשֵׂנוּ רַעֲנָנָה'—זֶה בֵּית הַמִּקְדָּשׁ, הַ[וָא] מ[ַה] ד[ְאַת] אָ[מַר] 'וְאֵת מֵנִיקְתּוֹ
בַּחֲדַר הַמִּטּוֹת. מַהוּ 'בַּחֲדַר הַמִּטּוֹת'? ר׳ אֶלְעָזָר וְר׳ שְׁמוּאֵל בַּר נַחְמָן. ר׳ אֶלְעָזָר אָמַר:
בָּתַּאִים. וְרַבִּי שְׁמוּאֵל בַּר נַחְמָן אָמַר: בַּעֲלִיּוֹת. וְלֹא פְּלִיגֵי. מָאן דְּאָמַר בָּתַּאִים, בִּימוֹת
הַגְּשָׁמִים. מָאן דְּאָמַר בַּעֲלִיּוֹת, בִּימוֹת הַחַמָּה.

'Our couch is in a bower'—this is the Temple, as it says 'and his nurse in
a bedroom'. What does 'in a bedroom' mean? R. Elazar and R. Samuel son
of Nachman. R. Elazar said: in the cubicles. R. Samuel son of Nachman
said: in the attic. And there is no difference of opinion between the two.
He who said in the cubicles [meant] during the rainy season. And he who
said in the attic [meant] during the sunny season.

The term חדר המיטות also serves as an appellation of the Temple in two locations in the liturgical poetry of Qalir:[121]
"זכר תחלת כל מעש", lines 17–18:[122]

זֵכֶר נְקוּבֵי מַטּוֹת / שְׁבוּעוֹת מַטּוֹת / נְדִידוּת הַמַּטּוֹת / לְאַמְּצָם יִזְכֹּר:
נוֹשְׂאֵי עַל מוֹטוֹת / אִם פָּץ לְהַמְטוֹת / נֶפֶץ חֲדַר הַמִּטּוֹת / לִכְפּוֹר יִזְכֹּר:

למען תהלות שם קדשך, lines 9–10[123]

לְמַעַן צִדְקַת הַמַּטּוֹת, תַּצִּיע [חֲדַר] הַמַּטּוֹת, לְמַעַנְךָ ה׳.

Specific mention of Joash's time in the Holy of Holies is found in *Tanḥuma* (ed.
Buber), *Va'era'* 16 (p. 31):

וְיוֹאָשׁ עָשָׂה עַצְמוֹ אֱלוֹהַּ, שֶׁנֶּאֱמַר [וְאַחֲרֵי] מוֹת יְהוֹיָדָע. אָמְרוּ לוֹ: אֱלוֹהַּ אַתָּה, אִלּוּלֵי
שֶׁאַתָּה אֱלוֹהַּ אֵלּוּ לֹא הָיְתָה עוֹשֶׂה שֵׁשׁ שָׁנִים בְּבֵית קוֹדֶשׁ הַקֳּדָשִׁים. כֹּהֵן גָּדוֹל לֹא הָיָה נִכְנָס
אֶלָּא פַּעַם אַחַת וְהָיוּ הַכֹּל מִתְפַּלְלִים עָלָיו שֶׁיִּכָּנֵס בְּשָׁלוֹם, וְאַתָּה עָשִׂיתָ שָׁם שֵׁשׁ שָׁנִים!
אִלּוּלֵי שֶׁאַתָּה אֱלוֹהַּ אֵלּוּ לֹא הָיְתָה חַי. בְּאוֹתָהּ שָׁעָה קִבֵּל מֵהֶם ...

121　These works by Qalir do not in fact contain any express mention of the Holy of Holies,
but it is far from likely that the various references to the Temple precincts are intended to
evoke its auxiliary facilities or sleeping quarters. See also Rashi to Cant 1:16:
הַמִּשְׁכָּן קָרוּי מִטָּה, שֶׁנֶּאֱמַר 'הִנֵּה מִטָּתוֹ שֶׁלִּשְׁלֹמֹה', וְכֵן הַמִּקְדָּשׁ קָרוּי מִטָּה, שֶׁנֶּאֱמַר בְּיוֹאָשׁ
'בַּחֲדַר הַמִּטּוֹת' אֲשֶׁר בְּבֵית ה׳, עַל שֶׁהֵם פָּרִין וְרָבִיין שֶׁל יִשְׂרָאֵל.
The Tabernacle is called a bed, as stated, 'there is Solomon's couch' and the Temple is
called a bed, as stated with Joash 'in the bedroom' that was in the house of the Lord, because [through them] Israel are fruitful and multiply.

122　Goldschmidt *RH*, p. 247. The poem is adduced by Pseudo-Rashi to 2 Chr 22:11 as support
for the argument that the Holy of Holies was indeed called the Bedchamber.

123　Text is per Historical Dictionary Project.

Joash made himself out to be a god, as stated 'after the death of Jehoiada'. They said to him: you must be a god, for if you were not a god you could not have survived six years in the holy of holies. A high priest enters only once (a year) and everyone would pray that he enters in peace, while you stayed inside for six years! If you were not a god you would not have remained alive. Upon hearing this, he consented ...

Similarly, in *Exod. Rab.* 8:2 (p. 202):

יואש מנין שעשה עצמו אלוה? כדכתיב: 'ואחרי מות יהוידע באו שרי יהודה וישתחוו
למלך אז שמע המלך אליהם'. מהו 'וישתחוו למלך'? שעשו ממנו אלוה. אמרו לו:
אילולי שאתה אלוה, לא יצאת לאחר שבע שנים מבית קדשי הקדשים. אמר להם:
כך הוא. וקבל על עצמו ליעשות אלוה ...

What is the evidence that Joash made himself out to be a god? As written, 'But after the death of Jehoiada, the officers of Judah came, bowing low to the king; and the king listened to them'. What does 'bowing low to the king' mean? That they made him to be a god. They said to him: If you were not a god, you would have not emerged [alive] from the holy of holies after seven years. He said to them: This is true. And he consented to make himself out to be a god ...

While this is no proof that TC was familiar with either of these two sources, we may suppose based on the availability of sources identifying the place where Joash was concealed as the Holy of Holies that this tradition made its way to additional sources and that one of these made its way to the author of TC. The various sources that we have examined associated the Temple with the "bedchamber" (*Cant. Rab.* and Qalir), and Joash's hiding place with the Holy of Holies (*Tanḥuma* and *Exod. Rab.*). TC, though, is the only source that clearly identifies the bedchamber as the Holy of Holies. It may be that the targumist's source was a TT unknown to us—and such a hypothesis can go further than simply explaining why חֲדַר הַמִּטּוֹת is translated as it is. TC to the present verse differs from TJ in several respects. TC translates ממצע where TJ has מגו; selects a verb form in the past tense, אתקטילו, where TJ has the participle מתקטלין; and chooses the word תורבינה rather than מינקת as in TJ. TC also adds to the verse's description of Joash the name of his mother, צביה מן באירא דשבע (based on 2 Kgs 12:2; 2 Chr 24:1). Even the form of the translation of the mother's name, צביה מן באירא דשבע, differs from the transcription given by TC himself for the same name where it appears in 2 Chr 24:1, צביה מבאר שבע. We saw previously that TC—significantly, in the story of Joash—was directly affected by traditions such as those in MS Reuchlin, and the author of TC may well have inherited the unusual translational choices in the present verse, as well as the translation בקדש קדשיא, from an alternate Targum to 2 Kgs 12:2 that is unavailable to us.

4.15 *The Foundation Gate, Study Center of the Sanhedrin (2 Chr 23:5)*

2 Chr 23:5

MT	הַיְסֹוד	בְּשַׁעַר	וְהַשְּׁלְשִׁית בְּבֵית הַמֶּלֶךְ וְהַשְּׁלִשִׁית ...	
TC	גברייה	בתרע	ותלתא בבית מלכא ותלתא ...	

הוא תרע בית אולפן סנהדרין

NJPS: another third shall be stationed in the royal palace, and the other third at the Foundation Gate.

Dost: (another) third (should station themselves) at the king's house, and (another) third at the warriors' gate." It is the gate of the house of instruction of the Sanhedrin.

TC provides two translations for שַׁעַר הַיְסֹוד of the Hebrew verse—תרע גברייה, *warriors' gate*, and תרע בית אולפן סנהדרין, *gate of the house of instruction of the Sanhedrin*—both of which stray far from the literal meaning of the word יְסֹוד, *foundation*. The present verse parallels 2 Kgs 11:6, where MT gives a different name for this gate: שַׁעַר סוּר, *Sur gate*. The version of the translation of this phrase included by Sperber in the main body of his edition of TJ is תרע גיניא, *gate of the gardens*, though several MSS of TJ have תרע גיבריא or תרע גיברא.[124] Qimḥi, in his commentary to 2 Kings, writes:

> בשער סור—ובדברי הימים: 'בשער היסוד'. ותרגם יונתן: 'בתרע גבריא', ויש נס־
> חאות: 'בתרע נטוריא'.

At Sur gate—and in Chronicles: בשער היסוד. Jonathan translates, *at the warriors' gate*, while there are versions (that read): *at the sentries' gate*.

Qimḥi's attestation of such a version of TJ 2 Kings is consistent with those MSS that have גיבריא rather than גיניא, and the first translation given the phrase שַׁעַר הַיְסֹוד in TC thus is simply TJ's parallel translation of the phrase שַׁעַר סוּר, an incidental but clear indication that the version of TJ to which the author of TC referred contained the text תרע גיבריא.

The second of TC's translations of שַׁעַר הַיְסֹוד identifies this gate as the place of study of the Sanhedrin. What cause did TC have for identifying the gate in

124 Sperber, vol. 2, p. 297.

such a way? The source apparently is a passage in *y. ʿErub.* 5:1 (22c, p. 474) that discusses the gate's various names:

דמר ר' אחא בשם שמואל בר רב יצחק: כמה יגעו נביאים הראשונים לעשות שער
המזרחי שתהא החמה מצמצמת בו באחד בתקופת טבת ובאחד בתקופת תמוז.
שבעה שמות נקראו לו: שער סור, שער היסוד, שער חריסית, שער איתון, שער
התווך, שער חדש, שער העליון. שור סור—ששם היו טמאים פורשין, הדא הוא
דכת[יב] 'סורו טמא קראו למו'. שער היסוד—ששם היו מייסדין את ההלכה, שער
חריסית—שהוא מכוון כנגד זריחת החמה, היך מה דאת אמר: 'האו[מר] לחרס ולא
יזרח'. שער האיתון—שהוא משמש כניסה ויציאה. שער התווך—שהוא מיוסד בין
שני שערים. שער חדש—ששם חידשו סופרים את ההלכה. שער העליון—שהוא
למעלה מעזרת יש[ראל] החיל ועזרת הנשים.

R. Acha said in the name of Samuel son of R. Isaac: The early prophets worked laboriously to allow for the sun to shine in the eastern gate on the winter solstice and the summer solstice. It had seven names: Sur gate, Foundation gate, Harisit gate, Iton gate, Tawwekh gate, New gate, Upper gate. Sur gate—for impure people would leave off there, as is written, 'Away (סורו)! Unclean! people shouted at them,' (Lam 4:15). Foundation gate—where they would establish Halakha. Harisit gate—for the sun would rise against it, for one says 'Who commands the sun (חרס) not to shine'. Iton gate—for it was the place of entry and exit. Tawwekh gate—for it was located between two gates. New gate—for the scribes devised Halakha there. Upper gate—for it was above Israel's court, the rampart and the women's court.

Two of the explanations given in TY for the gate's seven names indicate that halakhic matters were determined within it: halakhic rules would be established, and scribes would share halakhic novellae. What body comprised of scribes met adjacent to the Temple and was responsible for the establishment and innovation of things halakhic? Clearly the Sanhedrin.[125] The author of TC was familiar with the tradition concerning this gate and, being well-versed in

---

125   The members of the Sanhedrin are described as scribes by, inter alia, *Tg. Cant* 7:5, in its rendering of the Hebrew עֵינַיִךְ בְּרֵכוֹת בְּחֶשְׁבּוֹן עַל־שַׁעַר בַּת־רַבִּים, *your eyes like pools in Heshbon by the gate of Bath-rabbim*:

ספריך מלין חכמתא כפרקטנין דמיא וידעין לממני חושבני עובדי ומעברין שנין וקבעין רישי
שנין ורישי ירחין בתרע בית סנהדרין רבא.

Dost: Your scribes are full of wisdom, like fountains of water, who know how to reckon calculations of intercalations, and they intercalate years and affix the beginnings of years and the beginnings of months, (all) at the door of the house of the great Sanhedrin.

the affairs of Torah scholars as described throughout rabbinic literature, knew to identify this place of halakhic decision making as the location where the members of the Sanhedrin gathered to study.

4.16 *The Tablets in the Ark (2 Chr 32:31; cf. also 2 Chr 5:10)*

2 Chr 32:31

MT	לִדְרֹשׁ	עָלָיו	הַמְשַׁלְּחִים	בָּבֶל	שָׂרֵי	בִּמְלִיצֵי|	וְכֵן		
TC	למתבע	לותיה	דאשתלחון	דבבל	מלכא	רבני	במתורגמי	והיכנא	

MT (cont.)	הַמּוֹפֵת	אֲשֶׁר הָיָה בָּאָרֶץ	
TC	תימהא דהוה	בארעא	למחמי ית תרין לוחי אבניא דהוון

בארון קיימיא[126] דה' דאצנע תמן משה עם תרין לוחי אבניא דאתברו על חובי עגלא
דעבדו בחרב

(cont.)	לְנַסּוֹתוֹ	הָאֱלֹהִים	עֲזָבוֹ
TC	לנסיותיה	לאחמיותהון ולא אתנזק מטול	ארשייה מימרא דה'

(cont.)	בִּלְבָבוֹ:	לָדַעַת כָּל־
TC	בלביה:	למדע כל מא דהוה

NJPS: So too in the matter of the ambassadors of the princes of Babylon, who were sent to him to inquire about the sign that was in the land, when God forsook him in order to test him, to learn all that was in his mind.

Dost: So too, with regard to the interpreters of the leaders of the king of Babylon that were sent to him to inquire (about) the miracle that had happened in

---

An example of a practical legal determination by the head of the Sanhedrin that supports the description in the *yerushalmi* is preserved in *m. 'Or.* 2:11–12:

שאור שלחולין ושלתרומה שנפלו לתוך עיסה—לא בזה כדי לחמץ ולא בזה כדי לחמץ—
[ונ]יצטרפו וחימצו. ר' אליעזר או[מר]: אחר האחרון אני בא. וחכמ[ים] או[מרים]: בין שנפל
אסור [ב]תחילה בין בסוף, לעולם אינו אסור עד שיהא בו כדי לחמץ. יועזר איש הבירה היה
מתלמידי בית שמי, [ואמר]: שאלתי את רבן גמליא[ל] הזקן עומד בשער המזרח, [ואמר]:
לעולם אינו אוסר עד שיהא בו כדי לחמץ.

Leaven of common produce and [leaven] of heave offering which fell into dough, [and there is] not enough of either to leaven [the dough], [but] they combined and leavened [it]— R. Eliezer says, "I rule [on the status of the dough] according to the last [leaven which fell in]." But sages say, "Whether the prohibited [leaven] fell in first or last, it does not render [the dough] prohibited unless there is enough of it to leaven [by itself]."

Yoezer of the Birah was one of the disciples of the House of Shammai, and he said, "I asked Rabban Gamaliel the Elder who was standing at the Eastern Gate, and he said, "It does not render [the dough] prohibited unless there is enough of it to leaven [by itself].'"

126   The original text of MS V, as well as E, has קיימא. A later hand added a *yod* between the lines and diacriticized the word as a plural form. MS C reads קיימיה, a singular form with the third-person masculine singular pronominal suffix.

the land (and) to see the two tablets of stone that were in the ark of the covenant of the Lord, which Moses had placed there along with the two tablets of
stone that were broken because of the sins of the calf, which they committed
at Horeb, the Memra of the Lord allowed him to show them without suffering
harm, because He was testing him to know all that was in his heart.

In summarizing Hezekiah's endeavors and accomplishments, the Hebrew
verse notes the visit of a group of Babylonian emissaries who came הַמּוֹפֵת לִדְרֹשׁ
אֲשֶׁר הָיָה בָאָרֶץ, *to inquire about the sign that was in the land.* In the plain sense of
the verse, this "sign" is that mentioned in verse 24, in the context of Hezekiah's
recovery from his sickness.[127] 2 Kgs 20:12–13 and Isa 39:1–2 state that Hezekiah
received a gift from the emissaries of the Babylonian king Merodach-baladan
son of Baladan on the occasion of his recovery and, during their stay, showed
them all of his treasures. Hezekiah discussed the visit with Isaiah, told him אֶת
כָּל־אֲשֶׁר בְּבֵיתִי רָאוּ לֹא־הָיָה דָבָר אֲשֶׁר לֹא־הִרְאִיתֶם בְּאוֹצְרֹתָי, *they have seen everything
that is in my palace. There was nothing in my storehouses that I did not show
them* (2 Kgs 20:15), and in response was rebuked with a prophecy of nothing
less than the Babylonian Exile. Chronicles mentions none of this, but makes
do with stating that envoys of the Babylonian king came to observe the sign
and that this event was a divine test of Hezekiah. To this the Targum adds that
he showed them the Tablets of the Law and the shards of the original tablets.
What is the source of this statement, and why was Hezekiah considered to
have sinned by doing so?

Hezekiah's actions do not appear in the Talmud or in other known targumic sources, but are found in relatively late sources, such as *Pirqe Rabbi Eliezer*
and Seder *Eliyahu Rabbah*.[128] Following is part of a detailed depiction in *Pirqe
Rabbi Eliezer* 51 (pp. 249–250) that sheds light on the secret divulged to the
Babylonians by King Hezekiah:

... וראה את המלכים ונתגאה לבו, והראה להם את אוצרות מלכי יהודה ואת אוצרות
של בית קדשי הקדשים. ועוד, שפתח את ארון הברית והראה להם את הלוחות ואמר
להם: בזה אנו עושים מלחמה ונוצחין, שנ[אמר] 'וישמח עליהם חזקיהו ויראם את כל
בית נכותה את הכסף ואת הזהב ואת הנזמים ואת שמן הטוב ולא היה דבר אשר לא
הראה חזקיהו בביתו ובכל ממשלתו'. וכעס הב"ה עליו ואמ[ר] לו: לא דייך שהראית
להם את כל אוצרות מלכי יהודה ואת כל אוצרות בית קדשי הקדשים, אלא שפתחת

127 Japhet *OTL*, pp. 995–996.
128 The version in *Seder Eliyahu Rabbah* 8, p. 47, is much shorter than that in *Pirqe Rabbi
     Eliezer*, but they have in common the association of Hezekiah's sin with the sign given on
     the stairway of Ahaz upon Hezekiah's recovery.

להם את הארון והראית להם את הלוחות מעשה ידי! חייך, הם יעלו ויקחו את כל
אוצרות מלכי יהודה ואת כל אוצרות בית קדשי הקדשים, שנ[אמר] 'הנה ימים באים
נאם ה' ונשא את כל אשר בביתיך ואשר אצרו אבותיך עד היום הזה בבלה יובאו לא
יותר דבר'. ותחת הלוחות יהיו בניך סריסים בהיכל מלך בבל.

He saw the kings and his heart grew haughty, and he showed them the
treasures of the kings of Judah and the treasures of the holy of holies.
Moreover, he opened the ark of the covenant and showed them the tablets, and said to them: By these we go to war and emerge victorious, as
stated, 'Hezekiah was pleased by their coming, and he showed them his
treasure house—the silver, the gold, the spices, and the fragrant oil—and
all his armory, and everything that was to be found in his storehouses.
There was nothing in his palace or in all his realm that Hezekiah did not
show them.' (Isa 39:2). The Holy One blessed be He was angry with him
and said to him: Is it not enough that you showed them all the treasures
of the kings of Judah and all the treasures of the holy of holies, that you
opened the ark and showed them my own handiwork, the tablets? By
your own life, they will ascend and take all of the treasures of the kings of
Judah and all the treasures of the holy of holies, as stated, 'A time is coming when everything in your palace, which your ancestors have stored up
to this day, will be carried off to Babylon; nothing will be left behind' (Isa
39:6). Instead of the tablets your sons will be eunuchs in the palace of the
king of Babylon.

Pirqe Rabbi Eliezer unifies the respective versions of Kings and Chronicles as a
single account. *Pirqe Rabbi Eliezer* identifies the sign mentioned by the verse
contextually, as referring to the shadow on the stairway of Ahaz. According to
this source, only afterward did Hezekiah act haughtily by showing them all of
his possessions and opening the Ark to show them the Tablets. TC, meanwhile,
explains that they came to see the sign and that this sign was the Tablets themselves. Despite this conspicuous disparity, we may reasonably assume that the
explanation given by TC is fundamentally related to a basic tradition that arrived in *Pirqe Rabbi Eliezer* and *Seder Eliyahu Rabbah* via alternate channels.

4.17 *Manasseh's Affliction, Prayer, and Repentance (2 Chr 33:11–13)*

2 Chr 33:11

MT	וַיִּלְכְּדוּ אֶת־מְנַשֶּׁה בַּחֹחִים	וַיַּאַסְרֻהוּ	בַּנְחֻשְׁתַּיִם	וַיּוֹלִיכֻהוּ בָּבֶלָה:
TC	ואחדו ית מנשה בכירומנקייא	ואסרוהי	בשושלוון דנחשא	ואובלוהי לבבל:

ועבדו כשדאי מולוות נחשא

ונקבוהא נקבין נקבין דקיקין וסגרו יתיה בגווה ואציתו נורא חזור־חזור ליה

NJPS: [They] took Manasseh captive in manacles, bound him in fetters, and led him off to Babylon.

Dost: they seized Manasseh with manacles, and they bound him with chains of bronze, and led him away to Babylon. 12 The Chaldeans made a mule of bronze, and they pierced it with many fine perforations, and they shut him up within it. And they lit a fire all around it,

2 Chr 33:12

MT   וּכְהָצֵר לוֹ חִלָּה אֶת־פְּנֵי ה׳ אֱלֹהָיו וַיִּכָּנַע מְאֹד מִלִּפְנֵי אֱלֹהֵי אֲבֹתָיו:

TC   וכד עיק ליה תבע מן כולהון טעוותיה דעבד ולא אסתייע ארום לית בהון צרוך והדר

 וצלי קדם ה׳ אלהיה ואתכנע לחדא מן־קדם ה׳ אלהא דאבהתוהי:

NJPS: In his distress, he entreated the LORD his God and humbled himself greatly before the God of his fathers.

Dost: and when he became distressed he sought from all of them his idols that he had made, but it did not help him, for there was power in them. So he repented and prayed before the Lord, his God, and he greatly humbled himself before the Lord, the God of his fathers.

2 Chr 33:13

MT   וַיִּתְפַּלֵּל אֵלָיו וַיֵּעָתֶר לוֹ וַיִּשְׁמַע תְּחִנָּתוֹ וַיְשִׁיבֵהוּ יְרוּשָׁלַ͏ִם לְמַלְכוּתוֹ

TC   וצלי קדמוהי מן־יד כל מלאכיא די ממנן על מעלני תרעי צלותא דבשמיא

ואחדו אמטולתיה כל מעלני תרעי צלותא דבשמיא וכלהון כוי וחרכי שמיא

מן־בגלל דלא תתקבל צלותיה ומן־יד אתגוללו רחמי מרי עלמא דימיניה מתיחא

לקבלא חייביא דתייבין לדחלתיה ותברין יצרא דלבהון בתתובא

ועבד חרכא ומחתרתא בשמיא תחות כורסי יקריה

ושמע צלותיה וקבל בעותיה ואזייע עלמא במימריה ואתנפעת

מולתא מתמן ונפקת רוחא מביני כנפי כרוביא ונתביה בגזירת מימרא דה׳

וחזר לירושלם למלכותיה

MT (cont.)   וַיֵּדַע מְנַשֶּׁה כִּי ה׳ הוּא הָאֱלֹהִים:

TC   וידע מנשה ארום ה׳ הוא אלהא דעבד עמיה אתיא ותמהיא האנון

ותב בכל לבביה קדם ה׳ ושבק כל טעוותא ולא אשתעבד להון:

NJPS: He prayed to Him, and He granted his prayer, heard his plea, and returned him to Jerusalem to his kingdom. Then Manasseh knew that the LORD alone was God.

Dost: When he prayed before Him, immediately, all of the kings who were appointed over the entrances of the gates of prayer, which are in the heavens, went forth, and because of him they closed all of the windows of the gates of prayer, which are in the heavens, and all of the windows and openings of the heavens, lest his prayer be received. But immediately, the mercy of the Lord of the World, whose right hand was outstretched to receive the sinners who were returning to His fear and who were defeating the inclination of their heart with repentance, was aroused, and He made a window and a breach in the heavens beneath the His glorious throne. He heard His prayer and received His request, and the world trembled at His Memra. The mule was shattered, and he went out from there. A wind went forth from between the wings of the cherubim, and it blew him by the decree of the Memra of the Lord, and he returned to Jerusalem to his kingdom. So Manasseh came to know that the Lord is the God who did for him these signs and miracles, and he repented with all of his heart before the Lord, and he forsook all of the idols and served them no longer.

Manasseh's affliction and prayer figure in many aggadic sources.[129] Here we will consider and discuss a number of exceptional words and expressions that appear in the version given by TC that the targumist may have inherited from a prior source: ימיניה מתיחה ,נקבוהא נקבן נקבין דקיקין ,מולוות נחשא ,כירומנקייא ועבד חרכא ומחתרתא בשמיא ,לקבלא חייביא דתייבין לדחלתיה.

כירומנקייא: Handcuffs.[130] The word appears in a number of rabbinic sources in explanation of the Hebrew term בַּחַחִים, *with hooks* (e.g. Ezek 19:9).[131] The appearance of the term in TC cannot be coincidental, but reflects a word borrowed from the targumist's source document.

מולוות נחשא: A copper vat. The term appears in a number of rabbinic sources as an explanation of the Hebrew word בִנְחֻשְׁתַּיִם, *in bronze fetters* (e.g. Jer 39:7).[132] The targumist gave the word בִנְחֻשְׁתַּיִם the literal translation בשושלון דנחשא and then described the Babylonians as having enclosed Manasseh in a copper caldron. This word, too, thus appears to have been borrowed by the targumist from an external source.

נקבוהא נקבין נקבין דקיקין: In the telling of *Pesiqta de-Rab Kahana, Shuvah* 11 (p. 365), we find a similar expression:

---

129 A detailed list of sources is provided by Ginzberg, vol. 6, pp. 375–376, nn. 107–108.

130 Krauss *Lehnwörter*, p. 286; Sokoloff *JPA*, p. 275.

131 *Y. Sanh.* 10:2 (28c, p. 1321); *Pesiqta de-Rab Kahana, Shuvah* 11 (p. 365); *Ruth Rab.* 5:6 (p. 130).

132 Aside from TC, sources that use the word מולה for the caldron in which Manasseh was cooked include: *y. Sanh.* 10:2 (28c, p. 1321); *Pesiqta de-Rab Kahana, Shuvah* 11 (p. 365); *Ruth Rab.* 5:6 (p. 130); *Deut. Rab.* 2:20 (p. 204); *Esth. Rab.* 9:2 (p. 27).

'ויאסרהו בנחשתים'—מהו 'בנחשתים'? א״ר לוי בר חיתה: עשה לו כמין מולי של
נחשת ועשה אותה נקבים נקבים ונתנו לתוכה והתחיל מסיק תחתיו. וכיון שראה
צרתו צרה, לא הניח עבודה זרה בעולם שלא להזכירה.

'He was chained in בנחשתים'—what does נחשתים mean? R. Levi son of Hita
said: He made a kind of bronze caldron (מולי), perforated it, put him inside and began heating below. When he realized he was in dire straits,
there was not a form of idolatry he refrained from mentioning.

Though the version in this source is not identical to TC in all of its details (it
does not contain the verb נק״ב or the adjective דקיק), it is the only one of the
sources known to us that uses the term נקבים (for the perforations).[133]

ימיניה מתיחה לקבלא חייביא דתייבין לדחלתיה: An Aramaic translation of "His right
arm is outstretched to accept sinners who return to His fear." The phrase is
similar to one that appears in the *Ne'ilah* service: (אתה נותן יד לפושעים) וימינך
פשוטה לקבל שבים, *You offer a hand to transgressors and Your right arm is outstretched to accept repentants*.[134]

בשמיא ומחתרתא חרכא ועבד: This insertion functions as an interpretation of
the word וַיֵּעָתֶר of the Hebrew verse, *He granted his prayer*, which the various

---

133   Churgin *Hagiographa*, p. 262, also referred to this source. Below, for the sake of comparison, is the text of the *yerushalmi*:

... אמר ר׳ לוי: מולא שלנחושת עשו לו ונתנו אותו בתוכה והיו מסיקין תחתיו. כיון שראה
שצרתו צרה, לא הניח ע״ז בעולם שלה הזכירה.

... R. Levi said: they made a bronze caldron (מולא) for him, put him in it and began heating below. When he realized he was in dire straits, there was not a form of idolatry he
refrained from mentioning.

The similarity between *Pesiqta de Rab Kahana* and TY in both sentence structure and
terminology is evidence that the two sources have a single tradition in common.
Nonetheless, TC more closely resembles *Pesiqta de Rab Kahana* for the occurrence of the
expression נקבים נקבים, which of all the sources cited occurs only in these two.

134   Such a phrase appears as early as *Sifre Deut.* 30: וימינו פשוטה לקבל שבים, but see
Finkelstein *Sifre*, p. 49, where the word שבים is absent from many textual witnesses cited.
Goldschmidt *YK*, p. 763, noted that the text of *Ne'ilah* had been influenced by the appearance of the expression פש״ט יד in the Mishnah (though not in the context of welcoming
those who repent) instead of the earlier פר״ש יד. Cf. *Lam. Rab.* 5:5 (p. 156):

נבוכדנצר הרשע צוה לנבוזראדן רב טבחים וא[מר] ל[ו]: אלוה של אומה זו רחמן הוא וידו
פשוטה לקבל שבים.

Evil Nebuchadnezzar commanded Nebuzaradan, chief of the guards and said to him: This
nation's god is merciful and his hand is outstretched to accept repentants.

aggadic sources interpret as denoting digging (ויחתר). Thus *y. Sanh.* 10:2 (28c, p. 1321) describes:[135]

> והיו מלאכי השרת מסתמין את החלונות שלא תעלה תפילתו שלמנשה לפני הקב״ה ...
> מה עשה לו הקב״ה? חתר לו חתירה מתחת כסא הכבוד שלו ושמע תחינתו. הדא
> היא דכת[יב] 'ויתפלל אליו ויעתר לו וישמע תחינתו וישיביהו'. אמ[ר] ר' לעזר ביר'
> שמעון: בערבייא צווחין ל[ח]תרתה עתרתה.

The attending angels sealed the windows to prevent Menasse's prayer from ascending before the Holy One blessed be He ... What did the Holy One blessed be He do for him? He dug a furrow under His glorious throne and listened to his imploration. This is what it is written, 'He prayed to Him, and He granted his prayer, heard his plea, and returned him'. Said R. Lazar son of R. Simon: In Arabia the call a trench עתרתה [resembling the Hebrew וַיֵּעָתֶר—L.G.].

The form מחתרת is found in the context of this tradition in *b. Sanh.* 103a:

> א״ר יוחנן משום ר' שמעון בן יוחאי: מאי דכת[יב] 'ויעתר לו'? מלמ[ד] שעשה לו
> הקב״ה כמין מחתרת והטמינו מפני הדין לקבלו בתשובה.

Said R. Yohanan in the name of R. Simeon b. Yohai, "What is the meaning of the verse of Scripture, 'And he prayed to him and an opening was made for him' (2 Chr 33:13)? "It should say, 'and he was entreated of him'! "It teaches that the Holy One, blessed be he, made a kind of cave for him in the firmament, so as to receive him in repentance ..."

The purpose of the tunnel in BT differs from that in the Targum: in the former it serves to conceal and protect Manasseh, while in the Targum, as in TY and *Pesiqta de-Rab Kahana*, its purpose is to permit his prayer to be heard despite the angels' closure of all of the windows, represented in the Targum by the word חרכא.[136] Still, the resemblance between ומחתרתא בשמיא ... עבד of TC and מחתרת ... עשה לו of BT is indicative of literary influence. It may be that the targumist integrated the language of BT with elements of a parallel tradition

---

135 A similar version appears in *Pesiqta de-Rab Kahana*, op. cit.

136 An intriguing link between מחתרת and חרכא is intimated by the Pentateuchal Targums to the word מַחְתֶּרֶת in Exod 22:1. TO translates מחתרתא (similar to the form in BT; also TJ Jer 2:34); TN translates חת[ר]תא (similar to the form in the *yerushalmi*; cf. חתורתה of GT); but TPJ renders חרכא דבכותלא.

found in other sources. We have not identified any source containing all of the distinctive terms defined above, but the closest is *Pesiqta de-Rab Kahana*.

5   Expansions Lacking Known Sources

5.1   *Joktan and the Drop in Longevity (1 Chr 1:19)*

1 Chr 1:19

MT   וְשֵׁם אָחִיו יָקְטָן׃

TC   ושום אחוי יקטן   מטול דביומוי שריאו דבני-נשא שניהון לאתקטעא מן-בגלל חוביהון׃

NJPS: and the name of his brother Joktan

Dost: and the name of his brother was Joktan, for in his days the years of the children of men began to diminish on account of their sins

The above verse parallels Gen 10:25, but only in TC do we find this expansion regarding יקטן. *Gen. Rab.* 6 (p. 43) offers a different homily on the name יקטן:

> שהיה מקטין את עסקיו. מה זכה? זכה להעמיד שלש עשרה משפחות

> Because he would make little of his endeavors. How was he rewarded? He was rewarded by establishing thirteen clans.

An explanation closer to that in TC appears in a later composition, *Sefer ha-Yashar, Noah* (p. 13):

> ואת שם השני קרא יקטן לאמר המעטו והקטינו חיי בני האדם בימיו

> And the second he named יקטן, indicating that human lives decreased and diminished in his day.

Churgin suggested this latter tradition as the source employed by TC, because both discuss the idea that human life expectancy declined in his day.[137] My view is that there is no direct connection between the two sources, as *Sefer ha-Yashar* predicates its exegesis on the name יָקְטָן as derived from the root קט״ן, while the homily in TC is based on the root קט״ע.[138]

---

137   Churgin *Hagiographa*, p. 247.

138   TC's use of the root is somewhat surprising linguistically, but for this reason especially we may surmise that the targumist's exegesis is not based on *Sefer ha-Yashar*.

5.2 *The Toponym Dinhabah* (*1 Chr 1:43*)

1 Chr 1:43

MT	וְשֵׁם עִירוֹ	דִּנְהָבָה:
TC	... וְשׁוּם קַרְתָּא דְּבֵית מַלְכוּתֵיהּ דִּנְהָבָה וְאִתְיְהֵיבַת לֵיהּ מַגָּן:	

NJPS: and the name of his city was Dinhabah

Dost: Now the name of the city of his royal palace was Dinhabah, and it was given to him freely

All Pentateuchal Targums known to us end this verse with the name דנהבה, without adding any information about that place. TC alone gives an interpretation of the name, derived from the root יה״ב, and understands the word to mean *it was given*, i.e., which was given to him at no cost. No other source is known to me for this homily.

5.3 *The Sons of Shobal* (*1 Chr 2:52*)

1 Chr 2:52

MT	וַיִּהְיוּ בָנִים לְשׁוֹבָל אֲבִי קִרְיַת יְעָרִים הָרֹאֶה חֲצִי הַמְּנֻחוֹת:	
TC	וַהֲווֹ בְּנִין לְשׁוֹבָל רַב קִרְיַת־יְעָרִים תַּלְמִידַיָּא וְכַהֲנַיָּא דַּחֲזַיִן לְפַלָּגָא קוּרְבָּנַיָּא:	

NJPS: Shobal father of Kiriath-jearim had sons: Haroeh, half of the Menuhoth.

Dost: Now Shobal, the chief of Kiriath-jearim, had sons: the disciples and the priests who were qualified to distribute the sacrifices.

Each of the words הָרֹאֶה חֲצִי הַמְּנֻחוֹת is translated exegetically. The words הָרֹאֶה חֲצִי are interpreted in the sense of *those fit* (ראוי) *to partake*, and accordingly are translated דַּחֲזַיִן לְפַלָּגָא. The word הַמְּנֻחוֹת is exegetically associated with מִנְחָה, and thus translated as קוּרְבָּנַיָּא. This exegesis anticipates what awaits in the Targum to verse 54, where וַחֲצִי הַמְּנֻחֹתִי is rendered as כהניא דמפלגין מותר קרבניא. The words תלמידיא וכהניא, *disciples and priests*, similarly make their entrance here in anticipation of the Targum to that verse and the next.

5.4 *Moses' Descendants as Prophetic Disciples* (*1 Chr 2:53*)

1 Chr 2:53

MT	וּמִשְׁפְּחוֹת	קִרְיַת יְעָרִים	הַיִּתְרִי
TC	וְגִנְסַיָּא	דִּיתְבִין בְּקִרְיַת־יְעָרִים	לִיוָּאֵי בְּנֵי מֹשֶׁה דִּילִידַת לֵיהּ צִפֹּרָה יַתְרָאֵי

MT (cont.)	וְהַפּוּתִי וְהַשֻּׁמָתִי וְהַמִּשְׁרָעִי מֵאֵלֶּה יָצְאוּ הַצָּרְעָתִי וְהָאֶשְׁתָּאֻלִי:
TC	פּוּתָאֵי וְשׁוּמָתַאי וּמִשְׁרַעַאי מֵאִלֵּין נְפַקוּ תַּלְמִידֵי נְבִיַּיָּא דְּצַרְעָה וְאֶשְׁתָּאוֹל:

NJPS: And the families of Kiriath-jearim: the Ithrites, the Puthites, the Shumathites, and the Mishraites; from these came the Zorathites and the Eshtaolites.

Dost: The families who were living in Kiriath-jearim were Levites, the sons of Moses whom Zipporah bore to him: the Ithrites, the Puthites, the Shumathites, and the Mishraites. From these descended the disciples of the prophets of Zorah and Eshtaol.

This verse, like the preceding one, anticipates the Targum to follow. The groups discussed by the verse are included in the heading ליוֹאֵי בני משה דיילידת ליה צפרה, *Levites, the sons of Moses whom Zipporah bore to him*, in keeping with verse 55: הנון שלמאי בני צפרה דמתיחסין עם גניסת ליוֹאֵי דאתיין מזרעית משה, *these were (the) Shalmites, the sons of Zipporah, who were registered with the lineage of the Levites, who came from the clan of Moses*. The identification of these individuals as descended from Zipporah is buttressed by their description as הַיִּתְרִי, a term reminiscent of Jethro/Jether, father-in-law of Moses.[139] תלמידי נבייא דצרעה ואשתאוֹל anticipates verse 54: ותלמידי נבייא דמן צרעה. The phrase תלמידי נבייא is the typical translation in TJ of the scriptural expression בני הנביאים, found in the book of Kings. Aside from these two instances in TC, we are aware of no tradition asserting the existence of a prophetic school in Zorah and Eshtaol.[140]

5.5   *Aharhel as Hur (1 Chr 4:8)*

1 Chr 4:8

MT	וְקוֹץ הוֹלִיד אֶת־עָנוּב וְאֶת־הַצֹּבֵבָה וּמִשְׁפְּחֹת אֲחַרְחֵל בֶּן־הָרוּם:
TC	וקוֹץ אוֹליד ית ענוב וית צוֹבבה וגניסת אחרא' הוא חוֹר בוֹכרא דמרים:

NJPS: Koz was the father of Anub, Zobebah, and the families of Aharhel son of Harum.

Dost: Koz fathered Anub and Zobebah, the lineage of Aharhel, who was Hur, the firstborn of Miriam.

The present verse is associated with Miriam by various midrashic traditions. One of these, *Sifre Num.* 78 (p. 75), identifies the two names with which the verse ends as references to Miriam and Jochebed:

---

139   Contrary to the implication in Le Déaut-Robert, vol. 1, p. 45, n. 17 (subsequently followed by McIvor, p. 52, n. 45), rabbinic literature contains no homilies on the names פותי, יתרי, שומתי, and משרעי. Their citation of Ginzberg, vol. 3, p. 76, is valid with regard to the names תרעתים, שמעתים, and סוכתים, of verse 55.

140   McIvor diffidently suggested that this presumed study hall had its origins in a GT to Judg 13:25 that appears in Sperber, vol. 2, p. 76: ושריאת רוח נבואה מן קדם ה' (instead of במקום רוח גבורא מן קדם ה'). Though Samson's spirit of valor may be understood as a kind of embodiment of the prophetic spirit, I doubt that such a supposition could be the source of an aggadic tradition regarding disciples of prophets in Zorah and Eshtaol. The Targum's source will have to be identified elsewhere.

'אחרחל'—זו מרים, שנאמר 'ותצאן כל הנשים אחריה'. 'בן הרום'—זו יוכבד, שנאמר
'כל חרם בישראל לך יהיה'. נשאת מרים לכלב, שנאמר 'ותמת עזובה ויקח לו כלב
את אפרת ותלד לו את חור', 'ואלה היו בני כלב בן חור'.

'Aharhel'—this is Miriam, as stated, 'and all the women went out after her
(אחריה)' (Exod 15:20). 'Son of Harum'—this is Jochebed, as stated, 'Everything
that has been proscribed in Israel shall be yours.' (Num 18:14). Miriam became
married to Caleb, as stated, 'When Azubah died, Caleb married Ephrath, who
bore him Hur.' (1 Chr 2:19), 'These were the descendants of Caleb, the son of
Hur' (1 Chr 2:50).

A parallel tradition is found in *Exod. Rab.* 1:17 (p. 68):

'ומשפחות אחרחל בן הרום'—זה מרים. ולמה נקרא שמה אחרחל? על שם: 'ותצאן
כל הנשים אחריה בתפים ובמחלת'. ומהו 'ומשפחות'? זכה להעמיד ממנה משפחות.
'בן הרום'—שזכתה שיצא ממנה דוד, שרימם הקב"ה מלכותו, כמה דאת אמר: '[ויתן
עז למלכו] וירם קרן משיחו'.

'and the families of Aharhel son of Harum'—this is Miriam. Why was she
called Aharhel? Due to 'and all the women went out after her (אחריה)
in dance with timbrels' (Exod 15:20). What is 'and the families'? He was
fortunate to establish families through her. 'Son of Harum'—she was fortunate to have David be born through her, for the Holy One blessed be he
elevated (רימם) his kingship, as you say: 'He will give power to His king,
And triumph (וירם) to His anointed one.' (1 Sam 2:10).

The motivation for the exegesis given in *Sifre* and subsequently in *Exodus
Rabbah* is the desire to prove that the Israelite monarchy was established
through the agency of Miriam as fulfillment of וַיַּעַשׂ לָהֶם בָּתִּים, *He established
households for them*, in Exod 1:21.[141] Though the approach taken here by TC is
not identical to that of *Sifre* or *Exodus Rabbah* (Jochebed goes unrepresented
in TC, and Hur does not appear in the other works), but I believe that the tradition associating this verse with Miriam was sufficient to facilitate the exegetical turn taken by TC.

The targumist identified Miriam with Ephrat thrice in Chronicles (see
pp. 362–364, above). In one of these instances—four verses before the present
one—Hur is entitled בְּכוֹר אֶפְרָתָה:

---

141   See Kahana, vol. 3, pp. 547–548. Kahana hypothesizes that the tradition in *Sifre* is based
       on a full-fledged midrashic work on Chronicles including more details than are today
       preserved in book form.

1 Chr 4:4

MT אֵ֤לֶּה בְנֵי־חוּר֙ בְּכ֣וֹר אֶפְרָ֔תָה

TC אלין בני חור בוכרא דאפרת היא מרים

NJPS: These were the sons of Hur, the first-born of Ephrathah

Dost: These were the sons of Hur, the firstborn of Ephrath, who was Miriam

Ephrat having been identified with Miriam, חור, who is the firstborn of Ephrath, must be the firstborn of Miriam as well. Therefore, four verses later, when the targumist arrives at a verse whose midrashic baggage associates it with Miriam, he identifies הרום as מרים and הרום בן אחרחל as חור בן מרים and, influenced by verse 4 above, gives the translation בוכרא דמרים, *firstborn of Miriam*. TC thus reflects a midrashically flavored understanding, whether of the targumist's own invention or a received tradition, which resembles but is not identical to that in evidence in the midrashic works excerpted.

5.6   *Sheerah, Survivor of the Slain Ephraimites (1 Chr 7:24)*

1 Chr 7:24

MT וּבִתּ֣וֹ שֶׁאֱרָ֗ה וַתִּ֤בֶן אֶת־בֵּית־חוֹרֹן֙ הַתַּחְתּ֜וֹן וְאֶת־ הָֽעֶלְי֑וֹן וְאֵ֖ת אֻזֵּ֥ן שֶׁאֱרָֽה׃

TC וברתיה שאר׳   דאשתיירת מן קטיליא

ובנת ית בית־חורון ארעייה וית   בית־חורון עלאה וית אזן־דשארה:

NJPS: His daughter was Sheerah, who built both Lower and Upper Beth-horon, and Uzzen-sheerah.

Dost: His daughter was Sheerah, who was left from the slain, and she built lower Beth-horon, upper Beth-horon, and Uzzan of Sheerah.

We might infer that the homily on this woman's name is a product of its content and the unusual scriptural description of a woman who constructs cities. She is called שארה because she remained (נשארה). She is a builder of cities, perhaps because no one else was left to pursue such projects after the massacre of two-hundred thousand members of her tribe. In any event, if TC received this homily from some other source, its identity is unknown to us.

5.7   *Baara is Hodeshah (1 Chr 8:8–9)*

1 Chr 8:8

MT וְשַׁחֲרַ֗יִם הוֹלִ֛יד בִּשְׂדֵ֥ה מוֹאָ֖ב מִן־ שִׁלְח֣וֹ אֹתָ֑ם חוּשִׁ֥ים וְאֶֽת־בַּעֲרָ֖א נָשָֽׁיו׃

TC ושחרים אוליד בחקלי מואב מן   בתר דפטר יתהון

וותב ונסיבנון ית חושים וית בערה נשוהי:

NJPS: And Shaharaim had sons in the country of Moab after he had sent away Hushim and Baara his wives.

Dost: Shaharaim had children in the fields of Moab after he divorced and re-married his wives Hushim and Baara.

1 Chr 8:9

MT: וַיּוֹלֶד מִן־ חֹדֶשׁ אִשְׁתּוֹ אֶת־יוֹבָב וְאֶת־צִבְיָא וְאֶת־מֵישָׁא וְאֶת־מַלְכָּם׃

TC: ואוליד מן בערה היא חדשה אתתיה

דאתחדתא בנשואה ית יובב ית צביא וית מישא וית מלכם:

NJPS: He had sons by Hodesh his wife: Jobab, Zibia, Mesha, Malcam

Dost: From Baara, who is his wife, Hadashah, for a novel interpretation of the law was established through her marriage, He fathered Jobab, Zibia, Mesha, Malcam

These verses are interpreted in *y. Yebamot* and *Ruth Rabbah* as referring to Boaz and Ruth.[142] TY comments:

כת[יב] 'ושחרים הוליד בשדי מוא[ב] מן שלח אותם חושים ואת בערה נשיו'. 'שחרים'—זה בועז, שהיה משוחרר מן העונות. 'הוליד בשדה מואב'—שנשא את רות המואביה ... 'חושים ואת בערה נשיו'—וכי יש לך אדם שהוא מוליד את נשיו? אלא חש כנמר וביאר את ההלכה. 'ויולד מן חודש אשתו'—לא צורכא דלא 'ויולד מן בערה נשיו'? אלא על ידיה נתחדשה הלכה: 'עמוני' ולא [ע]מונית, 'מואבי' ולא מואבית.

'Shaharaim had children in the fields of Moab after he divorced and re-married his wives Hushim and Baara' (1 Chr 8:8). 'Shaharaim'—that's Boaz, for he was free of sins. 'had children in the fields of Moab'—for he married Ruth the Moabitess ... 'his wives Hushim and Baara'—does a man beget his own wives? Rather, he hastened like a leopard and eluci-dated the Halakha. 'He had sons by Hodesh his wife'—shouldn't it read '... by Baara ...'? Rather, through her was a new Halakha established: 'Ammonite' and not an Ammonitess, 'Moabite' and not a Moabitess.

Jastrow suggests a textual emendation in TC and inserts the word הלכה after דאתחדתא, thereby weaving, in effect, the aforementioned rabbinic sources into TC.[143] McIvor and Dost both follow Jastrow in their English translations of TC and take the verb אתחדתא as a reference to a new interpretation of the law

---

142   *Y. Yebam.* 8:3 (9c, pp. 869–870); *Ruth Rab.* 4:1 (p. 96).
143   Jastrow, p. 909.

that was introduced through her.[144] However, I don't see justification for this in the textual witnesses of TC or in the plain sense of the Aramaic text before us. True, the rabbinic sources above introduce the law as the object of renewal, but that does not mean TC must be read accordingly or that its text as appears before us is unintelligible. The subject of the verb אתחדתא in the manuscripts is Baara—not the law. Therefore it was she who was renewed in some manner, according to TC. In what manner was she renewed? The former verse in the Targum provides a simple answer to this question. Shaharaim remarried her.

Clearly, then, TC does not converge with the interpretation of TY and *Ruth Rabbah*. If the targumist was familiar with these sources, he may have chosen to ignore them because the chapter in Chronicles concerns the Benjaminites, rather than the descendants of Judah. Still, I have not found any other source that interprets the verses as does TC. Nonetheless, the influence exerted on TC by a Hebrew midrashic source may be intimated by the words דאתחדתא בנשואה. The word נשואה in this Aramaic text is most easily explained as the reflection of a Hebrew source, for the root נש״א appears in Aramaic only when a Hebrew usage lurks someplace in the background.[145] Therefore I presume that the author of TC was familiar with a Hebrew source in which the words חֹדֶשׁ אִשְׁתּוֹ were interpreted as intimating שנתחדשה בנישואיה, *she*—not the Halakha—was renewed by virtue of being remarried to Shaharaim.

5.8   *Phineas: Officer of the Tabernacle (1 Chr 9:20)*

1 Chr 9:20

MT	עִמּֽוֹ׃	הֽ׳	וּפִֽינְחָס בֶּן־אֶלְעָזָר נָגִיד הָיָה עֲלֵיהֶם לְפָנִים	
TC			ופינחס בר אלעזר סרכן הוה עליהון מלקדמין	

מן יומא דאתוקם משכן זמנא במדברא   ומימרא דה׳ הוה בסעדיה:

NJPS: And Phinehas son of Eleazar was the chief officer over them in time past; the LORD was with him.

Dost: Phineas son of Eleazar was an officer over them from the beginning, from the day when the tent of meeting was established in the desert and the Memra of the Lord was at his aid.

This verse served in rabbinic literature as a source indicating the divine spirit's departure from Phineas when he failed to act to save Jephthah's daughter.[146] Nothing in the Targum here, however, indicates such an implication. The

---

144   McIvor, p. 76, n. 10. Dost's translation appears above.

145   Cf. TN Deut 28:49; TPJ Exod 10:19.

146   *Gen. Rab.* 60 (p. 643); *Lev. Rab.* 37:4 (vol. 2, pp. 466–467). Unlike MT, the midrashic reading precedes לְפָנִים logically: לְפָנִים ה׳ עִמּוֹ, but afterward He was not with him.

expansion, מן יומא דאתוקם משכן זמנא במדברא, *from the day when the tent of meet-ing was established in the desert*, functions as a clarification more precisely de-fining the time signified by the literal translation, מלקדמין, *from the beginning*,[147] and invites us to ask why the targumist chose to relate that Phineas began his career as captain when the Tabernacle was constructed, rather than when God promised him a covenant of everlasting priesthood or some other time. Did TC rely on a midrashic source in making this decision? There does not seem to be any midrashic tradition that associates Phineas' role as captain with the construction of the Tabernacle. Rather, the targumist appears to have been motivated to make this comment by the verse's context. Let us now refer to 1 Chr 9:19–24:

19 וְשַׁלֻּום בֶּן־קֹורֵא בֶּן־אֶבְיָסָף בֶּן־קֹרַח וְֽאֶחָ֞יו לְבֵית־אָבִיו הַקָּרְחִים עַל מְלֶאכֶת הָעֲבֹודָה שֹׁמְרֵי הַסִּפִּים לָאֹהֶל וַאֲבֹתֵיהֶם עַל־מַחֲנֵה ה' שֹׁמְרֵי הַמָּבֹוא: 20 וּפִֽינְחָס בֶּן־אֶלְעָזָר נָגִיד הָיָה עֲלֵיהֶם לְפָנִים ה' | עִמֹּו: 21 זְכַרְיָה בֶּן מְשֶֽׁלֶמְיָה שֹׁעֵר פֶּתַח לְאֹהֶל מֹועֵד: 22 כֻּלָּם הַבְּרוּרִים לְשֹׁעֲרִים בַּסִּפִּים מָאתַיִם וּשְׁנֵים עָשָׂר הֵמָּה בְחַצְרֵיהֶם הִתְיַחְשָׂם הֵמָּה יִסַּד דָּוִיד וּשְׁמוּאֵל הָרֹאֶה בֶּאֱמוּנָתָם: 23 וְהֵם וּבְנֵיהֶם עַל־הַשְּׁעָרִים לְבֵית־ה' לְבֵית הָאֹהֶל לְמִשְׁמָרֹות: 24 לְאַרְבַּע רוּחֹות יִהְיוּ הַשֹּׁעֲרִים מִזְרָח יָמָּה צָפֹונָה וָנֶֽגְבָּה:

NJPS: 19 Shallum son of Kore son of Ebiasaph son of Korah, and his kins-men of his clan, the Korahites, were in charge of the work of the ser-vice, guards of the threshold of the Tent; their fathers had been guards of the entrance to the camp of the LORD. 20 And Phinehas son of Eleazar was the chief officer over them in time past; the LORD was with him. 21 Zechariah the son of Meshelemiah was gatekeeper at the entrance of the Tent of Meeting. 22 All these, who were selected as gatekeepers at the thresholds, were 212. They were selected by genealogies in their villages. David and Samuel the seer established them in their office of trust. 23 They and their descendants were in charge of the gates of the House of the LORD, that is, the House of the Tent, as guards. 24 The gatekeepers were on the four sides, east, west, north, and south.

Verse 19 tells of שֹׁמְרֵי הַסִּפִּים לָאֹהֶל, *guards of the threshold of the Tent*, as well as refers to מַחֲנֵה ה', *the camp of the LORD*; verse 21 mentions אֹהֶל מֹועֵד, *the Tent of Meeting*; and verse 23 contains the pleonasm לְבֵית־ה' לְבֵית הָאֹהֶל, *the House of the LORD, the House of the Tent*. All these references to that structure to-gether form a description that, in the eyes of the targumist, suggests that the discussion harks back to the Tabernacle in the wilderness, and he therefore

---

147 מלקדמין is a regular Aramaic equivalent of לְפָנִים in the Targums.

understood Phineas' description as captain over them לְפָנִים as referring to the very beginning of the Tabernacle's functioning. Phineas, then, merited mention here not due to a specific action that he performed once, but because he was the first captain of the keepers of the Tabernacle, and, this being the case, the beginning his tenure naturally must have coincided with the day the Tabernacle was inaugurated. This interpretation thus appears to be an innovation of the targumist, rather than a quotation from a pre-existing tradition.

5.9 *Expert Calculators of the Calendar (1 Chr 12:33)*

1 Chr 12:33

MT	לְעִתִּים	יֹדְעֵי בִינָה	יִשָּׂשכָר	וּמִבְּנֵי
TC	לעדניא	ידעי סוכלתנו	ישׁשׁכר	ומן בני
	רישׁי שׁנין ורישׁי ירחין	למקבע	חכימין	
	ירחיא ושׁניא	ולעברא		
	במולדא דסיהרא	סופיסטין[148]		
	מועדיא בעדנהון	למקבע		
	בתקופתא דשׁמשׁא		בקיעין	
	במזליא וכוכביא		אצרולוגין	

MT (cont.)	מָאתָיִם	רָאשֵׁיהֶם	יִשְׂרָאֵל	יַעֲשֶׂה	מַה־	לָדַעַת
TC		רבניהון	בית ישׂראל	למעבד	מה כשׁרין	למדע
		מאתן	רישׁי סנדריא			

(cont.)	פִּיהֶם:	עַל־	וְכָל־אֲחֵיהֶם
TC	פומהון:	עבדין פתגמי אוריתא וחכימין על מימר	כל אחוהון

NJPS: of the Issacharites, men who knew how to interpret the signs of the times, to determine how Israel should act; their chiefs were 200, and all their kinsmen followed them

Dost: Of the sons of Issachar, those who possessed understanding of the times, who were skilled at determining the beginnings of years and the beginnings of months, and at intercalating the months and the years, who were knowledgeable about the birth of the new moon, to affix festivals in their (appropriate) times, experts in the cycle of the sun, astrologers (who were educated) in the constellations and the stars, knowing what is fitting for the house of Israel to

---

148 MS V has the reading סופמטין; the other MSS, however, read סופיסטין, from σοφιστής. This word also serves as a term for Torah scholars in JPA poetry (see Sokoloff-Yahalom, p. 144, poem 17:30; cf. p. 102, poem 9:8; p. 306; poem 58:16) but in targumic literature appears only here. See Kister *Poetry*, p. 109.

do, their leaders, the heads of the Sanhedrin: 200, all of their kinsmen, (who) execute the words of the Torah and are wise according to the word of their mouth.

Many sources within the rabbinic tradition describe the tribe of Issachar as one of wise men who occupied themselves with Torah study, and the present verse had an important part in the construction of this concept,[149] which readily explains the targumist's decision to expand his translation of it and supplement the verse with descriptions in this vein.

It also is in keeping with the phrase יוֹדְעֵי בִינָה לַעִתִּים in the Hebrew verse that the expansion in TC emphasizes their calendric expertise more than their general Torah scholarship.[150] Nevertheless, it is difficult to escape the sense that the targumist expended more words here than required. In translating the Hebrew present form יוֹדְעֵי, he wrote five equivalent words (ידעי, חכימן, אצרולוגין, בקיעין, סופיסטין), and for the Hebrew עִתִּים, the targumist gave a long list of areas of knowledge (למקבע רישי שנין ורישי ירחין ולעברא ירחיא ושניא, עדניא, מזליא וכוכביא, תקופתא דשמשא, מולדא דסיהרא למקבע מועדיא בעדנהון).

Let us compare this treatment to BT's comments on a similar verse. In Esth 1:13, Ahasuerus addresses himself לַחֲכָמִים יֹדְעֵי הָעִתִּים, (to) *the sages learned in procedure (/times).* These wise men are thus identified in *b. Meg.* 12b:[151]

'ויאמר המלך לחכמים'—מאן חכמ[ים]? רבנן. 'יודעי העתים'—שיודעין לעבר שנים ולקבוע חדשים.

"And the king said to the sages ...:" *Who are the "sages"?* The rabbis. "... who know the times ..." *What Times?* Who know [when] to intercalate the years and [how] to set the months.

Had the targumist made do in the present verse with a short addition, e.g., חכימן לעברא שניא ולמקבע ירחיא, *skilled at determining the beginnings of years and the beginnings of months, and at intercalating the months and the years,*

---

149 See Ginzberg, vol. 5, p. 368, n. 391.

150 Cf. expansion in TPJ Gen 46:13 regarding the Issacharites, חכימן ומרי חושבנא, which may also allude to the practical mathematics of calendric calculations.

151 See *Esth. Rab.* 4:1 (p. 14) and *Tg. Esth I* 1:13–14, where these scholars are identified with the Issacharites on the basis of the present verse. Grossfeld *Esther*, p. 85, notes that the Issacharites' prayer, described there in verse 14, is not known from any other source, and apparently is an autonomous composition by the targumist.

it would be attributable to talmudic dicta such as that above.[152] Such statements do not, however, justify as lengthy a series of expressions as we find in the present verse. Let us consider the collection of calendric terms that appear together in TC. A similar list of terms to that found here that is not known from any talmudic source appears in just one Targum: TPJ Gen 1:14:

ואמר אלקים יהון נהורין ברקיעא דשמיא לאפרשא ביני יממא וביני ליליא ויהון
לסימנין ולזמני מועדין ולממני בהון חושבן יומין ולמקדשא רישי ירחין ורישי שנין
עיבורי ירחין ועיבורי שנין ותקופות שמשא ומולד סיהרא ומחזורין:

Clem: Then God said, "Let there be lights in the firmament of the heavens, to divide between the daytime and the nighttime, and let them be for signs and for appointed times of festivals, and by which to count the calculation of the days, and for sanctifying the new moons and the new years, the intercalation of months and the intercalation of years, and the solstice of the sun and the birth of the new moon and the solar cycle.

Only in TPJ above and in TC do we find מולד(א) (ד)סיהרא(א) and (א)ת(ו)תקופ שמשא(ד).[153] In each of the two Targums, these terms appear within a long list of similar terms, and in both the terms appear as part of an expansion triggered by a Hebrew *Vorlage* that alludes to the calendric sciences. Perhaps the expansions penned by these two targumists and the terms that they chose indicate that they lived in an environment and an era in which the calculation of the calendar was a much-discussed topic.

As demonstrated by Splansky, the author of TPJ had astronomical knowledge that places this work between the end of the eighth century and the beginning of the tenth.[154] This period—and more so that which followed—saw the eruption of conflicts over the precise calculation of the New Moon and adjustment of the halakhic calendar to conform to new, more precise scientific

---

152   Cf. *b. Sanh.* 87a: "ממד"—זה יועץ, ולקבוע חדשים שיודע לעבר שנים, *this refers to a counsellor"—who knows how to intercalate years and designate the appearance of the new moon;* Ibid. 110a: "קריאי מועד"—שיודעין לעבר שנים ולקבוע חדשים, *"Chosen for the appointed times" (Num. 16:2): For they knew how to intercalate years and designate the beginnings of the new months.*

153   This is not, of course, to say that the words תקופה and מולד as such were unfamiliar: תקופה appears in Scripture and מולד is documented in the Dead Sea Scrolls (see Ben-Dov, p. 392; Morgenstern, p. 143), but we find no phrases similar to those in TPJ and TC in the Talmud or earlier targumic works. The above verse in TPJ also contains the word מחזור, *cycle,* a hapax legomenon in targumic literature.

154   See detailed discussion emerging from TPJ Gen 1:16 in Splansky, pp. 99–105, and sources cited ibid.

observations concerning the solar year and lunar cycle. Hebrew works discussing these topics in detail were written in the tenth and eleventh centuries in the midst of a violent debate regarding the appropriate way to calculate the halakhic calendar.[155] Now let us add to the present verse 1 Chr 4:23, whose translation in TC is remarkably expansive:[156]

הנון תלמידי אוריתא ... ומיצבי עלמא ובנן ומשכללין ית חורבני בית ישראל עם שכינת
מלכא דעלמא בפולחן אוריתא ובעבור ירחיא ובקביעות רישי שניא ומועדיא ...
וסכמין מן שמיא על דעתהון ...

Clem: They were the disciples of the Torah ... (who) make the world stand sure, and rebuild and bring to an end the desolations of the house of Israel with the Shekhinah of the King of the World, by the service of the Torah, by the intercalation of months, and by the establishing of the beginnings of the years and appointed times ... and determined from heaven by their knowledge

The targumist writes here at great length, motivated by the goal of buttressing the authority of Torah scholars to establish how the calendar is to be calculated. Engagement in this activity is comparable to taking part in the creation of the world and earns special divine endorsement. The verse also illustrates that calculation of the calendar was a lively, relevant issue in the targumist's day.

TC contains no statements from which we might learn about the extent of astronomic knowledge during its author's time, and we thus cannot determine on the basis of this verse whether he lived while these debates raged or after they died down. Yet the very fact that these terms are used and the sheer number of terms in the verse reflect the change that took root in the Jewish world when the issue of the calendar became a lively, controversial one. Since time immemorial, astronomical calculations have been the province of the educated class, but beginning in the mid-Geonic Period and particularly in the tenth century, this occupation was a highly public one within Jewish society, and this state of affairs convincingly explains the great number of descriptions heaped on the Issacharites by the Targum.

---

155   One of the most famous conflicts on the matter was the early tenth-century dispute between R. Aharon b. Meir and R. Saadyah Ga'on.

156   A general discussion of the Targum to this verse, not focused on the subject of the calendar, appears above, pp. 269–277.

5.10   *Micaiah is Maacah (2 Chr 13:2)*

2 Chr 13:2

MT   שָׁל֧וֹשׁ שָׁנִ֛ים מָלַ֖ךְ בִּירֽוּשָׁלִָ֑ם וְשֵׁ֣ם אִמּ֗וֹ מִיכָיָ֛הוּ בַת־אוּרִיאֵ֖ל מִן־גִּבְעָֽה

TC   תלת שנין מלך בירושלם ושום אמיה מיכיהו ברת אוריאל מן גבעתא היא הות

מעכה ברת אבשלום ואמטול דהות אתא כשירתא אתהפכא למתקרי מיכיהו שמא דמעלי ושום
אבוהא אתהפך למתקרי אוריאל דמן גבעתא דלא למדכר שמיה דאבשלום

NJPS: He reigned three years in Jerusalem; his mother's name was Micaiah
daughter of Uriel of Gibeah.

Dost: and he reigned for three years in Jerusalem. The name of his mother was
Micaiah daughter of Uriel of Gibeathah. She was Maacah daughter of Absalom,
but because she was a righteous woman, it was changed to be called Micaiah, a
name that is excellent. The name of her father was changed to be called Uriel,
who was from Gibeatha, so as not to remember the name of Absalom.

In this verse, the targumist was confronted by a contradiction within the Book
of Chronicles, within Kings, and between Chronicles and Kings concerning the
name of the mother of Abijah son of Rehoboam:

2 Chr 11:20	וַתֵּ֥לֶד ל֖וֹ אֶת־אֲבִיָּֽה	מַעֲכָ֖ה בַת־אַבְשָׁל֑וֹם	וְאַחֲרֶ֣יהָ לָקַ֣ח אֶת־
2 Chr 13:1–2	וְשֵׁ֣ם אִמּ֗וֹ מִיכָיָ֛הוּ בַת־אוּרִיאֵ֖ל מִן־גִּבְעָ֑ה	... אֲבִיָּ֖ה	וַיִּמְלֹ֖ךְ
1 Kgs 15:1–2	וְשֵׁ֣ם אִמּ֔וֹ מַעֲכָ֖ה בַּת־אֲבִישָׁלֽוֹם:	... אֲבִיָּ֖ם	מָלַ֖ךְ
1 Kgs 15:9–10	וְשֵׁ֣ם אִמּ֔וֹ מַעֲכָ֖ה בַּת־אֲבִישָׁלֽוֹם:	... אָסָ֖א	מָלַ֖ךְ
2 Chr 15:16	אֵ֣ם׀ אָסָ֣א	מַעֲכָ֗ה	וְגַם־

The contradiction took shape as a result of an internal textual process in
the transmission of MT Kings that gave the same name for the mothers of
Abijah and Asa.[157] The ramifications of this textual change in Kings extend
to Chronicles in three places. The first two concern Abijah, as appears above
in 2 Chr 11:20; 13:1–2. The third instance, involving Asa, is in 2 Chr 15:16, where
Maacah is given as his mother's name, as in MT 1 Kgs 9:10, 13.

The targumist explains that the original name of Abijah's mother was
Maacah daughter of Absalom (son of David), but she earned a better name
by comporting herself in a praiseworthy manner. Because of her good deeds,
it was preferred not to mention that she was Absalom's daughter, lest she be
tarnished by his ill repute, and his name, too, therefore was altered. This improbable explanation clearly is not an appropriate one even for the internal
purposes of the Book of Chronicles, as Maacah appears in 2 Chr 15:2 with Asa

---

157   See Cogan *Kings*, pp. 392–393, 397–398; Japhet *OTL*, pp. 670–671.

in what the rabbinic tradition, which the author of TC received, understood as a particularly grievous context, viz., that Maacah would conjugate with the image of Asherah (on which see pp. 338–340, below). Because TC considers this to be the same woman, he is compelled to explain that although she did so for a time, she subsequently resumed her seemly ways and name:

2 Chr 15:2

TC: ומן־בתר דתבת מעכה אמיה למהוי כשירתא אהדר ית שמה מיכיהו בת אוריאל דמן
גבעתא מן־בגלל דלא למדכר ית שמה קדמאי דלא למתגניה ביה:

Dost: Once Maacah his mother returned to being righteous, he changed her name back to Micaiah daughter of Uriel, who was from Gibeatha, so that her former name would not be remembered so that he might not be shamed by it.

Though it is not explicit in TC in the above verse, the targumist's comments indicate that he interpreted אַם אסא as referring to Asa's *grandmother*.[158] The targumist's solution to the Micaiah/Maacah problem is not familiar from rabbinic literature, although the approach is in keeping with rabbinic exegetical techniques. Such an interpretation appears regarding the name of Absalom himself in *b. B. Bat.* 109b:

... 'ויהי נער מבית לחם יהודה [ממשפחת יהודה] והוא לוי והוא גר שם' ... וכי לוי
שמו? והלא יונתן שמו! דכת[יב] 'ויהונתן בן גרשום בן מנשה הוא ובניו היו כהנים
למשפחת הדני'. וכי בן מנשה הוא? והלא בן משה הוא! אלא מתוך שעשה מעשה
מנשה, תלאו הכת[וב] במנשה. הכא נמי, מתוך שעשה מעשה מנשה דקאתי
מיהודה, תלאו הכת[וב] ביהודה. א״ר יוחנן משום ר' שמעון בן יוחאי: מיכן שתולין
את הקל[ק]לה במקול[ק]ל. ר' יוסי בר' חנינה אמ[ר] מהכא: 'וגם הוא טוב תאר מאד
ואותו ילדה אחרי אבשלום'—והלא אדניה בן חגית ואבשלום בן מעכה? אלא מתוך
שעשה מעשה אבשלום, תלאו הכת[וב] באבשלום.

"And there was a young man out of Bethlehem in Judah, of the family of Judah, who was a Levite, and he sojourned there" (Judg 17:7). But was Levi really his name? Wasn't his name Jonathan, as it is said, "And Jonathan the son of Gershom the son of Manasseh, he and his sons were priests to the tribe of the Danites" (Judg 18:30)? *He said to him, "And following your reasoning,* was he really a son of Manasseh? Surely he was son of Moses, for it is written, 'the sons of Moses: Gershom and Eliezer" (1 Chr 23:15). But since he did the kind of deeds that Manasseh did, Scripture assigns

---

158   Thus also Qimḥi to 2 Chr 15:16.

to him descent from Manasseh. *And, here too,* since he did the deeds of Manasseh, who comes from Judah, the Scripture attributed to him descent from Judah." Said R. Yohanan in the name of R. Simeon b. Yohai, "On this basis it follows that corruption is blamed on the corrupt." R Yosé bar Ḥanina said, "It is on this basis: And he was also a very good looking man and he was born after Absalom' (1 Kgs 1:6). Now is it not the fact that Adonijah was the son of Haggith and Absalom was the son of Maacah? But because Adonijah did the kind of deeds that Absalom did, who rebelled against the kingdom, Scripture assigned him to the line of Absalom."

The Talmud excerpt above is not a direct source of the discussion here, but the sort of exegesis that we find in TC here accords with the spirit of the Talmud's comments above. It may be that TC here reflects a homiletic tradition that did not survive to our day. Alternately, the solution may be an original proposal by the targumist.[159]

---

159   Cf. the solution suggested by Samuel Masnuth (as well as Qimḥi):

ושם אמו מיכיהו בת אוריאל—היא מעכה בת אבשלום הנזכרת למעלה. ובספר מלכים שני שמות היו לה ולאביה ומיכיהו ומעכה קרובים בלשון והרבה נמצאים בזה הספר אדם אחד נזכר בשני שמות.

His mother's name was Micaiah daughter of Uriel—she was Maacah daughter of Absalom mentioned above. The book of Kings has two names for her and her father. Micaiah and Maacah are close in pronunciation and there are many instances in this book of a person with two names.

Pseudo-Rashi:

מיכיהו בת אוריאל—ולמעלה קורא לה שם אחר, "מעכה בת אבשלום", ובמלכים כתיב כמו כן "מעכה בת אבישלום"? מיכיהו בת אוריאל היה שמה, וכאן קורא אותה כן, לפי שהוא ספר הייחס של יהודה. ובמלכים שהוא ספר מלכי ישראל ויהודה קראה בשם כנויה "מעכה בת אבישלום"; ולפיכך כינו שמה משם גמור שלה מיכיהו—"מעכה". ושם אביה אוריאל—"אבישלום", לפי שעל שם כלתה נקראת, שהיתה אשת חיל, גברתנית, כדתיב "וגם מעכה אם אסא הסירה מגבירה". ומשום כבודה של כלתה קראה לחמותה על שם כלתה. כך מפורש בירושלמי.

Micaiah daughter of Uriel—above she has a different name, "Maacah daughter of Absalom, and in Kings it is spelled "Maacah daughter of Abisalom"? Her name was Micaiah daughter of Uriel, and that is what she is called here, for this is the geneology of Judah. In Kings, which is the book of kings of Israel and Judah she is called by a pseudonym, "Maacah daughter of Abisalom"; and this is why they changed her name from her real name Micaiah to "Maacah", and her father Uriel to "Abisalom", her appellation follows her daughter in law, who was a valiant woman and strong, as written "He also deposed Maacah mother of King Asa from the rank of queen mother" (2 Chr 15:16). Out of respect for her daughter in law, the mother in law was named after the daughter in law. This is the explanation of the Yerushalmi.

Viezel *Pseudo-Rashi*, p. 27, n. 21, reports that no such source has been identified in the *yerushalmi*.

5.11 *A Covenant of Salt (2 Chr 13:5)*

2 Chr 13:5

MT	לֹא עַל־יִשְׂרָאֵל	לְדָוִיד	מַמְלָכָה	נָתַן	יִשְׂרָאֵל	אֱלֹהֵי	הְ׳׀	הֲלֹא לָכֶם לָדַעַת כִּי
TC	על ישראל	ואשלטיה	לדוד	מלכותא	יהב	דישראל	אלהא	הלא לכון למדע ארום ה׳

MT (cont.)	מֶלַח: בְּרִית	וּלְבָנָיו	לוֹ	לְעוֹלָם
TC	מלח היכמה דמוי לית איפשר דמתמתקין	ולבנוי קיים	ליה	לעלם
	שלטנא מדבית דוד דתעדי	לית איפשר היכדין		לעלם
				עד עלמא:

NJPS: Surely you know that the LORD God of Israel gave David kingship over Israel forever—to him and his sons—by a covenant of salt.

Dost: Do you not know that the Lord, the God of Israel, gave the kingdom to David, and He made him to rule over Israel forever; to him and to his sons (it is) a covenant of salt. Just as it is impossible for the water of the sea to ever become sweet, so also it is impossible that you will remove the rule from those of the house of David forever.

TC explains the expression בְּרִית מֶלַח, *a covenant of salt*, with an analogy: just as the waters of the sea never can become sweet, the rule of the House of David never can come to an end.[160] The end of TC's comments is based on a formulation incorporated in the prayer recited by the high priest as reported in the Talmud,[161] based on TO Gen 49:10:

Gen 49:10

MT	מִיהוּדָה	שֵׁבֶט	לֹא־יָסוּר
TO	מדבית יהודה	שולטן	לא יעידי עביד

NJPS: The scepter shall not depart from Judah

Clem: One who executes rule shall not pass away from those of the House of Judah

TC chose to do without the participle עביד and substituted דוד for יהודה (a change that carries with it no essential difference in meaning, as David was a descendant of Judah) so that the terminology would suit the context of the verse.

The Hebrew expression בְּרִית מֶלַח appears in two places in Scripture: Num 18:19, where all sacrificial gifts are eternally bestowed on Aaron and his

---

160   On the various opinions regarding the authenticity of the Aramaic form מוי and the history of its development, see Dan, pp. 214–215, and sources cited ibid.

161   *B. Yoma* 53b; *Ta'an.* 24b.

descendants, and the present verse, where kingship is eternally given to David and his sons. It is clear from the context of both verses that the term בְּרִית מֶלַח refers to a covenant that cannot be abrogated, and it is thus explained by the Rabbis in many sources. The only Targum to Num 18:19 that gives an explanation of the expression is TPJ:

Num 18:19

MT עוֹלָם הוּא לִפְנֵי ה'   בְּרִית מֶלַח

TPJ הי־כמלחא דמבסים בשר קורבניא דקיים עלם הוא קדם ה'   ולא יתבטיל

NJPS: it is an eternal covenant of salt before the Lord

Clem: for an eternal covenant, and it shall not be nullified. Just as salt that seasons the flesh of the offerings that is an eternal covenant before the Lord,

TPJ explains the term as meaning that just as there never will be any change to the commandment to salt the sacrifices, so there never will be any change to the assignment of the priestly gifts to Aaron and his sons. This explanation is clarified in TPJ to a different verse, containing the phrase מֶלַח בְּרִית אֱלֹהֶיךָ, which is reminiscent of the present verse:

Lev 2:13

MT וְלֹא תַשְׁבִּית מֶלַח בְּרִית אֱלֹהֶיךָ מֵעַל מִנְחָתֶךָ עַל כָּל־קָרְבָּנְךָ תַּקְרִיב מֶלַח:

TPJ ולא תבטל מלח קיים אלקך מעילוי מנחתך מטול דעשרין וארבע מוהבתא דכהניא

איתגזרו בקיים מילחא בגין כן   על כל קרבנך תקריב   מילחא:

NJPS: you shall not omit from your meal offering the salt of your covenant with God; with all your offerings you must offer salt.

Clem: so that you not eliminate the salt of the covenant of your God from upon your grain offerings, because the twenty four endowments of the priests were decreed with a covenant of salt. Therefore, you shall offer salt upon all your offerings.

The analogies offered by TPJ were of no help to the author of TC in this case, because those in the two verses above in the Torah were tailor made to deal with priestly subjects, while our verse in Chronicles speaks of David's dynasty, which calls for another type of analogy. I have not yet found a source for TC's explanation of בְּרִית מֶלַח as suggesting this particular analogy to the sea. However, another midrashic explanation incorporating sea water into the expression 'a covenant of salt' is found in several medieval European sources. Rashi on Lev 2:13 explained that God made a covenant with the Lower Waters (i.e. Earth's seas) at the time of creation, guaranteeing that they will be used in the sacrificial rites in the Temple, through the salting of the sacrifices and

the libation of water during the Sukkot festival.[162] While this explanation and
TC do focus on sea water, it would be a stretch to claim that both are directly
related.

5.12   *The Sons of Joash Killed in Battle (2 Chr 24:27)*

2 Chr 24:27

MT	הָאֱלֹהִים	וִיסוֹד בֵּית	הַמַּשָּׂא עָלָיו	וּבָנָיו יֶרֶב (קרי)
TC	מקדשא דה׳	על דבית יהודה כד הוה מייסד בית־	מסקין מסין	ובנוי רמו

ואתקטלו בקרבא מטול חובי אבוהון [א]בר ממימר מלכא וכהנ

MT (cont.)	תַּחְתָּיו:	אֲמַצְיָהוּ בְנוֹ	וַיִּמְלֹךְ הַמְּלָכִים	סֵפֶר עַל־מִדְרַשׁ כְּתוּבִים הִנָּם
TC	באתרוהי:	בריה אמציה ומליך	מלכיא ספר פרשגן על	והאנון כתיבין

NJPS: As to his sons, and the many pronouncements against him, and his re-
building of the House of God, they are recorded in the story in the book of the
kings. His son Amaziah succeeded him as king.

Dost: Now without the authorization of the king and the priests, his sons proclaimed a raising of taxes upon those of the house of Judah when he was re-
building the temple of the Lord. So they were killed in the battle because of the
sins of their fathers. Indeed, these things are written in the copy of the scroll of
the kings. And his son Amaziah ruled in his place.

The targumist understood יֶרֶב הַמַּשָּׂא to mean that the sons of Joash "enlarged,"
i.e., levied, taxes,[163] and added that this action was a burden imposed by them
on their own initiative in addition to the taxes collected by the king and priests
(for Temple renovations). These sons, according to TC, were killed in battle due
to their father's sins.[164] The Hebrew verse certainly poses substantial exegetical
challenges, but the interpretation of TC strays so far from Scripture that how
the targumist traversed the distance from the words of the verse to such an
explanation is difficult to understand. Churgin drew the conclusion that the
supplemental material included by the targumist had its source, "apparently,
in a midrashic tradition."[165] I believe that Churgin's assessment was correct,
but I have not succeeded in locating the midrashic source here referenced by
the targumist.

---

162   For some other sources (all medieval European, as mentioned above) echoing a version of
this *derasha*, cf. Kasher *Torah Shelemah*, vol. 25, p. 110, n. 111.

163   BDB, p. 672, משא II, meaning 4.

164   It bears note that the idea of children's dying due to their forebears sins is discussed in
Hebrew scriptures, and hence in the Targum, four verses after the present one (2 Chr
25:4). I do not, however, see any cause for linking the two verses.

165   Churgin *Hagiographa*, p. 246.

6   Closing Remarks

The targumist used TPJ as his primary source in five expansions, while other expansions, too, bear indications of familiarity with TPJ. In four instances, an expansion in TC was found to bear a link to a tradition known to us from a Targum Tosefta in MS Reuchlin. In one case (pp. 285–299), the targumist employed a pre-existing expansion found in TJ, augmented it, and thus altered the characterization of King David. Elsewhere (pp. 336–337), TC expanded an already pre-existing expansion found in TJ with the purpose of clarifying it. The exegesis found in two expansions in TC was found to correspond to traditions recorded in *Tanḥuma*.[166] No indications were found of close familiarity with TY. One expansion may have its source in TY, but even that attribution is uncertain.[167]

Summary and Conclusions of the Last Two Chapters

In the last two chapters we devoted a separate discussion to each of the expansions that appear in TC. In so doing much new information came to light in the interpretation of each expansion in its location and context in the Targum. Now that this examination of the "micro" is complete, it is time to assemble the central items of information on the "macro" level arising from these discussions. This summary includes the information from both chapters, because having studied all the expansions—those tied to BT and those that aren't—it is now important to treat them all as a group that informs us about the targumist and his library.

1.   Nearly all of the nonliteral expansions in TC are based on rabbinic literature. Of the seventy-six expansions discussed, only twelve may stem from the targumist's independent exegesis.[168] Even in these cases there is no definitive proof that the interpretations given are the original work of the targumist, but we simply lack the ability to identify a still-extant exegetical tradition on which the author of TC based his comments.

2.   Authors of previous studies noted the reliance of Targum Chronicles on the Babylonian Talmud. With the present study, we demonstrate that this reliance is even greater than previously expressed. The place of BT in informing TC is, quantitatively speaking, substantially greater than that of all other rabbinic sources together, and in my view this great quantitative disparity is indicative of a corresponding qualitative disparity. The logical

---

166   pp. 432–434, 445–449.

167   pp. 461–463.

168   These twelve expansions are: Chapter 8: 5.1 (p. 470), 5.2 (p. 471), 5.3 (p. 471), 5.4 (pp. 471–472), 5.5 (pp. 472–474), 5.6 (p. 474), 5.7 (pp. 474–476), 5.8 (pp. 476–478), 5.9 (pp. 478–481), 5.10 (pp. 482–484), 5.11 (pp. 485–487), 5.12 (p. 487).

conclusion from the kind of reliance shown by TC on BT is that the latter was the most important source of rabbinic exegesis and scriptural interpretation in the targumist's library.

3. The fact that a source has been found in rabbinic literature for the vast majority of the expansions discussed reflects the targumist's technique. By all appearances, the targumist is not a consciously autonomous exegete, but the repository of a variety of midrashic traditions concerning the verses of Chronicles with which he was familiar. The impression one receives is that the targumist was well-versed in some of the aggadic traditions of scriptural exegesis and, on reaching a verse with whose aggadic appurtenances he was familiar, incorporated this knowledge in his Targum. It was not the targumist's intention, or at least his primary intention, that these aggadic insertions serve to resolve textual challenges that he himself faced and sought to lay to rest. Rather, composition of the Targum served him as an opportunity to preserve traditional exegesis with which he already was familiar. Stated otherwise, it does not seem that in the course of his work the targumist would find himself faced by a challenge contained in a verse and then embark on a search for a solution. Rather, on arriving at a verse that he knew to be interpreted by a given rabbinic tradition, the targumist would incorporate that tradition in his work. TC thus differs from TJ to Samuel and Kings, which does not make such an impression. Though one often finds specific points in TJ that that Targum has in common with rabbinic sources, its author did not have his eyes perpetually set on rabbinic exegeses for guidance. TC is something of an anthology with a perspective on the study of rabbinic lore that reflects its late date. This conclusion is buttressed by the targumist's tendency to integrate competing views found in rabbinic sources, as noted above (p. 78). TC is a link between the Targums of old (TO, TJ) and the exegetical work of the early medieval scholars, and in this it resembles TPJ and various other Targums of the Writings.

4. The strong link identified between TC and TPJ in chapters four and five is further bolstered by the findings of chapters seven and eight.

5. The similarity identified between several expansions and Targum Toseftot in MS Reuchlin demonstrates that the author of TC was exposed to various targumic traditions. This conclusion accords with our observation, noted in the context of the Table of Nations, that the targumist sometimes included alternative targumic traditions, which he marked ל"א, and apparently was familiar with Pentateuchal targumic traditions that are unavailable to us (see p. 172, above).

6. Dating the Targum: Several expansions in TC appear to indicate that the work was authored at a relatively late date:

a. Generally speaking, the direct reliance on TPJ, identified in chapters four and five and in the discussion of several expansions in chapters seven and eight, attests to the late date at which TC was authored, as TPJ itself is a very late Targum, relatively speaking.

b. Specifically, it is self-evident from two expansions reliant on TPJ, which TC employed secondarily, that even in their original form (and prior to their incorporation into TC) they were authored well after the rise of Islam (2.2, p. 387; 2.3, p. 392). One must assume that some time had to pass for those homilies that describe Islamic rule as a well-established reality to have been formulated, and then more time must be assumed for this late exegetical material to have made its way into TC.

c. The complexity of material concerning the calendar (2.6, p. 269; 5.9, p. 478) is in keeping with a date later than the early tenth century, when the particulars of the Hebrew calendar made their controversial appearance on the stage of general Jewish discourse.

d. The tradition about the Ten Tribes' exile to the Mountains of Darkness (4.9, p. 442) is not known to appear in sources dating to the first millennium CE, but first appears in literary sources in approximately the eleventh century. The composition of TC, then, should presumably be dated to a historical period close to that time.

e. The pleonasm ספרא דבי רב הוא ספרא דאוריית כהניא reflects a relatively late period, certainly no earlier than that of the Ge'onim.

The accumulation of these conclusions, together with that of this book's earlier chapters now allow us to answer—at least in part—some of the basic questions pertaining to the origin of Targum Chronicles.

CHAPTER 9

Conclusions

1 Summary

This book has examined Targum Chronicles from several vantage points, which converge and add precision to the picture that has emerged. Textual discussions, linguistic studies, exegetical analyses, intertextual comparisons, have all led to conclusions that provide a far more secure footing than previously available in our understanding of Targum Chronicles and its origins.

In chapter two I surveyed some of the main translation techniques employed by the targumist as well as tendencies of his revealed by his choices of expression. TC's author was well versed in the accepted translation techniques of his predecessors—the earlier Jewish targumists—and made extensive use of them. In the vast majority of cases reviewed it was found that TC did not introduce new translation techniques or methods, but rather continued in the beaten path of earlier targumic traditions. This is true with regard to merely technical choices as well as special modes of expression developed within targumic tradition for the purpose of honoring God in written expression. This informs us of TC's author's deep and comprehensive familiarity with targumic tradition. He aligned himself with the modes of expression of classical Targums, including those of religious-theological importance, and applied them similarly to his forerunners. He embedded many elements from his rabbinic heritage throughout TC. He abundantly included aggadic material from rabbinic literature, institutions and terms emanating from their milieu and shaped biblical characters into rabbinic-like sages. TC was composed, then, in the image and form of its predecessors.

In chapters three through six I explored TC's relations with Targums of biblical books containing parallel units to Chronicles, namely Samuel, Kings, Genesis and Psalms. TC made use of Targum Jonathan as a base-text for the parallel material in Samuel and Kings, but adapted this text according to several considerations, most notably the conversion of basic words that comprise the linguistic backbone of the dialect in which he was writing, as well as taking into account the textual variants between Chronicles and Samuel-Kings.

TC relied on several targumic traditions with regard to the parallel material in Genesis. Among them, Targum Pseudo-Jonathan is demonstrably the closest Aramaic Targum to TC in these units. A close affinity was established between TC and TPJ also outside the parallel units. They exhibit a similarity

© KONINKLIJKE BRILL NV, LEIDEN, 2020 | DOI:10.1163/9789004417632_010

in vocabulary in a dialect that blends many western and eastern elements together. In several instances, I also identified cases of direct literary dependence of TC upon TPJ. I also indicated that this direct literary dependence is of great importance in light of the recently identified indications that TPJ is a product of twelfth century Italy. A degree of similarity was established between the language of these Targums and the type of Aramaic found in the Piyyutim of medieval Ashkenaz.

In the course of my study I also identified many shared elements in the language of TC and Targum Psalms. A philological comparison of the parallel material Chronicles and Psalms confirmed the great similarity in the language of the two Targums, while also leading to the conclusion that neither composition used the other (as TC did with regard to TJ and TPJ) while translating these verses. Of particular interest was the appearance of the appellation הונגראי in both Targums as an equivalent of the ethnic proper noun הַגְרִי and the logical ramifications of this for the dating of these Targums was discussed, if indeed this appellation points to the Hungarian people of Europe.

In chapters seven and eight I collated seventy-six expansions in TC, which appear to preserve or rely upon an aggadic or halakhic tradition, and I attempted to identify their literary sources. This study required a discussion of the contents of these expansions, in the course of which many new details came to light with regard to these verses—verses that comprise the greatest exegetical challenge for a commentator of TC. As for its sources, TC was found to have made extensive use of the Babylonian Talmud. The Bavli was a direct source of TC in approximately half of the expansions. Other sources for these expansions were TPJ (as already noted earlier), traditions found in the Targum Toseftot of MS Reuchlin and also assorted Midrashim.

In the course of this book many verses in TC were elucidated with novel explanations. In many instances I arrived at more precise explanations of TC due to the understanding that this Targum is not a stand-alone composition that can be understood independently of other works. The ability to pinpoint the author's intention frequently involves regarding the Targum as a composition dependent on rabbinic literature.[1] Indeed, this book reveals the links between TC and its rabbinic sources to a greater extent than has been shown in earlier studies of this Targum and it highlights just how important recognizing the connection between these two literary collections is, and how the precise identification of literary sources may aid us in better understanding a Targum, its *Sitz im Leben*, and its place in the history of biblical exegesis.

---

1   On this point cf. Lasair, p. 450.

2   When Was Targum Chronicles Composed?

As this book reaches its end, the broad perspective we now have and the facts that have come to light allow us to offer answers for some fundamental questions pertaining to the date and historical provenance of Targum Chronicles that may point to new ideas regarding the origins of some other Targums as well. In this book's outset we noted Rosenberg and Kohler's work on TC, in which they upheld Zunz's view that TC is a Palestinian Targum and that its final composition was not later than the eighth century. Churgin stated that "clear signs of the author's date are not discernible in the Targum itself. It is clear that it was completed after the Talmud Bavli, for the targumist made use of many of its Aggadot. It is also clear that this Targum was composed in the land of Israel, the birthplace of all the Targums".[2] Subsequent scholars have relied on these studies. Now, however, the perspective afforded us by the findings of this book call for a reevaluation of some of the conclusions that were so commonly accepted regarding TC's background.

Contra Churgin, TC does contain signs that point to the time of its author. They may not be abundant, but they agree with each other, despite being independent—and this makes them all the more convincing. A later date of composition than previously accepted may be ascertained from the Targum's dialect, from its direct dependence on TPJ and from some expressions that are most easily explained in a period later than the eighth century. The language of Targum Chronicles is not solely western (Palestinian) Aramaic, nor solely eastern (Babylonian) Aramaic, but rather a dialect that knows both and weaves eastern elements into a primarily western framework. Kaufman named this dialect, 'Late Jewish Literary Aramaic' and it is found in TPJ and many of the Targums to the Hagiographa.

Throughout TC we discovered examples of direct literary dependence upon TPJ—not only in the units parallel to the Torah, but also in the selection of equivalents in non-parallel sections. Scholars of TPJ such as Foster, Shinan, Splansky, Kaufman and Cook have presented linguistic, literary and historical reasons for ascribing a relatively late date to TPJ—the inclusion of earlier material within it notwithstanding. This being the case, as late as TPJ is shown to be, TC must be regarded as even later. So, for example, when TC makes secondary use of expansions found in TPJ that depict, or are founded upon, a world in which the Islamic empire is already a longstanding fait accompli

---

2   Churgin *Hagiographa*, p. 236. This generalization about Targums is common among scholars, but has not been sufficiently proven when speaking about the entirety of targumic literature. See also de Sola Pool, p. 23, "as the home of the Targum and Midrash was Palestine (Judea)".

(1 Chr 1:20, 30), we should allow the evidence to speak for itself. Limiting the dating of this secondary use to the eighth century because of the decline of Aramaic as a spoken language in the Land of Israel after the rise of Islam is unwarranted and quite frankly has closed the minds of twentieth century scholarship from recognizing the wealth of data suggesting a later date of composition.

The data culled from TC fully accord with the findings of McDowell and those of my own studies with regard to TPJ. In addition to the dependence upon TPJ, which points to a relatively late date of origin for TC (no earlier than the twelfth century), we identified several expressions in the Targum that indicate a relatively late date. Mention of the Hungarians, a name which did not exist before the ninth century and which began appearing in Jewish literature in the tenth, pushes the *terminus post quem* of the Targum several centuries later than its heretofore accepted date. The convention of referring to the halakhic Midrash to Leviticus by both of its names (Sifra, Torat Kohanim; cf. pp. 305–306) is documented from the end of the ninth century. The detailed listing of calendrical terms (1 Chr 4:23; 12:33; cf. pp. 276; 478–481) conforms to the period after the controversy over the calendar from the ninth century till the eleventh century. The legend about the exile of the two and a half tribes in the mountains of darkness appears in very late sources, circa the eleventh century (cf. pp. 442–445).

Not all of these signs are of equal value. Some, were they to appear in TC without the others, would not be enough to substantiate a late date of origin. One might argue, for example, that the legend of the mountains of darkness appears in very late sources, but may have originated much earlier, and its appearance in TC does not prove that the targumist relied on these late sources. Two items, though, seem to me to be conclusive and tip the scales as hard evidence beyond reasonable doubt. These are TC's direct dependence on TPJ and its use of the word Hungarians.

The mention of the Hungarians, if interpreted correctly, leaves very little room for discussion of a pre-tenth century date of composition, for we know when this name was introduced historically and when this nation came into contact with other European nations. This expression alone, therefore, refutes claims that TC was composed in the seventh or eighth centuries—the commonly accepted date of composition in previous studies. As written above, pp. 227–228, it stands to reason that the targumist could have used this name after the Hungarians became known throughout Europe as marauders and ultimately settling peacefully in their land in the mid-tenth century.

As for the direct dependence of TC on TPJ, having accepted that TPJ relies on sources of the twelfth century (and according to McDowell the late twelfth century at that), I must necessarily conclude that TC cannot have been written before that. That means that even without allowing any passage of time between TPJ and TC, the *terminus post quem* of TC is the twelfth century. This does not contradict any of the data above. On the contrary, it creates a comfortable time setting for the author of TC to have included the various relatively late elements mentioned above in his Targum.

With regard to a *terminus ante quem* for TC, I remind the reader that this Targum remained virtually unknown to the classical medieval Jewish exegetes of Chronicles and apart from its own few manuscripts seems to have left no trace till the first edition of its printing in the late seventeenth century. Therefore, based on the evidence at this point in time, all we have to rely upon is the extant manuscripts of TC. MS V, the earliest of the known manuscripts, was written in 1294,[3] but some textual features indicate that this is a copy of the Targum based on an earlier text. Therefore, we must presume that some time passed between TC's composition and its inclusion in MS V, but I cannot determine how much time would have had to pass based on this consideration alone. A conservative approach would, therefore, set the *terminus ante quem* of TC in the late thirteenth century.

This leaves roughly one century in which TC seems to have been composed—from the latter part of the twelfth century to the late thirteenth. The conclusion that TC may have been composed in the thirteenth century calls into question our perception of the *Sitz im Leben* of Aramaic Targums in general, or at least some of them. Is it indeed conceivable that an Aramaic translation of a biblical book be written in so late an era, in which Aramaic was no longer the vernacular in much of the Jewish diaspora? Is the composition of Targum Chronicles a singular phenomenon? For what purpose was this Targum written in this late period and who was its intended audience? I will attempt to answer these questions and make sense of the conclusions of this study, but first I wish to state that the data I have presented in this book—challenging as they may be—cannot be ignored based only on the difficulties that the ensuing questions pose to what was accepted by past scholars, but not supported by evidence. It is the very essence of the scientific pursuit to follow evidence and reevaluate past theories based on new information.

3　The Hebrew date in the colophon of MS V is 15 Kislev, 5055, which corresponds to December 5th, 1294.

3   Where Was Targum Chronicles Composed?

From the time of Zunz, through Churgin, till Le Déaut, Robert and McIvor, scholars assumed—perhaps even took for granted—that Targum Chronicles was written in Palestine due to its shared linguistic affinities with the Palestinian Pentateuchal Targums and its expansive nature which bears a resemblance to their modus operandi. The lack of Arabic words in the Targum was understood as indication of its being composed before the rise of Islam, or at least before Aramaic was supplanted by Arabic as the main spoken language of the Jews in Palestine.[4] However, the data amassed in this book lead me to conclude that these opinions can no longer be held.[5]

When Kaufman first charted the contours of LJLA, he realized the data indicate that, contra Kutscher, these texts were not composed in Palestine.

> … I am no longer prepared to accept … that the presence of Aramaic traits of the Land of Israel dialect in a particular text could be explained solely by the Land of Israel origin of that text…. I suggest that there is a block of texts connected to scripture—Targum Pseudo-Jonathan, Targums of the Writings and others—that were composed from the start in an Aramaic dialect that used certain specific Western characteristics abundantly, but it is very likely these texts were not composed in the Land of Israel. So it is quite proper to consider this question: Why did this literary dialect use these features of the language of the Land of Israel? I am not willing or able to give the decisive answer to this question now, but what I do wish to emphasize is that we cannot answer our question with the simple response: "Their source is in the Land of Israel."[6]

Kaufman did not provide a definite location or time for the composition of these works, but he did mention Syria of the sixth to the ninth century as one possibility. Insofar as we have seen with regard to Targum Chronicles, other locations and a later period need to be considered. While I am not in the position to offer a precise street address for TC's author, I am comfortable saying that the data that has accumulated in the course of this study allow me to offer

---

4   Rosenberg-Kohler, p. 277; Le Déaut-Robert, vol. I, p. 27; McIvor, p. 18.

5   Even without taking all the other considerations into account, just the two expansions in 1 Chr 1:20, 30 alone are most conveniently understood, even in their original form, as coming into being after Islamic rule was already a well-established reality. Their appearance in TC reflects a yet even later stage in the existence of these exegetical traditions. Therefore, a far later date for TC than the initial rise of Islam should be a matter of common sense.

6   Kaufman *TPJ*, p. 6.

a general direction. We have established that the author of TC was very well versed in the techniques and traditions of earlier Targums. We have also demonstrated that, while the backbone of TC's language continues the language of the Palestinian Targums, it also absorbed a great deal of the eastern vocabulary, much in the way that is found in Targum Pseudo-Jonathan. Pseudo-Jonathan was also found to be the most influential of the Pentateuchal Targums for the author of TC. Our author was also fully acquainted with the entire Babylonian Talmud, which served as his primary source for biblical exegesis, as was demonstrated in the study of TC's aggadic expansions. This complex picture comprises the reality in which our author operated. He was a rabbinic scholar who was exposed in varying degrees to the works of both centers of Jewish scholarship—Palestine and Babylonia. His language reflected this dual influence. His main Pentateuchal Targum—TPJ—also reflects this mixed tradition and is now known to have relied on different sources in twelfth century Italy.

Italy also happens to be where we may find a convergence of the above-mentioned different trends. Ta-Shma described the geographic route through which crystallized what came to be known as the custom of the Jews of Ashkenaz: from Palestine, through Byzantium, then Italy, Germany and northern France.[7] As this tradition made roads into Europe, it also became more and more exposed to the Babylonian Talmud, which emerged as its primary authoritative halakhic source. The few extant manuscripts of Targum Chronicles of the thirteenth and fourteenth centuries, though scant and therefore of circumstantial character, hail from the same general area, written in Ashkenaz style, which conveniently accords with the picture that emerges here. Three particular items of data add a degree of salience to this argument:

1. In addition to TPJ's reliance on Italian sources, TPJ itself was made known to the world through Italy.[8] We do not have knowledge of its existence outside Europe.

2. The term, Hungarian, became common in western Europe, not in the Levant.[9]

3. The Aramaic Piyyutim used in European liturgy (Italy, Germany, northern France) bear certain similarities to the blend of west and east that is found in TPJ and TC.[10]

---

7   Ta-Shma, p. 13. See also Grossman, pp. 29–48, for the description of the migration of the Kalonymus household in the first part of the tenth century from Italy to Germany as one of the central forces behind the formation of the religious character of Ashkenazi Jewry and its heritage of Torah scholarship.

8   Maher *TPJ*, pp. 1, 12.

9   As mentioned above, p. 228.

10 As discussed above, pp. 219–220.

The evidence, then, seems to indicate the probability that Targum Chronicles was composed on European soil, with Italy appearing to be an entirely reasonable candidate for its place of composition, from where it may have arrived in Germany. This conclusion may come as a surprise to some, but it has been reached based on converging pieces of evidence.

4   Why Was Targum Chronicles Composed?

The role of Aramaic Targums as being composed to accompany the public reading of Hebrew scripture has led some to ignore other purposes Targums fulfilled. Simply stated, if Targum's sole purpose was to serve as a simultaneous translation of scripture during public readings,[11] why do the Targums cover the entire Hebrew Bible save Daniel and Ezra-Nehemiah, when large sections of the Bible are not read in synagogues in a public setting? Even the relatively early Targums, such as Targum Jonathan, are not merely a simultaneous translation, but also an interpretation.[12] Even more literal sections of the Targums do not necessarily mean they were intended for public readings only. York made a distinction between the role of a Targum when read out loud in a public reading in the synagogue and its role as a learning aid for Bible study at schools.[13] This latter role does well to explain the need for Targums on the vast sections of the Hebrew Bible that are not read as part of synagogue ritual. In fact, this distinction was already raised by Rosenberg and Kohler with regard to TC, which they concluded was written for the *bet midrash*—the study hall— and not for the synagogue.[14]

In his study of Pseudo-Jonathan, Shinan arrived at the conclusion that the purpose of TPJ was not for public recital in tandem with the Hebrew Torah— even though the entire Torah is read publicly—but was intended to serve as a study tool, a commentary on the Torah, that is actually a form of 'rewritten

---

11   Rashi on *b. Meg.* 21b, lemma וּבְנָבִיא: "Targum is only for explaining to women and unschooled men that do not know Hebrew, and the [language of the—L.G.] Targum is the vernacular of the Babylonians, and when translating the Torah we must repeat it so they will understand the commandments."

12   Cf. Lieberman *Greek*, p. 186, where he describes the first stage in the interpretation of a text as ἑρμηνεία, which means both translation and interpretation and is the precise literary parallel of Targum.

13   York examined various rabbinic statements pertaining to the Targums and concluded, "it seems to me that the Targum which had such an important role in synagogue services was also employed within the school system *per se*." (York, p. 83)

14   Rosenberg-Kohler, pp. 274–275.

Bible'.[15] Shinan pondered with regard to TPJ and asked a similar question as we face now with regard to Targum Chronicles, though he thought TPJ was much older than I:[16]

> Why would someone compose in the seventh-eighth (?) century an Aramaic work of this kind? This question will remain unanswered for the time being, but one can surmise that [TPJ]... is part of the literary summary brought about by the rise of Islam and the demise of Aramaic and the institution of Targum. When dealing with an individual composition, strange and exceptional, it seems that the need to explain the motives for its creation will never be completely fulfilled.

In a later publication Shinan displayed a degree of awareness of new studies indicating that TPJ was apparently later than previously assumed and no longer mentioned the seventh century as a possible time for TPJ's composition, moving it up to (but no later than) the middle of the eighth century. However, he did not change his basic attitude, according to which it is improbable that Aramaic works continued to be composed after the rise of Islam:[17]

> It seems to me that there is no reason to regard [the date of TPJ's composition] much past the middle of the eighth century, for the use of Aramaic, and the distribution of this language, diminished among the Jews with the rise of Islam and Arabic. An Aramaic composition—itself founded upon an Aramaic Targum—is more probable close to the beginning of the Muslim era than later on.

I, however, am far less troubled by this consideration than Shinan was. Whether I find it probable or not for a work to be composed in Aramaic centuries after the decline of Aramaic as a spoken language throughout much of the Jewish world, the evidence seems to be speaking for itself and it is saying quite clearly that TC was composed in second millennium Europe. So the question I must ask is not *if*, but rather *why*! Why did Jewish works in Aramaic continue to be written well after its decline as a spoken language?[18]

---

15   Shinan *TPJ Legends*, vol. 2, p. 356.
16   Ibid., p. 357.
17   Shinan *Embroidered*, p. 198.
18   I discuss this at greater length in my article, Gottlieb *Composition*.

Jewish works continued to be written in varying forms of an artificial and literary Aramaic—in Piyyut, in mysticism and in talmudic/halakhic commentary—centuries after it was no longer spoken by the communities in which these writings were composed. Aramaic poetry written in Europe in the first centuries of the second millennium are historical fact, as attested in the Machzor manuscripts of Pesach and Shavu'ot. So are countless scholarly commentaries on the Talmud and Halakha. If some contents of Targum Chronicles suggest that it was written in medieval Europe, I see no justification to contest this notion.

Seeing as the composition of Targum Chronicles in Aramaic does not necessarily presume an Aramaic speaking community, it is that much easier to relate to the mixed character of its vocabulary—including words from east and west and not seeming to reflect a living spoken language. It received its many Greek loanwords, its western elements and its eastern elements from precisely the heterogeneous literary heritage that was the reality of early second millennium Jewry in Italy and its surroundings. This also comfortably explains the lack of Arabic words in the Targum—though I don't regard this in itself to be sufficient proof that it was composed outside or before the rise of the Islamic empire.

My findings in this book, which conform with the linguistic data of Kaufman and Cook with regard to TPJ, indicate that Targum Chronicles is part of a larger group of Targums written in Late Jewish Literary Aramaic. TPJ was for TC not only a lexicon for determining equivalents, but also a model for the compilation of a targumic sequence into which are embedded many aggadic expansions. Shinan suggested that Pseudo-Jonathan was born of the need to summarize and bring to close a period in Jewish history. With regard to TC, I already posited above (p. 489) that the manner in which the targumist chooses to incorporate aggadic material leaves the impression that—far more than the desire to provide answers to difficulties he happened to encounter in the biblical text—he sought to gather and include Chronicles-related Aggadot he was aware of. If I am correct in my dating of Targum Chronicles, the targumist lived many centuries after the golden age of classical Targums, and in tandem with the golden age of a new genre of biblical exegesis—the running commentaries of medieval Europe that ultimately supplanted the age-old tradition of studying the biblical verses with Aramaic Targum. It was a time, however, in which Jews with good schooling were still expected to be well-versed in traditional Targum and it is for this reason that the classical exegetes could confidently refer their readers to targumic sources, knowing that this genre was still central in the Jewish curriculum of Western Europe. During this time, an erudite rabbinic Jew, knowledgeable in Targum, Talmud and Midrash sought to fill a

lacuna he detected in the Jewish library. The book of Chronicles had no traditional Targum or Midrash, so this author composed a work that combined both
modes of biblical study he was so familiar with: traditional Bible study accompanied by Aramaic translation and the talmudic-midrashic style of expanding and expounding the biblical verse. TC is a Targum, but its author never
expected it to be read as a simultaneous translation in a public reading. He
expected it to serve as a study tool for individuals studying the biblical book of
Chronicles. That is why it is also an anthology of much of the aggadic material
on Chronicles scattered throughout the vast reaches of rabbinic literature in
general and the Talmud Bavli in particular. This work was written in Aramaic
not because this was the language his co-religionists spoke regularly, but because Aramaic Targum was a traditional genre for the study of the Hebrew
Bible. The author's intimate familiarity with the techniques of his predecessors
serves as written testimony that this was the case.

5   Implications for Further Research in Targum Studies

The conclusions of this book should serve as something of a wakeup call for the
field of Targum studies. Scholars should no longer be forced to assume that the
phenomenon of Targum must be identified with an Aramaic speaking environment. Where the evidence points to a later, non-Aramaic speaking society, we
should not be deterred from arriving at the proper conclusions. Where signs of
apparent lateness are found in a Targum, we should not limit ourselves to the
seventh or eighth centuries as a *terminus ante quem* due to the rise of Islam
and the decline of Aramaic as a spoken language. It is conceivable that some
Targums were written after the decline of Aramaic as a spoken language, because it continued to be a scholarly language, recognized as a vehicle through
which rabbinic Judaism and traditional study of the Hebrew Bible were passed
down over the generations.

   In this book I documented in great detail the strong link between Targum
Pseudo-Jonathan and Targum Chronicles, but linguistic and stylistic links
were also identified between these two and several other Targums to the
Hagiographa, the most prominent of which were Targum Psalms and Targum
Job. The findings of this book inform us not only of Targum Chronicles, but
also of its place among the Targums. The implications of this book for our
historical understanding of the phenomenon of Targums invite further study
and research into the links between this group of Targums. There are also pre-
liminary signs that need to be further researched in other Targums, such as *Tg.
Ruth.* Cook described the language of TPJ and the Targums of the Hagiographa

as artificial and reflecting "a literary language concocted out of other literary languages and bearing no relationship to any known Aramaic vernacular".[19] An assessment such as this should lead to the conclusion that it was written in a time and/or place that Aramaic was no longer spoken, but used as a scholarly language.

It is possible that if more links are discovered among the aforementioned and other Targums we will have discovered a school of late targumists—perhaps inspired by Pseudo-Jonathan and partially motivated by the desire to complete the Targum collection by composing Targums for those biblical books that did not have a traditional Targum from the classical period. If established, this would mean that targumic literature is comprised of three main groups. Targums Onqelos and Jonathan on the one hand and the Palestinian Targums on the other hand. But in contrast to past opinion, this second group does not include Pseudo-Jonathan and several of the Targums to the Hagiographa. These would constitute a group of their own—the late Targums—a third group that was greatly influenced by the first two, but was composed much later, in an entirely different region, and sprang forth from a different *Sitz im Leben* than that of the first two. The precise contours of this third group has yet to be fully studied and defined and further research in this direction will constitute a considerable contribution to the field of Targum studies. At this point in time, though, it can already be said that Targum Chronicles will have played a pivotal role in reevaluating much about what we know with regard to the composition of Targums. It is, therefore, the hope of this author that this study will have played an important role in our understanding of Targum Chronicles and its place among the Late Targums.

---

19   Cook *TPJ*, pp. 277–278.

Bibliography

Primary Sources

Hebrew Bible: The Masoretic Text (MT) of the Hebrew Bible is cited according to *Mikra'ot Gedolot 'Haketer'* (based on the Aleppo Codex) and BHS (*Biblia Hebraica Stuttgartensia*, based on Codex Leningrad).

Targums for the Pentateuch (Torah)

Targum Onqelos (TO)	A. Sperber, *The Bible in Aramaic*, 4 vols. Leiden: Brill 1959–1973
Targum Neophyti (TN)	A. Díez Macho, *Neophyti 1: Targum Palestinense ms. de la Biblioteca Vaticana*, 6 vols. Madrid: Consejo Superior de Investigaciones Científicas 1968–1978
Fragments Targum (FT: FTP, FTV)	M.L. Klein, *The Fragment-Targums of the Pentateuch According to their Extant Sources*, 2 vols. Analecta Biblica 76, Rome: Pontifical Biblical Institute 1980
Genizah Targums (GT)	M.L. Klein, *Genizah Fragments of Palestinian Targum to the Pentateuch*, 2 vols. Cincinnati: Hebrew Union College Press 1986
Targum Pseudo-Jonathan (TPJ)	E.G. Clarke, *Targum Pseudo-Jonathan of the Pentateuch: Text and Concordance*, Hoboken: Ktav 1986

Targums for the Prophets (Nevi'im)

Targum Jonathan (TJ)	A. Sperber, *The Bible in Aramaic*, 4 vols. Leiden: Brill 1959–1973
Targum Toseftot (TT)	R. Kasher, *Targum Toseftot to the Prophets*, [Heb.] Jerusalem: World Union of Jewish Studies 1996

Targums for the Writings (Hagiographa, Ketuvim)

Targum Psalms (TP)	MS Paris 110, as per M. Cohen, *Psalms* (Mikra'ot Gedolot 'Haketer'), [Heb.] 2 vols. Ramat Gan: Bar-Ilan University Press 2003
Targum Job	D.M. Stec, *The Text of the Targum of Job: An Introduction and Critical Edition*, Leiden: Brill 1994
Targum Lamentations	A. Sperber, *The Bible in Aramaic*, 4 vols. Leiden: Brill 1959–1973

Targum Ecclesiastes (Qohelet)	A. Sperber, *The Bible in Aramaic*, 4 vols. Leiden: Brill 1959–1973
Targum Ruth	A. Sperber, *The Bible in Aramaic*, 4 vols. Leiden: Brill 1959–1973
Targum Canticles (Song of Songs)	A. Sperber, *The Bible in Aramaic*, 4 vols. Leiden: Brill 1959–1973
First Targum to Esther	M. Cohen, The *Five Scrolls* (Mikra'ot Gedolot 'Haketer'), [Heb.] Ramat Gan: Bar-Ilan University Press 2012
Second Targum to Esther	M. Cohen, The *Five Scrolls* (Mikra'ot Gedolot 'Haketer'), [Heb.] Ramat Gan: Bar-Ilan University Press; 2012 and at times the longer recension, based on the text found in the Comprehensive Aramaic Lexicon
Targum Chronicles (TC)	MS Vatican-Urbinati ebr. 1, taking into account other manuscripts and editions (primarily Le Déaut-Robert, see below), as mentioned throughout the book
Septuagint (LXX)	A. Rahlfs, *Septuaginta*, Stuttgart: Deutsche Bibelgesellschaft 1979
Peshiṭta	R.P. Gordon, *The Old Testament in Syriac According to the Peshitta Version*, vol. IV2, Leiden: Brill 1998 (other biblical books also according to the Leiden edition)
Vulgate	R. Weber, *Biblia Sacra Iuxta Vulgatam*, Stuttgart: Deutsche Bibelgesellschaft 1994
Antiquities	W. Whiston, *The Works of Flavius Josephus, Complete and Unabridged*, Peabody: Hendrickson Publishers 1987

Rabbinic Literature

Mishnah	MS Kaufmann A50
Tosefta	Zera'im-Našim according to S. Lieberman, *The tosefta according to Codex Vienna, with Variants from Codices Erfurt, London, Geniza Mss. and Editio Princeps (Venice 1521), together with References to Parallel Passages in Talmudic Literature and a Brief Commentary*, New York: Jewish Theological Seminary of America 1955–1988; other Sedarim according to M.S. Zuckermandel, *The Tosefta*, Jerusalem 1938

Mek. RY	H.S. Horovitz and I. Rabin, *Mekhilta de-Rabbi Yišmaʿel²*, Jerusalem: Bamberger and Wahrmann 1998
Mek. RSbY	J.N. Epstein and E.Z. Melamed, *Mekhilta de-Rabbi Šimʿon ben Yoḥai*, Jerusalem 1955
Sifra	A.H. Weiss, *Sifra de-bei Rab i.e. Torat Kohanim*, Vienna 1862
Sifre Numbers	H.S. Horovitz, *Siphre ad Numeros adjecto Siphre zutta*, Leipzig: Gustav Fock 1917
Sifre Deuteronomy	L. Finkelstein, *Siphre ad Deuteronomium*, [Heb.] New York: Jewish Theological Seminary of America 1969
Midrash Tanna'im	D. Hoffmann, *Midrasch Tannaïm zum Deuteronomium*, 2 vols. Berlin: Hirsch Itzkowski 1908
Seder Olam	C.J. Milikowsky, *Seder Olam: A Rabbinic Chronography*, [Ph.D. dissertation] Yale University, 1981
Megillat Taʿanit	V. Noam, *Megillat Taʿanit: Ha-nosaḥim, pishram, toldotehem*, [Heb.] Jerusalem: Yad Izhak Ben-Zvi 2003
Talmud Yerushalmi	Y. Sussmann, *Talmud Yerushalmi*, Jerusalem: Academy of the Hebrew Language 2001

Talmud Bavli (BT): Citations and references given according to the list of tractates below. Usually the text is according to the manuscripts chosen by the Historical Dictionary Project and the reading thereof. I compared most of these readings with the text of the Lieberman Project and that of Diqduqei Soferim Hashalem. Missing letters are provided in brackets. When any other version of the Bavli was given, I made note ad loc. in the book.

ʿAbodah Zarah—MS Paris 1337
ʿArakin—Vilna edition and MS Munich 95
Bava Qamma—MS Hamburg 165
Bava Meṣiʿa'—MS Hamburg 165
Bava Batra—MS Hamburg 165
Berakot—MS Oxford 366
ʿErubin—MS Vatican 109
Giṭṭin—MS Vatican 130
Horayot—MS Paris 1337
Keritot—MS Oxford b.1, 10–20
Makkot—MS Jerusalem, Yad Harav Herzog

Megillah—MS New York (Columbia) x 893-T 141

Menaḥot—MS Paris, כ״ח H 147A

Moʿed Qaṭan—MS New York (Columbia) x 893-T 141

Pesaḥim—MS New York, Enelau 271

Qiddušin—MS Vatican 111 and Diqduqei Soferim Hashalem edition (2012, Jerusalem)

Šabbat—MS Oxford 366

Sanhedrin—MS Jerusalem, Yad Harav Herzog

Soṭah—MS Oxford d.20, 26–63

Taʿanit—MS Jerusalem, Yad Harav Herzog

Tamid—MS Florence II.I.7

Temurah—MS Florence II.I.7

Yebamot—Vilna edition and Diqduqei Soferim Hashalem edition (1983, Jerusalem)

Zebaḥim—MS New York (Columbia) x 893-T 141

Semaḥot	E.P. Qaminqa, *Ebel Rabbati Hanniqra Massekhet Semaḥot*, [Heb.] Tel Aviv: Haʿoved Haddati 1949
Kallah Rabbati	M. Heiger, *Massekhtot Kallah*, [Heb.] New York: Debei Rabbanan 1936
ʾAbot de Rabbi Nathan	S. Schechter, *Avot de-Rabbi Nathan*², [Heb.] New York and Jerusalem: Jewish Theological Seminary of America 1997
Genesis Rabbah	Y. Theodor and Ḥ. Albeck, *Midrash Genesis Rabbah*, [Heb.] (Repr.) 2 vols. Jerusalem: Wahrmann 1996
Exodus Rabbah	A. Shinan, *Midrash Shemot Rabbah, 1–14*, [Heb.] Jerusalem and Tel Aviv: Debir 1984 Parashot 15 ff. in Vilna edition of Midrash Rabbah
Leviticus Rabbah	M. Margulies, *Midrash Leviticus Rabbah*³, [Heb.] 2 vols. New York: Jewish Theological Seminary of America 1993
Numbers Rabbah	Numbers Rabbah in Vilna edition of Midrash Rabbah
Deuteronomy Rabbah	Deuteronomy Rabbah in Vilna edition of Midrash Rabbah
Lamentations Rabbah	S. Buber, *Lamentations Rabbah*, Vilna: Rohm 1899
Ecclesiastes Rabbah	Parashot 1–4, in: M. Hirshman, *Midrash Qohelet Rabbah*, Diss. Jewish Theological Seminary of America, New York 1982 Parashot 5 ff. in Vilna edition of Midrash Rabbah

Ruth Rabbah	M.B. Lerner, *Aggadat Ruth and Midrash Ruth Rabbah*, Diss. Hebrew University of Jerusalem, 1971
Song of Songs Rabbah	Song of Songs Rabbah in Vilna edition of Midrash Rabbah
Esther Rabbah	Esther Rabbah in Vilna edition of Midrash Rabbah
Lamentations Zuṭaʾ	S. Buber, *Midrash Zuṭa on Song of Songs, Ruth, Lamentations and Ecclesiastes*, [Heb.] Vilna: Rohm 1925
Ruth Zuṭaʾ	S. Buber, *Midrash Zuṭa on Song of Songs, Ruth, Lamentations and Ecclesiastes*, [Heb.] Vilna: Rohm 1925
Pesiqta de Rab Kahana	B. Mandelbaum, *Pesikta de Rav Kahana*, [Heb.] 2 vols. New York: Jewish Theological Seminary of America 1962
Pesiqta Rabbati	M. Friedmann (Ish-Shalom), *Pesikta Rabbati, Midrasch für den Fest-Cyclus und die Ausgezeichneten Sabbathe*, Vienna 1880
Tanḥuma	*Midrash Tanḥuma*, Jerusalem 1971 (Repr. of editio princeps, Constantinople, 520–522)
Tanḥuma (Buber)	S. Buber, *Midrash Tanḥuma Haqqadum Wehayyašan*, [Heb.] Vilna 1913
Midrash Psalms	S. Buber, *Midrash Tehillim*, [Heb.] Vilna 1891
Midrash Samuel	B. Lifshitz, *Midrash Shmuel: based on the Constantinople Edition of 1517*, [Heb.] Jerusalem: Schechter Institute 2009
Seder Eliyahu Rabbah	M. Ish-Shalom, *Seder Eliyahu Rabbah Weseder Eliyahu Zuṭa*, [Heb.] Vienna: Fromme 1900
Pirqe Rabbi Eliezer	M. Heiger, *Pirqe Rabbi Eliezer*, [Heb.] 3 parts in *Ḥoreb*, New York 1944–1948
Midrash Aggadah (Buber)	S. Buber, *Midrash Aggadah*, [Heb.] Vienna: Abraham Punto 1894
Aggadat Bereshit	S. Buber, *Aggadat Bereshit*, [Heb.], Krakow 1903
Sekhel Tov (Buber)	S. Buber, *Midrash Sekhel Tov*, [Heb.] Berlin 1900–1901
Midrash Hagadol	M. Margulies, *Midrash Hagadol*, [Heb.] 5 vols, Jerusalem: Mosad Harav Kook 1947–1976
Sefer ha-Yashar	*Sefer ha-Yashar*, [Heb.] Warsaw: Joseph Lebensohn 1873

Yalquṭ   D. Heiman, *Yalquṭ Šimʿoni on the Former Prophets*,
                              Jerusalem: Mosad Harav Kook 1999
                              D. Heiman, *Yalquṭ Šimʿoni on the Latter Prophets*,
                              Jerusalem: Mosad Harav Kook 2010
                              Yalquṭ Šimʿoni on the Writings, Jerusalem 1975
                              (Repr. of Warsaw, 1877)

Tibat Marqeh   Z. Ben-Ḥayyim, *Tībat Marqe—A Collection of
                              Samaritan Midrashim*, Jerusalem: Israel Academy
                              of Sciences and Humanities 1988

Liturgical Poems by Yannai   M. Zulai, *Piyyuṭe Yannai*, [Heb.] Berlin: Schocken
                              1938

Seder Rav ʿAmram Gaʾon   E.D. Goldschmidt, *Seder Rav ʿAmram Gaʾon*, [Heb.]
                              Jerusalem: Mosad Harav Kook 1971

Responsa of Rav Naṭronai Gaʾon   *Teshuvot Rav Naṭronai Gaʾon*, [Heb.] Jerusalem:
                              Makhon Ofan 1994

Responsa of the Geʾonim (Miller)   Y. Miller, *Teshuvot Hageʾonim, Geʾone Mizrach
                              Umaʿarav*, [Heb.] Berlin 1888

Responsa of the Geʾonim (Harkavi)   A. Harkavi, *Teshuvot Hageʾonim*, [Heb.] Berlin 1887

Responsa of the Geʾonim (Musafia)   Y. Musafia, *Teshuvot Hageʾonim*, [Heb.] Jerusalem
                              1967 (Repr. of 1864)

Early Geʾonim   D. Kassel, *Teshuvot Geʾonim Qadmonim*, [Heb.]
                              Berlin 1848

Shaʿarei Teshuvah   *Sefer Teshuvot Hageʾonim: ʿim Hagahot ʾiye Hayam*,
                              [Heb.], Livorno 1869

Halakhot Gedolot   *Sefer Halakhot Gedolot*, Jerusalem: Makhon
                              Yerushalayim 1992

Commentary attributed to a   R. Kirchheim, *Ein Commentar zur Chronik aus dem
student of Saadyah   10ᵗᵉⁿ Jahrhundert*, Jerusalem 1966 (Repr. of 1874,
                              Frankfurt am Main)

Masnuth, Samuel   Commentary by Samuel Masnuth on Chronicles,
                              MS Vat. Hebr. 97 (5363 in the JNL manuscript
                              institute)

Abravanel   Y. Shaviv, *Perush Haneviim Lerabenu Yizhaq
                              Abravanel*, vol. 2 (Samuel), Jerusalem: Horeb 2009

Zacuto, Abraham   H. Filipowski, *Liber Juchassin ... Lexicon Biographi-
                              cum et Historicum ... Rabbi Abraham Zacuti*, Lon-
                              don and Edinburgh 1857

Meturgeman   E. Levita (Bachur), *Metourgaman*, Jerusalem 1967
                              (Repr. of 1541, Isnae)

Other Scholarly Literature

Alexander *ABD*

P.S. Alexander, "Targum, Targumim" *Anchor Bible Dictionary*, vol. VI, 320–331

Alexander *Rules*

P.S. Alexander, "The Targumim and the Palestinian Rules for the Delivery of the Targum", in [ed. J.A. Emerton] *Congress Volume: Salamanca, 1983*, VTSup 36, Leiden 1985

Alexander *Toponomy*

P.S. Alexander, *The Toponomy of the Targumim with Special Reference to the Table of the Nations and the Boundaries of the Land of Israel*, [Ph.D. Dissertation] Oxford 1974

Assis

M. Assis, "קטע של ירושלמי סנהדרין (פ״ה ה״א, כב״ ע״ג-פ״ו ה״ט, כג ע״ג", *Tarbiẓ* 46 (1977), pp. 29–90

Aufrecht

W.A. Aufrecht, "Some Observations on the Überlieferungsgeschichte of the Targums", in [ed. P.V.M. Flesher] *Targum Studies*, vol. 1, Atlanta 1992, pp. 77–88

Azuelos

Y. Azuelos, *The Angelology of the Aramaic Targums on the Pentateuch*, [Heb.] Tel Aviv: Resling Publishing 2016

Bacher *Apocryphon*

W. Bacher, "Ein Hebräisches Apocryphon", *Monatsschrift für Geschichte und Wissenschaft des Judentums* 18 (1869): 542–544

Bacher *JE*

W. Bacher, "Targum", *The Jewish Encyclopedia*, vol. XII, pp. 57–63

Bacher *Zwei Corruptelen*

W. Bacher, "Zwei Corruptelen. Ein Beitrag zur talmudisch-midraschischen Lexicographie", *Monatsschrift für Geschichte und Wissenschaft des Judentums* 25 (1876): 237–240

BDB

F. Brown, S.R. Driver, C.A. Briggs, *The Brown-Driver-Briggs Hebrew and English Lexicon*, Peabody: Hendrickson 2000[5]

Beattie

D.R.G. Beattie, *The Targum of Ruth: Translated, with Introduction, Apparatus, and Notes* [The Aramaic Bible 19], Collegeville 1994

Beck *I*

M.F. Beck, *Paraphrasis Chaldaica I Libri Chronicorum*, Augsburg 1680

Beck *II*

M.F. Beck, *Paraphrasis Chaldaica II Libri Chronicorum*, Augsburg 1683

Ben-Dov   J. Ben-Dov, "Scientific Writings in Aramaic and Hebrew at Qumran: Translation and Conceal-ment", in [eds. K. Berthelot and D. Stökl Ben Ezra], *Aramaica Qumranica, The Aix en Provence Collo-quium on the Aramaic Dead Sea Scrolls* [Studies on the Texts of the Desert of Judah 94], Leiden 2010, pp. 379–402

Ben-Ḥayyim   Z. Ben-Ḥayyim, "'erkhei Millim", [Heb.] *Tarbiẓ* 50 (1981), pp. 192–208

Ben Menaḥem   A. Ben Menaḥem, דברי הימים ראשונים ואחרונים עם תרגום רב יוסף, Vilna 1815

Bendavid   A. Bendavid, *Parallels in the Bible*, [Heb.] Jerusalem: Carta 1972

Berger   Y. Berger, *The Commentary of Rabbi David Kimhi to Chronicles: A Translation with Introduction and Supercommentary*, Providence 2007

Bernstein   M.J. Bernstein, "The Aramaic Versions of Deuteronomy 32: A Study in Comparative Targumic Theology", in [ed. P.V.M. Flesher] *Targum and Scripture: Studies in Aramaic Translations and Interpretations in Memory of Ernest G. Clarke*, Leiden 2002, pp. 29–52

Blau   J. Blau, "תיקונים מדומים בלשונות שמיות", *Journal of the Israel Academy of Sciences and Humanities* 4 (1969), [Heb.] pp. 1–10

Bowker   J. Bowker, *The Targums and Rabbinic Literature: an Introduction to Jewish Interpretations of Scripture*, London 1969

Boyarin *Memra*   D. Boyarin, "The Gospel of Memra: Jewish Binitarianism and the Crucifixion of the Logos" *Harvard Theological Review* 94 (2001), pp. 243–284

Boyarin *Border Lines*   D. Boyarin, *Border Lines: The Partition of Judaeo-Christianity*, Philadelphia 2004

Cashdan   E. Cashdan, "Names and the Interpretation of Names in the Pseudo-Jonathan Targum to the Book of Genesis", in [ed. H.J. Zimmels] *Essays Presented to Chief Rabbi Israel Brodie on the Occasion of his Seventieth Birthday*, London 1967, Volume I, pp. 31–39

Chester	A. Chester, *Divine Revelation and Divine Titles in the Pentateuchal Targumim*, Tübingen: J.C.B. Mohr 1986
Churgin *Hagiographa*	P. Churgin, *Targum Ketuvim*, [Heb.] New York 1945
Churgin *TJ*	P. Churgin, *Targum Jonathan to the Prophets*, reprinted from the 1927 edition in: L. Smolar & M. Aberbach, *Studies in Targum Jonathan to the Prophets*, New York-Baltimore 1983
Clarke	E.G. Clarke, *Targum Pseudo-Jonathan of the Pentateuch: Text and Concordance*, Hoboken 1984
Clem	E. Clem, translation of TO and TJ in: *Targums English* (Targ-E) v. 7.2—Electronic module in *Accordance*, Oaktree Software; Ibid., translation of TN in: *Targum Neofiti, Esther Sheni English* (Targ2-E) v. 2.3—Electronic module in *Accordance*, Oaktree Software; Ibid., translation of TPJ in: *Targum Pseudo-Jonathan English* (Targ3-E) v. 1.7—Electronic module in *Accordance*, Oaktree Software; Ibid., translation of FT in: *Fragmentary Targumim English* (TargF-E) v. 1.4—Electronic module in *Accordance*, Oaktree Software; Ibid., translation of GT in: *Genizah Targum Fragment English* (TargG-E) v. 1.3—Electronic module in *Accordance*, Oaktree Software
Cogan *Kings*	M. Cogan, *I Kings: A New Translation with Introduction and Commentary*, [Anchor Bible, Volume 10] Garden City 2001
Cogan *Nahum*	M. Cogan, *Nahum*, [Heb.—Miqra Leyisrael] Jerusalem: Magnes Press 2006
Cook	E.M. Cook, translation of *Tg. Ps*: *Targums English* (Targ-E) v. 7.2—Electronic module in *Accordance*, Oaktree Software
Cook *TPJ*	E.M. Cook, *Rewriting the Bible: The Text and Language of the Pseudo-Jonathan Targum*, [Ph.D. Dissertation] UCLA 1986
Curtis-Madsen	E.L. Curtis & A.A. Madsen, *The Books of Chronicles* [International Critical Commentary], Edinburgh 1910

Dan   B. Dan, *The Targum of Psalms: A Morphological Description*, [Heb.; Ph.D. dissertation] Hebrew University of Jerusalem 2008

Le Déaut-Robert   R. Le Déaut & J. Robert, *Targum des Chroniques* [Analecta Biblica 51], Tome 1–2, Rome 1971

Demsky   A. Demsky, "בתיה בת פרעה וקרוביה בנחלת יהודה", *Studies in Bible and Exegesis* 9 (2009) [Heb.], Ramat Gan: Bar-Ilan University Press, pp. 427–437

Dinur   B.Z Dinur, *Toledot Yisrael*, Second Series—Israel in the Diaspora, vol. 1 [Heb.] Tel Aviv, 1958

DJD   *Discoveries in the Judaean Desert*, Oxford 1955–2009

Dost   C. Dost, translation of TC in: *Targums English* (Targ-E) v. 7.2—Electronic module in *Accordance*, Oaktree Software

Dray   C. Dray, *Translation and Interpretation in the Targum to the Book of Kings*, [Studies in the Aramaic Interpretation of Scripture, Volume 5] Leiden 2006

Eisenberg   B. Eisenberg, *A krónikák-könyvének tárguma*, Budapest 1938

Elisséeff   N. Elisséeff, "Manzil", *Encyclopaedia of Islam, Second Edition*, Brill Online, 2012

Epstein   J.N. Epstein, *Prolegomena ad Litteras Tannaiticas: Mishna, Tosephta et Interpretationes Halachicas*, [Heb.] Jerusalem: Magnes Press 1957

Fassberg *Genizah*   S.E. Fassberg, *A Grammar of the Palestinian Targum Fragments from the Cairo Genizah*, Atlanta 1990

Fassberg *Infinitive*   S.E. Fassberg, "Infinitival forms in Aramaic", in [eds. J.C. Salmons—Sh. Dubenion-Smith] *Historical Linguistics 2005*, Philadelphia 2007, pp. 239–256

Finkelstein *Sifra*   L. Finkelstein, *Sifra on Leviticus according to Vatican Manuscript Assemani 66 with variants from the other manuscripts, Genizah fragments, early editions and quotations by medieval authorities*, [Heb.] vol. 1, New York: Jewish Theological Seminary of America 1989

Finkelstein *Sifre*   L. Finkelstein, *Siphre ad Deuteronomium*, [Heb.] New York: Jewish Theological Seminary of America 1969

Flesher *Introduction*	P.V.M. Flesher and B. Chilton, *The Targums: A Critical Introduction*, [Studies in the Aramaic Interpretation of Scripture, Volume 12] Leiden: Brill 2011
Flesher *Scripture*	P.V.M. Flesher, "Targum as Scripture", in [ed. P.V.M. Flesher] *Targum and Scripture: Studies in Aramaic Translations and Interpretations in Memory of Ernest G. Clarke*, Leiden 2002, pp. 61–75
Flusser	D. Flusser, *The Josippon*, Jerusalem: Mosad Bialik 1978
Foster	J.A. Foster, *The Language and Text of Codex Neofiti in the Light of other Palestinian Sources*, [Ph.D. dissertation] Boston University 1969
Fraade	S. Fraade, "Locating Targum in the Textual Polysystem of Rabbinic Pedagogy", *Bulletin of the International Organization for Septuagint and Cognate Studies* 39 (2006), pp. 69–91
Fraenkel *Pesach*	J. Fraenkel, *Machzor Pesach*, [Heb.] 1993, Jerusalem: Koren
Fraenkel *Shavuʻot*	J. Fraenkel, *Machzor Shavuʻot*, [Heb.] 2000, Jerusalem: Koren
Fränkel	S. Fränkel, "Die syrische Übersetzung zu den Büchern der Chronik", *Jahrbücher für protestantische Theologie* 5 (1879), pp. 508–536, 720–759
Geiger	A. Geiger, *Hamiqra Wetargumaw*, 1949, Jerusalem [Hebrew translation of: *Urschrift und Übersetzungen der Bibel in ihrer Abhängigkeit von der Innern Entwicklung des Judentums*[2], Frankfurt 1928]
Ginsburg	C.D. Ginsburg, כתובים—מדויק היטב על פי המסרה ועל פי דפוסים ראשונים, עם חלופים והגהות מן כתבי יד עתיקים ותרגמים ישנים, [Heb.] London: Society for the Circulation of Uncorrupted Versions of the Word of God 1926
Ginsburger	M. Ginsburger, *Pseudo-Jonathan (Thargum Jonathan ben Usiel zum Pentateuch) nach der Londoner Handschrift (Brit. Mus. Add. 27031)*, Berlin: S. Calvary 1903
Ginzberg	L. Ginzberg, *The Legends of the Jews*, volumes I–VII, Philadelphia 1909–1938

Goldschmidt *RH*   E.D. Goldschmidt, *Maḥzor Layamim Hanora'im*,
                           [Heb.] vol. 1 Rosh Hashanah, Jerusalem: Koren
                           1970

Goldschmidt *YK*   E.D. Goldschmidt, *Maḥzor Layamim Hanora'im*,
                           [Heb.] vol. 2 Yom Kippur, Jerusalem: Koren 1970

Goshen-Gottstein   M. Goshen-Gottstein, *Fragments of Lost Targumim*,
                           [Heb.] 2 vols., Ramat Gan: Bar-Ilan University
                           Press 1983–1989

Gottlieb *Composition*   L. Gottlieb, "Composition of Targums after the
                           Decline of Aramaic as a Spoken Language",
                           Aramaic Studies 12 (2014), pp. 1–8

Gottlieb *Vorlage*   L. Gottlieb, "The Hebrew *Vorlage* of Targum
                           Chronicles", *Aramaic Studies* 14 (2016) pp. 36–65

Gottlieb *Yetzer*   L. Gottlieb, "The Evil Inclination in the Targums to
                           the Writings", forthcoming in J. Aitken, I. Rosen-Zvi,
                           H. Patmore (eds.), *The Origins of the Origins of Evil*,
                           Cambridge: Cambridge University Press

Greenberg   M. Greenberg, "The Decalogue Tradition Critically
                           Examined", [Heb.] in B.Z. Segal (ed.), *The Ten
                           Commandments in History and Tradition*, [Heb.]
                           Jerusalem: Magnes Press 1986, pp. 67–94

Grossfeld *Bibliography*   B. Grossfeld, *A Bibliography of Targum Literature*,
                           vol. II, Cincinnati-New York 1977

Grossfeld *EJ*   B. Grossfeld, "Bible: Translations, Aramaic
                           (Targumim)", *Encyclopedia Judaica*, vol. 4,
                           Jerusalem 1971, col. 841–851

Grossfeld *Esther*   B. Grossfeld, *The First Targum to Esther*, New York
                           1983

Grossman   A. Grossman, *The Early Sages of Ashkenaz*³, [Heb.]
                           Jerusalem: Magnes 2001

HALOT   L. Koehler, W. Baumgartner, *The Hebrew and
                           Aramaic Lexicon of the Old Testament*, 5 vols.
                           Leiden: Brill 1994–2000

Hamiel   H. Hamiel, *Hamiqra Wetargumaw*, [Heb.] vol. 5,
                           book 2, Jerusalem 2009

Hayward *Islam*   R. Hayward, "Targum Pseudo-Jonathan and anti-
                           Islamic Polemic", *Journal of Semitic Studies* 34:1
                           (1989), 77–93

Hayward *Memra*   R. Hayward, *Divine Name and Presence: The
                           Memra*, Totowa: Allanheld, Osmun 1981

Hayward *Sacrifice*   R. Hayward, "Present State of Research into the Targumic Account of the Sacrifice of Isaac", *Journal of Jewish Studies* 32 (1981), 127–150

Hayward *TPJ*   R. Hayward, "The Date of Targum Pseudo-Jonathan: Some Comments", *Journal of Jewish Studies* 40 (1989), 7–30

Hayward *Transmission*   R. Hayward, *Targums and the Transmission of Scripture into Judaism and Christianity*, [Studies in the Aramaic Interpretation of Scripture, Volume 10] Leiden: Brill 2010

Heinemann *Terms*   Y. Heinemann, "להתפתחות המונחים המקצועיים לפירוש המקרא", [Heb.] *Lešonenu* 14 (1946), pp. 182–189

Hurvitz *BLL*   A. Hurvitz, *Ben Lashon Lelashon*, [Heb.] Jerusalem 1972

Hurvitz *LBH*   A. Hurvitz, "Biblical Hebrew, Late", *Encyclopedia of Hebrew Language and Linguistics*, vol. 1, 329–338, edited by G. Khan, 2013, Leiden: Brill

Hurvitz-Gottlieb   A. Hurvitz (in collaboration with L. Gottlieb), *A Concise Lexicon of Late Biblical Hebrew: Linguistic Innovations in the Writings of the Second Temple Period*, [Supplements to Vetus Testamentum 160] Leiden: Brill 2014

Hyman   A. Hyman, *Torah Hakethubah Vehamessurah: a reference book of the scriptural passages quoted in Talmudic, midrashic and early rabbinic literature*, [Heb.] 3 vols. Tel Aviv: Debir

Japhet *Authorship*   S. Japhet, "The Supposed Common Authorship of Chronicles and Ezra-Nehemia Investigated Anew", *Vetus Testamentum* 18 (1968), 330–371

Japhet *Ideology*   S. Japhet, *The Ideology of the Book of Chronicles and its Place in Biblical Thought*, 2009, Winona Lake: Eisenbrauns

Japhet *OTL*   S. Japhet, *I & II Chronicles: A Commentary*, Old Testament Library, London 1993

Jastrow   M. Jastrow, *A Dictionary of the Targumim, the Talmud Babli and Yerushalmi, and the Midrashic Literature*, New York 1903

Jellinek   A. Jellinek, *Bet Hamidrash*, [Heb.] 6 vols., Jerusalem 1938

Kaddari | M.Z. Kaddari, *A Dictionary of Biblical Hebrew (Alef-Taw)*, [Heb.] Ramat Gan: Bar-Ilan University Press 2006

Kadushin | M. Kadushin, *The Rabbinic Mind*, New York 1952

Kahana | M. Kahana, *Sifre Bemidbar*, [Heb.] 4 vols., Jerusalem: Magnes Press 2011–2015

Kalimi *Bibliography* | I. Kalimi, *Sefer Divre Hayamim—Bibliographia Memuyenet*, [Heb.] Jerusalem: Simor 1991

Kalimi *Interpretation* | I. Kalimi, "History of Interpretation: The Book of Chronicles in Jewish Tradition", *Revue Biblique* 105, 1 (1998) pp. 5–41

Kalimi *Journey* | I. Kalimi, *The Retelling of Chronicles in Jewish Tradition and Literature: A Historical Journey*, Winona Lake 2009

Kasher *Torah Shelemah* | M.M. Kasher, *Chumash Torah Shelemah*, [Heb.] Jerusalem, 1949–

Kasher *TT* | R. Kasher, *Targum Toseftot to the Prophets*, [Heb.] Jerusalem: World Union of Jewish Studies 1996

Kaufman *Akkadian* | S. Kaufman, *The Akkadian Influences on Aramaic*, Chicago 1974

Kaufman *Review* | S. Kaufman, Review of G.J. Kuiper, "The Pseudo-Jonathan Targum and its Relationship to Targum Onkelos", *Journal of Near Eastern Studies* 35 (1976), pp. 61–62

Kaufman *TPJ* | S. Kaufman, "התרגום המיוחס ליונתן והארמית היהודית הספרותית המאוחרת", [Heb.] *Iyune Miqra Upharshanut* 3 (1993, in memory of Moshe Goshen-Gottstein), pp. 363–383;
This article was translated into English:
S. Kaufman, "Targum Pseudo-Jonathan and Late Jewish Literary Aramaic", *Aramaic Studies* 11 (2013), pp. 1–26

Kaufman-Maori | S. Kaufman and Y. Maori, "The Targumim to Exodus 20: Reconstructing the Palestinian Targum", *Textus* 16 (1991), pp. 13–78

Kedar | B.Z. Kedar, "The Arab Conquests and Agriculture: A Seventh-Century Apocalypse, Satellite Imagery, and Palynology", *African and Asian Studies* 19 (1985), pp. 1–15

Kennicott   B. Kennicott, *Vetus Testamentum hebraicum, cum variis lectionibus*, vols. I–II, Oxford, 1776–1780 (repr. Hildesheim-Zürich-New York 2003)

Kister ARN   M. Kister, *Studies in Avot de-Rabbi Nathan*, [Heb.] Jerusalem: Hebrew University 1998

Kister *Poetry*   M. Kister, "שירת בני מערבא—היבטים בעולמה של שירה של עולמה", [Heb.] *Tarbiẓ* 76 a–b (2007), pp. 105–184

Kister *Style*   M. Kister, "Some Observations on Vocabulary and Style in the Dead Sea Scrolls", in [eds. T. Muraoka, J.F. Elwolde] *Diggers at the Well: Proceedings of a Third International Symposium on the Hebrew of the Dead Sea Scrolls and Ben Sira*, Leiden 2000, pp. 137–165

Klein *1 Chronicles*   R.W. Klein, *1 Chronicles: A Commentary*, [Hermeneia] Minneapolis 2006

Klein *Preposition*   M.L. Klein, "The Preposition קדם ('Before'): A Pseudo-Anti-Anthropomorphism in the Targums", *Journal of Theological Studies* 30 (1979), pp. 502–507

Klein *Anthropomorphism*   M.L. Klein, "The Translation of Anthropomorphisms and Anthropopathisms in the Targumim", *Vetus Testamentum Supplements* 32 (1981), pp. 162–177

Knights *Rechabites*   C.H. Knights, "Kenites = Rechabites?: 1 Chronicles II 55 Reconsidered", *Vetus Testamentum* 43 (1993), pp. 10–18

Knights *Reka*   C.H. Knights, "The Text of 1 Chronicles IV 12: A Reappraisal", *Vetus Testamentum* 37 (1987) pp. 375–377

Knoppers *vol. I*   G.N. Knoppers, *I Chronicles 1–9: A New Translation with Introduction and Commentary*, [Anchor Bible, Volume 12] New York 2004

Knoppers *vol. II*   G.N. Knoppers, *I Chronicles 10–29: A New Translation with Introduction and Commentary*, [Anchor Bible, Volume 12] New York 2004

Kohn   S. Kohn, "Das Land 'Hagar' in der hebräisch-mittelalterlichen Literatur", *Monatsschrift für Geschichte und Wissenschaft des Judentums* 30 (1881), pp. 145–161, 193–201

Kohut *'arukh*   A. Kohut, *Sefer 'arukh Hashalem*, [Heb.] 9 vols. New York: Pardes 1956

Kohut *Tosaphot*   A. Kohut, *Additamenta ad librum aruch Completum*, [Heb.] Vienna 1937

Komlosh, *Bible*   Y. Komlosh, *The Bible in the Light of the Aramaic Translations*, [Heb.] 1973, Tel Aviv: Debir

Komlosh, *EB*   Y. Komlosh, "תרגומים, תנ״ך", *Encyclopedia Biblica*, [Heb.] vol. 8, 1982, Jerusalem, col. 764–765

Krauss *Lehnwörter*   S. Krauss, *Griechische und lateinische Lehnwörter im Talmud, Midrasch und Targum*, Berlin 1898–1899

Kuiper   G.J. Kuiper, *The Pseudo-Jonathan Targum and its Relationship to Targum Onkelos*, [Studia Ephemeridis "Augustinianum" 9] Rome 1972

Kutscher   E.Y. Kutscher, *Hebrew and Aramaic Studies*, eds. Z. Ben-Ḥayyim, A. Dotan, G. Sarfatti, Jerusalem: Magnes Press 1977

de Lagarde   P. de Lagarde, *Hagiographa Chaldaice*, Leipzig 1872

Lasair   S. Lasair, "Current Trends in Targum Research", *Currents in Biblical Research*, 10, 3 (2012), pp. 442–453

Lendvai   P. Lendvai, *The Hungarians: A Thousand Years of Victory in Defeat*, London 2003

Levine   E. Levine, "Codex Urbinates Ebr. 1: a 'Targum' Text", *Biblische Zeitschrift* 24, 1 (1980), 95–100

Levy   J. Levy, *Wörterbuch über die Talmudim und Midrashim*[2], Berlin and Vienna 1924

Lewis   B. Lewis, *The Jews of Islam*, Princeton: Princeton University Press, 2014

Lieberman *Greek*   S. Lieberman, *Greek and Hellenism in Jewish Palestine*[3], [Heb.] Jerusalem: Mosad Bialik 1991

Lieberman *Studies*   S. Lieberman, *Studies in Palestinian Talmudic Literature*, [Heb.] edited by D. Rosenthal, Jerusalem: Magnes Press 1991

Lieberman *Tosefta*   S. Lieberman, *Tosefta Ki-Fshuṭah: A Comprehensive Commentary on the Tosefta*, [Heb.] New York: Jewish Theological Seminary of America 1955–1988

Liver   J. Liver, "יקטן", *Encyclopedia Biblica*, vol. 3, col. 762–763, Jerusalem 1958

LSJ   H.G. Liddell, R. Scott, H.S. Jones *A Greek-English Lexicon*, Oxford: Clarendon Press 1996

Maher	M. Maher, *Targum Pseudo-Jonathan—Genesis: Translated, with Introduction and Notes*, [The Aramaic Bible 1b] Collegeville 1992
Mandel	P. Mandel, "The Origins of 'Midrash' in the Second Temple Period", in [ed. C. Bakhos] *Current Trends in the Study of Midrash*, Leiden-Boston 2006, pp. 9–34
Mann	J. Mann and I. Sonne, *The Bible as Read and Preached in the Old Synagogue*, Volume II, Cincinnati 1966
Maori	Y. Maori, *The Peshitta Version of the Pentateuch and Early Jewish Exegesis*, [Heb.] Jerusalem: Magnes Press 1995
McCarter *I Samuel*	P.K. McCarter, Jr., *I Samuel: A New Translation with Introduction, Notes and Commentary*, [Anchor Bible, Volume 8] Garden City 1980
McCarter *II Samuel*	P.K. McCarter, Jr., *II Samuel: A New Translation with Introduction, Notes and Commentary*, [Anchor Bible, Volume 9] Garden City 1984
McIvor	J.S. McIvor, *The Targum of Chronicles: Translated, with Introduction, Apparatus, and Notes* [The Aramaic Bible 19], Collegeville 1994
McNamara *Testament*	M. McNamara, *Targum and Testament Revisited: Aramaic Paraphrases of the Hebrew Bible: A Light on the New Testament*, Grand Rapids: Eerdmans 2010
McNamara *TN*	M. McNamara, *Targum Neofiti 1: Genesis; Translated, with Apparatus and Notes*, [The Aramaic Bible 1a] Collegeville 1992
Melamed	E.Z. Melamed, *Biblical Studies in Texts, Translations and Commentaries*, [Heb.] Jerusalem: Magnes Press 1984
Milikowsky	H. Milikowsky, "'הפרסדיאות' שהושיב ירבעם: התפתחותה של גירסה", *Sidra* 7 (1991) [Heb.] pp. 45–48
Mizrahi	N. Mizrahi, "The History and Linguistic Background of Two Hebrew Titles for the High Priest", *Journal of Biblical Literature* 130, 4 (2011): pp. 687–705

Moore   G.F. Moore, *Judaism in the First Centuries of the
                         Christian Era—The Age of the Tannaim*, volumes
                         I-III, Cambridge 1927–1930

Moreshet   M. Moreshet, "הברייתות העבריות בבבלי אינן לשון
                         חכמים א'", *Sefer Zikaron La-Hanokh Yalon*, [Heb.]
                         edited by Y. Kutscher, S. Lieberman, M. Kaddari,
                         Ramat Gan: Kiryat Sefer 1974, pp. 275–314

Morgenstern   M. Morgenstern, "The Meaning of *beit moladim*
                         in the Qumran Wisdom Texts," *Journal of Jewish
                         Studies* 51 (2000): 141–144

Mortensen   B. Mortensen, *The Priesthood in Targum Pseudo-
                         Jonathan*, [Studies in the Aramaic Interpretation
                         of Scripture, Volume 4] 2 vols. Leiden: Brill 2006

Muñoz León   D. Muñoz León, *Gloria de la Shekina en los targu-
                         mim del Pentateuco*, Madrid: CSIC 1977

Neubauer   A. Neubauer, "Where are the Ten Tribes?", *The
                         Jewish Quarterly Review* I, 1 (1888) pp. 14–28

NJPS   *Tanakh: A New Translation of the Holy Scriptures
                         According to the Traditional Hebrew Text*,
                         Philadelphia: Jewish Publication Society 1985

Noam   V. Noam, *Megillat Taʿanit: Ha-nosaḥim, pishram,
                         toldotehem*, Jerusalem: Yad Izhak Ben-Zvi 2003

Oeming   M. Oeming, *Das Wahre Israel: Die "genealo-
                         gische Vorhalle" 1 Chronik 1–9* [Beiträge zur
                         Wissenschaft vom Alten und Neuen Testament
                         128], Kohlhammer 1990

Ohana   M. Ohana, "La polémique judéo-islamique et
                         l'image d'Ismaël dans Targum Pseudo-Jonathan
                         et dans *Pirqe de Rabbi Eliezer*", *Augustinianum* 15
                         (1975), pp. 367–387

van Peursen   W.Th. van Peursen, "Negation in the Hebrew
                         of Ben Sira", in [eds. T. Muraoka; J.F. Elwolde]
                         *Sirach, Scrolls, and Sages: Proceedings of a Second
                         International Symposium on the Hebrew of the
                         Dead Sea Scrolls, Ben Sira, and the Mishnah, held
                         at Leiden University, 15–17 December 1997*, Leiden
                         1999, pp. 223–243

Posen   R.B. Posen, *The Consistency of Targum Onkelos'
                         Translation*, [Heb.] Jerusalem: Magnes Press 2004

Rabinowitz   Z.M. Rabinowitz, *Ginze Midrash*, [Heb.] Tel Aviv 1977

Rahmer   A. Rahmer, *Targum shel Divre Hayamim*, Torun: Mann 1866

Rieder   D. Rieder, *Pseudo-Jonathan Targum ben Uziel on the Pentateuch*, [Heb.], 2 vols., Jerusalem 1985

Rofé   A. Rofé, *Angels in the Bible: Israelite Belief in Angels as Evidenced by Biblical Traditions*, [Heb.] Jerusalem: Carmel 2012

Rosenberg-Kohler   M. Rosenberg and K. Kohler, "Das Targum zur Chronik", *Jüdische Zeitschrift für Wissenschaft und Leben* 8 (1870): 72–80, 135–163, 263–278

Rosenthal *Inscription*   E.S. Rosenthal, "הכתובת מגבעת המבתר", [Heb.] *P'raqim: Yearbook of the Schoken Institute* 2 (1974), pp. 335–373

Rosenthal *Text*   D. Rosenthal, "על דרך טיפולם של חז"ל בחילופי נוסח במקרא", [Heb.] *The Isaac Leo Seeligmann Volume*, eds. Y. Zakovitch and A. Rofé, Jerusalem: Rubinstein 1983, vol. 2, pp. 395–417

de Rossi   J.B. de Rossi, *Variae lectiones Veteris Testamenti*, vol. I–IV, Parma 1784–1788 (repr. Amsterdam 1969)

Rudolph   W. Rudolph, *Chronikbücher* [Handbuch zum Alten Testament 21], Tübingen 1955

Saldarini   A.J. Saldarini, "'Is Saul also among the Scribes?': Scribes and Prophets in Targum Jonathan", in [ed. H.J. Blumberg et al.] *"Open Thou Mine Eyes ..." Essays on Aggadah and Judaica ...*, New Jersey 1992, pp. 239–253

Schorr   J.H. Schorr, "Textual Variants in Targum Chronicles" [Heb.] *Heḥalutz* 8 (1869) pp. 134–135

Seeligmann   I.L. Seeligmann, "ניצני מדרש בספר דברי הימים" [Heb.], *Studies in Biblical Literature*, eds. A. Hurvitz, S. Japhet, E. Tov, Jerusalem: Magnes Press 1996, pp. 454–474

Seow   C.L. Seow, *Ecclesiastes: A New Translation with Introduction and Commentary*, [Anchor Bible, Volume 18C] New York 1997

Shailat	I. Shailat, *The Letters and Essays of Moses Maimonides*, [Heb.] 2 vols., Jerusalem: Shailat Publishing—Ma'aleh Adumim 1995
Shinan	A. Shinan, "Dating Targum Pseudo-Jonathan: Some More Comments", *Journal of Jewish Studies* 41 (1990), pp. 57–61
Shinan *Embroidered*	A. Shinan, *The Embroidered Targum: the Aggadah in Targum Pseudo-Jonathan of the Pentateuch*, [Heb.] Jerusalem: Magnes Press 1993
Shinan *TPJ Legends*	A. Shinan, *Agadatam shel Meturgemanim*, [Heb.] 2 vols., Jerusalem: Makor 1979
Smelik	W.F. Smelik, *The Targum of Judges*, Leiden: Brill 1995
Smolar-Aberbach	L. Smolar & M. Aberbach, *Studies in Targum Jonathan to the Prophets*, New York-Baltimore 1983
Sokoloff *JBA*	M. Sokoloff, *A Dictionary of Jewish Babylonian Aramaic of the Talmudic and Geonic Periods*, Ramat Gan 2002
Sokoloff *JPA*	M. Sokoloff, *A Dictionary of Jewish Palestinian Aramaic of the Byzantine Period*[3], Ramat Gan 2017
Sokoloff *Syriac*	M. Sokoloff, *A Syriac Lexicon*, Winona Lake—Piscataway 2009
Sokoloff-Yahalom	Y. Yahalom and M. Sokoloff, *Shirat Bene Maarava: Jewish Palestinian Aramaic Poetry*, [Heb.] Jerusalem: Israel Academy of Sciences and Humanities 1999
de Sola Pool	D. de Sola Pool, *The Kaddish*, New York 1964
Sperber	A. Sperber, *The Bible in Aramaic*, vol. I–IV B, Leiden 1959–1973
Splansky	D.M. Splansky, *Targum Pseudo-Jonathan: Its Relationship to other Targumim, use of Midrashim, and Date*, [Ph.D. dissertation] Hebrew Union College 1981
van Staalduine-Sulman *Lamb*	E. van Staalduine-Sulman, "The Aramaic Song of the Lamb", in [eds. J.C. de Moor, W.G.E. Watson] *Verse in Ancient Near Eastern Prose* [Alter Orient und Altes Testament 42], Neukirchen-Vluyn 1993, pp. 265–292

van Staalduine-Sulman *TJ Samuel* E. van Staalduine-Sulman, *The Targum of Samuel*, [Studies in the Aramaic Interpretation of Scripture, Volume 1] Leiden: Brill 2002

Stec *Job* D.M. Stec, *The Text of the Targum of Job: an Introduction and Critical Edition*, Leiden 1994

Stec *Psalms* D.M. Stec, *The Targum of Psalms: Translated, with a Critical Introduction, Apparatus, and Notes* [The Aramaic Bible 16], Collegeville 2004

Ta-Shma I.M. Ta-Shma, *Early Franco-German Ritual and Custom*, [Heb.] Jerusalem: Magnes 1999

TAD B. Porten and A. Yardeni, *Textbook of Aramaic Documents from Ancient Egypt*, 4 vols., Jerusalem: Hebrew University 1986–1999

Tal A. Tal, "The Role of Targum Onqelos in Literary Activity During the Middle Ages", in [eds. H. Gzella, M.L. Folmer] *Aramaic in its Historical and Linguistic Setting*, Wiesbaden 2008, pp. 159–171

Talmon S. Talmon, "המה הקינים הבאים מחמת אבי בית־רכב": 1 Chron. ii, 55", *Israeli Exploration Journal* 10 (1960), pp. 174–180

Talshir D. Talshir, *Living Names: Fauna, Places and Humans*, Jerusalem: Mosad Bialik 2012

Tov *LXX* E. Tov, *The Text-Critical Use of the Septuagint in Biblical Research*[3], Winona Lake: Eisenbrauns 2015

Tov *TCHB* E. Tov, *Textual Criticism of the Hebrew Bible*[3], Minneapolis: Fortress Press 2012

Urbach E.E. Urbach, *The Sages: Their Concepts and Beliefs*, Jerusalem: Magnes Press 1986

Vannutelli P. Vannutelli, *Libri Synoptici Veteris Testamenti seu Librorum Regum et Chronicorum Loci Paralleli*, Tomus Prior, Rome 1931; Tomus Secundus, Rome 1934

Viezel *Author* E. Viezel, *"Ezra katav sifro veyahas shel divrey ha-yaamim 'ad lo ... uman 'askeh? Nehemia ben-Hakalya*: On the Author of Chronicles in Bava Batra 15a", *Jewish Studies Quarterly* 16,3 (2009), pp. 243–254

Viezel *Pseudo-Rashi* E. Viezel, *The Commentary on Chronicles Attributed to Rashi*, [Heb.] 2010, Jerusalem: Magnes Press

Weiss   R. Weiss, *The Aramaic Targum of Job*, Tel Aviv:
                          Tel Aviv University 1979
Weitzman   M.P. Weitzman, *The Syriac Version of the Old
                          Testament: An Introduction*, Cambridge 1999
White   R.T. White, *A Linguistic Analysis of the Targum to
                          Chronicles with Specific Reference to its Relationship
                          with Other Forms of Aramaic*, [Ph.D. dissertation]
                          The Queen's College, London 1981
Wilkins   D. Wilkins, *Paraphrasis Chaldaica in librum pri-
                          orem et posteriorem Chronicorum*, Amsterdam 1715
York   A.D. York, "The Targum in the Synagogue and in
                          the School", *Journal for the Study of Judaism in the
                          Persian, Hellenistic and Roman Period* 10 (1979),
                          pp. 74–86
Zakovitch   Y. Zakovitch, *Shir Hashirim*, [Heb.—Miqra
                          Leyisrael] Jerusalem: Magnes Press 1992
Zunz   L. Zunz, *Die Gottesdienstlichen Vorträge der Juden
                          Historisch Entwickelt*[2], Frankfurt 1892; references
                          to page numbers are according to the Hebrew
                          translation:
                          י״ל צונץ, הדרשות בישראל והשתלשלותן ההיסטורית[2],
                          ירושלים תשי״ד; נערך והושלם בידי חנוך אלבעק; תורגם
                          ע״י מ״א ז׳ק

Electronic Tools

Accordance   http://www.accordancebible.com
Comprehensive Aramaic Lexicon   http://cal.huc.edu/
Mikra'ot Gedolot 'Haketer'   https://www.mgketer.org/
The Historical Dictionary Project   https://maagarim.hebrew-academy.org.il
The Responsa Project   http://www.biu.ac.il/jh/Responsa
The Saul and Evelyn Henkind   http://www.lieberman-institute.com
Talmud Text Databank (The Saul
Lieberman Institute of Talmud
Research)

Index of Ancient Sources

Index of Modern Scholars and Sources